Social Policy in Brita

D1386134

Pete Alcock
with
Margaret May

Social Policy in Britain

Fourth Edition

palgrave
macmillan

First edition 1996
Second edition 2003
Third edition 2008
Fourth edition 2014

Published by
PALGRAVE MACMILLAN

Palgrave Macmillan in the UK is an imprint of Macmillan Publishers Limited, registered in England, company number 785998, of Houndmills, Basingstoke, Hampshire RG21 6XS.

Palgrave Macmillan in the US is a division of St Martin's Press LLC, 175 Fifth Avenue, New York, NY 10010.

Palgrave Macmillan is the global academic imprint of the above companies and has companies and representatives throughout the world.

Palgrave® and Macmillan® are registered trademarks in the United States, the United Kingdom, Europe and other countries

ISBN 978-0-230-34635-2

This book is printed on paper suitable for recycling and made from fully managed and sustained forest sources. Logging, pulping and manufacturing processes are expected to conform to the environmental regulations of the country of origin.

A catalogue record for this book is available from the British Library.

A catalog record for this book is available from the Library of Congress.

Printed in China

Contents

List of Boxes, Figures and Tables

Tables

How to use this book

This book is intended to provide a general introduction to social policy for students studying the subject at all levels of further and higher education. The main intended readership is students in higher education on the first year, or at the first level, of undergraduate degree courses in social policy. However, the book will be equally valuable to students studying social policy as part of a broader undergraduate programme in the social sciences, as part of NVQ, BTEC or A level courses in further education or as part of professional education courses in areas such as social work or nursing. It also aims to provide a comprehensive and up-to-date guide to the subject for students first encountering social policy at postgraduate level, or wishing to re-examine previous studies as part of a new postgraduate course.

The book adopts a comprehensive and yet topical approach, and aims to provide a clear and comprehensive guide to all the major issues that are likely to be encountered in the study of social policy. The primary focus of the book is on the UK and on the development and analysis of social policy in the country. Its primary intended readership, therefore, is students in UK universities and colleges. However, as is argued in the text, it is no longer feasible to restrict the study of social policy to the context and actions of only one nation state. The international context of British social policy is thus discussed, and in particular the growing impact of the European Union (EU) upon policy development in Britain. This provides a framework for the coverage of British policy development, however, rather than an extensive focus on comparative study or on the EU in particular detail. Students seeking a textbook on comparative social policy or on social policy in the EU should look to some of the increasing numbers of specialist texts now focusing on these issues and discussed in Chapter 7.

It is also no longer possible to deal comprehensively with the provision of social policy across Britain. First the terminology itself is in practice confusing. Britain and the UK are often used interchangeably to refer to the country governed by the UK Parliament at Westminster, although strictly speaking Northern Ireland is not formally a part of Britain, though it is part of the UK. However, in this book we will use both terms to refer collectively to all four UK nations. More significantly, in policy terms, the devolution of political and policy-making powers to Scotland, Wales and Northern Ireland since 1999 has led to significant and growing diversity in welfare provision across these separate countries within the UK (see Chapter 6). This is especially important in certain policy areas, such as education, health and social care, where devolved powers have led to major departures in policy and practice. The policy changes that have flowed from devolution are discussed throughout the book, with explanations of how and why these have developed. There is also some discussion of the political and policy context of devolution in Chapter 6.

Although focused on the UK, this book is likely to be of interest to readers outside of this national context. The policies and issues within British social policy discussed here are situated within a broader international and theoretical context; and this is likely to make the book of interest to students in other countries too, who wish to find a comprehensive and accessible guide to the development and analysis of policy within the UK that could provide a basis for comparative study.

Readers of this book may start at the beginning and carry on through to the end; however, many students of social policy following a course, or courses, of study will probably want to move backwards and forwards between the sections and chapters in order to explore the specific themes or issues that they are studying at any particular time. With this in mind, the contents of the book have been carefully divided between sections and chapters addressing different issues, and have been written so that any one chapter could be read in isolation from those around it, but in the expectation that the others would probably be used or referred to at another time. This is a book, therefore, that can either be read or used as a source of reference – or, perhaps most commonly, both.

The chapters have also been divided into subsections, with subheadings listed in the contents. These are intended to help readers to find quickly the particular issue on which they want to focus at any one time. However, where issues – or particular terms or concepts – are not listed in the contents, readers should use the index at the end. This provides page references to the detailed coverage of all specific concepts and empirical policy developments and is perhaps the quickest way of all to gain access to the book in order to find the answer to a particular question. To help the book to work as a tool for learning as well as a source of information, this fourth edition includes boxed summaries of the key points at the beginning of each chapter and suggestions of useful sources of further reading (including some key websites) at the end. The text is also interspersed with questions to help readers to assimilate the material covered and to reflect on some of the broader issues involved. These are distinguished as questions for *comprehension* and questions for *reflection*; and, as well as providing a stimulus for individual readers, they could also be used as learning tools by tutors or student groups.

Chapter 1 is a general introduction to the subject of social policy, the history of its development and some of the major changes in emphasis and focus that have been experienced within it. The term 'social policy' of course refers not only to an academic subject but also to the empirical basis of that subject, the policies that have been developed within society to meet welfare needs. The chapter also summarizes the development of British social policy in the context of the academic study of it. However, there is no comprehensive coverage of the history of British social policy here; and again readers wanting such coverage should look elsewhere.

Part 1 of the book outlines the structural context of policy delivery, highlighting the different sectors which provide welfare services and exploring the local and the international dimensions of policy-making and practice. Part 2 of the book provides an extended summary of the main areas of social policy provision across the UK, including the impact of devolution on these. This is additional coverage compared to that provided in the first edition of this book and it has been significantly expanded and updated for this new edition, in particular to include extended coverage of devolution and the policies developed by the UK Coalition government. Part 3 of the book explores some the key theoretical debates and empirical pressures that underpin policy development and policy practice, including some of the issues affecting the availability and use of welfare services, and concludes with a short overview of major developments and future prospects. Overall the text therefore provides a comprehensive introduction to the substance of social policy as well as to the themes and issues underlying its development and operation.

Inevitably in an introductory text there are limits to what can be covered in one book, of course. Readers wishing to look in more detail at particular issues or debates, or particular areas of service development or delivery, will need to move on to more specialist texts within these areas, such as those listed in the further reading; indeed, it is likely that they will be directed to do so by tutors. So, although this could be the first and most comprehensive text that students of social policy use, it will probably not be the only one.

Acknowledgements

I have been joined in the production of this fourth edition by Margaret May. Maggie has helped in particular in the rewriting of the chapters in Part 2 to take account of the extensive changes in social policy flowing from the change of UK government in 2010. She has also helped to extend the coverage of the book to include policy developments under the devolved administrations in Scotland, Wales and Northern Ireland. Without her contribution it would not have been possible to produce such an extensive and up-to-date text. Thus the book is now published as *Alcock with May*.

PETE ALCOCK

We should both like to thank Catherine Gray, and the other staff, at Palgrave Macmillan for her support and patience, as inevitably it took longer to produce this revised edition than we had initially anticipated. For the content we are now both jointly responsible.

PETE ALCOCK AND MARGARET MAY

The authors and publishers would like to thank the following publishers and organizations for permission to reproduce copyright material:

John McCormick for permission to reproduce Map 7.1 'Political map of the European Union' from J. McCormick, *Contemporary Britain*, 3rd edn (2012) (reproduced and adapted with the permission of Palgrave Macmillan and John McCormick); Wiley Publishers for permission to reproduce Figure 2.1 'Welfare spending in the UK, 1900 to 2015' from H. Glennerster 'Paying for welfare' in *The Student's Companion to Social Policy*, 4th edn (2012) edited by P. Alcock, M. May and S. Wright; Linda Hantrais for permission to reproduce Figure 7.1 'Social protection expenditure in EU member states, as a percentage of GDP and *per capita* in PPS, 2003' from L. Hantrais, *Social Policy in the European Community*, 3rd edn (2007) (reproduced with the permission of Palgrave Macmillan); The Institute of Fiscal Studies for permission to reproduce Figure 8.2 'Relative importance of spending on contributory, income-related and other benefits, 1979/80 to 2009/10' from W. Jin et al., *A Survey of the UK Benefit System* (2010); M. Marmot and the UCL Institute of Health Equity for Figure 9.1 'Life expectancy and disability-free life expectancy (DFLE) at birth, persons by neighbourhood income level, 1909–2003' from M. Marmott, *Fair Society, Healthy Lives* (2010); The King's Fund for permission to reproduce Figure 9.2 'Real net spending on the UK NHS at 2010/2011 prices and as a percentage of GDP' from J. Appleby et al., *How Cold will it be? Prospects for NHS Funding 2011–2017* (2009); Policy Press for permission to adapt Table 10.1 'Tenure of dwellings: England, 1914–2010' from A. Murie, 'Housing, the welfare state and the Coalition', in *Social Policy Review*, 24 (2012), edited by M. Kilkey, G. Ramia and K. Farnsworth.

This work contains public information licensed under The Open Government Licence v1.0.

Every effort has been made to trace all copyright-holders, but if any have been inadvertently overlooked the publishers will be pleased to make the necessary arrangements at the first opportunity.

List of abbreviations

ALMO	Arms-Length Management Organization
AQP	Any Qualified Provider
ASBOs	Anti-Social Behaviour Orders
ASI	Adam Smith Institute
BIS	Department for Business, Innovation and Skills
BMA	British Medical Association
BSP	British State Pension
BUPA	British United Provident Association
CAB	Citizens' Advice Bureau
CAF	Charities Aid Foundation
CCETSW	Central Council for Education and Training in Social Work
CCG	Clinical Commissioning Group
CDF	Community Development Foundation
CIC	Community Interest Company
CPAG	Child Poverty Action Group
COS	Charity Organization Society
COSLA	Convention of Scottish Local Authorities
CPI	Consumer Price Index
CPS	Centre for Policy Studies
CQC	Care Quality Commission
CSA	Child Support Agency
CSCI	Commission for Social Care Inspection
CSE	Certificate of School Education
CSP	*Critical Social Policy*
CSR	Comprehensive Spending Review
CTC	Child Tax Credit
CVA	Contextual Value Added
CVS	Council for Voluntary Services
DB	Direct Benefit Pension Scheme
DC	Defined Contribution Pension Scheme
DCLG	Department for Communities and Local Government
DCSF	Department for Children, Schools and Families
DEL	Department of Employment and Learning (Northern Ireland)
DES	Department of Education and Science
DfE	Department for Education
DfEE	Department for Education and Employment
DfES	Department for Education and Skills
DG	Directorate General
DHA	District Health Authority
DIUS	Department for Innovation, Universities and Skills
DLA	Disability Living Allowance

DoH	Department of Health
DPM	Department of the Deputy Prime Minister
DRA	Default Retirement Age
DSD	Department for Social Development (Northern Ireland)
DHSS	Department of Health and Social Security
DHSSPS	Department of Health, Social Services and Public Safety (Northern Ireland)
DSS	Department of Social Security
DTI	Department for Trade and Industry
DTLR	Department of Transport, Local Government and the Regions
DUP	Democratic Unionist Party
DWP	Department for Work and Pensions
EAC	Education and Employment Directorate (EU)
EAPN	European Anti-Poverty Network
EAZ	Education Action Zone
EC	European Community
EEC	European Economic Community
EMA	Education Maintenance Allowance
EMPL	Employment, Social Affairs and Inclusion Directorate (EU)
EPA	Educational Priority Area
ERM	Exchange Rate Mechanism
ESA	Employment and Support Allowance
ESF	European Structural Fund
ESRC	Economic and Social Research Council
ET	Employment Training
EU	European Union
FE	Further Education
FEFC	Further Education Funding Council
FHA	Family Health Authority
FND	Flexible New Deal
FSA	Financial Services Authority
FSA	Food Standards Agency
GCE	General Certificate of Education
GCSE	General Certificate in School Education
GDP	Gross Domestic Product
GHS	General Household Survey
GLC	Greater London Council
GNP	Gross National Product
GOR	Government Office for the Regions
GP	General Practitioner
GREA	Grant Related Expenditure Assessment
GSCC	General Social Care Council
HAZ	Health Action Zone
HA	Housing Association
HB	Housing Benefit
HCA	Homes and Community Agency
HEFC	Higher Education Funding Council
HEFCE	Higher Education Funding Council for England
HEI	Higher Education Institute
HMG	HM Government
HMRC	HM Revenue and Customs
HMT	HM Treasury
HO	Home Office
HSCIC	Health and Social Care Information Centre

ICA	Invalid Care Allowance
IB	Incapacity Benefit
IEA	Institute of Economic Affairs
IGO	International Governmental Organization
ILO	International Labour Organization
IMF	International Monetary Fund
INGO	International Non-Governmental Organization
IS	Income Support
JSA	Jobseekers' Allowance
JSP	*Journal of Social Policy*
KS	Key Stages
LA	Local Authority
LEA	Local Education Authority
LETS	Local Exchange and Trading Scheme
LGA	Local Government Association
LHA	Local Housing Allowance
LINks	Local Involvement Networks
LMS	Local Management of Schools
LSC	Learning Skills Council
LSE	London School of Economics
LSP	Local Strategic Partnership
MP	Member of Parliament
MSC	Manpower Services Commission
MWA	Mandatory Work Activity Programme
NA	National Assistance
NAO	National Audit Office
NAW	National Assembly for Wales
NCVO	National Council for Voluntary Organizations
NEET	Not in Education, Employment or Training
NEST	National Employment Savings Trust
NGO	Non-Governmental Organization
NHF	National Housing Federation
NHS	National Health Service
NHSCB	National Health Service Commissioning Board
NHSE	National Health Service Executive
NHSFT	National Health Service Foundation Trust
NHSIC	National Health Service Information Centre
NI	National Insurance
NIA	Northern Ireland Assembly
NICE	National Institute for Clinical Excellence
NICVA	Northern Ireland Council for Voluntary Action
NIE	Northern Ireland Executive
NIHCE	National Institute for Health and Care Excellence
NIHE	Northern Ireland Housing Executive
NPM	New Public Management
NSPCC	National Society for the Prevention of Cruelty to Children
NVQ	National Vocational Qualification
OCS	Office for Civil Society
OECD	Organization for Economic Co-operation and Development
OFFA	Office for Fair Access
OFSTED	Office for Standards in Education
OHE	Office of Health Economics
ONS	Office for National Statistics

OPCS	Office of Population Census and Surveys
OPEC	Organization of Petroleum Exporting Countries
OTS	Office of the Third Sector
PBR	Payment by Results
PCG	Primary Care Group
PCT	Primary Care Trust
PFI	Private Finance Initiative
PHE	Public Health England
PIP	Personal Independence Payment
QAA	Quality Assurance Agency
QTS	Qualified Teacher Status
Quango	Quasi-autonomous non-governmental organization
RAWP	Resource Allocation Working Party
RDA	Regional Development Agency
RPI	Retail Price Index
RSG	Rate Support Grant
RSL	Registered Social Landlord
RTB	Right to Buy
RVS	Royal Voluntary Service
SAT	Standard Attainment Test
SBWA	Sector Based Work Academy
SCE	Scottish Certificate of Education
SCIE	Social Care Institute for Excellence
SCVO	Scottish Council for Voluntary Organizations
SDA	Serious Disablement Allowance
SERPS	State Earnings Related Pension Scheme
SEU	Social Exclusion Unit
SfC	Skills for Care
SG	Scottish Government
SHA	Strategic Health Authority
SMI	Support for Mortgage Interest
SMR	Standardized Mortality Ratio
SNP	Scottish National Party
SPA	Social Policy Association
SQV	Scottish Vocational Qualifications
SSA	Standard Spending Assessment
SSD	Social Services Department
SSRC	Social Science Research Council
SWD	Social Work Department
SWP	Social Work Partnership
S2P	State Second Pension
TEC	Training and Enterprise Council
TUC	Trades Union Congress
UC	Universal Credit
UGC	University Grants Committee
UN	United Nations
UNICEF	United Nations Children's Fund
UNDP	United Nations Development Programme
VAT	Value Added Tax
VCS	Voluntary and Community Sector
WAG	Welsh Assembly Government
WCVA	Wales Council for Voluntary Action
WG	Welsh Government

WLB	Work Life Balance
WHO	World Health Organization
WP	Work Programme
WTC	Working Tax Credit
YOP	Youth Opportunities Programme
YTS	Youth Training Scheme

1

Introduction: The Development of Social Policy

SUMMARY OF KEY POINTS

- Social policy is a unique subject, but is closely linked to the other social sciences and studied by students undertaking a wide range of social science courses and professional qualifications.
- Over time the scope of analysis and debate in the subject has broadened, captured in the change in title from social *administration* to social *policy*.
- Academic study of social policy has always been closely linked to policy practice, with leading academics sometimes acting as advisers to government.
- The creation of the 'welfare state' by the post-war Labour government established public services to meet welfare needs.
- Criticisms of state welfare from the *New Left* and the New Right have argued that the continued expansion of state welfare is not sustainable. In the last quarter of the last century this seemed to be borne out as an economic crisis led to retrenchment in social policy planning and welfare expenditure.
- At the beginning of the twenty-first century a *Third Way*, between the left and the right, was championed by government in the UK.
- Following the economic recession of 2008/09 there has been pressure to reduce public spending on welfare provision in the UK, and elsewhere.
- Social policy can no longer be studied solely within national boundaries, and comparative analysis of welfare in different countries has revealed that in different countries there are different *mixes* of welfare services.
- It is how this 'welfare mix' operates, and changes, in Britain that is the core concern of students of social policy.
- This mix also varies within Britain now, as a result of the devolution of much social policy planning to the separate administrations in Scotland, Wales and Northern Ireland.

WHAT IS SOCIAL POLICY?

Social policy is an academic subject, studied by students on undergraduate and postgraduate degree programmes and in a number of areas of professional training. It is also studied by some students at A level or in further education; but for the most part social policy study takes place in universities and other higher education institutions. Social policy can be studied as a discrete subject, on a 'single honours' programme; but there are many other students (indeed the large majority) studying the subject as one element in a broader social studies programme, or as part of a related programme in sociology or political science or, as mentioned above, as part of a programme of professional training – for instance, in social work, health science, housing or planning.

Social policy is also, however, the term used to refer to the actions taken within society to develop and deliver services for people in order to meet their needs for welfare and wellbeing. Social policy is thus both the name of the academic subject and the focus of what is studied. Thus sociologists study *society*, whilst social policy students study *social policy*. This may seem confusing, but it need not be. Indeed the terminological link between what we study and we do makes clear the link between analysis and practice which is what attracts many people into social policy, as we shall discuss below.

Studying social policy alongside other subjects such as sociology or economics also raises questions about the extent to which social policy is a discrete subject, or discipline, as academics sometimes call them. It is likely that there will always be argument and debate about what constitutes an academic subject, and in social science, in particular, there is debate about the overlap between subjects such as sociology, economics, politics and social policy, and about what should be the core concerns of each. Certainly social policy overlaps with other subjects, such as these and others like social work or criminology; and this has led some to question whether social policy is an interdisciplinary field rather than a discrete academic subject. This is not a terribly fruitful debate, however, for disciplinary boundaries are disputed in all academic subjects, and interdisciplinary work is widely promoted across the social sciences.

In most British universities social policy in fact often shares departmental status with cognate social sciences such as sociology, or with professional education such as social work, and the teaching of these is generally closely related, with social policy included in all. And in research institutes specialists in social policy often work alongside sociologists, economists, statisticians and even lawyers. However, within this broader context some key features do delineate social policy. Where it differs from sociology, for instance, is in its specific focus upon the development and implementation of policy measures in order to influence the social circumstances of individuals rather than the more general study of those social circumstances themselves. And, where it differs from economics, is in its focus upon welfare policies, or policies impacting upon the welfare of citizens, rather than those seeking to influence the production of goods, materials and services.

What is more, if we move on to examine the historical development of social policy, we can see how these issues have been played out – how the attempt to provide a specific focus for study was embarked upon, how this led to boundary disputes with other subjects, how it was subject to external political influence and to internal theoretical debate, and how these events changed the nature of social policy itself. In fact, debates over the nature of social policy even resulted in a change in name for the subject from *social administration* to *social policy*, symbolized by the change of the professional association, representing academics and researchers in universities, from the Social Administration Association to the Social Policy Association (SPA) in 1987. This was a change that was not without conflict and disagreement (see Glennerster 1988; Smith 1988; Donnison 1994). Nor is it necessarily complete, and some university departments and qualifications are still referred to as social administration.

Within the British social policy tradition in particular, what has also distinguished social policy from some other social science subjects has been its specific, and driving, concern not merely to understand the world, but also to change it. In this tradition social policy is not only a *descriptive* subject, it is also a *prescriptive* one. This is in part because the early academic development of social policy in Britain was closely allied to the political development of *Fabianism*. The Fabians were both academics and politicians, and they wanted to utilize academic research and analysis in order to influence government welfare policy. Throughout much of the early part of last century the development of British social policy was often synonymous with the concerns and perspectives of the Fabians; and the subject largely shared Fabianism's benign view of the role of state provision within welfare policy. Social policy also shared the empirical focus of Fabianism, in particular its concern to measure the need for, and the impact of, state welfare provision.

The ideological and empirical alliances with Fabianism were, however, associated most closely with the social administration perspective of the subject, and with a concern with *what* is done by policy action, and *how* it is done, rather than *why* this is done, or indeed *whether* it should be done. This narrower focus has come under critical scrutiny as the academic subject has developed over the last 50 years or so. Of particular importance in this process of development was the work of Richard Titmuss, the first Professor of Social Administration, who was appointed at the London School of Economics (LSE) in 1950. In his inaugural lecture at the LSE Titmuss described social policy as 'the study of the social sciences whose object… is the improvement of the conditions of life of the individual in the setting of family and group relations' (1958). This included a commitment to prescription (improving living conditions) and to an understanding of social context. These concerns were taken up by Titmuss in his later work, which remains the most influential legacy of conceptual reflection and empirical analysis within the subject, both within the UK and beyond (see Alcock et al. 2001). Titmuss was especially concerned, however, to argue that the role of academic study was to explore the values that lay behind policy decisions and the research evidence that should shed light on these, rather than to extol the virtues of particular policy changes. It is this reflective approach which led him to challenge some of the narrower perceptions of the achievements of the Fabian-inspired welfare reforms of post-war Britain, and which still provides an inspiration to critical judgement amongst students of the subject today.

In the latter half of the twentieth century the narrow focus of the Fabian tradition upon how to improve existing welfare services thus began to come under increasing criticism and attack from different perspectives which sought to widen the questions asked by the subject and to challenge the underlying assumption of the benign role of the state in welfare provision. Furthermore, the narrow focus and assumptions of the social administration tradition have also been called into question by the increasing academic and political concern with *international* comparisons of welfare policy. For what international comparisons quickly reveal, as Titmuss again was influential in pointing out, is that welfare policies have not developed elsewhere as they have done in Britain; that different political assumptions in different countries have led to different patterns of provision; and, therefore, that different political assumptions could lead to different patterns of provision in Britain too.

The cumulative effect of these questions and challenges has been to bring about a significant shift in the focus of academic debate and political influence within the subject, which has been represented by the change in title from administration to policy. This has resulted in a shift from a subject that was, in Mishra's (1989) terms, 'pragmatic, Britain-centred, socially concerned and empirical', to one that is characterized by ideological division, theoretical pluralism and a growing internationalism. However, this shift, significant though it is, should not deter us from recognizing the continuities, as well as the discontinuities, in the development of social policy.

FABIANISM AND THE ROOTS OF SOCIAL WELFARE

The concern of social policy writers to contribute to the development of political change – as well as to analyse it – has been a key feature since its birth as a subject in Britain. Interest in it began to develop at a time when state policy towards the welfare of citizens was undergoing a radical revision and Fabian politics were seeking both to understand and influence this. The Fabian Society was formed in 1884, under the leading guidance of Sidney and Beatrice Webb who were firm believers that collective provision for welfare through the state was an essential, and inevitable, development within British capitalist society; Sidney Webb also held strong views on the moral values of social (or socialist) provision (Headlam 1892; Ball 1896).

One of the early examples of the influence of Fabian thinking was within the Royal Commission on the Poor Laws and the Relief of Distress, of which Beatrice Webb was a member. The Commission was established by the government, in 1905, to review the old Victorian approach to support for the poor. It signified a recognition by government of the need to overhaul welfare policies and the importance of social policy debate in shaping this process, and it increased the pressure on government to bring about the major changes in social security and other policies that were introduced in the ten years before the First World War.

Debate about the future direction of welfare policy was a central concern of the work of the Commission, and when it reported in 1909 the Commission produced both a Majority and Minority Report, as the members could not all agree about the role that the state should play as provider of welfare services. The *Minority* Report was largely written by the Webbs and argued for an extensive role for state provision. The *Majority* Report envisaged a greater, continuing, role for charitable and voluntary action. Nevertheless, both argued for significant reform and in retrospect there was as much in common as there was in conflict between them; and, as we shall see in Part 1 in particular, both state and voluntary action have played significant roles in the subsequent development of social policy.

Influential in the drafting of the Majority Report were Charles Booth and Bernard and Helen Bosanquet, leading members of the Charity Organisation Society (COS), which coordinated much of voluntary sector provision of social work and social services and the training of social workers. In December 1912, however, the COS's School of Sociology was merged with the LSE, founded by the Webbs, to form the LSE's new Department of Social Science and Administration. This was arguably the first academic base for the study of social policy and it provided a significant academic forum for developing the debates rehearsed in the Commission's deliberations. The first lecturer to be appointed to the new department in 1913 was Clement Attlee, demonstrating almost immediately the close link that the Fabians were concerned to secure between academic analysis and political change because, after the Second World War, Attlee became the Prime Minister of the Labour government which introduced many of the far-reaching state welfare reforms that the Fabian reformers had been calling for throughout the intervening period.

During the early part of the twentieth century the LSE Department of Social Science and Administration also received significant financial support from the private trusts of an Indian millionaire, Ratan Tata. This money was specifically tied to support for empirical research on policies for the prevention and relief of poverty and destitution. It therefore provided an impetus for the development of another significant aspect of the subject: its concern with empirical work on the need for, and impact of, social policy. In particular, the research funding supported the work of academics such as Tawney, and Bowley and Burnett Hurst, who were early pioneers in the theoretical and empirical investigation of poverty and inequality in Britain (Harris 1989).

During the period following the First World War, therefore, the department at the LSE contained the main themes of the subject of social policy in its early form. It was informed, and directed, by a strong ideological commitment to Fabianism, in particular the use of academic knowledge and research on social problems to create pressure on the state to introduce welfare reforms. The continuing influence of the old COS, however, also maintained a concern with the role of the voluntary sector in social service and, although diminished by the statism of the Fabian approach, this broader concern with non-state welfare provision has always remained a vital feature of political as well as academic debate in social policy.

Teaching at the LSE, although also informed by sociology and economics, remained firmly tied to the education and training of social services workers, however; and research work focused on the detailed investigation of the problem of poverty. Despite the high-profile political context of its birth in the early twentieth century, when the Webbs and the Bosanquets were influential in shaping the reform of Victorian welfare policy in Britain, social policy soon became more concerned with the pragmatic issues of education for practice and empirical research on established social problems (the social administration tradition).

THE WELFARE STATE

In the period following the Second World War this tradition reached what was perhaps its high-water mark with the creation of what has often been referred to as a 'welfare state' in Britain. The development of this welfare state owed much, in principle at least, to the influence of the Beveridge Report of 1942. Beveridge (himself Director of the LSE for a time between the wars) had been appointed by the wartime government to conduct a review of social security policy. However, when his report appeared, at around the time of one of the earliest allied victories at El Alamein, it included, alongside a detailed blueprint for the reform of benefits, a vision for a much broader role for the state in meeting collective welfare need, captured in his famous reference to the need for public action to remove the 'five giant evils' that had haunted the country before the war: *disease, idleness, ignorance, squalor* and *want*.

Beveridge's report was a best-seller, and it set the scene for debate about policy development after the war. Reforms were introduced by the post-war Attlee government to combat Beveridge's evils through state action:

- The National Health Service (NHS) to combat disease
- Full employment to combat idleness
- State education to fifteen to combat ignorance (actually introduced in 1944 by the wartime National Government)
- Public housing to combat squalor
- The National Insurance (NI) and Assistance schemes to combat want.

At the same time local authority (LA) children's and mental health departments introduced comprehensive social service provision too. All of these policy changes, and the subsequent development of them, are discussed in more detail in Part 2.

This was probably the most intensive period of social policy reform ever experienced in the UK. The head of the LSE Department of Social Science and Administration at the time was T. H. Marshall. In a famous treatise on citizenship (1950) he argued that the earlier development of civil and political citizenship in British society had been complemented in the mid-twentieth century by the creation of *social citizenship*. With the expansion of public funding for comprehensive state services it is easy to see how this embodiment of social citizenship and the new role that it included for the state as the provider of social services came to be seen as the creation of a welfare state.

Furthermore, the post-war welfare state appeared to have widespread political and ideological support. Although most of the reforms were introduced by the Labour government elected in 1945, when Labour were replaced by the Conservatives in 1951, the state welfare services were maintained in almost exactly the same form. The general assumption was that there was a political consensus over the desirability of state welfare provision within a capitalist economy. In 1954 *The Economist* magazine coined the phrase *Butskellism* to refer to this consensus, which was an amalgamation of the names of the Labour Chancellor of the Exchequer, Gaitskell, and his Conservative successor, Butler (also the author of the 1944 education reform) (Dutton 1991). This consensus seemed to represent an accommodation in Conservative thinking to the role of state intervention, referred to by Macmillan as *The Middle*

Way (1938), and a recognition in Labour thinking of the abandonment of the need for a future socialist revolution (Crosland 1956; Addison 1975). All the post-war governments and prime ministers are listed in Table 1.1.

Table 1.1 UK post-war governments and Prime Ministers		
1945–50	Labour	Attlee
1950–51	Labour	Attlee
1951–55	Conservative	Churchill
1955–59	Conservative	Eden/Macmillan
1959–64	Conservative	Macmillan/Douglas-Home
1964–66	Labour	Wilson
1966–70	Labour	Wilson
1970–74	Conservative	Heath
1974	Labour	Wilson
1974–79	Labour	Wilson/Callaghan
1979–83	Conservative	Thatcher
1983–87	Conservative	Thatcher
1987–92	Conservative	Thatcher/Major
1992–97	Conservative	Major
1997–2001	Labour	Blair
2001–05	Labour	Blair
2005–10	Labour	Blair/Brown
2010–	Coalition (Conservative and Liberal Democrat)	Cameron

The welfare state and the post-war consensus may be seen as significant achievements for social policy but they also presented the subject with something of a challenge, for in a sense they removed the need for further academic and ideological debate and therefore the main basis for future political influence. In the period following the introduction of the welfare state, social work practice and training became more and more concerned with the individualistic, psychoanalytical approach to social problems; voluntary sector activity began relatively to decline; and policy research became restricted to the narrow role of gathering facts to support the case for the gradual expansion and greater effectivity of the now-established agencies of state welfare. The success of Fabianism therefore meant that social policy debate ran the risk of being restricted to analysis and improvement of existing welfare services.

Such a narrow consensual approach was not without its critics, however (see Lowe 1990). In particular the work of Titmuss challenged the supposed comprehensive nature of the new state services and their assumed egalitarian consequences, pointing out that support also took place outside state services and frequently selectively benefited the rich rather than the poor, and directly questioning the concept of the 'welfare state' itself (see Alcock et al. 2001). Evidence of the limitations of state welfare was also developed by Titmuss's colleagues at the LSE. For instance, Townsend and Abel-Smith conducted research, which showed that, despite the welfare reforms to combat want, many people were still living in poverty in Britain in the 1950s and 1960s (Abel-Smith and Townsend 1965; Townsend 1979).

Influential though these criticisms were in questioning the success of the welfare state in meeting all the goals of its Fabian protagonists, they remained to some extent within an overall Fabian framework of academic and political debate that continued to dominate social policy. Titmuss and his colleagues were staunch supporters of the principles behind the state welfare services introduced after the war and their criticisms were intended to create pressure to improve these rather than to question their basic desirability. By the 1970s, however, changes in Britain's welfare capitalist economy were beginning to create the climate for a challenge to the assumed desirability of the maintenance and gradual expansion of the post-war welfare state; and more critical voices were beginning to develop within social policy debate to challenge the Fabian domination of debate and research.

COMPREHENSION QUESTIONS

- Why did social administration change its name to social policy?
- What is 'Fabianism', and to what extent did Fabian thinking dominate the development of British social policy in the last century?

REFLECTIVE QUESTION

- What are the implications for students and practitioners of the recognition that social policy is a *prescriptive* subject?

THE NEW LEFT

Towards the end of the 1960s and the beginning of the 1970s, the rapid expansion of higher education saw social policy becoming established as an academic subject in most British universities and expanding its research base with increased state and charitable support for an ever wider range of projects on the implementation of state welfare. In 1967 the professional association was established, and in 1971 a major academic journal for the subject was launched: the *Journal of Social Policy* (*JSP*).

However, the expansion of social policy also brought into the subject a wider range of academics and practitioners, not all of whom shared the Fabian perspective or the LSE roots of its earlier members. The late 1960s and early 1970s was a period of the renaissance of Marxist and other radical debate within the social sciences in most welfare capitalist countries, referred to by many of the leading protagonists as the *New Left*. The expanding base of social policy brought this debate into the politics and ideology of welfare too.

Marxist theorizing covered a range of different, and disputed, approaches to social structure and social policy but, in general, there was agreement among many that the achievement of the welfare state in post-war Britain and the Fabian-supported consensus on the gradual and unilinear growth of welfare protection were neither as successful, nor as desirable, as had been assumed. Pointing to the empirical work of Titmuss, Townsend and others, Marxists argued that the welfare state had not succeeded in solving the social problems of those in poverty and the broader working class and, in practice, operated to *support* capitalism rather than to *challenge* it (Ginsburg 1979). They argued, therefore, for a rejection of the consensual, Fabian, approach to the understanding of, and support for, state welfare and its replacement with a *political economy of the welfare state* (Gough 1979), which situated the explanation of the growth of state welfare in the needs of the capitalist economy for healthy and educated workers and the struggle of the working class for concessions from the capitalist state (sometimes referred to as the *social wage*).

By the 1980s the influence of the left was no longer a 'new' feature of the subject; theoretical debate between Marxists and Fabians about the desirability, or the compatibility, of their different approaches to the subject ranged widely (Taylor-Gooby and Dale 1981). In 1981 a new journal, *Critical Social Policy (CSP)*, was launched to provide a forum for such debates and for other alternative approaches to theory and research in social policy.

The New Left critics challenged the theoretical assumptions of the post-war consensus approach to state welfare, arguing for a conflict model that saw welfare reforms as the product of struggle and compromise rather than gradual enlightenment (Saville 1983). They also challenged the assumed desirability of state welfare services, arguing that for many working-class people welfare services such as council housing or social security were experienced as oppressive and stigmatizing. These criticisms were not only informed by Marxism: the pages of *CSP*, in particular, were also filled with academics and practitioners arguing that state welfare was also failing women, ethnic minorities and other oppressed or marginalized social groups (an issue to which we shall return in Chapter 17).

It is perhaps no coincidence that the New Left challenge to the Fabian domination of social policy was occurring at more or less the same time as the welfare state itself was also under threat from Britain's changing economic and political fortunes. The failure of economic growth in the 1970s discussed in Chapter 15 to continue to provide a platform for expanding state welfare was argued by Marxists to be an inevitable consequence of the inability to reform capitalism from within and was evidence that the process was beginning to experience a 'crisis' in which stark choices would have to be faced by social policy planners and politicians (see Mishra 1984). However, the crisis – if crisis it was – in state welfare of the 1970s not only attracted a critical reappraisal of the Fabian domination of social policy from the left, but it also provoked a counter-attack from right-wing theorists.

THE NEW RIGHT

Despite the overriding influence of Fabianism within social policy, especially during the immediate post-war period, right-wing critics of state welfare had always argued against the interference of state provision with the workings of a capitalist market economy (Hayek 1944). During the 1950s, through the work of organizations such as the Institute of Economic Affairs (IEA), the appeal for a 'return' to the classic liberal values of a *laissez-faire* state and self-protecting families and communities was kept alive, if rather marginalized from mainstream social policy debate. In the 1970s, however, the crisis in the welfare state created circumstances in which such right-wing critics of state welfare could present a more cogent attack on Butskellism. What is more, this academic attack was accompanied by a shift to the right in politics too, exemplified by the election of Margaret Thatcher as leader of the Conservative Party in 1975. Together these changes provided an opportunity towards the end of the last century for a new liberalism (neoliberalism) to rise to a prominence in academic and political debate that it had not achieved at any time in the previous 80 years.

Drawing on the work of right-wing American theorists such as Friedman (1962) and Murray (1984), the IEA (now *Civitas*) and others began to develop a neoliberal critique of state welfare and Fabian politics that both they, and their left-wing critics, began to refer to as the *New Right*. Not of course that these views were that new either, as we shall discuss in Chapter 14, they drew on classical liberal thinking from the nineteenth century and before. Their main argument was that state intervention to provide welfare services, and the gradual expansion of these which Fabianism sought, drove up the cost of public expenditure to a point at which it began to interfere with the effective operation of a market economy (Bacon and Eltis 1976). They claimed that this was a point that had already been reached in Britain in the 1970s as the high levels of taxation needed for welfare services had reduced profits, crippled investment and driven capital overseas – concerns which resurfaced after the 2008 recession.

Like the New Left, the New Right also challenged the desirability of state welfare in practice, arguing that free welfare services only encouraged feckless people to become dependent upon them and provided no incentive for individuals and families to protect themselves through savings or insurance (Boyson 1971). Furthermore, right-wing theorists claimed that state monopoly over welfare services reduced the choices available to people to meet their needs in a variety of ways and merely perpetuated professionalism and bureaucracy (Green 1987).

After 1979, once the Conservative Party under Thatcher's leadership came into power, these academic arguments found a sympathetic hearing from government ministers such as Keith Joseph and Rhodes Boyson. However, the more extreme forms of New Right thinking never completely dominated the Conservative governments of the 1980s and 1990s. Even under Thatcher the influence of the right (dubbed the *dries*) was to some extent counter-balanced by those more sympathetic to a continuing role for the state (the *wets*); and although, as we shall see in Part 2, significant reforms were made to many public welfare services, the basic principles of comprehensive public services for health, education, social security and social services remained largely intact. Thatcher herself was removed from power in 1990 and after that the Conservative government adopted a more pragmatic approach under John Major.

THE THIRD WAY AND THE BIG SOCIETY

By the 1990s, therefore, the domination that Fabianism had enjoyed over social policy had been overturned from two contradictory directions and, at the same time, its influence on government through support for the Butskellite consensus had been displaced by a political climate in which controversy was widely preached and the value of traditional academic analysis and empirical research openly questioned.

Furthermore, it was not just those from the left and right of the political spectrum who were challenging the consensual approach to welfare: other critical perspectives too were questioning the central role of Fabianism and the benign view of state welfare. Feminist writers began to question what they claimed was the male domination of academic social policy and the assumptions about unequal gender roles that were contained in much practical social policy provision (Wilson 1977; Dale and Foster 1986). In a critical reappraisal of social policy analysis throughout the post-war period Williams (1989) argued that both the gender and racial (or racist) dimensions of policy practice had been largely ignored by mainstream debate; and, as we shall see in Chapter 17, the importance of other social divisions has also now come to influence academic argument and policy development. This wider range of critical perspectives has also opened up a debate about the extent to which complex social organizations and social processes could ever be captured within the simplistic left/right dichotomies that had had such a dominant influence over policy debate throughout much of the last century. Within a modern (or perhaps a 'postmodern') society it was argued there are many contradictory and conflicting influences on social policy and no one approach can meet all needs in all circumstances (see Chapter 14).

The abandonment of old certainties had also influenced political and policy development by the beginning of the twenty-first century. When Tony Blair became leader of the Labour Party in 1994 he began a thorough review of past policy priorities, which led to a rebranding of the party as *New Labour* and a rejection of many of the state welfare commitments of past Labour governments. Drawing on a distinction developed by a Commission on Social Justice (Borrie 1994) appointed by his predecessor John Smith, Blair argued that New Labour should reject both right-wing pro-market approaches and old left support for monopolistic state services in favour of a *Third Way* for policy development, located between the state and the market (Blair 1998). When Labour came to power in 1997 this new approach quickly came to dominate both political debate and policy practice in the UK.

However, it was not just within the UK that a third way for welfare reform was promoted at the beginning of the new century. Some of Labour's early policy prescriptions owed much to the reforms developed by the Clinton administration in the USA. In Europe too Third Way principles were espoused, most notably by the Social Democratic government in Germany under Schröder, which referred to this as *Die Neue Mitte* (the new middle); and this approach largely survived Schröder's loss of power in 2006.

The Labour government's embrace of a third way in the UK was in part based on a recognition of a changed understanding of the more complex make-up of modern societies, drawing on the work of Giddens (1998, 2002, 2007), a close adviser to Blair. In part, however, it was also a product of a more pragmatic approach to policy-making and service delivery, captured by the government slogan 'what counts is what works'. Rather than assuming that services are best provided by the state (the old, Fabian, left) or the market (the New Right), the Labour government claimed to be concerned only with what was the most effective way to meet the needs of citizens; and this was a practical judgement based on empirical evidence of effectiveness rather than any ideological commitment to any particular form of provision.

As policies developed in the new century, there was increasing debate, therefore, about the extent to which the Third Way was a new philosophy for welfare provision in (post)modern society or merely an eclectic pragmatism within which different mixes of provision and organization might be supported at particular times or in different particular circumstances. This is a debate upon which social policy academics take both sides (see Powell 1999, 2002, 2008; Driver and Martell 2006; Page 2007). Nevertheless it is possible to identify some key themes that informed UK policy development under Labour:

- A shift from *negative* to *positive* welfare – the expectation that citizens should take some responsibility for planning and meeting welfare needs
- A focus on the funding of services by different providers rather than automatic provision by the state, with audit and inspection to ensure that basic *standards* are maintained
- A focus upon the needs, and the preferences or *choices*, of the consumers of welfare and a rejection of uniform and undifferentiated service provision.

When Brown succeeded Blair as Labour Prime Minister this policy direction continued largely unabated. It was also taken up to some extent by the Conservative Party in opposition once David Cameron became leader in 2005. Cameron was keen to distance the Conservatives from the New Right politics of the Thatcher era and position them as a centre-right party to challenge New Labour (Bochel 2011); and in the 2010 general election this proved successful – to some extent – as Labour lost the election and the Conservatives emerged as the largest party in the Commons. However, the Conservatives could not govern alone and therefore formed a Coalition government with the Liberal Democrats, the first formal coalition since the Second World War (Lee and Beech 2011).

Coalition with the Liberal Democrats further reinforced the Conservatives' move to the centre ground of British politics, reinforcing a reverse from the more conflictual politics that had developed in the 1970s and 1980s. Once he took over as Prime Minister, Cameron sought to promote the new political approach of the Coalition government particularly to welfare provision in England by referring to it as creating the *Big Society*. This was a concept he and the Conservatives had developed in opposition, although the Liberal leader, Clegg, also embraced it in government. Like New Labour's Third Way, it was intended to capture the Conservatives' rejection of both monopoly public services (the 'big state') and unfettered free markets, which some argued had caused the economic recession (see Chapter 15). However, like the Third Way, it was also rather vague and could be used to cover a range of policy developments.

Like New Labour, the Big Society embraced changes in the 'welfare mix' to encourage private and voluntary organizations to take over delivery of welfare services from the state, and an increasing focus upon consumer choice as the key driver for the development of provision. The Big Society also continued Labour's emphasis on the positive role of citizens in meeting their own welfare needs, but sought to extend this beyond policies to encourage job seeking (see Chapter 13) to promote citizen and community based initiatives to define and deliver a wide range of welfare services locally. Also referred to as 'localism' the Coalition policy agenda therefore aimed to shift the balance of power in policy-making and delivery away from central government and towards local citizens. As this was being developed at the same time as the severe reductions in public provision discussed in Chapter 15, however, some critics argued that the Big Society was little more than a cover for welfare cuts. Nevertheless, the Labour opposition also supported aspects of the Big Society, pointing out that many features continued initiatives they had developed in power

This provided further signs of a return to a more consensual middle ground in social policy in the early years of the twenty-first century. Although, as with the Butskellite consensus of the post-war years, it was not without difference and disagreement, in particular over the scale of reductions in public expenditure needed to respond to the economic crisis and the value of public provision within the Big Society. Following devolution there were also differences in Scotland, Wales and Northern Ireland, where the Big Society agenda did not catch on and support for public service provision remained relatively stronger.

COMPREHENSION QUESTIONS

- To what extent were the New Left and the New Right critics of state welfare arguing that public provision for welfare was incompatible with the effective operation of a capitalist market economy?
- In what ways is the Coalition's *Big Society* different from Labour's *Third Way*?

REFLECTIVE QUESTION

- Has a new consensus on welfare policy in the UK emerged at the beginning of the new century?

COMPARATIVE PERSPECTIVES

Throughout much of its early development social policy had remained, like many other academic subjects in the social sciences, concerned almost exclusively with policy change and policy implementation in Britain. This is perhaps understandable, for Britain has had a more or less self-contained social and legal order and a government with the power to introduce policies affecting the lives of all people in the country. British social policy students thus studied Britain, and the description of, and the prescription for, welfare policy focused primarily on Britain and its government. However, as we are all now very much aware, the lives of people in Britain are not only affected by the decisions and actions of British governments.

In the twenty-first century we live in what is an increasingly globalized world order, where the power and influence of major international companies is greater than that of many individual nation states. As we discuss in Chapter 15, no government, including the British one, can now operate independently of such global forces. Furthermore, as we shall see in Chapter 7, major decisions on economic and social development, affecting people in many countries, are taken on an international scale by bodies operating over and above the remit of national governments, such as the World Bank and the International Monetary Fund (IMF). Of particular importance for the UK is the European Union (EU) of which Britain is a member, and within which the decisions taken by the representative bodies of the EU have a direct impact upon policy development in its member nations. Social policies in Britain are thus no longer exclusively British – if indeed they ever really were – and the subject of social policy has been required to recognize, and to analyse, this broader international dimension.

Both left- and right-wing critics of Fabian social policy were, of course, able to point to the lessons that could be learned from policy development in other countries. Some of those on the left looked to the socialist countries of the Soviet bloc although, even before the collapse of Soviet socialism, others were drawing attention instead to the social democratic countries of Scandinavia as models for welfare reform in Britain. Those on the right used the Soviet bloc as a negative example, and argued rather for policy changes modelled on the market-oriented welfare provisions found in the USA. What was clear to all was that the welfare policies, or the welfare states, of other countries demonstrated that social policies did not *have* to be as they were in Britain. Recognition of the importance of international comparison radically changes the focus of debate within social policy; but it, too, is not without its problems and disagreements. For a start, much of the early development of social policy in Britain had been presented as a gradual extension of state welfare, as if driven by a kind of inexorable law of progress, and tempered only by questions of speed, not direction. International comparisons initially tended to be dominated by similar assumptions. The expectation was that other countries would be following the same pattern of state welfare growth as Britain, albeit perhaps at a different pace. This assumption of international congruity is sometimes called a *convergence* thesis, because all nations are assumed to be converging towards one common goal.

Although it is true that most developed countries have introduced policies to make some provision for the welfare of citizens, this convergence thesis can, however, only be sustained at a level of massive simplification. More detailed study of the welfare policies of other countries, even of Britain's nearby neighbours in the EU, reveals significant differences in the form, and the extent, of social policies, and in the political pressures that have given rise to them (George and Taylor-Gooby 1996; Bonoli et al. 2000; Taylor-Gooby 2004; Castles et al. 2010). By the 1980s social policy scholars in Britain and elsewhere were increasingly concerned to make such international comparisons, not merely in order to argue for the importation into Britain of models of welfare provision from other countries, but rather to demonstrate, at a more general theoretical and empirical level, the widespread diversity within welfare states. They sought, in effect, to challenge the convergence thesis with a celebration of difference, or a *divergence* thesis (Mishra 1990; and see Alcock and Craig 2009; Alcock and Powell 2011).

The development of comparative analysis in social policy can be traced back in particular to the work of Titmuss, who did much to promote policy development in other countries and developed an approach to comparative study of welfare states using three models drawn from the different value positions underlying their development (Titmuss 1974). Perhaps the most influential contribution to comparative analysis, and to the divergence thesis, however, has come from the Scandinavian academic, Esping-Andersen (1990). Esping-Andersen carried out a detailed study of the welfare states of a number of developed welfare capitalist countries, concluding that the different developments could be roughly grouped into different types of *welfare regime*, as we explore in more detail in Chapter 7. Esping-Andersen's regime approach has dominated comparative social policy study over two decades, and has revealed that comparative analysis can draw on both theoretical analysis and empirical data to help us to understand better the different ways in which policy develops in different contexts.

Comparative analysis is no longer just a concern for students of social policy at international level, however. Since the devolution of politics and policy-making to the new administrations in Scotland, Wales and Northern Ireland in 1999, different welfare regimes have been developing to some extent within the UK too. The impact of this devolution is discussed in more detail in Chapter 6, and the important differences in policy that have developed in the new century are mentioned throughout the text. It is important to remember though that these 'internal' differences can form an interesting basis for comparative understanding of how policies are changed and developed from what was before 1999 largely common base; and analysis of this UK dimension to policy divergence is now beginning to emerge (see Lodge and Schmuecker 2010).

THE WELFARE MIX

What the different forms of welfare regime to be found in other countries reveal, of course, is that welfare policies develop in different ways in different social, economic and political contexts. These differences also reveal a varying balance within different regimes between the place of the state in the provision of welfare, for example, with public welfare playing a major role in social democratic regimes such as Sweden and the private market playing a major role in liberal regimes such as the USA. It is not, however, only the balance between the state and the market which varies between different regimes. In corporatist regimes such as Germany, considerable emphasis is placed on the informal role of family structures in providing welfare support (for instance, in the care of children or the long-term chronically sick). In other regimes, such as the 'welfare societies' of some Mediterranean countries including Greece and Spain, many welfare services are provided by voluntary agencies including churches and other religious organizations.

In other words, in different welfare states there is a variation between the roles of different *sectors* in the provision of welfare services. We shall return in Part 1 to look at the roles of these different sectors, in Britain in particular, in more detail. However, it is important to recognize here that it is not just that the balance between the different sectors varies between different welfare states, or welfare regimes, but also that this balance may vary within any one welfare state over time (especially, of course, if that welfare state is experiencing a move from one regime to another). Indeed, it is primarily upon the balance between the roles of the different sectors of welfare that the nature of the welfare regime in any one country at any one time can be determined; and in all regimes there will inevitably be such a balance.

Despite the public welfare reforms which established the 'welfare state' in Britain in the 1940s and pro-market reforms of the New Right in the 1980s, welfare services in this country have in practice remained a mixture of state, market, voluntary and informal provision. Furthermore, the balance of this mixture has changed over time, with private market and other non-state forms of welfare growing in importance since the end of the last century. The general point is, however, that there has always been a balance between the providers of services. Some commentators have referred to this as a *mixed economy* of welfare, and argued that this welfare mix is actually a more accurate term to describe the overall nature of provision in Britain, and elsewhere, than the welfare state (Powell 2007).

The welfare mix has also now received formal political recognition in the Third Way policies developed by New Labour and the Coalition government's Big Society. Concern to encourage public services to be delivered by a range of providers has led to support for new forms of market provision (for private pensions), voluntary activity (delivery of health and social care by non-profit organizations) and informal welfare (continuing reliance upon family support for vulnerable citizens). The Labour Prime Minister, Tony Blair, argued that government should be 'a partner to strong communities' (1998: 7); and the Coalition government has pledged to put the Big Society 'at the heart of public sector reform' (Cabinet Office 2010a).

Most commentators would probably now agree that welfare services in Britain, as in all other welfare capitalist societies, are best described as a welfare mix, with different elements delivered in different measure by different means. The role of social policy analysis therefore is to study the development and operation of these measures and these means and to use theoretical argument and empirical research to seek to influence them. This requires:

- awareness of the structures and contexts within which social policies are developed and delivered
- knowledge of the aims and features of key areas of policy practice
- understanding of the theories and debates which underpin policy development and of the important issues which affect the availability and use of services.

It is these different dimensions of analysis that will be taken up in the next three sections of this book.

COMPREHENSION QUESTIONS

- What is the difference between convergence and divergence approaches to comparative analysis of developments in the international context for welfare policy?
- What is a 'mixed economy of welfare'?

REFLECTIVE QUESTION

- Does it make any sense now to refer to Britain as having a 'welfare state'?

FURTHER READING

There is no book dealing directly with the development of the study of social policy. However, Bulmer, Lewis and Piachaud (1989) provide an interesting history of the development of the work of the academic department at the LSE; and Alcock et al. (2001) collect together (with commentaries) the key works of its leading scholar Titmuss. Alcock et al. (2012) provides a wide range of contributions from leading authors on social policy; and Baldock et al. (2011) is a more detailed edited collection of chapters on key areas of welfare policy. There are also larger edited collections covering social policy analysis at an international level: Castles et al. (2010) includes new contributions from across the world and Alcock and Powell (2011) is a compendium of previously published material.

Powell and Hewitt (2002) is a good overview of changing conceptions of the welfare state. There are a number of books that aim to provide a history of the development of social policy provision in the UK. Fraser (2009) goes back to the early roots of policy before the nineteenth century; Lowe (2005) provides an overview of developments in the second half of the last century; and Glennerster (2006) focuses in more detail upon policy changes over the same period. Timmins's (2001) discussion of post-war welfare policy in the UK is a fascinating study of some of the politics behind the policy process and Hay and Wincott (2012) look at a range of influences on state welfare provision in Europe including the UK. There is a useful website which accompanies the Student's Companion to Social Policy (Brunsdon and May 2012) at www.blackwellpublishing.com/alcock4e/; and some introductory material on the subject is also contained on a site maintained by Paul Spicker at www2.rgu.ac.uk/publicpolicy/introduction/.

Government documents can be accessed through the general government website at www.gov.uk, or though the individual departmental sites listed in later chapters.

PART 1
Structures and Contexts

It is essential to understand how the development and delivery of welfare services are organized and structured – we need to know how social policy is implemented and by whom. The chapters in this section focus on the structures and contexts of provision in order to provide this understanding. The first four chapters cover the 'mixed economy' of welfare provision discussed in Chapter 1. The other two chapters explore the international and local contexts of UK policy development.

The chapter on the state concentrates on the structure and function of the state, including the policy-making process, and then looks more generally at the different roles that the state plays in welfare delivery and the limitations in operation and legitimacy which all states inevitably face. The chapters on market, third sector and informal welfare explain the continuing importance of these different forms of welfare delivery within the welfare mix as it has changed over the development of modern social policy. What is clear from this is how significant these different forms of welfare provision are, and yet how their structure and operation have changed over time, in particular in terms of their relationship with the state. In part an understanding of these different sectors of welfare includes also an appreciation of the ways in which changing public policies have sought to control and influence what is done within them. As with state welfare, there are also limits to the extent, and the effectiveness, of these different sectors of provision; and these too are critically discussed.

The next chapter examines the internal dimensions of policy-making and policy delivery within the UK. Devolution of powers from the central UK government to the separate administrations in Scotland, Wales and Northern Ireland at the beginning of the new century is now an important dimension of policy development, which has been having an ever more extensive impact on policy diversity within the UK. The extent of political and policy devolution is explained, and the ways in which this has led to a more diverse range of policy developments across the four countries are discussed. The chapter then goes on to explore the important role that local government has played, and continues to play, in social policy development and delivery in the country, and reveals that in practice a large part of social policy continues to be locally, rather than centrally, controlled.

British society is no longer simply a national phenomenon, however – indeed arguably it never was. The UK is part of a broader global social order, and this international context influences what happens here, both directly and indirectly. This global context is discussed and the role of comparative social policy analysis in helping us to understand it is briefly outlined. Britain's membership of the EU provides a particular, and more extensive, influence on national policy-making, however; and this is examined in more depth, discussing in particular the ways in which EU policy-making is now incorporated into UK policy practice.

2
The State

SUMMARY OF KEY POINTS

- State provision of welfare is an essential element of social policy, for only the state has the power and the legitimacy to act on behalf of all citizens.
- The provision of welfare through the state has operated both to support economic growth and protect citizens from some of the social problems caused by economic markets.
- The welfare reforms of the 1940s have sometimes been argued as leading to the establishment of the 'Keynes/Beveridge welfare state' in Britain.
- Expenditure on state welfare grew gradually both in absolute and relative terms throughout the last century, and in particular after the post-war reforms.
- The British state is made up of an executive (the Cabinet), a legislature (Parliament) and a judiciary (the courts). However, much control over policy is in practice held by civil servants working in government departments.
- Policy-making in the UK is partly devolved to the different national administrations and to local government.
- As well as acting as a *provider* of services the state also *commissions* and *regulates* other providers, and acts as a major *employer*.
- The continued expansion of state welfare has been questioned by ever-increasing demands for services and debate about the limits of public expenditure on welfare, with significant cuts planned in the early 2010s to respond to high levels of government borrowing.

THE 'WELFARE STATE'

The main focus of study and debate in social policy has been the 'welfare state'. As we discussed in Chapter 1, the Fabian pioneers of social policy in the early twentieth century were concerned first and foremost with developing academic research and political argument that would put pressure on the UK government to use the power of the state to introduce welfare reforms to respond to the social problems which they had identified. Their expectation was that if evidence could be produced to demonstrate that the capitalist economy was operating in ways that were leading to hardship or deprivation, it would be the duty of the state to intervene to alleviate or prevent this hardship. Their intention was that this intervention should take the form of services provided directly by the state, using resources collected from citizens in the form of taxation.

Quite how far the state should go in providing such services, of course, has always been a matter of debate and disagreement, both within social policy and beyond. However, after the introduction of public provision for education and social security in the early decades of the last century, the debate about state welfare has become very much one about *how much* state provision there should be, as opposed to *whether* there should be any. And as the textbooks on the history of the welfare state explain (Thane 1996; Harris 2004; Fraser 2009), throughout the first half of the century state welfare provision gradually expanded.

This growth was not a product only of the persuasive moral and academic arguments of the Fabian policy reformers: academic and moral argument does not necessarily bring about political change. Nevertheless, the hardship about which the Fabians argued was real and, for those who were its victims, it created a source of active social and economic discord. Britain's capitalist economy thus produced conflict between the poor working class and the rich and powerful; and this was a conflict that produced social movements, not just the theories and statistics of the academics.

The early part of the twentieth century saw the rapid development of such movements, in particular the trade union movement, designed to protect the interests of workers against their capitalist employers, and the Labour Party, supported by the unions, to pursue the collective demands of workers through winning political power within the electoral system. In the 1920s and 1930s the unions engaged in conflict with capital over hardship and deprivation at work; and the Labour Party achieved political power – for periods at least – in central and local government. In these ways the deprivation produced by capitalism created conditions of conflict and struggle from which intervention by the state became an achievable political goal. With Labour governments, in particular, the Fabian policy reformers had a base within the British political system at which to direct their arguments on the need for welfare reform.

However, the causes of the growth in state intervention for welfare in Britain do not lie only in the successful struggle of the working class and its Fabian middle-class allies, for welfare reform has always had a double-edged impact within capitalist economies. Improved state education, for example, provides employers with a better trained and more able workforce; and, as the development of machinery and the introduction of new technologies have made the process of production ever more complex, this has permitted industry to operate more efficiently. Improved housing and health conditions for workers have also improved their overall efficiency, and so have helped the development of the economy. Even social security benefits, although financed in part by contributions from employers, have helped to maintain the unemployed as a labour force in waiting to be rejected or re-employed as economic forces dictate.

The development of the welfare state, therefore, is not only the product of the attempt to remedy the failings in a capitalist economy but also of the recognition of new ways in which this economy might better be maintained and developed. On the one hand, therefore, social policy challenges the operations of capitalist economics, and yet on the other it helps these economies to develop and function more effectively. This dual character was identified by Gough in his seminal text on the political economy of welfare (1979); and more recently international analysis of the development of welfare provision across capitalist economies has revealed the continuing importance of state welfare provision to the economic performance of these countries (Pierson 2001; Goodin et al. 1999; Ellison 2006). The provision of public welfare is now an intrinsic feature of all advanced industrial economies.

In the period immediately following the Second World War these pressures for welfare reform, both from within capital and within the working class, appeared to all come together in Britain:

- A Labour government was elected, after a landslide victory, with manifesto commitments to reform capitalism through state intervention.
- Fabian academics and their allies occupied influential positions within the state: notably Beveridge, author of the report on social security reform, and Keynes, a senior economic adviser to the wartime government.

- British capitalism had experienced significant government intervention as part of the war effort, and it needed rapidly to adjust to the changing demands of peacetime production within a restructured world economy.

It is for these reasons that commentators argued that during this post-war period there was a *consensus* in Britain over the desirability of welfare reform between capital and labour, and between their 'representatives' within the major political parties, and that this consensus created a unique opportunity for the rapid development of the welfare state (Addison 1975).

The Labour government reforms of the 1940s are widely credited as providing the basis for the establishment of the welfare state in Britain, informed by the social policy prescriptions of Beveridge and the economic policy plans of Keynes (see Chapter 15). For this reason it is sometimes referred to as the *Keynes/Beveridge* welfare state. The post-war reforms encompassed a wide range of social and economic changes aimed at eliminating Beveridge's five evils (see Chapter 1); but three features in particular established a new role for the state within the British capitalist economy:

- The development of public social services
- The nationalization of major industries
- The commitment to full employment.

The development of *public social services* included the NHS, state education and the National Insurance (NI) scheme, discussed in Part 2. These were financed out of taxes and contributions from citizens and they recruited employees into state-run organizations to provide services to all who needed them, generally on a universal basis with free access. These state welfare services could be seen as almost 'socialist' in their aims and structures; and there were some on the left (and the right) who hoped (or feared) that they would be a first step towards a more far-reaching socialist restructuring of Britain's capitalist economy. As we shall see, however, Britain's welfare state, even in this immediate post-war period of expansion, was never socialist either in aim or in achievement; as in the earlier part of the century, state provision for health, education and social security operated as much to support the broader capitalist economy as to challenge it. It was also not comprehensive, and private and voluntary provision of many services remained alongside the new state services – sometimes even in competition with them.

The *nationalization* programme of the post-war Labour government also established a new role for the state within British society. Major industries such as coal and steel were taken into public ownership; they were run by state appointed managers, and their workers became state employees. The same happened to the main infrastructural services such as gas, electricity and public transport. Again, these nationalization measures could appear to be elements of a strategy for the 'socialization' of the entire capitalist economy. Certainly they significantly restructured British capitalism by introducing a large state sector no longer under the control of private ownership and the profit motive, and this led some commentators to argue that Britain had therefore been transformed from a capitalist economy into a *mixed economy* (Crosland 1956).

However, even the nationalization of major industries left the vast majority of British capital in private hands, and there was never any intention of carrying through a state takeover of all private firms. Furthermore, the nationalized industries had to trade and contract with private capitalist enterprises and, although they were supported and sometimes subsidized by the state, they were required to operate in the marketplace with profit and loss accounts like private companies. Indeed, the guaranteed operation of such major state industries and services after the 1940s provided both a stable physical and economic environment for private industry and a secure market for many private products. In the welfare field, for instance, the NHS provided a major boost to the development of private drug companies. Public ownership of these major industries and utilities was not sustained, however, and towards the end of the last century privatization measures returned them to the private corporate sector, albeit with continuing regulatory controls from government.

The commitment to *full employment* was in part based on a reaction to the high levels of unemployment experienced during the economic depression of the 1930s, as we discuss in Chapter 13. State intervention to promote employment fitted well with the wider role for economic policy recommended by Keynes. It was his belief that governments could, and should, use their role as employers and investors to encourage growth within market economies, as explained in Chapter 15; and one of the major triggers for such intervention was the commitment to maintain unemployment below an agreed minimum level.

Therefore, although the post-war welfare state transformed the capitalist economy in Britain, it did not replace it. The political consensus in favour of welfare reform through the state was as much a matter of compromise as a meeting of minds; it was predicated upon the assumption that state welfare reforms would support, and not prejudice, wider economic growth. What is more, as we discuss in Part 2, the development of state welfare did not entirely displace private provision in areas such as health and education, and the voluntary and informal sectors of welfare provision continued to operate. In welfare, as in manufacturing, post-war Britain became a mixed economy in which state provision was only a part of the overall picture.

This was a picture, nonetheless, in which it seemed that state welfare provision was able to grow ever more rapidly to meet more and more social needs as British society became increasingly affluent in the years following the war; expanding welfare could even be seen as part of an inevitable process of development within a capitalist economy. This can be seen most clearly in the growing size of state welfare as a proportion of economic activity in the country. As Figure 2.1 reveals, welfare expenditure has grown dramatically from around 2.5 per cent of GDP in 1900 to ten times that at the beginning of the new century, although this is now challenged by the government's commitment to reduce public spending in order to reduce government borrowing. Taylor-Gooby and Stoker (2011) point out that this is planned to reduce overall public spending as a proportion of GDP by around 5 per cent.

As a result of this growth in state welfare services significant social improvements have been achieved: for example, educational standards have risen, mortality and morbidity rates have declined, housing problems have been reduced, and basic living standards increased. However, as we explore in more detail in Chapter 15, such growth was far from inevitable. It was the product of international economic trends and national government policies, both of which can change. And when these have changed, for instance in the 1970s and the 2010s, the future of an ever-expanding welfare state begins to come into question, and the role of public provision may be subject to far more critical scrutiny.

WHAT IS THE STATE?

We probably all have some idea to what we are referring when we talk about the state and state involvement in welfare provision in a country such as Britain; but in fact the various institutions and individuals that comprise the state in a modern developed country together make up quite a complex constitutional picture. Furthermore, the various parts of the state are subject to rules and political conventions that sometimes define fairly closely the powers and responsibilities that they are able to exercise. We do not have room here to examine the complex constitutional processes of the British state, which has now been made more complex by devolution within it; but a brief overview of the main constituent parts, and the different functions that each fulfils in the implementation of economic and social policy, will provide us with some background understanding of both its scale and scope.

Many people perhaps assume that the state is the same thing as the government; and it is obviously the case that in a democracy such as the UK the government has overall power over, and responsibility for, the activities of the state, through the electoral mandate that it

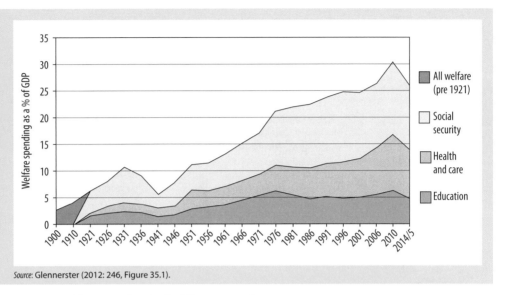

Source: Glennerster (2012: 246, Figure 35.1).

Figure 2.1 Welfare spending in the UK, 1900 to 2015

secures from the population. However, technically speaking, the government is merely the collective views of the majority of Members of Parliament (MPs) in the House of Commons. Parliament also includes the House of Lords, however; and this can, and sometimes does, disagree with the views of MPs. It has recently been reformed by the government in the Commons to reduce the role of hereditary peers and further reform is mooted to move towards a mix of elected and appointed members. All laws enacted by Parliament must be agreed by both Houses, and subsequently must be ratified by the Queen as the constitutional monarch, although in practice this is a formality as the monarch is a figurehead and plays no active part in the legislative process.

However, because of the system of political parties that contest elections in Britain, the government is in practice made up of the senior MPs from the majority party (two parties in the case of the current Coalition government). These meet regularly as a *Cabinet* under the leadership of the Prime Minister to plan future policies and the legislation required to implement them. The Prime Minister thus leads the Cabinet, which is comprised of MPs from majority party (or parties) in the Commons and government supporters in the Lords (see Figure 2.2). Most major policy decisions are made in the Cabinet, and are normally later approved by the majority of MPs in Parliament at Westminster. Policies are then implemented by state employees (civil servants) based in the different departments of the state, with each department being under the overall control of a Secretary of State, who is a member of the Cabinet.

In theory, then, policy is decided by the cabinet in *Westminster*, and is implemented by the civil servants in the departments based (mainly) in *Whitehall*. This Westminster/Whitehall division symbolizes the split between the democratic (policy-making) aspect of the state, and the bureaucratic (policy-implementation) aspect of it, although, as books that concentrate in more detail on the policy-making and policy-implementation process reveal, this division is far from a watertight one in practice: many MPs play little part in policy-making and some civil servants have much power and influence over it (Hill 2009).

Political scientists also often attach importance to the distinction that is made between the policy-making, or legislative, process, and the enforcement of the rights granted by this through the courts under the control of the *judiciary*. Where there is a dispute over the implementation

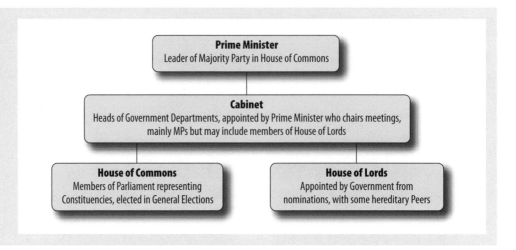

Figure 2.2 UK parliamentary structure

of policies in particular cases, or even over the powers of government to make policy, everyone has the right to go to court for a judicial ruling, although, given the cost of using the law, this is a right that in practice may only be open to those with significant financial resources or to those poor enough to qualify for state support through legal aid. The judges in court are bound to follow the rules laid down by Parliament and by previous legal rulings, through precedent; but in exercising judgement under these rules they are quite independent of the government and of the civil service, and they sometimes make decisions that government ministers or civil servants do not like. Like Westminster and Whitehall, however, the judiciary is part of a centralized state power within Britain. The policies that are developed and the rules that are enforced here are produced on behalf of, and are provided for, the whole of the population.

However, these central state institutions are not the only features of state power involved in the provision of welfare services in the country. State welfare is now developed and delivered within the devolved administrations operating at a new national level within the UK, and there is a significant range of policy delivered by local government (see Chapter 6). UK social policy is also affected by supranational developments within the EU, and beyond (see Chapter 7). In practice, these aspects are as important in determining the shape of the welfare state in the UK as the main arms of central government in London.

The devolved context of state policy-making in Britain is a peculiar product of the constitution of the country as a 'United Kingdom' of formerly separate nations. The UK thus comprises in effect the four *subnations* of England, Scotland, Wales and Northern Ireland (which itself is formally not part of Britain). These countries have always had some degree of legal and policy-making autonomy: for instance, Scotland has always had a separate legal system from that of the rest of the UK. However, significant areas of policy-making practice were devolved to separate administrations in these countries by constitutional changes introduced at the end of the last century, and since then these differences have become more pronounced. We return to discuss these in more detail in Chapter 6.

Scotland now has a separate elected Parliament with the power to legislate in a number of key policy areas, and this has led to some major differences in policy development there such as the abolition of fees for university students and the provision of free care services for frail older people. The Northern Ireland Assembly also has legislative powers in certain areas. It was suspended for a number of years at the beginning of the century following a temporary breakdown in relations between the major political parties in the province; but devolved administration was reinstated in 2007, since when the Assembly has been restored with leadership shared across the major political parties. In Wales the National Assembly initially had only secondary legislative responsibility in areas devolved by Westminster; but these powers were extended in 2006, with the creation of the Welsh Assembly Government (now the Welsh Government), and expanded in 2011 following a national referendum. In both Northern Ireland and Wales too, significant policy divergence has also taken place; and we discuss the main examples of this in Part 2. There is also significant devolution of administrative support for policy implementation with separate civil service structures supporting the different policy regimes in each of the three countries replacing the central control exercised by Whitehall (see Lodge and Schmuecker 2010).

Within England policy-making still takes place in the Parliament at Westminster; there is no separate English legislative body. However, as we discuss in Chapter 6, there was some element of devolution in the 2000s to the broader *regional* areas, such as the North West or the West Midlands, through the creation of Regional Development Agencies. However, these were discontinued in 2010, with regional planning only taking place within a small government office in each region. The role of *local* government has been of critical importance in the development of welfare in Britain. Local authorities (LAs) (or local councils) became subject to democratic election towards the end of the nineteenth century, and since then have played a major role in promoting state provision for education, health, housing and other social services. Indeed, in many ways the creation of the welfare state in the 1940s was really a period of the centralization and standardization within Whitehall of the welfare services developed, albeit unevenly, by local government in the first half of the century.

Public policy-making also operates at a *supranational* level in Britain as a result of the country's membership since 1973 of the EU. As we discuss in Chapter 7, the EU now provides an ever more influential international context for policy development in Europe; and, more immediately, policies and rules determined by the Commission and other EU bodies in Brussels now have a direct impact in all member states, including Britain. Membership of the EU requires all nations to adopt and implement the policy decisions taken by the partner nations, and this has had a cumulative effect in altering British social policy to fit in with broader European practices. In practice, however, as we will see, Britain has sometimes been a rather reluctant partner in the development of EU policy initiatives: for instance, it did not join the single currency (the Euro) when it was established in 2002 and, more recently, the Conservative Party has pledged to both renegotiate the terms of Britain's membership and conduct a yes–no referendum on membership in 2015.

COMPREHENSION QUESTIONS

- To what extent is there central state control over policy-making in the UK?
- What is the relationship between the civil servants (in *Whitehall*) and the politicians (in *Westminster*) in determining the development of state social policy?
- Why is the British welfare state sometimes referred to as the Keynes/Beveridge Welfare State?

THE FUNCTIONS OF THE STATE

PROVISION

Most discussion of state welfare is focused on the social services provided for people by the institutions or agencies of the state; in other words, where the function of the state is as the provider of services. State provision in Britain includes, for example, the NHS, the state education system and the social security benefits schemes. In all of these the state employs workers (doctors, nurses and teachers) based in publicly owned and operated institutions (hospitals and schools) to provide services to all citizens who are in need of, or are entitled to, them. To do this the state uses public money collected by government, largely in the form of taxes, to purchase buildings and equipment and to pay workers; and, depending on the area of provision the plans for spending this money have to be justified and agreed through the political process either at UK level, in the devolved administrations or locally. These spending plans are therefore a central – and potentially therefore a controversial – feature of government policy development.

Clearly such comprehensive provision of services is the most obvious, and arguably the most extensive, function of the state in welfare provision, but it is far from the only one. In addition to being a provider of welfare the state also fulfils other functions that have an equally direct and important impact on the development and implementation of welfare policy within the country.

COMMISSIONING

As well as using public money to provide welfare through public agencies, the state also provides public money to purchase, or commission, the provision of welfare services by commercial, third sector or informal providers. The role of state funding has always been important in the development of non-state welfare, including both direct subsidies, for example, grant funding to voluntary agencies such as the Royal Voluntary Service (RVS), or the Citizens' Advice Bureau (CAB), and indirect support, for example, exemption from taxation through Gift Aid for charities (see Chapter 4).

Whilst direct subsidies such as grants have been the traditional means of supporting non-state delivery of welfare services, there has been a significant move over the last decade or so towards contracts for the delivery of specific services from either private or third sector providers. Through contracts the state can provide funding for organizations to deliver specific services to agreed standards, and these can be specified through a process of commissioning led by the state (see Chapter 18). Here then the state is funding services and determining their form, but delivery comes from other providers.

REGULATION

Commissioning can shape and direct the delivery of private or third sector welfare provision. However, this can also be controlled more directly by legal regulation through the state. State regulation of welfare through the law is perhaps the oldest aspect of state policy intervention. Legal rules set the limits within which private markets have developed and third sector organizations have operated and, of course, regulation also determines the structure of state-provided welfare. As we discussed above, the courts and the judiciary are an important aspect of the use of state power. Through the enactment and enforcement of rules and procedures the state can control a wide range of welfare provision, even where it is not delivered or funded by any public body. Thus commercially provided pensions and health insurance, for instance, are closely regulated through statute law; and third sector bodies are subject to a range of legal controls such as those on the definition and extent of charitable purposes (see Chapter 4).

EMPLOYMENT

Finally, in its role in the provision of services, and in its roles in commissioning and regulating these, the state is also acting as an employer of those working in state institutions such as the courts or government departments. Indeed the state, through both central and local government, is by far the largest employer in Britain. And, of course, for those working for the state their welfare as employees – and any broader occupational protections, such as sick pay or pensions, which they enjoy – are determined by the state as an employer and the policies that it adopts towards its workforce. In addition in the immediate post-war period the state was often held to have a further responsibility, that of operating as a 'model employer' setting an example for others to follow. This notion fell out of favour in the 1980s though it gained greater government support in the 2000s when under the Labour governments public employers were urged to lead the way in developing equal opportunities, work–life balance and other policies.

In practice, however, as an employer, the state has a rather inconsistent record in Britain. Some state employees (for instance, senior civil servants) enjoy some of the best working conditions and most extensive occupational benefits of any employees in the country. However, there are others (for instance, cleaners or porters in schools or hospitals) who are on part-time contracts and levels of pay that leave them needing to claim support under the tax credit system or from 2013, the Universal Credit (UC) scheme, to top up their weekly incomes in order to meet their families' needs. At times of high employment and economic growth the poor conditions in some areas of public employment can make it difficult to recruit and retain staff, with shortages of teachers and nurses being experienced in the early years of this century – especially in parts of the country, such as the South East, where living expenses were higher. Conversely the major cuts in public services after 2011 led to the loss of state employment, especially at LA level, which impacted more severely in former industrial areas of the North and Midlands where public employment had become a more significant proportion of the local labour market.

THE LIMITS OF THE STATE

During the period of the gradual, and incremental, growth of state welfare provision in Britain, in particular in the decades following the Second World War, it seemed to most commentators – and certainly to those acting as protagonists for the growth of state welfare – that there were no limits beyond which state welfare might not extend. There seemed to exist a widely shared assumption that the greater identification of social needs would create the case for improved state services and that continuing economic growth would provide the resources that could be harnessed, through taxation, to pay for these. Thus, although there might be questions about the speed or emphasis of the development of state provision, there could be no doubt about its overall desirability, or viability.

In the last quarter of the last century, however, this assumption about the limitless role for the state began to come into question in Britain – and, indeed, in all other developed welfare regimes. Questions about the limits of the welfare state arose primarily as a result of two developments that may appear to be contradictory but, in practice, are inextricably inter-related.

First, despite the successes of state welfare in meeting welfare needs and reducing social problems, social policy research has continued to provide evidence of further needs and problems that could, or should, be the focus of additional state provision. Some of these problems might be argued to be the result of the failure of state welfare services to meet existing targets: for instance, Abel-Smith and Townsend's (1965) 'rediscovery of poverty' which identified over a million people, mainly pensioners, living below state assistance benefit levels in the early 1960s, and in the 1990s continuing high levels of child poverty resulted in the government committing to adapt policy to reduce this in the future. Others, however, are the product of the more general social and technological progress that has gradually overtaken past provision: for instance, expanding demand for higher education (HE) in universities, or for heart transplants or chemotherapy treatment in the NHS. Whatever the reasons, however, there is no shortage of evidence of the continued existence, and continuing growth, of needs which current state welfare provision does not meet.

Second, alongside the evidence of growing needs, there was recognition in the last quarter of the twentieth century, by both Labour and Conservative governments, that public expenditure on welfare could not simply be expanded indefinitely to meet increased demand. The economic recession of the 1970s and early 1980s forced first Labour and then the Conservatives to restrict, and in places to cut, state welfare expenditure. For Labour this was predominantly in order to reduce the economic 'burden' of public spending, although for the Conservatives, especially in the 1980s, cuts in public provision were also aimed at promoting expanded take-up of private market welfare services.

In fact, despite the cuts, public welfare expenditure continued to grow during these periods, as we saw in Figure 2.1; and this was something of a contradictory outcome for the more outspoken critics of state welfare in the Thatcher governments of the 1980s. Nevertheless, the controls introduced over state expenditure were real, and they did have an effect in restricting some of the planned expansions of spending. This continued throughout the 1990s; and a key element in Labour's successful election campaign in 1997 was a commitment not to seek rises in (especially income) tax and to remain within the previous Conservative spending limits for two years. And although Labour expanded welfare expenditure in the first decade of this century, the Coalition government has pledged to reduce it significantly again between 2011 and 2015 and beyond.

Retrenchment of welfare spending is not just a British phenomenon. There were cutbacks in planned welfare spending in a number of other European countries in the late twentieth century (Bonoli et al. 2000), including even the high spending social democratic regimes in Denmark and Sweden; and these have become more severe since the 2008 recession, especially in countries with high levels of public borrowing, such as Greece and Italy. As Ellison (2006) discusses, this is to some extent an international, or a global, trend; it is driven by international pressures on economic growth and promoted by major international agencies such as the World Bank and the International Monetary Fund (IMF). And by and large it is underpinned by a neoliberal approach (see Chapter 14) that sees extensive public spending and borrowing as threatening economic growth within competitive global markets. As Castles' (1999 and 2004) work reveals, however, this does not mean all countries follow the same patterns of growth and retrenchment; and this was true of responses to the 2008/09 economic crisis too (Farnsworth and Irving 2011).

Thus, although it is recognized that the cost of public services does impose constraints on welfare spending, the nature of these constraints in practice varies in different national contexts and can be subject to economic and political change over time. However, it is not only cost which can set limits to the extent of state welfare. In particular, as a provider of welfare services, there are limits on the ability of the state to recognize and to meet all social needs; and these limits apply, if less obviously, to the state's commissioning and regulatory roles too. State provision of welfare requires the departments of central or local government to identify social needs and then provide services that meet them. However, this is neither a non-controversial nor a one-way process.

Critics have argued that state welfare often fails to identify the welfare needs of many people: for instance, it is often accused of failing to address the needs of many of Britain's ethnic minority communities. Even where needs are identified, state welfare also sometimes provides services that do not adequately satisfy those needs, for instance, the tower blocks of council flats, discussed in Chapter 10, created as many housing problems as they solved and many were later demolished. Although such failings sometimes mean that needs go unmet, they may also lead, indirectly at least, to the development by people of alternative, non-state, forms of welfare service to fill the gaps left by inadequate state services: for instance, through the establishment of community-based, self-help groups in different communities or neighbourhoods, or through the development of housing cooperatives to build, or renovate, houses for rent and even to take over the management of these from LAs. However, although such alternative provision may complement state welfare, it may also create pressure for state provision to be expanded to meet these additional or new needs; and so in some cases non-state activity can led to an extension of public provision.

Moreover, even where they are successfully meeting a range of social needs, state welfare services can also acquire complex, and remote, bureaucratic structures that may alienate or exclude some potential service users (an issue to which we will return in more general terms in Chapter 18). In an influential book published in 1981, Hadley and Hatch argued that there was a contradiction here between the development of state bureaucracies and their ability to meet real social need; and that alternative forms of provision should be welcomed both by policy analysts and by citizens. Of course, as we discuss in Chapters 3, 4, and 5, alternative forms of welfare provision, through the informal, third and private sectors, have in any case continued to coexist, and to grow, alongside state welfare – recognition of their role in welfare was not a new discovery in 1981. And also, as we shall see, these other sectors of provision are not without their own problems and shortcomings. However, recognition that there must be limits to the ability of state provision to identify and meet all needs, or to anticipate and support or regulate the development of all community or private alternatives to state services, is significant in pointing to the limitations in the role of the state that arise from organizational and cultural factors, as well as simply from economic ones; and this is now widely accepted by politicians and policy makers.

There are not just limits to the *maximum* role of the state, however: there are limits to its *minimum* role too. In any complex society a state structure will be needed to organize, to support and to regulate the activities of citizens; and this applies to the provision of welfare as much as it does, for instance, to the control of crime. Although voluntary agencies or private companies may develop services for groups of people, only the state has the legitimacy and the power, politically and legally, to act on behalf of *all* citizens – sometimes referred to as the democratic mandate. Where regulation of the activities of non-state providers is required, for instance to guarantee minimum standards in private education or health care, only the state has the power to provide this. Where financial support is sought, as it often is, to help the development or maintenance of private or voluntary social provision, only the state can call on public resources to provide this. Where commercial, third sector or informal providers cannot, or will not, operate to provide for social needs, only the state can be required to step in.

There have been some extreme right-wing theorists who have argued for a 'return' to a society in which all citizens are able to provide for themselves without public welfare services – for instance, Murray (2006) suggested that all such services should be removed and replaced by an annual cash grant to all adults, from which privately provided services could be purchased. However, there is no evidence that such harmony and wellbeing has ever existed in the past, and certainly no advanced society has been willing or able to countenance the removal or replacement of all state welfare provision. More challenging in practice to the state's central role in welfare provision is the Coalition government's *Big Society* agenda in England, which seeks to promote voluntary and community determination and delivery of welfare services as an alternative to the 'big state' approach of post-war planning. As we shall see in Chapter 4, however, the Big Society may not in practice be such a new policy departure and state provision of and support for welfare services is likely to remain central within it.

Even where state provision is restricted to the role of a 'safety net', to catch those who slip between the gaps in private and voluntary provision, it is still there to prevent citizens falling through, and perhaps starving or freezing to death. Of course, in practice the safety net may not always work, but that has not been used as an argument for removing it: indeed, it is more likely to be used to argue for strengthening it. And even where alternative forms of independent provision are openly promoted and supported by government, they require state funding and regulation to guarantee minimum standards and ensure that all can access services.

As we discussed at the beginning of this chapter, therefore, the debate about the role of the state in welfare services in Britain, and indeed in other advanced industrial societies, is a debate about the *extent* of state welfare, not about the overall *need* for it. Welfare provision in modern capitalist societies requires the state to play a range of roles in the provision and control of social services. Of course, such state provision and control of welfare have their limits, both minimum and maximum; but the extent of those limits is the result of political processes, not some iron laws of market freedom or socialist development. The role of the state thus varies in different countries, and it changes over time, but in some form or other it is always there.

COMPREHENSION QUESTIONS

- To what extent does the burden of taxation set a limit on the scale of state welfare provision?
- What is the 'democratic mandate', and why is it thought to justify an indispensable role for the state in social policy provision?
- Is the 'Big Society' an alternative to the state?

REFLECTIVE QUESTION

- Should the state aim to provide comprehensive social services for all citizens?

FURTHER READING

A good introduction to the academic study of the role of the state is provided by Schwartzmantel (1994). Timmins (2001) provides the best, and most interesting, account of the development of the welfare state in Britain, although Glennerster (2006) is also a good summary of the post-war role of state welfare policy and a readable account can be found in Fraser (2009). The contributors to Powell (2007) explain the different aspects of the mixed economy of welfare in Britain and the role of the state within this. Ellison (2006) discusses the international context and the changing external pressures on welfare states in latter part of the last century and Jordan and Drakeford (2012) provide insights into the implications of more recent austerity measures. For a broader introduction to political processes and issues it is worth looking at one of the introductory political science texts, such as Moran (2011) and the online summaries in Brunsdon and May (2012) at www.blackwellpublishing. com/alcock4e/. Recent and current government information can be accessed at www.gov.uk and the websites for the devolved administrations: www.scotland.gov.uk, www.wales.gov.uk and www.niassembly.gov.uk.

3
The Market

SUMMARY OF KEY POINTS

- Markets, or commercial provision of welfare, exist in all countries, but the balance between the state and the market within the welfare mix varies significantly across different countries.
- The proponents of free markets argue that they constitute a natural social order and that state intervention will inevitably distort this by reducing choice and introducing inefficient monopoly providers.
- Critics of free markets argue that state intervention is needed to support and control market activity, to ensure that those who cannot afford market prices are not excluded, and to meet those needs which markets cannot address.
- Private market provision exists alongside public services in all areas of welfare in , including those such as health and schooling where public provision is free for all.
- In the 1980s a policy of 'privatization' encouraged the development of a wider range of market-based welfare, although basic state services were largely retained.
- Quasi-markets are an attempt to use market principles of choice and competition to shape state welfare practice. They were introduced in a number of British public services in the 1990s.
- Private investment in public services has been encouraged since the 1990s through joint capital programmes such as the Private Finance Initiative (PFI) and partnership funding for academies and free schools.
- In the twenty-first century under Labour and the Coalition, the state's role as service procurer and enabler has been extended and the contracting out of public services has expanded the role of commercial providers of welfare, especially in England.

THE COMMERCIAL SECTOR

The supply of social services through the welfare state is often discussed by commentators as public provision of welfare, and this is contrasted with *private* provision arranged by individuals, families or organizations outside the state. This distinction between public and private welfare is a bit misleading, however, because much private provision is public in the sense that it is in the public domain and available to any would-be purchaser, which is why fee-paying schools are sometimes referred to as 'public schools' (see Chapter 12). Private health care, for instance, is publicly available, and indeed is advertised as such on television. The public/private distinction might, therefore, be better used to distinguish between individual and family-provided services and those provided collectively to a range of people either through the state or by other agencies. We will return in Chapter 5 to examine this 'private' dimension in more detail; but such a distinction is not one widely used in social policy literature.

More commonly, social policy analysts distinguish between state and non-state services. This too can be misleading, however, if non-state is taken to mean exclusively profit-based, private market provision for, as we shall see in Chapter 4, not all non-state welfare provision is profit-based. There is in fact a vast range of non-profit or third sector organizations engaged in all kinds of welfare activity, and operating according to different aims and principles from both the state and the market sectors. We need to distinguish in addition, therefore, between these non-profit, third sector organizations and those operating for profit on a commercial basis, referred to in the US as 'for-profit' organizations. It is perhaps this commercial aspect that does serve best to distinguish these organizations from both the state and the voluntary sector, and from the private, informal, sector too.

Commercial organizations operate with budgets and balance sheets. They levy charges for services and use these to employ workers and invest in equipment to provide future services. They also generally seek to make a profit out of the difference between their charges and the costs of provision. For most commercial organizations it is the expectation of profit that is the motivating factor for the establishment and development of them by their owners or shareholders, who will benefit from the profit, although on some occasions charges may not exceed costs and no profit, in practice, is made. In fact there are many small (and not-so-small) commercial organizations that do not set out to make a profit. These include small residential homes, whose owners merely wish to recover their operating costs, as well as some major institutions, such as building societies providing mortgages to house buyers, which are mutually owned by their investors and borrowers and do not pass on profits to shareholders.

More recently this boundary has also been blurred by the development of *social enterprises* that operate as commercial companies but seek to reinvest some or all of their 'profit' in non-commercial social or environmental causes. There are debates about the extent to which these social enterprises should be seen as part of the private sector or the third sector, and in practice some of them operate across this boundary (Peattie and Morley 2008; Teasdale 2012). However, they have been growing in importance in the provision of welfare services, with the government directly encouraging public providers, such as health service trusts, to leave the public sector and establish themselves as independent social enterprises, sometimes under employee ownership schemes.

Nevertheless, even where they are not profit-seeking or like social enterprises use their profits for social ends, commercial organizations such as these can still generally be distinguished from both state and voluntary sector agencies by their financial structure, in particular by the charges they make for services, and the location of their operations within a competitive market. We might, therefore, most accurately call these organizations the *commercial* sector but, in practice, social policy commentators commonly refer to them as the *market*, especially when the market is being contrasted with the *state*.

To complicate matters commercially-based welfare includes a further form of provision, also often included in the notion of market welfare. This is the services and benefits or *occupational welfare* offered to employees as part of employer's human resource management strategies (Brunsdon and May 2007). Such provision, which is more common in large than small organizations, has traditionally been a feature of state as well as private and third sector employment (see Chapter 13). It may be furnished directly, but is often supplied by commercial agencies trading in welfare goods and services.

Market-based activity of course extends far beyond welfare services. Most goods and services in are exchanged through markets, and the labour market provides the main means of employment and subsistence for the majority of the population, either directly or indirectly. It was the growth of a market basis for production and distribution in the seventeenth and eighteenth centuries that established the basis for the development of capitalism in Britain, and for the creation of modern society in the nineteenth and twentieth centuries. And it was in this capitalist market economy that state welfare developed in the twentieth century, as we discussed in Chapter 1. Despite the development of state welfare, we all of us rely heavily on markets for a large part of our daily individual and social needs; and, as we shall see in Chapter 15, the economic development of markets, and the ability of states to control or manipulate them, are crucial factors in structuring the broader context in which social policy planning takes place.

Welfare state provision has thus influenced, and in some cases has altered, markets; but it has not displaced them. It is for this reason that commentators sometimes refer to modern economies with developed state welfare provision as *welfare capitalism*: a compromise, or collaboration, between the state and the market. Of course, the nature of this compromise – the relationship between state and market – varies significantly between different welfare capitalist countries (see Alcock and Craig 2009; Hay and Wincott 2012). In social democratic countries, such as Sweden, much welfare support is provided by the state, which takes an active role in controlling and regulating many aspects of commercial markets. By contrast, in the liberal USA many welfare services, such as health care, are provided on a private market basis and the state plays a much more residual role. In Japan occupational and commercial services are the 'front line' of welfare provision, and it is through the labour market that most social protection is delivered.

Furthermore, the relationship, or the balance, between state and market in any one country is not fixed, and it can change over time. In Britain since the 1980s, for example, the role of commercial market provision has expanded significantly at the expense of state provision as a direct result of government policy, in some cases by requiring state services to be put out to tender to commercial providers. In the former socialist countries of Eastern Europe rapid changes took place after the collapse of their communist regimes, which led to the replacement of previous state monopoly provision by private markets for a wide range of goods and services. Indeed, the changes in the balance between state and market are an intrinsic feature of the development of welfare provision in all countries, and are a major focus of the study of social policy.

THE CASE FOR MARKETS

Proponents of market-based welfare have often claimed that market provision is preferable to the use of state power. Indeed, some have argued that state intervention is not compatible with the successful operation of markets and that, where it is pursued, it results in 'perverse incentives' which disrupt the natural flow of market development, by encouraging people to rely passively on state support rather than seeking to provide for themselves through entry into market relations. These arguments received particular prominence in social policy debate in Britain in the 1980s, associated with the rise of the New Right (see Chapter 14, and Barry 1987; King 1987); but they are not new arguments. In fact they are based on long-standing liberal theories of the workings of markets, which go back to the ideas of Adam Smith in the eighteenth century.

In his book, *The Wealth of Nations*, Smith (1776) argued that in theory markets created a natural equilibrium within the social order, because individuals exercising free choice over the purchase of goods and services would create a demand for those services they wanted. This demand would be expressed in terms of the price that they would be prepared to pay for the service, and this would then attract suppliers to provide such a service in order to profit from the price charged. The profit motive would not lead prices to rise unduly, however, because high prices would attract large numbers of suppliers, who would then be in competition and would thus be required to reduce prices to reflect more closely the costs of production and the demand for the product. Therefore, in a situation of perfect equilibrium, all needs would be met by suppliers and all prices would reflect the legitimate costs of production.

Since the exchange of goods and services (buying and selling through the market) arise in any social order, supporters of markets claim that they constitute a 'natural' social order, and also that they are self-regulating, with new demands leading to new supply and inefficient providers being weeded out by their unacceptably high prices. Smith referred to this as the 'invisible hand' of the market mechanism. Its cause was taken up in modern welfare capitalist countries such as Britain by new neoliberals, such as Hayek (1944) and Friedman (1962); and it is at the heart of the classical economics argument that market incentives are needed to promote economic growth.

As a result of this, therefore, pro-market theorists also argue that attempts by governments to intervene in, or control, markets will be doomed to failure. Government support for inefficient producers will distort the price mechanism; state provision of services will create potential monopoly producers not subject to the influence of purchasers' choices; and state regulation of providers or purchasers will prevent their free choice of the most optimal forms of service provision. Hayek argued in the 1940s (at the height of political support for state intervention in the capitalist economy in Britain), that such intervention would be ineffective and self-defeating. In the 1960s, as Keynesian interventions in the economy began to come under question, the same theme was taken up by the American economist, Milton Friedman (1962).

Hayek, Friedman and others argued that the fundamental weakness of state intervention is the problem that no agents of the state, such as government ministers or senior civil servants, could have sufficient knowledge of the needs, wants and circumstances of the individuals living in a complex modern society to be able to judge when, or where, to intervene in the market, or what sort of goods or services to provide. The result is that interventions distort, rather than support, markets, and that state services become paternalistic and bureaucratic monopolies. This, they argued, was the cause of the economic crises experienced by welfare capitalist countries in the 1970s and 1980s, and also of the hostility found in these countries towards some of the unpopular features of state welfare provision, such as unresponsive local authority landlords and long hospital waiting lists. The solution to these problems, they argued, was a return to free-market provision through the removal of state intervention and the break-up of state monopoly services. However, in theory there are problems in relying on markets to deliver welfare provision in modern societies, as we shall discuss shortly. Classical economics has been challenged by Keynesian theories of state intervention to promote and manage market development (see Chapter 15); and in practice the operation of market provision has always relied heavily on the support of the state.

THE MARKET AND THE STATE

Even the most ardent supporters of the free-market provision of goods and services recognize that the state does have some role to play in supporting markets. In order for markets to function freely there must be laws concerning property ownership and contract rights, and these need to be enforced independently through the state. There must also be a policing function provided by the state, to detect and prevent abuses of the law, and there must be provision for defence of society against the threat to the markets of one country imposed by the imperialistic designs of external enemies. Even the liberals thus concede the need for state law, a police force, and national defence.

It is clear, however, that other state functions are also necessary in any modern economy: for example the provision of air traffic control and the development of motorways and trunk roads, broadband other infrastructure. Obviously for such functions it is quite possible for providers or governments to have a full understanding of people's needs, and of the importance of a centrally planned response to these. Furthermore, as we suggested in Chapter 2, there are many other state activities and services which operate in effect to *support*, rather than to *undermine*, the operation of a modern market economy:

- State provision (for instance, of education and health care) meets the long-term strategic demands for an adequately equipped labour force that individual employers alone could not efficiently replicate.
- State regulation ensures maintenance of minimum standards that private individuals could not be expected to monitor (for instance, in housing or pension provision) and ensures that competition takes place according to appropriate levels of quality and efficiency as well as price.
- State protection (for instance, for the unemployed or chronically sick) ensures that individuals do not suffer unduly where the market fails or is unable to reach all.

Furthermore, the limitations and contradictions of market provision in complex modern welfare capitalist countries mean state interventions are needed to prevent potential social problems and to protect all citizens:

- There is the ever-present danger of monopolies or cartels developing that would subvert the natural self-regulation of market operations (for instance, in the supply of gas and water or in the production of specialist drugs).
- In many areas where markets do operate consumers are clearly unable to make informed choices about how best their needs might be met: for instance, consumer ignorance of medical needs and practices or of higher education (HE) standards mean that free choice cannot in practice mean the freedom to choose anything on offer.
- Most importantly of all in our unequal society, free choice in the market will be constrained by consumer immobility and poverty; so, for instance, for most children the state will have to ensure provision of a local school, and for certain categories of people free or subsidized access to essential services will have to be guaranteed.

Perhaps the best example of a case where state provision, organized according to altruistic rather than profit-oriented principles, was argued to be superior in social and economic terms to market-based provision is Titmuss's comparative study of blood donation, *The Gift Relationship* (Titmuss 1970, 1997). In this he argued that the state-organized system of blood donation in Britain, which relied upon free donation of blood, was both safer and more effective than the market-based systems of countries such as the USA and Japan, which paid donors for their blood. This was because the financial incentive provided an inappropriate inducement where the primary concern, as here, was with the quality and consistency of the supply of blood across a range of blood groups, some of which were in scarcer supply than others. Thus Titmuss found that the blood banks in countries where donors were paid were much more likely to obtain and distribute contaminated blood, and to experience problems in securing donors in some areas.

It seems clear, therefore, that the free, and unregulated, market to which Hayek and Friedman aspired does not exist in practice in modern capitalist states, and what is more could not effectively be 'revitalized' within them. Nevertheless, market provision of many goods and services continues to be of major importance in these societies. There are of course two sides to this coin; just as markets in practice need the state, so in many ways does the state need markets.

From the purchase of clothing to provision of housing there is no doubt that individuals expect to have a large measure of choice over their lifestyle, and are prepared to 'shop around' in the market to secure this. In many welfare services the retention, or introduction, of elements of commercially-based provision has enhanced both consumer choice and consumer responsiveness, for example, in the marketization of optical services in the 1980s. Market provision also provides an attractive supplement to basic state protection for many people in certain areas of welfare: for instance, personal and occupational pension protection, or private rooms and additional 'hotel' benefits during hospital stays.

In these more general terms, therefore, the case for regulated market provision alongside state welfare is now widely accepted within welfare capitalist societies. However, the pure markets espoused by the neoliberals do not exist, and never have. Market freedom has always in practice needed to be balanced by state regulation, and state subsidy and protection, in order to guarantee effective service development and delivery.

COMPREHENSION QUESTIONS

- To what extent does the pressure of commercialism mean that all private sector providers must seek to make a profit?
- What are the relative merits of state and market provision as explored in Titmuss's study of blood donation?

REFLECTIVE QUESTION

- Does the profit motive inevitably distort the provision of welfare for social needs?

FORMS OF COMMERCIAL WELFARE

Within a complex welfare mix, such as that in modern Britain, the commercial development of welfare takes a variety of forms, some of which in practice overlap, in part at least, with aspects of state provision or with provision in the third or informal sectors. At the time of the creation of the modern welfare state in Britain in the 1940s commercial provision was consciously retained alongside public services, even in the areas of major universal provision, such as education and health:

- In education private schools (misleadingly called public schools) which charge pupils for attendance continued to operate on a fee-paying basis, and to attract pupils.
- In the health service doctors have been permitted to retain fee-paying patients who pay for special treatment in NHS hospitals (sometimes called *pay beds*) following a compromise between the government minister (Bevan) and the British Medical Association (BMA) when the NHS was first established.

What is more, in the 1950s, after the establishment of state welfare, commercial provision – as an alternative, or a supplement, to state provision – actually began to grow. As we discuss in Chapter 10, at this time private house building rapidly began to outstrip the building of public rented housing. At the same time occupational pensions providing additional pension protection for workers also began to grow, and by the mid-1960s over 12 million workers were members of such private schemes.

In the 1980s this growth was accelerated as the Conservative governments of the time adopted a policy of openly encouraging commercial provision as a substitute for state provision, sometimes described as a policy of *privatization* (Johnson 1990). The largest privatization measures of the 1980s were the highly publicized break-up and sale of the major utilities (gas, electricity and water) that had initially been developed by local, not central, government, as we discuss in Chapter 6. State industries, such as British Steel, were also sold to private shareholders, although here what really occurred was a *re*privatization as these had first been set up by state takeover of old private companies. In the welfare field privatization in the 1980s took a number of forms, including the replacement of state provision, the removal of state subsidies, and the withdrawal of state regulation:

- The sale of *council houses* to tenants, and later the wholesale transfer of estates to private landlords, was a significant, and high-profile, example of the shift of provision from the state to the market sectors, with over a million council houses sold to tenants, although many estate transfers in practice went to housing associations in the third sector.

- Private provision in health was directly encouraged, and began to grow. Between 1979 and 1989 for instance the proportion of the population covered by private *health insurance* grew from 5 to 9 per cent, and over 50 new private hospitals were opened.
- Similar changes occurred in education; between 1979 and 1991 the number of children in *private schools* increased from 5.8 per cent to 7.4 per cent.
- The introduction of sick and maternity pay transferred *social security* protection from the Department of Social Security (DSS) to employers.
- The use of charges increased, in particular *prescription charges* for drugs purchased as part of medical treatment under the NHS (these went up from 20p in 1979 to over £3 in 1990).
- The public regulation of services, such as *public transport*, was largely withdrawn, with these being thrown open to competition between various commercial providers.

Important and far-reaching though these changes were, however, they did not amount to anything like a full-scale privatization of welfare services and, although this had been called for by some commentators from the New Right, it is not at all certain that the governments of the 1980s considered it either feasible or desirable. For instance, although private education and health care grew, they remained very much a minority provision alongside the comprehensive state services in these fields; and by the 1990s it had become clear that what had happened in practice in Britain had been not so much a replacement of the state with the market but rather a change in the welfare mix, in which state welfare was retained and market provision was more widely, and more variously, developed.

This mix of market and state provision was subsequently embraced by the Labour governments of 1997–2010 – and encapsulated in its promotion of the Third Way. The Coalition government has taken this process further, especially in England, partly to cut public spending but also on ideological grounds. As discussed in Part 2 it is opening up public service delivery in many areas to competition from other providers, and, in a climate of economic and fiscal austerity, encouraging non-governmental provision, with the state extending its role in *commissioning*, *procuring* and *outsourcing* services and *enabling* or facilitating market-based developments.

What we have in the early twenty-first century therefore is a range of private welfare services coexisting alongside, or operating in partnership with, state provision:

- Direct purchase of services is available (for example, in the provision of houses, domiciliary and residential care or spectacles).
- Insurance-based protection operates in the fields of income and retirement protection, education, and health care.
- Occupationally-based welfare is widespread with many workers getting additional benefits, such as sickness and redundancy pay, and some pension cover and private health care, from their employers on top of their cash wage.
- Charges have been introduced to cover the costs of much provision previously provided free within the state sector (for example, for social care services).
- Private providers are delivering publicly funded services, such as residential care and employment support, under contracts with local government or state agencies.
- Private companies are operating in partnership with government to invest in capital projects for developments such as new hospital buildings, under so-called Private Finance Initiatives (PFI).
- Private companies can also form partnerships with public providers in service delivery, for instance, through investing in the educational Academies and Free Schools established to replace state schools.

Not all of these forms of provision are profit-making and their success in reducing the cost to the state also varies. In fact, many features of market-based provision cannot even exist on a break-even basis and effectively only continue to operate with the support of major subsidies from the state. Many personal and occupational pensions rely upon the indirect subsidies provided by the tax relief available on contributions; and direct means-tested subsidies are provided to support poorer users who cannot pay the full cost of commercial prices or charges, for instance, through housing benefits or free NHS prescriptions. However, companies investing in PFIs do expect to reap significant rewards from the operating costs of the hospitals and other investments that they have made, once these become fully operational (Holden 2009); and private providers of services such as employment support have costed these on a profit-making basis.

As a result, therefore, the market basis for provision of welfare services is now widely and securely established alongside the state, and third, sectors in Britain, as it is in all other welfare capitalist countries. Further than this, however, attempts have been made in recent decades to integrate some of the key features of market principles within the delivery of state services themselves. In Britain over the last decade or so this has taken the form of *marketization* and the widespread development of *quasi-markets* within the state welfare sector.

MARKETIZATION

The development of marketization within welfare provision in Britain is a relatively recent phenomenon. Most of the legislative changes were introduced at the end of the 1980s, but the provisions themselves largely came into force during the 1990s (Bartlett et al. 1998), and have been continued and expanded since, particularly in England. However, the idea behind quasi-markets is really quite an old one and is based on an attempt to combine in one form the advantages of both market and state provision of welfare:

- The advantages of markets are that they gear the allocation of resources towards consumer needs and preferences and that, in operating on a cash basis, they maximize cost effectiveness through price sensitivity. Compared to this, state provision is paternalistic, because consumers' needs cannot all be accurately identified and accommodated, and decisions are taken by professional providers; state provision is also potentially expensive because, since services are provided free of charge, neither providers nor consumers have any incentive to reduce costs.
- The disadvantages of markets, as we have just discussed, are that they cannot afford to meet all needs and require consumers to have knowledge and power to be able to exercise realistic choices between competing service providers. By contrast, state provision can guarantee that no one will be excluded from access to provision and minimum service standards will be provided even where consumers are unable themselves to monitor these.

Quasi-markets are based in state services and funding is guaranteed by the state, with access to services generally being free so no one is excluded on grounds of poverty. However, a division is introduced between the *purchaser* (or consumer) and the *provider*, so that purchasers can choose from which provider they will select a service, and providers are forced to gear their service provision to meet these consumer preferences. One example of this, although it has not been widely utilized in Britain, is the education *voucher*, which provides pupils (or their parents) with a voucher equivalent to the cost of schooling that can then be 'cashed in' at any school of their choosing. In HE the part provision of student fees plus access to guaranteed loans operates something like a voucher scheme for adults, permitting suitably qualified applicants wishing to go to university to choose a place on a course.

As we discuss in Chapter 12, since the implementation of the Education Reform Act of 1988, local management of schools has meant these now can accept any pupils they choose to, giving children and their parents some freedom of choice between schools. This choice has also been facilitated, in theory at least, by the requirement for schools to regularly publish information about their achievements and the school 'league tables' that are constructed from this. Local management is not a fully-fledged voucher scheme, however, as schools can also refuse pupils and LAs are still required to secure local places for all children.

As well as the education reforms of the late 1980s, quasi-markets were also introduced into health and social care services, as discussed in Chapters 9 and 11. Here the market operates through the split between purchasers and providers, initially in the NHS in the form of an *internal market*. Here hospitals and other major service providers, such as ambulance services, became organizationally and financially independent trusts, whose income depended on the services they provided; and commissioning bodies representing doctors and other community-based patient services contracted to purchase these services on behalf of health service users in their area. This policy has been extended in England where they now also have the ability to purchase services from outside the NHS from 'any qualified provider', although it has been abandoned in Scotland and Wales. In social care managers became responsible for negotiating and purchasing packages of care on behalf of their clients from a range of service providers, which could include commercial or third sector agencies operating under contracts with the state.

Unlike the working of quasi-markets in education, health and social care provision remains under the control of the welfare professionals who are acting on behalf of their clients, in part because of the difficulty which individual citizens would be likely to face in making complex decisions about the choice of medical treatments or care packages. However, as we discuss in Chapter 11, plans for direct payments and individual budgets put the decisions over the purchase of services more directly into the hands of users themselves (Needham 2011). This 'personalization' of service provision takes quasi-markets beyond the purchase of services between public agencies, in to a potentially free market for customer choice over what to buy on the market, although in practice not all customers are able to make completely free choices (Glasby and Littlechild 2009).

As we discuss in more detail in Chapter 16, therefore, there are some problems involved in paying for welfare services in this way. In particular there is the danger that such mechanisms can operate to introduce the distorted incentives of the private profit principle into public service delivery. However, quasi-markets also introduce some more practical problems into state services because of the commercial procedures that they inevitably require.

Both service procurement whether within a public programme or, as is increasingly the case, from external providers and budget management require legal and accounting, as well as computing skills, as does bidding for contracts against other providers. Doctors, social workers and other welfare professionals often do not have these skills and might understandably be reluctant to develop them. However, procurement and budget management are now central to much policy delivery in welfare services, and where they are not managed well then provision – and hence users – will be likely to suffer. Furthermore, procurement and budgeting exercises take time, and, as all accountants (at least) know, time costs money. When welfare professionals are involved in these tasks, they are not engaged in service provision; and in this way the operation of quasi-markets has introduced significant extra administrative (*transaction*) costs into welfare systems, many of which may be unknowingly disguised in unplanned and even unidentified service cuts. In practice, therefore, quasi-markets require additional resources and skills that state welfare services may not be well equipped to provide, for instance GPs may want to commission services on behalf of their patients, but may not be the best equipped to manage this business effectively. It may be that efficiency savings generated by market allocations can create the scope for these to be met within existing service provision, for example through the employment of specialist commissioning agents; but, where they are not, quasi-markets can prove to be an expensive means of importing price sensitivity into state services.

PROBLEMS WITH MARKETS

The neoliberal claim that a free-market economy will provide for efficiency and consumer sovereignty through self-regulation, even if it were attractive in theory, cannot realistically be applied to the welfare provision of modern welfare capitalist countries. Markets in such countries are too complex for individual consumers to negotiate and they are inextricably intertwined with state, and third sector, provision. So, although neoliberal theorists have pleaded for a return to a pure market economy, no government has in practice sought to pursue such a radical path.

Thus markets exist in welfare, as in the economy generally, alongside state and voluntary provision, as government support for public/private partnerships and a mixed economy of welfare providers now openly recognizes. In this context they frequently provide advantages in service development and delivery that could perhaps not be achieved in any other manner. Where consumers have resources and knowledge, their ability to choose (and the incentive for providers to improve services in order to secure that choice) provides a powerful motor for innovation and improvement. In the case of housing provision, for instance, it is this consumer sovereignty that has made owner-occupation so much more attractive to people than public renting.

In a mixed economy of welfare, markets have their advantages. However, they also have their problems. Even where they do not actually make a profit, the commercial operators within markets are inevitably driven primarily by financial considerations rather than service priorities since, through the charges they make for services, they must ensure they continue to retain the viability to operate. This means that all commercial operators are forced to levy charges that at least meet their costs. However, in the unequal social order in which these charges operate, some consumers will be better able to meet them than others. Wealthy people are able to opt out of public services and purchase alternative services or additional benefits; and yet people in poverty faced with additional charges are unlikely to be able to afford the services they may desperately need.

In an unequal society a pure market system will inevitably fail to meet the service demands of poor people in need. Indeed, it is just such market failure that motivated the Fabian reformers, and the trade union and political representatives of the working classes, to press for state welfare services to be introduced in the early part of the twentieth century. Unlike the drive for profit, which distributes market-based provision to those most able to pay, state services or state support can be allocated according to need. Thus state provision can ensure that people are not excluded from protection because of poverty, either through direct non-market provision to them or through the subsidization of poorer purchasers within markets. Even where they do operate to provide welfare, therefore, markets have to be supplemented by state provision.

However, markets do not only fail individual poor people; they also fail to meet certain welfare needs that may often be associated with poverty more generally. Because commercial operators must seek to ensure financial profitability, or at least viability, there are likely to be certain service areas that they will not be willing to enter at all.

This is largely true, for instance, of protection for unemployment. Unemployed people are outside the labour market and they, and their dependants, need financial support. Commercial provision of this support would only be likely if charges could be levied on employed people, on an insurance basis, to cover the costs of their potential unemployment. However, many employed people may be unwilling to pay charges to meet the support needs of the unemployed, especially if they themselves are unlikely to be threatened with unemployment. A scheme collecting charges only from those who did fear unemployment might not be sufficiently buoyant to meet the needs of all those unemployed, especially in periods of economic recession. For example, in the early 1990s the government sought to encourage private protection for the repayment of mortgage debts for those becoming unemployed by removing some of the state protection for this. However, few private insurance providers were willing to develop insurance protection for those most at risk of unemployment; such schemes as were developed offered only very limited and short-term financial protection; and, as highlighted in Chapter 10, only a small minority of home owners took out cover. Commercial provision for protection for the unemployed has thus not developed in Britain or in other welfare capitalist countries; and, although a variety of different schemes providing support for unemployment exist, they are all organized (and partly financed) by the state, on behalf of society as a whole.

Whatever the extravagant claims made by its protagonists, therefore, the fact remains that market provision cannot meet all the needs of all the people all of the time. It is for this reason that third sector organizations and state welfare services have developed in all modern market economies, even though their development has to some extent operated to supplement, rather than to displace, market-based services. Although different governments have emphasized different balances between this mix of non-state and public welfare provision, successful policy development in the future will need to ensure that markets continue or develop where they can genuinely provide a responsiveness and sensitivity which monopolistic state services could not do; and that they are replaced, or supplemented, where they threaten to exclude necessary services or needy consumers.

COMPREHENSION QUESTIONS

- To what extent did the privatization reforms of the 1980s replace state welfare with private provision?
- In what ways do quasi-markets aim to import market principles into state welfare services?
- Why is it argued that there are natural limits to the scope of markets in meeting welfare needs?

REFLECTIVE QUESTION

- Has marketization meant that public services are now delivered more effectively?

FURTHER READING

There are no books on the subject of private welfare in Britain at present, but Powell's (2007) collection on the mixed economy of welfare contains chapters on market welfare provision. Drakeford (2000) provides a good guide to the policy developments around privatization in the late twentieth century. Bartlett et al. (1998) is a critical discussion of the implementation of quasi-markets in the same period. Drakeford (2008) and Holden (2012) consider some of the issues arising from more recent developments.

4
The Third Sector

SUMMARY OF KEY POINTS

- The third sector includes voluntary and community organizations, charities, social enterprises and cooperatives. It is broader than, but includes, what has traditionally been referred to as the voluntary and community sector.
- The third sector overlaps with the other sectors and in particular has a complex and changing relationship with the state.
- All voluntary organizations require funding and many have complex packages of finance from a range of different sources.
- In 2010 UK charity income was around £37 billion and had grown significantly over the previous decade.
- Voluntary organizations vary in aims and structure; they are thus uneven in their distribution and sometimes narrow in their focus. They do not guarantee a comprehensive approach to service provision.
- 'Umbrella' or infrastructure agencies play an important role in supporting and representing voluntary organizations and the sector more generally.
- Public support for the third sector from central and local government has continued despite the development of state welfare services.
- Voluntary organizations are being encouraged to bid to take over the delivery of some public services.
- Government policy has included active promotion of partnership working between the state and voluntary organizations, including the development of a formal *Compact* to govern relations and considerable investment of public resources to support capacity building and organizational development.
- The Coalition government sees voluntary and community organizations as a central part of its Big Society agenda in England, although state funding for the sector has been cut.
- Policy-making in the devolved administrations has largely developed on similar lines to that in England.

DEFINING THE THIRD SECTOR

The focus of debate and policy development on the relative roles of the state and the market in the provision of welfare services has meant that the size and the scope of voluntary organization in the development and delivery of welfare has sometimes not been fully appreciated in the study of social policy. These are significant omissions since the third sector in the UK, and in other welfare capitalist countries, has played a key role in policy practice, often in the very areas where state and market provision is least effective. As we shall see, the complex and varied nature of voluntary activity makes it very difficult to arrive at any accurate assessment of the scale and scope of the third sector.

Nevertheless the scale of the sector is significant. Focusing just on recognized UK charities, the total gross income of the sector in 2010 was just under £37 billion, and their total assets were worth around £90 billion. The National Council for Voluntary Organisations (NCVO) (Clark et al. 2012) calculate that there may be as many as 900,000 organizations of various kinds within the wider third sector, and they employ around 765,000 workers, 2.7 per cent of the UK workforce.

In historical terms, too, the role of the third sector is of central importance in the development of welfare provision. The collective provision of both self-protection and altruistic service to others preceded both the state and the market; and both state and market forms of welfare have built on structures and practices developed by voluntary organization and activity (Harris 2010). Indeed the development of public provision, in particular the 'comprehensive' services of the post-war welfare state, was based in places more or less directly on previous forms of provision from voluntary organizations, for instance, the friendly societies (NI) and voluntary hospitals (NHS). And since that time voluntary organizations have continued to grow and develop alongside state welfare services, as we shall return to discuss below (see Finlayson 1994; Lewis 1995).

Voluntary and community organizations vary in size and shape, from neighbourhood parent and toddler groups to major service providers such as AgeUK. They were once famously described by Kendall and Knapp (1995) as 'a loose and baggy monster'. It is almost impossible to generalize about their structure or their activities, or to come up with a definition or description that will fit all cases; but we can provide some definitional parameters to shape our study of the sector, even if only negatively by specifying what is not encompassed within it.

Voluntary organizations are *not* part of the state provision of services, either at central or local level. They are *not* constituted by statutory legislation, although their activities are of course affected by legislation. They are *not* directly accountable to elected state representatives either nationally or locally; their employees, where they exist, are *not* officers of government or LA departments. Voluntary organizations are thus in one sense *private* bodies but they are *not* part of the private market or commercial provision of welfare, primarily because they do not operate exclusively with a concern for profit and loss. Commercial organizations seek to make a profit out of their activities, or at a minimum to cover their costs; thus they charge for the provision of services (at least in most cases) and pass profits made on to owners and shareholders. Voluntary organizations are *not* motivated solely by the pursuit of profit and although many develop business plans and even charge for services, for the large part they do this in order to support their broader social mission. This includes social enterprises, which are established as businesses, but use the proceeds from this to support social (and sometimes environmental) goals rather than distributing these profits to shareholders.

As they are not part of the state, voluntary organizations are sometimes referred to as *non-government organizations* (NGOs), and this is often the term used to refer to international organizations operating in developing countries where they are independent of the local state. Because they are not generally established by state legislation, they are sometimes also referred to as the *non-statutory sector*, and in the USA, in particular, their distinction from commercial organizations has led to them being referred to as the *non-profit sector*. It was also in the USA that the notion of the *third sector* developed – after the first (market) and second (state) sectors.

This was also the term used by the UK Labour government in the 2000s, which established an Office for the Third Sector, based in the Cabinet Office (see below) and under which, as discussed later, third sector policy became the responsibility of the devolved administrations. However the term was dropped by the Coalition government and the Cabinet Office base retitled the Office for Civil Society. As we shall see though there is some debate about whether civil society is synonymous with the third sector; and in this chapter we will generally use the latter term to cover both voluntary and community activity and organizations such as social enterprises and cooperatives, which are not straight commercial ventures.

This intermediary role between the public, market and family sectors and between the formal and informal, public and private, and profit and non-profit features of provision, is sometimes presented in diagrammatic form to reveal how this notion of the third sector distinguishes it from other aspects of welfare provision. In this model third sector organizations are identified as formal, non-profit, private agencies and they occupy a space between the state, the market and the family (see Figure 4.1).

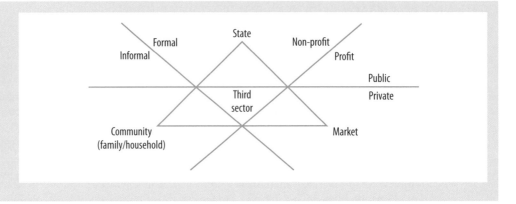

Figure 4.1 The intermediary role of the third sector

The relationships between the third sector and the other forms of welfare provision are critical to an understanding of the distinctive features of voluntary action. In practice, however, these relationships are far from clear-cut and the boundaries between the different sectors are porous or overlapping. In Figure 4.1 the sector is placed in between the state, the market and the community. In each of these areas there are organizations operating on or across these boundaries – delivering state services with public money (as we shall see below), operating commercially as social enterprises charging fees, or acting largely to coordinate informal community action. Evers and Laville (2004) have discussed these 'inter-sectoral landscapes' and argued they create 'tension fields' for voluntary action, for instance, those on the boundary with business will be under pressure to operate according to commercial criteria and those on the boundary with government will be restricted by public policy and statutory control. More recently Billis (2010) has taken up this issue of boundary overlap to argue that what have been created as a result of these tension fields are *hybrid* organizations, which are no longer purely part of the voluntary and community world.

The location of the sector amidst a complex of relations between the state, the commercial market and the individual has more generally been discussed by social theorists as the sphere of *civil society*. Civil society is a more generic notion than voluntary action and organization, and has been identified by many authors as encompassing more generally that set of relations within society not governed by either statutory control or market forces (see Deakin 2001). From this perspective civil society is a reference to the social relations that exist within society, outside of those based on economic exchange in the market or under statutory regulation by the state. This includes, but extends beyond, voluntary action and voluntary organizations.

Whatever the importance of this broader civil society context, however, the focus of this chapter is on third sector organizations and their narrower role in the provision of welfare within society. And, however they are defined or located, third sector organizations are *organizations*. Even the neighbourhood parent and toddler group requires organization. There have to be meetings, which require notification and premises. There has to be a membership list to know who to invite to the meetings. This will require a secretary and perhaps a chair and other officers. All this requires organization and results in a body that is something much more than the informal support and services provided by families and neighbours, without any organizational structure, that we discuss in Chapter 5. These organizational aspects of voluntary activity are important in determining its development (and sustainability), in shaping the way in which it operates to deliver services and in structuring its relationships with other sectors.

ORGANIZATION AND FUNDING

The difficulties of defining the third sector also extend to difficulties in describing it. This is because of the wide range of organizational forms and activities included within it. It is partly as a result of this that the term voluntary sector can be misleading, because the form and centrality of volunteering itself varies. The unpaid time, freely given, of volunteers could be seen as the essence of voluntary activity. It is virtually the sole resource of many organizations, in particular smaller community-based ones; and, if it could be costed in financial terms, or in comparison with full-time paid employment, it would probably reveal significant additional economic value within the sector. However, not all volunteering takes place *within* the third sector: for example state welfare agencies such as social care departments make quite extensive use of volunteers to supplement the statutory services they provide through the use of public money.

Any organization operating at more than a neighbourhood level is going to find it difficult to survive by relying solely on volunteers. Volunteers, no matter how well meaning, can only give up so much of their time since they are also likely to have jobs or family commitments. The Coalition government has claimed that it wants to encourage more volunteering, but survey evidence suggests levels of voluntary activity are actually quite static (Staetsky and Mohan 2011).

What is more, volunteers, no matter how capable, are likely to have limited skills; but large organizations require secretaries, accountants and managers. Where these organizations are providing complicated services, specialist skills or training for staff may be required. If some specialist tasks can be carried out by paid workers on a full-time or a part-time basis, the organization may be better able to both meet its service goals, and make better use of its volunteer labour. Also volunteers are not entirely a 'free good'; they need to be managed and supported, and, in some cases, trained – for instance, Citizens' Advice Bureaux (CABs) run an extensive training programme for their volunteer advisers. Organizations may need to employ staff to manage and train volunteers therefore.

Large international or national voluntary organizations, such as Oxfam or the NSPCC, employ a wide range of paid staff both to run the organization itself and provide services to users, and some of these may be well paid. They have salary and career structures, and provide training and development for their workers. However, many smaller local organizations also employ paid staff. For example, most CABs have at least one paid, and trained, manager and advice worker, as well as relying heavily on the commitment of volunteer advisers.

Of course the employment of paid workers means organizations need the financial resources at their disposal to pay them. To do this organizations require more than just the efforts of volunteers. Those with paid workers may differ to some extent from those without because of their need to secure regular funding to support their work; but in fact even organizations relying entirely on voluntary effort usually require some financial resources to pay for equipment and materials, which these days may mean a telephone or a computer and broadband connection, and to pay for premises in which to work or meet. Thus the funding that voluntary organizations can secure may be a central feature in determining their shape and structure, as well as their ability to deliver the services they are aiming to provide.

In principle at least the first source of funding for voluntary organizations is *giving*, or charitable donation. Just as some people may be willing to give their time to a particular local or national group, others may be willing, and able, to give money. Charitable giving has been the financial mainstay of many major voluntary organizations in Britain and elsewhere for over a century. The nineteenth century pioneers of voluntary social service agencies relied largely upon such charitable sources, coordinated by the Charity Organisation Society (COS) (Humphries 1995; Lewis 1995); and over the last century the scale of charitable donation expanded significantly.

Although private altruism is the essence of charitable giving, not all donors are individuals; and not all donations are entirely altruistic. Private corporations also donate large sums to voluntary organizations, in part as a genuine support to their activities; but in part also, in some cases, to improve the profile or reputation of the corporate donor, or even to establish or promote their commercial business activity. Such charitable giving, both individual and corporate, is also now frequently coordinated and directed; for instance, the Charities Aid Foundation (CAF) acts to provide advice and support to both UK donors and voluntary organizations looking for support.

The status of charities, however, is a particular – and a particularly important – one within British social policy because recognized charities enjoy significant tax concessions, which act as a form of indirect public subsidy to them. Charities using certain premises do not have to pay local property taxes; and more generally they can benefit from what is now called 'Gift Aid' under which they can claim back from the government the equivalent to the standard rate income tax that has been paid by donors. This is now a significant indirect public subsidy to charitable organizations, and their beneficiaries, worth about £2.6 billion in 2010 (Clark et al. 2012).

For a long time the determination of charitable status depended upon an obscure legal statute of 1601 that limited charitable status to organizations performing specific services for specific groups of beneficiaries (Brenton 1985). In 2007, however, this was replaced in England and Wales by the Charities Act 2006, which followed an earlier similar reform in Scotland in 2005. These provide for a new definition of charitable status based primarily on the provision of public benefit. However, this is not clearly defined in the legislation and has been left to the determination of the Charity Commission, the body that has formal responsibility for monitoring the legislation and regulating charitable organizations in England and Wales. Similar bodies now also exist in Scotland and Northern Ireland, although registration in Northern Ireland had still not commenced fully in 2013.

Charitable giving for altruistic purposes to provide services for others can be distinguished from making payments into voluntary organizations that are intended rather as a form of *self-protection*. Collective self-protection through pooled donations was a form of voluntary organization that developed significantly in Britain in the nineteenth century, for instance, in order to provide income protection for workers in times of sickness or temporary unemployment. Unlike insurance protection on the private market, this involved a joint commitment to collective self-protection for specific groups of workers and their families, into which contributions would be made in the expectation of future support at times of need. The *friendly societies*, as these organizations came to be known, were an important feature of the early development of social security protection outside the state. Their model of mutual self-protection was later copied and incorporated into the national insurance scheme proposed by Beveridge (see Chapter 8), however; and after this they largely disappeared from the scene.

Friendly societies were not the only form of organizations based on mutual contribution and support. This was also the model behind the cooperative movement, which also began in the nineteenth century; but has expanded and prospered since. Cooperatives are business organizations owned and managed by their members. These members could be producers, as in the large agricultural and manufacturing cooperatives that operate in some European countries, or they could be consumers, as in the cooperative retail outlets more common in the UK. Many cooperatives are separately registered as Industrial and Provident Societies, and operate as a distinct part of the third sector. But this model of *mutualism* is now more widely copied, for instance in the John Lewis department store chain and by some health care providers who have opted out of NHS control to operate as independent organizations. This form of mutualization is now actively promoted by government, with the Coalition in England for instance upholding it in part as a third sector alternative to public service provision with mutually owned providers delivering services funded largely by contracts with public agencies (HMG 2011b).

Charity and mutual support are key features of voluntary action and core elements in the funding of many third sector organizations. However, they are no longer the only significant sources of funding for many. In 2010 donations and fees from individuals at £14.1 billion were closely followed by public funding at £13.9 billion as the major sources of funding for charities in England and Wales (Clark et al. 2012). The state may fund voluntary organizations in a number of different ways and for a number of different reasons. As we mentioned, exemption from payment of taxes is a form of state support for charities; however, money is also given directly to organizations to help them provide services or employ workers.

The majority of public funding for third sector organizations does not in practice come from central government, but rather from LAs. They have for some time provided public financial support for many voluntary and community organizations operating within their area, from play schemes and tenants' associations to advice centres and social care services. This funding was in the past often provided in the form of grants to voluntary groups to underwrite or subsidize an agreed range of activities. More recently, however, it has generally taken the form of more formal contracts for the delivery of specific services. Indeed the growth in public funding for the sector from £8.6 billion in 2001 to £13.9 billion in 2010 was entirely comprised of a more than doubling of such contract income (Clark et al. 2012).

What is more public support, from local government in particular, does not always take the form of cash payments. Assistance may also be provided in kind (for instance, through free use of LA premises, such as schools, or free access to council equipment or mailing facilities), or through the provision of paid workers to support voluntary groups, for instance, community social workers who may help to set up and to manage community-based activities.

State funding is thus a major feature of the resource base of many third sector organizations in the UK; and this pattern is common throughout other similar developed nations. Indeed back in 1990 Kramer commented that, 'In fact, there is no country today where there is a substantial voluntary sector, that is not dependent on governmental support to a greater or lesser degree'. Although it is important to remember that it is still only a minority of, mainly larger, organizations who benefit from this, at least directly.

In addition to state support and charitable donations, many third sector organizations also rely on earned income and returns on investments as a source of income. Earned income, investments and fees accounted for around £9 billion of the sector's income in 2010 (Clark et al. 2012). Although they are non-profit organizations, many charities and other voluntary organizations do in practice engage in market-based activity to provide funding. A number charge for some of the services that they provide and use this income to pay staff and provide services. Others may have assets such as properties or capital funds invested in financial institutions that can also provide a significant source of income.

In addition to this there are those organizations which engage more directly in (quasi)commercial activity to provide income that is then reinvested to develop new business. This includes the service charities, such as Oxfam or Cancer Research UK, which run small high street shops selling second-hand or specially produced merchandise to provide income that can be used in service provision.

Such direct business activity within the sector has expanded more rapidly over the last decade or so with the growth, and growing recognition, of *social enterprises*. These are independent firms engaged in social or environmental activity that reinvest all or a majority of their income from commercial work in pursuing these community goals. They include the organization behind the magazine sold by homeless people, *The Big Issue*, and the restaurant chain set up by celebrity chef Jamie Oliver, *Fifteen*. Many social enterprises are registered as limited companies, but they can also be constituted as Community Interest Companies (CIC) under a separate registration designed to support their growth and development.

The great appeal of earned income, of course, is that to some extent organizations can have more control over these sources than over donations, or grants and contracts from the state. Control over resources, or lack of it, is a more general problem for many organizations, however; and this is particularly true where, as is often the case, funding in practice comes from a number of different sources. Mixed funding streams mean that there is no need to rely on one funding agency, particularly important for organizations with significant support from public sources that are under threat; but they also mean there may be a need to maintain different procedures and deliver different outputs to satisfy different funders. What is more, the balance of these sources may well change over time, so that what the organization does, and what it is, is forced to shift as new funding sources come on-stream or disappear.

COMPREHENSION QUESTIONS

- What did Kendall and Knapp mean by their description of the sector as 'a loose and baggy monster'?
- What is the difference between the third sector and the voluntary sector?
- What are the advantages and disadvantages for organizations of grant and contract funding from public sources?
- Why has earned income become a more important source of income for third sector organizations?

REFLECTIVE QUESTION

- Should third sector organizations engage in commercial activity?

THE STRUCTURE OF THE SECTOR

The third sector is a vast and varied collection of organizations composed of different groups of people pursuing different aims at different levels of society: 'a loose and baggy monster'. Indeed, the variety is so great that some have argued that it is impossible to arrive at a consistent definition or description of it. Alcock (2010) argued that it had only a 'strategic unity' defined by its relationship with the other sectors, rather than any intrinsic internal unifying structure. Others have sought to identify unifying characteristics, however. For instance the international study of third sector organizations developed at the Johns Hopkins University in the US to compare the size and structure of these activities across a number of developed countries (Salamon and Anheier 1997; Salamon et al. 1999) identified organizations by four linked themes: formality, independence, non-profit distribution and voluntarism. They then used these to develop an International Classification of Non-Profit Organizations (ICNPO), which in fact constituted a list of twelve different fields of non-profit activity including areas such as culture and recreation, health, social services, and religion.

This is quite a long list; and it is a list rather than a definition. However, it does draw our attention to one way of understanding the structure of the sector, by recognizing and identifying the different 'subsectors' that might in practice exist within it. Even here, given the diversity of the sector, it is not possible to come up with an exhaustive typology; but we can develop some distinctions between different types of organization, based on functional goals and activities, as in Box 4.1.

BOX 4.1 Types of third sector organizations

Protective organizations set up by their members for mutual self-protection or benefit. These include the nineteenth-century friendly societies and the twentieth-century credit unions, and also more ad hoc self-help groups such as those providing support for drug or alcohol users and mental health patients. The organization of these protective associations is focused internally on maintaining their effective operation. The motivation for participation is self-interest.

Representative organizations promote or represent the self-interest of members but do this through external activity, in particular promoting their needs and campaigning for improved services from other sources. These include small lone parent groups such as a local Gingerbread group; but they would also include some of the largest, and most powerful, third sector organizations, such as the trade unions.

Campaigning organizations do not act specifically on behalf of their members but campaign more generally on issues that affect large numbers of people throughout society. These organizations are motivated primarily by altruism rather than representation, although in some cases it may be altruism with a clear political message. They include the Child Poverty Action Group (CPAG), campaigning for children living in poverty in Britain, and Greenpeace or Friends of the Earth, campaigning for worldwide environmental change.

Service organizations are also generally motivated by altruism, in particular the charitable motive of giving in order to help others. Many of the largest and most successful third sector groups continue to be those whose aim is to provide services to others in need. These include international agencies such as Oxfam and national organizations such as the RVS and the NSPCC, as well as others that may also have a religious dimension, such as Christian Aid or the Salvation Army, now generally referred to as *faith groups*. They also include the many small and diverse neighbourhood activities designed to help local people in need.

Culture and leisure organizations are mainly focused on providing a forum for members to share cultural interests or participate in leisure activities, and they would include a music collective or a local football team, or a faith group acting to promote religious culture. However, there are larger organizations providing public access to culture and leisure too; for instance the Royal Opera House is a registered charity.

Social enterprise organizations, as we explained above, are businesses also set up to pursue a social purpose and with a commitment to reinvesting the bulk of their surplus into this mission. As mentioned the homeless person's magazine *The Big Issue* and the restaurant chain *Fifteen* are both social enterprises, although the boundaries between some social enterprises and small businesses may be a blurred one in some cases.

As with funding differences, of course, these functional features do not constitute watertight boundaries between organizations. Some campaigning organizations may include a mixture of representative and altruistic activities, and they may also provide services to members or to others. This is true, for instance, of the CPAG, which has branches representing local people but which campaigns primarily at national government level, and also provides advice and advocacy services both to its own members and to non-members who use its handbooks and its Citizens' Rights Office. Nevertheless, the boundaries do provide us with something of a guide to the different aims of voluntary and community organizations, and these differences can be supplemented by comparing the levels at which different organizations operate. As we have seen, some voluntary organizations work at an international level while others operate at a national level, although in the UK they may have separate organizations for England, Scotland, Wales or Northern Ireland.

Thus far we have been discussing individual voluntary organizations; but organizations do not exist or operate in isolation; indeed, many work within networks or broader groups. For instance, all CABs are members of a national association called *Citizens' Advice*. National federations of voluntary organizations are in fact quite common; but there may also be local federations to which several organizations belong, for example, many cities and towns have local federations of tenants' associations representing all the associations from estates across the area.

National or local federations based on particular types of organization provide what we might call *vertical* networks with the sector, representing and linking organizations operating within particular fields of activity. However, most local areas also have more general umbrella organizations representing a wide range of (indeed, potentially all) voluntary local groups, usually known as the local Council for Voluntary Services (CVS) or some similar title. Such umbrella federations provide a *horizontal* integration across the sector within a local area. And similar horizontal agencies operate at national level too, providing support services for the sector as a whole and often playing an influential role in major national policy planning. The leading national body in England is the NCVO, and there are similar agencies representing the sector in Scotland, Wales and Northern Ireland; but there are many other umbrella agencies, including the Association of Chief Executives of Voluntary Organizations (ACEVO) for sector leaders, and the National Association for Voluntary and Community Action (NAVCA), which itself is comprised of local CVSs.

THE HISTORY OF VOLUNTARY ACTIVITY

Third sector organizations representing people and delivering services preceded the development of both state and market provision of welfare in Britain and in other welfare capitalist countries, yet they have also survived the development of these newer sectors and have continued to accommodate and adapt their activities alongside them (Harris 2010). Thus even the major protagonists of state welfare have recognized the significant and continuing role played by the third sector. In the early part of the twentieth century, for instance, the Webbs (strong supporters of state welfare) talked about the continued importance of a voluntary sector operating alongside state welfare provision. They contrasted two ways in which such a partnership might operate, although they made it clear that they preferred the second model:

- The 'parallel bars' approach, where the state and the third sector each provided separately for different social needs
- The 'extension ladder' approach, where voluntary activity was developed as a supplement to the basic state services that were guaranteed for all.

Beveridge, too, became an advocate for the third sector, when he wrote in 1948 that state provision should not stifle the initiative and enterprise of citizens for voluntary action (Beveridge 1948).

As we have seen, the state welfare services that developed in the first half of the twentieth century drew heavily on third sector models and organizations: for instance, on the friendly societies for social insurance. The establishment of the 'welfare state' following the Second World War saw the replacement of the friendly societies with state welfare agencies for major social needs such as social security. However, comprehensive state welfare provision in the 1940s did not signify the end of third sector activity. New local organizations, such as the CABs established earlier in 1939, continued to flourish and some important new national organizations, such as the Marriage Guidance Council and the Samaritans, were set up.

Indeed, once state welfare had been established in the latter half of the twentieth century, it operated to provide a new and different impetus for voluntary organization. This included groups campaigning against the state to challenge or extend state provision, such as the CPAG, as well as those working in partnership with the state to develop and deliver new forms of public service, such as MIND, the mental health charity.

By the 1970s, therefore, rather than state welfare displacing the third sector, state support was being used extensively to foster its expansion and further development (see Kendall 2003). It was in this context that an independent committee was set up by the Rowntree Memorial Trust, headed by Lord Wolfenden (1977), to review the future role and function of the sector in the UK. Its main conclusions were that the sector would have an important role to play in the future development of welfare services and, consequently, that this should be the subject of strategic planning by government and would require the support of public funds. In 1980 the government introduced a Local Voluntary Action programme, based in a Voluntary Service Unit in the Home Office to provide support for voluntary organizations (Rochester 2001).

In the 1980s, however, the Conservative governments' commitment to reduce public expenditure and to 'roll back' the boundaries of state welfare provided a broader, if less direct, support for the growth of the sector. Government commitment to transfer service provision from the state provided an opportunity, and an incentive, for voluntary and community organizations to secure state support for such work, albeit under strict contractual constraints. This was particularly the case in the area of health and social care as a consequence of the community care reforms introduced in the 1990s and discussed in Chapters 9 and 11. Community care meant a change in the role of public service agencies, particularly LA SSDs, from the providers of services to the purchasers, or enablers, of packages of support, which might include elements delivered by voluntary agencies to the clients placed with them, under agreed arrangements which would channel public funds to support these. As enablers, therefore, LAs and other agencies were expected to work in partnership with providers in the private and third sectors, and in practice this was expressed through the establishment of legally binding contracts to deliver agreed packages of care.

This new contractual basis marked a significant departure from the previous grant regimes under which many organizations had been supported by local and central government. Contracts generally specified much more closely what was to be delivered with the public funding provided and how organizations were to be held accountable for delivering this. It has sometimes been referred to as a move to a 'contract culture', however; and some have argued that this could challenge the independent mission of organizations and lead to a form of 'isomorphism' in which they come to resemble the statutory agencies that they have replaced (Paxton et al. 2005; Macmillan 2010). Nevertheless the use of contracts as a basis for transferring the delivery of public services to voluntary organizations has continued and expanded under both Labour and the Coalition, particularly in England.

The moves towards contracting were not the only policy changes affecting voluntary organizations in the 1990s, however. In 1994 the Prime Minister, John Major, gave his personal support to a new programme to promote volunteering more generally through the 'Make a Difference' initiative (see Davis Smith 2001). At around the same time the NCVO commissioned a major inquiry into the future of the voluntary sector in England (Deakin 1996), and a similar review was commissioned in Scotland (Kemp 1997). Both commented on the growing strength and depth of voluntary action and the critical role that the sector was by then playing in policy development and delivery, and argued that relations between the sector and the state should be conducted on a more formal basis, perhaps through some formal agreement or concordat.

THE NEW POLICY ENVIRONMENT

Once they came into power in 1997 Labour acted quickly to take forward the ideas outlined in the Deakin and Kemp reports and began to develop a number of initiatives to promote voluntary action and improve relations with the state that, after 1999, were paralleled by the devolved administrations. In an earlier review of the changing policy context Kendall (2003) argued that public support for the sector could, like umbrella organizations, be distinguished between vertical and horizontal dimensions. In respect of service delivery at least, the vertical support of specialist agencies was more important. However, it was the horizontal dimension that expanded most dramatically in the early years of this century, leading to a step change in government concern and support for voluntary action.

Initially Labour expanded the support and coordination for the sector provided through the Home Office; but in 2006 this was revamped and much extended through the creation the new Office of the Third Sector (OTS), based in the Cabinet Office. The OTS was also a consolidation of government support for the sector, incorporating also the Social Enterprise Unit from the DTI. It was based at the centre of government and had a wide remit both to ensure coordination of internal Departmental engagement with the sector in England and support and promote it through formal relationship building and management of the new funding programmes discussed below. In 2010, as noted earlier, the Coalition government retitled the OTS the Office for Civil Society (OCS), in an attempt to reject the third sector label; but it remained within the Cabinet Office as the central focus for relations with the sector.

In the 2000s Labour moved quickly to develop what it called a 'partnership' with the third sector (Lewis 2005). The concordat idea recommended by the Deakin Commission was taken up and implemented through the establishment by the Home Office (1998) of a formal *Compact* in England to govern relations between the sector and the state, and developed as part of a more general drive to improve partnership working between the state and other welfare sectors (see Glendinning et al. 2002). The Compact idea was also implemented by the devolved administrations in Scotland, Wales and Northern Ireland, and it was followed by the establishment of local compacts between local government and third sector representatives (see Craig et al. 2002). Since 2010 the Compact has also been retained by the Coalition government, although financial support for it was withdrawn and in practice it has had a much lower profile.

Labour introduced a range of major funding programmes to support third sector organizations, in particular those seeking to take on public service delivery contracts, for instance through the *Futurebuilders* and *Change-up* funds created by the OTS – although these were not continued by the Coalition. There was also support for a rather different role for third sector organizations, however, in promoting civic renewal and more active citizenship by providing places for volunteering and community action, especially, it was hoped, for those experiencing social exclusion.

There may be something of a contradiction here between the role that voluntary organizations can play in promoting civic renewal and social inclusion and the responsibilities they have also been encouraged to undertake for delivering public services. Strict contractual terms to secure service delivery may not mesh well with attempts to include vulnerable people in voluntary action. Of course, it is in practice probably different types of organizations that engage in promoting civic renewal from those that deliver public services. As we mentioned above, the third sector is a diverse and divided entity.

This is a problem for policy engagement with the sector, however; and it is one that has been accentuated even further with the shift in emphasis following the formation of the Coalition government in 2010. The new government was keen to distance itself from its predecessor, and this was captured most clearly in the commitment to create a *Big Society* in which third sector organizations would in practice play a leading role (Cabinet Office 2010a). The Big Society rhetoric has been an important element of the new politics of the Coalition government, and has been directly promoted by the Prime Minister, David Cameron. However, it is not clear exactly what is meant by the Big Society, and some critics pointed out that it was little more than a cover for cuts in public expenditure (Coote 2010).

Nevertheless there have been some new commitments, including further extension of the opportunities for organizations in England to be commissioned to provide public services (HMG 2011b), the introduction of new agencies such as Big Society Capital as an independent investment bank for the sector, new measures to encourage volunteering such as the National Citizens Service for 16-year-olds, and further support for community engagement through the training of community organizers.

In practice, however, these programmes continue many of the themes developed under Labour, which was also committed to introducing the investment bank and expanding third sector involvement in public service delivery. What is more these programmes are operating in a much reduced public spending climate and within the context of a political commitment to reduce, or replace, the role of the state in supporting the sector more generally. The support for the sector developed by Labour and symbolized by the creation of the OTS, may be something of a high water mark in relations between the sector and the state, therefore, with the Big Society leading to more distance being created between them.

The devolution of policy-making to the administrations in Scotland, Wales and Northern Ireland has significantly changed the landscape of social policy development and delivery within the UK, as we discuss elsewhere in this book. This is particularly the case with third sector policy, because here devolution of policy has also reinforced the already separate development and coordination of the sector in these three countries. As mentioned earlier the main sector umbrella organization, the NCVO, is actually an English agency. There are separate national umbrella agencies in the other countries: for instance, the Scottish Council for Voluntary Organisations (SCVO), the Wales Council for Voluntary Action (WCVA) and the Northern Ireland Council for Voluntary Action (NICVA).

Since 1999 these agencies have been able to engage directly with the parliaments and assemblies of the devolved administrations. In all three countries similar agencies to the OTS/OCS have been established, for instance, the Third Sector Division in Scotland. In practice largely similar policy regimes were initially developed in each. However, this was in part no doubt a product of the fact that Labour was in power in all four countries throughout most of the 2000s, in Northern Ireland through direct rule until 2007. Since the 2010 general election and the 2011 elections in the devolved administrations, however, this has changed, with the Conservatives and Liberal Democrats having little profile outside England. The Coalition's Big Society agenda has not been shared by the devolved administrations since 2011 therefore, although in practice commitments to involvement in public service delivery and community engagement are still common across all (see Alcock 2012).

CONTRADICTIONS AND CHALLENGES

The great strengths of voluntary action – its variety and spontaneity – are also to some extent its greatest weaknesses. Voluntary and community organizations and social enterprises have largely developed on an ad hoc basis, as activists and innovators have turned their ideas into collective action. The distribution of such activists and entrepreneurs, however, is both uneven and unplanned. There may be an excellent community play scheme or independent advice centre in a local area; but it is equally likely that there may not be. The NSPCC provides an important additional service to protect children in need; but there are other needy groups for whom no such charitable body exists. A social enterprise like *Fifteen* may transform the lives and prospects of its workers, but this is a drop in the ocean of need for training and employment development.

Furthermore, some organizations receive much more popular support, and charitable donations, than others; for example, animal charities regularly feature amongst the most popular causes for individual donations, whereas support for migrants and asylum seekers never does. Third sector activity is thus not comprehensive, or even equitable; it is partial, patchy and sometimes unreliable, and against the good initiatives must be contrasted the major gaps.

Exclusion and discrimination can also be problems within organizations as well as across the sector; and here, arguably, is an even more serious dilemma. Not all voluntary organizations are outward looking. Some can be quite narrowly focused and dominated by a few powerful individuals and their individual interests. Because voluntary activity relies, in essence, on voluntary participation this can often mean many are excluded either passively (because they do not take part) or actively (because they are told that they are not wanted). And this exclusion, too, can be structured by race, gender, class or other social divisions. Indeed, it may be argued that most voluntary organizations exclude some potential activists, or potential beneficiaries, through social divisions of one kind or another, which could create significant problems for the role they might be expected to play in promoting civic renewal and social inclusion.

Nevertheless the third sector has been strongly supported by both academics and policy makers, from Hadley and Hatch (1981) to Putnam (1993, 2000), and now occupies a central role in political dialogue and policy planning. This central role is borne out too by international comparison. In countries such as the USA, with more limited state welfare provision, the non-profit sector, as it is often called there, is large both in scale and scope. In many European countries with well-developed welfare states the sector also has crucial roles to play. In the Netherlands, for instance, although welfare services such as education and health are largely funded by the state, they were developed and initially administered by independent bodies based around the 'pillars' of religious affiliation and membership of organizations linked to the Catholic or Protestant churches. Religious organizations, especially those based in the Catholic Church, are also important in providing services in the Mediterranean countries such as Italy and Spain.

The third sector is varied, flexible, innovative, non-bureaucratic, accessible and, perhaps most significantly, cheap; but it is also unpredictable, unstable, incomplete and sometimes oppressive and exclusionary. It has developed largely on an unplanned basis, and, despite the massive increase in public support for it since the turn of the new century, remains independent of government control and wary of government interference. Social policy planning must recognize this, and also recognize the limitations that inherently flow from it. The government may now wish the sector to play a central role in creating its new Big Society; but organizations and activists may not take up this challenge in quite the way politicians and policy makers might want. Voluntary action will always seek out, and challenge, the gaps and contradictions in state welfare policy; and this capacity for innovation cannot be directed from above.

COMPREHENSION QUESTIONS

- Compare and contrast the 'parallel bars' and 'extension ladder' approaches to state support for voluntary activity.
- What is the 'Compact' and why was it introduced?
- Why did Labour governments invest so much public expenditure in horizontal support for the sector in the first decade of this century?
- What is the Big Society and how are third sector organizations expected to play a role in it?

REFLECTIVE QUESTION

- Does public funding threaten the independence of third sector organisations?

FURTHER READING

Kendall (2003) provides the most comprehensive coverage of the third sector in the UK and in particular its relations with government, although Kendall and Knapp's (1996) earlier introductory text is also worth looking at. Evers and Laville (2004) is a good guide to European debates on the sector, and Kendall (2009) includes comparative analysis of different European policy regimes. Billis's (2010) latest collection of papers is a good source of contemporary debates, including on the issue of hybridity. The journal *Voluntary Sector Review* publishes academic research on the sector. Deakin (2001) discusses the broader concept of civil society as a space for voluntary action. Detailed information on the shape of the sector in England can be found in the NCVO *Almanac* (Clark et al. 2012), which is now available through the NCVO website below, with similar material on the SCVO, WCVA and NICVA sites. Recent government policy developments can be accessed on the Cabinet Office website, www.cabinetoffice.gov.uk. There are also a number of useful independent websites servicing different aspects of the sector, including the NCVO, www.ncvo-vol.org.uk, and the CAF, www.cafonline.org.uk; and academic research can be found on the Third Sector Research Centre's website, www.tsrc.ac.uk.

5
Informal Welfare

SUMMARY OF KEY POINTS

- Informal welfare is family, friends and neighbours providing a range of services through helping networks.
- The continuing existence of informal care and support is assumed by the other provider sectors in the planning of welfare provision.
- Informal care is not organized or regulated and in practice is based on individual dedication and goodwill or reciprocal commitments.
- Informal care is sometimes referred to as 'community care', although in practice this means care within communities, not care by communities.
- The form and structure of informal welfare is affected by changes and developments in the other sectors.
- Support for childcare, especially of very young children, has grown but is still limited despite commitments to 'family friendly' provisions.
- The availability of family members to provide informal care has been affected by broader demographic and social changes.
- The needs of carers may not be the same as those they care for.
- Social security benefits are available for those unable to enter paid employment because of caring responsibilities, and other forms of support have also been developed, though these are not extensive.
- Support for the personal and care costs of adults needing long-term care varies across the devolved administrations.

THE IMPORTANCE OF INFORMAL PROVISION

Analysis of the structure of social policy provision focuses our attention on the different ways in which welfare services are provided and the varying mix of providers within any particular social context, as we have seen in the other chapters in Part 1. However, despite this broadened focus, it remains the case that until recently debate about the different sectors of welfare paid relatively little attention to what is, in volume terms at least, the major provider of social services: the informal sector. Although, as Means and Smith (2008), have pointed out, there is now recognition that it has played the 'dominant', if often 'invisible', role in all welfare regimes.

The unorganized and unrecorded activities of family, friends and neighbours in caring for and supporting each other has always been the underlying social fabric upon which all other welfare activity is based. That such care and support will be provided is something we take for granted as academics and policy makers and, more importantly perhaps, that we take for granted as members of society too. It is of course understandable that we should do so and in practice it is desirable – indeed, even essential – that we should be able to. There is an implied reciprocity and mutual interdependence in all interpersonal relationships that could never fully be planned, predicted or neatly pigeonholed. However, taking such support as given should not prevent us from recognizing its importance in broader social policy terms, or from analysing, and acting upon, its interrelations with other forms of support in other sectors.

It is precisely because informal support has always been there in the past and, we trust, always will be in the future, that we must seek to understand its scope and its problems, and make sure that what we take for granted, we do not also ignore or unintentionally exploit. In practice the state welfare services that were developed over the last century in Britain largely took as given, or more positively were predicated upon, the support and care provided informally by families and communities. In other words, certain responsibilities were – and still are – presumed to exist within particular restricted groups: for example, education policy assumes parents will be available to support children outside the school day and school year; health policy assumes both minor acute conditions and chronic sickness or disability can be provided for informally at home; and social security assumes some family members will pool resources and support one another.

Without the informal services provided at home and in the neighbourhood, state, commercial and third sector providers would not be able to operate in the way they do – or, indeed, in many cases would be unable to operate at all. Informal provision is thus crucially important. It is also massive. Because it is not organized or recorded, it would be impossible to measure the size of the informal sector, although, as we shall see later, some attempts have been made to count the numbers involved in giving and receiving some aspects of informal care. However, the fact that we cannot measure informal welfare activity does not mean it does not have any costs. As Wright (1987) pointed out in an early study of the economics of informal care for the elderly, it is in fact very costly. It is costly immediately in terms of the time provided by carers and supporters; and it is costly indirectly in terms of the lost earnings and opportunities this caring work imposes on them, which are sometimes referred to as *opportunity costs* (Joshi 1988).

Recognition of the costs involved in the informal provision of services is an important part of social policy analysis of them. It also suggests important policy responses. In some cases these costs could, and perhaps should, be covered by others, or at least subsidized. For instance, this could be done through the provision of income in the form of social security benefits for informal carers, and this does, to some extent, take place. Informal service providers could also be supported and assisted in their tasks by a range of other means and measures, and we shall discuss these shortly.

Where such support is provided, however, informal provision is clearly going to overlap with support from the state, or from the private sector where these means are purchased on the market. As we discussed in Chapter 4 it also overlaps with third sector provision; and, where these overlaps exist, the distinction between informal support and organized services in the other sectors becomes blurred. The relationship with voluntary activity, in particular, can be a complex one: for instance, when does a baby-sitting circle cease to be neighbourly support and become an organization? There are problems, therefore, in defining precisely what we mean by the informal sector; and, even if these definitional problems cannot be entirely resolved, they must be addressed.

WHAT IS INFORMAL CARE?

In fact it is the question of overlap that is perhaps the most important difficulty faced in seeking to define what we mean by the informal sector. As we discussed in Chapter 3, public provision is often contrasted with private provision in social policy debate. Although the latter is sometimes taken to mean commercially provided welfare in the market, it can also include informal services provided privately at home. Private provision thus includes the informal sector, although it is not conterminous with it.

However, there is a danger in perceiving informal provision simply as private welfare. The public–private dichotomy can be a misleading one, especially where it is used to suggest that somehow private provision is not a matter of public concern or that it cannot, or should not, be the subject of public policy. Feminist critics, for example, have pointed to attempts to reduce family relations to such a private (or personal) sphere and have argued strongly that such relationships are not in reality separate from broader socioeconomic structures. As they have often put it, 'the personal is also political'. And, as Ungerson (1987) signified in the title of her book on informal care, *Policy is Personal* too. Just as it is unhelpful to define commercial services as private, so it is inaccurate to perceive the informal sector as a separate private sphere.

A more significant feature of the informal sector, for definitional purposes at least, is its unorganized (or, more accurately, *non*-organized) nature. State bureaucracies and businesses organize the services they offer to their users, or customers. Indeed, it is just this organization, and the bureaucracy accompanying it, that has often been a feature of the criticisms that have sometimes been levelled at these sectors. Voluntary organizations aim to avoid these structural constraints; but, even where they are controlled and managed by their users, they are nevertheless organizations. In contrast, the provision of care and support on an informal basis is not organized, either by an external agency or by those providing the service themselves. There are no rules or regulations governing what is to be done or how it is done. There is no enforceable contract or even a formal goodwill agreement: there is only the willingness to care and the expectation to benefit.

This is not to say, however, that services provided informally are not both reliable and predictable. Indeed they are usually both, and often more so than those supposedly provided under strict legal rules and statutory obligations. The willingness to care and the expectation of support are the two sides of the reciprocal nature of most informal services; in practice this reciprocity ensures we do care for others because we know that others will care for us, even if this may be a different 'other' at a relatively distant time. *Reciprocity* is thus at the heart of informal care and support; and reciprocal relations between individuals are not generally amenable to formal organization or control, for then the obligation moves from the individual to the structural level. Of course, as with all definitions in this area, the distinction is a blurred one; support provided by a neighbour may, for example, be incorporated into a package of care through a social worker, thus including it within a form of state service. However, insofar as the commitment to provide the support moves from an individual offer to a structural obligation, the service moves from the informal to the state, or perhaps the voluntary, sector.

The non-organized provision of informal care and support is usually based within families or communities: thus the informal sector might be identified with the relationships within families and communities. As a definitional base, however, this too provides us with some difficulties. For a start, the definition and structure of family relations is constantly changing. Despite appeals in some quarters and at some times for a return to 'traditional' family values, family relations have always been in a state of flux. Relationships change: people marry earlier (or now later, or not at all), have fewer children, or separate and divorce; and definitions change: those whom we might have included within our (extended) family in the past may now be regarded rather differently as distant relatives, from whom support would not be expected. If the informal sector is based on families, then what exactly does this mean?

Much the same problems arise with the notion of community. What we mean by community is in practice contested and the nature of communities differs significantly – from the local neighbourhood, to the church group, to the migrant workers' collective. Although commentators and policy makers often refer to 'the community' and talk, usually in complimentary terms, about things such as community schools or community policing, quite different things are often meant, and understood, by these references to community structure. As we discuss in Chapter 11, policies to encourage the 'community care' of people with mental or physical health problems are based, at least in theory, on the assumption that there are community structures in contemporary British society that will automatically provide a supportive and caring environment to cater for the needs of such people. This expectation has been taken up by the Coalition government in its promotion of the Big Society, and, more specifically, in the development of local care networks and neighbourhood involvement in caring, a more community-oriented role for social workers, and training for community organizers, discussed in Chapters 4 and 11.

However, it is in fact doubtful whether such close-knit and caring communities have ever been widespread in UK society; and certainly they do not exist in this simple form now. There are community activities and organizations in which people may, or may not, be involved or to which they may feel allegiance; but these are constantly changing structures from which allegiance may be withdrawn or transferred. Also communities can be political and cultural, such as the anti-bypass campaign or the local arts group, rather than geographical and social. Many such community structures are quite ill-equipped – and indeed inappropriate – as a base for informal social services.

In practice, therefore, it is usually the family, friends and neighbours of those in need who provide services rather than any broader community group. They can sometimes constitute what one American commentator called 'helping networks' (Johnson 1987); and these networks may provide a range of support and care services, but they do not do so on behalf of any given community structure.

Families in particular, of course, provide care and support, at least for those within the close family group (whether that is a lone parent or a three-generation household). Friends we choose, and presumably they choose us. They may expect to give, and receive, support; as the old saying goes, 'a friend in need is a friend indeed'. Neighbours we probably do not choose; but they are likely to know us and know of our needs for care and support. Friends and neighbours can undertake a wide range of informal services, including shopping, cooking, gardening, providing transport or even just keeping a watchful eye (surveillance), albeit only in a minority of cases: for instance, Rossiter and Wicks (1982) once calculated that only around 8 per cent of the elderly received regular support of this kind from neighbours, while more recent studies point to the lack of neighbourly contact experienced by significant numbers of older people. Drawing on evidence from research into informal care, Johnson (1987) listed five categories of social service regularly provided on an informal basis:

- Personal care – washing, dressing, feeding, etc.
- Domestic care – cooking and cleaning
- Auxiliary care – gardening and odd jobs
- Social support – visiting and companionship
- Surveillance – keeping an eye on vulnerable people.

Family members may provide services in all these categories, but friends or neighbours are more likely to provide those in the last two or three only.

Thus, here we have a classification of the types of activity involved in informal social services and some idea of who might be involved in providing these. As far as a definition of the informal sector goes, this may be as good as we can get: it is family, friends and neighbours providing a range of individual services through unorganized helping networks, with those offered by friends and neighbours being more restricted and variable than the support supplied by family members.

THE DEVELOPMENT OF INFORMAL CARE

The informal provision of care and support preceded the development of modern social policy and to some extent it has remained outside the formal service planning process. The point about informal welfare provision is that it is not planned or organized like other sectors.

However, it is affected by developments within the formal welfare sectors; indeed, these have been crucially important in shaping the context within which informal activity takes place, and the expectations that both service providers and recipients have of it.

Many voluntary organizations have grown out of informal activity. These include the baby-sitting circle that becomes the local mother and toddler group, or the squatters' group that becomes a campaign against homelessness. The boundaries between the third and informal sectors remain constantly blurred and, in particular, changes in the size and scope of voluntary and community activity are likely to relieve, or accentuate, pressure on informal service providers to take on caring or supporting roles. Furthermore, these changes occur both over time and across different places.

The development of commercial welfare services has also affected the informal sector. The wider range of services available commercially can displace informal care. Those with resources have always been able to buy the personal care they need (for example, through the employment of nannies and nurses); and, with growing affluence, this commercial replacement of informal care is utilized by a broader range of the population, for instance fee-charging early years or out-of-school care, albeit still more by the better-off. Commercial services can also, however, support informal activity. Adaptations to homes, such as a stair lift; personal aids, such as an electric wheelchair; or help with domestic and personal tasks can make the provision of informal care much less onerous; and there is now a large market for such domiciliary services. Commercial savings schemes and health insurance policies can secure financial support if, or when, a need for informal care arises and, as discussed in Chapter 11, the Coalition's care funding reforms in England are intended to stimulate such provision. Again, these services are likely to be more widely used by the better-off; nevertheless, their impact on the size, and shape, of the informal sector is extensive.

Most importantly of all, however, the development of state welfare services has affected the informal sector in a wide manner of ways; and changes in public provision have continued to alter the relationship between the two. To a large extent much of the early development of the welfare state was predicated upon an attempt to remove the burden of informal care and support for all welfare needs from the individual and replace it with collectively organized services provided by all, and for the benefit of all. State health and education services took responsibility for much of the provision of these away from the family who, perforce, would have provided more of them before. The development of state social work services resulted in the provision of more and better quality public residential care for children and adults in need of extensive support, of day care and drop-in services for those with more limited needs, and of counselling and advice for those uncertain of how to secure the assistance they need.

During the post-war period the establishment of state welfare in Britain saw a major extension of public social services, which were intended, in part at least, to ensure that collective provision should replace the informal demands made on family, friends and neighbours in the past. However, since then the pendulum of policy planning has to some extent swung away from state provision and back towards an explicit expectation of, and reliance upon, informal sector care. Within two decades of the establishment of post-war state services, criticisms began to emerge of the discomfort, insensitivity and even brutality of state institutional care (for example, Townsend's classic 1962 study of homes for older people); and belief in the undesirability of 'total institutions' has since become widespread. Indeed both children's and care homes are still sometimes viewed negatively with a mixture of fear and pity.

Perhaps the most negative images of state collective care, however, have been reserved for mental hospitals. Here a state service has often been seen in popular culture primarily as a threatening place, to be avoided almost at all costs. Such negative imagery has resulted in a move away from such residential care in social policy planning. In Italy, in the 1970s, this shift was a stark one; all large mental hospitals were closed down and their patients transferred to community-based care schemes. Policy change, though not as rapid in Britain, moved in the same direction, particularly following the community care measures of the 1990s, discussed in Chapter 11. Such community care can avoid the insensitivity, and the stigma, of state residential provision; it can also be more flexible and adaptable to the particular needs of different people, although it can also still require the support of organized services within the home.

However, the shift towards community care is not just a product of political and policy rejection of the value of public residential provision: it is also the result of financial pressure on state services and a narrower economic assessment of the (apparent) costs of these different models and sectors of care. State residential care is expensive to provide and large amounts of public money are needed to purchase and maintain institutions and pay their staff. Community-based care provided informally by family, friends and neighbours has much less of an impact on the public purse, especially where, as has often been the case in Britain, the state services to support such care have themselves been restricted by lack of resources. Of course, as we have already pointed out, informal care in the community is costly in other ways; in particular it imposes costs on those individuals who do the caring work. However, this does not register in the economic or political calculations of the resourcing of community care; and thus the shift back to the informal sector has been assumed to create much-needed savings in state welfare provision. These savings have been experienced as an increased pressure on the informal sector, resulting directly from developments within the state sector that are likely to intensify as the Coalition government's deficit reduction plans take effect.

COMPREHENSION QUESTIONS

- What are the 'opportunity costs' of informal care, and to what extent would it be desirable to try and quantify these?
- To what extent has the expansion of public, commercial and third sector care services reduced the demand on the informal sector?

REFLECTIVE QUESTION

- Can communities care?

SUPPORTING INFORMAL CARE

Although the welfare services provided informally vary widely in form and scope, the most significant feature of the sector, especially from a social policy perspective, is the role played by the provision of individual care in the home. Caring services can encompass a range of activities; in particular they include the personal and domestic tasks outlined above. These forms of care are provided by adults (usually parents, and especially mothers) for their young children; but they are also provided by adults (and occasionally by children) for other adults, in particular those who through illness or disability are unable to care adequately for themselves.

Until recently care for children was often not discussed in social policy debates, largely because it was taken for granted that parents can, and do, provide such care. In practice, however, it is generally mothers, rather than fathers, who provide the bulk of care for young children and who, in particular, forgo paid employment in order to do so. As we have pointed out, the long-term consequences can be significant in terms of their lost opportunities for receipt of wages and for career experience and enhancement. When children are older and can go to school this lessens to some extent the burden of care at home, but the limitations of the school day and year mean that it can still be difficult for mothers to combine childcare with full-time employment.

Due to these pressures on family-based care the provision of collective childcare has become a more significant issue for social policy in recent decades. This is recognized in moves to an extended school day for children and their parents; but it is particularly before school age where collective provision has been significantly expanded. As we outline in Chapter 12, parents of three- and four-year-olds and disadvantaged two-year-olds in England, Scotland and Wales are now entitled to free part-time early learning provision in a variety of settings. These include not only day nurseries but registered child minders. Provision for longer hours and care for school-age children, however, has to be paid for by parents and, though tax credit assistance is provided for those on low incomes, the level of such support has been cut back

The cost of such care is widely recognized to be among the highest in the EU and means working parents often rely on informal care, particularly that provided by grandparents. It is also seen as a significant constraint on women's employment and has led to debate over ways of reducing the burden on parents. Some favour the provision of free universal childcare; but the Coalition government's planned voucher scheme for some working parents in England offers more targeted assistance (see Chapter 12) – although this will take some time to be fully implemented.

To support parents recent governments have also invested in the 'family friendly' and 'work–life balance' measures described in Chapter 13. These provide entitlement to flexible working and parental leave, including greater recognition of fathers' roles through paternity and shared leave arrangements, and encouragement and guidance to employers on the need to support employees as parents and recognize their family commitments in workload and career planning. Whether purchased from a full-time live-in nanny or for a few extra hours a week from a neighbour or friend, however, private childcare services supplement the informal provision of care in families, and may overlap with it. Many private arrangements such as baby-sitting can be extremely informal. Of course, such private arrangements are not new; they have always been a central feature of the family-based informal care of children, although one often overlooked, and inadequately supported.

More generally, though and perhaps unfortunately, policy planning for childcare in the informal sector has traditionally concentrated not on the complex working arrangements many families successfully make for the care of their children, but on the failure of some families to provide care adequately, and the consequent need for state intervention to ensure the harm done to children in such cases is minimized, as discussed in Chapter 11.

However, while the bulk of informal care is provided for young children, a significant, and growing, proportion concerns that for vulnerable adults. In practice, this is largely provided by close family members, especially partners and adult children, and usually without formal support from either the state or the other sectors of welfare. The 2011 Census showed that in England and Wales, for instance, 5.8 million people, the same proportion of the population (10 per cent) as in 2001, provided unpaid care for someone with an illness or disability. Of these 2.1 million (37 per cent, compared to 32 per cent in 2001) were giving 20 or more hours of care a week (ONS 2012b).

It is feminist commentators, in particular, who have elevated the issue (and the problems) of informal care for adults on to the policy agenda. As they have pointed out, it is often women who provide such care and experience many of the problems related to it (Finch and Groves 1983; Ungerson 1987), with women, as Parker (1990) pointed out, disproportionably carrying a significant, yet hidden, burden and being 'more likely to give up their jobs, lose more money and experience more stress than are male carers'. However, it would be wrong to assume that all informal care in the home is carried out by women, and overall female carers only slightly outnumber males, though amongst the over seventy-fives this balance changes (Arksey and Glendinning 2012).

The contradictions that underlie this burden were brought out sharply in the title of an early overview of informal care, Finch and Groves' (1983) *A Labour of Love*. For women especially, the fusion of labour and love is manifest in the double meaning of the word care. Care can mean caring *about* someone and it can also mean caring *for* them. The provision of much informal care is predicated on the assumption that, because we care about someone, we can also therefore be expected to care for them in times of need. This is an assumption that may be strongly held, most significantly by those in need of care, and those who feel obliged to care for them. Here the presumed, and yet unplanned, reciprocity of the informal sector can begin to take on a coercive, and even an oppressive, form. The costs of caring for a vulnerable or dependent adult can be great, both immediately and indirectly over the longer term (Joshi 1992). It can also, unlike childcare, frequently be a long (and ultimately depressing) ordeal, ending only with the death of the recipient of the care. Yet the provision of such care is widespread and vitally important at both an individual and a broader social level. It is also an area of provision that has grown rapidly, and is likely to increase in the future, with larger numbers of older people and people with disabilities surviving within the population.

However, while the demand for informal care is growing, the 'helping networks', in particular the families, that provide it are changing in ways that are likely to reduce their capacity to do so in the future and which have led to concerns over a potential 'care gap'. There has been a continuing decline in the number of younger single people able to provide informal care, particularly single daughters; and at the same time family size has fallen with the result that there are fewer children to provide a future pool of potential carers. The numbers of childless people has also risen, whilst changes in family stability have further reduced the potential supply of carers, with increased numbers of divorces meaning that previous family obligations are frequently severed. Families may also be more geographically dispersed either within the UK or further afield.

Perhaps most significant though is the growth of women's (especially married women's) participation in the labour market, discussed in Chapter 13, and the continuing economic policy pressure for women to enter and remain in work. Of course, some married women do give up paid employment in order to provide informal care. But this is a hard financial, as well as emotional, decision which many are having to face, and which many decide to refuse to make. These refusals may, of course, lead to a growth in the market provision of such care (perhaps even in organizations employing women as paid carers); but such a shift away from the informal towards the market sector is both uncertain and fraught with difficulties, especially for those too poor to purchase support services. Moreover other labour market changes, especially the pressure for people to work longer (also arising from demographic ageing) or care for grandchildren as well as older relatives are likely to affect the availability of carers, particularly since the newly retired provide much of both forms of informal care.

A shift from informal to market-based caring services may not, of course, necessarily be an unhelpful development for those requiring such care. The inclusion of 'community care' in recent policy planning seems to have been informed by an almost unquestionable belief in the desirability of informal, individual, care as against collectively provided services, founded largely on the criticisms of the worst of state residential provision. Yet, as early research showed (Qureshi and Walker 1989), much depends upon the dedication and commitment of the carer, and upon the support services available to supplement their informal provision, both of which can vary dramatically.

Support for community care initially focused almost exclusively on its advantages from the point of view of the recipients, the *cared for*, and largely ignored the problems experienced by *carers* within the informal sector. Yet, as Twigg (1989) argued, appreciation of carers' circumstances and carers' needs may lead to a rather different emphasis in policy planning. For instance, carers may be perceived as *resources* for service provision, as *co-workers* with those in other sectors, or as *co-clients* with the person they are caring for. More recently, it has been argued carers might also be viewed as *experts*, working with professionals to assist care recipients (Arksey and Glendinning 2012). These varying perceptions lead to different ways of supporting carers, all of which have been variously pursued – sometimes simultaneously. They have also, however, added to the concerns expressed by disabled people's and other organizations over the tendency to equate the needs and therefore the service requirements of carers and service users.

One of the most fundamental problems facing carers is the source (and the adequacy) of their income, especially where they are excluded from paid employment as a result of their caring work. Since 1975 there has been a social security benefit specifically designed to provide an income for carers. Now called the Carers' Allowance, it is paid to those over 16 not in full-time education or receiving a pension, and earning below a minimal amount (£100 in 2013), who provide 35 hours or more of care a week to someone who receives a qualifying disability benefit. However, it has long been one of the lowest UK benefits and those without any other source of income are still left depending upon Income Support and its replacement, the UC.

Even this low benefit was not provided for married and cohabiting female carers prior to 1986, because of the assumption they could be provided for by their male partners. The discriminatory perspective that informed this assumption reveals much about past (and perhaps still present) policy assumptions about the structure and workings of the informal sector that have been highlighted by feminist writers.

Caring work is thus frequently associated with financial dependency upon inadequate social security benefits. It can also affect a carer's ability to save for their own future, adding to the immediate pressures of caring work on a low income. Recent governments have, however, provided some assistance through protections in the BSP, which are set to be extended under plans for the new single-tier pension referred to in Chapter 8. Again, however, many carers may not fully benefit from this.

As Glendinning (1992) pointed out, moreover, caring work is also associated with *interdependency* between the carer and the cared for. This is true at the formal level, with, as noted above, entitlement to the Carers' Allowance being predicated on the latter receiving the middle or higher rate DLA, a problem that significantly reduces take-up levels of both benefits because of the complexities involved in claiming them, and one that may be compounded as Personal Independent Payments replace the DLA.

Attempts have also been made to support carers in other ways, with the four countries of the UK initiating a succession of Carers' Strategies, most recently following the elections of 2010 and 2011. They also adopted similar policies including funding to promote local respite and employment services and encouraging employers to recognize carers' needs. At a UK level the Labour government attempted to support this through legislation providing a right to request flexible working first for parents of disabled children (in 2002) and in 2007 for eligible carers of adults. Provisions for carers' assessments and services in their own right were also introduced across the UK. In practice, however, the impact of these initiatives was limited.

More recent attempts have been made to strengthen this support, notably in England through the 2013 Care Bill, which followed the 2012 Care White Paper (HMG 2012a) discussed in Chapter 11. Alongside the promotion of 'replacement services' to enable carers to continue working, this is intended, for the first time, to entitle carers to support on the same basis as adults with care and support needs, including LA provision of a support plan. For many in the sector, however, financial concerns remain paramount. Where care is provided within family relationships, it may well involve a pooling of resources within the household; thus all sources of income, however inadequate, are likely to be used to support all family members. As a result the caring relationship can come to dominate the financial arrangements of the whole household – and, of course, their financial prospects for the future too.

As we discuss in Chapter 11 financial support for the provision of long-term and especially residential care to vulnerable adults in England has been reviewed by a series of bodies starting with the Sutherland Commission (1999). It recommended a separation between the costs of providing personal care to be met by the state for all, and more general living and housing (or 'hotel') costs, to be paid by individuals, perhaps with some means-tested support. Its recommendations, however, were only adopted by the devolved administration in Scotland, which introduced state funded personal care for over sixty-fives meeting defined categories of need in their own or residential homes; although in 2011 the Welsh administration introduced a capping scheme for non-residential care.

However, these provisions may well come under pressure from the general squeeze on public sector funding since 2011. Meanwhile in England support for vulnerable adults and their carers remained means-tested and targeted on those who could not afford private market domiciliary or residential services. But, as explained in Chapter 11, following another review (Dilnot 2011), the Coalition government has set in train measures to cap the cost of social care, excluding food and accommodation from 2016, and to establish a new deferred payments scheme for residential care from 2015.

For those funded by the state further changes are also under way. Since the 1990s their care has largely been provided by their LA in partnership with NHS agencies (see Chapter 11) and generally depended on the packages of care negotiated by social workers (care managers). These could include the provision of domiciliary services (home helps and 'meals on wheels') to assist both cared for and carers at home. However, the move to *personalization* is set to enable service users and carers to determine the support they require, and is being developed in Scotland, Wales and Northern Ireland as well as England, where it is being promoted alongside a renewed emphasis on care by as well as in the community and the promotion of local care networks (HMG 2012a).

The continuing embracement of 'community care' in the planning and development of services for vulnerable adults has placed it at the centre of policy practice therefore. But, the demand for care services is growing inexorably, in particular as the proportion of older people in the population grows; and this is putting pressure on public finances, which are also experiencing major cutbacks, in particular at LA level in some parts of England. Whatever the merits of the planned changes to long-term care funding in England and the broader spread of personalization, concern therefore remains over the support offered for informal carers, over the potential 'squeeze' between labour market pressures and the demand for caring, and over the extent to which the UK may face a care gap in future.

COMPREHENSION QUESTIONS

- What is meant by 'family friendly' policy planning, and to what extent can it reduce the demand for informal care of young children or of adult care?
- To what extent have the needs of *carers* been overlooked in policy planning in the informal sector?
- How have governments responded to the potentially growing demands for informal care?

REFLECTIVE QUESTION

- Should we be expected to care for those we care about?

FURTHER READING

Two early texts which put policy on informal care into a broader perspective and developed a feminist critique of past policy development were Finch and Groves (1983) and Ungerson (1987). Commentary on recent policy on community care can be found in Means and Smith (2008) and Arksey and Glendinning (2012), and can be tracked for England at www.doh.gov.uk and at the websites of the devolved administrations (see Chapter 6). Carers UK and the Carers Trust are independent bodies representing and campaigning on behalf of carers, and more information can be found on their websites at www.carersuk.org and www.carers.org.

6 Devolution and Local Control

SUMMARY OF KEY POINTS

- The UK is only in part a 'United Kingdom'. There is significant devolution of policy-making powers to separate elected governments in Scotland, Wales and Northern Ireland.
- Devolution of policy-making has been extended further over the last decade with a referendum on Scottish independence planned for 2014.
- Local government became established in Britain by the end of the nineteenth century. However, Britain retains a relatively unitary and centralized state structure.
- Local councils played a key role in the development of much economic and social policy provision, although the extent of local government powers was in decline throughout much of the last century as the balance between central and local control of policy planning shifted.
- Local authority income is made up of local taxes (Council Tax), charges for services and grants from central government. The balance between these has changed significantly over time.
- In the 1980s cash limits and cutbacks in government grants were used to control local government, leading to conflict with central government over the extent of local autonomy over service planning.
- Further reductions in local autonomy have followed from the contracting out of some local services and transfer of housing and schools to independent providers.
- New initiatives in local governance have meant a shift in the role of local councils from service provision to that of *enabling* authorities working in partnership with a range of other local agencies.
- In England the Coalition government has introduced renewed commitments to 'localism' with the aim of devolving greater policy-making powers to LAs, and encouraging further 'double devolution' of powers to local communities.

DEVOLUTION OF POLICY-MAKING

Most discussion and analysis of social policy in Britain focuses upon policy-making at the national level and the role of the national government in determining and delivering public policy. However, policy-making and delivery do not just take place at a national level. As we discuss in Chapter 7 there are external international pressures on UK policy development, which restrict the power and freedom of the British government. There are also restrictions on national policy-making which flow from structures and pressures within the UK, however. Indeed the British state has always had an internal political structure within which political power and policy-making authority does not always reside at a national level; and in recent times this devolved structure for policy-making and delivery has become more accentuated and more diverse across a range of geographical and political dimensions.

For a start, as we mentioned in Chapter 2, the UK is only to some extent a 'United Kingdom'. It is comprised of the separate nations (or subnations) of England, Scotland, Wales and Northern Ireland – although the size of these varies significantly, with England the largest by far (see Table 6.1). These separate nations have always had some level of autonomy from the British government in Westminster and Whitehall; for instance, in Scotland there has always been a separate legal system with different courts and a separate judiciary operating under significantly different legal principles, at least in some areas of law. Towards the end of the last century, however, there was increased pressure from Scotland, Wales and Northern Ireland for greater autonomy from the UK government in policy-making and service delivery.

Table 6.1 Four UK nations compared in 2011		
Nation	*Population*	*Percentage of UK Population*
England	53 million	84
Scotland	5.2 million	8
Wales	3 million	5
Northern Ireland	1.8 million	3

Source: 2011 Census, Office for National Statistics (2012b).

The UK government had always had separate offices overseeing public policy in Scotland and Wales, and in Northern Ireland there were a number of separate administrative structures controlling policies such as housing and education across the province; but these offices had largely been responsible for policies decided by the national government in Westminster. In 1999, however, the new Labour government moved beyond administrative separation to introduce genuine devolution of policy-making powers to separate elected bodies in these three countries, following referenda held to secure support for this. In Scotland this took the form of a new Scottish Parliament with legislative powers in certain designated areas (see Box 6.1).

In Wales devolution was more complex, due in part to evidence of less support for separation here. An elected National Assembly was initially set up with lesser secondary legislative powers. However, in 2006 the Government of Wales Act replaced this with a new Welsh Assembly Government (WAG) with ministerial appointments and a greater separation of powers. Provision was also made for primary legislative powers to be devolved as in Scotland, following a referendum. This took place in 2011 and led to a two to one majority for such a change and the Welsh Government (WG) now also has power to legislate on all devolved areas.

Both it and the Scottish Government (SG) now occupy high profile buildings in Edinburgh and Cardiff. Elections are held for each every four years, using systems of limited proportional representation. Throughout much of the first decade after devolution both were led by Labour, sometimes in coalition with the Liberal Democrats. In 2007, however, the Scottish National Party (SNP) secured a narrow majority in Scotland and in Wales Labour formed a coalition with the Welsh nationalists (Plaid Cymru).

BOX 6.1 Legislative powers devolved to the separate administrations in Scotland, Wales and Northern Ireland

Scottish Government
- health
- education and training
- local government
- social work
- housing
- planning
- tourism, economic development and financial assistance to industry
- some aspects of transport, including the road network, ports and harbours
- law, the prosecution system and the courts
- the police and fire services
- the environment, natural and built heritage
- agriculture, forestry and fishing
- sport and the arts
- statistics, public registers and records

Welsh Government
- agriculture, fisheries, forestry and rural development
- ancient monuments and historic buildings
- culture
- economic development
- education and training
- environment
- fire and rescue services and promotion of fire safety
- food
- health and health services
- highways and transport
- housing
- local government
- National Assembly for Wales
- public administration
- social welfare
- sport and recreation
- tourism
- town and country planning
- water and flood defence
- Welsh language

Northern Ireland Assembly
- health and social services
- education
- employment and skills
- agriculture
- social security
- pensions and child support
- housing
- economic development
- local government
- environmental issues, including planning

- transport
- culture and sport
- the Northern Ireland Civil Service
- equal opportunities
- justice and policing

In Northern Ireland an elected Assembly, also with restricted legislative powers, was established as part of the power sharing agreements flowing from the Good Friday peace process in 1998. However, the Assembly was suspended in 2002 as the leading political parties in the province, the Democratic Unionist Party (DUP) and Sinn Fein, could not agree on power sharing. It was subsequently re-established in 2007, and a range of legislative powers devolved to the Assembly and the Northern Ireland Executive (NIE), based in the Parliament Buildings at Stormont. There was a further round of Assembly elections in 2007, which were dominated by the DUP and Sinn Fein, and led to the appointment of a new DUP First Minister and a Sinn Fein Deputy First Minister.

The different initial constitutional position in the three countries was the product of the different political and institutional structures already operating within them and, initially at least, the varying strength of feeling on devolution expressed in referenda held there before formal devolution took place. They make understanding the different political and policy developments within the UK an ever more complex issue, and this is discussed only briefly here therefore. Parry (2012) provides a useful summary of the policy consequences of devolution, and more detailed analysis of the major issues can be found in Lodge and Schmuecker (2010).

In Scotland and Wales there are separate coordinating bodies implementing devolved policy powers, the SG and WG, supported by a range of departments or directorates with responsibility for different areas of policy. In Northern Ireland the NIE coordinates separate functional departments such as education, employment and health, with strategic oversight provided by the Office of the First Minister and Deputy First Minister. Although Labour dominated the politics of all three countries in the early years, as mentioned above, nationalist parties made more headway in 2007 (in new elections in Northern Ireland). In 2011 a further round of elections was held in all three with the SNP extending control in Scotland, Labour maintaining a narrow advantage in Wales, and the DUP and Sinn Fein again dominating in Northern Ireland. By this time though the Conservative-led Coalition government was in power in Westminster, and so for the first time there was a significant difference in political control across all four nations.

The range of policy matters devolved to the separate administrations is broadly similar. Major international policy-making powers, including defence, are still held by the UK government in Westminster as is budget-setting and fiscal policy which we discuss in Chapter 16. However, most areas of social policy, including education and training, health, social care, housing and planning, local government and aspects of employment policy have all been devolved – the major exception being social security (see Box 6.1).

In these policy areas devolution led quite quickly to some significant departures in policy development, and these differences have continued to grow over the last decade, as revealed in Part 2. For instance, in all three devolved administrations NHS prescriptions are provided free of charge to all patients, whereas charges remain for many patients in England. In Scotland provision has been made for free higher education tuition and universal free long-term care for vulnerable adults and Wales too has extended support for its citizens in these areas. Scotland has also strengthened its separate school system and in Wales non-selective comprehensive education has been openly pursued. Conversely in Northern Ireland secondary education has traditionally been selective and segregated by religion, and despite policy change this is still widespread.

With the 2010 and 2011 elections leading to different public control in all countries it is likely that policies will diverge even further in the future. In 2012 the SG, led by the SNP, announced they planned to hold a referendum in Scotland to seek endorsement for a move to leave the United Kingdom and establish Scotland as an independent country. The UK government agreed this referendum would take place in 2014, and both governments committed themselves to implement the majority view. Provisions giving the WG limited tax raising powers are also being considered.

Devolution to Scotland, Wales and Northern Ireland leaves unresolved, of course, the question of what should happen about policy-making within England, the largest country in the UK with 84 per cent of the population. In practice nothing much has really changed here, with the British Parliament being the legislative body for England on those issues where elsewhere power is devolved to the new national governments. This has led to some political conflict over the role Scottish, Welsh and Irish MPs in Westminster should play in determining legislation on social policy issues to be applied only in England (the so-called West Lothian question), which was accentuated for a while when a Scottish MP, Gordon Brown, became the Prime Minister in England.

However, the size of England itself has led to increasing concern about the extent to which policy-making and delivery could also be devolved here. After 1997 the Labour government began to develop some new elements of policy of devolution within England; for instance, the introduction of the new office of the Mayor in London. This resulted in the pursuit of some new high profile policy initiatives here, such as congestion charging on roads in the capital. Other local areas have also been given the power to establish mayors, and in 2011 the Coalition government sought to extend this further. However, in practice, only a small number have taken up the opportunity; and even here none have the extent of power wielded in London, where the mayor's office is the only base for policy planning across the capital.

Devolution of policy planning was also extended to some degree to regional level in England under Labour. This built on the Government Offices for the Regions (GORs) which had been set up to coordinate some aspects of policy development and delivery at regional level within the country, and led to the creation of Regional Development Agencies (RDAs). The RDAs were comprised mainly of local councillors and leading business people from across the region and operated primarily to promote and support regional economic development. The Coalition, however, was not convinced that this additional tier of governance was effective, or affordable, and abolished them after the 2010 election, passing any remaining powers back to local government.

COMPREHENSION QUESTIONS

- How has devolution changed the context and content of social policy-making in the UK?
- What is the West Lothian question, and why does it challenge the authority of the Westminster government over English policy development?

REFLECTIVE QUESTION

- Has devolution led to the end of the British welfare state?

THE CENTRAL–LOCAL DIMENSION

The recent moves towards the devolution of policy-making in the UK, including the now aborted regional level, has largely been the result of a top-down transfer of power from central government. However, a longer historical review of the development of public services in

Britain reveals it is local initiatives that have frequently been the driving force behind the establishment and extension of many major services, and that the local administration and delivery of services is still a major operational feature of modern welfare provision. Indeed in many ways it would be more accurate to say that modern British welfare has its roots in the initiatives and activities of local, *rather* than central, government.

The history, and current state, of the relationship between central and local government in the development of welfare services is, however, a complex – and at times a conflictual – one. In particular in organizational terms, the extent of devolution of power and responsibility that can be made to the local level is fraught with difficulties and contradictions. For instance, if local administrators have the power to determine the shape, or size, of local services, how can consistent standards of service for users be maintained between different areas? And, if local responsibility for services is based upon the power of locally elected representatives, does this not provide a basis for political conflict between local and central government? Both of these are problems that have dogged the relationship between the two in Britain at least since the latter half of the twentieth century, as we shall see. As a result the central–local dimension of social policy development is both complex and fraught and, as a consequence of this, it is also constantly changing, and this complexity has intensified following devolution.

In examining the central or local balance of policy control, however, it is important to distinguish between the local administration and delivery of welfare (or other) services and the local government of such services. Of course, most welfare services are delivered, and thus *administered*, on a local basis, even where all aspects of policy and practice are determined directly by central government. Citizens using services on a day-to-day basis are likely do so through their local area office. However, for services that are governed nationally, this local administration of central welfare services is merely an organizational feature of the structure of delivery to users, who need a local point of contact with those providing them. For instance, the Jobcentre Plus provides a local office from which working-age claimants can pursue their entitlement to social security benefits, and in health Clinical Commissioning Groups (CCGs) in England, the Area Health Boards in Scotland and Health Boards in Wales are locally focused.

As we discuss in Part 2, in a number of policy areas there has more recently been a commitment to introduce collaboration and even partnership working across these different local administrative structures and those of local government, and this is an issue to which we shall return in Chapter 18. However, not all of these bodies operate within the same geographical boundaries as local government (or as each other) and so practical discontinuities have often hampered the development of effective local partnerships.

The local *government* of welfare services means these are the direct responsibility of a set of politicians elected by the local population, operating with powers and duties that are quite separate from those of national politicians in the central state, and which may even conflict with these. For instance, LA housing has been planned, designed and built according to policies set by local politicians, sometimes against central government priorities; and education services, although they are constrained by statute to provide certain standards in teaching and learning, have traditionally been controlled by local councillors who can set the policy priorities for development and delivery of these within their area – although in both of these fields local control has been weakened further over recent years (see Chapters 10 and 12). Local government is therefore a separate sphere within the state, with a guaranteed constitutional status, referred to by one commentator as the 'local state' (Cockburn 1977).

In fact, most welfare capitalist countries have local, as well as central, state machinery as a constitutional feature of their political make-up, and these enjoy clear, yet delineated, powers over both policy development and implementation. The central–local political divide is a widespread international phenomenon; and in comparative terms this divide can take a number of different forms. In particular it is important to distinguish between two broad categories of central–local structure:

1. *Unitary* states have a central government that has historically been the major political base of the country and has the exclusive power to legislate and thus determine the broad structure of policy throughout the country, although in unitary states some powers and responsibilities are usually devolved by legislation to local government. Leaving aside for a moment the devolution of powers to Scotland, Wales and Northern Ireland discussed earlier, the UK is an example of a unitary state; and within the UK central and national government politicians have greater power and influence than local politicians.

2. *Federalist* states are generally the product historically of the coming together of a number of smaller administrative regions, each initially with their own autonomy; and, although there is now a central government covering all such regions, this autonomy is preserved to some extent, for example, by the retention of law-making powers by local regions. The USA is the major example of a federalist state, where law-making powers over major aspects of social policy are retained by individual States despite national union. Here, by contrast, the power of local State politicians is such that they are considered some of the most important political actors within the country.

However, even between unitary states the extent and amount of devolved power and control varies significantly. For instance, in Europe, countries such as France and Germany have devolved control to local government to a much greater extent than is the case in Britain, with the German *Länder* appearing in some cases to have almost as much power as American States. In fact, in comparative terms Britain is not just a unitary state, it is one of the most centralized amongst advanced industrial nations; and it has become more and more centralized as its welfare services have developed.

THE DEVELOPMENT OF LOCAL GOVERNMENT

The history of local government in Britain, in the context of social policy, is one of structural stagnation, and yet policy initiative. It is also a story of rapid local growth followed by a gradual loss of powers to central government, although this is a much more complex and fluctuating picture than it is sometimes presented as being. For instance, especially since the Second World War, the loss of powers has been accompanied by a significant growth in local government expenditure; and particularly in recent years the centralizing thrust of national government policy has been counteracted by the extension of local political activity into new and innovatory areas and a renewed commitment to promote 'localism' in decision making wherever possible. As Stoker (1991) argued in his textbook on local government, the view of its development as a history of decline is at best a one-sided one.

The rise of local government in the UK was initially closely linked to the growing impact of industrialization. The creation of new, large, urban populations led to local problems, to which the existing minimalist central state was unable to respond. The initial reaction of central government to this was to establish bodies at a local level, such as the Poor Law Boards and the Improvement Commissioners, to deal on an ad hoc basis with different social problems as they arose. In 1835, however, elected municipal councils were established in the new urban towns and cities. As the century progressed, these authorities gradually acquired responsibility for a range of local social services, such as health and housing. At the same time, however, the ad hoc bodies continued to grow, in particular through the establishment of School Boards to run local primary schools.

In 1888 local government was extended by the establishment of county councils in rural areas and municipal borough councils in the larger non-industrial towns. A separate London County Council covering the whole of the London metropolitan area was also established, providing some much-needed coordination over local services within the capital. Between 1894 and 1899 this structure of local government in England, Wales and Ireland was completed, and in places revised, in particular through the creation of new multi-purpose authorities (district councils) operating below county councils in rural areas and with responsibility for a separate set of powers and services. Similar developments also took place in Scotland. Thus throughout much of the UK there were, by the end of the nineteenth century, two tiers of local government, with a larger county council including within it a number of smaller district and parish councils with various powers over different services. In the larger urban towns and cities, however, there was unitary political control within the municipal borough council.

The structure that emerged from the 1890s was thus a complex – and frequently overlapping – one. Nevertheless, it remained throughout the first three-quarters of the twentieth century and was not reformed until 1974 (1975 in Scotland), following the recommendations of the Maud Committee of 1967. In Northern Ireland, however, legislation in 1973 limited the powers of local councils, with responsibility for services such as education, housing, health and social care being transferred to other, non-elected, bodies. Since then, however, further structural reform has taken place in the rest of the UK on a number of occasions with some elected authorities being abolished in the 1980s and a range of others restructured or abolished since.

In the early part of the twentieth century, however, despite an unchanging structure, local government initiative and influence within social policy grew dramatically. During this period the functions of local government also changed and expanded:

- Control of health, highways and housing remained but the latter grew significantly in importance after the development of LA housing for rent in the 1920s.
- Local councils controlled and developed major infrastructural services such as gas, water and electricity.
- In 1902 the School Boards were abolished and control over education passed to LAs.
- In 1929 LAs acquired responsibility for Poor Law relief and local hospitals and their responsibilities for children were expanded.
- Finally, by the late 1940s local government had acquired more general control over all physical development through responsibility for town and country planning.

The first half of the last century was therefore a period of municipal enterprise and development, influenced by the pioneering work in the late nineteenth century of Joseph Chamberlain who, as leader of Birmingham, the largest authority in Britain, oversaw a massive growth in local services and proudly boasted that the lives of all citizens of the city had been 'improved' by the council's achievements. The model of Birmingham was followed in particular by a number of other larger municipal authorities, for whom the power, for example to build housing, allowed them to transform both physically and socially the circumstances of local people. This resulted in a massive growth in the extent of local government activity; and between 1900 and 1938 LA expenditure increased fourfold.

The period up to the beginning of the Second World War is sometimes referred to as the heyday of local government in Britain, because it was a period of almost uninterrupted expansion on all fronts and was followed after the war by gradual loss of many of the functions that had been created and developed in this early period. In one sense this is clearly true:

- Control of gas and electricity was lost in 1947.
- Control over mainstream health services was lost in 1948 when these were transferred to the NHS.
- Control over water services was lost in 1962.
- Control over ancillary health services was lost in 1974.
- In the 1980s control over housing, education and personal social services was much restructured and reduced, an issue to which we shall return later.

This loss of local government services during the post-war period was all the more significant because this was the period of the major growth of state welfare in Britain. For the Labour government of 1945–51 in particular, the vision of social policy development was one of national, rather than local, responsibility for the welfare of citizens. This can be seen most obviously in the establishment of the NHS, which took much responsibility for health provision away from local government, and of the social security system (NI and NA), although many functions here had effectively been lost in the 1930s.

In practice there was little effective voice from local government within the post-war Labour government and the implicit distrust of the local state to deliver national services evenly on a high-quality basis was undoubtedly compounded by the rather outdated structure within which it was trapped. Yet, although there was pressure from some quarters to update this structure, it was never accorded sufficiently high political priority during the welfare reform years of the early post-war period (Stoker 1991).

However, the centralizing tendencies of this era can be over-exaggerated. Of the five major welfare services, three (education, housing and social care) remained – or, in the case of social care were placed – in LA hands. For instance, as we discuss in Chapter 12, the Education Act of 1944 was the first of the welfare reforms and it placed almost total control over the establishment and running of primary and secondary schools on local government. This situation was to lead to conflict in the 1960s and later, when central government sought to change the structure of secondary education in particular, and many LAs refused to implement the required changes.

Before the reforms of the post-war period, education and housing had already become established as the major items of *expenditure* for local government (Dunleavy 1984). Throughout the 1950s and after, the rapid growth of these services fuelled a continued growth in local spending, with the result that, even though functions were lost, LA expenditure continued to increase, both absolutely and in proportion to overall national expenditure growth. Between 1955 and 1975 LA expenditure increased threefold, and rose from 28 to 30 per cent of overall public expenditure. Furthermore, much of this expenditure was represented by an increase in employment in LA services (Stoker 1991). In terms of Keynesian economic policy, therefore, local government remained a central feature of both service delivery and the generation of economic growth.

Alongside the continued increase in LA expenditure in the immediate post-war period, however, was a shift in its financial base although this had already begun to take effect before the war. LA expenditure was, and still is, financed by income from three sources:

- Local taxation raised by councils; initially these were *rates* paid by property owners and based on property values, but since 1993 they have been replaced by a similar *council tax* (apart from Northern Ireland where a revised rates system remained).
- The *charges* that authorities make for some of the services they provide, such as education courses, planning applications or domiciliary care services.
- A share of national taxation revenue to cover some of the costs of local services, provided by *grants* from the UK government for England and the devolved administrations for the rest of the UK (under the overall budgetary system discussed in Chapter 16).

Originally the local development of services had been financed primarily out of local taxation through the rates, with central government money constituting only a minor source of income, and charges (providing around 30 per cent) somewhere in the middle. The role of charges has remained more or less constant, although the range and scale of charges began to grow in the 1990s. But the relative balance between rates and grants has changed dramatically, with central government grants replacing rates as the major source of income by the 1950s. The reason for this was the greater importance of national services, locally governed, such as education and housing, within local expenditure; and central government's concern to ensure adequate provision was secured in all areas. However, the consequence of this was to provide central government, potentially at least, with much greater control over local government through the provision of central grants. This was a factor that was to become of major significance in the changing relationship between the two in the 1980s and since.

Between the 1950s and the 1970s, therefore, the gradual expansion of the welfare state was mirrored by a gradual expansion, and enhancement, of the role of local government. Not only did the numbers of teachers, planners and social workers grow, but so too did their professional prestige and influence. With the support of their increasingly powerful public sector trade unions, LA employees enjoyed secure employment and extensive (and some would say paternalistic) control over local services. So, although functions had been lost, it is these post-war years that were perhaps the real heyday of local government, at least in the social policy field.

Towards the end of the 1970s, however, this began to change. As we have seen, the major fuel for local government expenditure and influence was by this time the provision of welfare services. The freezing, followed by cutbacks, of these services after the onset of recession in the 1970s was therefore bound to lead to pressure for reductions in LA spending and LA influence. Cash limits were set for all public expenditure, including house building and education spending; and in the 1980s these cash limits became cash cuts. The attempts by central government to secure reductions in local government expenditure on welfare service in the 1980s led, in practice, to major conflicts between them fuelled by the party political differences between Conservative central governments and the Labour controllers of many of the major LAs. And as a result a number of significant changes in the relationship between central and local government were introduced in the 1980s, in particular to restrict central financial support for local government services.

Throughout the earlier post-war period central support had taken the form of a *Rate Support Grant* (RSG) from central government to supplement local rates and to ensure service spending commitments could be met. The problem with this was that it left the determination of local commitments in the hands of local government, and thus cuts in the RSG would tend to be perceived by local government, and local people, as cuts in service commitments. Thus it was replaced after 1980 with a regime of financial support determined on a standardized basis through the use by central government of a list of indicators of local service needs. This was called the *Grant Related Expenditure Assessment* (GREA). It was determined directly by central government and, in a climate of cuts, was frequently well below the assessments of need made within authorities by local politicians.

The initial response of many authorities to the reduced levels of central support through GREAs was to increase local rates in order to maintain services at the levels that they felt were necessary. This, however, meant the government's overall targets for reduced public expenditure were still not being met because, in effect, they were thwarted by the continued spending of LAs. Central government therefore sought to control their powers to expand expenditure through increased local rates.

Initially this led to *rate capping* (setting a limit on the amount of increase in the local rates); but this was difficult to enforce in practice, and unpopular with local electorates. And eventually, apart from Northern Ireland, the whole rating system was replaced by a new form of local taxation, the *community charge* (or 'poll tax'), which was paid by all individuals living in the area, who, it was thought, would thus be less willing to vote to elect high-spending authorities. In fact, however, the community charge proved to be a hopelessly ineffective and widely unpopular form of local taxation. It was difficult to collect money from all individuals and it provoked popular resistance to payment in many areas. It came into force in 1990, but in 1993 had been replaced by a *council tax*, based, as the rates had been, on payments made by all property owners or occupiers, with a separate business tax on local businesses. Rates of business tax are set by central government, but LAs can set their own rates for council tax, although these are no longer used to challenge central spending targets as they were in the 1980s, and only raise around a fifth of local government revenue.

Since the 1990s the GREA has been replaced by a series of different central funding streams with similar aims to control levels of local government spending. Across the UK they are usually referred to now as *block grants*, with, for instance, a four block model being introduced in England in 2006–07 based on four elements of assessment of local needs. Under the Coalition government's austerity measures since 2010 reductions in local government block grants have borne the brunt of the new spending restrictions. In England LAs were expected to cut local spending by around 25 per cent over the Spending Review period, and in practice this is likely to be greater in some areas than others, because changes in the formulae have meant grant reductions are larger in some of the big cities, with significant areas of social deprivation, than in smaller towns and rural councils. LA spending elsewhere in the UK was also under pressure, and the Coalition government made clear this cumulative scaling back was set to continue well into the next parliament.

During the 1980s, however, local government did not just experience reductions in its expenditure base; there were also attempts to remove important aspects of its provision primarily through measures requiring or encouraging the privatization of LA services; and in England particularly this process has continued further since.

Privatization began, most dramatically, in 1980 by the granting to council house tenants of the right to buy (RTB), discussed in Chapter 10, followed later by provisions for whole estates to opt out of LA control. As we discuss in Chapter 12, powers and responsibilities were also shifted from LAs to local schools; and in England since the 2000s this has been taken much further with the encouragement of schools to opt out of local control altogether through the Academy programme and, more recently, the establishment of independent, Free Schools.

In addition to this opting out, LAs in the 1980s and 1990s were also required to offer certain services, such as cleaning or refuse collection, to commercial operators through a process by which contracts for the delivery of local services were put out to tender on the private market, and this has been extended further since. In some cases these contracts were 'won' by the LA workforce, in competition with commercial tenders. However, on occasions they were not; and in such cases provision was removed from direct local government control.

Unlike the earlier losses of functions in the 1940s, this reduction in the scope of local government in the 1980s and early 1990s was somewhat piecemeal in its effect, with the extent of opting-out and contracting-out varying from one authority to another. In general it was also nowhere near as extensive as some of the protagonists of the 'contract culture' on the political right (both in and out of government) might have hoped, and in many cases most services remained in the hands of local government. Nevertheless, it was a further accentuation of the gradual trend towards a reduced role for the local control of service provision.

The right for housing estates and schools to opt out of local control, however, remained and, as we discuss in Chapters 10 and 12, led to some significant transfers out of council control, which are likely to be accelerated further in England under the Coalition government. Compulsory competitive tendering for service provision though was abandoned in the 2000s and replaced by a new duty on authorities in England and Wales, with parallel legislation in Scotland and Northern Ireland, to secure *Best Value* in the provision of local services. This was a judgement of quality as well as quantity (or cost) and was intended to lead to a gradual overall improvement in service standards. Authorities were intended to pursue the joint goals of economy, efficiency and effectiveness, to compare services with local public and private providers and consult with local businesses and communities, and to introduce measures to audit performance (see Chapter 18). Further, in keeping with broader trends towards competition and pluralism in service delivery, the expectation was that this would continue to lead to a mixed economy of service provision in which the best services could be delivered by private or voluntary sector providers rather than local government departments.

The commitment to Best Value has been continued by the Coalition and devolved administrations, although the former particularly has been concerned to ensure it leads to only 'light touch' interference or direction in local planning, in keeping with more general commitments to 'localism', discussed below. Across the UK legislation in 2012, however, introduced a further requirement on LAs to ensure that they, alongside other public service agencies, took account of social value, as well as economic cost, in the commissioning of services, although how this social value was to be defined and measured was not specified.

LOCAL AUTHORITY STRUCTURES AND POWERS

Despite the changes to LA structures introduced since the 1970s, it remains a complex, and for many local citizens perhaps a confusing, picture. This is in large part because it is the product of historical process, rather than logical planning; and it has remained dominated more by current vested political interests than by any future vision of the proper role for localism.

In reality, of course, what might properly constitute the 'local' area for the purposes of devolved government or community control is far from clear. The local dimension is perhaps best seen as something of a continuum rather than a clear-cut distinction; it ranges from the small village or neighbourhood community (where in theory at least everybody knows everybody else), through the parish or small town, to the city, county or metropolitan area, and then to the region, although, as mentioned, the regional dimension has now been removed from government structures in England, and in Scotland, Wales and Northern Ireland the picture is not so complex (see Table 6.2).

Table 6.2 The varying scale of local government					
Smallest ⟵			⟶		*Largest*
Neighbourhood	*Parish*	*District*	*City*	*County*	*Region*
Belgravia	Beverley	Bedford	Birmingham	Berkshire	East Midlands

There has never been local government at neighbourhood level in Britain, although, as we shall see in Chapter 18, there is now a significant amount of policy delivery aimed at neighbourhoods in some areas, and this is now a central element of the Coalition government's commitment to promoting localism in England, with the Department for Communities and Local Government (DCLG) supposedly actively promoting political activity and policy-making within local communities. At parish level, however, local councils have existed in rural areas since the nineteenth century and most remained after the local government reforms of 1974, although their powers are very limited (Elcock 1982). In England District Councils cover all towns and some smaller cities, and usually share the powers of local government with the County Council, which extends over a number of district areas. Larger cities, however, often have single authorities that enjoy the full range of local powers.

Thus the structure of local government does not follow the simple logic of devolution of different powers down to different local levels on a consistent basis. In particular, since the changes made by the abolition of the metropolitan counties in the major urban areas, such as London and Merseyside, in the 1980s, there has been a somewhat arbitrary divide in England between those large industrial towns and cities, such as Newcastle or Oldham, and the London boroughs, such as Islington or Tower Hamlets, which have unitary authorities providing all local government services, and those more predominantly rural areas where powers are divided between a district council (responsible for housing and local infrastructure) and a larger county council (responsible for welfare services such as social care and education). In Scotland and Wales, however, all the larger regional and county councils have been removed and replaced with smaller unitary authorities (see Table 6.3). In Northern Ireland, as mentioned earlier, local government has considerably fewer policy powers, with policies on education, social care and housing being determined by separate national departments within the NIE, although there are plans to develop a more active local government structure within the province in the future.

Table 6.3 Local government structure in the UK		
Two tier authorities – England		
County Councils		27
District Councils		201
Single tier authorities		
London Boroughs	32	
Corporation of London	1	
Metropolitan Districts	36	
English Unitary Authorities	55	
Isles of Scilly	1	
Scottish Unitary Authorities	32	
Welsh Unitary Authorities	22	
Total		179
England Wales & Scotland Total		407
Northern Ireland District Councils		26
Grand Total		433

Despite the loss of services to central government mentioned earlier, education, housing and social care have for the large part remained in local government hands. In addition to these LAs also have responsibility for a range of other service provision, which, in part at least, is encompassed within the field of social policy. These include leisure services (such as sports facilities, museums and parks), consumer protection, maintenance of highways and street lighting, and emergency services (such as policing and fire fighting). The latter, however, are under the control of separate bodies sometimes covering more than one authority in urban industrial areas. The Metropolitan Police (in London) and the Police Service of Northern Ireland (formerly the Royal Ulster Constabulary) are separately controlled by statute. In 2012 elected Police and Crime Commissioners were introduced to take over strategic planning of policing in England and Wales.

The structural divisions between LAs, and the distribution of powers to local government, do in themselves pose problems for the management and delivery of services, however. For a start the delineation of LA areas is inevitably a controversial issue. Lines must be drawn on a map between authorities, and wherever they are drawn they are likely to lead to boundary problems. For instance, families living near the boundary of one authority might wish to send their children to a school nearby in a neighbouring authority. Prior to the education reforms of 1988 they would not have been able to do this; and today they still may not, in practice, if the school or the neighbouring authority will not accept children from another local council. Similarly, an urban LA wishing to demolish inner-city slums and rehouse their inhabitants in new housing estates in the countryside may be unable to build such houses because the neighbouring countryside it wishes to use is part of a different authority. In some cases neighbouring authorities are able to cooperate successfully over issues that cross their respective boundaries – in London in particular this is common and essential – but it does not always happen; and in practice it requires both careful management and political support.

In England cooperation between authorities is essential in rural areas where powers are shared between county and district authorities. To many local people here, the difference between the county and the district authorities in their area may be an obscure, and even an unjustifiable, one. All they know is that they need to contact different officers in different council buildings, probably in different towns, in order to make use of different local services; and, if the officers of these two authorities whom they contact turn out to know little or nothing about the structures or workings of the other (a not uncommon problem), this is unlikely to extend the popularity of local government to local service users. If they are in conflict (which sometimes they are), it is likely to make the practice of local accountability both a negative and a frustrating one.

At a more general level, however, LAs do cooperate through collective organizations that provide a national voice for local government in political and policy debates and support for individual councils across a range of issues such as employment practices and partnership working. In England and Wales this is provided by the Local Government Association (LGA), though the Welsh LGA operates an autonomous body within Wales. In Scotland and Northern Ireland there are separate organizations: the Convention of Scottish Local Authorities (COSLA) and the Northern Ireland Local Government Association.

LOCAL GOVERNANCE AND THE ENABLING AUTHORITY

The declining powers and influence of local government over the last 20 years or so have been accompanied by a decline too in the apparent support for local democracy. The turn-out in local elections has generally decreased, and is well below that in national elections with only one-third or less of those entitled to vote doing so (far fewer than in most other European countries). It is even difficult in some cases for parties to find candidates to stand for election in their local wards, so that in a small number of wards councillors are sometimes elected unopposed. This low turn-out and shortage of councillors is accentuated in some authorities where one political party has enjoyed a long period of unchallenged political dominance. Here local democracy has become simply the practice of local party politics. This has occasionally led to high-profile cases of corruption amongst local politicians who have abused their powerful positions to pursue their own financial interest; but more commonly it has often meant local policy-making and service delivery have become dominated by the senior officers of the LA departments, with elected members largely acting as 'rubber stamps' for the policies developed by local officials.

At the end of the last century this led some commentators to talk about a 'democratic deficit' within local government, where electoral democracy was no longer acting as an effective control over the development and delivery of local services and the role of local democratic control required some rethinking (King and Stoker 1996). Critical to this rethinking has been the notion of a move from local government to local governance as the guiding principle of local democracy and local service delivery (Clarke and Stewart 1999; Stoker 2003).

The idea of *governance* is in fact much broader than the operation of local democracy in the UK. It has been used to describe a more general recognition within political science and political practice that the factors influencing the exercise of policy-making powers are (and should be) more than just the responsibility of elected politicians. It has been widely adopted in the USA and been central in influencing thinking about public policy-making and public management in the UK, especially after 1997, as we discuss in Chapter 18 (and see Newman 2001). The critical issue, for local governance, however, is the acceptance that responsibility for public services does not necessarily imply direct provision of these, or direct accountability of providers to elected local councillors; rather, the role of local government is that of ensuring appropriate services are delivered to meet the needs of local citizens, exemplified in the Best Value mandate and the new localism agenda.

This requires a new approach to policy planning and the development of positive measures to assess local need. Rather than assuming existing services are effective, councils have commissioned audits of need and engaged in consultation with local users and citizens. It also requires collaboration and partnership working with other local providers of services (public services such as the NHS, as well as commercial and third sector bodies), and a recognition that it is through appropriate management and the development of a mix of service providers that the needs of local citizens will best be met. Overall this has been characterized as a shift in the role of authorities from that of providers to that of *enablers* (Clarke and Stewart 1988, 1999).

As enablers LAs work with other public, private and voluntary agencies in their area, both informally and formally, through partnership bodies and interagency agreements. The structure and operation of these relationships vary from authority to authority though there are many common features. For instance, joint working is required by local care and health service agencies over community care provision (see Chapter 11), and in England in 2002 LAs in receipt of Neighbourhood Renewal funding were required to establish Local Strategic Partnerships (LSPs) to bring a range of local agencies together to oversee economic and social development planning.

These LSPs were an interesting example of the differences between local governance and previous models of local democratic control. Within these partnerships LAs were only one party, and decision making was based upon consensus and collaboration between a number of different interests, all of which could have some measure of influence or control over local policy provision. They were later introduced in many LA areas even where there was no formal requirement; and they have continued, despite the ending of Neighbourhood Renewal funding, although their focus has generally become more restricted to local economic development.

Another dimension of this shift in local government has been a move away from the emphasis on electoral democracy (somewhat discredited by the poor turn-out in local elections) towards the promotion of 'deliberative democracy'. This too is a complex issue extending far beyond UK local government; but in simple terms the idea is that the involvement of local citizens in service development and the accountability of providers to users should be pursued through the establishment of methods of direct consultation with local people, rather than (only) through the electoral process. Such consultation can take a variety of forms including local committees of residents, service fora where representatives of local user groups can meet, and citizens' panels or citizens' juries where the views of a random sample of local people can be gauged. The Local Government Act of 2000 required all authorities in England and Wales to engage in such formal consultation with local interests and encouraged the establishment of local fora to act as the settings for democratic debate.

The 2000 Act also imposed other changes on local government, requiring all councils to move away from their previous organization and management based upon separate committees responsible for different service departments to the establishment of central 'cabinets' with overall strategic and planning powers, perhaps working with a local directly elected mayor. Most authorities have been slow to move towards the mayoral model, although there have been some high-profile mayors elected, most notably in London. The greater centrality of planning and decision making has significantly altered the structure and practice of local government democracy, however, making LAs more like strategic planning agencies than local parliaments, although this is likely to be challenged by renewed commitments to localism being developed in England under the Coalition government.

COMPREHENSION QUESTIONS

- What is the difference between the local administration of welfare services and the local government of these?
- To what extent has the history of local government been one of a gradual decline in local autonomy over policy planning?
- How did central government seek to control local government spending in the 1980s and to what extent was it successful?

REFLECTIVE QUESTION

- Should local authorities be encouraged to cooperate more with each other?

CENTRALISM OR LOCALISM?

Within any democracy political conflict is inevitable: indeed arguably it is desirable, for it is evidence of healthy political debate and development. However, the separate electoral base for local government from central government creates a specific context for potential political conflict between the two, since there are likely to be a range of issues, particularly those relating to local government powers and resources, over which they may not agree. Furthermore, these conflicts are likely to be exacerbated in a party political electoral system, where at different times different parties may be in control of different levels of central and local government.

Despite this potential, however, the history of local government is not in particular a story of party control and party conflict. Even by the late 1960s only around 50 per cent of LAs were under party political control (Stoker 1991), with the majority of these being in the larger urban areas. Since then , however, local government has become much more widely party politicized and now control of virtually all councils is the subject of party political struggle and competition, although this often has to be followed by compromise and cooperation if the election is 'hung' and no one party is successful in winning enough council seats to exercise overall control.

If, however, party control is a relatively new phenomenon for many rural authorities, it is a much more established tradition in the larger urban areas. Following the lead in municipal development taken by Birmingham at the end of the nineteenth century, many of the larger city authorities elected parties into power based upon radical manifestos for local development. The Labour Party in particular was instrumental in using such local government manifestos as an early base for demonstrating the potential achievements of democratic socialism. In cities such as Sheffield, where Labour exercised control on an almost uninterrupted basis from the 1920s, a programme of 'municipal socialism' based on public house building and infrastructural improvement was pursued by the new council regimes of the first half of the century (Blunkett and Green 1983).

Of course the local pursuit of municipal socialism would be likely to bring such Labour councils into conflict with Conservative-controlled central governments. In the 1920s, for instance, conflict arose in a direct form within the London Borough of Poplar (now Tower Hamlets) where the Labour council was pursuing a policy of paying higher wages to its workers and higher levels of poor relief to its benefit claimants. This led to legal action being brought against the council as a result of which some councillors were eventually imprisoned, and, although a rather extreme example of central/local conflict, political challenges by LAs to central government policies have continued and are sometimes referred to as *Poplarism* (Ryan 1978; Holman 1990).

For instance, in the 1960s there was conflict between the Labour government and a Conservative authority over comprehensive schooling in Tameside, near Manchester (Finch 1984), and in the 1970s between the Conservative government and a Labour authority over increases in council house rents in Clay Cross, in Derbyshire (Elcock 1982). In the 1980s, the politicization of local government, and the conflicts between local and central government, reached new levels, however. In particular, in the large urban councils, where Labour had traditionally been in control, there was a dramatic move to the left in many areas at the same time as the central government, under Conservative control, moved to the right.

Commentators referred to this shift as the development of a new *urban left*, committed, as their predecessors in Poplar in the 1920s had been, to the development of a kind of 'local socialism' (Boddy and Fudge 1984). This urban left was in control of many authorities, most notably perhaps in Sheffield, under the leadership of *Blunkett*, and in Greater London, under the leadership of *Livingstone*. These two figures in particular became dominant spokesmen for the new local politics of Labour. Blunkett wrote about the renewed importance of local democracy (Blunkett and Green 1983; Blunkett and Jackson 1987); and Livingstone was instrumental in extending the range of local government activity in London to cover economic development, support for minority groups and local anti-poverty initiatives. Both also remained prominent in national and local politics, Blunkett becoming a key member of Labour cabinets from 1997 to 2005, and Livingstone becoming a Labour MP and then the first elected Mayor of London.

The conflict between central and local government in the 1980s was not a struggle of equals, however; and, as with the Poplarism of earlier eras, it was a conflict that central government was ultimately better placed to win. As we discussed above, throughout much of the post-war period central government had been extending its powers over local government; and in the 1980s this was taken further, primarily though the changes in funding formulae mentioned above – and in the case of the Greater London Council (led by Livingstone) and other large urban authorities by their abolition and the transfer of power to smaller local councils.

The Labour governments from 1997 to 2010 saw increases in funding for local government as part of the more general expansion of public welfare expenditure, and this period saw something of a reduction therefore in conflict between central and local government in England. Elsewhere in the UK the smaller size of the devolved administrations combined with simpler local government structures and the new emphasis on liaison also made for greater harmony. As mentioned above authorities were required to reorganize their internal structures to improve effectiveness. They were also subject to indirect central control through the range of performance targets and audit regimes discussed in Chapter 18, in particular the Audit Commission, which had overall responsibility for monitoring and advising on LA expenditure in England, until it was abolished by the Coalition in 2012.

Significant new streams of funding developed in England by Labour, however, were focused on smaller local areas, for example the Neighbourhood Renewal Fund, which targeted additional resources onto neighbourhoods identified as having high levels of local deprivation. These initiatives also generally sought to engage local citizens and communities in the planning and delivery of new investments, and were accompanied by other measures to encourage LAs to engage more closely with local communities in the development of local service provision that were paralleled elsewhere in the UK. In 2006 the then Minister for Communities and Local Government, David Miliband, expressed his support for moves to shift power from councillors and officers to local communities, working in and through local voluntary and community organizations. He referred to this as *double devolution*; and the notion was taken further in a book on the subject, by Mulgan and Bury (2006), which promoted greater powers for local government to raise funds and the introduction of new rights for neighbourhoods and local communities.

This was a trend supported both by the devolved administrations, with Scotland for example introducing a more consultative localist approach to planning in 2007, and, most significantly, by the Coalition government after 2010. The new Secretary of State for Communities and Local Government in England, Eric Pickles, was an open supporter of double devolution, or what he increasingly began to refer to as *localism*, which he claimed was one of the government's major policy priorities. Localism was part of its broader political support for the 'Big Society' (see Chapter 4), and included within this was an initiative to create 'Vanguard Communities' in Liverpool, Windsor and Maidenhead, Sutton and Eden Valley in Cumbria, where citizens and communities would be encouraged to by-pass local agencies and act directly to introduce new initiatives such as local broadband infrastructure or the take-over of local shops and pubs.

In practice the community action in these vanguard areas never really took off, and Liverpool formally withdrew from the programme claiming that cuts in LA budgets made it impossible to undertake such new initiatives. Nevertheless the broader commitment to localism was continued with the introduction of the Localism Act of 2011. This ostensibly was a move to promote local government in England by giving LAs powers to do anything they wanted to which was not specifically prohibited by other legislation, and more generally returning powers from central to local government by removing 'red-tape' and bureaucracy.

However, in practice the main thrust of the Act was in promoting double devolution, by giving local citizens and communities rights and powers to act against their LAs. Planning restrictions were removed to allow planning to take place at neighbourhood level. Local communities were given the 'right to buy' local assets from their local council, and the 'right to challenge' the council to put local services out to tender. New rights were also given to LA employees to make proposals to take the services they ran out of council control and provide them through independent social enterprises. The Act also introduced changes to local democracy, giving large cities the right to establish locally elected mayors and local residents the right to instigate referenda on local issues, although in practice most cities rejected elected mayors and local referenda have not proved popular.

The Localism Act was accompanied, however, by the wide-ranging cuts to LA funding mentioned above, as part of the overall commitments to reduce public expenditure discussed in Chapter 15. The combined effect of these changes, particularly in England, is likely to be an overall weakening of local government, rather than a renewal of it, with the powers and resources of local councils being 'hollowed out' through lack of resources and the shift of decision making to neighbourhood level. It is this neighbourhood localism, not local government in the traditional sense, that is at the centre of the Coalition's renewed commitments to the local in the 2010s; and this may be taken further if pilot projects to develop 'community budgeting', where local service budgets are devolved to smaller neighbourhood levels and debated by local fora of community groups and user organizations, are developed more generally.

These further shifts from central to local government could potentially see significant departures from the gradual centralizing tendencies of social policy development in the last century, therefore. Their supporters claim the moves towards a new localism place policymaking closest to those who are most engaged in providing and using services. It also, however, introduces other potentially significant problems. One of the major reasons for central government's greater control over local services in the twentieth century was the concern of national politicians to ensure consistent services and minimum standards could be provided for all – that education, social care and other services would be guaranteed for the citizens of Bermondsey and Belgravia, regardless of local circumstances and resources. This was based on a concern that inequities could arise in different areas with different political and economic resources, sometimes referred to as the 'post-code lottery'.

This is a lottery in which, as ever, there can be losers as well as winners. Greater power to local neighbourhoods, or local councils, can mean that these are used to reduce local public services as well as enhance them – and some citizens may bear a greater proportion of the costs of these changes than others. It is, however, to some extent an irresolvable dilemma, for greater centralization can lead to standardization and a potential decline to only basic minimum provision. It is perhaps for this reason that the balance between central and local control has fluctuated so much over the development of social policy in Britain; and current trends towards greater localism may not in the longer run prove to be the end of this particular story.

COMPREHENSION QUESTIONS

- Why was there conflict between central and local government in the 1980s? Why did central government 'win' this conflict?
- What are 'enabling authorities', and to what extent has the development of these improved the delivery and accountability of local welfare services?
- What form has localism taken in the early twenty-first century, and why has it apparently been so popular?

REFLECTIVE QUESTION

- How can we resolve the problem of guaranteeing consistent service provision with the placing of decision-making power close to service users and providers?

FURTHER READING

A good discussion of the impact of devolution on policy at national level within the UK is provided by Birrell (2009); and Lodge and Schmuecker's (2010) collection provides useful information on a range of recent developments. The history of the development of local government is covered in Stoker (1991). Wilson and Game (2011) provide the most comprehensive guide to current structures and issues. Bovaird and Loffler's (2009) collection provides a good overview of the management and governance of local services, and for a broader discussion of local governance and citizen relations see Durose et al. (2009). The website of the Department for Communities and Local Government (DCLG) houses documents on regional and local government in England, see www.communities.gov.uk. For developments in the devolved administrations see their separate websites: www.scotland.gov.uk, www.wales.gov.uk and www.northernireland.gov.uk. The Local Government Association has a useful website, www.lga.gov.uk. COSLA has a website at www.cosla.gov.uk, and for Northern Ireland see www.nilga.org. More general discussion of local government issues can be found at www.lgiu.org.uk.

7

International and European Influences

SUMMARY OF KEY POINTS

- Global economic forces now influence economic and social policy in all countries, although the extent of this influence is disputed by commentators.
- Global agencies play an influential role in determining the development of social policy across the world.
- Comparative analysis of different 'welfare regimes' has extended understanding of the international context of social policy.
- Policy transfer is the adoption of policy ideas from one country into another.
- The European Union (EU) was initially developed to promote economic collaboration in Western continental Europe and has since extended across much of Europe.
- Social policy regimes within the EU are diverse, but member states are committed to elements of joint planning and coordinated practices.
- EU social policy has developed in phases with shared policy planning becoming more extensive in each stage.
- EU social programmes target support to regions within the Union with acute social and economic problems, thus leading to a redistribution of resources across (and within) member states.
- Since joining the EU in 1973 Britain has often been a reluctant partner in European initiatives, and the two main political parties have been divided in their views on membership.

THE GLOBAL CONTEXT

The primary focus of this book is on social policy in the UK. Most social policies affecting the lives of UK residents have been developed by the British government, or at a local level by other agencies and, more recently, by the devolved administrations; and by and large social policy has been studied at these levels. As explained in Chapter 1, however, in both economic and social terms Britain is no longer, if it ever was, an isolated national entity.

The lives of its population are affected by international social and economic forces; and the ability of the UK administrations to develop policies to respond to these is constrained by their relations with other nations, both politically and economically. Furthermore, the policies pursued are likely to be informed by the knowledge and experience of developments in other countries. We are not only affected by the actions of our international friends and neighbours; we can also learn from them. Thus social like economic policy in the UK has an international context.

As the recession of 2008 revealed economic development now takes place on a global scale, increasingly powered by the growth of China and other emergent economies and trading by multinational conglomerates such as Apple or Samsung that produce and distribute goods and services across the world. The scale of their operations is immense (the larger corporations have annual turnovers much greater than those of many countries) and their power and influence is a significant factor in shaping the economic climate internationally and in the countries where they operate (or do not!). This *globalization* of economic activity has led some to argue that transnational economic forces have become the prime determinants of economic and social policy in all nations, because they must adapt their domestic policies to ensure that they can compete in worldwide markets.

The argument about the extent to which global economic forces shape national policies is a complex one, however (Hirst et al. 2009; Holton 2011). Looking at developments at the close of the last century some commentators held globalization had forced a significant restructuring of social policy in all states (Mishra 1999); others though contended there was little evidence that national policy-making had been significantly altered, or brought greater convergence amongst advanced industrial societies (Pierson 2001). This debate is still ongoing, though hedged by many qualifications and, more recently, by differing views on the impact of the 2008 recession and the trade-offs between welfare provision and maintaining a competitive edge in world markets (Farnsworth and Irving 2011; Hay and Wincott 2012).

In reality of course the situation is highly complex, with governments recognizing the need to adapt to global economic forces, but varying political traditions and welfare structures leading to differing responses (Swank 2010). This process is often referred to as 'path dependency' and we shall return shortly to discuss the extent to which different national settings can themselves help us understand the cross-national influences on social policy formation. But it is important too to recognize another contextual factor, and that is the role of international economic and social policy agencies.

For some time such agencies have sought to influence, or even determine, policy making transnationally, most obviously perhaps through the United Nations (UN), which was established after the Second World War to prevent future international conflict and promote international relations. Although remaining largely a political and strategic body, it has developed a range of initiatives to promote and support international social policy activity, such as the United Nations Development Programme (UNDP) and the United Nations Children's Fund (UNICEF). Although mainly operating in developing nations it has also had an impact in industrialized states including the UK, particularly through its reports on child poverty levels (UNICEF 2007; Adamson 2012).

In addition to the UN there is a range of other international governmental organizations (IGOs) with interests in seeking to support, and steer, social policy across nations. These include the Organisation for Economic Co-operation and Development (OECD), the International Labour Organization (ILO) and the World Health Organization (WHO). All of these gather data about policy development across their member nations (providing useful sources of information for comparative policy analysis), but also seek to use this knowledge to guide national policy: for instance, through the WHO's work in preventing the spread of disease and setting standards for health promotion.

Whilst the WHO and the ILO focus specifically on social policy there are other agencies that, though mainly concerned with economic development, also have the power to wield both a direct and an indirect influence on welfare planning. For a start the world's most powerful countries now meet regularly to plan and coordinate international economic policy development at a general level through what are referred to as the G8 and G20 Summits. More specifically there are the World Bank and the International Monetary Fund (IMF), which can support international investment and development within nations (World Bank) or to nations (IMF). In doing so, as in Britain in the 1960s and 1970s (see Chapter 15), they generally have a clear view about the social policy priorities they wish to promote (Deacon 2007; Yeates 2008).

These agencies now play an influential role in shaping social policy across the globe, and, although much of their activity focuses on the developing nations and former communist states, it would be unwise to underestimate their influence, especially indirectly, in richer countries such as the UK. This is also true of the many international agencies that are not established or supported by governments, but nevertheless operate to sway social policy and respond to social needs worldwide (Yeates and Holden 2009). Generally referred to as international non-governmental organizations (INGOs), these include major charities such as Oxfam, Christian Aid and the Red Cross, which influence policy and practice across the globe. Like IGOs they operate in both developed and developing countries with Oxfam, for instance, having an extensive anti-poverty programme in the UK.

The global context of social policy development is thus one in which international forces and agencies are exercising an increasing influence on policy development and delivery in all nations. The pressures of globalization do not, however, mean an inevitable process of convergence with all national policies moving towards a common denominator set by the World Bank or the IMF. But, as recent UK governments recognize, they do mean policy-making within individual nations must respond to this international context and the challenges and opportunities that flow from it. It is, of course, partly for this reason that comparative analysis occupies such a key role in academic study today, helping us to understand the ways in which social policy across the UK relates to, and is influenced by, developments in other countries.

WELFARE REGIMES AND POLICY TRANSFER

Comparative research is now a well-developed element within the study of social policy and encompasses a number of different levels of analysis (May 2012). There are studies that provide a guide to the policy context in different countries (Alcock and Craig 2009), explore aspects of social policy across two or more countries (Lewis 2009; Clasen 2011; Dodds 2013) or examine international trends in policy planning (Castles et al. 2010). There are also those who have sought to provide a theoretical framework for analysing (and measuring) the varying types of social policies found in different societies in order to explore the extent to which we can explain (and predict) national developments by setting these in an international context.

As in much else Titmuss was one of the first social policy academics to attempt to produce such a framework with his three 'models of welfare' (Titmuss 1974; Alcock et al. 2001):

- Model A – the residual welfare model
- Model B – the industrial achievement-performance model
- Model C – the institutional redistributive model.

This categorization was subsequently developed by the Scandinavian academic Esping-Andersen (1990). Based on empirical research using data on welfare activity in 18 advanced industrial countries from the OECD and other international agencies and an analysis of political trends in a number of exemplar nations, he constructed a tripartite typology of what he called '*welfare regimes*'. In particular he argued that three key features could provide a guide to the differences between welfare states. These were:

- Decommodification – the extent to which welfare protection was provided by non-market providers
- Stratification – the extent to which access to welfare was determined by social class
- The public–private mix – the relative roles of the state, market and family in supplying welfare.

From this he drew up a rank order of the states that he examined according to their score on a decommodification index and argued these could be broken down into three distinct clusters (regimes) with different types of welfare provision resulting from variations in the political contexts of particular countries. The three he identified were the social democratic, corporatist and liberal regimes, which he held were exemplified by Sweden, Germany and the USA respectively (see Table 7.1).

Table 7.1 Characteristics of welfare regime ideal types			
Regime	Social Democratic	Corporatist	Liberal
	Sweden	Germany	USA
Political base	Broad-based compromise	Employer/Worker coalition	Free market
Service type	Universal	Occupational	Residual
Public expenditure	High level	High level	Low level
Labour market	High employment, high wage	Low employment, high wage	High employment, low wage

Esping-Andersen's typology has continued to dominate comparative analysis of social policy primarily because it provided a framework for comparison to be made between structures and trends according to fixed and measurable criteria, whereas much previous research had merely described the welfare characteristics of different countries. He himself later used the model to examine the ways in which different regimes were responding to the pressures of globalization in the early 1990s, and concluded they did respond in different ways, challenging the convergence thesis mentioned above (Esping-Andersen 1996).

Others have also adapted and developed his approach, extending it to other national and international contexts. This has led a number of authors to argue that there may in practice be more than three regime types across the developed world. For instance: Leibfried (1993) and Ferrera (1996) suggested there might be a fourth within Europe associated with the more limited public welfare nations of the 'Latin Rim' (Spain, Portugal and Greece); Castles and Mitchell (1991) identified another type in the largely means-tested welfare systems of Australia and New Zealand; whilst two other regimes were charted in the former communist countries (Deacon et al. 1992) and south-east Asia respectively (Jones 1993). These analyses have since both been re-addressed (Castles et al. 2010) and linked to other theorization on capitalist diversity (Schroder 2013), while regime analysis has also been extended to developing countries and the notion of global or 'metawelfare regimes' (Abu Sharkh and Gough 2010).

There have also been those who have highlighted limitations in Esping-Anderson's theoretical framework and database and questioned regime theorization more generally. For instance, Lewis (1992) and others argued Esping-Anderson ignored gender dimensions within welfare provision and their inclusion could have altered the construction of his regimes. His approach has also been criticized on other grounds, particularly its focus on state social security systems rather than other provision.

Nevertheless the welfare regime approach has become well established within social policy analysis, and the fact that commentators continue to argue about extensions or criticisms of Esping-Andersen's work suggests his basic approach remains influential (Castles et al. 2010; Powell and Barrientos 2011; Ferragina and Seeleib-Kaiser 2011). Whatever its shortcomings welfare regime theory enables us to compare the structures and characteristics of different welfare systems. This can help us understand welfare arrangements in our own country and can also mean lessons might be learnt about future policy development from those regimes that have approached similar problems in different ways, and perhaps with more success. Policy development in one country, such as the UK, can therefore be influenced by our knowledge of development elsewhere. However, this does not just happen at a general level; it can also take place with specific policy ideas and initiatives, where these are developed in one country and then copied elsewhere.

This copying is now referred to as *policy transfer*, and has become an important feature of comparative policy analysis and political theory (Dolowitz and Marsh 1996; Dolowitz et al. 2000; Dodds 2013). Of course, policy 'borrowing' is far from new – for example the social insurance system developed by Bismarck in Germany in the late nineteenth century was imported by many other countries over the next century and the British NHS of 1948 provided a model for state health services across the world. It is only more recently, however, that such transfers have been studied as a form of policy-making, their advantages and drawbacks more widely discussed and the possibility of their being a way of legitimizing planned change explored.

In recent decades there have been some important examples of policy transfer openly pursued by UK governments. The short-lived Child Support Agency, introduced by the Conservatives in the early 1990s, was modelled in part upon similar provision in Australia and the close ideological links between the Blair and Clinton administrations led to the adoption of a number of American initiatives including the New Deal and the working tax credit discussed in Chapters 8 and 13 (Dolowitz 1998; Deacon 2000). More recently the Coalition government too has drawn on developments elsewhere, notably in education where some of its reforms were 'plundered' from provisions in Singapore, Sweden and Finland as well as the USA (Gove 2011).

Within the UK devolution has added another dimension to such policy diffusion (Lodge and Schmuecker 2010). But Britain also has close geographical and cultural links with continental Europe and the latter part of the last century in particular saw increasing policy transfer and development within Europe too. Of course this is now dominated by the policies and practices of the European Union (EU), which provides a formal and far more powerful supranational control over economic and social policy planning within its member states and within which the UK government represents the whole country.

COMPREHENSION QUESTIONS

- In what ways do global agencies now shape international social policy?
- What did Esping-Andersen mean by 'welfare regimes'? How has this notion been developed by subsequent comparative social policy analysts?
- What is 'policy transfer', and how has it influenced policy development in the UK?

REFLECTIVE QUESTION

- Will international pressures lead to an inevitable 'convergence' of policy regimes over time?

SOCIAL POLICY IN EUROPE

The EU is not the only international agency influencing social policy in Europe. The *Council of Europe* is a broader-based body, founded in 1949 with 10 Western European member countries, which by 2012 comprised 47 nations including the post- Soviet states. It acts to promote

Source: McCormick (2012).

Figure 7.1 Political map of the European Union

human rights amongst its members and established a European Court of Human Rights with supranational authority. It has also sought to influence social policy through the establishment in 1961 of a Social Charter embodying rights for workers and citizens that member nations can (but do not have to) take up. Because of its largely voluntary coordinating role, however, the Council has not been as important in influencing social policy in Europe as the EU, which operates like a club within which members must agree to share in policy-making and abide by the rules developed.

The EU emerged from the reconstruction of Western Europe after the Second World War. To prevent the political and economic competition that might generate further wars, the major nations of continental Western Europe decided to join together to share and plan economic development. Since then they have been joined by most other Western European nations, including Britain, and, more recently, by many post- Soviet states, with membership swelling to 28 states in 2013 (see Figure 7.1).

What started out as a community of nations sharing economic planning has developed into a single European market for goods and services, capital and labour, and a European

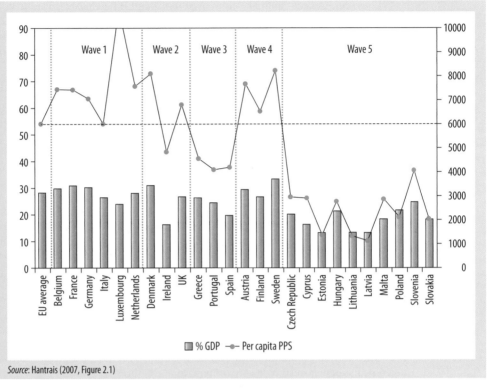

Source: Hantrais (2007, Figure 2.1)

Figure 7.2 Social protection expenditure in EU member states, as a percentage of GDP and per capita in proportionate personal spending, 2003

legislature and bureaucracy responsible for a wide range of initiatives affecting the member states, 17 of whom have also adopted a single European currency, the *Euro* (forming the *Eurozone*). Moreover since its establishment in the 1950s the EU has grown not only in scale but influence, and since Britain joined in 1973 has shaped the way economic and social policy has developed here, too.

There is now an extensive literature on social policy within the EU examining both its development and policy-making trends in the member states. What these various studies show is that analysis must take account of the distinctive understandings and structures of social policy in the constituent countries since the EU encompasses a number of welfare regimes. There are a number of dimensions to this *diversity* as it is generally called. But broad variations can be seen simply by looking at differences in overall spending levels and the relation of these to GDP, which, as Figure 7.1 reveals, became more pronounced when the EU expanded in the first decade of this century.

Such diversity is in part a product of the different ways in which social policy is conceived within the member nations. In Britain it has traditionally been associated with the planning and delivery of the major welfare services, such as education and health. In some other European countries, however, social and employment policy formed linked elements of social provision from the beginnings of their welfare systems. Here social legislation has long encompassed employment relations, working conditions including health and safety, vocational training, family support and other activities that are clearly policy driven and affect the lives of all people, but which have not been subject to social policy analysis, or in some cases until recently policy planning in Britain (May 2006; and see Chapter 13).

These differences can make comparison difficult. They have also led to conflicts over the scope of EU action; for instance, attempts to regulate employment rights under the rubric of health and safety measures have led at times to opposition from some countries, particularly the UK. However, the more general welfare regime differences pose more significant problems for the broader development of EU policy-making.

One of the original aims of its founder nations was the eventual *harmonization* of welfare provision within a single European model, perhaps as a precursor to a *federal* European state that could plan social and economic policy across the then member nations. This is still the hope of some EU members, but one that some argue has become less feasible as the Union has expanded and diversified. Furthermore, the hope that there might be a gradual shift towards the corporatist, labour-market and family-based protection of the north-western continental countries seemed to be undermined at the turn of this century by moves towards more liberal or residual regimes in Britain and Ireland and the inclusion of the more limited and underdeveloped regimes of the Eastern European states.

In the more immediate term, therefore, the goal of harmonization was effectively replaced by a policy of convergence: a more limited commitment to the development of shared, pan-EU social policy initiatives around particular issues of cross-national importance or in areas where standardization of practices would ensure fair competition between nations within a single economic market.

However, even this form of convergence is contradicted to some extent by another key EU principle: *subsidiarity*. This is based on the German practice of seeking to devolve decision-making and initiative-taking to the smallest possible local base, thus encouraging participatory activity rather than top-down state paternalism. This strategy is supposedly now being replicated throughout the EU. However, it places constraints on common action and has often been understood by some member states (notably the UK) to mean that policy decisions taken by national governments are preferable to EU directives, which in effect means federalist tendencies can be resisted at a national level.

Harmonization and subsidiarity are political principles. They have been important in shaping policy-making within the EU, but they have not been the only factors. The primary aim for its initial establishment was the pursuit of collaborative economic development, as we discuss below; but economic growth also created pressures for social policy planning to deal with the consequences of change.

One of the outcomes of economic planning taking place at a European level was the concentration of the power, and the advantage, of economic development into a small central core within the EU, sometimes referred to as a *golden triangle* based between Frankfurt, Paris and Milan. As this happened the more peripheral regions, including parts of Britain, experienced relative economic decline. This could only be countered by the use of EU-wide initiatives to redirect resources and investments towards these areas, and, as we outline later, this has become a key feature of EU social policy and has led to a growing role for the EU in promoting regional economic and social development.

The concentration of economic power and benefit is not, however, the only broader social policy implication of collaborative economic development within the EU. There were also fears that employers seeking to reduce costs would transfer capital resources around the Union in order to employ workers with the lowest pay and conditions and the least expensive social protection – a process sometimes referred to as *social dumping*. Over time this could lead to a general downward drift in conditions and protections throughout the EU if all countries or regions ended up trying to compete with each other by lowering standards. Avoiding this requires EU-wide commitments to minimum standards and enforceable rights for workers, and has been a major factor in promoting the regulation of employment and other rights, though this has become more difficult since the accession of the former communist states.

A converse tendency is the accompanying fear of *social tourism*. Workers, or more especially non-workers, in disadvantaged regions with poor social protection may be encouraged to exercise the rights which they enjoy within the EU to move within it to seek improved employment prospects and social protection elsewhere. This too has become more pronounced since the beginning of this century, which has seen significant movement of labour from Eastern member states into lower paid, and often less regulated, employment in the more affluent Western countries.

Thus those nations with better social protection may face increased demand from the mobile population of countries with less well-developed social services. This is a fear that has in part been responsible for restrictions on social security entitlement in the UK for those not 'normally resident' within the country. However, only enforceable pan-EU planning and standards can counter these tendencies effectively across the Union, providing yet another source of pressure for integrated social policy development.

When viewed in this light, the greater integration of social policy across the EU's member states seems to be an inevitable process and, from the point of view of the majority of workers and citizens throughout the Union, a desirable one. For, without the attempt to guarantee common social standards, there may be pressure on all governments to reduce protection to secure short-term economic advantage. Economic concentration has therefore inevitably been followed by social concentration and an ever more extensive role for EU social policy-making, as the development of the Union reveals.

THE DEVELOPMENT OF THE EU

The history of the EU is primarily a story of the gradual development of European cooperation from the limited goals of the original six members in securing some shared political vision and economic regeneration after the ravages of the Second World War, to the federalist ideals of a European superstate that could be one of the world's most powerful economic blocks – and its most progressive social regime. This is a process during which the European Economic Community (EEC), as it was first called, has both expanded and increased the extent and depth of its activities and aspirations. This expansion has seen it grow from six to 28, members (Table 7.2). It may also expand further, with Iceland, Turkey, and several Balkan and ex-Soviet states having expressed an interest in joining.

Table 7.2	EU member states 2013
1957	France, West Germany, Italy, Belgium, the Netherlands, Luxembourg
1973	UK, Ireland, Denmark
1981	Greece
1986	Spain, Portugal
1995	Austria, Sweden, Finland (Norway voted not to join)
2004	Czech Republic, Cyprus, Estonia, Hungary, Latvia, Lithuania, Malta, Poland, Slovakia, Slovenia
2007	Bulgaria, Romania.
2013	Croatia

Before the EEC was established by the *Treaty of Rome* in 1957 its six founding members had already embarked on limited joint economic planning to deal with the socioeconomic consequences of industrial change in the form of the European Coal and Steel Community, set up in 1951 by the *Treaty of Paris* (Table 7.3). The Treaty of Rome, however, established a far more extensive base for joint economic development. Its 248 Articles covered a wide range of matters of shared concern or commitment. Moreover, though it focused on economic policy, Articles 117–28 upheld cooperation on employment matters, training, working conditions and social security and the principle of equal pay and provided for the harmonization of social security arrangements to support migrant workers and a *European Social Fund* (ESF) to promote employment and worker mobility (Hantrais 2012).

Table 7.3 European Union treaties	
1951	Treaty of Paris
1957	Treaty of Rome
1986	Single European Act
1992	Treaty of Maastricht
1997	Treaty of Amsterdam
2001	Treaty of Nice
2007	Treaty of Lisbon

The Treaty of Rome began what can be categorized as the *first* phase of development of social policy within the EEC/EU. This period ran from 1957 to 1972 and was characterized largely by the promotion and regulation of movement between labour markets within the new community. Such social policy activity as existed was closely tied to the broader aims of economic development within the six member states with no specific social goals being pursued (hence the focus on labour mobility).

The *second* phase, from 1973 to 1984, following the first expansion of the Community, saw more extensive concern with employment related social rights. There were, for instance, attempts to harmonize and upgrade basic employment entitlements particularly in the areas of health and safety and equal pay and equal treatment for women and men. This period also saw the implementation of the Community's first social action programme which was begun in 1974 with a view to developing common objectives for member states' social policies without standardizing the approach taken or limiting their powers. In keeping with the EC's primary concerns, it centred on labour-market issues. Outside the formal treaty commitments, however, it was supported by all the members and resulted in a number of important community-wide initiatives, including an anti-poverty programme and the creation of community agencies to monitor and report on social issues, such as the European Foundation for the Improvement of Living and Working Conditions established in Dublin in 1975.

The *third* phase of development was set by the accession of the French politician, Jacques Delors, to the Presidency of the Commission, and ran from 1985 to 1992. He is credited with developing a *social dimension* or '*espace sociale*' to encourage convergence and supplement the EC's focus on economic development. It was based particularly on facilitating the development of minimum EC-wide workers' rights by promoting discussion between employers and trades unions (referred to as *social dialogue* between the *social partners*). So at the same time as economic planning was drawing closer together – notably through the commitment of most members to a European exchange-rate agreement (the European Monetary System, EMS) – social commitments to workers' rights were also placed on the EC agenda, and the scope of Community-wide social programmes and initiatives widened.

In 1985 high-level talks on socioeconomic issues were held at Val Duchesse in Belgium and in 1986 the Single European Act was signed by all the EC members. The Act emphasized a commitment to social cohesion as a corollary to economic cohesion and in its wake EC activities in the social field were considerably expanded, especially through the *structural funds* (outlined below). The idea of social rights for citizens within the Community was taken further in 1989 by the drafting of the *Community Charter of the Fundamental Social Rights of Workers*.

This was analogous in some ways to the Social Charter developed by the Council of Europe, and similarly focused primarily upon rights at work. It echoed the continuing domination of economic over social issues within the EC and the fact that the labour market remained the major focus of social policy in the most powerful nations of continental Western Europe. It too was not legally binding. But, with the exception of the UK, in 1989 it was adopted by all the member states and has sometimes since been referred to as the social dimension of the Single European Act.

The 1980s also saw a much-increased use of EC structural funds, a second action programme and other initiatives including further anti-poverty schemes. These were designed to secure social policy goals and, in particular, to mitigate the problems stemming from industrial restructuring and the concentration of economic growth in the core of the Community. Knowledge about the effects of economic change also became a more important feature of the EC agenda, not least because of the increased activity of Community agencies such as the statistical office, the Dublin Foundation and some of the newly established *Observatories*. Together they began to provide more extensive and detailed information about social and economic trends, both within and across member states, adding to pressure for further action.

Concern over these trends became more significant in the *fourth* phase that began in 1992 with the creation of the Single European Market and the signing of the *Maastricht Treaty*, which transformed the EC into the EU. The single market was the logical conclusion of the plans for economic cooperation that had commenced in 1951 and, with national trade and tariff barriers removed, it meant goods, labour and capital could move freely from one member state to another.

There was, however, some opposition to the extensions of EU policy influence within the Maastricht Treaty fuelled in part by concerns that pressure for more extensive economic and political union might grow. Denmark initially voted against adopting it. But the most vociferous opposition came from the UK, then led by Prime Minister John Major, who secured an arrangement permitting the UK to opt out of the creation of the single European currency envisaged by the treaty. He also secured an opt-out from endorsing the Social Chapter, which (through a separate Protocol to the treaty) committed member states to implementing the Social Charter. As we shall see, the UK has always been a somewhat reluctant participant in moves towards greater harmonization of economic and social policy planning within the EU, and, though the Treaty formalized the subsidiarity principle, the preceding negotiations made it clear that not all member states were always going to be able to agree on the pace and direction of policy change.

This disagreement did not, however, prevent the Union pressing ahead with economic and social policy reform, including the publication of two keynote White Papers, on Growth and Competitiveness and Social Policy (EC 1993, 1994). The first centred on ways of increasing employment through economic restructuring. Whilst maintaining the prioritization of job creation and employment rights, the latter also argued the EU should work to common goals and, more generally, preserve and develop the European social model. It led to the development of a series of social action programmes and attempts to improve employment conditions, especially for women (Hantrais 2007).

After the 1997 UK election the Labour government adopted a participatory stance towards EU policy-making. It quickly endorsed the EU Social Charter and, in 1997, signed the *Treaty of Amsterdam*, which incorporated this and a number of other social policy measures. It included commitments to promote economic and social progress, high employment and sustainable development through strengthening economic and social cohesion, and to developing a coordinated strategy for employment. This last was furthered through the adoption of EU employment guidelines at the 1997 Luxembourg summit. However, Britain did not join with the majority 11 member states in the establishment of formal monetary union in January 1999, or join the euro, introduced in January 2002, nor did Denmark and Sweden. It did, however, sign up to a new *Charter of Fundamental Rights of the European Union*, secured by the Treaty of Nice in 2001.

Thereafter though the development of the EU entered a *fifth* phase, prompted by the expansion in membership in 2004 and 2007, in preparation for which the Amsterdam Treaty was mainly designed, and culminating in the enforcement in December 2009 of another treaty, the 2007 *Lisbon Treaty* (the Amended Treaty on European Union). As we discussed earlier the extension of the EU further accentuated its diverse nature, bringing a wider range of socioeconomic standards and a more varied spectrum of political opinion and power. But, though the Amsterdam Treaty provided for more streamlined decision-making, only slow progress was made on meeting the need for a new constitution to govern the affairs of the enlarged union and a draft constitution was voted down in referenda in France and the Netherlands in 2005. However, after further protracted negotiations the Lisbon Treaty provided for changes to the EU's system of governance (see below).

On the social policy front it reasserted the goal of promoting economic and social development and ensuring moves towards economic integration were paralleled in other areas. It also reaffirmed the EU's role in encouraging cooperation, particularly over strategies for employment, tackling social exclusion and securing adequate social protection. While not incorporated directly the treaty made the Charter of Fundamental Rights legally binding, though a separate Protocol stipulated its 'judiciable rights' did not pertain to the UK, Poland and the Czech Republic.

In many ways the long-drawn-out constitutional negotiations held back possible social policy developments, which again remained closely tied to the wider attempt to stimulate growth spelt out in the EU's ten-year Lisbon Strategy in 2000. Though much social policy effort focused on support for the new member states, the 2000s saw a number of significant developments, including attempts to coordinate employment policy through the European Employment Strategy and, with more impact, the extension of equal opportunities provisions and new rights at work (see Chapter 13). This period also saw the development of provisions encouraging work–life balance, wellbeing in the workplace and lifelong learning and the promotion of measures addressing new issues such as demographic ageing as well as schemes to combat social exclusion.

Since 2009, however, EU development has entered a *sixth* phase, with the implementation of the Lisbon Treaty coinciding with the aftershocks of the banking crisis and the global recession, and the ensuing financial crisis in the Eurozone. The problems in the Eurozone eventually necessitated a series of 'bailouts' and the imposition of austerity measures on heavily indebted countries, particularly Greece, but also Portugal, Spain, Italy and Ireland (see Chapter 15). For the EU economic issues inevitably dominated political debate and led to a new 'Europe 2020' strategy for economic renewal (EC 2010) supported from 2013 by a Social Investment Package. In social policy terms the focus was primarily on countering high, especially youth, unemployment in many member states, whilst continuing to promote consideration of social protection, education and employment-related matters.

The Eurozone crisis, however, led to attempts to foster closer integration not only of economic but fiscal policy across its member countries, including agreement in late 2012 for developing a single supervisory banking regime, seen by some as the beginning of a Eurozone 'banking union' and greater coordination of tax and employment policies. The UK Prime Minister, David Cameron, negotiated protections preventing the UK from being marginalized when key decisions were made under these provisions, which were to be implemented by 2014. But the growing attention given to aspects of closer harmonization by many EU states added a new twist to earlier debates, particularly in the UK, about the possibility of developing a 'twin', or even, a 'multi-track' approach to policy-making within the Union.

To what extent and how moves towards greater harmonization develop, signifying yet another phase in the EU's evolution and, possibly, necessitating another treaty, is a hotly disputed and still unfolding issue with debate again driven more by economic than social policy concerns. For the UK, however, these developments have contributed to renewed controversy about its relationship with the EU, as we will discuss later.

THE INSTITUTIONS OF THE EU

The problem for realizing a single planning framework is that the EU and its predecessors were formed by the coming together of separate states, and it is still predominantly run (or governed) by the representatives of the member governments. The EU is an association of member nations rather than a separate political entity like the Federal government of the USA, with a system of governance now determined by the constitution agreed at the 2007 Lisbon Treaty. The forum where these representatives come together is the *Council of Ministers*, comprising the member states' heads of government, accompanied (depending on the issues being considered) by another minister. It meets twice a year, usually in Brussels, and makes the major decisions regarding the EU's policies and priorities. Its president is appointed by qualified majority for a two-and-a-half-year term, renewable once; and, unless the Treaty specifies majority or qualified voting, its decisions are taken by consensus.

While the Council determines policy, it is generally initiated by the *European Commission*, which operates as a kind of civil service for the Council and is the only institution with the powers to propose EU legislation. Apart from policy initiation it is responsible for setting long-term priorities and the EU budget, developing guidelines on employment policy, implementing and monitoring EU legislation, and reporting on general social trends and member states' social policies. An early example of its role in the social policy field was the Council's approval of Commission recommendations in the 1970s for binding EU provisions on equal pay and equal treatment between women and men that forced some member states (such as the UK) to alter their legislation to bring it into line.

The Commission comprises an extensive administrative network based in Brussels and Luxembourg led by 28 Commissioners, one from each EU state and responsible for a specific policy area, and headed by a President nominated by the Council. They are appointed for a five-year term and expected to work for the Union's and not any national interest. The Commission's day-to-day work is undertaken by departments, or Directorates-General (DGs), with responsibility for different aspects of EU policy development and implementation, the main ones in the social policy area being the DGs for Employment, Social Affairs and Inclusion (EMPL) and for Education and Culture (EAC). It has also established a number of other bodies to develop, implement or monitor policy across the union. These include the EU statistical service, *Eurostat*, research *Observatories* comprising academic representatives from all member states (such as the European Employment Observatory) and various European *Centres* (such as the one for the Development of Vocational Training, CEDEFOP, based in Greece).

If the Commission is the EU's civil service, then the *European Court of Justice* (ECJ) founded in 1952 is its judiciary. Sitting in Luxembourg, it acts as the guardian of the treaties and the enforcer of EU law and in areas covered by that law is the highest court in the EU, outranking courts in the member states and operating as an autonomous legal system. It comprises one judge from each member state, appointed for six-year terms and supported by eight Advocates-General. All citizens, and member states, can use the court; and, if the court finds a country to be acting in breach of treaty commitments, that country must change its laws to comply, as happened in the UK following the equality legislation in the 1970s mentioned above.

In terms of constitutional theory we might expect that the *European Parliament*, sitting in Strasbourg and Brussels, would be the legislative body of the EU especially as, since 1979, its members have been directly elected by all EU citizens (every five years), with the number of MEPs reflecting a country's population and capped at 750 overall by the Lisbon Treaty. The member governments have ceded little real political power to it, however, and continue to exercise control over all major policy-making through the Council of Ministers. Under the Lisbon Treaty, however, it gained more influence over the content of legislation. Legislative proposals have to be agreed jointly between the two before becoming law, with the parliament having powers to reject a proposed measure. Commissioners' appointments also have to be approved by the parliament, which has powers to sack the whole Commission and jointly approve the EU's annual budget.

The other major EU social policy institution is the *Economic and Social Committee*, which comprises representatives of employers, workers and other interest groups throughout the community. Founded in 1957, its prime role is to provide a forum for consultation and representation on a range of social and economic issues, including EU legislative proposals. In effect, it has something of a 'watchdog' role within the complex set of institutional checks and balances which seek to ensure policy-making follows the wishes and interests of a broad spectrum of the population across the union. It is also an example of the formal commitment within the EU to a corporatist approach that seeks to involve major interests (the social partners) in policy-making.

In a large, complex supranational body like the EU policy-making is, not surprisingly, complex, protracted and often the outcome of extensive negotiation and 'horse-trading'. Successive increases in membership have also brought changes in decision-making processes and the introduction of qualified majority voting in a range of areas including employment, though unanimous voting applies to the areas of social protection and social security.

EU legislation is also complex. Whilst the various treaties provide the basis for all EU action (referred to as *primary legislation*), their objectives are enacted through different types of *secondary legislation*. The most binding measures are *Regulations*, which take immediate effect, apply across the EU and do not require confirmation by national parliaments. The other forms of binding legislation are *Directives* (such as those on parental leave and working time) and *Decisions*. The former require national enactment within a set timeframe but are formulated in broad terms, setting goals that all member states must achieve, but giving them flexibility to determine how. The latter in contrast are binding only on those to whom they are addressed such as a particular member state or organization.

Concerted policy-making is also encouraged through a range of non-binding policy statements suggesting lines of action, the most important being *Recommendations* and *Opinions*, and consultative documents such as Green and White Papers. Policy development within the EU, however, also takes place through two other formal routes. Firstly, since 1992 the social partners have had powers to negotiate framework agreements for the Council to adopt; and, though not extensively used, these have led to some EU-wide agreements, such as the parental leave directive.

Secondly, policy-making within the EU has also been shaped by the development of *soft legislation* through a framework for cooperation termed the '*open method of coordination*'. This provides for the setting of common objectives, or agreement on particular targets and guidelines, and it requires member states to produce national action plans in the area of employment and social exclusion. It also provides for monitoring of these and, in effect, enables member states to share good practice, benchmark and compare their actions. Though its effectiveness is far from clear (Buchs 2008), it forms part of the context for social policy development in the EU, including the UK whose reports also cover the devolved governments (HMG 2012b).

EUROPEAN SOCIAL PROGRAMMES

As the EU developed the Council and, more especially, the Commission focused increasingly on the EU-wide implications of the economic development the Union was fostering. Their concern centred particularly on the deleterious social consequences of economic change and their inequitable distribution between and within member states noted earlier. What is more, the findings of the Observatories and Centres examining social trends in the EU created pressure within the Commission to redress these repercussions. The result has been an increasingly extensive set of community-wide measures agreed by the Council and designed to counter, or at least alleviate, the social costs of economic restructuring and reduce national and regional disparities.

The most important of these have been the *European Structural Funds*, which initially comprised three strategic funds:

- The *European Social Fund* (ESF), launched in 1958 to facilitate employment and training initiatives.
- The *European Agricultural Guidance and Guarantee Fund* (FEOGA) founded in 1962 to assist in rural change and development.
- The *European Regional Development Fund* (ERDF), established in 1975 to improve infrastructure in depressed regions.

To maximize their impact these funds were expanded and coordinated following the Single European Act. The Maastricht Treaty led to further extensions and the creation in 1994 of a *Cohesion Fund* aimed to encourage economic convergence in the build-up to the EMU and provide infrastructure aid for less-developed member states. In effect, the funds came to operate as one general programme for employment, infrastructure and agricultural change providing support for projects initiated or supported by national governments in areas of established social need.

Spending on the funds is set by the EU's seven-year budget cycle and support allocated according to objectives agreed by the Council and against which specific regions within countries are designated as priority areas. In the last century there were seven such objectives, distributing resources across a wide range of areas across the member states. But in 2000 these were reduced to three and changed again in 2007 to meet the restructuring pressures posed by the expansion of the EU and promote the goals of economic, social and territorial cohesion (Table 7.4).

Table 7.4 The European structural funds: general objectives 2000–2013	
2000–2006	*2007–2013*
Objective 1 – the most deprived areas	Convergence objective – to accelerate the convergence of the least developed member states and regions
Objective 2 – areas facing industrial decline or other structural problems and in need of economic diversification	Regional competition and employment objective (including regions not covered by the convergence objective)
Objective 3 – assistance with modernization in education, training and employment.	
	European territorial cooperation objective

The new entrants to the EU already faced more serious socioeconomic problems than most of the poorer areas of Western Europe and membership accentuated the gap between them and the prosperous 'golden triangle'. One of the consequences of this has been significant labour mobility towards the West; and to reduce these disparities, from 2007 support has focused more directly on reducing economic and social differences across the EU, through regional redistribution.

Spending on the structural funds has thus grown since the 1990s; and the budget at EU level for the Structural and Cohesion Funds for 2007–2013 was €347 billion, about a third of the total EU budget, with €76 billion going to the ESF (BIS 2012). From 2014 to 2020 the funds are to operate in a more flexible and integrated way under a 'Common Strategic Framework' aimed to drive international competitiveness and growth whilst delivering programmes geared to the specific challenges faced by different regions. In the context of the problems in the Eurozone and public spending cutbacks more generally, however, the budget for the funds set in 2013 was, like those of the member states and the EU overall, an 'austere' one.

BRITAIN IN THE EU

As we have seen the UK was not a member of the Coal and Steel Community or the EEC. Moreover its attempts to join the latter in the 1960s were vetoed by France, so when it eventually joined in 1973 it was after a decade of waiting. Thus it might be expected that there was widespread political support for membership and future European cooperation. However, this was not the case.

The Labour Party, which was in government from 1974 to 1979, was split over the issue of EEC membership. Partly in order to quell these divisions, the Prime Minister, Harold Wilson, organized a referendum in 1976 on the question of whether or not to continue membership. This resulted in a significant majority in favour of continuation, thus isolating Labour's anti-Europeans. Their opposition was partly based on the EEC's predominantly economic focus and narrow labour market concerns. When this began to change with the development of a stronger social dimension in the 1980s, the party (then in opposition) adopted a much more united policy of support for the EU, which largely continued after its return to power in 1997.

During the 1980s the Conservative Party in government, however, began to divide over Europe. A significant, and vocal, minority of its MPs became overtly hostile to the extending powers and influence of the European Commission, particularly in the social policy field. Some of this animosity was shared by the Prime Minister, Margaret Thatcher, who led Britain into a far more oppositional role within the Council of Ministers, frequently speaking out against new policy initiatives and far-reaching federalist plans and blocking some initiatives. Britain did not join the European Exchange Rate Mechanism in the 1980s, preferring to pursue a separate monetary policy; and, though membership was agreed in 1990, the government quickly withdrew when the 1990s recession began to bite (see Chapter 15). British reluctance to participate in further EU development continued under Major with the opt-out arrangements over the single currency and the Social Chapter discussed earlier.

Between 1997 and 2010 Labour's more positive approach meant that for the first time since joining in 1973 the UK had a government largely committed to maintaining an active role in EU policy-making and ensuring its economic and social development was closely linked to that of its co-members. Social policy initiatives such as the Social Charter were implemented and EU Directives on, for instance, working time, paid holiday entitlements, and discrimination in the workplace were implemented (see Chapter 13). It also meant the Prime Minister and other ministers were more willing to discuss and agree to further programmes for social action in the Council of Ministers, and hence to a continued extension of EU social policy provisions.

Nonetheless the UK did not join the single currency in 2002 and Labour held to the view that it would only do so when the indicators revealed it was in the country's economic interest and a majority supported it in a national referendum. The combination of financial problems in the Eurozone and the election of the Conservative-led Coalition in 2010, however, has brought a change in tone and reopened controversy over the UK's place in the EU, which has also been reflected in the increased popularity of the anti-EU political party, the UK Independence Party (UKIP). Eurosceptics within the Conservative Party have pressed for a renegotiation of Britain's relationship with the EU and the 'repatriation' of various powers, especially over employment matters. In 2013 the Prime Minister, David Cameron, called for a more flexible, diverse and accountable EU and committed the Conservative Party, if elected in 2015, to negotiate a new settlement and membership terms, and to hold an 'in–out' referendum on these early in a new Parliament. Pro-Europeans of all parties on the other hand, whilst acknowledging the need for reform within the EU, strongly oppose any 'exit' strategy and are concerned about the emergence of a 'two-tier' (rather than a multi-track) EU.

The outcomes of these debates remain a matter of speculation, however, and whether moves to a closer union within the EU will be advancing after 2015 is also unclear, as are any implications for social and employment policy. Hitherto experience of EU membership has been linked to a one-way street: one may be able to slow down or even stop, but once in the street one cannot turn round and go back; but whether recent Eurozone problems have challenged this direction of travel remains to be seen.

COMPREHENSION QUESTIONS

- To what extent is the EU is an organization of nations rather than citizens?
- What are the EU structural funds and how have they sought to redistribute resources between and within member nations?
- What are the advantages and disadvantages of closer union within the EU?

REFLECTIVE QUESTION

- Why has Britain been such a 'reluctant' member of the EU?

FURTHER READING

Alcock and Craig (2009) provide an accessible introduction to the international context of social policy development. The impact of globalization across a range of social policy dimensions is explored by Deacon (2007), Yeates (2008) and Kennett (2008). Dodds (2013) provides a comparative analysis of different policy areas, whilst the compilations by Castles et al. (2010) and Alcock and Powell (2011) cover a range of comparative studies including regime analysis. The most useful book on the development of EU social policy is Hantrais (2007). McCormick (2011) provides a useful guide to its workings. Updates on EU developments can be accessed at www.ec.europa.eu/social and its magazine, *Social Agenda*. Useful websites on global social policy are: www.globalpolicy.org and www.worldforum.org.

Part 2
Key Policy Areas

All students of social policy need some understanding of the core areas of policy delivery – that is those services which are provided by government, or by private or third sector organizations, in order to meet our major needs for welfare and well-being. In practice the range and extent of welfare service provision is massive and we could not hope to cover all aspects of this in one book. Also the organization and operation of the different services is complex and detailed. We can only hope to provide a summary introduction here therefore. There are dedicated texts covering particular services in more depth, and the key examples of these are listed in the further reading at the end of each chapter. Those wanting more detail on particular services are thus advised to consult these.

Nevertheless this section does include a summary of the history and development of the core welfare services, their current structure and operation, and some of the key issues and policy debates arising in them. Each of the chapters here include a summary of the recent historical development of policy provision, emphasizing how important it is to understand the ways in which past policy decisions have influenced current and future policy practice. Current provision is also summarized, including the recent developments and future plans of the UK Coalition government and the devolved administrations in Scotland, Wales and Northern Ireland. Nevertheless policy change continues, and readers are encouraged to use the web-based resources outlined in the further reading to keep up to date with future changes, in particular the websites of the major government departments responsible for each service area, which contain all government publications and statistics, and are regularly updated.

Social policy study has often focused on the five main services areas – social security, education, health, housing and social services. There are substantive chapters on each of these. There is also a chapter on employment. Employment policy is important in part because it responds to one of the 'five giant evils' (idleness) identified by Beveridge in his 1942 report and discussed in Chapter 1. However, it has also come to occupy a central role in government attempts to tackle a wide range of social needs such as poverty in the UK and in other developed economies. This means that there is no extensive coverage of some other social policy issues such as family policy; crime, criminal justice and community safety; or environmental and transport policy. All these, and other, policy areas do affect our welfare and wellbeing of course; but a book on social policy must draw the limits of substantive coverage somewhere; and these are beyond the scope of this book.

8
Social Security

SUMMARY OF KEY POINTS

- Social security involves the redistribution of resources within society. This takes place through market, voluntary and informal transfers as well as the provision of state benefits.
- Public expenditure on social security has been rising both in absolute terms and as a proportion of GDP.
- Social security is administered by independent agencies under the overall control of the Department for Work and Pensions (DWP).
- Redistribution through benefits may be horizontal or vertical, and the difference between these also leads to different principles for provision based on insurance or assistance.
- The development of social security policy has seen shifts between insurance and assistance benefits, with means-testing becoming more prevalent in recent decades.
- Benefit entitlement varies for different groups of claimants including pensioners, single parents, the unemployed, the long-term sick and disabled and those on low wages.
- Non-take-up of benefits is a significant problem, especially for means-tested support.
- Means-testing of benefits also leads to unemployment and poverty traps.
- The 1997–2010 Labour governments introduced new pension provisions, increased benefits for families with children and expanded the role of tax credits to encourage claimants to move from 'welfare to work'.
- The Coalition government has cut social security spending and instigated further changes designed to shift claimants into work.
- A Universal Credit system is being phased in and other measures to simplify provision and increase private savings are planned, but social security reform remains a complex and highly contested process.

WHAT IS SOCIAL SECURITY?

Social security is the term normally used to refer to the range of policies aimed at transferring cash resources between individuals and families in the UK. In practice though, these transfers cover a wide range of public and private redistribution and social security is not necessarily used to cover all of them. It is worth reflecting briefly on the term itself therefore, for the words used convey something of the means and ends that govern policy in the area:

- *Social* implies that what is going on here is collective, or at least collaborative; it is an activity that is intended to involve and impact upon individuals in their relations with others.

- *Security* implies that what is being provided is intended to secure people's position within those social relations, and indeed secure social structures for all more generally.

These are powerful and positive connotations and to some extent they have provided the underpinning for ideological support for social security policy since the last century. However, in recent times these have sometimes taken on a different tone: for example, with social security criticized as a drain on the public purse, and the position of 'being on the social' seen as having a devalued social status.

It is perhaps obvious, and inevitable, that social security should have negative as well as positive connotations, for in practice some may see it as a benefit and some as a cost. But the images conjured up by some critics – most starkly perhaps in certain elements of the popular press – can make the development and implementation of policy in this area more difficult. For instance, opinion poll evidence, which has generally demonstrated strong support for public spending on health and education, indicates both far less support for increasing social security expenditure and a hardening of attitudes to benefit recipients since the 1990s (Rowlingson et al. 2010; Clery 2012), which is arguably now helping to drive policy changes (Taylor-Gooby 2013).

In the USA a number of public income transfers are referred to as *welfare*; and it is generally the case that these provisions and their receipt are viewed in negative terms, with recent attempts being made by governments there to cut benefit dependency. These negative overtones have been imported into Britain, with social security since the 1980s being frequently referred to as 'welfare', often with a pejorative subtext. In fact there is a distinction in the USA between welfare policy, which technically refers to certain benefits targeted on poor families, and social security, which is a form of income insurance to which the majority of employees contribute.

In Britain, and in the rest of Europe, there is a similar distinction between targeted *social assistance* and contributory *social insurance* provision, which we will discuss in more detail shortly (and see Walker 2005). There has also generally been more public support for insurance-based protection. But, although both are still referred to as social security, 'welfare' is now widely used as an umbrella term for state benefits, as in the 2012 Welfare Reform Act, a rebranding that many argue has facilitated significant shifts in support.

Whatever form it takes, however, social security is concerned with policies governing cash transfers, or the *redistribution* of resources within society. Such transfers take place across all dimensions of social activity. In Part 1 we distinguished between the state, market, third and informal sectors of welfare and redistribution takes place in all four:

- Informally money is passed across generations and within communities.
- Voluntary organizations operate to redistribute cash and goods, from Oxfam's international aid to local soup kitchens for rough sleepers.
- Companies offer opportunities for investment, and protection for retirement, sickness, mortgage costs and other contingencies.
- Government provides cash benefits and other support both nationally and locally.

There is also a significant amount of financial support provided by employers for their employees, including pension schemes and sick pay. These could be regarded as part of private market protection although the government and other public sector employers are among the major providers of these forms of provision, which are generally referred to as *occupational* welfare.

The redistribution occurring within the different sectors of the policy terrain is a crucial element in the provision of 'social security', for we all at various points in our lives depend upon support from one or more of these sources. However, in social policy debate social security is usually taken to mean state, or public, provision for protection through redistribution and it is mainly this support that we will discuss in the rest of this chapter. Nevertheless it is important to note that policy-making increasingly focuses upon the interrelationship between the protections provided within different sectors. For instance, planning for pensions is based upon an explicit partnership between state, occupational and self-provision, with most future retirees being expected to invest in workplace or personal schemes from which they will receive pensions alongside support from the state.

ORGANIZATION AND ADMINISTRATION

Public provision of social security is now the major part of social expenditure organized through the state to provide for the needs of citizens. Of course, in one sense it is not public *expenditure* as money is not spent by government officers but *transferred* between citizens. As we shall explain the nature and direction of these transfers is extremely complex and over-lapping, with almost all people receiving benefits at some points in their lives and many cur-rently receiving them at the same time as paying contributions through National Insurance (NI) and taxation. And when the impact of tax transfers as well as social security payments is taken into account, which, as we shall see, has generally not been the case in UK social policy planning, this picture becomes even more convoluted.

Nevertheless the provision of social security benefits is recorded as public expenditure and is by far the largest element, amounting to just under a third of government spending, close to education and health combined (see Figure 16.1) and in 2010 it accounted for 13.7% of GDP (see Figure 2.1). What is more, as Figure 8.1 shows, social security expenditure has grown in both absolute and real terms almost continuously since the 1980s.

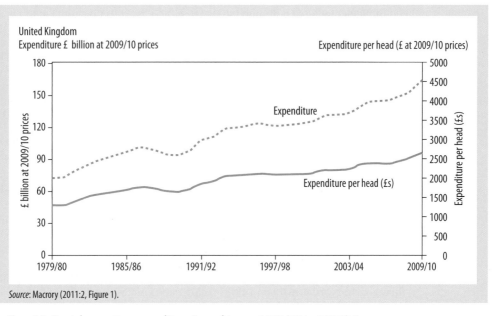

Source: Macrory (2011:2, Figure 1).

Figure 8.1 Social security expenditure in real terms 1979/80 to 2009/10

Expenditure figures such as this need to be treated with some caution for what is counted in total benefit expenditure can include (or not) a number of different elements. For instance, some totals (including Figure 8.1) exclude support for housing benefit paid through local, not central, government; while since 1999 the replacement of some means-tested benefits by tax credits paid through HM Revenue and Customs (HMRC), formerly the Inland Revenue, has removed the cost of support in this area from the social security budget. However when expenditure on these tax credits is added in then the overall cost of social protection rises to the £220 billion in 2013/14 revealed in Figure 16.1.

Furthermore, increases in expenditure are the product of a wide range of different factors. In recent times these include the rising numbers of pensioners, fluctuations in unemployment levels and the growth of lone parent families, as well as changing government policies such as the introduction of tax credits. They are not, by and large, however, a product of higher levels of benefit payment. These, as we discuss later, have largely been restricted, particularly when compared to rising average income levels, and there is extensive evidence suggesting they often to do not meet claimants' basic needs. Furthermore since the 1980s many benefits have been subject to income tax, reducing the support provided.

In part the pressure to contain benefit levels is a product of concern over the overall growth in social security expenditure resulting from these other factors. In the 1980s the Conservative governments sought, largely unsuccessfully, to contain most areas of public expenditure, particularly social security through measures restricting entitlement to some benefits, notably those for unemployment and invalidity or incapacity. Despite this, total expenditure passed the then £100 billion mark in the 1990s, and, notwithstanding the 'removal' of tax credits has, as seen above, continued to rise. High levels of expenditure of course encompass support that all citizens at different times benefit from to some extent; and, for a while, concern over controlling public spending growth shifted to debate about how best to distribute state support to meet the broader aims of government policy. With the cuts in public expenditure introduced from 2010, however, policy-making has again focused on reducing the social security bill.

Unlike some of the other areas discussed in this book, social security policy is developed and implemented on a common basis across the UK, with no significant powers devolved to the administrations of Scotland, Wales and Northern Ireland. Historically formal responsibility for the management of both budgets and benefit delivery has rested with variously named ministries, but since 2001 lies with the Department for Work and Pensions (DWP) in Great Britain. In Northern Ireland benefit administration and payments are overseen by the Department for Social Development (DSD), which is also responsible for housing and urban regeneration. However, since the 'Next Steps' initiatives of the late 1980s and early 1990s the delivery of most benefits in the UK is managed by independent agencies (sometimes referred to as quasi-autonomous non-governmental organizations – quangos).

Initially this was primarily the Benefits Agency. This, however, was replaced in 2002 by Jobcentre Plus, providing benefit and employment services to claimants of working age (Jobs and Benefits Office in Northern Ireland, administered by the Social Security Agency), the Pensions Service, administering benefits for pensioners, and the Disability and Carers Service for disabled people and carers. As mentioned above, tax credits are administered by HMRC, which also collects and manages NI contributions and is responsible for child benefits. In Britain a separate Child Support Agency (CSA) was established to administer maintenance payments from absent parents. But following prolonged criticism in 2008 in mainland Britain this was incorporated into the Child Maintenance and Enforcement Commission, only for its functions to be returned later to the DWP as part of the Coalition's abolition of a range of Quangos. In Northern Ireland child maintenance issues since 2008 lie with a division in the DSD.

To most claimants these agencies may feel little different to government offices, and they are staffed by government officers working to procedures and regulations determined by Parliament. However, since the late 1990s there have been significant moves to improve customer relations in benefit delivery. From a time when claimants waited for hours in seats bolted to the floor and then shouted through plastic screens to nameless officers with no direct access to their individual files, administration of most benefits has moved to a personal contact model, backed by computerized data storage, helplines and internet-based information as well as face-to-face advice. In addition under an initiative called ONE the agencies sought to provide a 'one shop' service for each claimant with the aim of simplifying the process of claiming all their benefits.

For those of working age this was referred to as the 'single gateway' and incorporated advice on training and job search as part of Labour's 'work first' approach connecting social security and employment policies in what was seen as a mutually supportive strategy (see Chapter 13). From 2008 these provisions were extended to a wider range of benefits and non-statutory providers contracted to support people to move into employment. More individualized provision remains a key government aim and, in practice, for those of working age not in employment now means a work-focused interview with Jobcentre Plus or an external employment service provider to discuss work issues before claims for financial aid are dealt with. Further ways of streamlining benefit administration, both to improve the service for claimants and cut costs are, as will be discussed later, under way, particularly through the Universal Credit (UC) scheme for working age adults, which will be managed by the DWP, with HMRC relinquishing responsibility for tax credits.

Simplification, however, is often contradicted by the fact that responsibility for administering some provisions, notably housing and council tax benefits, lies with local, rather than central, government (and in the case of housing with the Northern Ireland Housing Executive (NIHE)). Local government administrative procedures are quite different, and sometimes much slower. Local authorities (LAs) are also responsible for the provision of a range of other cash transfers (such as free school meals) and subsidized access to local services (such as public transport and leisure facilities). In practice this support is aimed at those who also receive some of the major national social security benefits, and so the experience of many claimants remains one of confusion and disjuncture in the pursuit of their rights to public support. With 30 different benefit programmes run either by one of nine central departments or an LA in Britain (HoCPAC 2011), this complexity has long been recognized by policymakers and is the focus of some of the initiatives discussed later. It is, however, a product of the diverse and multifaceted needs that social security is seeking to address and, hitherto, moves to reduce complexity have had little success (Howarth 2005).

For the most part claimants have a right to the benefits they receive, although there has long been debate about the extent to which they should be provided as of *right* subject to clear written rules and regulations, as opposed to under *discretion*, where social security officers are required to make individual judgements about the financial needs of each claimant. The earliest form of social security in the UK, the Poor Law, was based upon the latter approach and this continued to play a central role in the delivery of many means-tested benefits until the last two decades of the twentieth century. Discretionary payments create administrative and budgetary problems, however (how should different needs be assessed and how can spending be anticipated and controlled?), and have now largely been removed from mainstream social security provision. Until recently the main exception to this was the cash limited provision under the Social Fund established in 1988 allowing discretionary payments for exceptionally costly items, generally in the form of loans deducted from a claimant's benefit (Grover 2011). From 2013, however, this form of support gave way to localized, even more discretionary 'last resort' assistance schemes administered by LAs in England and the devolved administrations elsewhere.

Nonetheless the existence of rights to most social security benefits means that potential claimants can be given clear advice about their entitlements. This is primarily done through leaflets, online and media information prepared by the DWP. However, as we shall see, the rules governing entitlement to the wide range of benefits available are highly complex, with detailed regulations running into hundreds of pages, which officers themselves require specialist training to understand. Most claimants are likely to have only a vague idea of their legal rights, and ignorance and confusion over these is one of the major reasons why some fail to claim all the benefits to which they may be entitled, an issue we return briefly to later. Advice can be sought from social security staff, of course, including via telephone information lines. However, help may also be available from specialist *welfare rights* workers.

These are employed by LAs or third sector advice agencies to provide independent advice and assistance for claimants, and many agencies also include volunteer advisers. Most are not lawyers, and there are few lawyers who specialize in social security as it is not a lucrative area of legal practice; but specialist welfare rights workers have become an important source of independent support for social security claimants and have developed a range of strategies to support and encourage the claiming of benefits (see Alcock 2006), although some of these are threatened by recent public spending cuts.

The rights base of current benefit arrangements does, however, provide an important legal foundation for the delivery of social security policy (see Dean 1996). It means that if claimants are unhappy with the decisions taken by social security officers they can challenge these through a legal appeal. Claimants have a right to appeal against most benefit decisions to a Social Security and Child Support Appeal Tribunal, although many cases may be resolved before reaching a formal hearing; and then, subject to the ordinary rules about appeals, there can be further recourse to the courts in the UK and European Union. Pursuing an appeal requires an understanding of legal rules and procedures, and here welfare rights workers may also offer assistance. Not surprisingly, perhaps, relatively few social security cases make it into the court process; but on occasions important issues have been subject to appeals and judicial decisions have altered the interpretation of regulations to the benefit of claimants, underlining the symbolic importance of the role of rights in policy delivery.

COMPREHENSION QUESTIONS

- How and why has the balance of social security expenditure changed over the last 20 years?
- Which bodies are responsible for the administration of state benefits in the UK and how is this likely to change over the next decade?
- What are the advantages and disadvantages of the idea of *rights* to benefits?

REFLECTIVE QUESTION

- Should we be concerned about the rise in social security expenditure?

PRINCIPLES

At the heart of social security policy are the principles which underlie the payment of benefits and tax credits and, more generally, the transfer or redistribution of resources which these aim to achieve (see Walker 2005). In broad terms we can distinguish between two fundamental principles that might inform cash transfers within society:

- *Horizontal redistribution*: the transfer of resources across people's life cycles. It is based on the assumption that at different points in our lives we may be more likely to need income support. This is particularly the case in childhood (and for the parents of children) and in retirement, as during working age most individuals are likely to be in paid employment and therefore able to make contributions and/or pay taxes. Thus horizontal redistribution provides support at times of need (child benefit and pensions) paid for by contributions made at times of (relative) plenty, and is a form of support from which we may all expect to benefit and towards which we all may contribute.
- *Vertical redistribution*: the transfer of resources from rich to poor within society. Within an unequal distribution of income and wealth there may be those at the bottom who do not

have enough resources to support themselves and their dependants adequately, and those at the top who have more than they need. Resources can (and arguably should) therefore be transferred from those who have more than enough to those who have too little. Unlike horizontal redistribution, however, there is a difference between those who pay, and may never benefit, and those who benefit, and may never pay.

There are important ideological, political and economic differences between these two approaches and they result in disparate ways of financing and delivering benefit support. However, in practice both have informed the development of social security in Britain and remain at the centre of provision today. Analysis reveals that it does redistribute from rich to poor, with the value of cash benefits including tax credits received being highest for those at the bottom of the income distribution, and that it also redistributes across the life cycle, with all income groups benefiting from some element of redeployment over their lifetime (see Hills 2012).

The differences between horizontal and vertical redistribution lead to different methods of financing social security payments, and determining benefit entitlements, and these too can be divided into two broad approaches:

- *Social insurance*: this is linked to horizontal redistribution and the idea that those in work make contributions that are then redistributed to those at other stages in their life cycle. Workers therefore pay social security contributions, and these are collected with contributions from employers into a national insurance fund from which benefits are paid to those unable to work. Social insurance benefits typically cover circumstances such as retirement, sickness or disability, and unemployment (usually conceived of as a temporary period whilst seeking further work). Benefit entitlements are linked to the payment of contributions, with only those meeting specified contribution conditions able to claim and the amount paid therefore generally unaffected by a partner's earnings. It has some similarities to private insurance therefore, although in most social insurance schemes contributions are used to meet current benefit needs rather than being invested to cover the demands which might be made by future claimants (sometimes referred to a 'pay-as-you-go' funding). Because of this funding base, social insurance payments are often referred to as *contributory benefits*.
- *Social assistance*: this is linked to vertical redistribution and the idea that benefits should be targeted only on those who need support because they are poor. Here provision is paid for by taxes on those with adequate incomes (usually including some element of progression with those on the highest incomes paying the most) and benefits paid to those who can demonstrate they are in need. This involves the application of 'means-tests' in which the financial circumstances of potential claimants are investigated to ensure they do not have sufficient other sources of support. Means-tests mean these benefits are income-related, and they can be used to redistribute resources across a range of different income levels, but within social security provision this is generally limited to those at the very bottom of the scale. Moreover entitlement may (as in the UK) depend on family resources, including savings as well as income. Assistance benefits are therefore also referred to as selective or targeted social security schemes. In addition to income, social assistance is also often dependent on satisfying other conditions and failure to meet these may carry sanctions or penalties. For instance in the UK, as in many other countries, working age adults without responsibility for caring for young children or disabled adults have to be available for and actively seeking employment.

Social insurance and social assistance provide the ideological and organizational basis upon which most social security provision is founded throughout much of the developed world and in most countries they operate alongside each other. This has also been the case in Britain since the early part of the last century, and the very different principles informing them are a source of much complexity and confusion, particularly for claimants, many of whom in practice rely on support from both. Social assistance has, however, played a larger role in the UK than in northern and continental European countries where there has been a greater emphasis on income maintenance rather than poverty relief. Indeed the UK relies more on means-testing than most developed economies (NAO 2011). There have, however, been changes in the balance of coverage between them, with insurance becoming more widespread in the middle part of the last century and assistance more dominant since the 1980s, a development we consider later.

As in other countries there is, though, another form of benefit in the UK. This is not based on contributions or income and hence is often referred to as *contingent* or *categorical*. It is also sometimes known as a *universal* benefit, as it is paid to everyone falling within a designated social group recognized as facing particular costs or needs. Such benefits include financial help for people with specific disability needs and also for the cost of child rearing. Historically the main non-contributory, non-income related provision in the UK was Child Benefit payable to all parents or guardians of children. Since 2013, however, as will be mentioned later, this has become to some extent income related. Table 8.1 summarizes these differing principles:

Table 8.1 The principles behind social security provision		
	Who should pay?	*Who should benefit?*
Social Insurance	Employers and employees	Contributors
Social Assistance	Taxpayers	People deemed to be poor
Contingent/Universal Benefits	Taxpayers	People with particular needs

THE DEVELOPMENT OF SOCIAL SECURITY

The history of social security policy in the UK is long and complicated and we can only provide a brief overview here (for more detailed summaries see Alcock 1999a, 1999b and Spicker 2011). Most commentators trace current provision back to the *Poor Law*, which dominated British social policy before the twentieth century. It was basically a locally administered social assistance scheme providing support on a discretionary basis to those who could establish that they were effectively destitute. The Poor Law system aimed to control and discipline the poor, and the support it provided was deliberately designed to be below that enjoyed by the lowest-paid workers – referred to as the principle of 'less eligibility'. The effects of this, amongst others, were to give dependence upon social security an undesirable and stigmatized status – and reinforce a negative image of the role and scope of public support.

In the early part of the twentieth century the Poor Law was gradually replaced by social insurance-based protection for unemployment, sickness and pensions (see McKay and Rowlingson 1999; Spicker 2011). However, not all those in need of support were covered and so assistance-based Poor Law provision remained, renamed Public Assistance in the 1930s. In 1942 a fundamental review of social security commissioned by the wartime government was produced by William Beveridge. His report (1942) is still the only comprehensive review of social security in Britain; it was influential throughout the developed world, and formed the basis of the post-war reforms that still frame provision in the UK.

In essence Beveridge proposed that social security should be organized and delivered on a social insurance model, called *National Insurance* (NI). However, he recognized that the contributory model might leave some in need who did not fulfil the NI criteria and so he recommended assistance provision be continued as a 'safety net' for those outside the new NI scheme. Renamed *National Assistance* (NA), the intention was that this means-tested support would play a minor and declining role within the social security system, but this proved to be far from the case.

In the 1950s some 1 million claimants remained dependent upon NA. This rose to 2 million in the 1960s, 4 million in the 1970s, 8 million in the 1980s; and by the 1990s those dependent upon income support (IS), as assistance support was now called, reached 10 million. With lower unemployment, the transfer of tax credits to HMRC, and the replacement of some provision by other benefits (discussed below) the numbers claiming IS subsequently declined. This did not, however, dent the shift in the balance between means-tested and NI-based support. As Figure 8.2 reveals, by 2009/10 contributory benefits accounted for less than a half of benefit expenditure. Since 1978/79, moreover, real expenditure on these had grown by 73% compared with a rise of 580% on income-related (means-tested) benefits (Jin et al. 2010).

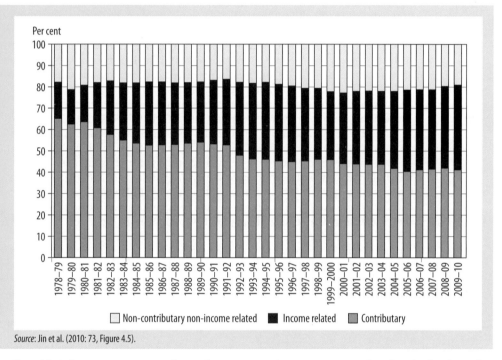

Source: Jin et al. (2010: 73, Figure 4.5).

Figure 8.2 Relative importance of spending on contributory, income-related and other benefits, 1979/80 to 2009/10

One of the reasons for the expanding role of social assistance in the latter part of the twentieth century was the limited protection in practice provided by the NI scheme. However, means-tested provision was itself expanded both in scale and scope. In the 1960s NA became Supplementary Benefits, and in the 1970s new means-tested benefits to provide support for low-income families in work and assistance with housing rents were introduced. From the 1980s the Conservative governments embraced the principle of means-testing to 'target' state support only upon those in proven need. These benefits were renamed Income Support (IS), Family Credit and Housing Benefit (HB) and an integrated model for administering them under a single means-testing framework introduced.

The Labour governments of 1997 to 2010 continued many of these policies, albeit within the context of the notion of a 'new contract' between the individual and the state for social protection (DSS 1998a). In practice much of this new contract relied upon individuals of working age seeking employment, facilitated by Labour's welfare to work strategy (see Chapter

13). To sustain this, but also as part of a more general policy to ensure resources went to those most in need, means-testing was expanded further and support for low-income families in work converted from a social security benefit into a tax credit. It was also extended to a much wider range of low incomes and expanded to cover childcare costs. Tax credits also provided support for those without children. At the same time, however, NI provision for state pensions remained a key feature of support for all in old age, and insurance benefits for short-term unemployment and longer-term sickness and incapacity were retained.

ENTITLEMENT TO SUPPORT

Social security provision in Britain is a product of these developments and the shifting balance of the different principles that underlie benefit entitlement. Hence provision does not follow a logical framework but rather reflects these different historical trends. Determining individual entitlement and calculating weekly benefit payments is therefore a specialist task for social security officers and welfare rights workers, and the best sources of accurate advice on this are the various handbooks and guides produced each year by the Child Policy Action Group (CPAG). Benefit and tax credit rates also themselves change on an annual basis following the decision of the government either to maintain their value against inflation or to increase (or reduce) this, with the new rates coming into effect at the beginning of the tax year in April.

The gauge for measuring inflation has also varied. Governments from the 1980s based it on rises in prices rather than earnings. But, as part of the Coalition's broader expenditure cuts, in 2011 the measure used for benefits other than the basic state pension (BSP) and pension tax credit was switched from the Consumer Price Index (CPI) to the Retail Price Index (RPI), lowering the amount paid. More recently in the light of continuing fiscal problems there has been pressure to apply an earnings-related index and, as seen below, from 2013 increases for most working age benefits and tax credits were limited to 1 per cent a year for three years.

Understanding social security provision is further complicated by the fact that the government is in the process of overhauling it. Initially, as will be seen, this involved changes in entitlements and payment levels for new working-age claimants. But it also embraces pension reform, new provisions for those with disabilities and the phasing in by 2017 of a Universal Credit (UC) scheme. As indicated above this is intended, amongst other aims, to create a simpler, more comprehensible structure. During the transitional phase, however, 'outgoing' provisions will, for varying periods, coexist with the new arrangements as well as continuing provision (see Table 8.2).

RETIREMENT BENEFITS

Of these NI Benefits remain a major feature of social security, primarily because they include the BSP, which is paid to all those over state pension age who have a record of contributions to the NI scheme. One of the reasons this expenditure remains high is because with longevity reaching record levels the number of older people is growing both absolutely and in relation to the rest of the population (see Table 17.2); and there are now over 12 million pensioner claimants in the UK. This is a phenomenon common to most developed countries, and indeed is less pronounced in the UK than in some others; and it has led many governments to seek to control potential future expenditure on pensions.

The cost of state pensions also rose in the last century, however, because the BSP was increased in line with the higher levels of wage inflation and from 1978 increasing numbers became entitled to an earnings-related supplement (SERPS) based on their contributions. In the 1980s the government sought to contain this growth in expenditure by uprating benefits in line with prices, leading at a time of wage inflation to a reduction in the relative value of the BSP. Labour compensated for this to some extent by increasing it above price inflation, but did not restore a regular link with wages with its expenditure implications. The Coalition,

Table 8.2 Benefit entitlements in 2012 and changes from 2013

Benefit Type	Entitlement Base	Main Benefits 2012	Provision from 2013
National Insurance Benefits (Funded by employer and employee contributions)	Individual's Contribution Record	Basic State Pension (BSP)	All retained*
		Contributory Job-Seekers Allowance (JSA)	
		Contributory Incapacity Benefit (IB) Contributory-based elements of Income Support (IS)	
Social Assistance Benefits (Tax-funded)	Means-tested (Individual's/Household's income and assets)	Pension Credit Income Support (IS)	Retained Replaced by UC
		Income-based Job Seekers Allowance (JSA)	Replaced by UC
		Incapacity Benefit (IB)/Employment and Support Allowance (ESA)	Replaced by UC
		Severe Disablement Allowance (SDA)/ Employment and Support Allowance	Replaced by UC
		Housing Benefit (HB)/ Local Housing Allowance (LHA)	Replaced by UC
		Council Tax Benefit (CTB)	Localized
Contingent (Universal) Benefits	Non-contributory + non-income related	Child Benefit (CB)	Income-related
		Disability Living Allowance (DLA)	Replaced by Personal Independence Payment
		Winter Fuel Allowance Over 60s Bus Pass Over 75s TV Licence	Retained Retained Retained
Discretionary Benefits	Regulations + judgments	The Social Fund	Replaced by Local Assistance Schemes
Tax Credits (Fiscal transfers)	Income related/means-tested (Individual's/Household's income and assets)	Child Tax Credit (CTC)	Replaced by UC
		Working Tax Credit (WTC)	Replaced by UC
Other Assistance	Income related/means-tested (Individual's/Household's income and assets)	(Examples) School meals; free prescriptions, eye tests, dental care	Retained

* BSP to be reformed from 2017 (see below)

however, in contrast to other benefits, adopted a different stance, introducing a discretionary 'triple lock' system uprating BSP and pension tax credit annually by the highest of increases in earnings, prices or 2.5%.

The Conservative governments of the 1980s also tried to reduce pension costs by encouraging people to make their own provision and promoting personal and occupational schemes, particularly through enabling employers providing schemes that met certain criteria to contract out of SERPS and maintaining pension tax reliefs. Labour took this policy further in a series of measures seeking to reduce reliance on the state through a public/private partnership approach and encouraging voluntary supplementation of the BSP (DSS 1998b). These included the withdrawal of SERPS, its replacement by a supplementary or second state pension (S2P) targeted only on lower-paid former workers and paid at lower rates together with a new stakeholder pension scheme. It also legislated to raise the state pension age for women from 60 to 65 to meet that of men by 2020.

Further reforms were instigated following the findings of the Turner Commission (2006) established by the government to consider options for future pension policy. It outlined the fiscal pressures flowing from demographic change (see Table 17.2) as well as the large numbers without adequate non-state cover and the changes in private sector occupational schemes that were making them more risky for employees as private sector organizations switched from providing defined benefit (DB) to defined contribution (DC) schemes (see Table 8.3).

Following this Labour took more steps to minimize the potential burden of pensions on the public purse and increase 'top-up' savings. These included lifting the state pension age of women and men to 67 by 2020, other provisions to encourage people to work for longer, changes to public sector pensions and provisions for abolishing the default retirement age (DRA) operated by many employers. Most crucially a new workplace pension scheme aimed at low-paid workers along with a system of auto-enrolment for all workers was launched for implementation in 2012, starting with large employers.

Both of these measures were taken up by the Coalition. As a result, in a staged process, by 2018 employees earning above a certain level must be enrolled into an employer scheme that conforms to a minimum standard, with the National Employment Savings Trust (NEST), a private sector scheme established by the government, supplying a low-cost default option. Minimum and maximum employer and employee contributions set by law are also being phased in. Individuals, however, have the right to opt out at any time, and make their own arrangements, though they will be re-enrolled every three years. The outcome is a complex mix of pension provision in the UK, summarized in Table 8.3.

Labour had also sought to enhance support for those already retired, especially those totally dependent on the BSP. This provided an inadequate income for many, with significant numbers having to seek supplementary means-tested support and many, particularly, women lacking the NI contributions to claim a full pension. In 2003 Income Support (IS) for pensioners was replaced by a Pension Credit to which all state pensioners were entitled, and, from 2008, the qualifying years for BSP for women and men reduced to 30 years. The Pension Credit was intended to ensure an income equivalent at least to means-tested IS levels and by the beginning of this decade nearly 3 million pensioners received these credits. Such provision is means-tested, however, and not paid in full to those with other sources of income or capital support. There is also evidence that around a third do not claim their entitlement (DWP 2013), an issue to which we return below.

UNEMPLOYMENT, SICKNESS AND DISABILITY BENEFITS

Pensions account for the vast bulk of NI expenditure, but contributory benefits still remain for unemployment and sickness. Unemployment cover is provided by the Jobseekers' Allowance (JSA), which replaced Unemployment Benefit and IS for the unemployed in 1996. It provides six months' non means-tested support for those who meet the NI contribution conditions. As the name suggests, it is linked to agreements by claimants to take steps to return

Table 8.3 Key pension provisions in the UK in 2013		
Pension provider	*Funding base*	*Type of pension*
The state	NI contributions (taxation)	Basic State Pension (BSP) Additional State Pension [State Earnings Related Pension Scheme (SERPS); Second State Pension (S2P)] (+ Pension Credit)
Employers	Employer + employee contributions (tax-subsidized)	Defined Benefit (DB) Schemes (providing a guaranteed pension based on an employee's salary, usually either the final or career average salary)
	[some schemes employer funded]	Defined Contribution (DC)/money purchase schemes (providing a pension based on the contributions made and investment return generated; employers pay a defined percentage of earnings with the sum accumulated converted into an annuity on retirement).
NEST	Employer + employee contributions (tax-subsidized)	DC scheme
Financial Service Companies	Individual Purchase (tax-subsidized)	Personal Pensions (DC schemes) Annuities

to work, which we discuss in Chapter 13. JSA is no longer solely an insurance benefit, however. After six months, claimants remain on it and subject to the same job search requirements, but their benefit becomes means-tested (Non-contributory JSA), with any other resources (including the income of a spouse or cohabitee) leading to a reduction in overall entitlement. In practice this means-tested JSA was largely a retitling of IS which had for some time been payable to unemployed claimants not covered by NI benefit. As will be seen below receipt of JSA is also subject to sanctions and is undergoing further change.

Sickness cover was once a major feature of social security protection and remains a legal right. But in the 1980s support for short-term sickness, up to six months, was transferred to employers who are required to provide at least a minimum level of payment for workers off work due to sickness. Beyond six months claimants with chronic sickness or disability moved on to NI protection through Incapacity Benefit (IB), providing that they met the contribution conditions and a medical test of their inability to work. The numbers claiming IB rose from around 400,000 in 1981, to 800,000 in 1991, and 1.7 million by 2006. In part this was because many long-term IB claimants had become so detached from the labour market that they were unable to return to it, especially in areas where overall unemployment was high (Alcock et al. 2003).

These problems were addressed in a further set of reforms that came into effect from 2008 and owed much to another independent inquiry conducted for the government, the Freud Report (2007; see too Chapter 13). These included the requirement that all IB claimants engage in work-focused interviews under a 'Pathways to Work' scheme operated by non-state providers as well as Jobcentre Plus and the replacement of IB and IS for new claimants by an integrated benefit, the Employment Support Allowance (ESA). In addition all claimants became subject to a new Work Capability Assessment.

Under this those judged unable to work receive a higher rate of benefit and exemption from the work-focused conditions; others are in effect on JSA and helped and encouraged to find appropriate work, including from 2012 being mandated onto voluntary work placements (see Chapter 13). The Freud Report also led to parallel changes in IS provisions for lone parent claimants. Here, to encourage lone parents to work, in 2008 the government limited IS for those whose youngest child was 12. This 'age cap' was lowered to five in 2011 with the result that those with children at school now move on to JSA instead and have to seek employment. Again, as we outline later, further changes are in the pipeline.

HOUSING BENEFITS

IS and Income-Related JSA are in effect a minimum income scheme for British citizens. They are only payable to those out of full-time employment (defined as 16 hours a week) and are reduced if there are any earnings over a minimum level or any significant capital holdings. They do not cover housing costs, however, although, subject to some restrictions, interest payments on mortgage debts are covered. Claimants paying rent, however, could claim Housing Benefit (HB), which is a means-tested contribution to rent that, together with council tax benefit, is available to claimants and low-paid workers. Both are administered by LAs, quite separately from the other benefits discussed above, leading to confusion for many claimants. For public sector tenants HB can cover all rental costs for those on minimum incomes, and is generally simply deducted from tenants' rent accounts. This was also the case for private sector tenants until 2008, when HB was replaced by a Local Housing Allowance (LHA) set at a fixed level, based on local rental market values, and paid directly to tenants who must make up the difference if their rent is above the amount paid. Both HB and LHA, however, have recently been curtailed in various ways, as we discuss in Chapter 10.

OTHER MEANS-TESTED BENEFITS

IS and Income-Related JSA claimants are also entitled to a range of other so-called 'passported benefits'. These include free school meals for their children, other LA provisions and health benefits (such as free prescriptions, eye tests and dental care), although whether all claimants realize the full extent of their entitlements is questionable, as we will explore below. Until recently, as noted earlier, claimants might also be able to receive loans under the Social Fund and may still be helped by support from the devolved governments and in England by discretionary LA assistance schemes, though these are likely to be limited in scope.

TAX CREDITS

For those in low-wage employment means-tested support is also available. These in-work benefits include the housing and council tax benefits charted above; but since 1997 support for those on lower pay has increasingly taken the form of tax credits payable through employers and administered by HMRC. This has been a significant shift in the operation of means-testing and is used more in the UK than elsewhere in Europe. Initially it involved a number of different credits devised to support low-income families, cover some childcare costs and assist low-paid disabled workers. In 2003 these were replaced for all low-paid workers over 25 by a generic Working Tax Credit (WTC). It is supplemented for those with families by a Child Tax Credit (CTC) plus, where appropriate, a contribution to childcare costs.

WTC was a key element in Labour's welfare to work strategy, intended to make low-paid employment more attractive to all as we discuss in Chapter 13. The childcare provisions extended entitlement significantly, and were a major feature of its more general, and widely publicized, promise to end child poverty by 2020 and halve it by 2010. This was a major and unprecedented policy commitment, not least because it extended well beyond the remit of contemporary governments. Its effects, however, were mixed, bringing a significant fall in child poverty levels, against international trends (Waldfogel 2010), but missing the 2010 target.

The abolition of child poverty was therefore made a statutory duty under the 2010 Child Poverty Act, with the strategies for achieving it being the responsibility of the government for

England and the devolved administrations. In England, however, the emphasis is now less on income support and rather on strategies to promote social mobility and improve children's life chances (DfE 2010a; DPM 2011), although somewhat different approaches are being developed in Scotland and Wales (SG 2011a; WAG 2011a; and see NIE 2011), with the latter in 2013 appointing the first UK minister charged with tackling poverty.

CONTINGENCY BENEFITS

In addition, as mentioned earlier, there are some contingency benefits in the UK. Of these Child Benefit, received by some 7.7 million families for over 13 million children in 2010, remains the most significant. The great value of this universal benefit is that parents do claim it, no stigma is associated with its receipt, and of course, its contribution to the cost of rearing future generations could be regarded as a valuable public investment for all citizens (see Atkinson 2011). Critics, however, argue that, as with all universal services, it is 'wasting' public resources to pay benefits to wealthy as well as poor parents; and the Coalition government introduced measures to link payment to incomes by clawing the benefit back from families containing higher-paid earners. Since 2013 families with at least one higher-rate taxpayer are no longer eligible, and for those just below this threshold the benefit is paid at a reduced rate.

Certain benefits to meet the needs of older or some disabled people are also universal, in the sense that they are not subject to contribution conditions or means tests. These include the lump sum winter fuel allowance and over 60s bus passes for older people and, until recently, the Disability Living Allowance (DLA) introduced in 1993, for those with care or mobility needs. DLA was paid, following medical assessment, to those under pensionable age, including children, to cover the costs associated with personal care and mobility needs, and for pensioners there was an equivalent Attendance Allowance. Payments under these schemes were, however, generally set at very low level and, though claimant numbers rose from the late 1990s, many did not claim their entitlement. In 2013 Personal Independence Payments replaced DLA for those aged 16–64.

COMPREHENSION QUESTIONS

- What are the relative advantages and disadvantages of social insurance and social assistance as the bases for entitlement to social security support?
- How and why has a public/private partnership in pension provision been encouraged by governments since the beginning of this century?
- What are tax credits and how did they expand the role of means-testing within social security?

REFLECTIVE QUESTION

- Can universal benefits be justified in an unequal society?

PROBLEMS WITH BENEFITS

It is perhaps not surprising to find that there are problems with the operation of social security in meeting its aims of horizontal and vertical redistribution; although, of course, quite what constitutes a problem rather depends upon one's point of view here. There are some who argue the whole system operates to control and discipline citizens rather than support and protect them (see Jones and Novak 1999). Few in social policy would take such a stance, but most commentators recognize the system, perhaps inevitably, has drawbacks as well as significant merits. And many would agree that some of the problems which claimants or administrators experience pose major challenges to the notion that it provides an effective form of security for all.

The first, and perhaps most worrying, problem is that of *non take-up*. Because social security benefits are so varied and entitlement regulations so complicated many potential claimants do not understand or realize their full entitlement: that is, they do not take up their right to benefit. This has been a longstanding problem within social security, and is not unique to Britain (Van Oorschot 1995, 1996; Walker 2005). It also varies between different types of benefit with high take-up levels of universal and contributory benefits and lower claims for means-tested ones. Of course, estimating take-up levels is a rather inexact science; we can only guess at what those who do not claim might be entitled to.

However, the DWP does make regular attempts to estimate take-up for the major means-tested benefits, calculating these by caseload (numbers claiming) and expenditure (amount of money claimed). For IS and IS-related ESA these generally hover around 78–90 per cent, although they are below this for income-related JSA at 47–59 per cent and for Pension Credit at 62–73 per cent (DWP 2010a). For tax credits there are similar patterns (HMRC 2011), with higher take-up rates for CTC (79–84 per cent by caseload and 86–92 per cent by expenditure), than WTC (with 55–59 per cent and 72–81 per cent). These may look like high figures, but they mean that one-fifth or more of some of the poorest claimants do not get the benefits to which they are legally entitled; and for other means-tested benefits, especially smaller payments such as school meals, the proportions of non-claimants are much higher. Moreover low take-up makes it difficult to target assistance on the most needy.

The reverse problem is that of *fraudulent claims*: that is, people claiming money to which they are not entitled. Such fraud, where proven, is a criminal offence and can lead to prosecution and even imprisonment. However, very few criminal cases are actually brought. Much more significant is the more general concern with relatively minor cases of unreported overpayment or concealment of circumstances by claimants. In recent years successive governments have been concerned that levels of minor benefit fraud have been increasing and adding significantly to the overall social security bill. As with non-take-up, of course, these figures are only estimates, and although the government sometimes claims that billions of pounds are lost through fraud, the various attempts that have been made to 'crack down' on fraudsters and tighten up delivery have, hitherto, not generally resulted in significant savings (Sainsbury 2003).

Both of these problems are particularly associated with means-tested benefits. So, too, is the other major problem, that of *perverse incentives*, or what Walker (2005) calls economic (in)efficiency. Because means-tested benefits are paid for family needs, including housing costs, the amount to which a family may be entitled could be greater than the wage a potential breadwinner might be able to earn, especially during economic downturns. This is called the '*unemployment trap*', because it may have the effect of removing the positive incentives to take work and trapping individuals on unemployment benefits. It was a serious problem in the latter part of the last century and one which Labour sought to address through tax credits paid to those on low wages with the aim of ensuring that overall income in work was above IS levels.

However supplementing low wages by means-tested tax credits creates another problem: the '*poverty trap*'. This is a result of the withdrawal of such means-tested support when wages rise, coupled with the increasing liability to tax and NI contributions. The effect of these deductions is to impose a high 'marginal tax' on additional income; in other words, loss of means-tested credits together with other liabilities can mean as much as 80 or 90 per cent of any wage increase is forgone. This too can create perverse incentives, so that it may be better (or little worse) to remain on low wages rather than seeking to increase these (for instance, by undertaking more work or seeking promotion). It also has the effect of trapping those on low wages in poverty; and across a wide range of low incomes the effect of tax credits means take-home pay is more or less the same whatever the initial income might be.

What is happening here is a kind of flattening of wage differentials at the lower end of the income scale, and hence it is sometimes now referred to as the 'poverty plateau'. It is an important by-product of recent policies that can have a significant impact on both employment policy and social security support and one not confined to the UK (Walker 2005). In addition to this issue there are concerns that such in-work benefits constitute a subsidy to employers sustaining low wages and high levels of 'in-work poverty', whilst their complexity can lead to both over- and under-payment.

It is significant that all of these problems in social security provision occur in the delivery of means-tested benefits. It is also no coincidence. Because means-tested benefits are targeted on those who are poor, they must be subject to intricate regulations intended to ensure only those who need support receive it. These rules are difficult for many of those in need to understand, and they are also easier to abuse (perhaps not always maliciously). They also require that support be withdrawn when circumstances improve, leading to the poverty trap. Many of these problems do not apply in the same way to contributory or universal benefits; and increasing reliance on means-testing to target resources rather than social insurance is compounding the problem therefore. There has long been pressure to reverse the rise in means-testing and revive contributory-based provision (CSJ 1994; Cooke 2011); but it is often seen as a cost-effective form of support (NAO 2011) and is now part of a wider policy development within social security.

RECENT POLICY DEVELOPMENT

As in all other welfare capitalist countries social security provision in the UK is, in large part, the product of commitments developed by earlier governments. Past social policies in any area constrain future developments. But in social security this is perhaps particularly the case, for those currently relying on benefits or on low wages may have had no opportunity to make alternative provision for support. Recasting the system is therefore a complex, and inevitably a gradual, undertaking. However, this does not mean that it cannot be attempted; and indeed social security is one of the areas where change continues to be a significant and high-profile feature of government agendas.

From its formation in 2010 the Coalition took up many aspects of Labour's work-oriented strategy. It also though moved much further and initiated reforms intended to transform the social security landscape. These included deep cuts in social security spending and measures to curb future growth (HMT 2010) amounting to £18 billion annually in the period up to 2015, with further cuts expected thereafter (HMT 2012a). The first tranche of changes included a three-year freeze on some benefits, tighter eligibility criteria, greater conditionality, and reductions in tax credits and other benefits such as HB and LHA (see Chapter 10). Heavier sanctions were introduced to JSA for repeated job refusals or leaving employment without good reason, and more stringent, privately run work-capability assessments imposed on those claiming IB or ESA, which was also subject to means-testing after one year and other new rules, and, as outlined earlier single parents moved onto JSA once the youngest child was five. In a further round of reforms they were also expected to prepare for work once their youngest child was three, whilst people on JSA were to sign on weekly and have English language skills.

Future benefit and tax credit upratings were also cut back. Initially these were linked to the RPI, with the lower increases this typically entails; but from 2013 uprating for most working-age benefits and tax credits was limited to 1 per cent for three years, in effect cutting the real value of support, particularly for the poorest working households (Hood et al. 2013). In 2013 an overall benefit cap also came into force, affecting single and couple households apart from those with someone in receipt of DLA, the support component of ESA or WTC.

This meant that benefits over the capped limit, including Child Benefit, would not be paid, leading to potentially significant reductions in income, especially for larger families.

These changes were part of a wider package to counter 'welfare dependency' including a new *Work Programme*, examined in Chapter 13. They were also the prelude to a fundamental restructuring of support in and out of work for those of working age though the UC scheme intended to be fully operational by 2017 (DWP 2010b). As mentioned above, this is intended to simplify the social security provision by assimilating the main means-tested benefits (IS, Income-Related JSA, Income-based ESA and HB) with the tax credits paid to those in work (WTC and CTC) into one benefit intended to ensure that 'work always pays' (see Table 8.2). The expectation is that the UC will be supported by a new 'real time' information system, projected to cut fraud and error and to incentivize work, by moving the majority of claims onto an online basis, which can regularly update claims and provide a 'better off in work' calculator.

Future changes to the UK's pension system are also under way, again with a view to simplifying provision whilst containing costs and promoting personal responsibility. The planned rise in state pension ages has been speeded up, with that for women joining men's at 65 in 2018 and increasing for both to 66 by 2020 and 68 or higher thereafter, following periodic review. In addition there are plans to merge the BSP and S2P into a universal, flat-rate, single tier state pension for those reaching state pension age from 2017 (DWP 2011a, 2013).

This is intended to improve provision for women, low-wage earners and the self-employed and, more generally, to minimize means-tested supplements and provide a 'foundation' for personal long-term saving. Whether these developments or the advent of workplace auto-enrolment discussed earlier will secure an adequate retirement income for future pensioners and incentivize top-up saving, however, is far from clear; and much depends on the development of commercial schemes and the robustness of employment based provision.

Alongside these changes the Coalition and its counterparts in the rest of the UK also sought to develop their responses to the 2010 child poverty legislation (DfE 2011a; DPM 2011; HMG 2011a; SG 2011a; WAG 2011a; NIE 2011a). In England the government focused particularly on strategies to promote social mobility, which some feared downplayed the importance of income as the measure to be used. This raises more general questions about the role of social security and the extent to which a commitment to combat poverty should underpin policy. Here academic and political agreement is hard to reach (see Alcock 2006). There is no agreed policy base for setting benefit levels in Britain, although this is not the case in all other countries (Veit-Wilson 1998).

Research in the 1990s suggested benefits were insufficient to meet the needs of those dependent on them and lift them out of poverty (Gordon et al. 2000; Pantazis et al. 2006). Labour's policies did go some way to improve the incomes of the poorest households, though they did little to dent income inequality (Muriel et al. 2010; Joyce and Sibieta 2013; Hills et al, 2013). However, recent studies have pointed to the difficulties likely to be faced by benefit recipients and have predicted a rise in child poverty and increasing inequality (Brewer et al. 2011; Aldridge et al. 2011). Increasingly attention has also turned to considering the implications of continuing fiscal austerity and the possibility of further changes in Britain's social security system, including another round of benefit cuts, increased conditionality and proposals to link benefits more closely to people's contributions.

Of course social security is not just aimed at preventing poverty. It also, as we have discussed, meets the aims of horizontal redistribution across the life cycle and income protection for those who have left work. What is more poverty prevention extends far beyond the provision of cash benefits, as in their different ways, Labour's policies to stem social exclusion (DWP 2006a) and the Coalition's new Social Mobility and Child Poverty Commission (DPM 2011) indicate. Policy development to combat poverty requires much more than social security reform therefore; and social security reform is not just directed at combating poverty. Debate over its future is likely to reflect these complexities as well as the new challenges posed by the continuing pressure on public expenditure.

COMPREHENSION QUESTIONS

- Why is non take-up of means-tested benefits so prevalent?
- What are the 'unemployment trap' and the 'poverty trap', and why is it argued that these create perverse incentives for low-paid workers?
- What is the Universal Credit and why is it being introduced?
- Why is pension reform still under consideration?

REFLECTIVE QUESTION

- What should be the primary aim of social security policy?

FURTHER READING

The most comprehensive book on the historical development of social security in the UK is McKay and Rowlingson (1999). More recent coverage of its history and the key issues in social security policy can be found in Millar (2009) and Spicker (2011). Ditch (1999) contains contributions on the history and principles of social security. Walker (2005) is an excellent, though detailed, guide to the concepts and ideas that underpin policy, setting these in an international and comparative context. Alcock (2006) is the main academic text on poverty and anti-poverty policy. *The Journal of Poverty and Social Justice* is a specialist academic journal featuring articles on social security. The DWP website, www.dwp.gov.uk, carries most government documents and information on benefits; information on tax credits can be found on the HMRC website, www.hmrc.gov.uk. A useful website for data on poverty is www.jrf.org.uk and a guide to the main think tanks can be found in Brunsdon and May (2012) at www.black-wellpublishing.com/alcock4e/.

9
Health

SUMMARY OF KEY POINTS

- Health policy aims both to improve health and treat illness; at times these may lead to different priorities for policy development.
- Measuring health needs is complex. Mortality and morbidity rates are used for this. They show improvements over time, but continuing inequalities between different social groups and areas.
- The National Health Service (NHS) was established in 1948 on a tax-funded, universal basis, free at the point of use.
- The NHS has been reorganized frequently with different structures now found in the four jurisdictions of the UK.
- There are also significant variations in some aspects of health policy across the devolved administrations.
- Promoting health and wellbeing at individual and social levels is now supported by governments across the UK.
- After a period of substantial growth, expenditure on the NHS is being reined back, renewing debates over sources of funding and the rationing of services.
- Although the NHS is largely free, there are charges for some services, particularly in England.
- Commercial and third sector organizations deliver services outside the NHS and also sell medical insurance; and in England particularly the use of private finance for capital investment to supplement public spending has grown.

HEALTH AND ILLNESS

Our health is one of the most precious features of our lives as human beings. This applies at an individual level: we all want to enjoy good health. However, it also underpins our collective interests since healthy citizens make for a more successful and prosperous society. Viewed negatively, this message is even more emphatic: poor health is debilitating and costly. It is not surprising therefore that health has long been a central concern of social policy across the world, and remains at the core of welfare planning in the UK. But at the heart of this concern is a fundamental dilemma that underpins much of the debate about how to develop and deliver health services. This can be summed up in the question: Should the focus of policy be health and wellbeing or illness?

In part this is a definitional question. It is not necessarily clear what is meant by good health or 'wellness'. For instance, should we all aspire to the fitness standards of professional sportspeople, or are inactive, overweight office workers in good health if they are not suffering from any obvious debilitating condition? And what do we mean by illness? It can range from the common cold to terminal cancer, and one is clearly more serious than the other. Furthermore, illness might be distinguished from disease, with the latter implying the medical diagnosis of a known infection or disability and the former the unspecified symptoms experienced by individuals who feel unwell. For practical purposes this distinction is captured to some extent in the way in which absence from work for sickness is treated in the UK, with the first seven days being recorded as the self-diagnosed symptoms of the individual, but longer periods requiring medical certification by a doctor. The medical diagnosis of particular conditions is of course a complex and highly specified science, but the more general terminology of health and illness is far from clearly agreed or consistently used.

More significant perhaps are the very different models of health services and the different philosophies and practices underlying these that flow from a concern with illness rather than health. In the UK there is what is still generally referred to as a National Health Service (NHS), though since devolution some argue there are now four variants (Connolly et al. 2011), of which more shortly. Critics, however, have sometimes dubbed it a national *illness* service, because it has largely focused on diagnosis and treatment, particularly in hospitals, with relatively few resources directed towards preventing healthy people from becoming ill. This has been challenged by some of those working within, and outside, the NHS; and, as we shall discuss, the promotion of public health has become more prominent in recent years, though it is still the case that less than 4 per cent of NHS funds are devoted to preventive measures (Marmot 2010).

However, there is a more general consequence of the focus on treating illness: it has meant that provision has largely developed as a demand-led service. This can be seen in the General Practitioner (GP) model that dominates *primary health care*. When we think we may be ill we go to a doctor, who confirms that we are (or not), provides a diagnosis and (in most cases) prescribes some form of treatment. This may involve *community health services* such as district nursing or physiotherapy. But in more serious cases the GP may refer us to an acute or *secondary* service (usually a hospital), and for complex conditions we may be sent to a specialist or *tertiary* service. And in emergencies we may go directly to hospital, generally to an accident and emergency (A&E or casualty) department. In all instances, however, it is the citizen's circumstances that determine the services provided and drive the need for resources to meet these.

When the NHS was launched it was assumed that access to health care for all would reduce sickness levels and so demand for, and expenditure on, health services would gradually fall. Ironically, as we shall see, for a range of reasons the reverse has been the case. Whatever the explanation, however, there is no doubt that demand has driven up supply and continues to outstrip the ability of NHS providers to meet all needs. So in practice, the provision of health services is often a process of rationing, as graphically revealed in concerns over the lengths of waiting lists for treatment or the availability (or not) of expensive medicines.

HEALTH NEEDS

However it would not be correct to characterize provision as entirely based on attempts to ration health services in response to consumer demands. Budget setting necessarily requires planning by service providers and occupies a crucial place in health policy development. In England the Department of Health (DoH) and its counterparts in the devolved administrations (see Tables 9.1, 9.2) provide a general steer over the identification of health needs and the allocation and prioritizing of resources, and the various entities managing services are required to establish and respond to health needs in their areas, a responsibility that, as will become clear, has increased in recent years

However, determining health needs is far from straightforward, not least because of the definitional problems outlined above. In practice the most widely used measures are mortality rates: that is, the ages at which people die or the number of deaths per 1,000 in the population. Mortality data can provide a measure of life expectancy that can be used on a comparative basis over time or across different sections of the population. This is generally done through the use of Standardized Mortality Ratios (SMRs) that compare death rates within particular groups with a national average, controlled for variables such as age and sex, giving a measure of above or below the average. Of course mortality rates measure death, not health or illness. Therefore attempts have also been made to gather data on morbidity, the experience of illness. The problem here is what to count as illness and this varies: for instance, some measures use health service visits, others self-reporting or absence from work, although all have limitations.

In general the evidence from mortality statistics is highly positive, with more people staying healthier for longer. Average male and female life expectancy in the UK rose between 1900 and 2010 from around 45 and 49 to 78.2 and 82.3 years respectively (ONS 2011a) and is predicted to rise further, with around a third of those born in 2012 likely to become centenarians (ONS 2012a). This is not just a product of improved health services, of course: better diets, working and living conditions have probably had a greater influence. Indeed one of the major problems in health policy is the difficulty of establishing causal links between measured improvements and policy interventions.

Moreover, though the overall message is encouraging, the improvements are not evenly distributed across the population with longevity and morbidity rates varying between different socioeconomic groups as well as by gender and ethnicity, and also having a geographic or spatial dimension. Such disparities have long been recognized, but their scale was tellingly revealed in a government commissioned study, the Black Report of 1980. This pinpointed the many factors underlying health inequalities, attributing them primarily to differences in people's material conditions. Its findings were confirmed by a further study, *The Health Divide*, which the Conservative administration of the time refused to publish, leading to its independent release along with a reprint of the Black Report (Townsend et al. 1988). But despite mounting evidence of growing differentials throughout the 1980s official research into health inequalities was stopped and its proposals ignored.

However, on its election in 1997 Labour appointed another independent inquiry headed by Lord Acheson to revisit the issue. Measuring health inequalities is conceptually and methodologically highly complex. But the Acheson Report (1998) demonstrated an incontrovertible link between poor health and social class, and stark differences in life expectancy at birth between the most and least deprived groups and areas that had increased since the 1980s. Despite the resultant policy initiatives (outlined below) a raft of studies reiterated these findings and the persistence of health inequalities across the UK (Shaw et al. 2008). Partly in the light of these Labour in 2008 commissioned a further independent review in England led by Professor Sir Michael Marmot (2010).

Whilst highlighting the general improvements in health across all social groups, it too revealed continuing inequalities in life expectancies and risk of disability, which varied according to people's social position and neighbourhood incomes and also within areas (see Figure 9.1). Those in the richest neighbourhoods, for instance, were likely to live seven years longer and have 17 years more of a healthy, disability-free life than those in the poorest. Life expectancy also varied between the countries of the UK, with England having the highest (78.6 and 82.6 years for men and women in 2008–10) and Scotland the lowest (75.8 and 80.4 respectively) with that in Glasgow varying by up to 28 years between the richest and poorest areas (ONS 2011a; Reid 2011).

Underlying the evidence of the link between social status and health, however, is the issue of cause and effect, sometimes referred to as the 'artefact' problem: are people ill because they are poor, or poor because they are ill? This raises questions about the appropriate policy response to health inequalities and ill-health more generally; issues complicated by differences in access to health care and in the case of geographical targeting by the fact that many healthy

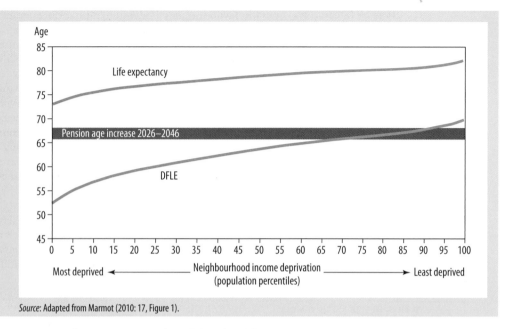

Age

Source: Adapted from Marmot (2010: 17, Figure 1).

Figure 9.1 Life expectancy and disability-free life expectancy (DFLE) at birth, persons by neighbourhood income level 1999–2003

people live in deprived areas and many unhealthy people outside them. More generally, however, it underlines the dilemma highlighted earlier about the extent to which policy-making should focus on illness or health improvement.

THE DEVELOPMENT OF THE NATIONAL HEALTH SERVICE

Governmental policies to combat poor health can be traced back to the nineteenth century when, for example, legislation from the 1848 Public Health Act on sought to tackle poor sanitation and living conditions. It was in the early twentieth century, however, that state health services began to develop more systematically, inspired in part by the revelation that many of those recruited to fight in the Boer War were found to be unfit. In 1919 a Ministry of Health was established; and, when national insurance for sickness was developed after 1911, free access to GPs was provided for certain groups of workers. By the 1940s some 21 million, half the population, were covered and two-thirds of GPs were participating in the scheme (Ham 2009). In the nineteenth century institutional provision for sickness had been dominated by the Poor Law workhouses and infirmaries; but in 1929 these were transferred to local authorities (LAs) to be developed into a local hospital service, alongside the commercial and voluntary hospitals that had also grown by then, and the 'lunatic asylums' for the mentally ill which had developed since the 1800s.

In the 1930s a series of reports, including studies by the British Medical Association, the collective voice of GPs and hospital doctors, highlighted the shortcomings in this patchwork of provision and recommended greater coordination. With the outbreak of war national planning emerged out of national need. Public and voluntary hospitals were combined in an Emergency Medical Service and in 1942 Beveridge's influential report on social security argued that a comprehensive national service should be formed after the war to combat the evil of disease. In 1944 proposals for this were developed; legislation passed in 1946; and in

1948 the NHS came into operation with the stated intention of providing equitable access to health care (Webster 2002).

The introduction of the NHS was a seminal moment in the development of British social policy, enshrining as it did the principles of a comprehensive, nationally-owned, tax-funded service, free at the point of use and provided equally to all citizens on the basis of need. As the first health scheme offering free medical care to the entire population in any Western society (Klein 2010) it became a model of universal provision that has remained largely unchallenged in the UK and provided a basis for state action in many other countries. Its establishment is often credited to the Labour minister, Aneurin Bevan, who steered it through Parliament; and there is no doubt that his vision and skilled political manoeuvring were critical in ensuring support, particularly from the medical profession who were concerned about the loss of autonomy that it might entail. However, there was cross-party backing for the NHS (the initial proposals came from the wartime coalition government), which has continued since.

As we saw above, the initial expectation was that the NHS would lead to a reduction both in general health needs and health inequalities; and indeed there was a concern that many needing help would not use it. However, service use increased, and a report by the Guillebaud Committee in 1956 suggested more funding was required. Spending on the NHS subsequently grew as did its share of GDP (see Figure 9.2), trends that, as we summarize later, accelerated under the 1997–2010 Labour governments, which doubled expenditure in real terms, but have fallen since.

Yet while the principles and funding base of the NHS have remained largely intact as its scope increased, its delivery has been subject to almost continuous change as different governments, including the devolved administrations, have sought to reshape it according to their changing policy agendas. Originally it was structured on a top-down tripartite basis comprising executive councils (administering GPs, dentists, opticians and pharmacists who retained their independent, self-employed contractor status), regional hospital boards (overseeing hospital management committees) and LAs (managing school, community, public health and ambulance services) – all under the direction of the Ministry of Health. This lasted until 1974 when, to provide more coordinated provision, Regional and Area Health Authorities and District Management Teams assumed responsibility for all health services with Family Practitioner Committees (FPCs) contracting primary care professionals.

Then in 1982 this system was streamlined. In England District Health Authorities (DHAs) became the major administrative units with FPCs directly responsible to the then Department of Health and Social Security (DHSS) and different configurations in the rest of the UK, with Northern Ireland retaining the integrated health and care system introduced in 1974, paving the way for further variation after devolution. In the 1980s, moreover, the NHS came under criticism from some on the New Right, such as the Adam Smith Institute, which advocated replacing it with a private insurance system. Nevertheless the Conservative government continued to assert that the NHS was 'safe in our hands', and retained the principles of a universal free service, but with further significant organizational changes.

In public services generally the 1980s saw the increasing influence of what came to be called the 'New Public Management' (NPM, see Chapter 18). For the NHS, as other services, this meant making it more businesslike and efficient through target setting and budget planning. Following a report in 1983 by Roy Griffiths (the managing director of Sainsbury's), it also meant specialist managers rather than clinicians became responsible for key decision-making. This was a significant development, for the autonomy they enjoyed extended to administrative control which now passed to non-medical managers, who, it was argued, could develop a more coordinated response to service development and patients' needs.

The other change was a more overt promotion of private health care as an alternative to NHS provision. As we shall see, this had continued alongside the universal NHS, though attracting only a minority of patients. In the 1980s, however, support for market competition as a means of improving choice and accountability to users gained government backing. Commercial markets could never provide these for most NHS users of course. But the Conservatives turned to a different means of achieving these goals, based on the ideas of an American academic, Enthoven (1985), who argued markets of a kind could be created within health services by encouraging providers to compete for patients, thereby driving up standards, accountability and value for money (in theory at least).

Following the 1989 White Paper, *Working for Patients* (DoH 1989), the 1990 NHS and Community Care Act established a *quasi-market* on these lines. Like similar changes in social care (see Chapter 11) this formed part of a general shift towards the marketization of public services discussed in Chapter 3. It also led to another restructuring (Table 9.1) splitting the NHS between:

- *Purchasers* – District Health and Family Health Services (DHAs; FHAs) managed by the Regional Health Authorities, with provision also made for GP practices to become fundholders, receiving a budget based on patient registrations from which they could contract directly with suppliers, and
- *Providers* – quasi-independent non-profit-making NHS Trusts offering acute hospital, ambulance, mental or community health services.

The idea was that contracts for specific treatments for individual patients would focus service delivery on user needs. In practice, however, this proved unworkable and more generic 'service agreements' were reached between the two wings. These mostly replicated existing practices, with critics pointing out that, though the new internal market increased health service managers' powers, far from improving efficiency, it brought new *transaction costs* as time and money was taken up in budgeting and procuring. The purchaser/provider split was only completed in 1996, accompanied by further variations in the make-up of the health authorities, and, following the 1997 election, Labour embraced many of its key features, as a means of delivering more choice and control to NHS users, though, as we will see, after 1999 the devolved administrations began to take a different course.

COMPREHENSION QUESTIONS

- Why is the NHS sometimes referred to as a national illness service?
- Why were professional managers brought into the NHS in the 1980s?
- What is an internal market, and why was it introduced within the NHS in the early 1990s?

REFLECTIVE QUESTION

- Would it be better to focus resources on preventing rather than curing illness?

A PATIENT-LED HEALTH SERVICE

KEY DEVELOPMENTS IN ENGLAND 1997–2010

Labour's commitment to remaining within the public spending limits set by its predecessor for its first two years meant few additional resources were available to support significant change. Nevertheless in a White Paper, *The New NHS* (DoH 1997), it outlined six principles for reform including setting national standards and restoring public confidence in the

NHS. The paper also promised there would be no return to the centralized bureaucracy of the past or a continuation of the Conservatives' divisive market system. Rather, as in other areas of social policy, a 'third way' based on partnership and performance was proposed with the aim of shifting the balance away from hospitals to a more strategic patient- and primary-care-led service. This, it was hoped, would also enable collaboration with LAs in delivering social care (see Chapter 11). As in social care, however, Labour retained the internal market and, after 2003, sought both to strengthen it and increase private sector involvement.

Initially though its reforms involved modifying the purchaser/provider split into what was described as a collaborative separation between planning and provision (Table 9.1). GP fund-holding was withdrawn and GPs formed into geographically-based primary care groups (PCGs) responsible to HAs, which were expected to work in partnership with LAs particularly over social care. Then, following a revised plan (DoH 2000), the shift towards patient- and primary-led care was taken further and the internal market expanded. By 2002 PCGs were replaced by 303 PCTs, which became the key budget holders and commissioners, regional offices were disbanded and HAs merged into 28 strategic health authorities (SHAs) responsible for managing the work of both commissioners and providers. Moreover reorganization did not stop there and in 2004 another 'improvement' plan to 'put people at the heart of public services' (DoH 2004a) led to a more competitive-based NHS and greater plurality in provision (see Table 9.1).

On the purchasing side PCTs became responsible for over 80 per cent of NHS spending and the commissioning of most health services, including the use of commercial and third sector agencies as well as NHS trusts. It was anticipated that this would result in around 15 per cent of services being delivered by non-state providers. This role demanded closer partnership working with other agencies and greater strategic reach. Hence in 2006 PCTs were reconfigured into 152 larger bodies, most coterminous with LA boundaries, and the SHAs reduced to ten.

These reforms also gave greater freedoms to hospital and other provider trusts, enabling them to convert to Foundation Trusts (FTs), operating as independent legal entities overseen by a Board of Governors with financial autonomy and powers to raise money from the public and private sectors and reinvest operating surpluses. They were also released from performance management by SHAs, becoming accountable instead to a new financial regulator, Monitor, and inspection by a new Healthcare Commission.

This round of restructuring was accompanied by other reforms aimed to expand patient choice, increase provider competition and get the best value from public spending on the NHS. From 2004 the intention was that money would 'follow the patient' through a payment by results system under which NHS providers were paid a fixed tariff for each course of treatment. More visibly from the patient perspective, various 'Free Choice' measures allowed them to select 'any willing provider' for elective treatment, aided by a 'Choose and Book' referral system and the use of non-NHS treatment centres. Attempts were also made to strengthen service procurement through the introduction of practice-based and then 'world class' commissioning with support from private sector agencies. However, the bulk of purchasing remained within the NHS and hospitals' long-standing clinical authority meant they still largely drove priority setting. Partnership working with LAs also proved elusive (see Chapter 11) and was not eased by the many changes in the NHS.

Nevertheless in 2007 the government appointed the Health Minister, Lord Darzi, to lead a review of the next stage of reform. Its report (DoH 2008) recommended refocusing on the quality rather than the volume of care and was taken up in a new five-year strategy (DoH 2009a). This promised to accelerate the pace of reform and build a more person-centred NHS with greater patient choice and quality-improvement incentives. It proposed to do so by gradually tying hospital income to patient satisfaction, enabling the best hospitals and GP services to expand, abolishing GP boundaries for patient registration and introducing personal

Key Dates	Regional Authorities	Commissioners	Providers	Advisory and Performance Management Agencies
1991–1996	Regional Health Authorities (14)	District Health Authorities (100+) Family Health Service Authorities GP Fundholders	NHS Trusts (Hospital, ambulance, mental health, community) Primary care services (GPs, Dentists, Pharmacists, Opticians) Independent providers	1990 Audit Commission
1996–1999	NHSE Regional Offices (8)	Health Authorities (100) GP Fundholders		
1999–2002		Health Authorities (100) Primary Care Groups		1999 NICE Commission for Health Improvement
2002–2006	Strategic Health Authorities (28)	Primary Care Trusts (303)		2004 Health Commission 2004 Monitor
2006–2011/13	Strategic Health Authorities (10)	Primary Care Trusts (152)	NHS FT Trusts (c 115) NHS Trusts (c 125) Primary Care Services Independent providers	Monitor 2009 Care Quality Commission
2013		Clinical Commissioning Groups (212)	NHS FT Trusts* [NHS Trusts] Primary care services Independent providers	NICE NHS Commissioning Board Clinical Senates Monitor Care Quality Commission Health watch England Local Health watch Health and Wellbeing Boards Chief Inspector of Hospitals

Table 9.1 The structure of the NHS in England 1991–2013

* Phasing in

health budgets akin to those in social care (see Chapter 11). However, 2010 brought a change in government.

LIBERATING THE NHS: RECENT DEVELOPMENTS IN ENGLAND

Some of the Darzi propositions were developed after the 2010 election by the Coalition, as part of a further fundamental restructuring of the NHS. Its proposals, outlined in the White Paper, *Liberating the NHS* (DoH 2010a), combined Conservative calls for greater private sector input and the Liberal Democrats' commitments to increasing local accountability (Timmins 2012). There was some initial popular criticism of these proposals, and so the government deferred their introduction, providing for a 'listening pause' and the appointment of the NHS Futures Forum (DoH 2011a, 2011b), which led to some modifications in the Health and Social Care Act of 2012. This provided for a substantial shift in power and accountability towards a decentralized, patient oriented service, although overall responsibility remained with the Secretary of State.

On the purchaser side the most fundamental reform was the phased replacement of PCTs by 212 Clinical Commissioning Groups (CCGs) controlling 80 per cent of the NHS budget from 2013 and with incentives for more active commissioning and powers to use outside support (Table 9.1). This was accompanied by the introduction of personal health budgets for patients with continuing conditions. As in social care (see Chapter 11) these aim to increase patient choice and control over the selection of services; and this was extended to include the right to register with any GP and to choose consultant-led teams for outpatient and some mental health and diagnostic services. More broadly, LAs were also given a greater role, becoming responsible for working with CCGs and other agencies to determine local health priorities and promote joined-up services.

On the provider side the Act enshrined the government's aim of establishing a less centralized system with a plurality of competing suppliers. All hospitals were therefore to become semi-autonomous FTs with greater freedom to earn money by treating private patients. To generate a level playing field between suppliers the Act also established the status of 'any qualified provider' from which patients could choose (Monitor 2012a); and from 2012 community services too were opened up to competition from non-state providers, with PCTs or CCGs expected to externalize their remaining provision.

As with other Coalition policy changes, these will take time to work through. However, whereas Labour's reforms were cushioned by rising expenditure, they are being implemented in a climate of significant public expenditure cuts. It is far from clear, therefore, whether in practice they will lead to more efficient, user-driven service commissioning and much may depend on the involvement and effectiveness of new non-state providers and their calculations. What is more there is growing divergence here between England and the rest of the UK where there has been less support for the Coalition government's competition strategy.

KEY DEVELOPMENTS IN NORTHERN IRELAND, SCOTLAND AND WALES

The structure of the NHS outside England had begun to diverge in the 1970s, in large part to reflect the smaller scale of national planning in the other UK countries. Nevertheless, by 1996 the purchaser/provider split was common across the UK, with an initial emphasis as at first in England under Labour on cooperation (Table 9.2). In Scotland PCTs and in Wales local health groups were overseen by health authorities established in 1999 and the number of acute trusts reduced. Political uncertainties in Northern Ireland, however, meant proposals for a simpler integrated health and social care system did not materialize.

Following devolution health policy and spending on the NHS from block grants became the responsibility of the three separate administrations (Table 9.2) though to begin with only Scotland had full law-making powers (see Chapter 6). As with other services the political situation meant provision in Northern Ireland was at first largely framed by that in England and in practice held back after 2007 (Gray and Birrell 2012; Horgan and Gray 2012), although a slimmer structure was instituted in 2009 (see Table 9.2). Unlike England, however, whilst the purchaser/provider split was retained in the province, the emphasis remained on cooperation rather than competition, as a means of developing a more patient-centred, community-based service (Compton 2011; DHSSP 2012).

Embedding patient-focused, primary-care-led provision was also the prime goal of

Table 9.2 The structure of the NHS in Northern Ireland, Scotland and Wales 1999–2013: key components

	Northern Ireland	Scotland	Wales
National Management (2012)	Department of Health, Social Services and Public Safety	Health and Social Care Directorate	Department for Health, Social Services and Children
Commissioners/ Providers	Health and Social Service Boards (4) Health and Social Services Trusts (19) 2008 Health and Social Care Boards (4) 2008 Health and Social Care Trusts (5) 2009 Health and Social Care Board Local Commissioning Groups (5) Health and Social Care Trusts (5)	1999 Health Boards (15) NHS Trusts (28)	1999 Health Authorities (5) Local Health Groups (22) NHS Trusts (14) Primary care services 2003 Local Health Boards (22) NHS Trusts (14) Primary care services
Local Management		2004 Area Health Boards (15) 2004 Community Health Partnerships (c 40) 2007 Area Health Boards (14) Community Health Partnerships (c 40)	2009 Health Boards (7) NHS Trusts [Ambulance, Velindre (cancer); Public Health Wales]
Advisory and Performance Management Agencies	[NICE]* 2003 Regulation and Improvement Authority	2003 NHS Quality Improvement Scotland 2011 Healthcare Improvement Scotland	[NICE]* 2003 Healthcare Inspectorate Wales

* Recommendations considered for implementation.

successive Scottish and Welsh administrations. The internal market, particularly patient choice for its own sake, however, was seen as a barrier to needs-based planning and equitable provision. Instead the NHS was restructured on non-competitive lines (see Table 9.2), the principled basis of which was frequently asserted in both countries (CIPFA 2008; Keating 2009).

In Scotland strategic authority and significant budgetary control was moved in 2004 to 15 Local Health Boards, including LA representatives, responsible for both funding and provision and in which the role of managers was reduced to give health professionals more control than in England, with sub-committees of community health partnerships set up to promote more holistic provision. Further reform provided for an elected element in the Boards' membership from 2009, and in 2012 the Boards and LAs were required to form health and social care partnerships as a prelude to further integration of provision (see Chapter 11). Although there was some support for private sector involvement in service provision initially, this policy was later dropped, and since 2011 the SNP-led government has explicitly banned contracting for hospital cleaning and catering, excluded commercial companies from primary medical care services, and committed itself to maintaining a publicly delivered service (Poole 2012; Scott and Wright 2012).

In Wales the devolved administrations also dismantled the internal market, although at a slower pace as a result of the lesser powers initially devolved. Here a 'Welsh way' based on public provision and collaboration rather than competition has now been promoted however (Greer 2004; Sullivan 2005). As in Northern Ireland, FTs were not introduced, and from 2009 the Health and Social Care Board oversaw the planning and delivery of all local health services (Table 9.2). Like the SG since 2011 the WG has also reaffirmed support for non-marketized, community-based provision with professionals working in clinical networks, and acute care concentrated in centres of excellence (Bevan Commission 2011; WG 2011a, 2011b).

Quite how significant the differences in policy following devolution really are is contested by commentators. Some emphasize similarities (Smith and Hellowell 2012), and are critical of limited differentiation (Poole 2012); but others point to the divergence now found within the NHS in the UK (CIPFA 2008; Greer and Rowland 2008; Ham 2009). And this may well become more pronounced following the political changes flowing from the 2010 and 2011 elections.

RAISING STANDARDS, INVOLVING USERS

Raising the level of NHS provision was a cornerstone of Labour's health policy in England in the early twenty-first century. To do so it developed a range of mechanisms mirroring the wider shift towards performance management in welfare services discussed in Chapter 18. In the NHS this meant a new approach to medical accountability (Ham 2009) as spending was increasingly tied to evidence of improvements, with a battery of performance measures monitored by new regulatory agencies. One of the early priorities was the setting of targets for primary and acute services guaranteeing that patients could see a doctor within 48 hours and receive outpatient treatment within 26 weeks, and limiting waiting on trolleys for hospital care to 12 hours. Specific commitments were also made to cut accidents, to reduce the death rate and prevalence of illness from heart disease, cancer and mental health by 2010, and improve the treatment of long-term conditions.

To secure these changes new agencies were created to monitor standards, complementing the established roles of the Audit Commission and National Audit Office (see Table 9.1). These included the National Institute for Health and Clinical Excellence (NICE), founded in 1999 to provide guidance on cost-effective treatments. Tighter inspection of providers was introduced, initially under the Commission for Health Improvement, but from 2004, this was replaced by two regulators: Monitor, overseeing FTs; and the Healthcare Commission, inspecting private as well as public sector providers – although in 2009 the latter's functions were transferred to another new agency, the Care Quality Commission (CQC). This monitoring was backed by the development of national standards for different conditions and patient groups set out in service frameworks; and providers were subject to new performance measures: a star-rating scheme in 2000, followed in 2005 by Annual Health Checks, and in 2009 by the CQC's essential standards system and an increasing emphasis on patient satisfaction surveys.

These developments were largely paralleled elsewhere in the UK where, after devolution, new national healthcare standards and monitoring bodies were established (Table 9.2). The devolved administrations did not, however, develop public reporting systems as in

England, though they increasingly emphasized user involvement as a means to improve performance.

In England, in particular this was seen as the key focus of policy development, Labour's aim being that patients should be able to choose the health services they needed with resources flowing to the providers who best meet their needs. However, delivering genuine user involvement in service development is not easy to achieve, as we discuss in Chapter 18. In health care it has proved particularly problematic, not least because many, if not most, patients have limited knowledge of the services they need and tend to rely on professional judgements. What is more control over many key services has continued to lie with hospital providers. These were supposed to be responsive to patients through PCT commissioning; but, as noted earlier, this was often weak and did not challenge the dominance of hospital provision.

Nevertheless Labour introduced several innovations extending users' access to health services. A nurse-led telephone help line, *NHS Direct*, was introduced in 1998 (replaced in 2013 by the 111 service), followed by a web-based NHS Direct in 1999, NHS Digital Television in 2004, and in 2007 the NHS Choices website, offering information and advice not only about individual health but healthcare services in general, including comparative information on providers. There was also provision to facilitate patient and citizen participation in service planning and monitoring, including the establishment Local Involvement Networks (LINks) in 2008, though these had few powers and a largely voluntary membership.

These measures aimed to put users at the forefront of provision. But the advice given would only be helpful, especially in serious cases, if the resources needed followed patient demands; and this could add to tension between expectations and funding which is far from easy to resolve. Although the principles of the NHS were clear, the 1948 Act did not incorporate a legally enforceable set of entitlements to health care. Some attempt was made to address this through the 1991 Patient's Charter, the first document summarizing the service standards patients should expect. It focused largely on waiting times though, as did Labour's update for England issued in 1997 and amended in 2001, when, significantly, an outline of patients' responsibilities was also added (DoH 2001).

Following the Darzi Review, however, the first NHS Constitution for England was published in 2009. This was backed by legislation requiring NHS providers take it into account and providing for its regular renewal. It set out the rights and responsibilities of patients, the public and staff including: informed choice for patients, access to predominantly free nationally approved treatments, and patients' responsibilities for their own health (DoH 2009b). Scotland and Wales have also developed similar measures with the 2011 Scottish Patient Rights Act and promised legislation in Wales.

Evidence suggests that significant progress was made in meeting the key performance indicators in England established under Labour, including, hospital waiting times and general patient satisfaction (Dixon and Ham 2010), although data differences make it difficult to compare this with the devolved jurisdictions. Despite higher per capita spending and staffing, however, there was less progress here on efficiency levels, partly because additional resources were less tied to targeting and public reporting (Connolly et al. 2011). In general, however, where data were available there appears to have been little difference in terms of value for money (NAO 2012).

The Coalition has also been committed to raising standards and expanding choice within the NHS, although this has involved a move towards more of an outcomes-based strategy, centred on a new Commissioning Outcomes Framework holding CCGs in England to account on a range of health outcome indicators including patient reporting (DOH 2010b). Linked to this have been the introduction of other more localized elements of public and patient accountability and an adapted regulatory structure to accord with a marketized remodelling of the NHS (Table 9.1).

The CQC, the main watchdog, has been retained, NICE's remit extended to social care, and Monitor's role altered to become the economic regulator of the new provider market, with responsibilities ranging from safeguarding choice and competition to licensing all NHS-funded services and regulating prices (Monitor 2012b). In addition following inquiries into the mistreatment of patients at Mid Staffs NHS Trust and failings at other hospitals (Francis 2013; Keogh 2013) the CQC's inspection regime was toughened, and a new ratings system and Chief Inspector of Hospitals established. As part of its broader reforms the government also established a new NHS Commissioning Board (NHSCB) to allocate resources to CCGs and hold them to account along with Healthwatch England, a new national agency based in the CQC, to act as a voice for users and carers and deal with complaints. At the same time LINks were replaced by Local Healthwatch bodies, led by LAs to promote further public involvement. The continued expectation is that such involvement will lead in time to overall health improvement, although for the large part that remains to be seen, and may depend much more on what happens outside of traditional NHS services.

COMPREHENSION QUESTIONS

- Why did PCTs become the major organizational focus of health service delivery in England?
- What are FTs and how are they expected to improve the management and delivery of acute services?
- To what extent are the Coalition government's NHS reforms in England a departure from previous policy planning?

REFLECTIVE QUESTION

- Should patient choice be the key driver of NHS services?

PROMOTING HEALTH AND WELLBEING

Policy action to improve people's health stretches back to the early nineteenth century legislation to outlaw insanitary conditions mentioned earlier. LAs played a key role in developing much of this new provision and, even after the NHS reforms of 1948, they retained overall responsibility for public health until these were reassigned to the NHS in 1974 (see Chapter 6). At around the same time in 1976 NHS spending was adjusted to address growing concern over geographical variations in access to health services through a formula devised by the Resource Allocation Working Party (RAWP). This directed additional support to under-provided areas according to a needs-based allocation model that, with refinements and differing formulae in the devolved administrations, has been retained since.

The RAWP approach was in effect a response to the demand-led, illness model of health service development. It also, however, reflected concern over continuing health inequalities and the potential for self-care schemes to address these (DHSS 1976). Though improving public health remained a secondary concern within the NHS (Hunter et al. 2010), its roles in preventing illness and disease, and in reducing reduce health inequalities and the costs of ill-health (by ensuring that minimum standards are applied to all), were increasingly canvassed. And since the 1990s public health policy has crept up government agendas for health reform. This has involved an extension of traditional preventive clinical measures such as immunization, monitoring and, in particular, screening programmes, together with a new interest in health promotion and wellness services.

These aim to support the creation of a healthier society and reduce health inequalities by fostering wellbeing and tackling the potential causes of poor health. There is considerable debate in health policy circles, however, about the relative significance of these and hence the scope and focus of government action. This is compounded by the paradox that provisions aimed at the public in general can heighten rather than counter health inequalities (Buck and Frosini 2012).

Biomedical factors and access to health care influence health outcomes, but so too do lifestyle choices. This has led to the development of policies exhorting, and enabling, people to alter their behaviour (for example changing diets, quitting smoking or exercising more frequently). However, there are also broader social dimensions to these issues, such as poor housing or working conditions and income poverty; and these lead to different forms of intervention (the 'social model' of public health), including for instance higher taxes on tobacco and alcohol, regulation of food standards and broader measures to improve living standards.

Of course, in practice both individual and socioeconomic factors can contribute to poor health and this has been reflected in recent policy across the UK. The emphasis placed on them though has varied. Governments have often sought to concentrate on the more visible individual-level aspects and what are described as 'downstream' health service-based measures, rather than broader 'upstream' interventions in social and economic conditions (Graham 2007).

In the late twentieth century a renewed interest in public health was signalled by a White Paper in 1992 that set targets for improvement in a number of areas, primarily based on a lifestyle approach (DoH 1992). This had little impact (Baggott 2010). But it was taken up by Labour after 1997, which initially adopted a broader-based strategy (Secretary for State 1998) and appointed the first Minister for Public Health in 1998. In the same year, NHS authorities were asked to develop health improvement programmes and partnership-based Health Action Zones (HAZ) were established in 26 areas of high need (Barnes et al. 2005); and, following the 1998 Acheson Report a White Paper boldly titled, *Saving Lives: Our Healthier Nation* (DoH 1999) re-emphasized the reduction of health inequalities as a major policy goal alongside health improvement more generally.

The policies developed by Labour ranged beyond the NHS as part of its more general aim of combating social exclusion (see Hills et al., 2002). They were often modelled on a target-based strategy, involving national goals to, for instance, stem the major causes of early death, particularly cancer, heart and circulatory disease and pledges to cut inequalities in infant mortality and life expectancy at birth by 10 per cent by 2010. Partnership working was also encouraged, particularly in areas of high deprivation, and when the HAZs were disbanded SHAs, PCTS and LAs were given a greater, more general public health role (DoH 2003a). The Food Standards Agency was established in 2000 and two Treasury commissioned reports on health funding by Sir Derek Wanless, the former Nat West Banker (2002 and 2004), led to further measures to improve public health, for instance, the banning of cigarette advertising in 2003 and of smoking in public places in 2007. Following the second Wanless Report, however, policy-making increasingly focused more on behavioural change (DoH 2004b) and the development of health education campaigns to cut smoking, alcohol and drug use and counter the rising incidence of obesity, complemented by the promotion of wellness services in the workplace (May and Brundson 2007; Black 2008).

These new measures to promote health and wellness in practice met with mixed success (Baggott 2012). Overall life expectancy improved and many targets such as those for cancer and heart disease were met (Thorlby and Mabin 2010). But evidence also suggested that despite some improvements, the healthy living messages were heeded most by those in higher socioeconomic and educational groups (Buck and Frosini 2012), with the result that the health gap in general was not dented. In the light of this the Marmot Review was established in 2008 to advise on a new post-2010 strategy.

This took a social determinants approach, arguing that preventive action was a matter of social justice as well as health promotion, that required long-term policies based on what it termed 'proportionate universalism', framed nationally but allowing for local planning and action across the life course. Its recommendations were in line with international developments (WHO 2008), and chimed with studies such as Wilkinson and Pickett (2009) that had pointed to a strong correlation between a country's level of economic inequality and its social outcomes including ill-health rates, suggesting that high levels of inequality adversely affect the whole society not just the poor. In the event, however, the response came from the Coalition government, which quickly after its election published a new White Paper, *Healthy Lives, Healthy People* (HMG 2010a).

The White Paper adopted the Review's concepts of a life course framework and proportionate universalism and pledged to 'improve the health of the poorest fastest'. It also promised whole-of-government action to improve early years provision, education and working conditions and foster active ageing and sustainable communities. The main focus in practice, however, was on lifestyle problems, the scale of which were depicted in an accompanying document (HMG 2010b), and, as in other policy fields, on local action and empowering individuals to take responsibility for their own health. More specifically it stated the Coalition's aims were to maintain choice and adopt a non-intrusive approach using a 'ladder of interventions' to nudge people into change before resorting to regulation.

To develop this strategy a new dedicated DoH executive agency, Public Heath England (PHE), was established in 2013 and at local level lead responsibility for public health returned, with ring-fenced funding to LAs. They were given freedom to develop locally geared services under the strategic direction of Directors of Public Health transferred from the NHS and in liaison with new local Health and Wellbeing Boards (Table 9.1). Funding levels were held at 4 per cent of NHS spending, however; and provision itself was to be commissioned from commercial and third sector agencies.

More generally health professionals were now expected to promote healthy living in their encounters with patients (DoH 2012a), and Labour's target-based system was replaced by an outcomes framework (DoH 2012b) including health premiums to reward LAs for progress in meeting them and provisions for local and national reporting on these. New obesity, alcohol and tobacco strategies all emphasized local decision-making (DoH 2011c; Cabinet Office 2010b); and Public Health Responsibility Deals were designed with food and alcohol retailers, to promote healthy living, and with employers, to encourage health in the workplace (DoH 2011d).

The use of outcome measures and the further development of health promotion and wellness services has also been implemented by the devolved governments. Following devolution public health policy in Northern Ireland has largely followed a similar trajectory to that in England, though organizationally there was less upheaval. Public health remained within its integrated health and care system, supported from 2009 by a separate Public Health Agency, but framed from 2011 by a somewhat different policy orientation to that in Scotland and Wales where provision too remained within the NHS.

From the outset post-devolution public health policy in Scotland was grounded in a more robust commitment to the social model of health and the use of the state than in England (Poole 2012). This has been marked by a range of anti-poverty programmes, the evolution of a new structure for NHS Scotland, the setting of wider targets to reduce health inequalities, and the development of local community health partnerships. Towards the end of the 2000s there was also a reassertion of government responsibilities for public health and commitments to develop more 'upstream' measures to combat health inequalities (SG 2008, 2010b). And these have been taken further since 2011 (Smith and Hellowell 2012), for instance, with the introduction of minimum alcohol pricing and the replacement of community health partnerships with health and social care partnerships (see Chapter 11).

The 2011 election also added to the differential developments in Wales where its (and the UK's) first public health strategy was initiated by the then Welsh Office in 1989. This was largely ineffective, but the issue of health improvement was taken up after devolution, initiating a distinctive approach to public health in Wales (Baggott 2004; CIPFA 2008). This has included a greater stress on improving public health and, initially, on counteracting the socioeconomic sources of health inequalities than England (NAW 2001; WAG 2003b), as well as a strengthening the role of health improvement in the new Local Health Boards (Table

9.2). A unified public health structure, One Wales, was established in 2009, followed by the setting of a range of health gain targets. Local Health Boards were given an explicit public health remit and have provided the base for a distinctive Welsh strategy of state-led promotion of the health of citizens (WG 2011a, 2011b; and see Drakeford 2012).

Despite the variations that have flown from devolution, reducing differentials in ill-health and promoting wellness have remained common issues across the UK and these have renewed debate over how they might be best addressed, particularly since the health of the UK population continues to lag behind many comparable countries (Dorling 2013). More generally this has added to the dilemma raised earlier about whether the focus of policy should be on illness or health, and the priority to be attached to public health within the overall health-spending envelope.

COMPREHENSION QUESTIONS

- Why has public health moved up the policy agenda in recent years?
- Why has it proved so difficult to narrow the health gap in the UK?
- In what ways have the health promotion policies of the devolved nations differed from those in England?

REFLECTIVE QUESTION

- Is health and wellbeing a social or an individual responsibility?

PAYING FOR HEALTH SERVICES

The last two decades have seen significant, and ongoing, changes in the organization of health services in the UK. This created upheaval and concern for many staff and may also have engendered confusion amongst patients and citizens more generally. The basic principle of a publicly funded NHS free at the point of delivery remains, however, and indeed has been reaffirmed by governments of all complexions. For many citizens this may be more important than the organizational shifts; what matters to most is whether the health service is there when they need it. However, the ability of the NHS to meet all potential health needs has always been limited and, as we said earlier, has always involved a process of rationing.

Rationing is primarily affected, of course, by budget restrictions and allocations to different services. Since 1997 these are set by periodic spending reviews with the devolved governments determining allocations outside England. As noted earlier spending on the NHS has grown since its foundation, from £447 million in 1949 (Ham 2009) to £127 billion in 2010/11, a tenfold increase in real terms outpacing the rise in both GDP and total public expenditure in the UK (see Figure 9.2).

However, health needs have also intensified, so increased budgets have not in practice been a protection from rationing. Moreover the resources provided have reflected the agendas of different governments and the state of the economy. After rising steadily in the immediate post-war years the rate of growth lessened from the late 1970s and 1980s, for economic and ideological reasons (see Chapter 15). After the 1999 Comprehensive Spending Review, however, Labour promised to boost spending on the NHS and, in 2000, to raise it to the European average. It also commissioned the Wanless report (2002) on future health service funding referred to earlier. This identified a range of factors likely to increase demand, notably:

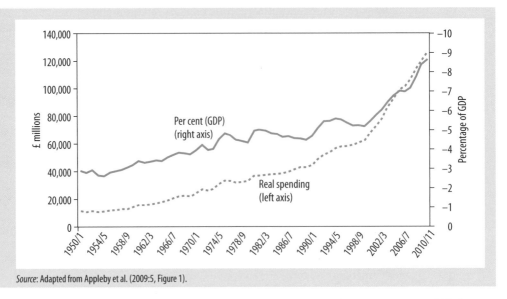

Source: Adapted from Appleby et al. (2009:5, Figure 1).

Figure 9.2 Real net spending on the UK NHS at 2010/11 prices and as a percentage of GDP

- Demographic changes, particularly population ageing
- Medical and technological advances and the rising costs of treatments
- Social changes, especially rising expectations for treatment and good health.

It also outlined different spending scenarios depending on the extent to which life expectancy and public expectations rose and showed a need for substantial spending increases over the long term and higher rates initially to enable the UK to catch up with other countries. Wanless's recommendations were accepted by Labour and the 2002 spending review committed it to an unparalleled five-year increase to expand capacity and staffing and improve NHS salaries. What is more this was paid for in part, by a 1 per cent increase in NI contributions introduced in 2003, the only major increase in direct taxation then made by Labour. Under its aegis spending rose by an average of 6.4 per cent each year until 2009/10 (Crawford and Emmerson 2012), by which time the NHS consumed 9 per cent of GDP, taking the UK above the EU and OECD average (OECD 2009).

Historically and currently England accounts for about 83 per cent of NHS spending, but that by the devolved administrations has also climbed. Labour planned lower but still high growth up to 2011 (see Figure 9.2); but after the 2008 recession, it was clear this was likely to be unsustainable in subsequent years; and since the early 2010s the NHS across the UK has faced one of the most serious funding situations since its creation in1948.

The 2010 Spending Review (HMT 2010) provided relative protection for NHS spending, including a rise of 0.4 per cent annually up to 2015, although capital expenditure was cut by 17 per cent. In real terms this meant the NHS budget was roughly the same as in 2010 across the UK (Dilnot 2012) with further efficiency savings of £20 billion planned in England, resulting by 2012 in staff redundancies and tighter criteria for some treatments. More recently, as discussed in Chapter 15, while the NHS remains relatively protected, the government has warned that fiscal constraints mean austerity is likely to continue beyond 2015 (HMT 2012b; HMG 2013). At the same time, however, the pressures outlined by Wanless are set to increase bringing renewed public concern over access to health care and adding to questions over priority setting within the NHS, and between it and other services, especially social care.

Most of current, and likely future, NHS expenditure goes on acute services in hospitals (63 per cent), followed by mental health, community health, learning disability and maternity (14, 12, 4 and 3 per cent respectively) (Ham 2009). As might be expected salaries and wages account for around two-thirds of total spending, with the NHS employing around 1.7 million people (1.4 million in England) in 2010 making it the largest employer in the UK. The primary source (around 80 per cent) of this funding is taxation, with some 17 per cent coming from NI contributions and the rest from charges for services, sometimes termed 'co-payments', together with receipts from land sales and other minor sources such as car parking (OHE 2012).

Not surprisingly given the NHS was intended to be a free service, charges have always been a controversial issue. They were first introduced for prescribed medicines and some optical and dental provision in 1951, prompting Bevan's resignation. Subsequently prescription charges have been increased, most notably in the 1980s, when payments for optical and dental services were also expanded. Since the early 1990s these have largely been provided by opticians and dentists who combine private treatment with the delivery of NHS services. Indeed there are some dentists who provide no NHS treatment and many optical services, including the supply of spectacles, are now largely fee based.

The increased scope and scale of charges also led to exemptions from charges for those on low incomes and groups such as pensioners and children to ensure payments did not deter them from seeking help. This has introduced an element of means-testing and targeting into the (supposedly) universal NHS, although in practice the range of exemptions meant most patients did not pay charges. This remains the case in England. However, prescription charges were abolished by the Welsh administration in 2007, followed by Northern Ireland in 2010 and Scotland in 2011. Scotland has also introduced free sight and dental checks and ended car parking charges on NHS-owned sites, whilst Wales and Northern Ireland have extended entitlements to eye and dental tests, leaving the highest charges in England.

Charging, with its implications for equality of access, remains a politically sensitive issue. However, in the light of pressures of demand and spending constraints, extending co-payments has been supported by a number of organizations, as has higher taxation (Friends Provident/Future Foundation 2012; Crawford and Emmerson 2012) and increased private provision (Davies 2011). Particularly in England non-state resources have already been brought into the NHS in several ways. In the 1980s hospitals were required to put catering, domestic and laundry services out to tender and this led to a widespread transfer of provision to commercial enterprises. The use of agency nurses also grew steadily. Subsequently, as outlined above, Labour gave FTs powers to borrow in private markets and enabled PCTs to commission services from external suppliers, leading to a significant increase in NHS funded private treatments for some procedures in England (Kelly and Tetlow 2012). More recently the Coalition's reforms too are geared to stimulating a plurality of providers and also provide for NHS Trusts to sell their services overseas under the aegis of Healthcare UK.

Moreover since the 1990s NHS trusts have been encouraged to engage in joint capital programmes through the use of private finance initiatives (PFI) and much of the new hospital building of the 2000s was financed in this way. The repayments, however, have caused financial difficulties for some hospitals and others face substantial future problems. However, this form of financing health provision has been limited in Scotland and halted in Wales and, as noted earlier, the administrations in both, especially since 2011, have also opposed other forms of commercial involvement.

Overall, as yet, private funding within the NHS remains small. So, too, does the level of private spending and investment in health services outside it, especially when compared to countries such as the USA. However, private health care has retained a significant role and private spending accounts for around 18 per cent of health expenditure in the UK (Laing and Buisson 2012). Private health care can be provided in separate, commercially run hospitals, which are mainly concentrated in England. But it can also be offered by NHS hospitals, with separate beds or units set aside for paying customers. These can buy additional services, such as private rooms, but can also pay for accelerated (and perhaps superior) treatment. It is this issue in particular which has caused controversy in recent times, with such patients being able in effect to jump waiting lists and private care being marketed as doing just that. Of course, private medical treatment can be extremely expensive and few could afford the necessary fees. Hence it is largely purchased through private medical insurance (PMI), coverage of which has hovered between 10 and 11 per cent of the population since the early 1990s, with some two-thirds of policies bought by employers as part of their welfare packages for key staff (see Chapter 13).

There are a number of providers of such schemes. The problem with many, however, is that, to keep subscriptions low (and attract custom), the range of services covered is often limited, with the most extensive and expensive hospital treatments not included. There is also an incentive for providers to seek to attract only those least likely to make heavy demands on the scheme, so the chronically sick and other groups in need are sometimes excluded (referred to by economists as 'cream-skimming'). In short, therefore, PMI often does not offer comprehensive cover and those with insurance also rely on the NHS. The NHS supports private provision in another sense too, since the staff that treat private patients and work in private hospitals have by and large been trained and gained experience within it. Indeed a private health care system in the UK that had to train and support its professional staff could not survive with current rates of investment. Hence despite the existence since 1948 of a free, universal state service, health care in the UK, and indeed the NHS itself, continues to be based on a mixture of public and private funding. Moreover, especially in England, this mix has broadened since the turn of the century and is set to both widen further and become more complex.

However, in health policy, as in many other areas, there is something of a contradiction contained in this joint pursuit, especially if patient choice shifts resources away from some providers, who are then unable to meet those standards. This is compounded in health policy by the dilemma touched on throughout this chapter between the provision of services that promote health and those that treat illness. Within the NHS the latter, especially the large hospitals, have traditionally had the greater influence; and this may well remain the case whatever the exhortations of policy-makers for resources to be shifted closer to patients.

At the same time, in a context of fiscal constraint and rising demand, the problem of rationing is likely to intensify, as revealed in media reports of difficulties in accessing new drugs or restrictions on procedures for hip and knee replacements. Mitigating these demands partly depends on the feasibility of raising NHS productivity and the politically sensitive reconfiguration of local services. But it may lead to pressure to raise taxation or shift the balance between it, NI contributions and individually funded treatments.

In practice much depends on the difficult questions of rebalancing health and social care provision (see Chapter 11) and how to prioritize and ration NHS services, an issue which may become more visible following the establishment of CCGs in England. Financial autonomy will give them, and FTs, the freedom to control and prioritize their expenditure; but it will also mean that they have to accept responsibility for remaining within their budget allocations – and for implementing rationing to achieve this.

The freedoms and flexibilities that now characterize NHS funding, in England in particular, have their disadvantages as well as their advantages, therefore. Recent changes have moved the pressures between demand and choice on the one hand, and financial accountability on the other, down to those managing and delivering health services; but they have not removed the hard decisions that inevitably accompany the need to reconcile these or the problems of how to determine and prioritize the most cost-effective treatments, and the reconfiguration of services to optimize these.

COMPREHENSION QUESTIONS

- What have been the main trends in spending on the NHS since 1948?
- How is private involvement in the NHS intended to help the development and delivery of state health services?
- What are the main challenges now facing the funding of the NHS across the UK?
- How will devolved budgets and patient choice change the way in which services are rationed?

REFLECTIVE QUESTION

- Could we ever remove the rationing of health care services?

FURTHER READING

The best general text on the history and development of health services in the UK is Ham (2009). Klein's (2010) book on the policy and politics of the NHS is a useful guide to the broader history and context of provision, and Baggott (2010) looks at current issues in public health policy. Glasby (2012) is a good summary of the interface between health and social care. Government documents can be found on the departmental website at www.doh.gov.uk, and the devolved administration websites (see Chapter 6). Another useful website is the King's Fund, www.kingsfund.org.uk and a guide to other think tanks can be found in Brunsdon and May (2012) at www.blackwellpublishing.com/alcock4e/.

10
Housing

SUMMARY OF KEY POINTS

- Housing policy aims to balance private housing markets with public housing needs.
- Fluctuations in the supply of and demand for housing have strongly influenced policy-making leading to major shifts in approach over time.
- Housing provision is structured by the existence of tenure divisions, the main forms being owner-occupation and renting from public, private and registered social housing providers.
- Exploitation of private tenants set the scene for the development of housing policy in the early twentieth century.
- At the end of the First World War government accepted responsibility for providing homes for all households requiring adequate housing.
- Owner-occupation began to grow with the increasing availability of mortgages, becoming the major tenure in the second half of the century.
- Public rented provision expanded rapidly after the Second World War, but declined from the 1980s with Housing Associations (HAs) and other registered providers becoming the main suppliers of social housing.
- After shrinking for most of the last century private renting has recently risen.
- Private and social housing rents have increased since the 1980s, with tenants on low incomes entitled to means-tested support, although this has recently been cut and integrated into the Universal Credit (UC).
- House building has fallen significantly since the late twentieth century.
- Labour's housing policy in England reflected a commitment to raising basic standards, increasing choice for tenants and owners and, belatedly, boosting supply.
- Housing policy under the Coalition government in England has moved towards a more marketized approach and been closely linked to changes in welfare support.
- Tackling homelessness has become a major concern for policy-makers, although the approaches taken now vary across the UK.
- Devolution has led to increased differences in housing policy within the UK.

HOUSES OR HOMES?

Having a home is a basic human need; we all need somewhere to live. For those without a home life is barely tolerable; and for society (especially a modern welfare state) a continuing problem of homelessness is an indictment of its ability to meet one of its citizens' key welfare needs. Yet homelessness remains a significant issue in the UK, with people still sleeping rough on the streets of some towns and cities because they do not have a home to go to. In general terms the study of housing policy is the study of the ways in which this need for housing is met (or not).

We will return to look at responses to the problem of homelessness later. However, more general interventions aiming to control the availability of and access to housing have been a feature of social policy for over a century, and have occupied a critical, albeit fluctuating, role in public debate. Indeed, it is probably fair to say that policy change here has been more marked than in any of the other major areas discussed in this book. This has led critics to sometimes suggest housing has been like a 'policy football', kicked one way and then another; although, if the analogy holds, it is a game in which there have been a few 'own goals'. Nevertheless policy-making has influenced the structure of provision and public investment, and regulation has been central in this.

Provision is not just the result of governmental action, however, for housing is not only about homes, it is also about markets. Houses are provided as commodities in a market, within which the principles of supply and demand operate to a large extent to determine who owns houses, who buys them and how much they cost. House ownership, however, is a rather complex legal and economic issue. Technically ownership rights apply to land rather than buildings (though in practice, of course, the two are inseparable), and, more significantly, these may be held outright (freehold) or shared (leasehold). The latter means the (freehold) owner of a house can rent (lease) it to someone else in return for payment. The effect of this, in simple terms, is to create different kinds of provision, generally referred to as *tenures*:

- Owner-occupied housing, where the property is bought for a capital sum from the builder or a previous occupier (usually with the aid of a mortgage, as we explain later)
- Rented housing, where the dwelling is let by an owner, who retains a legal interest in it and collects rent payments from the occupier.

The latter is provided with varying tenancy arrangements by different types of owners, the main ones in the UK being:

- Private landlords
- Local Authorities (LAs) providing public housing (initially called council housing)
- Independent, non-profit Housing Associations (HAs) and other regulated suppliers (registered providers in England, registered social landlords in Wales and Scotland; registered HAs in Northern Ireland).

Provision by the last two, especially since legislation in 2008, is generally referred to as *social housing* and can also include low-cost homeownership, though this is a small proportion of the market.

Markets for housing have long operated for both owner-occupation and private renting. Going back to the nineteenth century the aristocracy and new middle classes lived in houses they owned, usually designed for them by renowned architects. These were expensive to build, generally solid and well-proportioned, and many can still be seen today in the countryside and better-off parts of towns. For the vast majority of people, however, buying or building their own home was financially impossible, and most lived in accommodation rented from someone else.

The massive population growths and shifts which accompanied the Industrial Revolution meant those (few) people who owned land in the new urban conglomerations could benefit by building houses to rent for the new working classes. This private rented market expanded rapidly during the nineteenth century. But, though it meant housing was provided, it resulted in high levels of exploitation by the (rentier) landlords. Most of the dwellings built for rent were small, badly constructed, unsanitary and generally overcrowded, with many poorer families having to manage in one or two rooms.

Philanthropic attempts at improvement had little impact and by the turn of the century it was clear the private rental market had not delivered adequate or sufficient housing. As we discuss later the subsequent history of housing policy is largely the story of how governments have sought to both regulate and provide alternatives to it. This led to a decline in private letting and the growth of LA houses to rent, bifurcating the rental sector. The other major development was the emergence of a new market for owner-occupiers made possible, as we will explain, by the spread of mortgages enabling people to borrow money to buy a home. This meant landowners could exploit their property by building houses for sale, rather than rent, thus ensuring a faster and securer return on their investment.

Housing markets have therefore been structured by tenure divisions. But like all markets they have been driven by the profit motive and in seeking to capitalize on their holdings, those who own houses (or land) have not necessarily responded to housing needs. Governments have sought to meet these, but have had to do so through intervening in, or providing alternatives, to that market. Housing policy in practice therefore has been about the relationship between the operations of private markets and the meeting of public needs. It is complicated, moreover, by overlaps with economic policy and, particularly in this century, by the extent to which the funding of private housing has become part of a global financial market.

As indicated above the outcome has been significant shifts in the balance of provision between the different tenures, though these vary locally. In England for instance (see Table 10.1) the last century saw a contraction of private renting, increasing owner-occupation, a rise and then fall in LA provision, and a growth in the role of HAs. But from the turn of this century whilst the latter trends deepened and HAs overtook LAs as the main social housing provider, home ownership fell for the first time since the 1980s. This was paralleled by a resurgence of private renting, with the number of households in such accommodation rising from 2.2 to 3.7 million between 2001 and 2010 (DCLG 2012). Broadly similar trajectories can also be found in the rest of the UK (NIHE 2012a; SG 2012b; WG 2012b); and recent studies suggest these trends are likely to continue over the next decade, with homeownership falling to just over two-thirds and private rental growing to a fifth or more of tenures in England (Whitehead et al. 2012).

Past policy changes affect current policy options therefore; but, past changes in housing policy leave another legacy since, by and large, many of the properties built for rent or sale in the past are still with us. Unlike most other commodities houses are generally built to last and today's houses are largely those left by yesterday's builders and owners. Moreover this is a cumulative heritage and a walk around any city or town will reveal the different types and ages of housing currently in use – and, indirectly, tell us much about how and why it was developed when it was.

Table 10.1 Changes in the distribution of housing tenure in England (and Wales, up to 1971) 1914–2010 (percentages)				
	Owner-occupation	LA Rented	Privately Rented	HA Rented
1914	10		90	
1939	32	10	58	
1953	32	18	51	
1971	53	28	18	1
1981	60	27	11	2
2001	70	13	10	7
2010	66	8	17	9

Source: Adapted from Murie (2012:61, Table 3.1).

Indeed some of the UK's housing stock is amongst the oldest in Europe (Andrews et al. 2011) with, for instance, only 21 per cent of homes in England built since 1980 and 22 per cent constructed before 1919 (DCLG 2012). This inheritance is something of a mixed blessing. Some old houses are lavishly sized and proportioned and, especially when renovated, provide some of the most expensive homes around. Others, particularly those initially built to rent, still constitute some of the poorest quality housing on the market. In the past many older houses were deemed unfit for human habitation and demolished. But in recent times the emphasis across the UK has switched to upgrading them and securing provision of a suitable quality for all. Nevertheless in England for example 27 per cent of all dwellings and 37 per cent in the private rental sector in 2010 failed to meet the government's decent home standard (DCLG 2012).

Whatever its quality for most people their home is a house or bungalow. Twenty per cent of dwellings, however, are flats, though this ranges from eight per cent in the owner-occupied to 39 and 46 per cent in the private rental and LA sectors in England (DCLG 2012). In England, and in the devolved jurisdictions, most publicly rented flats are largely purpose-built blocks from the latter part of the twentieth century. Private rental provision is more mixed, however, including, as we discuss later, both a high proportion of converted properties and expensive high quality units built in many city centres over the last three decades.

Housing policy is concerned with the ways in which societies meet their citizens' needs for homes. In general this is about balancing the supply of houses in the market with households' demands. Over the past hundred years this balance has fluctuated between a broad surplus of houses over households and the converse, with consequent changes in policy-making. Measuring both supply and demand though is far from straightforward and all calculations are to some extent necessarily crude approximations of the pressures people face in their search for a home.

SUPPLY AND DEMAND

Housing supply is affected by both the *quantity* and *quality* of accommodation. Views on the former vary, and can change over time as tastes and expectations alter (for example for fitted kitchens or second bathrooms), and new issues emerge. Setting acceptable and affordable standards for policy-making purposes is therefore a complex task. In England the current official gauge is based on the minimum decent homes standard set by Labour in 2000, revised in 2006 to incorporate new health and safety ratings and meet the need for more eco-friendly, energy-efficient housing. Similar, though somewhat tighter, standards were also introduced elsewhere in the UK along with targets as in England for social landlords to meet them.

Alongside quality, however, the quantity of housing available also matters. By the early twentieth century for instance there were large numbers of rented houses, but many were of poor quality. At the end of the First World War this became a major political issue, captured in the slogan 'homes fit for heroes' and prompting, as will be seen, the development of public housing. At this time supply was mainly about quality. During the Second World War, however, house building stopped, 450,000 houses were destroyed and 3 million damaged by enemy bombing. The immediate post-war decades therefore saw an insufficient quantity of dwellings (and initially building materials too), triggering the largest house building programme ever undertaken in the UK.

This meant that by the 1970s there was calculated to be a crude surplus of houses across the country. By the turn of the century, however, demand was outpacing provision, a process that intensified as house building stalled in the wake of the 2008 recession and continuing demographic change, sparking concerns over a 'housing crisis'. In England for instance the government predicted an annual growth in new households of 232,000 between 2008 and 2033, double the annual rate of house building between 2000 and 2010 (DCLG 2010a;

Montague 2012). Significant shortfalls were also identified in Wales and Scotland, though less so in Northern Ireland (Pawson and Wilcox 2011).

What is more this was partly a regional phenomenon with economic changes leading people to move to areas with greater employment opportunities. However, houses do not move with households, with the result that supply began to vary significantly in different areas, with empty and hard-to-let properties in the older industrial areas of the UK and shortages in growth areas, most notably in the South-East of England, especially at the lower end of the market. House prices in such areas consequently became relatively much higher, leaving young adults in particular unable to purchase a home.

However more general demographic and cultural changes also affect demand. Rising life expectancy means there are more elderly, often single-person households, young people too are living as singletons or childless couples for longer and more couples are separating or divorcing, dividing what was one household into two. Rising birth rates over the last decade have added further to these pressures, and there are also other less predictable changes flowing from migration and immigration, with the latter increasing significantly between 2001 and 2011 (ONS 2012b). These developments in demand and supply are the major factors influencing the housing market, driving up rents and house prices in places where prospects are good and large numbers want to live (so-called 'hotspots'), and leading to low demand and empty properties elsewhere (often in areas with other significant socioeconomic problems). They are also the issues that most concern policy-makers as they seek to ensure decent housing is available for all, at prices they can afford and that also meets more recent concerns over environmental sustainability.

COMPREHENSION QUESTIONS

- What have been the main tenure changes over the last hundred years?
- How and why has the balance between supply and demand for housing altered since the turn of this century?

REFLECTIVE QUESTION

- Can we ever expect housing policy to cater for the demand for decent homes for all households?

PAYING FOR HOUSING

The cost of housing is determined by two factors: the initial building or 'bricks and mortar' costs and those of renting or purchasing the property from the legal owner. The outlay involved in building a new house is beyond most people's means. But once built maintenance costs are comparatively low, especially if it has been well constructed; and, as houses can last for decades (or more), may decline in relative significance over time. To put it another way, capital spending on house building can provide a long-term return: for individuals the investment provides a home (potentially) for life and in conditions of rising prices a valuable one, and for governments or private speculators an asset that can be rented or sold to recoup building costs.

RENTS AND RENT ASSISTANCE

As most people cannot afford to build their own homes it is the way in which owners (governments, organizations or individuals) seek to recover their costs (or make a profit) that determines what people have to pay to access housing. Private, public and social landlords will want to recoup their capital investment (sometimes called the historic cost) and the maintenance costs through rent payments. But private landlords in particular also expect to make a profit. Over time the size of this profit, and hence the rent charged, is likely to be decided more by the market demand for housing than the original cost of building or repair. For instance in a market of short supply rents will rise, and vice versa. In the case of publicly owned and rented dwellings and those provided by other social landlords the profit motive does not apply and traditionally these landlords set below market or 'social rents'. However, as we shall see, there has been pressure at different times to raise these beyond the historic cost and closer to private market rents and this is now a key feature of housing policy, particularly in England.

One of the main problems with rising rents is the fear that many would-be tenants may not be able to afford them and this has led to varying measures for financial support and legal regulation of housing provision (see Table 10.2). These have included regulation of private rents and government subsidies to LAs aimed either to reduce the historic cost of building houses (*capital subsidies*) or the costs of managing and maintaining them (*revenue subsidies*). These *producer* or *supply-led* subsidies were crucial to the development of state provision and, particularly after the Second World War, led to a gradual increase in overall public spending on housing. This was extended from the 1970s to include grants to facilitate HA provision.

Table 10.2 Main past and current forms of state support for housing in the UK		
Tenure Sector	Support for Householders (demand-side/ consumer subsidies)	Support for Providers (supply-side investment/subsidies)
Owner-Occupation	Mortgage Interest Relief Housing Benefit Mortgage Interest Relief Discounted Right to Buy (RTB) New Entrant Support Schemes Shared-Ownership Schemes	Tax Relief/Incentives Underwriting Schemes
Private Rental	Rent Controls Secure Tenancy Regulations Housing Benefit/Local Housing Allowance/ Universal Credit (HB; LHA; UC)	Tax Relief on Administrative Costs Underwriting Schemes
Public (LA) Rental	Social/ Affordable Rents Secure Tenancy Provisions HB/UC	Capital Subsidies Specific Subsidies (e.g. for slum clearance) Revenue Subsidies
HA/Registered Social Housing Rental	Social/Affordable Rents Secure Tenancy Provisions HB/UC	Capital Grants Low Cost Loans

Towards the end of the last century, however, the Conservative governments abandoned rent controls and subsidies for providing public housing. They were replaced by *consumer-* or *demand-led* support in the form of *Housing Benefit* (HB), a means-tested social security payment for low-income tenants unable to meet the market costs of their rents. Unlike most social security benefits (see Chapter 8), HB was administered by LAs in mainland Britain and the NIHE in Northern Ireland. This was partly because it was based on the *rent rebates* initially developed by LAs as a way of ensuring all tenants could meet what may be relatively high rents. Such rebates were first introduced by some authorities in the 1940s and their use expanded in the 1960s. In 1972 the Housing Finance Act made provision of this means-tested assistance mandatory; and parallel legislation in 1973 extended rebates (or allowances) to poor tenants in private lettings. This provided for the first time a form of subsidy to tenants (and landlords) in this sector, and also consolidated support for HA tenants.

In 1982 this system of rebates and allowances was replaced by a single HB scheme, paid directly to landlords, providing a 100 per cent rent subsidy for tenants on income support (IS) and a contribution towards rent costs for those on low wages, tapering off as wages rose so those with the highest rents and lowest wages received most. At the same time the subsidies for both building and maintaining LA housing were further reduced; and in 1989 the Housing and Local Government Act brought further, complex changes in England and Wales, requiring LAs to establish 'ring-fenced' Housing Revenue Accounts along lines set by central government.

This resulted in an increase in rents since many authorities had sought to hold them down in the past. The removal of private sector rental controls in the 1980s also brought rent rises; and the effect of both was to drive up the cost of HB, which by the mid-1990s had swollen to around £12 billion a year in Britain (Malpass and Murie 1999). This was evidence not only of a continuing increase in state spending on housing, despite Conservative assertions that public expenditure should be reduced, but of a massive shift in its nature, from subsidizing 'bricks and mortar' to subsidizing poor tenants. One of the other consequences, however, was a further increase in market rents, since low-income tenants were in effect shielded from these and had no incentive to seek cheaper accommodation while landlords had little reason to offer it (or employers to raise wages).

Over the next decade the high cost of HB and the problems caused by supporting poor tenants in this way become a major issue. The payment of the full cost of rents in this way was also out of line with most European and other comparative nations, which generally used fixed subsidies and required all tenants to contribute to their housing costs (Kemp 2006). With over 80 per cent of public expenditure on housing by the early 2000s going to subsidize tenants, compared to the reverse in the mid-1970s, there was also concern that it had contributed to the a general slowdown in new building and done little to spur private landlords to improve their properties (Stephens et al. 2005).

In the new century both Labour and the Coalition have sought to stem this ballooning benefit bill. In 2008 HB for private sector tenants was replaced by a flat-rate *Local Housing Allowance* (LHA), fixed at the median point of rents in the local market and payable to the tenant not the landlord. This was intended to stimulate a more competitive market even for those unable to pay the full costs of renting through widening the range of offerings. Likewise paying it directly to tenants was expected to give them greater choice and control and incentivize them to move to cheaper accommodation (DWP 2006b); and there were plans to extend this principle to HB for public tenants too.

In practice, however, the reform did little to dent the housing support bill, which by 2010 covered almost a fifth of the population and had climbed to £21 billion (Andrews et al. 2011; HMT 2010). Concern was heightened by growing awareness of LHA levels for those renting larger properties in expensive areas, especially in London, which was the subject of some hostile media coverage. Labour planned to cap support to the cost of houses with five bedrooms and to review LHA more generally from 2011 (DWP 2009a).

Following the 2010 election these ideas were taken up by the Coalition government as part of wider moves to decentralize policy. In England the 2011 Localism Act ended the revenue subsidy regime for LA rented housing, which had already been restructured under Labour and was set for further reform (DCLG 2010b), extending the move from 'bricks and mortar' to means-tested tenant support. However, this was accompanied by the deep cuts to public support more generally.

These included capping LHA levels at the 30th percentile of local rents, national caps for different-sized properties, a room-only allowance for single people under 35, and restricting uprating of support to the Consumer Price Index (CPI) rather than average private sector rents. Uprating for working-age HB claimants was also linked to the CPI and restrictions placed on those occupying properties larger than their household required (popularly dubbed the bedroom tax). From 2013 both LHA and HB upratings were further fixed at 1 per cent for three years, amounting in effect to a cut and a considerable saving on the overall social security bill. Working-age claimants, other than those on disability benefits, were also subject to an overall benefit cap. These and other restrictions also applied to the inclusion of HB and LHA in the Universal Credit to be introduced by 2017, discussed in Chapter 8, with further cuts anticipated following extended fiscal restraints in 2012 (HMT 2012a; HMG 2013).

Support for LA and HA tenants was also changed in other ways in England. The Localism Act empowered LAs to let properties to new tenants on fixed terms of a minimum of two years rather than indefinitely; and HAs were encouraged to apply flexible tenancies to new lets of around five years. HAs can also use a new 'affordable rent product' to let properties at rents of up to 80 per cent of local market rates. The intention is that all of these measures will secure greater 'fairness', choice and improve stock management within the social rented sector by moving from a 'one size fits all' provision to one where better-off tenants transfer to the private market and others move to different lets as their needs change (HMT 2012a). Meanwhile HAs are expected to rely more on rental income and commercial sources to fund new housing, while in the private sector the hope is that landlords will adjust their rents downwards and, again, that households will be able move as their circumstances change.

Unfortunately, the overall housing shortage has so far meant private rents have continued to rise and as a result, despite the cuts, so have benefit costs (NHF 2012). It also seems that over time landlords' responses might vary regionally, with those in high-demand areas less willing to let to LHA recipients, forcing people to move to cheaper localities, and increasing spatial segregation. Adding to this are fears that restrictions on HB could lead LAs, especially in London, to place homeless households in cheaper accommodation further afield.

MORTGAGES AND MORTGAGE ASSISTANCE

As we have seen, owner-occupation gradually replaced renting as the dominant UK tenure during the twentieth century. In part this was because of the problems associated with rising rents and concern over the scale of public subsidies to tenants. But it was also due to other changes that opened up homeownership to a wider range of the population. The main barrier to buying a house is the capital cost of purchase. This is the case both with new properties being sold by builders and older houses for which owners expect a market price. Most people will never have the money to pay such sums. However, the early part of the century saw the spread of a legal mechanism permitting them to borrow and repay the necessary capital – the *mortgage*.

In simple terms this is a loan of capital that is repaid, with interest, over a period of (usually) 20 or 25 years. Normally such loans would be too risky for lenders (what happens if changing events mean borrowers cannot repay?). But in the case of mortgages the house that is purchased is pledged as security for the loan so, if borrowers default, lenders can repossess and sell it to recover the unpaid loan. For the lender therefore the risk is removed, provided of course the loan is not for more than the market value of the house. For the borrower a sum large enough to buy a house can be accessed and repaid gradually over a long period, albeit with interest and dependent upon maintaining the monthly payments.

It was not just the existence of mortgages that promoted owner-occupation, however (indeed, the legal device is an old one); it was also the growth of new providers. These were the *building societies*. They were initially founded in the nineteenth century as mutual investment and lending organizations 'owned' by *borrowers*, who repaid their mortgages and interest, and *investors*, who deposited money in return for interest payments. Though they grew rapidly from the early twentieth century, the societies were rather conservative bodies that only granted mortgages to buyers in secure, well-paid employment purchasing homes at reasonable prices in safe sections of the market. However, in the 1980s, as part of the wider deregulation of financial services (popularly called the 'big bang'), the government removed controls on granting and servicing loans, creating a new market in mortgages. Banks began to compete with the societies, which became less restrictive (with many converting into or merging with banks). In effect control over mortgage lending disappeared and most people wanting to borrow to buy were able to do so.

The surge in owner-occupation was fuelled by *Mortgage Interest Tax Relief*, which, under provisions stretching back to the nineteenth century, meant those earning enough to pay tax had their payment reduced by the amount of mortgage interest they paid (Table 10.2). This was a direct subsidy to owner-occupiers and one that largely benefited those who paid most tax and borrowed large sums. In the 1970s and 1980s, as house prices rose, the cost of tax relief also mounted, adding to the consumer subsidies for housing that, as has been seen, also rose in the rented sector due to HB. And finally, amid fears that it was contributing to an economically damaging housing boom (Sinfield 2013), it was gradually phased out in the 1990s.

The expansion of owner-occupation and mortgage lending brought a range of other concerns, which we return to below. In particular, however, it created a problem for mortgagees who lost their jobs and moved on to social security benefits. To prevent such households becoming homeless when lenders foreclosed on their loans the social security system had initially covered the interest payments of claimants on IS and certain other income-related benefits in a comparable way to the payment of rents through HB and LHA (Table 10.2). This support was not, however, extended, as HB was, to low wage earners, creating an unemployment trap for some homeowners who could be better off out of than in work. From 1992 it was paid directly to the lender in the form of *Support for Mortgage Interest* (SMI) or as part of a claimants' benefit.

There were concerns about the growing cost of this support too and in the late 1990s the amount paid was heavily reduced, with new mortgagees being expected to take out private insurance or risk losing their home. Despite this most mortgages remained uninsured and, following the collapse of credit in 2007/08, the government secured temporary assistance for those in difficulties. The Coalition maintained this safeguard; but the emphasis of policy reverted to self-protection, with SMI being reduced and then rolled into the UC. Self-provision, however, still only covered a fifth of mortgages, leading to calls from some for compulsory insurance funded by borrowers, lenders and the state (see Stephens 2011).

COMPREHENSION QUESTIONS

- What are the advantages and drawbacks of HB and LHA as a means of subsidizing the costs of rented housing?
- Why was mortgage tax relief abolished?

REFLECTIVE QUESTION

- Should we expect all citizens to bear the full cost of providing for their own housing needs?

HOUSING POLICY IN THE TWENTIETH CENTURY

As we have indicated housing policy in the UK is largely a product of the last century. Although there was some philanthropic provision based on need, for much of the Victorian era a *laissez-faire* approach dominated official thinking and, apart from measures to safeguard public health, housing was largely left to the market. But from the 1900s, as the private sector's failure to provide adequate rented accommodation became apparent, government policy began to intervene in the structure of provision.

This was partly a consequence of the emergence of town planning as a means of improving the environment in which people lived, notably through the Garden City movement that helped inspire the 1909 Housing and Town Planning Act. During the First World War, however, the cost and availability of existing housing became more pressing issues, symbolized by rent strikes by working-class tenants in Glasgow. The first response was the imposition in 1915 of controls on private sector rents (Table 10.2). These were initially intended as a temporary measure but once introduced proved difficult to remove without risking rent inflation and problems for tenants unable to pay more. So controls remained in force in various forms for much of the century, resulting according to commentators in the decline shown in Table 10.1 for without higher rents there was little inducement for landlords to invest in the sector.

By 1918, however, the policy climate had altered again, bringing a further long-lasting development. Crucially the government accepted it had a responsibility to meet the need for new homes and this meant, for the first time, large-scale public investment in building new houses to rent. The 1919 'Addison Act', popularly known by the name of the minister behind it, introduced the first subsidies for LAs to provide houses for rent discussed earlier (Table 10.2). This measure was later withdrawn. But over the next two decades further subsidies were provided and many, especially larger, metropolitan authorities built houses aimed primarily at working-class tenants, often of a higher standard than those offered by private landlords. Housing quality became a more prominent issue in the 1930s when capital subsidies were refocused on 'slum clearance' and the replacement of rundown private rented dwellings, contributing to the decline of this tenure.

Public sector building between the wars added an average of 50,000 dwellings a year to the housing stock (Malpass and Murie 1999). In the 1930s in particular, however, it was outstripped by private construction for sale. Prompted by low interest rates and the availability of mortgages from the expanding building societies, this averaged around 200,000 a year mainly for higher income households. Then, as noted earlier, the Second World War caused an acute housing crisis. Its end saw the election of a Labour government committed to providing state services to meet citizens' basic needs, a vision captured in Beveridge's five giants (see Chapter 1). For it and Bevan, the minister for housing as well as health, this meant LA provision of high quality homes to rent for all social groups, not just those on low incomes.

In line with this thinking virtually all building was initially concentrated in the public rented sector, with restrictions on private building for sale, in part because of the overall shortage of materials and labour. In consequence over the ensuing two decades almost 3 million LA dwellings were built, a million more than in the private sector (Mullins and Murie 2006). By the late 1960s LAs accounted for almost a third of dwellings in the UK, amounting to the largest state housing sector outside Eastern Europe (Glennerster 2009). During the early post-war years the quality of LA building was also high, conforming with national standards, sometimes called 'Parker Morris' standards after the chairman of the committee that recommended them.

However, from the late 1950s subsidies for LA building were cut and redirected once again to slum clearance. This shift was accentuated by the development of new low-cost system-building, with the result that much new public housing took the form of blocks of flats either replacing inner city slums or on the outskirts of urban areas. Some were well designed and constructed winning architectural awards; but many were not. And, as they largely housed people displaced from the slums, rather than adding significantly to the overall stock, they turned LAs once more into the role of providing largely for the working classes. Moreover some blocks were so poorly built that by the 1980s they too had to be demolished. Most dramatically, a gas explosion, which caused one side of a tower block at Ronan Point in London to collapse in 1968, revealed the fragility of such provision and signalled the end of public and political confidence in system-built, mass public housing.

These changes in the role of public provision were also connected to developments in private housing. Once the Conservatives replaced Labour in the 1950s they lifted the restrictions on commercial development, which from the early 1960s began to surpass public building. One of their reasons for promoting private construction was their belief that housing policy should include support for owner-occupation as a key element of provision, with mortgage interest tax relief initially providing an instrument to achieve this. From the 1960s, believing rebuilding was largely accomplished, Labour too focused more on LA house improvements and supported owner-occupation, confirming its central role in housing policy.

The 1980s saw a further principled policy shift as Conservative governments sought more directly to switch the balance of provision from public to private ownership and from a centrally managed to a market-based system (Mullins and Murie 2012). As outlined earlier this was partly realized through cutting subsidies for LA building, limiting their powers to borrow for construction and maintenance and deregulating both mortgage lending and private renting. More prominently it was achieved through the introduction in 1980 of LA tenants' 'right to buy' their homes (RTB) with the aid of a guaranteed mortgage and substantial discounts, a policy initially opposed by Labour, though it gradually came to endorse it. Over the decade this led to some 2 million dwellings (out of 6.5 million) in mainland Britain being moved into the owner-occupied sector and, as these tended to be the better properties, to a decline in the quality and popularity of the remaining stock, an issue we return to later.

Critics of RTB argued it was motivated more by political considerations than a concern with housing need. Tenants who became owner-occupiers (at a discount) were thought likely to vote for the party driving this policy, undermining their former LA landlords, many of whom were Labour controlled. More generally, however, it accorded with the Conservatives' anti-state stance and was one of the more successful examples of their attempts to 'privatize' elements of public provision. This was, moreover, taken further by the 1988 Housing Act, which gave tenants the power to 'opt out' of LA ownership *en masse*, if a majority voted to switch their tenancies to a private sector or registered social landlord (RSL). The result, alongside the fall in new LA housing, was a significant growth in the non-profit rented sector, with many LAs encouraging tenants to agree to the transfer of stock to HAs, or RSLs, as these were now sometimes called.

RECENT HOUSING POLICY

The Labour governments of 1997 to 2010 embraced the notion of a mixed economy of housing provision, including support for the RTB and the encouragement of stock transfer to RSLs. In keeping with their 'third way' philosophy they took a pragmatic approach that did not assume either market or public sector domination. Following devolution, however, housing policy (within the block grant system) became the responsibility of the new administrations in Scotland, Wales and Northern Ireland, though, as in other areas, Wales initially had less legislative freedom (see Chapter 6). However in all three countries this new-found autonomy was limited by fiscal policy and other key functions affecting provision and the appeal of different tenures also remained at UK level, the most important being mortgage regulation and housing support through the social security system.

Since 2001 benefit policy has been overseen by the DWP in Britain and, since 1999, the DSD in Northern Ireland, which also has overall responsibility for housing and urban regeneration (Table 10.3; and Chapter 8). In England policy-making has been located in variously titled departments, but since 2006 with the Department of Communities and Local Government (DCLG), and its counterparts in Scotland and Wales. In England the Homes and Community Agency (HCA) established in 2010 regulates HAs and oversees capital support for the construction of affordable homes for rent and sale outside London (where investment and strategic planning rests with the Mayor). HA regulation lies with parallel bodies in Wales and Scotland and with the NIHE in Northern Ireland, which took over public housing in 1971 to counteract religious discrimination in allocations. The NIHE, however, is to be split into a regulatory and social enterprise landlord from 2015 (DSD 2012). Elsewhere LAs remain responsible for provision subject to national guidelines.

Table 10.3 The administration of housing in the UK in 2013			
England	*Scotland*	*Wales*	*N. Ireland*
Department for Communities and Local Government (DCLG)	Governance and Communities Directorate	Local Government and Communities Directorate	Department for Social Development (DSD)
LAs [/Mayor of London]	LAs	LAs	Northern Ireland Housing Executive (NIHE)
Homes and Community Agency [Housing Corporation 1964–2008; Tenants Service Authority 2008–2011]	Scottish Housing Regulator	Regulatory Board for Wales	NIHE

In England the Labour governments aimed to reduce benefit dependency, and improve choice and standards, especially in social housing. This was spearheaded by the decent homes standard instigated in 2000 referred to earlier and its target of upgrading all social housing by 2010, later adjusted to the risk-based standard set in 2006 (DETR/DSS 2000; DCLG 2006). Choice in renting for LA tenants was also promoted, although more generally choice in housing continued to depend to a large extent on the overall balance between supply and demand.

Somewhat belatedly Labour recognized that the underlying problem facing housing policy was the continuing, and growing, shortage of supply – described by Mullins and Murie (2006) as a 'rediscovery' of housing policy. In a Green Paper in 2007 (DCLG 2007a) it set targets for 3 million new dwellings by 2020, with 2 million of these by 2016, including 180,000 'affordable' homes to promote social housing. These were backed by new funding and regulatory, bodies, the Homes and Community Agency and the Tenants Service Authority (DCLG 2007b). This supply-side strategy was thrown into crisis following the 2008 recession, however. To sustain construction a 'kickstart' programme to boost social housing was introduced, but overall house building plummeted and by 2010 was at its lowest peacetime level since 1923 (NHF 2011).

In 2010 the Coalition thus inherited an improved public stock (DCLG 2012) but continuing concern over housing shortages, particularly for first-time buyers. Its response was framed within the context of the public expenditure cuts and its commitments to the promotion of market-based, and localist, approaches to policy development. There were thus cuts in benefit support, as discussed above, and reductions of over 60 per cent in capital spending on housing (HMT 2010), with commentators suggesting that these could amount to a redesign of housing within the welfare state (Ellis 2011; Murie 2012). In England this also meant scaling back the decent homes programme, and reduced support for HAs, with regulation moved into the Homes and Community Agency (Table 10.3). There was also further support for stock transfers as we discuss below. These were accompanied by major changes to the planning system to remove the targets and regional planning system outside London, developed under Labour, and replace them with a less regulated regime under the 2011 Localism Act and a more flexible National Planning Policy Framework.

Nevertheless the continuing slump in building forced the government to resort to more direct incentives to reboot the market and 'get Britain building again', not least because of the 'spillover effects' both for the economy and other public services (HMG 2011c). Its approach centred primarily on under-writing schemes to subsidize private, particularly large, house building firms (Hull and Cooke 2012), particularly through a 'help to buy' programme that some feared would raise prices rather than supply. There was also some attempt to stimulate construction for rent by both commercial landlords and HAs and a New Homes Bonus for LA building. However, in practice future house building will depend too upon the broader state of the economy and the scope for significant private sector investment. Given this questions still remain about who should fund new house building: in particular the private sector's capacity to meet the housing gap without support, and whether there should be a renewed commitment to funding new public housing.

In many ways similar trends can be found in the devolved administrations, not least because they are subject to the same systems of benefit support. Initially policies here paralleled those in England (Mullins and Murie 2006) with decent home standards and targets for meeting them being developed in all three countries leading to significant improvements in their social housing (Pawson and Wilcox 2011). Within their devolved budgets, however, housing gained less priority than other services, especially in Wales; but from the mid-2000s concern over potential shortages prompted housing reviews and the promotion of new building.

Though constrained by the Coalition's capital cuts improving housing supply and conditions remain core objectives in all three jurisdictions. But, while supportive of owner-occupation the housing strategies advanced by recent administrations varied from that in England. As we explore below, particularly in Wales and Scotland, these have pursued a less marketized approach based on maintaining consultative national planning and coordination between LAs encompassing, in Wales, a cross-tenure 'system stewardship', and in Northern Ireland a tenure neutral approach (SG 2011c; WG 2012c; DSD 2012).

COMPREHENSION QUESTIONS

- Why did the two world wars have such a significant effect on housing policy in the UK?
- How, and why, did public subsidies for housing shift from 'bricks and mortar' to people?
- What was the main focus of housing policy in England between 1997 and 2010? To what extent has this changed since?

REFLECTIVE QUESTION

- How would you account for the rising demand for new homes?

HOUSING PROVISION

OWNER-OCCUPATION

As has been seen by the end of the last century owner-occupation had become the most popular tenure in the UK; and this was a pattern repeated in many advanced industrial societies (Randall 2011). Across the UK both economic and cultural pressures supportive of homeownership were, and remain, strong. Once mortgages became widely available most households were in a position to borrow money to acquire not only a home, but an appreciating asset. This was particularly the case over most of the last four decades when house prices generally outstripped overall inflation (Dolphin and Griffith 2011). Indeed, despite the problems considered below, the financial returns on investing in housing has been one of the great success stories of economic development, with some making a comfortable living simply out of buying and selling houses in a rising market. Those who could afford a mortgage would therefore have been well advised to get one. That was just the advice many were given and it is not surprising so many took up the RTB, which we discuss later.

Owner-occupation has also benefited in the past from a relatively benign fiscal regime, with no capital gains levy on first homes or taxation of their imputed rental value so that in effect, like social housing tenants, homeowners were subsidized by the state (Perry 2012). For many, the returns were substantial (Lowe 2011) including the possibility of trading up to a more expensive property with the capital gains this brought or taking out loans or a second mortgage freeing money (housing equity) to buy other goods, help with children's education or university fees or even purchasing another property to let. In a context of less secure occupational pensions and minimal state support, it also offered the prospect of a more secure retirement. In effect property ownership became not only a financial asset rather than a home, but a 'kind of personal welfare state' (Glennerster 2009).

Homeownership is not without its problems, however; both for households and the economy. For a start owners can encounter difficulties not faced by those who rent. These include maintenance costs, which for older or badly constructed properties can be significant and for low-income owners difficult to meet. Some of the worst housing in the UK is therefore owned by poorer, frequently older, people who cannot afford its upkeep. For the most part, however, the problems associated with it are linked to the cost of houses especially in times of high demand and rapidly rising prices.

These can affect the deposit, mortgage, and repayment levels and mean many buyers have to borrow large sums and may overreach themselves. Where circumstances change for the worse, borrowers may get into arrears and ultimately lenders may repossess and sell the property to recoup the loan. In the early 1990s for instance repossessions reached over 75,000 a year (Malpass and Murie 1999). While they then fell back as economic circumstances improved, the 2008 credit crisis threatened another rise, though this was tempered by the measures referred to earlier.

Repossession means lenders get their money back, though for the borrower it often marks the end of their homeowning aspirations. It only works for the lender, however, where the value of the house exceeds the outstanding loan. Generally speaking this is the case since lenders are careful to get houses valued before agreeing a mortgage and only lend a proportion of its total value. However when house prices rise especially rapidly, as in the late 1980s and early 2000s, lenders and borrowers may be less cautious with 100 per cent mortgages being agreed. Initially in the 1980s such lending was made possible by the abolition of earlier restrictions. But increasingly it was fuelled by the development of new financial mechanisms, particularly securitization, enabling mortgage providers to borrow money to lend to purchasers as we discuss below. When markets fall as in the 1990s or collapse as in the late 2000s owners can be left with a property worth less than the amount borrowed (referred to as 'negative equity'). This may be only a temporary setback, especially if the market recovers. But where repayments cannot be maintained they can be left both homeless and heavily in debt with no means of escape. The cultural and policy attractions of homeownership begin to wane in circumstances like this.

The ability of borrowers to repay their mortgages depends on their household income and the size of the loan and in a rising market people may be pressured into borrowing as much as they can to secure the best possible home. There is another variable affecting repayments, however, and that is the rate of interest charged by banks and building societies on loans. Mortgage lenders usually reserve the right to vary this as general economic circumstances change and particularly for those with large loans even small fluctuations can substantially alter the monthly repayments. Rising mortgage rates can therefore affect homeowners' capacity to pay off their loans, keep their homes and meet other commitments. Indeed, mass homeownership has meant mortgage rates have become so central to people's spending power that the government, through the Bank of England, uses bank lending rates (which largely determine mortgage rates) as a means of regulating the wider economy, increasing them to curtail spending when inflation is rising and reducing them to encourage consumption when demand is weak. It is telling evidence of the role owner-occupation now plays in the UK and many other societies and the extent to which it has become a significant factor in economic performance and policy.

This and the wider problems associated with homeowning were starkly highlighted by the global credit crisis that led to the recession of 2008 (see Chapter 15). High levels of mortgage lending, sometimes up to 125 per cent of the value of the property and with repayments only covering interest charged and not reduction of the overall debt, were lent to an ever wider proportion of the population, sometimes occupying poor quality housing (FSA 2009). This happened in the USA too, where it was referred to as the 'subprime' market, and was supported by complex financial packages supposedly guaranteeing lenders protection against mortgage defaulters. However, defaults did take place and the non-viable nature of subprime mortgages was exposed, triggering the wider crisis in bank lending.

This led to the bank bailouts discussed in Chapter 15, and a return to much stricter mortgage lending practices, backed by the development of tighter regulation of the mortgage market with new rules fully operational from 2014 (FSA 2012). However, this has led to much more restricted access to the owner-occupation market, especially for new (first time) buyers, who often have to find large cash deposits before they can access mortgage finance (Pawson and Wilcox 2011). Despite historically low interest rates, with new house building also failing, as explained above, this pressure on owner-occupation has been one of the reasons for the recent growth in the private rented market revealed in Table 10.1 and discussed below, and has also led to a rise in the age of new owner-occupiers.

Easing the pressure on access to owner-occupation was a central plank of the Coalition's strategy in England and led to an expansion of earlier schemes promoting more flexible forms of purchase including the help to buy programme and low-cost shared-ownership schemes. In Scotland similar shared-ownership initiatives were developed with public support and extended to all first time buyers in 2012. Various 'new entry' measures have also been promoted in Northern Ireland and Wales, although here, as in the rest of the UK, policy-making has also centred on the rental sectors (SG 2007b; NIA 2008; WAG 2005; WG 2012c).

PUBLIC RENTED HOUSING

The story of this sector in the UK is one of rise and fall. As indicated earlier it initially grew following the introduction of subsidies enabling LAs to build houses for rent, and expanded rapidly after 1945 when such provision dominated the response to the housing shortage. Built on the outskirts of large cities and in the planned 'new towns', this was generally of good quality and intended for all social groups. And, though building costs were relatively high, LAs kept rents down to ensure as many as possible could afford them. Indeed up to the 1980s such was the popularity of public rented housing that they had to ration access.

Generally this was done through the use of *waiting lists*, in effect, putting all applicants in a queue, often determined not just by the time of submission but various measures of housing need with families and homeless people being accorded greater priority. In some LAs this was based on a formula, usually a 'points system' with more points and a higher position going to those in most need. But in others it was more discretionary and judgemental and there were accusations that this could lead to discrimination and unfair treatment (Merrett 1979; Henderson and Karn 1987). With changes in provisions for homeless people in 1977 (considered below) and the waning popularity of the sector, allocation systems became more complex and varied though much depended on the demand for different types of property, with some becoming so hard to let they were left empty.

After the initial post-war boom LA building was channelled into slum clearance and the associated system-building described earlier. The poor quality of much of these city centre blocks partly accounted for the sector's declining popularity and was compounded by the fact that those allocated to them were generally from the private rented dwellings they replaced. Inevitably many were low-income households and this accentuated a link between public housing and social class that stretched back to earlier requirements that it be geared to the needs of the working class. With the growth of owner-occupation public renting was coming to be seen by many, not least its tenants, as a second-class tenure for those who could not afford a mortgage.

The introduction of RTB in 1980 cemented this secondary role. This was partly because, as noted earlier, it was mainly better-off tenants in the quality properties that bought their houses, leaving much of the stock concentrated in inner cities and larger estates. Furthermore there were far fewer sales in areas of high unemployment and deprivation (Forest and Murie 2010) and, more generally, LAs were prohibited from investing the receipts in new building or improvements.

The effect was to accelerate the process by which the remaining stock became a tenure of poor quality housing for low-income households, a development referred to as *residualization* (Cole and Furbey 1994). This process was intensified by the removal of subsidies for building and maintenance discussed earlier and the consequent near-disappearance of new and neglect of existing provision. By the early 2000s a third of LA tenants were in the poorest 20 per cent of the income distribution (Hills 2007) and included a high proportion of households with no earners due to retirement, ill-health, caring responsibilities or unemployment.

Although the RTB was the most significant policy change, it was not the only development. The 1980 Housing Act also introduced a 'tenant's charter', strengthening LA tenants' entitlements by, for instance, securing their right to indefinite, lifetime tenures, restricting the grounds for eviction and empowering them to alter and exchange their homes with other tenants. In 1988, as we outlined earlier, the government went further, giving them the right to transfer their tenancy to a private or registered social landlord, starting a process that by the late 1990s replaced RTB in reducing LA provision. Such transfers required the support of a majority of the tenants to be affected and initially were not as popular as their protagonists hoped. Large-scale transfers were, however, initiated by LAs wanting to shift their management responsibilities, usually to HAs.

These expanded more rapidly in England after 1997, in part because of the greater financial backing and flexibility given to registered social landlords (RSLs). This option was taken up in many areas; but in some, reflecting both fears of rent rises and loyalty to public sector landlords, it was voted down. From the turn of the century other means of transforming the management of public rented housing were introduced however, including the creation of arms-length management organizations (ALMOs), where rented housing remained in the public sector, but passed to quasi-independent agencies. As there was no transfer of ownership these only required consultation and, aided by the extra funding, gained widespread backing, covering nearly half of LA housing by 2010 (HMG 2011c) and making public housing a 'thing of the past' in many areas (Pawson and Mullins 2010).

The Labour governments of the 2000s were also concerned with the potential problems flowing from the residualization of public rented housing and its association with the notion of 'sink estates'. They sought therefore to upgrade the stock and promote greater tenant choice and more mixed tenure provision (DETR/DSS 2000) by, for instance, encouraging transparent allocation systems and a choice-based letting scheme launched in 2001.

In establishing this LAs had some discretion. But in essence the scheme meant upcoming LA (and HA) vacancies were publicly advertised enabling applicants to view and bid for properties according to their circumstances and preferences, those with the most critical needs being given priority. It was widely upheld as a means of developing 'viable communities' as well as extending choice (DCLG 2007b) and by 2010 operated by the majority of LAs albeit often for only a proportion of their properties. Its development was linked to a complex and lengthy process of rent restructuring aimed to ensure that by 2015/16 LAs and HAs charged similar rates for properties of similar size and value in similar areas (DCLG 2007c).

Since 2010 the Coalition has continued a number of the measures introduced by Labour. Rent restructuring was progressed and choice-based letting furthered by the introduction of an all-England 'swap' scheme. As noted earlier, the subsidy changeover too was completed, allowing LAs to keep their rental incomes to manage their housing and, within stringent borrowing limits, invest in new buildings. Benefit reforms have also provided for housing support to be paid directly to tenants aimed at improving choice and encouraging self-responsibility.

Public spending on housing has been cutback, however, and a more marketized approach to public housing pursued, as a 'springboard' to other tenures. This was most clearly signalled by the introduction under the 2011 Localism Act of the fixed term tenancies (of two years minimum), the expectation that rents should be raised for high-earning tenants and to reduce under-occupancy, the 'rejuvenation' of RTB, and the encouragement of further estate transfers.

Many of these initiatives have not, however, been pursued in the rest of the UK where devolution has led to different developments in public housing. In Northern Ireland the NIHE remained both the key determiner of provision and the largest public landlord in the UK with responsibility for a common allocation scheme for all social housing. As such and in the context of wider political concerns it adopted a largely conservative stance, resisting most attempts at stock transfer and other changes to housing management and reducing RTB discounts. HAs, however, became the main suppliers of new housing and, as noted earlier, the NIHE is to be divided into a strategic agency and a social enterprise landlord under a policy framework similar to England's (DSD 2012).

RTB discounts were also reduced in Scotland and Wales and, though the administrations here sanctioned stock transfers, they did not promote ALMOs or private finance initiatives (Wilcox et al. 2010). In Scotland particularly while there were large large-scale transfers, notably in Glasgow, most were to small community-based HAs. To secure them legislation in 2001 established a common tenancy system across the social rented sectors. But from the mid-2000s the transfer process slowed as LAs gained 'prudential' borrowing powers and were encouraged to widen their provision to include so-called intermediate rentals and, as noted earlier, shared-ownership schemes.

Welsh administrations also sought to diversify LA provision and, increasingly, to protect it. Though negotiations enabling LAs to retain their rental income proved protracted, this strategy was furthered from 2011, particularly through the development of national rent setting for LA and HA housing (WG 2011c). The 'affordable rent' initiative was not introduced in Wales and the right to buy has been suspended. More radically the Scottish government aimed to scrap it and similarly did not plan to develop affordable rents or remove security of tenure for LA (or HA) tenants. There is thus significant difference now in policy towards the public rented sector across the UK, adding to controversy over its future more generally and the extent to which it should operate as safety net or have a wider role.

REGISTERED PROVIDERS AND SOCIAL LANDLORDS

The provision of rented housing by independent non-profit organizations dates back to the nineteenth century and the activities of philanthropic agencies such as the Peabody Trust, established in 1862. Perhaps the best known of these early providers was Octavia Hill, who focused particularly on housing schemes for those most in need, and was a prominent member of the Charity Organization Society (see Chapter 1) which, as in other policy areas, saw such provision as a (more desirable) alternative to public housing. To a significant extent, therefore, the growth of the latter from the 1920s was paralleled by a decline in the scale and profile of non-profit provision, much of which concentrated on developing supported housing for groups with particular needs.

Whilst this remains a key activity, the role of non-profit organizations, now called HAs, began to expand again from the middle of the century. Initially this was precipitated by the 1961 and 1964 Housing Acts which made government loans available to them for providing low-cost renting and, under the latter, created the Housing Corporation, a quango linking HAs and government departments. In 1974 state assistance was expanded through the provision of generous grants to support them in building and renovating accommodation for rent, subject to registering with the Corporation and meeting certain criteria, including charging below market rents. The main spur to their growth, however, was the 1988 Housing Act, which also established separate regulatory bodies in Scotland (Scottish Homes) and Wales (Tai Cymru), powers remaining with the NIHE in Northern Ireland.

As has been seen the act gave LA tenants the right to transfer their tenancies to HAs and, more generally, obliged them to similarly offer assured tenancies on all their lettings. At the same time, though the level of grant aid was cut, they also gained the power to top up it up with private borrowing, a facility denied to LAs and which had the added advantage of not counting as public expenditure. Combined with the lack of investment in public building these developments meant HAs came to play an increasing role in the housing market, replacing LAs as the major providers of new social rentals in the 1990s (Table 10.1; Pawson and Mullins 2010).

In 1996 new legislation rebranded associations as RSLs, although this term applied to a wider range of organizations than those approved under the 1974 Act, including the new bodies set up by LAs to administer rented dwellings transferred under the 1988 legislation. By then, however, they were under increasing pressure to rely more on private rather than state funding, leading many, especially larger, HAs to branch out into other forms of provision to pay their commercial lenders and subsidize their social lettings, though these too were raised (adding to the HB bill). Such diversification often involved merging into larger entities, participation in other public-funded programmes and the provision of care homes, student and key-worker accommodation and shared-ownership schemes.

The development of what is often described as a 'hybrid' role (Mullins 2011) accelerated in the 2000s as governments, particularly in England, continued to encourage HA expansion supported by private borrowing; and, as highlighted earlier, the creation of ALMOs augmented the sector. Partly in recognition of these trends the 2008 Housing and Regeneration Act relabelled RSLs as registered providers. It also split the Housing Corporation between the Homes and Communities Agency and the Tenants Service Authority, the former becoming responsible for their regulation and funding (Table 10.3).

Since 2012 the Coalition government has continued and extended the sector's role, particularly in new housing and LA stock transfers. It has also, however, sought to strengthen HAs' commercial base, driving it to fund new provision largely through higher borrowing, partnership working, tenancy changes and increased rents (HMG 2011c); and to promote this expansion in 2011 the Homes and Communities Agency and the Tenants Service Authority were merged again and the new single regulator's powers tightened (Table 10.3).

Some of these developments were paralleled in the rest of the UK where, again partly because of their ability to raise private funds, HAs gradually became the main suppliers of new social housing. With grant aid now provided by the devolved administrations, regulation was initially undertaken directly. But after various changes in 2010 this task passed to a Regulatory Board in Wales and the Scottish Housing Regulator, which also became responsible for monitoring LA housing (Table 10.3). As noted above, Scottish HAs are generally smaller and more community-based than their counterparts elsewhere. Whatever their form, however, the role of HAs in providing and managing new social housing has continued across the UK, with the expectation (especially in England) that this would increasingly be commercially funded.

PRIVATE RENTED HOUSING

Whilst other tenures grew over the last century, private rented housing shrank dramatically (see Table 10.1). This was not just a relative decline: the overall numbers of private rented dwellings also fell as scores were demolished in slum clearances and others sold to owner-occupiers, who promptly renovated them and raised their market value. For many, particularly tenants, this was no bad thing. Private landlords had long exploited their position, providing poor quality homes at high rents and those who could afford to buy or move into social renting in most cases undoubtedly improved their housing conditions. It is perhaps for this reason that successive governments until recently did little to reverse the sector's decline.

Policy-makers did not entirely ignore it, however. Indeed from 1915 governments at various times sought to regulate rents and protect tenants from arbitrary eviction. In the 1950s, when these controls were relaxed, rents soared and tenant harassment gained public notoriety through the activities of one particularly unscrupulous London landlord called Rachman. In response in the 1960s more extensive regulation provided for 'fair rents' set by government officers. Such controls were blamed by some critics, however, for removing any incentive for landlords to enter the market; and in the 1980s Conservative governments gradually withdrew them and introduced new tenancy arrangements. These permitted landlords to evict tenants, if they wished, at the end of a fixed (shorthold) period of six months and an additional two-month notice, a form of tenancy that became the norm in much of the UK, though Scotland retained its separate provisions for different tenancy lengths.

Decontrol again led to rent rises although, as discussed above, HB now provided some protection for poorer tenants and by the late 1990s there were signs of a revival of the sector. This was marked by provision by large companies, particularly, of new apartments in popular inner-city locations targeted at young professionals, and by buy-to-let landlords renting older properties to a younger (often student) market. For both sets of tenants such renting was often seen as a flexible 'staging post' to owner-occupation (Rugg and Rhodes 2008). In contrast the more traditional end of the market catered for poorer and older tenants in low-quality older properties, sometimes renting from landlords little better off than themselves.

With the fall in new buildings for sale, tighter mortgage conditions, rising house prices and rents from the mid-2000s, the growth in private renting accelerated, particularly in pressure spots such as London. It was largely propelled by the continued rise in buy-to-let provision, which benefited from the availability of interest-free mortgages and appeared to offer better returns than other forms of saving. In consequence, the sector remained dominated by small landlords, with only 1 per cent of the stock owned by institutions compared to between 10 and 15 per cent in most European countries (HMG 2011c).

By 2010 provision in England neared that of the social housing sectors combined (Table 10.1) and, as noted earlier, despite including some of the lowest-quality dwellings was widely predicted to become the main rental tenure by 2020. This growth, moreover, meant private landlords now catered for a less transient market and, increasingly, for more households with children and those often described as a new 'generation rent', with incomes too high for social housing but insufficient for homeownership (Alakeson 2011).

Not surprisingly after years of neglect these developments reignited interest in the sector, leading to a review of its role (Rugg and Rhodes 2008) and in 2009 to an attempt to attract institutional investment in expanding provision. Prior to the 2010 election the Labour government was also planning tighter oversight of the sector through landlord registration, regulating letting and managing agencies and tightening tenancy agreements; and since then the Coalition has emphasized support for 'a thriving' private rented sector in meeting people's housing needs (HMG 2011c). However it has opposed further regulation, including calls for longer tenancies and the reintroduction of rent controls and, as outlined earlier, cut LHA, focusing instead on boosting provision, particularly through more supportive planning arrangements and encouragement of institutional investment (Montague 2012).

The revival of private renting elsewhere in the UK has also sparked a new interest in increasing provision, particularly by large developers. In Scotland, with its different tenancy system, private landlords were subject to mandatory licensing in 2006. With their increased powers the 2011 Welsh administrations also adopted a 'distinct, less laissez-faire' approach (Edwards et al. 2012), providing for mandatory licensing of landlords and letting agencies and more flexible, longer tenancies (WG 2011c, 2012c). Mandatory registration was also planned in Northern Ireland along with a partnership scheme to develop 'quasi' social housing (DSD 2010).

Whether recent trends signify a lack of realistic alternatives or a resurgence of a private market in rented housing is open to speculation. They also, however, point to potential tension between the sector's further development and continued support for owner-occupation as the preferred tenure type, and raise questions about whether either of these markets can provide adequate housing for low-income earners and others in acute housing need.

COMPREHENSION QUESTIONS

- To what extent has public sector housing become a 'residual' provision for those unable to secure accommodation in the private market?
- What are HAs and can they provide a new future for rented housing?
- How would you account for the changing fortunes of the private rental sector and how significant is its recent revival?
- Why are young people finding it more difficult to move into owner-occupation than previous generations?

REFLECTIVE QUESTIONS

- Should we be concerned about the domination of owner-occupation in the provision of housing?
- Should social housing be allocated solely on the basis of need?

HOMELESSNESS

Homelessness is central to any assessment of housing policy since where people are homeless it is because in a sense housing policy has failed. However, it is far from clear exactly what is meant by homelessness and, as a result, how policy-makers should respond to it. It can mean literally having no place to sleep tonight – sometimes referred to as rooflessness or, more recently, rough sleeping. Reducing the numbers in this situation in England became a priority for Labour and its interventions led to a two-thirds fall by 2006 though numbers rose again in the late 2000s (Pawson and Wilcox 2011). The Coalition has similarly pledged to reduce this highly visible form of homelessness, through a 'no second night out' scheme and has also reformed the system for gauging its extent, which had been criticized as underestimating the problem (DCLG 2011).

However, people may be homeless even though they have a bed for the night, if that bed is insecure or inadequate. This applies to those living with family or friends in overcrowded, uninhabitable or dilapidated housing, or threatened with eviction, domestic conflict or violence. We may regard many in these circumstances as homeless, but there has generally been no direct policy response to such problems and no legal right for those affected to access a home. Until 1977 such homeless people were simply placed on LA waiting lists, albeit perhaps towards the top because of their desperate need. In that year, however, a statutory duty was placed on LAs to provide housing for certain categories of homeless persons, although, because of a concern they might otherwise be unable to meet this duty, support was restricted to those with priority needs. Hence only families with children deemed unintentionally homeless were entitled to require LAs house them, with other groups having a right to receive advice and assistance.

Nevertheless the act was a significant policy change and in 1988 it was consolidated into the general duties of LAs in the provision of public housing. However, the existence of a legal right did not automatically mean houses were available for all homeless people. In some urban areas, particularly London, there were frequently more homeless people than empty LA properties. In these circumstances authorities were sometimes forced to house people temporarily in 'bed and breakfast' (B&B) accommodation (generally cheap and crowded rooms in down-market hotels).

In England tackling homelessness again become a major policy concern in the 2000s, when Labour ended the use of B&B for long-term accommodation for families and set targets to halve the numbers of all households in temporary accommodation by 2010, which were met (Pawson and Wilcox 2011). Legislation in 2002 also introduced a more coordinated response to the problem, including extending the definition of priority need to cover young people, prison leavers and those fleeing domestic violence, and the provision of preventive/housing options services by LAs. From 2008 the latter were expanded, contributing to a sustained fall in recorded homelessness (Pawson and Wilcox 2011).

This preventative approach was reaffirmed by the Coalition, though not its centrally-driven target-base (DCLG 2010c). The 2011 Localism Act, moreover, reversed the 2002 legislation, allowing closed waiting lists and greater LA discretion over allocations. It also enabled them to fulfil their homelessness duties by offering suitable fixed-term tenancies without the applicants' consent.

Homelessness has also been viewed as a priority by the devolved administrations since 2000, bringing increasing divergence in provision here too. The most radical approach was pursued in Scotland following a commitment in 2003 phasing out priority need conditions and ensuring practically all homeless people had a right to rehousing by 2012 (McKee and Phillips 2012). This resulted initially in a rise in statutory homelessness, which subsequently fell as more preventive services came on stream. Northern Ireland too saw the gradual development of a preventative strategy (NIHE 2012b). Such provision was central to Welsh policy from the outset, however, and was extended further after 2011 along with a new commitment, as in Scotland, to abolish the intentionally homeless test, switch LA duties to preventive action, and end family homelessness by 2019 (WAG 2009a; WG 2012c).

As we noted at the beginning of this chapter, the problem of homelessness is at the sharp end of housing policy and recent initiatives suggest it has become a key concern across the UK though addressed in different ways. However, with rough sleeping, statutory homelessness, the use of temporary accommodation and overcrowding rising again in the early 2010s (Fitzpatrick et al. 2012), it also remains a significant problem, adding to pressures for rethinking housing policy for those in acute need and more generally.

COMPREHENSION QUESTIONS

- How have legislative provisions for homeless people changed over the last half century?
- To what extent do the devolved administrations in Northern Ireland, Wales and Scotland treat homeless people differently to England?

REFLECTIVE QUESTION

- Should everyone in the country have a right to be provided with housing?

FURTHER READING

Mullins and Murie (2006) and Lund (2011) provide good overviews of the development of housing policy. Lowe (2011) offers a stimulating discussion set in a comparative context. Current trends are usefully summarized in Pawson and Wilcox's (2011) annual surveys at www.york.ac.uk/res/ukhr. Government papers can be viewed on the DCLG website www.communities.gov.uk for England and the websites of the devolved administrations (see Chapter 6). Local government publications can be viewed at www.lga.gov.uk, and a guide to the main think tanks can be found in Brunsdon and May (2012) at www.blackwellpublishing.com/alcock4e/.

11
Social Care Services

SUMMARY OF KEY POINTS

- Social care encompasses individual services and social work for vulnerable children and adults in need supplied by local authorities (LAs) in partnership with other statutory, commercial and voluntary agencies.
- The early development of social care was dominated by voluntary provision, and only in the welfare reforms of the 1940s were statutory services established in LAs.
- In 1971 provision for children and adults was consolidated into generic Social Service Departments (SSDs); but the 2000s saw a return to separate services in England and in some Scottish LAs.
- Devolution has brought increasing divergence in some aspects of policy.
- High-profile media reporting of child abuse has on occasions created pressure for changes in policy and practice, yet agencies constantly have to deal with large numbers of children at risk.
- Work with child offenders has fluctuated between welfare and justice approaches and both continue to influence policy-making.
- Both child and adult provision are based on a mixed economy of care involving commercial and voluntary providers and an emphasis on partnership working.
- There has been a significant move away from residential care to community care for adults, and to fostering in children's services.
- Adult care has shifted to a system in which users are more actively involved in planning, designing and purchasing services.
- There is mounting pressure to establish effective arrangements for funding and meeting adult care needs.

WHAT IS SOCIAL CARE?

Social care is a complex and diverse area of social policy. This in part reflects the range of services provided; but it is also a product of the main terms used to describe them, which commentators sometimes confusingly employ in different ways. As a result there is probably no single, common approach; but for the purposes of clarity we will distinguish the major terms and the activities they generally refer to, and use them in this way throughout the book. The main distinction is between four core terms:

- *Social care* is the umbrella term for the provision of non-medical individual support to vulnerable, sick or disabled adults unable to provide fully for themselves and aimed to help them maintain their independence. Such support is provided by other members of society on an unpaid basis (generally by family members) or on a paid basis by care workers in a person's home or a residential establishment. Social care is, of course, provided to children, but until recently the term denoted support for adults. It is often linked to health needs and hence sometimes referred to as *health and social care*. The care provided informally by family members is a significant part of overall welfare provision as we discussed in Chapter 5 and recent legislation has entitled carers to various forms of support.
- *Social work* is the professional activity carried out by social workers employed by LAs, other statutory bodies, commercial and third sector organizations. Such workers are trained to degree level and often have further specialist qualifications. They have to be registered with the Health and Care Professions Council in England, or its counterparts in the rest of the UK (see Table 11.1), undertake regular updating and conform to professional codes of conduct. They act on behalf of their employers to identify children or adults who might need support or protection as a result of their circumstances, and, where possible, aim to provide this or, more generally, to assist them in securing it from other agencies. For adults social workers are largely engaged in this 'facilitating' role, as we discuss below. In their work with children in need they more often aim to protect those at risk, in extreme cases by removing them from their family home.
- *(Personal) Social Services* is the generic term for the provision of social care and social work, particularly by public agencies to those within a defined area who need extra support. Traditionally it also encompassed a wider range of services provided on an individual or community basis, including community work and welfare rights advice. For the most part this range of services is provided, directly or indirectly, by departments or sections of LAs. Their overall organization however, varies between the countries of the UK (Table 11.1) and, as outlined later, is in the process of being restructured.
- *Children's Services* is used to refer to general provisions for children and young people, particularly those in need, and more specialist *child protection* services for those at risk of abuse or neglect. Such services may be overseen by LA departments that also manage those for vulnerable adults and hence the terms 'Social Services' or 'Social Care Services' are often used to apply to provision for both groups (Table 11.1).

THE STRUCTURE OF CARE SERVICES

Currently most, but not all, English LAs have separate children's and adults' services departments, though the titles used vary – and they may both still be referred to colloquially as 'Social Services'. Directors of the former are taxed with education as well as child care, whilst responsibility for adult care is often combined with services such as housing, adult education or leisure. In Northern Ireland, where organizational differences preceded devolution, adult and children's services are commissioned by the Health and Social Care Board and managed by regional Health and Social Care Trusts which also cover health services. Responsibility for both services in Wales lies with LA SSDs, though more collaborative, regionalized provision is under way. In Scotland support is mainly channelled through LA social work departments (SWDs), some being child or adult specific, though gradual integration of the adult services with adult health under Health and Social Care Partnerships in each LA area is planned.

Table 11.1 The administration of care services in the UK in 2013

England	N. Ireland	Scotland	Wales
Department for Education (DfE) Department of Health (DoH)	Department of Health, Social Services and Public Safety (DHSSPS) Health and Social Care Board	Health and Social Care Directorate	Department for Health, Social Services and Children
LA Adult Care Services LA Children's Services LA Adult and Children's Services	Health and Social Care Trusts	LA Social Work Departments (generic/split)	LA SSDs
Performance Management			
Ofsted Care Quality Commission (CQC) [Commission for Social Care Inspection (2004–2009); Social Services Inspectorate (1985–2003); SS1/Audit Commission Joint Review Team (1996–2003); National Care Standards Commission (2000–04)]	Office of Social Services	Social Care and Social Work Improvement Scotland [Scottish Commission for the Regulation of Care (2002–2011); Social Work Inspection Agency (2002–2011); HMI Education 1999–2011)]	Care and Social Services Inspectorate Wales
Social Work Regulation and Care Workforce Development *[1970–2001 Central Council for Training in Social Work (CCETSW)]*			
Health and Care Professions Council [General Social Care Council (2000–2012)] Skills for Care for Adult Services Department for Education (DoE)/ Teaching Agency [Children's Workforce Development Council (2005–2012)]	Northern Ireland Social Care Council	Scottish Social Services Council	Care Council for Wales

However it is structured one of the central features of social care is its focus on individual needs. This contrasts with other major policy areas such as education, which is concerned with the provision of learning, or social security, which focuses on the distribution of financial benefits. Social care, however, covers a range of needs, and in effect is driven by these rather than a predetermined service framework. For this reason, notably in the USA, it is sometimes termed human services. More critically it is often described as a 'crisis' or, in Baldock's (2003) terms, a 'residual' service, available to those who could not be helped by more specific providers. Individuals supported by care services are still therefore sometimes referred to as *clients*; though following extensive criticism this notion has given way to that of service user (see Glasby 2012).

The conception of social care suggests that, like the NHS (see Chapter 9), it is largely a demand-led area of social policy; and, to a significant extent, both social work and care services are based on processes of identifying and responding to the needs of individuals (or families). Where needs are growing therefore, we would expect provision to expand; and a broad review of public spending on LA social services indicates this is indeed the case. Gross expenditure on adult and children's services in England for instance grew from £7.5 to £12.8 billion between 1994/95 and 2001/02 (DoH 2007a). By 2009/10 council spending on children's services almost doubled again (CIPFA 2011), though this was partly due to the Sure Start programme (see Chapter12). Spending on adult care also continued to climb (see Figure 11.1), although slightly more slowly if Supporting People (SP) funding was excluded.

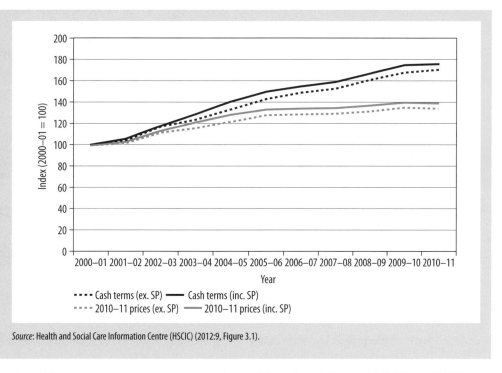

Source: Health and Social Care Information Centre (HSCIC) (2012:9, Figure 3.1).

Figure 11.1 Gross current expenditure on adult social services in England 2000/01 to 2010/11

As with other services, overall funding is set at UK level; and this pattern of growth has taken place under Conservative governments ostensibly aiming to contain spending, as well as Labour administrations committed to expanding services. In part this is a product of rising needs, and even with rising expenditure, there is no guarantee that all needs can be met – indeed demand for social care has continued to outstrip provision, an issue we will return to later. Since devolution, however, allocation of spending is decided by the separate administrations in Scotland, Wales and Northern Ireland, which also determine the policy framework.

In England strategic responsibility for adult services lies with the DoH, and for children with the DfE (Table 11.1). In Scotland policy development for both domains is vested in the Scottish Government (SG), which has tended to rely more on guidance than new legislation. In Wales, policy-making rests with the Welsh Government (WG), although in child protection its powers were initially confined to producing regulations and guidance; and in Northern Ireland it is set by the DHSSPS, though like social policy generally it has had a low priority (Gray and Birrell 2012). Each country has its own, often revised, quality assurance structures (Table 11.1) and, as we will highlight, different approaches to some aspects of provision.

Direct responsibility for managing social care in mainland Britain sits, however, with LAs. Their funding is determined by grants from the national administrations together with local council tax and charges made for certain services, with funding for the Trusts in Northern Ireland coming from the DHSSPS (see Chapter 6). These constitute a fixed budget from which support for local citizens must be provided. For care services managers across the UK, therefore – and, indeed, for social workers – delivery involves prioritizing needs within predetermined and limited resources. Determining allocations across all those needing support is no easy task, especially since these vary significantly and, in effect, must be treated on an individual basis, sometimes termed the 'casework' approach. In practice in England children take up about a quarter of total gross expenditure on social services (HSCIC 2009), with adult social care absorbing nearly a third of LA spending, over half of which goes to supporting over 65s (Table 11.2). Within this though, older people's circumstances vary greatly and include needs that are in practice extensions of those experienced as working age adults (see Glasby 2012).

Table 11.2 Expenditure on adult personal social services in England 2010–11	
Service Users	*Percentage of Total Expenditure*
Older people (65+)	55
People with a learning disability (aged 18–64)	25
People with a physical disability (aged 18–64)	10
People with mental health needs (aged 18–64)	7
[Other services	3]

Source: Adapted from HSCIC (2012:1).

It is primarily the various local departments that have to manage these budgetary dilemmas, although this is increasingly done in partnership with other entities in what is, to a greater extent than other policy areas, a mixed economy of funding and provision. As we discussed in Chapter 5, the bulk of care is provided informally; but services are also provided by other statutory bodies such as health authorities, and, increasingly, by commercial and third sector agencies. They are also purchased directly by users.

Child protection, for instance, originated in the work of nineteenth century voluntary organizations such as Barnardo's and the National Society for the Prevention of Cruelty to Children (NSPCC), many of which still operate today. Adult residential care too has always been in part delivered by commercial and non-profit organizations, and their provision has grown significantly since the 1990s, as have commercial and third sector enterprises supplying non-residential children's and adult care services. As we discuss below across the UK many of these are now delivered on a contractual basis by such providers, and they are also increasingly involved in service planning.

THE DEVELOPMENT OF CARE SERVICES

Contemporary provision can be traced back to the ideals and innovations of Victorian philanthropists. This included the work of the so-called 'childsavers' (Platt 1969), who influenced the establishment of the voluntary agencies mentioned above. More generally the work of the Charity Organisation Society (COS) in providing a mixture of assistance and moral guidance to people in need underpinned the development of formal, individually-based social work in the last century. It established the first School of Sociology to provide formal training for social workers in 1902. This later merged with the social policy department at the LSE (see Chapter 1); and similar provision also developed at other universities, such as Birmingham.

State provision for children and adults in need in the nineteenth century largely took the form of the Poor Law. As we noted in Chapter 8, this was primarily designed as a response to destitution, and a pretty harsh one at that. However, many people were destitute because of illness, disability or vulnerability and in practice the Poor Law Guardians were expected to provide for these too. The review of the Poor Law by the Royal Commission of 1905 resulted in disagreement about the future development of social security and social care policy between the philanthropic model of the COS and the (Fabian) public service approach championed by the Webbs (see Chapter 1). For social care this remained a largely unresolved issue and, although there was a limited expansion of public provision for children and adults outside the increasingly disparaged Poor Law, philanthropic and commercial provision remained of central importance for many.

It was only with the rapid expansion of state welfare under the 1945 Labour government that public care services really developed on a comprehensive basis. In part this was a product of Labour's commitment to public provision. It was also, however, a response to a media outcry over a tragedy which exposed the failure of society to protect its most vulnerable members. This was the death in 1945 of a child, Dennis O'Neill, at the hands of his foster parent. The ensuing independent inquiry, the Monckton Report, argued such tragedies could only be prevented by the recruitment of social workers trained to identify and prevent child abuse and in 1946 a government report, the Curtis Report, recommended public agencies be created to employ such personnel.

On a number of occasions since, as we shall see, similar high-profile tragedies have exposed the vulnerability of both children and adults in modern society, and resulted in public debate about the role of state provision, leading in some instances to policy reform. It is an unfortunate irony that care services generally only reach the public eye when their ability to identify and prevent harm have failed so dramatically; and unfortunate, too, that the changes which often follow end up being driven by short-term political pressure rather than longer-term planning.

In the late 1940s, however, longer-term planning was very much in vogue. Following the Curtis Report the 1948 Children Act led to the establishment of LA children's departments employing social workers with the specific task of identifying and protecting children at risk of cruelty or abuse. In the same year LAs in mainland Britain were also required to establish health and welfare departments to provide residential and domiciliary care for vulnerable adults, when the Poor Law basis for such provision was finally abolished by the National Assistance Act. The welfare authorities established in Northern Ireland, however, had a more comprehensive remit.

These new structures provided the basis for the development of social work as a professional public service over the following decades. In 1968 provision in England and Wales was reviewed by the Seebohm Committee, which recommended they be merged to form a single point for offering personal social services – sometimes referred to as a *fifth social service*, after education, health, housing and social security. Implicit in this was the vision of holistic provision delivered by generic social service professionals who could identify and respond to individual need across the life cycle and who would also be better placed to attract resources and plan ahead.

Its recommendations were realized in 1971, when the separate departments were amalgamated into SSDs and, following other reviews, into SWDs in Scotland, whilst in 1973 Northern Ireland established integrated Health and Social Service Boards. In parallel in 1970 professional qualifications and training for social workers were reformed and a new regulatory body, CCETSW, established (see Table 11.1). From 1974 local government restructuring in England and Wales resulted in a smaller number of larger LAs with a wider range of powers and responsibilities, enhancing the scale and scope of SSDs.

These big new departments offered the prospect of comprehensive provision for individual needs. However, there was something of a contradiction in this broad brush approach to the individual nature of needs for care, and the 1980s saw the beginning of a retreat from genericism. This became more formalized following reforms in that decade and the 1990s. In 1989 the Children Act in England and Wales and parallel legislation in 1995 in Scotland and Northern Ireland introduced tighter controls over child protection procedures and in 1990 the National Health Service and Community Care Act in England and Wales and related measures elsewhere made sweeping changes to services for vulnerable adults, which we examine later. In general, however, their effect was to increase specialization between adult and children's services and to expand commissioning from non-state suppliers.

In England these processes were maintained by Labour after 1997, which further encouraged LAs to outsource rather than provide services and, in 2004, passed the Children Act, following which most SSDs in England divided into the separate departments described above. To improve provision it also, however, promoted greater partnership working between them and other children's or adult care providers, introduced new planning requirements and service standards and subjected suppliers to regular inspection to ensure these were maintained.

For Labour these measures constituted part of its wider goal of modernizing public services through improved management and service coordination and the injection of a further element of market discipline, as we outline in Chapter 18. Parallel quality assurance regimes were established by the devolved administrations (Table 11.1), though in general their approach was less market-oriented. As in England, they also promoted greater inter-agency working, particularly between adult social care and health, a process furthered by joint management in Northern Ireland where the system was streamlined from 2007.

The intention of these moves was to improve the services offered to local people by the different providers; and, as we shall see, the role of users, including carers, in determining service development and delivery was made a key element of provision. However, within these too there were contradictory pressures and outcomes. The separation of SSDs in England and, more widely, resource constraints meant LAs across the UK have increasingly focused only on their statutory responsibilities. What is more the spread of commissioning, specialization and partnership working, led to a 'hollowing out' (Glendinning and Means 2006) of the LA's role as envisaged by Seebohm. The effect, particularly in adult care, was to narrow the range of services provided and the loss of much of the generic preventative work with communities and local groups that might have been provided in the past, and in England particularly provision once again effectively divided into separate services for children and adults.

- Why are personal social services sometimes referred to as a 'residual service'?
- Why was a generic approach to provision of social services developed in the 1970s, and what has happened since?

- Should budget constraints be used as a reason to refuse access to social care services?

CHILDREN'S SERVICES

The prevention of harm to children, and the protection and support of those who cannot be adequately provided for within their family, has always been a core focus of social care. It is also the area that receives most public and media attention, often triggering pendulum swings in policy between supporting children in their families and removing them to protect them from abuse. As we saw the death of Dennis O'Neill was a key factor in the establishment of LA children's departments and in 1973 the battering to death of seven-year-old Maria Colwell, after being returned to her parents from foster care, reignited concern over child protection services.

Since then further tragedies have captured media attention and led to policy reform across the UK. The murder in 2002 of eight-year-old Victoria Climbié by relatives caring for her, despite regular contact with social workers and other professionals, forced far-reaching changes. And in 2007 the death of a toddler, Peter Connelly (known as Baby P), also known to be at high risk, at the hands of his mother, her boyfriend and their lodger prompted further shifts in policy and practice. More recently similar cases such as that of Daniel Pelka in 2012, and revelations of sexual abuse of children in care and runaways from care homes have added to the pressure for reform (APPG 2012).

Unfortunately such tragedies are far from new and it was in response to similar events that the NSPCC was established and continues today. However, the grounds for social services intervention in such cases are far from clear-cut. In 1987 social workers in Cleveland took into public care a number of children thought to be at risk of sexual abuse by their parents, based upon evidence from physical examinations by clinicians. This attracted widespread publicity and criticism of those involved for heavy-handed overreaction that was upheld in the official inquiry that followed. The conclusion that many might draw – and many social workers in particular – is that social workers are 'damned if they do act' and 'damned if they do not'. In all such cases it easy to be wise retrospectively, but social workers are required to make judgements before problems arise, and to do so in thousands of cases every year.

The 1989 Children Act sought to clarify the responsibilities of SSDs and social workers in England and Wales for the prevention of harm and abuse of children. With similar measures in Scotland and Northern Ireland in 1995, it established a common framework of principles and processes that still underlie child protection across the UK. This upholds the notion that the welfare of the child should in all cases be the paramount concern, but that parental responsibility should be maximized and families involved as much as possible in children's care, with courts also playing a greater role in decision-making in critical cases.

Legislative provisions cannot identify when children are at risk of harm, however; and inevitably protection remains a matter of professional judgement. As with the establishment of children's departments in 1948, therefore, policy has focused upon the process, rather than the content, of provision and the legislation required LAs to maintain child protection registers of all children 'at risk' in their area. Since 2004 in England and Wales these registers have given way to information collected from child protection plans. There are concerns about under-reporting in these, and data collection differences between the four UK jurisdictions; but they provide an indication of the numbers at risk of abuse or neglect. These had declined steadily from the 1990s; but more recently, partly in response to the 'Baby P' case mentioned above, they have risen sharply across the UK, from 34,623 in 2007 to 50,552 in 2011 (42,700 being in England (NSPCC 2011).

In line with the ethos of the 1989/95 legislation most children at risk remain with their families, with social workers supporting and monitoring the care their parents provide. However, where there is fear of significant harm they have the power to take children 'into care', and potentially therefore away from home. In these circumstances formal parental responsibility is transferred to the LA, or another agency, and the children are 'looked after' by them. Again, after falling over the last three decades, the numbers being looked after have recently climbed, in England for instance to 65,520 in 2011, the highest number since 1987 (DfE 2011e).

The majority of these (74 per cent in 2011) were cared for by foster parents, who are paid and supervised by LAs to provide care for such children. Around 10 per cent are cared for in children's homes, and the others in various settings or by their parents under LA super-vision. Although children's homes were once LA owned, only a minority (around 25 per cent) now are, with large equity based companies becoming the major providers (Listowel 2012). These patterns are common across the UK, although LA ownership is higher outside England.

The regulation and remit of children's services, however, have changed substantially since the 1990s and are in the process of changing again. Initially this resulted from the inquiry into Victoria Climbié's death. Conducted by Lord Laming (2003) it concluded there had been a 'fragmentation' between potential crisis intervention and more general, 'soft end', social and educational services, which left professionals unclear about the extent of their responsibilities. The ensuing Green Paper, *Every Child Matters* (DfES 2003a), led to a shift in the focus of child protection and a reconfiguration of child care services in England, billed as the most radical since 1948 (Hudson 2006). It also led to restructuring in the rest of the UK and a general, principled move from a narrow, procedural emphasis on child protection to a broader concern with prevention, early intervention and the safety and needs of all children (Stafford et al. 2011).

The starting point was the 2004 Children Act, which provided for greater collaboration between agencies working with children in England and Wales, complemented by investment in preventative and early years services. Labour had already moved in this direction in England, with its original Sure Start programme (see Chapter 12) and the Children's Fund, a targeted scheme to promote health, education, safety and opportunity for school-age children up to 13. Promoting children's welfare and wellbeing generally and a cross-agency partnership approach were also the key principles upheld by the Green Paper, which set out five outcomes for 0–19-year–olds, each with substantial resource implications: being healthy, staying safe, enjoying and achieving, making a positive contribution, and economic wellbeing.

To promote these English LAs were required to establish Directors of Children's Services to work alongside a lead Council member and take strategic responsibility for children's needs. This included managing both their care and education and bringing together statutory and non-statutory agencies. To ensure more effective cross-agency working, statutory Local Safeguarding Children Boards replaced area child protection committees in England and Wales. In consultation with other providers, English and Welsh LAs were also to produce annual Children and Young Person's Plans (CYYPs) and the Act imposed a new 'duty to cooperate' between 'partner agencies' in delivering children's services. The preferred mechanism for this in England was the creation of Children's Trusts; in Wales they took the form of

CYP Partnerships. In addition a national service framework was launched setting standards for improving provision (DoH/DfES 2004; DoH 2007b).

Subsequently most English SSDs, as noted earlier, split in two and also established Trusts, initially on an informal basis. Following criticism (Audit Commission 2008) legislation in 2009 placed these on a statutory footing, mandated them to produce CYYPs, extended the duty to cooperate and enabled the pooling of 'partners'' funds. The expectation was, as with adult care discussed below, that these measures would facilitate joint planning and commissioning and enhance arrangements for identifying and caring for children and young people needing additional help, with social workers liaising with health visitors, schools and other services.

The Laming inquiry also prompted reviews of provision in Wales and Northern Ireland and influenced another in Scotland, although developments here were also sparked by another tragic death, that of 11-week-old Caleb Ness. This too led to the reform of child protection and a new, preventative, integrated children's policy framework (Scottish Parliament 2008) and contributed to a review of social work (Scottish Executive 2006). Whilst retaining joint children's and adult services Wales and Northern Ireland also produced overarching frameworks and furthered collaborative working (WAG 2004; NIE 2006) including in Northern Ireland statutory regional Safeguarding Boards, and, more recently, provisions for a National Independent Safeguarding Board and regional board in Wales. Policy-making in Wales has also been underpinned by a strong children's rights agenda (WAG 2000, 2004) extended by the 2011 Rights of Children and Young Persons Measure, an approach also emphasized in Scotland.

Across the UK these developments were reinforced by new guidance and regulatory changes (Table 11.1). In England Ofsted became responsible for inspecting all agencies involved in delivering children's services including multi-agency working, a process complemented by the co-location of child care services and education in the then Department for Children, Schools and Families in 2007, and the appointment in 2005 of a Children's Commissioner. This followed the lead set in 2001 by Wales, and quickly adopted by the other devolved administrations. Social workers too were subject to greater regulation through separate registration bodies established in 2001, along with the Social Care Institute for Excellence (SCIE) to promote knowledge and good practice more generally. In addition from 2003 they were required to have a graduate status qualification, and workforce planning was given a new priority, for instance through two new development agencies in England (see Table 11.1).

These changes were only bedding down when Peter Connolly's death precipitated another review of child protection in England, closely followed by another after the 2010 election. The first, again by Lord Laming (2009), led to a strengthening of the government's guidance. Many of the issues identified, however, were failures of practice rather than policy, particularly in the areas of social work training, recruitment and supervision. In response the government set up a Taskforce in 2008 and in 2010 the Social Work Reform Board to ensure these were fit for purpose. Like Labour the Coalition accepted the task force's recommendations (HMG 2010c) and instigated a ten-year reform programme, including revamping the social work degree, establishing a National College of Social Work and, for the first time, Children's and Adult's Chief Social Workers for England as well as wider workforce planning. It also transferred the GSCC's functions to a new regulator, the Health and Care Professions Council (Table 11.1).

Following the second review (Munro 2011) the Coalition, while upholding the 'duty to cooperate', sanctioned a less prescriptive, rule-bound, one size fits all approach to child protection in England (DfE 2011f). For instance, statutory guidance and central oversight by the renamed DfE have been rationalized and the requirement that Children's Trust Boards produce CYPPs removed, and instead LAs are to design more flexible partnerships and formulate plans if and as they see fit according to local circumstances (DfE 2012d). It has also, however, tightened the inspection process (Ofsted 2012).

These changes are still being progressed alongside the NHS reforms in England discussed in Chapter 9 and in a context of substantially reduced LA budgets (LGA 2012). Here they are leading to greater organizational variation and marketization. For instance, some LAs have separated children's services and education, others have reunited them with adult care or are experimenting with combined children's services with other LAs, and many have developed different planning formats (NCSL/ADCS 2011). Further, some are shifting to commissioning services from external agencies, including new independent Social Work Partnerships (SWPs) and concentrating only on their statutory obligations.

For the Coalition, like Labour before it, greater flexibility and pluralization are seen as the route, not only to early help, but improved outcomes for children once in care and it has similarly sought to improve both preventative, and residential and fostering services. To meet long-standing concerns over the educational and employment outcomes of looked after children, Labour promoted greater LA involvement through 'corporate parenting schemes', while individual budgeting and greater involvement of children in decision-making followed a Green Paper in 2006 (DfES 2006) and the 2008 Children and Young Person's Act.

In addition to other measures strengthening fostering and support for care-leavers, both Labour and the Coalition also aimed to boost adoption. This involves the irrevocable transfer of parental rights and responsibilities to 'new' parents and at one time was quite widely used to provide an alternative family for unwanted and abandoned children, and was popular with married couples unable to have children. Over the latter part of the twentieth century, however, adoptions declined dramatically as birth control and abortion reduced unwanted births, and the stigma surrounding single parenthood lessened. In the mid-1970s there were over 20,000 adoptions a year in England and Wales, mostly of babies and young children. But by 1998 this had fallen to 4,614, most of whom were toddlers or older children (ONS 2010).

Labour attempted to raise adoptions in England and Wales by setting targets, increasing support for adopters and, in 2002, providing for adoption by cohabiting couples, including gays and lesbians. Though the numbers rose temporarily, they then fell again, reaching a low of 4,472 in 2010 (ONS 2011b). In the light of this, the Coalition issued an action plan to speed up the process, including a national gateway (DfE 2012e). Similar policies have also been pursued in varying ways by the devolved administrations, with Wales, for example, planning a national adoption service.

In addition to child protection, however, there are two other important dimensions to LA services for children in the UK. The first is LA responsibility for those who come into contact with the public authorities because of criminal offending behaviour. Under criminal law under 10s (8 in Scotland) are presumed not to be responsible for their actions. Beyond this age, while children can, and do, commit crimes, until they are 18 they are dealt with under separate procedures and in separate courts, or in Scotland in hearings that have been part of LAs' social work services since 1968.

How to respond to the problems, and needs, of child offenders has been a matter of significant policy debate and disagreement for a long time, however; and the contradiction between helping children and controlling criminal behaviour was captured by the French critical theorist, Donzelot (1980) in his study, *The Policing of Families*. In the 1960s a *welfare* approach was promoted, under which child offenders would generally be cared for by LAs as part of their social work functions. Since the 1980s there has been a shift to a greater emphasis on a *justice* model under which punishment and deterrence were deemed more appropriate. In reality, however, both principles continued to inform policy and practice, though in Scotland the former appears to have become stronger with the Children's Hearing system, updated in 2011, maintaining a more welfare-based approach. Since 2011 the WG also used its legislative powers to promote a 'children first' approach based on diversion rather than custodial interventions (Drakeford 2012).

In England the Labour governments of the 2000s extended custodial and surveillance measures, particularly new anti-social behaviour orders (ASBOs), curfews and parenting orders, and developed various intensive family intervention projects to help families with multiple problems (DCFS 2010) – an approach emulated in Scotland and elsewhere. These measures encouraged inter-agency collaboration with social workers working alongside other professionals to tackle youth crime and support young people and their families in addressing the problems that led to offending behaviour (Muncie 2009). This is something of a 'policing' role for social workers; and, in carrying it out they are working with, and within, the criminal justice system. It has also been developed further in England under the Coalition, including a 'payment-by-results' scheme for the most troubled families, and a fast track punishment system to replace ASBOs with criminal behaviour orders and crime prevention injunctions (HO 2011, 2012).

The other area of LA responsibility for children is, as indicated earlier, the oversight, development and delivery of wider support services for families and children, particularly early years provision and support for higher need groups. As we discuss in Chapter 12 these have been progressively extended since the early 1990s, with LAs acquiring new responsibilities to ensure the availability of places and provide information and advice for parents and providers as well as approving and monitoring these. Here too similar investment and provisions have been made in Scotland and Wales and enhancing preventive and early intervention services remain a priority across the UK, though with different emphases on state and non-state provision, and developing in Northern Ireland at a slower pace (Gray and Birrell 2012).

The aim of the changes flowing from *Every Child Matters* and more recent policy-making has been to create more integrated services for children and families at LA level. These mirrored to some extent the reforms of 1948, and, although radical in some ways, were also a return to these principles. In England and in some parts of Scotland they also marked the end of the comprehensive departments established in the 1970s, although this was also driven by the changes to adult services discussed below. The underlying intention has been to foster a more preventative approach and promote the welfare of all children, although the impact of this has been mixed and LA provision has varied (Churchill 2011). This resource-intensive development, however, may be difficult to sustain in a climate of financial retrenchment, with cutbacks leading to more targeted initiatives, a narrower focus on child protection and more outsourcing.

COMPREHENSION QUESTIONS

- What were the key recommendations of *Every Child Matters*, and why did they take the form they did?
- How has the Coalition government sought to change child protection and children's services?
- What is the difference between the *welfare* and *justice* approaches to provisions for children with criminal offending behaviour?

REFLECTIVE QUESTION

- When should children be removed from their home to protect them from harm?

ADULT SERVICES

State provision of services to vulnerable adults can also be traced back in their modern form to the establishment of the LA health and welfare departments that took over this responsibility from the Poor Law in 1948. Unlike the centrally-directed universalist NHS, however, these services were not provided free at the point of use but remained means-tested, creating a funding difference that has, as we discuss later, become a major policy issue.

In practice the users of these services vary tremendously, and to a significant extent have unique needs. Nevertheless major user groups can be identified, and provision has largely been developed around these (Table 11.2), although some have needs that bisect such groupings (Glasby 2012). This classification can also be misleading in other ways too, for elderly people do not need care services because they are old. Many older people do not need individual help, but those who do because of chronic sickness, disability or mental illness, can get categorized together as older people for accounting and statistical purposes, introducing an element of *ageism* (see Chapter 17) into adult services. Users also often have overlapping health and social care needs, and securing concerted provision from health authorities and LAs has vexed successive governments.

Provision under the Poor Law was dominated by the institutional approach that governed nineteenth-century public service philosophy and was symbolized by the workhouse. This in effect provided a crisis service for those in need of care. By the 1950s workhouses had disappeared, but many vulnerable adults (including significant numbers of older people) were still being looked after in residential establishments, many run by LAs. In 1962 Townsend's study, *The Last Refuge*, exposed the poor, uncaring nature of some of this provision and fuelled a shift towards supporting vulnerable people in their own homes and being cared for within the community, referred to as *community care*. As in children's services, further accounts of ill-treatment have intermittently fuelled policy change, most recently media exposure in 2011 of abuses at a residential unit in Bristol for people with learning difficulties and subsequent highly critical inspections of other homes (CQC 2012).

Debate over the relative merits of residential and community care, the most appropriate forms of each and ensuring their quality continues to dominate adult care policy. The issues extend across all user groups; for instance, the last three decades of the twentieth century saw a large-scale shift of provision for those with mental health needs from psychiatric hospitals (many of which closed down) to community-based settings. They also extend across the range of service providers and within the public sector across the organizational divide between care and health. A significant amount of care for chronically sick adults is provided in hospitals; and it is in part in order to move such patients out of hospitals that domiciliary care has been so strongly promoted.

The changing balance of residential and community care for adults is thus a complex, and to some extent a contradictory, story which has resulted in some dramatic changes in the scope and nature of provision. In the 1980s the pressure to reduce hospital and LA residential care was met by a major expansion of commercial and voluntary homes. This was largely financed by public funds because providers were able to receive means-tested social security benefits for those residents (in practice a large number) entitled to them under a regulatory change made in 1980. The result was a surge in the number of places and social security spending.

For the Conservative government of the time, which had pledged to reduce social security expenditure, this was a serious embarrassment. In 1989 it published a White Paper outlining a radically different approach to the public funding of adult care. This was implemented through the 1990 NHS and Community Care Act and associated guidance. The government's aim was not only to cut social security costs, however. It was also part of a more general reform of public services designed to introduce an element of competition between different providers, and promote domiciliary services as the preferred care option (Means and Smith 2008).

The act transferred responsibility for what was now referred to as community care to LA SSDs, along with some of the money that would otherwise have been paid in benefits. Eighty-five per cent of this, however, was to be spent on non-statutory rather than LA provision. SSDs were also expected to work closely with NHS agencies to develop a comprehensive local service for adults, which could be specified in 'service level agreements' between them. Whether effective collaboration took place in all circumstances is questionable, however, as the 'bed-blocking' scandals at the turn of the century revealed. This is the problem caused when hospital beds could not be allocated to patients on waiting lists because they were occupied by chronically sick adults who could be provided for in residential or community settings, but for whom no places were available. It is a telling example of the difficulties experienced in planning for community care across different organizations and budget streams, particularly for people with cross-cutting needs, and is one of the factors that led to further changes.

The community care reforms also changed the role of both LAs and social workers in adult social care. LAs became responsible for planning and commissioning rather than directly providing services. Social workers, now referred to as 'care managers', took on an enabling role and became responsible for assessing people's needs and arranging appropriate care packages from one or more public, commercial or voluntary providers. In part this remained a casework task. But it also entailed financial brokerage because care managers were responsible for purchasing services and hence managing (and rationing) the (fixed) budget held by their departments and other agencies. In taking such decisions they had to take into account the financial constraints imposed by such budgets.

What is more, though there had always been a mixed economy of care, the shift to community care forced a large-scale switch from state to commercial and third sector suppliers and away from residential care, trends that continued throughout the 2000s. In England, for instance, by 2010, of the 1.7 million receiving care services only 0.2 million received residential care (Macrory 2011) and only 31 per cent of the 1.75 million social care jobs were in the public sector, whilst 46 per cent and 23 per cent were in the commercial and third sectors respectively (SfC 2010a), which by then provided over three-quarters of adult care services (SfC 2010b). Similar shifts have occurred in the rest of the UK, although, especially in Scotland, publicly provided care has remained more significant (Bell 2010).

The need for improved coordination of these varying providers was, as in children's services, a major factor in mounting pressure for further reform across the UK, particularly in surmounting what some termed the 'Berlin Wall' between health and care services. In England it culminated in another White Paper (DoH 2006), followed by a further reconfiguration of adult social care and the beginnings of another change in social work roles.

This included a more strategic approach to cooperative working, with performance targets against which providers could be held to account, mirroring the developments in other service areas discussed in Chapter 18. As in children's services, LA Directors of Adult Social Care were established and charged with developing partnerships with health authorities and other providers. This included the formation of joint commissioning frameworks, linking LA departments and the then Primary Care Trusts (PCTs), made easier where the two were geographically coterminous (see Chapter 9).

They were expected to work together through specialist teams, local area agreements and integrated care plans for users. Their budgets and planning cycles were also made more flexible so commissioning could be 'practice based', with GPs and PCTs in the leading role. In addition a common regulator, the Care Quality Commission (CQC) took over from other authorities in 2009 (Table 11.1). Similar attempts to knit the two services together were made in Scotland through the establishment of community health partnerships and in Wales through joint working arrangements, which (potentially) were encouraged by the structuring of social and health care in Northern Ireland.

Labour's reforms also encompassed another key component of its modernization programme, the greater involvement of users in service design, commissioning and evaluation. This included a pledge to increase control of their care for individual users, signalled in a Green Paper and the concordat, *Putting People First* (DoH 2005, 2007c). As mentioned above, adult care had from the 1990s largely been organized by social workers who assembled care packages from different providers, subject to the budget set by LAs or PCTS. The concordat, however, ushered in measures entitling users to choose, purchase and manage the services they felt best met their requirements.

Central to this were provisions for direct payments, which would allow users to buy services instead of relying on those contracted for them by care managers. These had been sanctioned for younger disabled people by a private member's act in 1996 and subsequently extended along with the requirement from 2001 that LAs offer them as an option to all users. Such payments were not problem-free, and did not always provide the support needed; but research suggested they did enable users to live more independent lives (Rummery 2006). And so, in what was described as 'the most important and exciting' development in adult social care since the 1940s (Glasby and Littlechild 2009), Labour promised to provide personal budgets for most users by 2011. These could be taken as a direct payment or a service managed by the LA or a third party with users determining the purchasing.

This move to 'self-directed' care was part of a broader shift towards *personalization* and *co-production* in public service provision, which we discuss in Chapter 18 (and see Needham 2011). It has also been taken up by the Coalition government in England, as part of more general commitments to devolved decision-making and greater marketization in social care, spelt out in a White Paper in 2010. This espoused a more consumer-driven, preventative, outcomes-oriented service based on seven principles: personalization, partnership, plurality of provision, protection against abuse, high productivity providers, and greater worker autonomy (DoH 2010c).

Personal budgets are at the heart of this new policy drive, and were to be rolled out, preferably as a direct payment, for all adult care users by 2013. Realizing their potential in a period of fiscal austerity may, however, prove difficult and some fear they might devolve risks as well as responsibilities to users, and in practice mask cuts in provision. Nevertheless over time they are likely to transform the delivery of adult social care and LAs have been given the lead role in growing new competitive, user-driven care markets, including micro, social and mutual enterprises, and encouraging niche and bespoke traders. This is to be achieved through cutting block contracts and most remaining public provision, with the separation of commissioning and supply becoming 'the norm' (DoH 2010c), in effect completing the reforms of the early 1990s.

Thus the 2012 Health and Social Care Act provided for the phased implementation of new Any Qualified Provider arrangements (see Chapter 9), and the 2011 Localism Act empowered third sector organizations and others to challenge LAs if they believed they could provide services differently or better. As in child care, there is also encouragement for the transfer of adult social work services to SWPs, while to facilitate choice and an efficient market under the 2013 Care Bill LAs are to ensure access to advice and information as a 'universal service', which could be supplied by a range of providers (DoH 2010c).

More generally, the development of adult social care has continued to depend on a closer integration with health care provision, although in practice this is still patchy and geographically varied (Audit Commission 2011). New mechanisms for partnership working were included in the 2012 Health and Social Care Act which placed a statutory duty on LAs and the new CCGs to work together to promote local health and wellbeing (See Chapter 9; and DoH 2010c, 2011e). This requires LAs to take the lead in producing Joint Strategic Needs Assessments (JSNAs) and Joint Health and Wellbeing Strategies (JHWSs), developed though the new, locally accountable Health and Wellbeing Boards. To sustain more seamless provision pooled budgeting has also been enhanced, sharing of back-office functions encouraged, and new guarantees and projects for coordinated patient care introduced, along with the transfer of some, albeit limited, resources from the NHS to LAs.

Furthermore from 2012, as outlined earlier, social work regulation was transferred to the (retitled) Health and Care Professions Council and NICE (see Chapter 9) renamed the National Institute for Health and Care Excellence, with its remit extended to social care. The government has signed an agreement with social care providers (DoH 2010d) and, as in other public services, established a new outcomes-based performance management system, including local accounts and reporting through the Health and Wellbeing Boards (DoH 2011e, 2012c). Following the revelations of abuses in adult care homes referred to earlier there has also been a tightening of the operation of the CQC and a requirement for LAs to establish Safeguarding Adults Boards (DoH 2011f).

Personalization of adult care is also leading to workforce redesign and the remodelling of job roles aimed to generate a less task-oriented, more user-driven working culture. As indicated earlier self-directed care packaging, with users shopping around for tailored support and contracting staff, implies changed responsibilities for social workers, particularly greater demand for information and advice and brokerage support. For domiciliary care staff more generally it heralds a growth in the numbers working as Personal Assistants (PAs) employed directly by users or a wider range of agencies, entailing familiarity with different employment regulations and, as for new all staff, new ways of working.

Social work training is being reformed, with the changes impelled by concerns over children's services also incorporating the new demands in adult care. Historically, apart from professionals such as occupational therapists, care staff had little or no training or specific qualifications. This has been changing since the early 2000s, however, and more recently the Coalition has revamped the qualifications and training system, expanded care apprenticeships and established, from 2013, a system of assured voluntary registration with the Health and Care Professions Council. Significantly its workforce development plans stress not only the new skill sets needed by PAs (DoH 2011e) and others, but LAs' role in cross-provider workforce commissioning (SfC 2010a, 2010b) and wider training in preventative and community work and network building (SfC 2011). Again linking with the government's wider agenda, they also emphasize the role of LA commissioners in promoting support both within, and by, the neighbourhood, and allowing for such 'support circles' in service planning (SfC 2011).

The Coalition's policies were reaffirmed and extended in a second White Paper in 2012 (HMG 2012a) and the 2013 Care Bill. In line with the Law Commission's (2011) recommendations, this will establish a new, consolidated legal framework, including the establishment of local adult safeguarding boards, and will introduce the principle of placing individual wellbeing at the heart of social care services. This is intended to ensure that LAs develop more pre-emptive cost-saving approaches and aim to fit services around users' needs. There is a new preventative duty on LAs, to provide all users of council-funded support (and their carers, see Chapter 5) with care and support plans, with users also entitled to receive a personal budget.

Prevention and personalization have also been embraced in the rest of the UK, though at a different pace and with a distinctive terminology and slant. After a slow take-up in the 2000s individual budgets have become central to the self-directed support agenda instigated in Scotland in 2010 (SG 2011d) and became an entitlement following legislation in 2012. In Wales they are being developed under the banner of 'citizen-centred care' and similarly form part of a long-term strategy to foster user-led services (WAG 2009b; WG 2012d), including legislation in 2012 compelling LAs to provide information and advice services and an increasing emphasis on prevention.

Policy in both also involves renewed attempts to synchronize care and health services and a shift to prevention and outcomes-based inspection. In 2011 the Scottish government set up a new regulator, Social Care and Social Work Improvement Scotland, and plans to replace community health partnerships with strengthened health and social care partnerships with pooled budgets and a jointly accountable officer delivering to national outcomes cutting across health and care (SG 2012c). From 2012 Welsh LAs and Health Boards have, like their English counterparts, to produce joint local health, social care and wellbeing strategies and assessments, together with care plans for individual users, and legislation promoting closer integration is also under way. Wales has also established a National Independent Safeguarding Board for children and adults and a single code of practice for social services, with LAs as well as non-statutory providers having to register with the Care and Social Services Inspectorate.

In Northern Ireland, although the government is now committed to self-directed services, development has been slower with care policy generally given low priority and, despite its integrated structure, often health-dominated and poorly joined-up (NIE 2011b; Heenan and

Birrell 2011). Partly due to the concerns in England it has, however, embarked on a new social work strategy (NIE 2012) and tighter regulation, making registration with the Northern Ireland Social Care Council compulsory for all care staff. Registration has also been extended to all staff in Scotland and widened in Wales.

Across the UK, however, given the complex nature of health and social care and the range of providers now involved, questions remain as to the most effective form of concerted action, with some now arguing that a full integration of the two services may be the way forward (see Glasby 2012). The form and outcomes of personalization too are still uncertain, as are its affordability and the likelihood of meaningful change for users. In England especially the emergence of more diverse care markets and reliance on engaged neighbourhoods also pose new questions about the capacity of local communities to provide care.

What is clear, however, is that adult services now come from a diverse range of public, commercial and non-profit providers who offer, in theory at least, more user-driven responses to care needs, including for those with most extreme needs hospitals, and residential and nursing homes. However, the thrust of policy development remains as since the 1990s the promotion of care in, and by, the community. For the most part in practice, however, this means care in users' homes or that of the family member caring for them (see Chapter 5); and such family care frequently requires supportive assistance. This can include *day care*, so those needing assistance can get out of the house during the day, and *respite care*, providing longer periods of alternative support to relieve both carers and those being cared for.

More generally public, commercial and non-profit agencies all supply *domiciliary care* services, such as assistance with bathing, dressing, housework and meals, to support vulnerable adults living at home, whether or not they are cared for by relatives. LAs can also provide other forms of help such as home adaptations; indeed, since the 1970 Chronically Sick and Disabled Persons Act they have been obliged to provide these, although what *is* required is for the LA to judge. Over the last decade new models of care have been added to domiciliary provision, including: live-in carers or shared-living (where a paid carer or house-sharer provides support), extra care housing, assistive technology, telecare, re-ablement arrangements (helping individuals to resettle on discharge from hospital), and peer and neighbourhood support schemes.

The quality of care services and the high staff turnover generally, however, remain a source of concern with domiciliary and residential services in England for instance recently subject to extensive criticism, leading to tighter inspection (EHRC 2011; CQC 2012). Ultimately, however, their availability and effectiveness depends on adequate resourcing, and this problem of how to pay for adult care services remains at the heart of policy planning and debate.

COMPREHENSION QUESTIONS

- What is community care, and why did it become a policy priority in the 1990s?
- Why has integrated working between adult care and health services proved so difficult to achieve?
- What is meant by 'personalization' in adult social care?
- In what ways are the Coalition's policies changing adult social care provision in England?

REFLECTIVE QUESTION

- To what extent should service users be encouraged to determine their own care needs without professional support?

FUNDING ADULT CARE

Publicly funded adult care, including personal budgets, is needs- and means-tested, though the approach taken varies across the UK. Eligibility is determined first by LA assessments of an individual's need for care. In England since 2003 these have to comply with a national framework within which LAs have discretion as to which of four levels of need (critical, substantial, moderate, low) they fund (DoH 2003b). Scotland operates a different tool, but with the threshold used again varying by LA. Northern Ireland, however, applies a single threshold, and Wales is also developing a single national eligibility system and portable assessments (ICSS 2011; WAG 2011d).

LAs can provide free support; but in practice many services are subject to charges with eligibility for exemptions determined by a financial assessment, as discussed in Chapter 6. Central government has long encouraged such charging by assuming a certain income from user payments in the financing of LAs' community care budgets, with social workers increasingly becoming resource controllers (Bailey 2011).

These issues were considered in a review of funding for social care in1999 by the Sutherland Royal Commission (Box 11.1). It distinguished between the living and care costs of those needing long-term care, proposing the latter should be provided free, with living costs subject to means-testing. The government rejected this recommendation, however, and in England the use of charging together with means-testing has continued. Residential care has, though, become subject to national regulations, with (in 2012) individuals having more than £23,250 in assets expected to pay their own fees, with housing included in this assessment, as long as no dependant is living in the home, forcing some to sell their homes to pay for the costs of their care.

LAs also design charging policies for domiciliary care, within national guidelines; and, as a result provision has diverged according to their differing weightings of needs assessments, priorities and resources – leading in effect to 152 different English care systems (Dilnot 2011) and, for users, a postcode lottery in access to public-funded care. This has also contributed to a growth in self-funding, which by 2010 accounted for around 45 per cent of residential care places, with a further 25 per cent being partly-funded by relatives or others (CQC 2011) and a substantial market in fee-paying domiciliary care, much of it unregulated.

Free personal care was also rejected by the Northern Ireland government in 2009, despite some support for it. In Scotland, however it has been provided for the over 65s in residential care and their own homes since 2002, with only direct living costs met by individuals. This has been a high profile commitment in Scotland and has proved highly popular (Sutherland 2008). Successive Welsh administrations have favoured a similar move. Until recently though they had no powers to override LAs' right to charge, but since 2011 a national system capping weekly non-residential care service charges at £50 for all users has been introduced (ICSS 2010; WAG 2011d).

The question of who should pay for the costs of adult social care remains a critical policy issue, however, especially in England where a succession of studies have highlighted the problem and, more recently, the increasingly restricted nature of LA support (HoCHSC 2010; CQC 2011; Beresford et al. 2011). What is more it is a mounting problem as costs are bourgeoning due to rising demand, especially from a growing elderly population but also from increasing numbers of younger adults with complex needs. Recent projections suggest for instance that by 2035 a quarter of England's population will be over 65, with the fastest growth rate being amongst the over-85s (see Table 17.2). The numbers of adults with a learning disability will also have grown by a third (ONS 2012c; Humphries et al. 2010). UK public spending on long-term care was projected to rise from 1.2 to 1.7 per cent of GDP between 2009 and 2029, an increase of 40 per cent (Dilnot 2011). Not surprisingly this has been the subject of a range of policy reviews and reform proposals, as summarized in Box 11.1.

> **Box 11.1 Key reports and policy documents on long-term care in England**
>
> - 1999 (Sutherland) Royal Commission on Long Term Care *With Respect to Old Age: Long Term Care: Rights and Responsibilities*
> - 2006 (Wanless) Social Care Review, *Securing Good Care For Older People: Taking a Long-Term View* (King's Fund)
> - 2008 Consultation Paper/National Debate, *The Case for Change: Why England Needs a New Care and Support System* (DoH)
> - 2009 Green Paper, *Shaping the Future of Care Together* (DoH)
> - 2010 White Paper *Building the National Care Service* (DoH)
> - 2011 Law Commission *Adult Social Care*
> - 2011 (Dilnot) Commission on the Funding of Care and Support, *Fairer Care Funding*
> - 2011 Consultation/Engagement Exercise, *Caring for our Future: Shared Ambitions for Care and Support* (DoH)
> - 2012 White Paper *Caring for Our Future: Reforming Care and Support* (HMG)
> - 2013 Care Bill

For most individuals, however, the likelihood of needing such care is unpredictable and its funding poorly understood. Furthermore the range of policy options is wide and extends from the universalistic schemes pursued in some countries (Glendinning and Bell 2008) to market-based measures, varying in their approach to individual contributions, the starting-age for these and the use of housing assets. They include various permutations of:

- Raising inheritance and/or capital gains tax
- Changing tax relief for pensions
- Removing entitlements for universal and categorical benefits (see Chapter 8) for better-off older people
- Provisions for disability-linked annuities
- Voluntary private insurance
- State-backed insurance (covering some costs, topped up by voluntary insurance)
- Comprehensive, compulsory state insurance
- A tax-funded state–individual partnership (providing free or income-related support or a mix of both).

Despite the pressure for reform, therefore, agreeing a way forward has proved problematic, with governments often reluctant to undertake policy changes that will commit future administrations to large-scale financial support. The most recent review, the Dilnot Commission (2011), would have required £3.6 billion of government funding by 2026. It included: capping individual lifetime care contributions, excluding general living costs, at £35,000, restricting annual contributions to between £7,000 and £10,000, and raising the capital threshold at which the full cost of residential care becomes payable to £100,000. It also called for free lifelong care for all disabled children and, yet again, better integration of health and care services.

In 2013, however, the Coalition government's 2013 Care Bill finally laid out a new national funding scheme for England, based to some extent on the Dilnot Commission's recommendations and providing lifelong free care for those who turn 18 with eligible needs. To ensure those who have saved for their old age do not lose all their savings, this allows for the establishment by 2016 of a lifetime cap on contribution that individuals will have to make to care home costs. Initially set at around £72,000 for those over state pension age the cap will be adjusted annually in line with inflation and, as recommended by Dilnot, does not include living costs which will be set at a standard amount. However, from 2015 people will have a legal right to postpone paying care home costs during their lifetime through an LA administered deferred payment scheme, with LAs recouping the charges from their estate on death.

The government also plans to raise the threshold, including property, for full payment of residential care from £23,250 to £118,000 from 2016 (DoH 2013). The aim of these changes is to provide national minimum eligibility standards so that costs are consistent across England; and linked to this, individuals will be entitled to ask for an assessment for care. The intention is that they will make it easier for people to take out private insurance to cover future care costs, which will be simpler to predict, and will encourage providers to offer new ways of providing these (DoH 2013).

These new measures are intended to inject much needed certainty in planning adult social care, for individuals, LAs and providers, and to ensure that most financial support remains targeted on those with the greatest needs and least wealth. The governments in Scotland, Wales and Northern Ireland will need to determine to what extent they will follow the new path being taken in England, especially given the increasing pressure on public budgets produced by their currently more generous policies; and it is not clear yet how they will respond to the continuing challenge of paying for social care. Across the UK, however, difficult decisions lie ahead for policy-makers and care funding is likely to remain a major policy issue.

COMPREHENSION QUESTIONS

- How, and why, have the policies for adult social care differed across the separate administrations in the UK?
- Why has it proved so difficult to reach policy agreement on long-term care funding?

REFLECTIVE QUESTION

- To what extent should individual citizens be expected to provide for their own future needs for long-term care?

FURTHER READING

A good general introduction to the evolution of children's services is provided by Frost and Parton (2009) while Stafford et al. (2011) provide a detailed survey of child protection across the UK. Means and Smith (2008) is the established text on the development of community care. Glasby (2012) offers a stimulating and accessible introduction to the issues involved in the delivery of adult health and social care; and Beresford et al. (2011) offer a user perspective. Needham (2011) discusses the new policy issues of personalization and co-production of services. Current developments in children's and adult services can be tracked at www.dfe.gov.uk, www.doh.gov.uk and www.dclg.gov.uk. Information for Scotland, Wales and Northern Ireland can be found on the websites of the devolved administrations (see Chapter 6) and a guide to the main UK think tanks can be found in Brunsdon and May (2012) at www.blackwellpublishing.com/alcock4e/.

12
Education

SUMMARY OF KEY POINTS

- There are two contrasting views of education: liberal education and training.
- Education is a major contributor to the development of human capital and is regarded as a continuing need for all citizens.
- There are different levels of education provision: early years, primary, secondary, further, higher and continuing, though the last three are increasingly seen in terms of lifelong learning.
- Education policy has been devolved to the administrations in Northern Ireland, Scotland and Wales and in some respects developed on different lines within the UK.
- Public schools still offer private education to a minority of children from wealthy backgrounds.
- Universal state education up to 15 was introduced in 1944.
- From the late 1960s comprehensive schools replaced the *tripartite* system of secondary education.
- A national school curriculum was introduced in 1988 and more power devolved to schools. Recent reforms have changed the former and enabled schools in England to become self-governing Academies.
- School education aims to guarantee minimum standards and especially in England to provide choice for parents and pupils.
- Further and higher education (FE, HE) have expanded significantly since the late twentieth century, bringing changes in their funding and governance and, particularly in England, increasing marketization. Continuing education has also become more important.
- Concerns over equality of opportunity in education have led governments to target extra resources on certain schools or categories of learners.
- Concerns over standards have led to new modes of quality assurance and performance management.

WHAT IS EDUCATION?

Education is about learning and teaching; and education policy is concerned with the ways in which these are organized and delivered in order to ensure that all citizens have the appropriate opportunities to learn. However, at the heart of education policy is a distinction, and perhaps a conflict, over what should be the primary aims or functions of individual learning. This is the distinction between education as the acquisition of knowledge (liberal education) and education as the acquisition of skills (training):

- *Liberal education*, sometimes presented as the 'traditional' basis for policy, is the notion that education should be provided to equip citizens – and especially children – with knowledge for its own sake (we should all have the opportunity to know something about the world in which we live), and in order to develop cognitive capacity (learning, and testing, helps us to develop our minds). In such a model knowledge is based upon a traditional curriculum (history, geography and science), and achievement is measured by the levels of understanding reached, with an undergraduate and, increasingly, a postgraduate degree being the ultimate goal (at least for some). In the most extreme form of this approach the content of education is of little importance compared to the level of qualification reached: for instance, the study of Latin and ancient Greek was once widely considered evidence of high academic achievement despite the fact that virtually no one communicated in them.
- *Education as training* in contrast stresses the content of education and the practical utility of the knowledge acquired. In this approach education should be geared to providing citizens with skills and competences that will be of value to them in their working lives and of value to society more generally by ensuring that the population is equipped to perform the tasks needed to sustain and enhance economic and social development. In such a model the content of the curriculum is as important as the level of ability reached, and greater emphasis is placed upon vocational knowledge and skills. Vocational training may also be valuable to adults and linked to labour market experience. In part because of this link, unlike European and many emerging economies, it has traditionally had a low status and priority in UK policy although, as we shall see, there have been moves to raise its profile in recent times.

In practice, however, the distinction between liberal education and training is far from clear cut, and to a large extent the two approaches can be pursued in tandem: for instance, one could study Latin alongside computer science. What is more, supporters of both models agree about the importance of some core elements of provision, particularly the role of the 'three Rs' (Reading, wRiting and aRithmetic – not in fact all Rs at all), in underpinning all learning and teaching. Nevertheless within educational debate there have been changes in the balance of emphasis between the two and this has had consequences for policy development.

Of most recent significance here were the policy debates of the 1970s. At the beginning of the decade a series of documents by right-wing critics of education policy, collectively known as the *Black Papers*, argued that basic literacy and numeracy skills (the three Rs) were being neglected and called for reforms to address this problem. The issue was taken up by the Labour Prime Minister, James Callaghan, who initiated what he called a *Great Debate* about the direction of education policy, in which he claimed there were: 'complaints from industry that new recruits from schools sometimes do not have the basic tools do to the job that is required' (Callaghan 1976, in Finch 1984). Following this a Green Paper (Secretary of State for E&S 1977) was issued outlining the case for schools to pay more attention to developing an understanding of industry and the economy, and provide pupils with practical skills.

The Conservative governments of the 1980s shared many of these concerns and strove to extend training in technical skills through initiatives such as City Technology Colleges directly supported by industry. In practice though few were established, while the National School Curriculum, introduced in 1988 (see below), confirmed the continuing centrality of many traditional subjects and approaches. Nevertheless the concern to raise the status of vocational provision had an enduring effect, shifting education policy towards the enhancement of skills as well as knowledge. This was captured in the increasing focus upon education as investment in *human capital*, that is the idea that high standards of education, covering knowledge and skills, are of benefit to individuals and the society in which they live, and that public outlay in such 'capital' is an essential priority for government.

In a Labour Party conference speech in 1996, the future Prime Minister, Tony Blair, claimed that the three social policy priorities for a Labour government would be 'education,

education, and education', because investment in improved educational standards was crucial to broader economic and social development. This view was reinforced by a series of reports highlighting the UK's productivity, qualifications and skills deficits compared to competitor countries (Moser 1998: Ketels and Porter 2003; Leitch 2006) and the need to ensure the prospective and existing workforce were equipped to meet the challenges of a fast-changing, increasingly globalized, knowledge-based economy. It also chimed with research emphasizing the importance of early years learning and, more broadly, the role of an 'active' or 'social investment' state in countering unemployment and enabling individuals to support themselves (Esping-Andersen et al. 2002; Morel et al. 2011).

Following Blair's pledge the Labour governments of 1997–2010 instigated a series of measures to raise basic standards, especially in schools, supported by substantial additional investment in state education more generally. As we shall discuss, its drive to improve educational performance also entailed expanding provision for young children and support for education for all, particularly through what was termed *continuing* or *lifelong learning*. Raising educational standards across society to boost the UK's economic competitiveness remains a key policy objective for the Coalition government, although it has also emphasized more traditional elements of the curriculum and greater self-provisioning by those over school age.

Education, however, is one of the areas where policy-making was devolved and though sharing these concerns, the administrations in Scotland, Wales and Northern Ireland, have often taken a different approach to that of Westminster governments. Scotland has long had a distinct educational system (Patterson 2003) and, since devolution, its policy-makers have extended this in various ways. Devolution has also brought changes in aspects of provision in Wales and Northern Ireland and since the elections of 2010 and 2011 differences within the UK have become more marked, with further divergence in the pipeline.

THE STRUCTURE OF PROVISION

Educational policy across the UK, as in other societies, provides for a range of learners in a variety of settings that can be classified into six broad levels or tiers.

EARLY YEARS PROVISION

Sometimes referred to as nursery education, preschool or foundation years learning (DfE 2012a), this is offered to children before the commencement of formal compulsory education, which in Britain begins in the year in which a child is five and in Northern Ireland at four. Attendance is therefore voluntary and until recently state provision was locally determined and often patchy. There was also a lack of clarity over provision seen as directly 'educational' and that supplying 'childcare' for working parents. From the 1990s, however, early years learning came to be seen as taking place in a range of settings, and, in 2006, with the aim of developing an integrated framework the Childcare Act removed the legal distinction between the two in England.

A more coordinated policy was also established elsewhere and state support expanded significantly across the UK. By 2012 English, Scottish and Welsh local authorities (LAs) were required to ensure places were available for all three- and four-year-olds whose parents want early years provision. Children in this age group are entitled to a free part-time place (15 hours a week) until they reach school age and 'disadvantaged' two-year-olds in England and Wales have a similar entitlement. It can be taken up in an LA maintained nursery school or unit, children's centre, commercial or voluntary run day nursery or playgroup, or with a childminder, though the balance between these varies nationally and locally. Provision is not a requirement in Northern Ireland, but is governed by a target of securing one year of preschool experience for all children whose parents want it that has largely been met. Each country has also developed an early years curriculum that providers must adhere to, with Wales giving extra support to those offering bilingual or Welsh medium provision.

PRIMARY EDUCATION

Until recently education across the UK continued to the age of 16. Under legislation in 2008 bringing England into line with many other countries, young people are now required to engage in education, training or workplace training until they are 17 (18 from 2015), although occasionally parents can make arrangements for their children to be educated at home. For the first seven years, up to the age of 11 (12 in Scotland), this is called primary education and usually takes place in separate infant (5–7) and junior schools (7–11), with children entering in the school year (September to September) in which they reach this age. The vast majority attend the school nearest their home and most schools admit all local children although, as we shall see, there are some specialist and also some private schools. Though with differing frameworks following devolution, primary education across the UK is geared to providing children with basic skills, particularly in literacy and numeracy, and teachers in these schools are trained specifically in such work.

SECONDARY EDUCATION

At the age of 11 children move into secondary education, and this almost always involves a change of school, although in some localities it is further complicated by a period of attendance at separate 'middle schools' from 9 to 13. Secondary schools also generally take local children, but they are normally larger and cover a wider area. At one time, as we shall see, children were selected for different schools on the basis of an assessment of ability and this still continues to some extent in some areas. Until recently there was selection in Northern Ireland, involving religious as well as academic segregation and, though the centrally-run assessment was removed in 2009, many schools still operate ability-based selection schemes.

State primary and secondary schools in England, Wales and Northern Ireland are governed by national curricula and assessment systems, although in England, as explained later, Academies and Free Schools do not have to teach the national curriculum. These stem back to the common national curriculum imposed in 1988 that split school learning into four key stages (KS), with external standard assessment tests (commonly termed SATs) at the ages of 7, 11 and 14 and public examinations at 16. But since devolution Welsh administrations have pursued a particular approach to curriculum development, delivery and assessment and moved to teacher-based testing prior to the exams at 16, as have those in Northern Ireland. Scotland, which has long had a separate system, has favoured non-statutory curriculum guidelines, revised in 2012, and giving LAs more flexibility. It has also maintained a different assessment system with formal exams spread out over the school years. In England testing at 7 and 14 also became teacher-based and the curriculum subject to several revisions, with, as outlined later, a new slimmed down scheme phased in by 2014. Alongside it is a new curriculum (DfE 2011b) for children with special needs, most of whom, as in the rest of the UK, attend state primaries and secondaries, though there is also a range of special schools.

Overall, however, secondary education is geared towards the preparation of children for public examinations, which are in effect a standard measure of their abilities and achievements. Until recently, apart from Scotland, the first formal assessment was the modular General Certificate in School Education (GCSE). Starting in the 11th year of schooling and ending in the 12th, at around 16, this was graded from A* to G, largely on a coursework basis, with A* to C being vital for moving onto further study. From 2015, however, a primarily exam-based GCSE graded 9 to 1 is planned for England, with the first examinations to be held in 2017. The Welsh government, however, aims to retain the modular structure and introduce 'Wales-only' GCSEs in four core subjects, whilst provision in Northern Ireland is still being reviewed.

Across the UK many schools also offer courses under the National Vocational Qualification (NVQ) scheme (SQVs in Scotland) which provides a common framework for vocational provision first developed in the late 1980s. Some of these are recognized as equivalent to a GCSE. Secondary schools also provide education (in sixth forms) up to the age of 18 in order for children to sit a higher standard of public examinations and a growing number of such 'all-through' secondary schools in England specialize in particular subject areas.

Outside Scotland these assessments are the GCE Advanced Subsidiary (AS) and Advanced (A) level examinations. Taken at age 17 and 18 respectively, they are graded from A* to E and used by universities and colleges as entry criteria for undergraduate study. In England from 2015 these too will become more exam-based, with a revised curriculum, and, unlike the GCSEs, these changes are to be implemented in Wales and Northern Ireland too. Since devolution Wales has introduced a Welsh Baccalaureate encompassing core skills and vocational as well as academic routes, as an alternative to A levels, and a related scheme for 14–19-year-olds, both of which are also set for reform (WG 2012a). And Scotland too has more recently introduced a Scottish Baccalaureate, in addition to its separate qualification structure. Here the longstanding system of Standard Grades taken at 15 or 16 was replaced in 2013 by National 4 and 5 schemes as part of a new National Qualification scheme. Still largely teacher-assessed this continues to lead onto Highers at 17 and Advanced Highers at 18.

FURTHER EDUCATION

Across the UK, however, young people can opt, usually at 16 or over, to transfer to an FE College, or into employment-based training, and from 2013 14–16-year-olds in England can also study in FE Colleges offering a combination of vocational and academic subjects. The colleges' main provision, however, encompass A levels/Advanced Highers, the Welsh and Scottish Bacs and a wide range of other (more vocational) programmes such as NVQs/SVQs. In some localities there is also the option of studying at a sixth form college and, in a new development in England, since 2012 it is also possible to study at a technical academy, studio school or university technical college, all of which offer vocationally-oriented programmes for 14–19-year-olds. In addition, many FE colleges now offer degree-level programmes.

HIGHER EDUCATION

This is more specialist education provided for adults in universities and other HE institutions (HEIs). Most students pursue an undergraduate degree (usually called a Bachelor of Arts, BA, or Bachelor of Sciences, BSc., which represents a throwback to what was once a largely male preserve) in a specialist area, such as social policy. An undergraduate degree course generally lasts for three years if completed on a full-time basis and four years in Scotland (though those with A levels or Advanced Highers can enter in the second year). Most universities also provide higher, and more specialist, postgraduate awards (at Masters level, either MA, MSc) and also research-based awards (in particular the Doctor of Philosophy, or PhD, which is a generic term for research in any area). Many 18-year-olds who achieve sufficiently high grades in their A level exams go on to study for university degrees, although universities also admit students at all ages and with a range of different educational backgrounds.

CONTINUING OR LIFELONG LEARNING

Whatever people's choices at 18 they are under increasing pressure to develop their knowledge and skills throughout their working lives and facilitating this has become a policy priority. Both HEIs and FE colleges, for instance, offer a wide range of full, part-time and short academic and professional courses for those who wish to qualify for or further a particular career, update their skills or change direction. Private providers also offer professional or work-related courses of varying types and lengths. And employers may supply or support vocational training, though this is very uneven compared to that in Europe and elsewhere.

Post-compulsory education also encompasses provision for (re-)learning basic literacy and numeracy skills, which may have been missed at school, and preparation for FE or HE through part-time GCSEs and A levels or alternative 'access' qualifications. Alongside these there is also provision geared more to personal development or leisure activities, enabling people of all ages to continue to enhance their knowledge, skills and interests. The prime policy concern, however, is work-related and here again, as we will discuss later, devolution has brought policy differentiation within the UK.

FUNDING AND ADMINISTRATION

Overall spending on education is determined by the Westminster government. That in the devolved administrations is funded by a block grant, spent as they see fit (see Chapter 6). In keeping with the policy commitments to education as an investment in individual and social development, compulsory education across the UK is provided by the state free at the point of use and funded out of general taxation; and this has been the case for over a hundred years. Non-compulsory education, however, is treated less like a public good. In the case of early years learning, though some get tax credit support, parents have to pay for provision beyond the child's free entitlement (and for childcare more generally), though further support is being planned from 2015 on (see below and Chapter 5). FE and HE is largely provided and funded by the state, but students are required to pay fees that contribute towards the cost of their education, as discussed below. More generally, postgraduates and those undertaking professional, work-related or self-development study usually have to self-fund, though some may be helped by the state or their employers.

Responsibility for state education in England is currently split between the Department for Education (DfE) covering provision up to 19 and the Department for Business, Innovation, and Skills (BIS) covering higher and continuing education (see Table 12.1) with funding for post-compulsory education channelled through the Skills Funding Agency and the Higher Education Funding Council. In Northern Ireland FE and HE policy-making and funding is located in the Department for Employment and Learning with schools overseen by the Department of Education. Policy-making in Wales and Scotland is determined by single departments, supported by the HE, and the FE and HE Funding Councils respectively, and agencies for skills development (that in Wales being advisory) (see Table 12.1).

Until recently school education (including early years learning) was administered nationally in Northern Ireland, but is now overseen by Education and Library Boards. Historically elsewhere it was managed by Local Education Authorities (LEAs), which are departments of local government established early in the last century. As discussed later and in Chapter 11, from 2004 education and other LA children's services in England were merged into one directorate or department with varying titles, though these are still often referred to as LEAs.

Since the 1980s, however, more powers over curriculum development have been taken by central government and financial and managerial responsibility devolved to schools, which were also, in 1988, given the opportunity to 'opt out' of LEA control, though most did not. The Coalition has taken this process further, legislating for schools in England to become self-governing Academies financed centrally rather than locally through the Education Funding Agency, an arm of the Department for Education established in 2012. Scotland and Wales, however, have not followed this route and remain committed to LEA controlled provision.

As indicated above, not all education in the UK is provided and funded by government, however. Firstly, in an educational market that is set to expand there are a range of fee-charging early years providers, operated by both commercial and not-for-profit agencies, with parents meeting the costs not covered by the state or relying on informal child care. Secondly, there are a number of fee-charging schools that operate outside the state education system.

These private or independent schools are often, misleadingly, called 'public schools', although in practice most only admit pupils who meet their selection criteria and whose

Table 12.1 The organization of educational provision in the UK in 2013

England	N. Ireland	Scotland	Wales
Department for Education (DfE)	Department of Education	Learning and Justice Directorate	Department for Education and Skills
Department for Business, Innovation and Skills (BIS)	Department for Employment and Learning		
		Skills Development Scotland	[Wales Employment and Skills Board]
Education Funding Agency			
Skills Funding Agency			
Higher Education Funding Council for England		Scottish Funding Council for Further and Higher Education	Higher Education Funding Council for Wales
Local Authority Children's Services Directorates (Local Education Authorities)	Education and Library Boards	Local Education Authorities	Local Education Authorities
Performance Management			
Office for Standards in Education (Ofsted)	Education and Training Inspectorate	HM Inspectorate of Education	Estyn (HM Inspector of Education and Training)
Quality Assurance Agency	Quality Assurance Agency	Quality Assurance Agency	Quality Assurance Agency

parents are able to pay the fees. Overall around 6–7 per cent of pupils attend such schools, although this proportion varies significantly in different parts of the country and very few attend in Scotland (Chitty 2009). They operate at primary (sometimes called preparatory) and secondary level, are frequently single sex and may provide for pupils to board during term time. Some have a long history and a high public profile, such as Eton and Harrow boys' schools on the outskirts of London. Many also have high standards of pupil achievement in GCSEs and A levels, in part because they can afford to have small classes and pay teachers high salaries. They have also, of course, traditionally been the preserve of the middle and upper classes, who can afford them. And there is an element of self-selection here with many pupils becoming wealthy adults, whose children also then attend these schools.

Despite a number of measures to reform and expand state education, private schooling has remained a significant sector of provision; and on occasions governments have sought to use public funds to intervene in this middle-class enclave. In the post-war decades some schools received public funding under a 'direct grant' scheme and could admit (usually the brightest) local children supported by scholarships from their LEA; but this was abolished in 1975. A similar arrangement introduced in the 1980s provided government-funded 'assisted places' for children from poorer backgrounds although this too was largely restricted to those meeting high academic entry requirements. This was phased out by Labour, though recently various bursary schemes have been reintroduced.

To ensure that pupils attending them are receiving adequate and appropriate education these private schools are now subject to many of the same regulatory procedures as state schools and, in England, are encouraged to link with state providers. Beyond them, and subject to varying regulations, lie an array of other fee-charging providers, ranging from individuals or agencies offering additional home tutoring to commercial training organizations and private universities.

COMPREHENSION QUESTIONS

- Why have successive governments extended compulsory schooling?
- How is education provision in the UK structured?

REFLECTIVE QUESTION

- Should private education be permitted when state-funded places are available for all pupils?

EDUCATION IN SCHOOLS AND EARLY YEARS PROVISION

THE DEVELOPMENT OF STATE PROVISION

State provided education in Britain can be traced back to the nineteenth century, when local schools for what would now be classed as primary provision were established in many areas. Some were small independent enterprises supported by parents; but most were linked to churches or chapels that provided the necessary financial support and also influenced the curriculum to promote the teaching of Christian beliefs and values. Organized religion has retained an influence over the management and curriculum of many schools, particularly in Northern Ireland. But after 1870 local School Boards were established with powers to fund schools from local rates and in 1880 attendance from the ages of 5 to 10 became compulsory. In 1901 the school leaving age was raised to 14 and, in 1902, one of the earliest of the twentieth-century welfare reforms transferred responsibility for school management to LEAs.

The early part of the century subsequently saw an expansion of state secondary schooling although many children received their education in extended primary schools. This was changed by one of the most important reforms of school education in the UK, the 1944 Education Act. Introduced by R. A. B. Butler, a Conservative minister in the wartime coalition government, it is sometimes referred to as the Butler Act, but it was supported by Labour and became part of the post-war welfare settlement, reaffirming the role of the state as the provider of free education for all children.

POST-WAR EDUCATION POLICY

With parallel legislation in Scotland and Northern Ireland the 1944 Act 'nationalized' much of the previously disparate publicly supported provision in England and Wales and confirmed LAs as the agencies for the management and development of school provision. Most importantly, it raised compulsory school attendance to the age of 15 (extended in 1972 to 16) and provided for a new structure of separate local secondary schools. Though it did not specify their structure, the legislation led to a *tripartite system* with different schools providing for particular pupil groups. The principle behind it was one of selection, with children in the last year of primary education, at the age of 10 or 11, sitting an examination (called the *11 plus*) on the basis of which they moved to one of three settings:

- Grammar Schools, hitherto the traditional form of secondary provision, catering for those with academic ability and preparing them for public examination at 16 (then the General Certificate of Education, GCE) and 18 (A levels)

- Secondary Technical Schools focusing on those with more technical abilities and preparing them for a more vocational career
- Secondary Modern Schools providing for those with 'practical' abilities.

The notion of allocating pupils according to aptitude or ability had obvious attractions. However, it was dogged by fundamental problems of both principle and practice and quickly attracted widespread criticism.

In principle the idea of selection at the age of 11 was problematic. The 11 plus examination, based on English, Mathematics and 'Intelligence Testing', was not a satisfactory basis for determining children's future abilities as the later progress of many confirmed: some grammar school pupils left at 15 or 16 without public qualifications, whilst growing numbers of secondary modern school pupils gained GCEs (Lowe 2005). There was also considerable disquiet, not least among parents and children, that future life chances and career opportunities should be so heavily dependent upon testing at 11.

In practice the notion of distinctive, yet equivalent, provision did not materialize. As the continuation of pre-war secondary education in many areas, the grammar schools inherited buildings, resources and staff that the newer technical and modern schools could not match. They attracted the top teachers and it quickly became clear that in most respects they were the 'best' schools. Thus attendance at grammar school became a coveted goal; and that at a secondary modern a sign of failure. This was compounded by the non-development of technical schools in many areas.

The 11 plus examination therefore became a pass or fail hurdle, with middle-class parents coaching and encouraging their children or sending them to private schools when they did not gain a grammar school place. This reproduced something of a traditional class divide within what was purportedly a meritocratic regime, undermining the supposedly egalitarian goals of state education. What is more, access to grammar schools varied geographically and also by gender, with girls doing on average much better in the 11 plus than boys (Chitty 2009).

In the wake of widespread criticism in 1965 the Labour government required LEAs in mainland Britain to draw up plans to replace tripartism with *comprehensive* secondary schools. Its aim was to give the same educational opportunities to all children in single (large) local secondary schools, although within these pupils could be 'streamed' into separate classes according to ability for particular subjects. Over the next decade most secondary schools became comprehensives, though selective provision continued in Northern Ireland.

Some LEAs (apart from Scotland), however, resisted this comprehensivization and, following the election of a Conservative government in 1979, the requirement was removed. Thus state grammar schools and selection at the age of 11 continued in some areas, whilst the provision introduced in 1988 for schools to opt out of LEA control enabled others to become state grammar schools. And of course, private schools remained for those who could pay. Nevertheless for the vast majority of children in mainland Britain since the 1970s secondary education has taken place in comprehensive schools catering for all those aged 11 to 16 or 18 in a local area.

The 1960s also saw a reawakening of concern over other issues, prompted by a series of government committees:

- The 1959 *Crowther* Report, which led to an extension of the school leaving age and the introduction of a new range of public examinations at 16 which all pupils could take: the Certificate of School Education (CSE). In 1986 this was merged with the GCE, mainly taken by a minority of the brightest pupils, to create the GCSE.
- The 1963 *Newsom* Report, which recommended that more effort be made to develop provisions for pupils with lower abilities.
- The 1967 *Plowden* Report, which focused on primary education, particularly the concern that some children in some schools were not doing as well as their peers. It argued this was due to cultural and social factors as well as school provision and proposed 'positive dis-

crimination' targeting additional resources to schools in deprived areas to boost performance, a policy that we discuss in more detail later.

These relatively formal reviews were followed in the 1970s by the more controversial Black
Papers and the Great Debate, discussed earlier, which shaped school policy over the next two
decades.

POLICY DEVELOPMENT IN THE LATE TWENTIETH CENTURY

The Conservative governments of the 1980s wanted to reduce LEA control and introduce
marketization and, where possible, privatization into school education. Starting with legislation
making it possible for parents across the UK to voice their school preferences, these policies
culminated in the 1988 Education Reform Act. This undermined the role of LEAs from two
directions. From above more direction was provided by central government, most notably the
imposition of the national curriculum and external attainment tests outlined earlier. From
below more power was given to schools to manage their affairs, most notably the devolution
of financial management to head teachers and governing bodies, under what was called the
Local Management of Schools (LMS).

LMS did not only include budgetary control; schools were also freed from LEA allocation
of pupils. This was part of a more general and lasting attempt to introduce market principles
of choice and competition into state education (or rather quasi-markets as commentators
called them; see Chapter 3). Under the legislation parents could in theory send their children
to the school of their choice through a system of notifying or placing their requests with LEAs.
To facilitate this, schools were required to publish information about their pupils' performance, and the government also initiated the publication of 'league tables' of public examination
results. The market in school places did not quite work like this in practice, however, for
schools could also take admissions decisions themselves, with the effect that some (better)
schools became oversubscribed and others (poorly performing) could not attract sufficient
pupils. Because from 1988 public funds were distributed to schools on a per capita basis this
meant weaker schools could become trapped in a downward spiral of falling rolls, results and
budgets.

The legislation thus significantly altered the principles and practice of school education,
with more control devolved to individual schools within a centrally prescribed curriculum
and a significant element of competition introduced into the system. A similar approach was
taken to early learning provision where, in the light of increasing concern both over children's
needs and those of working parents, a voucher system for part-time places for four–year-olds
was introduced in 1996, along with a goal-oriented curriculum (SCAA 1996).

POLICY DEVELOPMENT IN THE EARLY TWENTY FIRST CENTURY

In their drive to improve state education, the Labour governments of 1997–2010 extended
this process of quasi-market choice in England, although, as discussed later, this was not followed by the devolved administrations. Labour's policies, however, also entailed a renewed
recognition of the importance of concentrating more directly on the relationships between
children, families and schools, a development, particularly in early years provision, that was
paralleled elsewhere in the UK.

In England Labour launched the first ever Child Care Strategy in 1998, revised in 2004,
obliging LAs, as noted earlier, to ensure sufficient pre-school places for parents who wanted
them, largely through facilitating non-statutory provision. In addition the Sure Start
Programme, which we will return to later, provided more targeted support for disadvantaged
under-threes. These initiatives became part of a more radical policy heralded by the Green
Paper, *Every Child Matters* (DfES 2003a), to coordinate support for children across education
and care services (see Chapter 11). These included the creation of a separate government
department for school education and the new LA structures referred to above, with childcare

becoming a statutory LA duty in 2006. Early years provision also became subject to a new framework, the Early Years Foundation Stage. Parallel measures were pursued in Scotland and Wales, though with a different, play-based curriculum in the latter (WAG 2003a). Change in Northern Ireland, as in other areas, however, was slow and, despite successive proposals, not framed by a national childcare strategy (Horgan and Gray 2012).

Labour's school policies were intended to ensure provision contributed to wellbeing for all children, and that all benefited equally from it. Here its key objectives were to lift standards whilst increasing choice, and, in the process, secure both social justice and greater social mobility. Underpinning these aims was a concern to maintain competitiveness in world markets, a concern which some viewed as moving education policy away from being a pillar of the welfare state and narrowing its role (Tomlinson 2005).

Nevertheless, under Labour public investment in education across the UK was boosted substantially, especially after 2003, moving to above the OECD average by 2009 (OECD 2012a; Chowdry and Sibieta 2011). Teachers' salaries were increased (up 20 per cent in real terms), as were the numbers of teachers and support staff such as classroom assistants and efforts made to boost recruitment through, for instance, the Teach First scheme. School buildings and equipment were improved and a huge further upgrading planned under the Building Schools for the Future programme. Alongside these measures Labour sought to raise basic standards and educational attainment more directly through changes to the curriculum and its delivery. These included developments such as literacy and numeracy hours in primary schools and, more broadly, the introduction from 2008 of a more teacher-led curriculum for 11–14-year-olds and the abolition of tests at 14.

Though prompted by the same concerns and goals, the devolved administrations have often adopted a different tack and pedagogy. Wales saw the development of a more experientially based curriculum, the abolition of external testing in primary schools and the introduction of the Welsh Bac (Rees 2007). Scottish administrations too developed a distinctive curricular framework and testing programme which maintained a high confidence in the state system (Chitty 2009) and was updated in 2012. Crucially both countries also upheld a commitment to locally maintained and administered comprehensive schools and opposed the extension of parental choice. There are now no selective state schools in Wales. Scottish administrations have abolished self-governing status and given LAs greater powers to turn down place requests. And in Northern Ireland too there have been more recent attempts to limit selective secondary education.

In England, however, Labour sought to increase competition and parental choice by moving away from the 'one size fits all comprehensive' (DfES 2001). Extra resources were provided for those choosing to specialize in certain subjects, such as languages, sport, sciences or business, an option taken up by many, partly in the expectation that it would influence parental choice. However, this was (and is) also influenced by other factors, most notably performance tables. Better performing schools are in practice more attractive to parents, can quickly become over-subscribed, so that they choose pupils not the reverse. Some did (and continue to do) so on a geographical basis, largely mirroring the former LA allocations. But this has often meant housing in catchment areas for popular schools has become more expensive, in effect advantaging the children of the (largely middle-class) parents who could afford to live there.

It is not just geography that influences access to popular schools. As mentioned earlier organized religious groups have continued to maintain managerial control over some schools, and these are able to use religious commitments as criteria for selection, although some critics have argued that this is also used as a cover for academic selection. Religious selection has long played a major role in school selection in Northern Ireland and despite moves to encourage integration, remains a key factor in school applications. In England Labour also encouraged an increase in the sponsorship of schools within the state system by different faith groups.

Here it also adopted a range of other measures to lift standards and enhance choice, including encouraging private as well as faith-based sponsorship, enabling schools to opt for independent trust status (DfES 2005), and replacing 'failing schools' by Academies that could use private investment to improve provision or be sponsored by private schools. These initiatives in particular have been taken by the Coalition leading some to observe its schools policies were 'virtually interchangeable' (Chitty 2010). However, they have been developed in a very different economic climate and increasingly from a different ideological base, with far more emphasis on breaking up monopoly provision by the state and increasing school autonomy. Even though the schools budget was relatively protected, real-term spending has been cut, and Labour's school building project abandoned.

Most fundamentally the 2011 Education Act opened up the Academies programme to all schools – heralded as equivalent to the right to buy council housing in the 1980s discussed in Chapter 10 (Gove cited in Vasagar 2011). Under this all primary, special and secondary schools can now convert to self-managing, centrally-funded Academies. This means that they are then released from LA controls, and can vary the curriculum, school day, pay and employment, and set admissions, though they must still comply with statutory duties on assessments. In 2012 they were also given rights to employ staff without qualified teaching status (QTS). This brought them into line with both private schools and the new Free Schools, a further type of state-funded primary or secondary institution launched in 2011.

Free Schools have even greater powers to determine the subjects to be taught, their delivery and teachers' conditions and can also employ non-qualified teachers. They can be initiated by parents, teachers, faith groups, third sector bodies and even commercial firms. All of these featured in the first tranches of applications for such schools, which also included bids by private schools to set themselves up as Free Schools or open associated ones. To add to this diversity the 2011 admissions code also allowed good schools to expand (and unpopular ones contract) and, for the first time since 1964, existing grammar schools to grow (through satellite provision).

Change in the school landscape in England has been swift under these initiatives and the related development of new vocationally-oriented institutions for 14–19-year-olds. By mid-2012 well over half of secondaries were operating as Academies and most others and primaries were expected to convert. This contrasts sharply with the rest of the UK, however, especially Scotland and Wales where the post-2011 governments have reaffirmed the already strong antipathy to market-based policies and private-sector involvement in schooling (see WG 2011a).

Whether increased competition stemming from this diversity will raise standards and increase the supply of good quality schools accessible to low as well as higher income families in England as the government hopes is as yet unclear. There are concerns though that it may lead to less inclusive, more fragmented and segmented provision (Benn 2011; Mortimore 2013). There are also concerns over the implications of the increased scope for commercial enterprises within the state system signified not only by a new market in educational services once supplied by LEAs, but also the emergence of 'edu-chains' running Free Schools and Academies, with further pressure to allow profit-making companies to take over state schools.

The Coalition has also initiated further measures to raise school standards in England, including the introduction of a streamlined national curriculum focused more on traditional subjects and the new GCSE system and A levels referred to earlier. A new performance measure, an English Baccalaureate for those who gain GCSE grades A★ to C in certain core subjects was introduced in 2010, followed in 2013 by proposals for a 'techbac' and new 'secondary-ready' tests at 11. Beyond these the *Importance of Teaching* White Paper (DfE 2010), led to a higher bar for entry into the profession and an expanded Teach First scheme, and to the introduction in 2013 of performance-related pay for schoolteachers in England and Wales.

These reforms were accompanied by a continuing commitment to pre-compulsory provision (Field 2010; Allen 2011; DfE 2011a, 2012a). Part-time entitlement was implemented on a more flexible basis and granted to disadvantaged 2-year-olds and measures encouraging more private sector involvement and a social investment market developed (Allen 2011; HMG 2011a). Additionally a tax-free voucher scheme to assist some working parents and carers with childcare costs for children under 12 was to be phased in from 2015, starting with those under five. The devolved administrations too have continued to develop their early learning provisions, with Wales for instance furthering its 'Scandinavian style' approach (Drakeford 2012; Arnott and Ozga 2012), though, as we discussed in Chapter 6, like policy-makers in England, they are being pressed to move further and develop free universal early years services.

COMPREHENSION QUESTIONS

- Why was comprehensive secondary schooling introduced and why, despite this, do some state grammar schools still remain?
- What is meant by 'higher standards and more choice', and why have they been central to school education policy since the beginning of this century?
- What are the implications of the spread of Academy schools in England?
- Why has early learning provision become a key priority for policy-makers across the UK?

REFLECTIVE QUESTION

- Should parents be able to choose which state school to send their children to?

FURTHER AND CONTINUING EDUCATION

Further and continuing education have traditionally been associated with the acquisition of the vocational qualifications and skills needed for particular employment. Unlike many European countries, however, this was seen predominantly in *voluntaristic* terms as an employer and individual rather than a state responsibility and many workers received little formal post-school training (May 2006). For young employees throughout much of the twentieth century this largely took the form of *apprenticeships*, under which some received on-the-job training and part-time education leading to specific, industry-based, qualifications.

In the latter part of the century such training and education became more widely available in FE colleges; and, in the wake of the economic and labour market changes discussed in Chapters 13 and 15, the apprenticeship model began to decline, accelerated by the employment support schemes of the 1970s and 1980s. The rapid growth of vocational provision in FE, however, left a welter of differing provisions and in 1986 a National Vocational Qualification (NVQ) framework was established. FE colleges subsequently focused on NVQ courses, together with A levels for young people unable or preferring not to study in secondary schools and also for adults.

From 1997 Labour sought to extend vocational education as part of a wider bid to boost the skills and qualifications of the workforce. Following the Kennedy Report (DfEE 1998) provision in England was expanded with a view to widening participation, helping the unemployed (see Chapter 13) and enticing the many employees with no post-compulsory education back into learning. To these ends Labour introduced the first national skills strategy (DfES 2003b) and, in a policy that gained added momentum following the Leitch review (2006), set targets to raise skill levels, and entitled 19–25-year-olds to receive free training to NVQ level 3 (equivalent to A level) and employed adults to pursue their first level 2 qualification.

The expansion of FE-based training was paralleled by the promotion of skills development more generally through the Sector Skills Councils, set up in 2002 across the UK, and the UK Commission for Employment and Skills created in 2006. There was a reinvigorated apprenticeship scheme, the Train to Gain programme in England, linked to the promotion of a 'skills pledge'. Under this as well as basic skills training employers were expected to offer their staff training to NVQ level 2 by 2010, with a possibility of statutory requirements being introduced in the event of non-delivery, whilst legislation in 2009 introduced a right to request time off for training for employees in mainland Britain. From the mid-2000s, however, policy was also increasingly driven by concern over the rising numbers of young adults not in education, employment or training (NEETs; see Chapter 13), which led in particular to legislation raising the participation age in education and training in England to 17, with a further move to 18 by 2015.

Despite record spending and improvements in the workforce's skills base the UK did not keep pace with other countries or raise its position internationally (UKCES 2010). This long-standing trend remains a key policy issue for the Coalition, which has stressed the need to match standards from school age on not only with other OECD countries but also China and Pacific Asia. However, it has moved to a consumer-led skills strategy and a policy of co-investment by learners and employers with less emphasis on boosting workforce qualifications and more on informal learning and skills acquisition through other means (BIS 2010a, 2010b, 2011a, 2011b).

Overall funding for FE and continuing education has been cut by a quarter since 2010. Labour's targets and Train to Gain programme have been scrapped and free training entitlements restricted. And, following yet another review (DfE 2011c) vocational education for 14–19-year-olds has been reformed (DfE 2012c), allowing young people as mentioned earlier to move from school to other state providers at 14. For adults public resources are to be targeted into funding for 19–24-year-olds to take GCSE or equivalent level 2 or level 3 qualifications (BIS 2011d) and, while promoting more apprenticeships, the Coalition's strategy centred on 'shifting responsibility' towards self-development. Increasingly people over 24 were expected to invest in their own training, aided by new loan and Personal Records schemes, the establishment for the first time of an all-age National Careers Service and the restructuring of FE colleges.

These were originally established and managed by LAs, but their operation has been subject to frequent change, with funding in England undertaken centrally in the 1990s but that for 16–19-year-olds returned to LAs in 2001. With some administrative changes, the Coalition retained this division with the Education Funding Agency (in the DfE) responsible for training for 16–19-year-olds and a new Skills Funding Agency (within BIS) responsible for overseeing adult training including apprenticeships (see Table 12.1). FE colleges themselves were given greater autonomy, though in an increasingly competitive market, in which 'failing' ones face possible replacement, potentially by private providers, whose expansion is being encouraged, and all having to raise their fees (BIS 2010b, 2011d).

With different structures in the rest of the UK (see Table 12.1) post-devolution policy has been driven by the same overarching aims and a concern to redevelop provisions such as apprenticeships. Policy-makers in Northern Ireland, however, have focused more on the problems of raising a skills base lower than the rest of the UK (DEL 2010, 2012), whilst Scotland aimed to improve skills utilization as well as upskilling and the regionalization of FE (SG 2007a, 2010a, 2011b). It also placed more emphasis on lifelong learning, encouraging collaboration within FE and with HEIs, and promoting FE's broader social role. Wales too has developed a more integrated approach, favouring 'all-through' institutions, provider cooperation rather than competition, grant support for learners, and local planning (WAG 2008a, 2008b; Keep et al. 2010). These differing approaches have been reinforced since the 2011 elections but, as in England, all are constrained by the cuts in public funding.

HIGHER EDUCATION

University education dates back to the Oxford and Cambridge university colleges, created in the thirteenth and fourteenth centuries, and the four universities established in Scotland in the fifteenth and sixteenth. Until the end of the nineteenth century, however, it was a privilege largely restricted to (mainly male) upper-class young people from private schools. Around the turn of the century a number of new universities were established in major cities, such as

Birmingham and Manchester and also in Wales. Sometimes called 'redbricks' because of their buildings, these encouraged further provision although HE remained a largely middle-class preserve, not least because of its costs.

Admission was also restricted by entry criteria established by the universities, measured from the early 1950s by 'A' level exams. Following the post-war expansion of secondary education the numbers meeting these rose and successive governments sought to increase access, both to meet the aspirations of young people and wider economic and social goals. This was facilitated by the introduction in 1962 of LA funding (maintenance grants) for all students gaining a university place, and the 1963 Robbins Committee recommendations to extend provision from 8 to 17 per cent of the 18–21 age group.

This massive change required more institutions as well as places and in the 1960s a number of universities were created, some from pre-existing colleges of advanced technology, others from scratch, with all universities receiving central government funding via the University Grants Committee. From the mid-1960s, however, the then Labour government channelled growth into polytechnics. Established and run by LAs (although with national funding) these concentrated on less elitist and more vocational provision, often delivered on a part-time basis. The only new university created was the Open University, a UK-wide distance-learning venture for part-time students incorporating the then novel use of television.

The polytechnics and the new universities contributed to a gradual growth in places throughout the 1970s and 1980s, although it remained the case that a higher proportion of those from middle- than lower-class families undertook undergraduate study. Towards the end of the century, therefore, there was another sustained attempt to expand and broaden access. This involved the removal of the 30 polytechnics from LA control in 1988, giving them university status in 1992 and bringing these so-called 'new universities' under the same national funding and regulatory regime as the 'old universities'. This is now the Higher Education Funding Council (HEFC) in England, with its counterparts in Scotland and Wales and the Northern Ireland Department of Employment and Learning (Table 12.1).

All universities and HE colleges (of which there were also by now a significant number) were also incentivized to accept more students by shifting funding for teaching to a per capita basis. In 1997 a second official review, the Dearing Report, recommended increasing the proportion of young people going to university to one-third and extending provision for older adults and disadvantaged groups. Labour accepted this and then committed itself to a participation rate of 50 per cent of those aged 18–30 by 2010 with increased access for individuals with no family experience of HE. The need for such expansion was widely endorsed and in 2006 the Leitch Review recommended four in ten adults be educated to degree level by 2020.

Across the UK these developments led to a further growth, including an expansion of larger colleges, some of which then gained university status. In all four jurisdictions it also meant increased encouragement for those from disadvantaged groups to enter HE through various *widening participation* initiatives. In England this was formalized in 2004 through the Office for Fair Access (OFFA). Encouraging entry from low-income and other traditionally underrepresented groups proved difficult to achieve though, and participation rates remained lower than in other sections of the population.

The advent of mass higher education led, however, to increases in public funding, and pressures for cost containment. The per capita funding paid to universities for students was gradually cut back therefore, and in 1990 maintenance grants replaced with loans (repayable from future earnings). But the major change was the introduction of tuition fees for students, in order to share the costs of HE between its beneficiaries and the state. In 1998 means-tested tuition fees were introduced and in 2006 variable fees up to an annual ceiling of £3,000, repayable by graduates from income-contingent loans, were instituted along with provisions for discretionary university support for students. The Scottish Parliament, however, decided not to introduce these fees for students studying there, creating a major fault line in HE policy in the UK.

Subsequently there was pressure from some institutions for the ceiling to be raised and the Browne Review (2010) set out a case for a more demand-led basis for HE funding in

England. It was followed by far-reaching changes designed to stimulate an undergraduate market and place students at the heart of the system (BIS 2011e). Most significantly this included the introduction in 2012 of new tuition fees (of up to £9,000) for students in England covered by loans to be paid back out of future earnings after graduation.

The introduction of these up-front fees meant that direct funding of teaching by HEFCE was restricted to a few strategic, and more expensive, subjects, with most courses financed through the student fee. This has led to greater competition between HEIs, with unrestricted places for students with high grades and extra places for others at lower-charging 'value for money' institutions, a process furthered by the creation of ten new universities in 2012 and measures allowing external degrees to be taught in FE colleges and promoting private sector provision. However, in practice most universities charge the full £9,000 fee for all courses. To stimulate this market, as in other services, providers also have to supply prospective students with information on their performance and the standards to expect in return for fees paid.

Only time will tell if this marketization and the associated incentives to boost access will achieve their desired effects of better outcomes for students, although universities are now required to provide widening participation strategic assessments and to establish access agreements monitored by OFFA. The Scottish and Welsh administrations, although facing similar cost pressures, have pursued different funding policies, however, and have aimed to maintain a less pro-market model (WG 2011a; SG 2012a). Domiciled Scottish (and non-UK EU) students studying at Scottish universities were exempted from the new fee system; and in 2012 the Welsh administration provided tuition fee grants for Welsh domiciled undergraduates studying in the UK to cushion them against the rises. Domiciled undergraduates studying in Northern Ireland were also given some support.

Underlying these developments is a more general debate about the purposes of university education, and who should pay for it and post-compulsory education more generally. This includes fundamental questions over the extent to which education is an individual privilege leading to enhanced career opportunities for which those who benefit should contribute to the cost, or part of a public commitment to create a skilled workforce and a socially richer society from which all benefit – and for which all should pay. This is the human capital argument referred to earlier – put more sharply: doctors, lawyers, and even teachers, can expect reasonable salaries; but we all need these and other well-qualified professionals. Who should therefore bear the cost of their training?

COMPREHENSION QUESTIONS

- Why has there been a shift towards skills training in FE colleges since the latter part of the last century?
- What are the advantages and disadvantages of expanding access to higher education?
- How and why does HE policy vary within the UK?

REFLECTIVE QUESTION

- Is post-compulsory education a public or a private good?

EQUALITY AND SELECTIVITY IN EDUCATION

Particularly since the Butler reforms of 1944 there has been concern within policy circles about the extent to which educational provision should be governed by the principle of equality. If public education, free to all, is a public good, then should not all benefit equally from it? The answer to this question, however, raises a number of dilemmas that have significantly influenced policy-making, most importantly those arising from the distinction between two different approaches to equality in education:

- Equality of *opportunity* – should all have the same chances to succeed and reach their potential by making sure all have equal access to education?
- Equality of *outcome* – should all receive the same service and achieve the same results by making sure that educational provision itself is more equitably provided?

In practice both have informed policy development: the shift to comprehensive schools was driven in particular by a belief that all secondary pupils should get the same curriculum and teaching; and yet differentials in achievement at GCSE, A and (especially) university levels mean those better able to benefit from provision can in fact gain more from it. What is more the retention of grammar schools with selective entry in some areas means a more restrictive notion of equality of opportunity also operates for some, concerns over which have been accentuated by the institution of Academies in England.

Of course, it would be unlikely that all could be expected to achieve the same results in all circumstances, and the current joint, and yet contradictory, focus on standards and choice in school education suggests that confusion still remains, with equality of outcome applying mainly to support for basic standards only. Even these limited commitments raise other problems, however. If some pupils are achieving lower standards than their peers, is this because they have lower innate abilities or because the opportunities afforded them have not been equal to those available to others? Evidence that there are links between overall performance and social class, family background or attendance at particular schools suggests that this may, at least in part, be down to the opportunity factor.

The issue of whether all pupils are receiving the right kind of support and encouragement in education was a major concern of the government reports of the 1960s, particularly the 1967 Plowden Report, referred to earlier. This led to the creation of Educational Priority Areas (EPAs), where additional public resources provided for more teachers and work with parents (including pre-school parents). The EPAs were relatively short-lived. But the idea of focused additional support was later revived by Labour in England after 1997, through Education Action Zones and, more significantly, the Sure Start programme. Initially this provided targeted, integrated services for under threes and their families in disadvantaged areas through a network of Children's Centres. Following the *Every Child Matters* Green Paper (DfES 2003a), however, it broadened to encompass basic services for all families, including free part-time early years learning. Analogous provision was also developed in the rest of the UK, along with other measures to raise school performance and children's opportunities.

In England best practice was promoted by identifying 'beacon schools' to act as models for less successful ones around them. At the other end of the spectrum a system of 'special measures' to improve 'failing schools' was introduced, followed by the Academies scheme, mentioned above – although this too was not taken up by the devolved administrations. Labour also tried to lift staying-on rates among young people from low-income families by introducing a means-tested education maintenance allowance (EMA) to help meet the living costs of 16–19-year-olds who continued in FE. This was withdrawn in England by the Coalition in 2011, but was retained in the rest of the UK, with some reductions in Wales. In its place in England a Pupil Premium was introduced, along with an Education Endowment Fund, to give schools extra funding based on the numbers of pupils from disadvantaged backgrounds.

There are some other dimensions to the question of equal opportunities and treatment in education, however. First there is the issue of gender. Since the sex discrimination and equal treatment legislation of the 1970s girls and boys have been provided with equal access to education, formally speaking at least; although before this it was not uncommon for a different curriculum to be offered, with (for instance) boys studying carpentry and girls home economics. Nevertheless formal gender equality does not necessarily lead to practical equality of treatment. For a start it is still quite common for some schools to offer only single sex education, with girls and boys therefore experiencing different institutions and teachers, a separation which supporters argue can be of benefit to both. Even within mixed schools, however, there is evidence of differential achievement, with boys doing better in science and technology and girls in literature and arts; although more recently the evidence points to a general tendency for girls to outperform boys at all ages in their school careers, leading to (unresolved) questions about how best to provide equality of opportunity for both.

There is also evidence of differential performance of some black and ethnic minority children in UK schools, and this too has prompted policy debates about how best to address issues of equality of opportunity here. In 1985 a government committee report on the education of children from ethnic minority groups, the Swann Report, argued that underachievement by non-white pupils was an issue for the education system and was linked to the more general disadvantage and discrimination experienced by non-white people in Britain. It recommended that 'greater sensitivity' (DES 1985) needed to be shown to the particular circumstances and needs of ethnic minority children. Like many subsequent reports it also argued that more attention should be paid in education generally to the emergence of an ethnically diverse society. With pupils from an ethnic minority in state schools in England rising to over a fifth by 2010 (DfE 2011d), addressing these concerns has remained a key issue for successive governments.

In practice, however, the extension of parental choice and the geographical segregation of many ethnic minorities have led to greater segregation rather than diversity within the school system in many areas, with certain ethnic and immigrant groups becoming predominant in particular schools (OECD 2012a). This has been compounded to some extent by debate over the desirability of faith-based schools, which can in effect provide specialist education for particular religious and ethnic groups, and can lead to an exacerbation of divisions between social groups. There are also fears that, particularly in England, wider social divisions are being reinforced through the inequalities within the early years market (Daly 2010) and may be further compounded by the spread of Academies and Free Schools.

STANDARDS AND PERFORMANCE MANAGEMENT

The ongoing debate about equality of opportunity within the education system has resulted in an increasing emphasis on the measurement and maintenance of educational standards. The notion of a set of standards against which educational achievement can be objectively assessed has been a key feature of provision throughout most of the modern era. This is just what the tests and examinations that all pupils and students know so well are designed to ensure. In particular, national public examinations at 16 and 18 have for some time been established as the main goal, and measure, of educational achievement across the UK.

This is true for pupils, but also since the turn of the century for schools, particularly through the new levers of accountability, national curricula, testing and inspection. In England these include requirements to publish information about levels of achievement in public examinations that can be used to compare performance in league tables published by the press and lead to competition between schools. Scotland, Wales and Northern Ireland all ended the publication of official school performance tables post-devolution, though in 2010 the Welsh government instigated a form of banded, value-added secondary school results. In England, while including contextual value added (CVA) measures taking account of children's differing backgrounds, Labour upheld their publication and the Coalition have further revised and extended their use. Moreover schools are subject to other performance measures such as pupil attainment in the English Bac and tougher overall exam targets, and, more generally, tighter inspection, covering nurseries and the performance of pupils receiving the pupil premium.

The use of performance indicators is not confined to schools and has also been applied to post-compulsory, including HE, provision, with the press regularly producing league tables of universities and reporting on the annual student surveys first introduced by Labour. There is also a range of measures designed to ensure that the process of providing education is properly managed and delivered, as part of a more general concern with 'quality assurance' in public services, discussed in Chapter 18. Responsibility for quality in education is vested in the Office for Standards in Education (Ofsted) in England and in similar inspectorates in Scotland, Wales and Northern Ireland (Table 12.1). These aim to ensure that all schools, state-funded early years providers and colleges are visited on a regular cycle, and their reports are made publicly available. Quality assurance also extends to HE with the Quality Assurance Agency (QAA) overseeing monitoring of teaching across the UK, and HEFCE acting in effect as the market regulator in England.

Whether quality assurance procedures or other recent policy changes, especially in England, really do lead to improvements in the setting and maintenance of standards in education is a controversial issue, however. Many teachers and lecturers have been critical of inspection processes that they claim are unnecessary and divert resources (predominantly their time) into bureaucratic procedures that are not necessarily accurate measures of performance. Concerns have also been expressed about the value and reliability of the measures used and the distorting effects on teaching. Nevertheless minimum standards and independent assessment have become a key feature of educational policy in England and in the devolved administrations since the turn of the century.

ANCILLARY SERVICES

Education policy is primarily concerned with the delivery of learning and teaching. But it has long been recognized that effective learning may depend not only upon teaching but other forms of support. Indeed from the early days of formal school education it was realized that healthy and well-fed pupils were more able to learn effectively. Schools were thus encouraged, and later required, to provide meals at lunchtime for their pupils and milk at break times. The compulsory provision of milk was abandoned in the early 1970s. But subsidized school meals remain (for those pupils choosing to take them); and are free for those on certain social security benefits, and from 2014 for all infant school children aged 5 to 8.

LAs in mainland Britain and the Education and Library Boards in Northern Ireland have also long provided a range of other services to support school attendance, including free transport for those living too far to walk to school and free or subsidized school clothing for parents on low incomes. More targeted support and assistance to children experiencing difficulties attending school is provided by LA educational welfare services (or may be procured separately by Academies in England). However, these have become something of a 'policing' service ensuring attendance and this can be enforced by fining parents and, in England in extreme cases, by imprisonment, a policy introduced in 2000.

This rather punitive approach reflected growing concern for the future of children who miss out on schooling and both Labour and the devolved administrations pumped extra support into projects for tackling persistent truancy and school exclusion (the exclusion by schools of disruptive pupils). In England these were one of the first priorities assigned to the Social Exclusion Unit established in 1998 and included the introduction of parenting contracts. Support for school attendance for younger children was also part of a broader policy commitment under the *Every Child Matters* strategy (see Chapter 11) aimed at opening facilities beyond the school day and providing additional extra-curricular activities for pupils.

Improving attendance, particularly through engaging parents remains a UK-wide commitment, though the Coalition has focused more on schemes targeted at families identified as having multiple problems and strengthening schools' disciplinary powers. Truancy rates across the UK, however, have remained stubbornly high leading to continuing debate and regular reviews of this issue.

LA advisory services have also included careers guidance, but this too has been subject to restructuring. In England it included the Connexions service set up in 2000 to provide support for those at risk of dropping out and careers advice more generally for teenagers, which became an LA responsibility in 2008. Though LAs' statutory duty to provide services to enable young people to participate in education and training has been maintained, careers advice has now moved back into schools, which are expected to procure their own support often from the private sector. Young people also have access to the new National Careers Service for England offering online, telephone and face-to-face advice. This is similar to provision in Scotland and Wales where integrated all-age, all-ability services (Careers Scotland; Careers Wales) have been in place since 2001 (Watts 2010). Northern Ireland also has an all-through service, established in 2005.

In different ways therefore the notion of education as an investment in human capital and a concern to ensure the equality of opportunity has remained a central element of education policy across the UK. However, it is challenged by reductions in public resources and, in England at least, greater encouragement of market-style approaches at all levels of provision.

COMPREHENSION QUESTIONS

- What is the difference between equality of outcome and equality of opportunity and how have these influenced education policy in recent years?
- What have been the main changes of direction in support services for schools under the Coalition government?
- What are 'failing schools' and how are they helped to succeed?
- How do ancillary services seek to promote education in schools?

REFLECTIVE QUESTION

- Should parents be subject to formal sanctions for not ensuring that their children attend school?

FURTHER READING

The best text on the development of education policy in the UK is Chitty (2009). The collection of papers in Halsey et al. (1997) also provides a good overview of many of the key issues and Jones (2002) provides a more detailed history of post-war provision. Tomlinson (2005) is a clear guide to the policy context within which education provision has developed and Ball (2013) provides a stimulating overview of many key policy debates. The two government departments covering education in England have their own websites: www.gov.uk/dfe and www.bis.gov.uk, with the devolved administration websites providing similar services (see Chapter 6). Topical features on education policy can be found on *The Guardian* website at www.educationguardian.co.uk and in a range of think tanks in Brunsdon and May (2012) at http://www.blackwellpublishing.com/alcock4e/.

13
Employment

SUMMARY OF KEY POINTS

- Employment policy was not one of the major public programmes developed in the welfare reforms of the 1940s, but it has since become a key area of social policy.
- Responsibility for employment policy alongside social security policy lies mainly with the UK government and has not been devolved to the other administrations.
- Policy-making has fluctuated between supply-side and demand-side approaches to the promotion of employment.
- Labour markets have altered dramatically over the past half-century and become more diverse.
- Women's participation in paid employment has increased gradually since the 1950s.
- Since the 1970s governments have pursued more interventionist policies to promote employment, with recent administrations making welfare to work a policy priority.
- EU policy has been significant in expanding employment rights in the UK.
- Employment protection has grown in scale, including health and safety, working conditions and provisions against discrimination at work.
- Employment regulation also covers collective labour arrangements and the rights, and limits, of trade union action.

DEVELOPING EMPLOYMENT POLICY

When Beveridge (1942) listed the 'five giants' of social evil that he hoped would provide the foci for state welfare after the war *idleness* was included as one of these. Like many policy-makers he had been concerned by the social and individual costs of high unemployment during the inter-war depression and saw the waste of experience and potential that this represented as one of the main targets for state action (Beveridge 1944). As we shall see, the evil of idleness did largely disappear in the decades following the reforms of the 1940s. However, this was not the product of any direct commitment to a specific employment policy or public spending to support it as happened in response to the other evils considered in Part 2; rather it was the product of more general economic growth, supported on occasions by Keynesian-style stimulation of demand (see Chapter 15).

The study of social policy in the UK has therefore sometimes overlooked employment as distinct from unemployment as a dimension of state intervention, and concentrated instead upon the major areas of social expenditure, social security, health, education, housing and social services. However, this spending-driven approach ignored the importance of employment to the pursuit of wellbeing in society, and the wide range of measures that governments have developed to promote and regulate it. It also contrasted with the way in which employment policy was viewed in many other advanced economies, especially in northern and continental Europe (May 2006). Here and in other EU countries it became a central concern, particularly through the use of relatively strict regulatory frameworks to ensure that employment relations supported, rather than undermined, the welfare of working citizens. This has also been a major area of EU strategy that has increasingly affected policy in the UK, as we saw in Chapter 7.

This neglect has more recently been addressed in social policy study in the UK. Today most analysts and, more importantly, most politicians, recognize the role the state can play in the employment arena, and, in general, policy measures now cover two broad areas:

• The promotion and support of paid employment
• The regulation of individual and collective employment conditions.

It should be noted though that for much of the last century state action was generally conceived in terms of employment for men rather than women.

However, the growing centrality of employment policy within public planning became more prominent under the Labour governments at the beginning of this century. Support for employment was one of their highest-profile policy commitments, signified by the term used to describe a number of distinct but interrelated initiatives, *welfare to work*, a notion which has remained central to the Coalition government's policy agenda too.

The important role employment policy now plays in social policy can also be seen in recent organizational changes. In the 1990s the Department of Employment was merged with the Department of Education to create a Department for Education and Employment (DfEE), the intention being (in part at least) to link education and training to the needs and demands of the labour market. In 2001, however, this was broken up and responsibility for employment policy merged with social security in the Department for Work and Pensions (DWP). Aspects of employment policy, including UK-wide employment relations, and skills development in England though remained with other departments becoming the responsibility of the Department for Business, Innovation and Skills (BIS) in 2009. As with social security, employment policy is not an area where much autonomy has been devolved and the DWP has a UK-wide brief as does BIS for employee relations.

Skills and training policy and some aspects of economic development, however, are devolved responsibilities. Departmental direction of these has also been subject to change in Scotland and Wales, and since 2011 these are located in the Directorates of Learning and Justice and Enterprise, Trade and Investment in Scotland and the Department for Education and Skills in Wales. In Northern Ireland policy is overseen jointly by the Departments for Employment and Learning and Social Development, established in 1999.

For the UK as a whole, however, the central role of welfare to work in policy planning was most clearly marked by the creation in 2002 of a new agency to administer both employment support and social security benefits for all citizens of working age, *Jobcentre Plus* (Jobs and Benefits Offices in Northern Ireland). This replaced the Benefits Agency for working-age claimants and the Jobcentres run by the Employment Service (see Chapter 8). It remains the hub of the Coalition's welfare to work strategy although, as we will outline, it has a long history dating back to the beginning of the last century.

POLICY CONTEXT

As with other areas of welfare, employment interventions have been influenced by the wider policy context within which they have been developed. This is a complex and changing environment, but within it the influence of broader political and ideological perspectives can be identified. In particular we can contrast the influence of two different strands of thought and practice:

- *Regulation* – this approach draws on labourism and social democracy and is closely associated with the politics and concerns of the working classes. Labourist policy-makers are more politically committed to government intervention to protect workers and support employment. Social democratic thinking more generally is also underpinned by the belief that governments can, and must, act to regulate social relations (including employment relations) and promote virtuous economic development within capitalist economies. Labour governments in particular therefore have frequently championed workers' rights and the pursuit of 'full employment'; and this was certainly true of the administrations of 1997–2010.
- *Laissez-faire* – this approach draws on nineteenth-century liberalism and the neoliberalism of the New Right in the late twentieth century (see Chapter 14). It is based upon the assumption that any interference by government in the workings of the free market is likely to lead to imbalances and inefficiencies, and hence to economic and social problems (*laissez-faire* in French means 'leave alone'). This applies to the labour market as much as any other market, and hence neoliberals have argued in recent times that governments should not interfere in the regulation of employment conditions or promote employment opportunities. Such thinking underlay some of the rhetoric of the Thatcher administrations of the 1980s, although it did not in practice mean these withdrew entirely from either regulating or supporting employment. Such thinking is also reflected in the deregulatory stance taken by the Coalition government, though it similarly coexists with a more interventionist approach to some aspects of employment policy.

Historically then there has been something of battle between these opposing conceptions of the role of the state, although of course the reality of policy-making has generally remained somewhere between the extremes of *laissez-faire* and full employment.

Despite the rhetorical support which the *laissez-faire* approach enjoyed from most governments in the nineteenth century, policy intervention in labour market relations can be traced back to the early decades of that century with the introduction of the Factories Acts and other statutes restricting the working hours of some employees and controlling the employment of women and children in particular industries. These measures were taken much further by the Liberal governments of 1906–14, which also inaugurated other significant developments in state welfare (Fraser 2009). In 1909 further forms of employment protection were introduced, including the setting of minimum wages in some industries and the establishment of state 'labour exchanges' providing information and advice about employment opportunities to unemployed workers. They were the first significant step towards interventions to promote employment and in different guises have remained a major feature of policy practice, now in the form of Jobcentre Plus.

The turn of the last century also, however, saw the expansion of the trade union movement. Trade unions were independent organizations of workers, generally based on specific trades or industries, whose aim was to promote and protect the conditions of their members through collective action, or the threat of it. The movement was instrumental in the establishment of the Labour Party, which it was hoped would pursue workers' rights through political and legal reform; but its primary concern was to press employers to enter into collective agreements to guarantee basic rights and improve wages for their workers. The unions thus provided an avenue for employment protection outside the instruments of the state; and this alternative means of policy development has led even Labour administrations to weigh up how much employee protection should be a matter for government and how much should be left to private bargaining. It has also created pressure for additional policy intervention to control the activities of trade unions themselves, an issue considered at the end of this chapter.

In the 1920s and 1930s economic depression led to high levels of unemployment. There were also major conflicts between employers and trade unions, with the UK's only general strike being called in 1926. However, government employment policy remained relatively limited and concentrated on using social security administration to ensure those claiming unemployment benefits (now referred to as 'the dole') were 'genuinely seeking paid work'. This was in contrast to developments elsewhere, notably the 'New Deal' policies in the USA, where high public expenditure was used to create work opportunities for some of the unemployed.

However, the experience of idleness in the 1930s did influence political thinking during and after the Second World War. Wartime production needs soon reduced the scale of the dole queues; and policy-makers began to talk directly about the responsibility of peacetime governments, too, to promote full employment actively. Beveridge's (1942) report on social security reform was predicated on the explicit assumption that support for the unemployed would be linked to government commitments to ensure full employment and that jobs were available for all those (men) able to work. At the same time Keynes's (1936) economic advice to policy-makers was that full employment would ensure demand for goods and services and hence economic growth, and should therefore be supported by the state through increased public expenditure if necessary. In 1944 Beveridge and Keynes's thinking received official support in a White Paper on Employment Policy, outlining commitments to pursue high and stable levels of employment after the war.

In the subsequent three decades these commitments were largely met and the level of unemployment generally remained under 500,000, or 2–3 per cent of the working population (see Figure 13.1). In large part this was due to economic growth across the industrial world in the 1950s and early 1960s, with the consequent demand for labour prompting successive governments to encourage immigration from the UK's ex-colonial Commonwealth partners. However, in the mid-1970s there was again economic recession and, with unemployment rising to over a million, the effectiveness of Keynesian economic policies began to be openly questioned by the supporters of monetarism (see Chapter 15).

With the election of the Conservatives under Margaret Thatcher in 1979 Keynesian economics was abandoned, and with it the post-war commitment to seek to maintain full employment through public investment. In contrast the Thatcher administrations were strongly influenced by the neoliberal view that governments should not intervene in labour markets to stimulate demand for employment; and during the massive economic upheaval of the 1980s unemployment rose rapidly to over 3 million, or more than 10 per cent of the workforce (Figure 13.1).

The 1980s and 1990s thus saw a shift away from the post-war economic policies that had helped to support full employment. However, it did not result in an abandonment of employment policy. Indeed, the Conservative governments made substantial changes to individual and collective employment regulations; and as we highlight below, expanded policies to promote training and work experience. More significantly their policies marked a shift in the broad focus of employment policy from a concern with control over the demand for labour to its supply (see Box 13.1).

It is debatable, of course, whether either approach can be effective on its own and governments concerned to create and support paid employment need to pay attention to both. The policy balance between the two has though changed over time, and since the 1980s has shifted significantly towards a supply-side approach. Labour's welfare to work policies, which we consider below, were largely based on this strategy, as are the Coalition's.

As Figure 13.1 indicates, up to the 2008 recession, employment policy since the 1990s was accompanied by historically low unemployment and increased employment, with 2.5 million more people in work than in 1997 and almost 75 per cent of working age adults in work, one of the highest levels in the developed world (Freud, 2007). Of course this was not solely the product of the supply-side policy interventions explored below. The economic growth of the early 2000s examined in Chapter 15, also created demand-side pressures for

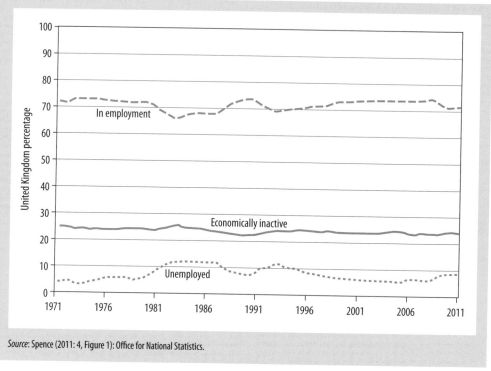

Source: Spence (2011: 4, Figure 1): Office for National Statistics.

Figure 13.1 Economic activity and inactivity rates 1971–2011

more jobs. Nevertheless, as Figure 13.1 also shows, many working-age adults remained out of work. Indeed the headline unemployment figures, which record only those seeking work and claiming benefits, concealed significant numbers of people considered economically inactive due, for example, to ill-health, disability, early retirement or full-time unpaid caring responsibilities.

BOX 13.1 Demand and supply side employment policies

- *Demand-side* policies for employment are concerned with the provision of employment opportunities within the labour market and the belief that these can be expanded (or contracted) by government investment in labour-intensive production either in the public or private sectors – in short, the provision of jobs for workers.

- *Supply-side* policies for employment are concerned with equipping potential workers for the labour market through public investment in the provision of skills training and job experience programmes for the unemployed, in the expectation that well-equipped workers will be able to secure a place in the labour market – in short, the provision of workers for the jobs.

The numbers of these 'hidden unemployed' has grown since the latter part of the twentieth century, particularly amongst men who, often because illness or disability, had become 'detached' from the labour force (see Alcock et al. 2003). For instance, the numbers dependent upon Incapacity Benefit (IB) escalated from around 800,000 in 1982 to 2.6 million in

2007 (Freud 2007). Demand-led increases in employment often did not benefit these ex-workers, because new jobs were generally not located in the former industrial areas where they lived and employers were often unwilling to take on staff with disabilities or health problems.

Nevertheless promoting employment remained a key policy for the Labour governments, and they committed the state to promoting 'full employment' for working-age adults, setting a new target of moving towards an 80 per cent employment rate, which meant getting significant numbers of former and 'non' workers into employment (DWP 2007). This was based in part on recognition of the social and individual costs of unemployment (Sinfield 1981), but also on the belief that employment offered the best route out of poverty – in short 'the best welfare policy of all is work' (DWP 2006b).

Following the 2008 credit crunch, however, the policy context changed again. In the UK, despite the worst recession since the 1930s, the immediate fall in employment was less than in the early 1980s and 1990s (DWP 2009b; Spence 2011). Nonetheless there was a significant rise in unemployment, which reached a 16-year high of 2.67 million at the end of 2011 and has hovered at close to 8 per cent since 2008. Moreover employment levels held up partly because of a sharp rise in part-time work, which for some indicated growing underemployment (TUC 2012) and rising in-work poverty, shored up by tax credits that have also since been subject to cuts (see Chapter 8).

As in the past, unemployment after the recession was higher in some regions, amongst older workers, those with low qualifications, and for ethnic minorities and women (Gregg and Wadsworth 2011). The brunt of the rise in unemployment, however, was born, as elsewhere in Europe, by 16–24-year-olds, almost one in five of whom were unemployed by the end of 2011, leading to concerns about the 'scarring' effects on a 'lost generation' (ACEVO 2012; ILO 2011). The response to this, as we outline below, has been a reassertion of supply-side welfare to work policies (Deacon and Patrick 2012; Wright 2012), although in a context where the demand for employment may be much weaker.

As we discussed in Chapter 7, the UK's membership of the EU has meant it is required to subscribe to EU-wide directives on policy; and, in consequence, the EU has become a significant influence on UK employment policy. In practice the UK has sometimes been a rather reluctant participant in these policies and in the 1992 Maastricht Treaty the Major government secured the right to 'opt out' of provisions for the regulation of workers' rights across the EU. In 1997, however, under the Treaty of Amsterdam, Labour reversed this arrangement, bringing the UK within the broader EU policy framework.

Employment regulation has always been a central feature of EU economic and social planning. This is in large part a product of its commitment to securing open and fair economic competition across member states and hence developing a 'level playing field' in which the rights and protections offered to workers are similar. This is intended to support the free movement of labour and prevent 'social dumping' whereby countries providing the lowest pay and conditions can seek to attract investment away from those requiring higher (and therefore more expensive) forms of employee protection.

EU employment provisions cover a number of areas including health and safety, working hours, equal treatment of women and men, protection against discrimination and the right to work (and receive social security protection) in any member state. Many of these rights are enshrined in the 'Community Charter of the Fundamental Rights of Workers', sometimes referred to as the *Social Charter*. It ensures a measure of equal competition for employers and employees; but also provides the framework for a common employment policy across the Union. Despite initial resistance, this has significantly influenced policy in the UK, with most of the key elements of the Charter being embedded in employment measures by the end of the last decade. It has also meant UK policy has and continues to be shaped by related initiatives, such as the EU Employment Strategy.

LABOUR MARKETS

Governments' ability to commit themselves to policies to secure full employment has always depended, as we have seen, on the broader economic climate within which these policies are required to operate. Changes in the economic context affect all social policies; but in the case of employment policy the relationship is a direct one for levels of employment, and workers' pay and conditions are inherently affected by changes in production processes and overall economic performance. The development of economic policy in the UK is discussed in Chapter 15, and we do not have the space here to detail the ways in which labour markets have altered as a result of broader economic shifts. However, it is worth outlining briefly the key changes affecting the development of UK employment policy.

To some extent these are a product of what is often summarized as a shift from *Fordist* to *post-Fordist* modes of production and beyond this the emergence of a globalized, *knowledge-based* economy. Under Fordism economic activity was dominated by the mass production of consumer goods that required large numbers of manual workers (and their managers) working on specific tasks in big factories, as pioneered by the Ford motor company in the USA. Workers thus acquired core skills early and remained in relatively secure jobs throughout their working lives. This model led economic development in the advanced economies for much of the last century, accompanied by *Taylorist* management practices through the setting of productivity-based targets and rewards for all workers.

In the latter part of the century, however, these patterns began to disappear. Manufacturing became more automated and performance driven and production was often transferred to countries with lower wage levels. Employment in the UK and other mature economies became concentrated instead in service work and in the design and development of new (often computer-based) technologies. This required more flexible contractual commitments and working hours (more jobs are part-time or temporary); and technological change meant skills had to be updated throughout a working life. Such post-Fordist processes have accelerated since the turn of this century and have been accompanied by further changes, particularly the growth of knowledge-based and creative industries.

Employment opportunities have been altered by these developments, creating what is sometimes called an 'hour-glass' labour market marked by the expansion of both high-wage non-routine analytical work and lower level unskilled manual work, and the contraction of routine middle level jobs (Hackett et al. 2012). Developments in areas such as banking and other financial or knowledge-based services have benefited some workers. But for many, especially in personal services, employment has become less secure, often part-time and frequently poorly paid. More generally, it has also become more demanding (Green 2009) and, especially outside the public sector, employment contracts have become more individualized and varied, with implications for social security as well as employment policies (Brown and Marsden 2011). Recent research suggests these trends are likely to continue (Brewer et al. 2012) and some analysts point to a possible acceleration with some forms of 'knowledge work' being moved 'offshore', and further polarization between a highly rewarded, skilled minority and larger numbers in low-paid routine work (Brown et al. 2011).

Labour markets have become more diverse in other ways too. The full employment policies of the immediate post-war era were in principle geared to male workers, under a model of family life in which men were 'breadwinners' and women unpaid 'carers', a view endorsed by Beveridge's (1942) social security scheme (see Chapter 17). Of course, this never represented reality for many men and women, and large numbers of women (both single and married) have always been in paid employment and their families reliant on their wages (Crompton 2006). However, alongside more general changes in family structure in the latter part of the twentieth century (including a decline in the birth rate and increases in divorce and lone parent families), there was a significant rise in the proportion of women in the UK workforce, from below 30 per cent in the 1950s to over 45 per cent in the early 2000s when nearly 70 per cent of working-age women were in employment (Duffield 2002). Since then women's employment rate has levelled off slightly to 66 per cent in 2011; but this has included an increase in the numbers of mothers with dependent children in the workforce, which reached 66 per cent in 2010 (Spence 2011).

The patterns of female employment, however, have remained very different to men's (Pascall 2012). For a start, despite the equal pay and sex discrimination legislation mentioned below, women on average still earn 16 per cent less than men, with the pay gap being higher for those in part-time jobs (Platt 2011). In part this reflects a persistently segregated labour market in which women are concentrated in different areas (for instance, in food and drink manufacture, catering, health and social care), and tend to occupy lower level, poorly paid posts. It also, though, reflects a continuing 'motherhood penalty' and the extent to which much of the expansion in women's employment has been in part-time work and welfare services (see Chapter 17).

This is a changing picture, of course; and since the turn of the century there have been a stream of initiatives designed to enable women to access and remain in higher status employment and move up organizational hierarchies, including the work–life balance provisions summarized below. Nevertheless gender differences remain a significant feature of the policy context (Scott and Crompton 2010) and ones that have highlighted other forms of differentiation in the UK labour market, such as the difficulties also faced by many members of ethnic minority groups in entering high level work and their greater vulnerability to unemployment (Platt 2011). Along with changes in the age structure of the workforce these labour market trends have contributed to continuing concern over unemployment and a widening of employment policy in the UK.

WELFARE TO WORK

THE DEVELOPMENT OF WELFARE TO WORK POLICIES

Throughout most of the last century policy measures were in force to encourage and assist those seeking to enter (or re-enter) the labour market. Assistance came from the labour exchanges or jobcentres, and encouragement from the expectation that people seeking social security support should make themselves available for work. The requirement to be available for work can be seen as a threat as well as an encouragement, however; and there has been much dispute over whether it means unemployed workers must take any job offered to them and what the consequences should be if they do not.

The state has long had powers to impose temporary benefit reductions on those refusing a reasonable offer of work or leaving employment without good cause. In practice, however, the conditions attached to unemployment benefits to incentivize job-seeking have varied over time, and have often been at their most draconian at points when labour market demand was weak and levels of unemployment high. This was particularly true of the 'genuinely seeking work' test applied in the 1930s and the conditions attached to the Jobseekers' Allowance (JSA) in 1996 which required claimants to enter an agreement to take positive steps to search for work with sanctions for non-compliance (Alcock et al. 2003).

Historically, however, the social security system did not provide direct assistance to people finding it difficult to gain paid employment. Indeed it operated more to underpin the market basis of employment than as an intervention in that market on behalf of those experiencing difficulties with it. But in the last quarter of the twentieth century, at a time when the economic restructuring outlined above was beginning to affect employment patterns this situation began to alter as more specific schemes were introduced to provide training and work experience for unemployed workers, targeted in particular at those groups finding it hardest to secure entry into a changing market.

The decline of traditional manufacturing employment from the early 1970s also resulted in the collapse of the training and apprenticeships that had accompanied such work, making entry into the labour market for school-leavers with limited academic qualifications much more difficult (see too Chapter 12). These unemployed young adults were one of the target groups for the programmes introduced by a new national agency established by the Conservative government in 1973, the Manpower Services Commission (MSC). It began a range of employment support schemes that have grown in scale and intensity since, though responsibility for managing them has shifted several times and is now overseen in mainland Britain by the DWP.

The most significant was the Youth Opportunities Programme (YOP). This provided training and work experience for 16–19-year-olds and in effect substituted public support for the old private apprenticeships. However, because YOP placements were publicly funded and temporary they did not guarantee access to paid employment, and at the end of the experience many trainees were little better off in labour market terms than they had been before. This has become an intrinsic feature of many subsequent employment support schemes, which similarly seek to equip workers for employment in a market where jobs may still be scarce. In simple terms employment support is not employment. Indeed, it may even be that the work experience provided in such placements can reduce the number of opportunities available as employers seek to take on (publicly subsidized) trainees rather than paid workers – a problem referred to as job displacement.

Similar concerns arose over its 1983 replacement, the broader Youth Training Scheme (YTS) that in the 1990s became the Modern Apprenticeship, and over parallel programmes that were developed for the long-term unemployed, those out of work for six months, a year or more. Their numbers also grew in the 1970s and 1980s prompting the launch of a Community Programme providing a range of work placements, which subsequently changed to the Employment Training scheme.

WELFARE TO WORK POLICIES 1997–2010

When Labour came to power in 1997 it did so pledged to replace much of this provision with a *New Deal* in which training and work experience would be aligned with a renewed commitment to help key groups amongst the unemployed gain entry to the labour market. Indeed the New Deal was initially the only element of its social policy reforms to receive additional public support, from a 'windfall' tax on the private utilities that helped to fund new programmes tailored for particular groups of social security claimants:

- Young people: 18–24-year-olds on Jobseekers Allowance (JSA) for over six months
- Long-term unemployed: over 25s claiming JSA for over 18 months
- Lone parents: with children over five, and over three months on benefit
- Partners of the unemployed: where partners have been on benefit for over six months

- Disabled people: on incapacity benefit (IB) or other disability benefits
- 50 plus: over 50s and their partners on benefits for over six months.

These New Deals varied in principle and practice, but all were premised on the view that working-age benefit entitlements carried with them a duty to engage in employment-related activity. They also heralded a new, extended role for the social security system in preparing claimants for and connecting them to the labour market alongside direct benefit administration (Finn 2011). The New Deal for young people comprised a 'gateway' period of intensive individualized support from a personal adviser in Jobcentre Plus aimed to enhance their job 'readiness' and search skills. It was followed by participation in one of four options: subsidized employment, full-time education/training, voluntary, or environmental task force work. This was in effect mandatory, there being no 'fifth option' of remaining on benefits (DSS 1998a) with support for those refusing to join the scheme being cut.

The over 25s programme too was mandatory and similarly structured; and, in 15 Employment Zones where unemployment levels were especially high, it was supported by specialist agencies contracted to provide support services on a payment by results basis. Initially the New Deals for the other groups were voluntary and centred on personal adviser support or, in the case of disabled people, job broker support provided outside the Jobcentre Plus network by public, commercial or third sector agencies. In 2003, however, a mandatory Pathways to Work scheme was instituted for new IB claimants.

In 2006, at a time when unemployment levels were low, the Labour government launched a further tranche of reforms aimed at raising the employment rate to 80 per cent by shifting people 'off benefits and into work' (DWP 2006b). These were also partly inspired by EU initiatives, as discussed in Chapter 7. They included support for single parents through tax credits and early years provision (see Chapters 8 and 12), and measures to move individuals with ill-health or disabilities into employment, following a review commissioned from the banker Lord Freud (2007; and DWP 2007).

From 2008 work-related requirements were extended to lone parents with children over seven (lowered in 2011 to age five). They were also attached to the new Employment Support Allowance (ESA) for disabled people, alongside a tighter Work Capacity Assessment (see Chapter 8). And the following year the different New Deals were bundled together into a single Flexible New Deal (FND) (DWP 2009b), with provision of the Pathways to Work contracted out to external providers whose payment hinged largely on job placements sustained for more than 13 weeks. To deal with rising unemployment following the 2008 recession, Labour also, however, introduced a number of special schemes, including a £1 billion Future Jobs Fund.

WELFARE TO WORK POLICIES SINCE 2010

The Coalition government took forward a number of the plans for delivery of welfare to work policy being developed by Labour (though not the Future Jobs Fund), backed by claims of radical new approaches to challenging worklessness (DWP 2010c); and indeed Lord Freud become a Minister for Welfare Reform in the new government. In tandem with the benefit cuts and the Universal Credit outlined in Chapter 8 this entailed further tightening the work-related conditions and sanctions attached to working-age benefits and expansion of their scope. There was also further marketization of employment support services.

The centrepiece of the Coalition's bid to 'get Britain working' was the Work Programme (WP) for the long-term unemployed (DWP 2010d, 2011b). Launched in mainland Britain in 2011 this replaced Labour's group-specific and FND schemes with a universal system aimed at breaking the cycle of benefit dependency and getting over 2.4 million people back into work over a seven-year period. While including a voluntary element, participation became mandatory for 18–24-year-olds after nine months on JSA, those over 25 after 12 months (and for some after three months) and those on ESA deemed close to being fit for work. It is also mandatory for lone parents with children (now over five) who, like all those who refuse to participate, face possible benefit losses.

Delivery has been contracted to 18 prime providers, 15 of which were commercial enterprises, who will use 'supply chains' of some 900 subcontractors, including some third sector organizations, to deliver specialist aspects of provision, including the tailored, personalized support that was a cornerstone of Labour's programmes. The WP is funded, however, almost entirely on a 'payment by results' (PBR) basis with providers paid on a sliding scale according to the length of time participants once placed stay in work and the unemployed group they come from – a model that may well be applied in other service areas too (see Chapter 18).

The intention is that the payments to contractors come from savings made as a result of reduced benefit dependency; and within this they are required to meet minimum performance levels determined by government estimates of job outcomes for the participant groups, with an element of market share being shifted from low to high performing providers over the five-year contract period. However, there are fears that, within a continuing weak economy, providers will face problems and the targets set for them may have to be relaxed. Indeed from 2013 the WP is being supplemented by a mandatory Community Action Programme for those who have completed two years on the WP but failed to find employment.

Alongside the WP the government also introduced a Mandatory Work Activity Programme (MWA) aimed at those deemed by Jobcentre Plus as requiring additional support in developing work habits. This required claimants, including some on ESA, to undertake four-week unpaid work experience placements in community-benefiting organizations or risk losing their benefits. Running beside it were other initiatives designed to support people needing additional help as well as the tighter sanctions for JSA claimants discussed above (and see Chapter 8). Faced with rising unemployment, particularly among young adults, the Coalition also launched extra measures including a three-year £1 billion Youth Contract for mainland Britain for extra voluntary work experience places for 18–24-year-olds before they enter the WP, followed by a wage incentive scheme for employers offering 18–24-year-olds from the WP jobs lasting for 26 weeks or more.

Wage incentives have also been made available to support new apprenticeships in England, and extra places have been funded in new Sector Based Work Academies (SBWAs). These are FE colleges or private agencies providing voluntary pre-employment training leading to a guaranteed job interview. In the longer term, however, perhaps the most fundamental development has been the continuation of Labour's policy of raising the education participation age to 17 and, from 2015, to 18 (see Chapter 12).

As mentioned, employment policy has remained a UK-wide domain and most of the welfare to work and related measures instigated by both Labour and the Coalition have applied also to the devolved jurisdictions. Education and skills policy has been devolved, however; and in the areas where they could exercise powers successive administrations in Scotland, Wales and Northern Ireland developed cognate job creation, apprenticeship and training schemes to reduce unemployment. These were similarly expanded in the immediate aftermath of the 2008 recession and redeveloped following the 2011 elections.

Provisions in Scotland for instance have included support for extra apprenticeships to reduce youth unemployment and a 'training for all' commitment for 16–19-year-olds, and in Wales there was a replacement for Labour's Future Jobs Fund (SG 2011e; WG 2011a; Drakeford 2012). The Northern Ireland government maintained its Pathways to Work and Steps to Work employment support system on lines similar to those elsewhere in the UK, and introduced a programme similar to the Youth Contract to cut the number of NEETs (DEL 2012).

MAKING WORK PAY

As with Labour's New Deal, however, the WP was only one plank in the Coalition's employment policy, and both governments also incorporated measures designed to ensure that those on low wages are no worse off in work than on benefits. Probably the most significant of Labour's initiatives here was the introduction in 1999 of the *statutory minimum wage* for all employees, the first time that a national pay floor had been introduced in the UK, though this was common in other industrial countries. While opposed by many in the Conservative Party at the time it has since become an accepted component of employment policy. The rate is set at different levels, on an hourly basis, for those aged over 21, 18–20, under 18 and the first year of an apprenticeship, and is determined annually by the Low Pay Commission. More recently, however, campaigners have also argued for a 'living wage', set at a higher level; and this has been adopted for its employees by the Scottish government and by other bodies.

The second dimension of making work pay under Labour was the introduction of the working and child tax credits to subsidize low wages, considered in Chapter 8. These have been retained by the Coalition and incorporated into the Universal Credit scheme, although the level of many tax credit elements has been cut.

In addition to supporting the low paid, Labour also introduced a series of measures to support the workforce more generally, including both its skill strategy in England (see Chapter 12) and, more broadly, provisions intended to enable individuals to combine work with other commitments. Initially the focus of this was on promoting *family friendly* employment, but it was later expanded into the wider notion of *work–life balance* (WLB), with a range of new rights for staff with caring and family responsibilities seen as meeting organizational as well as employees' needs (see Table 13.1). The extent to which these WLB measures have marked a fundamental shift in the family work nexus, in particular for women, has been questioned (Millar and Haux 2012), however, as have the moves to elevate paid employment over caring work within the family, which it is argued may not be a desirable, or achievable, aspiration for all (Arksey and Kemp 2006).

Table 13.1 Main work–life balance measures 1997–2010	
Type of Support	*Key Legislation*
Child Care/Early Years Learning Entitlements	(see Chapter 12)
Leave Entitlements	1999 Employment Relations Act • Extended maternity leave • New right to time off for adoption • New right to reasonable time off to deal with emergencies 2002 Employment Act • Extended paid maternity leave (from 18 to 26 weeks) • Introduced paid paternity leave (2 weeks) • Introduced adoption leave 2006 Work and Families Act • Extended paid maternity leave (to 39 weeks) • Provided for maternity leave (paid and unpaid) of one year 2010 Additional Paternity Leave Regulations • Provided for an element of shared parental leave
Flexible Working	2002 Employment Act • Introduced right to request [but not necessarily be granted] flexible working for parents of children under six or disabled children under 18 2006 Work and Families Act • Introduced right to request flexible working to carers of adults 2008 Employment Act • Introduced right to apply to work flexibly to parents of all children under sixteen and imposed duty on employers to consider requests seriously

Labour also extended statutory holiday leave and provided for more flexible retirement arrangements, as well as extending training opportunities (as noted in Chapter 12); and these policies were largely taken forward by the Coalition, including plans to augment paternity and shared parental leave. The default retirement age of 65 was abolished to encourage working for longer, the right to request flexible working was extended to all employees with 26 continuous weeks service (HMG 2011d), and workplace health care provisions also encouraged (DWP/HWW 2011).

WORK FIRST

Welfare to work measures continue the focus on supply-side approaches to employment policy discussed above; and critics have argued that, however desirable in principle, they will be less likely to lead to improved levels of employment if the demand for jobs is weak. There is evidence that this was the case early in this century in those parts of the country, such as the former coalfield and manufacturing areas of the North and Midlands of England, South Wales and Central Scotland, where economic growth was limited. It also applied to some extent to youth unemployment. Although Labour claimed success in reducing this (Freud 2007), some commentators had argued that in an expanding labour market many, especially young adults, would probably have found work anyway (Brewer and Shephard 2005), and that the more serious problem of 16–18-year-olds not in education, employment or training (NEETs) had not been significantly tackled (Audit Commission 2010). There was also evidence that, particularly in some parts of the country, the New Deal measures encountered a 'revolving door' problem, with people moving rapidly in and out of short-term employment (Lindsay 2007). There were also concerns about the type of work accessed and the impact of payment-by-results leading contractors to focus on the 'easiest to place' (van Berkel and Borhgi 2008) – sometimes referred to as *creaming* (a focus on those with good work experience) and *parking* (deferring support for those most difficult to help) (see Rees et al. 2013).

These concerns raise more general questions about the broad goals that have underlain employment policy in the UK since the turn of this century. As a number of commentators have pointed out, welfare to work policies here were to some extent modelled on policies developed in the USA, as part of similar strategic commitments to reducing welfare dependency and promoting employment (Deacon 2000; Garnham 2007). Here compulsory participation in publicly funded work placements has been much more widespread, in some States extending to the lone mothers of all young children, and often based on a moral belief in the value of paid employment. Such compulsory employment participation is sometimes referred to as *work first* or, where employment is compulsory, *workfare*.

This can be contrasted with the policies developed in Scandinavian and some continental European countries where entry into paid employment has not been treated as the only viable option. and the support provided for those outside the labour market has included a wider range of social activity including voluntary work and unpaid caring responsibilities. These programmes are sometimes referred to as *social activation* and are based upon very different understandings of the role of employment support in post-Fordist economies (see Lodemel and Trickey 2001; Bonoli 2010; Clasen and Clegg 2011). In the UK welfare to work policies initially included elements of both workfare and social activation, although it was far from clear that the different principles underlying them could operate side-by-side. But the work first approach became increasingly dominant in Labour's policies and has since been extended by the Coalition.

Despite the apparent cross-party consensus on supply-side interventions, however, recessionary pressures have reopened questions about their effectiveness and desirability. Some commentators have again criticized the emphasis on paid work as against other forms of social activity such as caring; and others have argued that the focus on work readiness and employability deflects attention from the low demand for employment and the barriers presented by factors such as the lack of universal childcare and the continuance of discriminatory practices.

There are also continuing concerns over the displacement effects of current provisions, particularly unpaid work experience, which can trap people in insecure low-paid work requiring tax subsidization.

COMPREHENSIVE QUESTIONS

- How do Fordist and post-Fordist labour markets differ?
- What is 'job displacement' and why is it a potential problem within supply-side policies to promote employment?
- To what extent is the Work Programme a continuation of the New Deals?
- Why has work–life balance become a key area of employment policy in the UK?
- What are the differences in principle and in practice between *workfare* and *social activation*?

REFLECTIVE QUESTION

- Should we aim to encourage all adults of working age to enter paid employment?

EMPLOYMENT PROTECTION

Social policy discussion of employment issues in the UK has tended to focus on unemployment rather than more general interventions affecting the workforce (May 2006). However, measures to promote employment protection have a longer history and cover a wide range of provisions. As mentioned earlier, they can be traced back to the early nineteenth century Factories Acts, which controlled hours and conditions of work for some employees in certain industries. These protections were extended in the early twentieth century, for instance under the Trade Boards Act of 1909 which also established minimum wage levels in some industries, enforced by Wages Councils.

Subsequent decades saw the development of further provisions for health and safety at work that were extensively expanded from the 1960s (May and Brunsdon 2007). These included measures setting safeguards and standards for various workplaces (such as fire precautions and safety guards on machines) enforced by public officials that culminated in the 1974 Health and Safety Act and the establishment of the Health and Safety Executive. They also extended to compensation for injuries sustained at work or specified diseases contracted as a result of exposure to certain workplace risks.

The 1960s and 1970s also saw the introduction of a wider range of individual employment rights securing some minimum standards beyond those employees could negotiate within their employment contracts. These covered compensation for unfair dismissal or redundancy, rights to information about terms and conditions of employment, paid sickness and maternity leave and rights to equal pay and equal treatment for women and men. Individual employment rights were also the subject of EU policy, flowing from the Commission's concern to combat 'social dumping'; and measures regarding health and safety, equal pay, and maximum weekly working time were all incorporated into British legislation to comply with EU directives. As seen in Chapter 7, the Conservative governments of the 1980s and early 1990s remained concerned though about what they saw as a 'burden' on business here. They resisted various EU initiatives and reduced some UK-based protections, including abolishing the Wages Councils.

From 1997 however, the Social Charter guaranteeing a range of employment protection for all workers was incorporated into British law, and the Labour governments progressively expanded a range of other employee rights. These included the WLB measures, mentioned above, and provisions for workplace consultation, contributing to what was argued to be a 'regulatory revolution' in UK employment policy and a 'juridification' of employee relations (Taylor and Emir 2009; Dickens and Hall 2009). Nonetheless by comparison with other OECD countries the UK remained one of the least regulated labour markets (OECD 2008).

EU directives have also required governments to introduce measures to ensure equal treatment for women and men at work, although legislation to enforce equal pay and outlaw sex discrimination at work had been initially introduced in the UK in the 1970s. Both of these provisions gave employees who could demonstrate that they were being discriminated against or treated unfairly the right to bring a legal claim against their employer. Enforcement therefore lay with the victims. This model also applied to race and disability legislation, which was similarly overseen by separate agencies in mainland Britain. It was extended in the 2000s to religion and belief, sexual orientation, gender assignment and age, and retained in the consolidating 2010 Equality Act. An overarching Equality Commission for Northern Ireland was established there in 1988, and in 2007 enforcement of all anti-discrimination legislation in Britain was passed to the Commission for Equality and Human Rights. Nevertheless the effectiveness of these measures has continued to depend upon the ability and willingness of the victims of discrimination to act, and the limited remedies available (mainly financial compensation) if they did. Pay differences and discrimination in employment have therefore continued (see Chapter 17).

Since 2010 the Coalition government has pursued a 'lighter touch' approach (HMG 2011d) and established a five-year Employment Law Review to consider labour market legislation across the employment life cycle, with a view to reducing the need for regulation. The employment tribunal system has been reformed, the qualifying period and compensation for claims of unfair dismissal cut, provisions for 'settlement agreements' to speed up dismissal procedures introduced, alongside a new 'Employers Charter'. In a less direct form of deregulation the government has also introduced provisions for employees to give up key employment rights in return for tax-free shares in their company. Further measures that could reduce other employee protections including the EU Working Time Directive provisions remain under consideration, and restrictions on aspects of industrial action by trade unions are also potential areas for future change.

As discussed earlier there has always been some dispute over the extent to which statutory employment protection should underpin (or undermine) bargaining over contractual relations between employers and trade unions acting on behalf of individual workers. In practice this is less of an issue than it was on occasions in the last century, with most trade unions now regarding statutory protections as a floor from which they can seek to negotiate greater protection for their members. More contentious, however, is the scope of measures aiming to control union action and seek a balance between collective and individual employment rights. Employment relations legislation has at times been controversial, with unions claiming that (particularly Conservative) governments have used it to prevent them acting in support of their members; and in the 1980s restrictions on trade union action were introduced by the Thatcher governments.

More generally, however, regulation of collective action has become an established element of employment law, covering such issues as the right to join (or not join) a union, union recognition, the procedures to be followed by trade unions before instructing their members to take industrial action, and the extent to which different forms of action are a legitimate means of pursuing a grievance or dispute with an employer. Whilst Labour retained much of the 1980s legislation, it introduced a statutory recognition procedure and also encouraged a social partnership role for unions (Brown 2011), although some of these measures may now be reviewed by the Coalition.

Employment protection has always occupied something of a secondary status within debate about, and study of, employment policy and this continues today with many social policy writers focusing on employment promotion rather than other developments.

Nevertheless policies to ensure minimum standards of job security, workplace health, working conditions and remuneration are an essential counterpart to provisions aimed at promoting paid employment, especially from a supply-side approach. It is arguably only if jobs offer sufficient security, protection and reward that potential future workers could be justifiably coerced into taking them on. Thus many would contend that employment policy requires government to intervene in the regulation of the labour market and encourage quality work as well as promoting increased participation within it.

COMPREHENSION QUESTIONS

- In what ways have statutory employment measures sought to protect the interests of workers?
- How does legislation seek to prevent discrimination at work?

REFLECTIVE QUESTION

- Should governments intervene to regulate individual employment relations?

FURTHER READING

There is no single comprehensive text on employment policy in Britain. A number of the issues considered in this chapter are covered in the suggested reading on social security for working-age people in Chapter 8. Deacon (2002) explores the theoretical arguments behind recent policies for employment promotion and Clasen and Clegg (2011) provide examples of policy developments in a range of different advanced industrial countries. The best guide to employment protection is produced by the Trades Union Congress, which also provides information on workers' issues and rights: see www.tuc.org.uk. Government papers can be found on the departmental websites at www.dwp.gov.uk, www.bis.gov.uk and the websites of the devolved administrations (see Chapter 6). Useful websites for employment issues are those of the Institute for Employment Studies: www.employment-studies.co.uk and the Chartered Institute of Personnel and Development, www.cipd.co.uk.

Part 3
Theories and Debates

The aim of this section is to provide readers with an appreciation of some of the broader theoretical and empirical influences on the development and operation of social policy. Ideologies are important because they structure the way in which we see the world and the ways in which we therefore analyse and understand it. Ideology influences all social perception; but there are some key ideological perspectives, or frameworks, which have had more direct impact on the development and analysis of social policy. Chapter 14 focuses specifically on these, providing a brief guide to their core principles and the policy implications which flow from these.

Economic development underpins all social relations through production, distribution and employment. The economic context has also been critically important in setting the context for, and limits to, government policy-making. Chapter 15 discusses the way this economic context has developed in Britain over the recent past and explores the consequences that this has had for policy-making and hence for welfare provision, including recent economic changes and future prospects. Welfare services must also be paid for, therefore; and the different ways in which funding for services is organized is discussed in the next chapter, which also reveals that this leads to benefits and costs for different groups within society.

Indeed, whatever the aims and intentions of the policy-makers, the real impact of policies depends upon how these are delivered within society and who does, or does not, use or benefit from them. In particular this includes the ways in which social divisions restrict the ability of social policies to provide equally for all. We live in a society divided by class, gender, ethnicity and other divisions; and the evidence discussed in Chapter 17 reveals that these divisions have significant implications for the different experiences of welfare for these different social groups.

Chapter 18 focuses more generally on analysis of, and policy development on, the delivery of welfare – in particular the contrast between the interests of the *users* and those of the *producers* of welfare services. Concern with the delivery of welfare services is also now a major area of policy intervention in its own right, however; and the recent development of management, inspection and audit of services is explained and summarized.

The book closes with a final chapter which looks at the past development of social policy and outlines the many major changes to British society that have flowed from this. The focus then shifts to the future and the social, economic and political trends that are likely to influence policy development. Although, as Chapter 1 explains, social policy is largely a *prescriptive* subject (analysts do seek to influence policy development), this chapter does not contain any plans or prescriptions for the future. Rather it is an exercise in 'crystal ball gazing' – although, as with any such speculation, the visions revealed are always likely to be rather hazy ones, and future events may in the long run turn out differently.

14

Ideologies of Welfare

SUMMARY OF KEY POINTS

- Ideologies structure our views of the world. They are *critical* and *prescriptive*, leading to disagreement and debate about what should be done. Those influencing social policy are called 'ideologies of welfare'.
- Ideologies of welfare have often been located along a continuum from *left* (pro-state) to *right* (pro-market) positions, although not all can be contained within such a simplistic framework.
- Neoliberalism argues that state provision of welfare is incompatible with free market economic growth and leads to a 'dependency culture', although few supporters advocate complete withdrawal of state welfare support.
- Support for the Middle Way was part of the *Butskellite* 'consensus' on welfare that emerged in the mid-twentieth century and also underpins aspects of the Coalition government approach in the new century. They support collective welfare provision in partnership with market-based economic growth.
- Social democrats believe that capitalist societies can (and should) be reformed to meet the welfare needs of all citizens. Social democracy is generally distinguished from democratic socialism, which advocates the ultimate replacement of all capitalist relations.
- Marxists argue that state welfare provision within capitalism is inherently unstable and will lead to failure and conflict, although socialist alternatives have not proved viable in practice.
- New social movements challenge the left/right orthodoxy of welfare ideologies by pointing to other social divisions and socioeconomic issues that underpin welfare policy and practice.
- Postmodernists argue that single ideological frameworks cannot provide an effective basis for analysis of complex societies, and that ideological analysis should concentrate upon how such frameworks are constructed and influence policy development.

IDEOLOGY

The concept of ideology is one of the most important in social science. However, it is also one of the most contested, and one of the most misused and misunderstood. For instance, ideology is sometimes taken to mean the adoption of a false or inaccurate perception of the real world; this is then contrasted with the true perspective, which is supposedly provided by scientific inquiry. This is not the sense in which ideology is normally understood in social policy debate, however; and it is not the sense in which it is used in this book. We use ideology more broadly as a concept that refers to the systems of beliefs within which *all* individuals perceive *all* social phenomena. In this usage no one system of beliefs is more correct, or more privileged, than any other.

In this sense, therefore, all of us have ideologies: they are our own systems of beliefs that shape and structure the way we see the world, and make judgements about it. And, of course, each individual's ideological perspective is different and unique. We do not all agree with one another about everything. Indeed, it is our disagreements and differences that make debate and development both desirable and possible. If we were all the same it would not only be a dull world; in terms of social development, it would also be a dead one. Thus individual ideologies differ, and they are a source of debate and conflict. They are also both *critical* and *prescriptive*: we know what is wrong with what we see, and we know what should be done about it. As a result of this they are therefore *partial* and *value laden*; we do not know or understand everything but we do know what we like and do not like.

Ideological perspectives therefore condition the way in which all of us perceive the world in which we live, and they do so in a way that leaves all of us with a more or less restricted and biased perspective on it. If this seems to be a rather depressing starting point, it should not be judged so. No one can know everything or be right about everything; but that does not mean that we do not know anything or that our views are always only a product of our own personal values. Our individual ideological perspectives are limited and biased, and they are unique; but they are not isolated. As individuals we are also part of broader social structures from which we receive the support we need to survive, and through which we give support to others. Our individual systems of belief are also part of broader ideological perspectives from which we draw the ideas and values which we use to form judgements, and to which we may contribute ideas and values of our own.

Individual ideologies are constructed within wider ideological perspectives in which views are shared and debated, and within which shared views are held and disseminated. Such broader ideological perspectives may be held by relatively small social groups and may focus specifically upon particular issues, for example, the neighbourhood campaign group whose members all wish to preserve the character of their area and oppose new development plans. However, they may also be much wider in both scale and scope, enlisting adherence or support from the majority of people throughout the country (or even across countries) and addressing a range of social issues from a particular perspective. Such broader ideological perspectives influence the way individual ideological views are formed and developed, and through this influence those individuals, or groups, who are in positions of power are able to shape the world in which we live. Indeed it is *because* ideologies shape the social world that we debate so passionately about them, and within them. The power of ideology cannot be overestimated in social science; and, as we shall see, in social policy ideologies of welfare have shaped and structured all perceptions of welfare policy and the development of all policy planning.

It is important to recognize here, however, that ideological perspectives not only determine which policies we propose to develop or support but also influence how we view, and judge, policy developments that have already taken place. Take, for example, the introduction of the right of all tenants to buy their council houses by the Conservative government in 1980. For many commentators with a right-wing political perspective, including some members of that government, this was seen as a victory for the rights of individual freedom and self-determination over the paternalistic control of state welfare bureaucrats. For some other Conservative politicians, and for some social policy commentators, it was seen as a necessary development within housing policy to accommodate more rationally the 'mixed economy' of welfare and the overlap, or partnership, between state and private sector provision. For some on the political left, however, the sale of council houses was a dissipation of public assets and a betrayal of one of the major planks of the welfare state.

No one of these ideological judgements is any more right or wrong than any of the others, although they are all perspectives on the same policy development. They are merely different judgements from different ideological standpoints. Of course, there are some views (such as racism) which many people may find offensive; but even here not all (particularly racists) agree – and, in any event, they do not exhaust the different ideological views that might be held. However, views such as those outlined above are not just the product of idiosyncratic individual attitudes: they are quite widely shared ideological views and are based within broader perspectives on welfare policy from within which similar judgements would probably be made about other policy initiatives. In other words, they are part of broader ideologies of welfare.

At this broader social level, however, the size and scope of ideological perspectives will vary dramatically. A perspective shared by the majority of people in a country will be rather more important than one shared by a small group of friends and neighbours. In their discussion of ideologies of welfare, George and Wilding (1994) discussed this point and argued that *major* ideological perspectives must possess certain characteristics in order to be regarded as of particular social importance. They outline four such characteristics:

- *Coherence* – ideological perspectives must have an internal logic and theoretical consistency
- *Pervasiveness* – ideological perspectives must be current and relevant, as old perspectives may have lost their social base
- *Extensiveness* – ideological perspectives must be widely shared within, or across, societies
- *Intensiveness* – ideological perspectives must command the support, and commitment, of those who share them; they must really be believed.

Therefore an ideological perspective is a shared view, or set of views, with a clear social impact. Of course not all ideological perspectives focus on, or even address, social policy issues; indeed, most do not. We are not concerned here, however, with all ideologies, but only with those that do address welfare issues and focus on description, and judgement, of policy development, and prescription for future policy reform. These we can call *ideologies of welfare*.

THEORY AND POLITICS

If ideologies of welfare are widely shared and coherent perspectives on policy and reform, this raises the question of what, if any, is the distinction between such ideological perspectives and theoretical analysis and debate of welfare issues. What about theories of welfare? In practice (and in theory!) the distinction between ideology and theory is not a clear or watertight one, and neither is it uncontested. Sometimes the two concepts are used more or less interchangeably: one person's theory is another person's ideology. However, it is probably fair to say that some broad differences in usage and understanding do exist, even though these would not be universally accepted.

A theoretical perspective may exist within a broader, and looser, ideological one. However, theoretical discourse is likely to be less partial and less value laden than ideology, and to be more comprehensive and logical. A theoretical perspective has more than an individual coherence: it has a systematic logical structure that is allied to a descriptive, rather than a prescriptive, approach to policy issues; it is generally presented in academic terms, for a largely academic audience. Theorists are not generally seeking to popularize or to persuade, but rather to describe and to convince; and they aim to convince only those who share their academic interests and can follow their academic arguments.

Theories of welfare are therefore produced by, and for, a relatively narrow group of academics and their students. In contrast, although ideologies of welfare are more partial, political and prescriptive, they are also more popular. While few people would claim any knowledge of, or support for, a theoretical approach to welfare, many would no doubt hold, and debate, ideological perspectives on welfare (or at least on welfare issues). Thus, although we are not all academics or theorists, we do all have, and share, ideologies of welfare. Or, to put it another way, we may not know about – or even understand – the welfare pluralist case against unaccountable state monopoly providers, but we do know that we want independent advice about the refusal of our claim for a social security payment. Theories of welfare are therefore narrower and more academic than ideological perspectives; it is for this reason that we focus here on the broader category of ideology. Both theory and ideology, however, are also linked to *politics*. As we discussed in Chapter 1, social policy is a prescriptive subject: it focuses on the development and implementation of political changes. Inevitably, and in most cases avowedly, therefore, it seeks to intervene in, and influence, political debate. Ideologies of welfare are linked to the politics of welfare, and different political allegiances and practices are based in different ideological perspectives.

Commentators have frequently attempted to compare ideologies of welfare according to their location within a continuum of political preferences. George and Wilding did this in 1976 in their first book on ideology and social welfare. In their later text (1994) they produced a table summarizing a total of ten separate analyses of ideologies of welfare. These various analyses identify a range of different numbers of perspectives and also sometimes give these perspectives different names. In practice, however, many analysts place the different perspectives that they identify at different points within a continuum moving from the political left to the political right, in particular in terms of their support for (or opposition to) the role of the state in welfare provision.

Thus on the *left* are socialists or Marxists, who believe the state should play the major, or exclusive, role in the provision of social policy; on the *right* are anti-collectivists or liberals, who believe individuals should be free to provide (or not) for whatever needs they wish. In between are the Fabians, the social democrats, the reluctant collectivists and others. Of course, not all ideologies of welfare can be so readily classified along such a left to right political continuum, as we shall see later. Nevertheless, the link between ideology and politics in social policy, and the central role played in both of debate about the relative roles of the state and the market, means that political differences here are also likely to represent ideological differences, and vice versa.

However, although ideology and politics may be linked, they are not the same thing. Ideology is concerned with ideas, ideals and principles; politics is concerned with pragmatism and results. Thus debate and study of the politics of welfare focuses not primarily upon differing perspectives and approaches, still less on the differing explanations that are the concern of theory, but rather upon events and achievements. Thus both Deakin's (1994) book on *The Politics of Welfare*, and Page's (2007) book *Revisiting the Welfare State*, examined the changes in British welfare policy following the creation of the welfare state in the latter half of the last century, pointing out how the changes in policy were the result of changes in the power and influence of different political perspectives. Timmins (2001) examined the links between political debate and policy change over this period in more detail, taking analysis up to the start of the new century; and more recently Bochel (2011) has brought together analysis of the arguments underpinning the politics of the Conservative Party in the 2000s, which are now at the heart of the Coalition government in the UK. In all writing on the politics of welfare, however, the differences in view are contrasted in terms of their impact on the development and implementation of policy.

During the first two decades following the war, however, the appearance of political consensus over the future direction of policy development, characterized by the notion of *Butskellism* (see Chapter 1), suggested that such political differences had been superseded. Commentators argued that this also implied that ideological differences had disappeared (in particular, the differences between left and right over the role of the state) and that future political conflict would be 'a fight without ideologies' (Lipset 1963). This *end of ideology* thesis proved to be a little premature, or over-simplistic, however, for ideological disagreements did remain and, in particular after the early 1970s, they were represented again in political debate and conflict over the future direction of reform, with a significant divide opening up between the Conservative right and the Labour left over the appropriate future direction for policy development.

At the beginning of the twenty-first century theoretical debates and political disagreements remain at the centre of discussion about the way social policy should be developed, and these are underpinned by ideologies of welfare that provide very different understandings of the ways in which welfare and wellbeing should be identified and addressed within modern society. As we shall see, these different ideologies of welfare also extend beyond the more traditional left to right continuum of support (or not) for state welfare to embrace ideological perspectives that emphasize other divisions and disagreements, and even to suggest that traditional ideologies can no longer provide viable explanatory frameworks in the complex (post)modern world that we now occupy.

COMPREHENSION QUESTIONS

- Why did George and Wilding argue that ideological perspectives must contain certain characteristics?
- What is the difference between ideology and politics?
- Are some ideologies of welfare more popular than others; and, if so, why is this?

REFLECTIVE QUESTION

- Could there be and 'end' to ideology?

NEOLIBERALISM

As we discussed in Chapter 1, the pro-market, anti-state ideological perspective of the New Right developed widespread support in Britain in the 1970s and 1980s, and also in some other countries such as the USA. This newfound political influence became associated with the Conservative governments under Thatcher in the 1980s and, together with the rapid growth in the numbers of commentators contributing their ideas to the government at that time, it made the New Right *new*. However, in practice these ideas, and the broader perspective from within which they are drawn, are not all that new and indeed were largely an attempt to adapt classical nineteenth-century *laissez-faire* liberalism to late twentieth-century circumstances (see Chapter 15). The New Right is thus also known as *neoliberals* or *market liberals*.

Many of the recent neoliberal theorists of social policy draw directly, and explicitly, upon the writings of Hayek, who had been consistently developing the case for market liberalism throughout the period of the establishment and growth of the post-war welfare state (Hayek 1944, 1960 and 1982). Hayek's argument was that there was a fundamental contradiction between the operation of markets and the intervention of the state, and that state intervention would inevitably lead to market dysfunction. He also argued that state intervention involved an unwarranted interference with the freedom of individuals to organize their own affairs and, therefore, that intervention was only justified if its aim was to protect individual freedom, for example, the use of the criminal law to protect private property.

Hayek's preference for market over state was also shared by the other main source of New Right theory and ideology, the American writer Milton Friedman (1962). Friedman too argued that, left to their own devices, markets would naturally protect individuals because consumer sovereignty would ensure producers adapted their services to meet consumer needs; but that, if the state intervened to seek to meet needs directly, this would distort the working of the market and lead to an economic collapse, in which both state and individuals would suffer.

Throughout the post-war period the ideas of Hayek and Friedman were propounded in Britain by a right-wing 'think tank', the Institute of Economic Affairs (IEA), but theirs was very much a minority voice against the welfare 'consensus' of the time. In the 1970s, however, the onset of inflation and rising unemployment and the collapse in the world economy appeared to demonstrate that the predictions of market distortion and dysfunction through state intervention were correct; and the IEA found a new confidence in, and a new audience for, proposals for rolling back the boundaries of state welfare and restoring the free market. Other voices also joined with the IEA in the chorus of anti-state criticism. In 1974 the Centre for Policy Studies (CPS), another think tank, was formed by Margaret Thatcher (later Conservative Prime Minister) and Keith Joseph (one of her close political allies); and in 1979 an independent right-wing policy centre, the Adam Smith Institute (ASI), was also established. Together these organizations, and their newfound political allies, gave neoliberal thinking a powerful push towards the centre stage of ideological debate.

The main plank of neoliberal thinking on welfare is its opposition to extensive state intervention to provide public services; in effect, opposition to the very idea of a 'welfare state'. The welfare state is undesirable, neoliberals argue, on economic, ideological and political grounds, and also, because it is undesirable in theory, it is unworkable in practice.

In *economic* terms they argue the welfare state is undesirable because it involves interference with the free working of market. This leads to a failure of markets to develop properly, because state monopolies dominate many areas of provision (for example, rented housing). More pertinently perhaps, however, it also leads to a crippling drain on private market wealth (and therefore investment) because of the ever-growing fiscal demands of public expenditure to meet the costs of expanding state welfare services. State intervention thus leads to economic recession as, it was claimed, was realized in Britain and elsewhere in the 1970s; and economic growth is only restored by cutting public expenditure and reducing the role, and scope, of the state as, it was alleged, was successfully achieved in the 1980s. What is more, it follows from this, therefore, that future economic growth can only be sustained if welfare is further and further contained, as the austerity policies of the Coalition government from 2011 also assume.

The *ideological* objections of neoliberals to state welfare centre around their concern over the supposed problems of *perverse incentives* and the *dependency culture*. By providing welfare services for all through the state, it is argued, individuals are effectively discouraged from providing these for themselves or for their families. Indeed, people are not only discouraged, they are effectively trapped into wholesale reliance upon the support of others (the dependency culture). This is most clearly revealed in the 'problem' of perverse incentives, an idea associated in particular with the work of the American theorist, Charles Murray (1984, and see Deacon 2002). Murray focused primarily upon the operation of social security protection, which, he argued, by providing everyone with a guaranteed basic standard of living, made it attractive for some people to opt for this rather than seeking to provide for themselves through paid employment. This is particularly the case with means-tested benefits, where entitlement is related to individual income levels, so that increases in income merely lead to loss of benefits. This has long been recognized in the problem of the *poverty trap*, discussed in Chapter 8 (and see Deacon and Bradshaw 1983, Ch. 8). Murray's argument gives it a different ideological slant, focusing on the moral perversity of state dependency and its effect in driving people out of the labour market. The British Conservative MP, Rhodes Boyson (1971), put it rather more pejoratively when he argued that the welfare state 'saps the collective moral fibre of our people as a nation'.

The *political* undesirability of the welfare state for neoliberals is best exemplified through an examination of what they refer to as *public choice theory*. This too has its roots in US scholarship, especially in the writing of a group of theorists called the 'Virginia School' (Buchanan 1986). Public choice theory involves the application of microeconomic calculation to party political behaviour (in itself a rather dubious exercise); and in particular it involves the analysis of politics from the assumption that all political actors are motivated only by self-interest. Despite its dubious assumptions, however, the argument is an important and a persuasive one. The main point is that within established welfare states all social groups will inevitably press for state support for their needs to be met, and that this pressure is likely to be supported by state welfare bureaucrats for whom expanded welfare services mean an extended power base, and also by politicians who can make themselves electorally popular by promising to legislate to meet more and more welfare needs. Thus no one in the political process has any interest in controlling the expansionary tendencies of state welfare, with the result that it acquires the momentum of a runaway train (with, it is argued, ultimately much the same disastrous consequences for all on board).

State welfare is thus seen by neoliberals to be economically distorting, ideologically perverse and politically uncontrollable. It is also, they claim, in any event hopelessly *impractical*. State provision of welfare services assumes that politicians and bureaucrats within the state machinery can be trusted with the provision of welfare services to all. Even if these people could be trusted ideologically and politically (and of course New Right protagonists do not believe that they could be), how could they be trusted in practice to know what sort of welfare services different people want or need? In a large and diverse society, they argue, it is simply not possible to know how to meet all social needs. The result of this is, at *best*, that people act themselves to tailor or extend state services through private adaptations; and, at *worst*, that standardized services are provided which meet the real needs of no one (for instance, the stories of council houses all painted alternately with red and green doors, or concerns over 'bog-standard' schools).

Nevertheless, although neoliberals argue that state welfare is neither desirable nor practical, they are not necessarily prepared to countenance its complete disappearance. Even Hayek envisaged some role for state welfare, primarily as a selective and residual provision for those unable to provide for themselves on the private market, although Friedman's position was rather different (see George and Page 1995; George, 2012). Most of recent neoliberal theorists have also argued that such a 'safety net' state welfare sector will in reality still be needed (and therefore, presumably, still be desirable), although Murray (2006) has argued for an alternative policy in which all public welfare is replaced by a simple annual grant to all adults, with which they can purchase welfare services from any available providers. Despite this and other anti-state rhetoric, however, neoliberalism remains for the most part within the bounds of the mixed economy of welfare, which is found in practice in all modern welfare capitalist countries.

It has been argued by some that neoliberalism has been challenging the balance of the mixed economy in such countries because of the influence of international agencies such as the World Bank and the IMF on the development of welfare policy across the globe. The IMF forced the UK government to change its social and economic policy plans in the 1970s in response to the rise in oil prices and consequent recession (see Chapter 15); and both it and the World Bank have been influential in shaping welfare policy in the former communist states (see Deacon et al. 1997) and, more recently, responses in many countries to the 2007/08 credit crunch. However, although neoliberalism may dominate thinking in these agencies, their influence is far from irresistible, and their impact in different countries varies significantly (Ellison 2006) and is not always consistent (Deacon 2011).

Indeed even during the Thatcher governments of the 1980s in the UK, the Prime Minister and her closest followers had to wrestle with those within the Conservative Party (as well as those outside) who wanted to retain universal state services, so that reform was restricted to the restructuring of the management and operation of welfare services and the more direct encouragement of separate private provision alongside these. Of course, in a sense this merely reveals in practice our previous point about the importance of the difference between ideological perspectives and real political practices. It also reveals that, whatever the predilections of governments and other policy agencies, there are always other ideological perspectives at play.

COMPREHENSION QUESTIONS

- Why do neoliberals argue that state welfare undermines economic growth?
- What is 'public choice theory' and what are its implications for the politics of welfare policy?

THE MIDDLE WAY

The term 'Middle Way' is taken from the title of a book on social and economic policy written in 1938 by the Conservative politician (and Prime Minister in the 1950s), Harold Macmillan. It is used by George and Wilding (1994) to refer to a perspective which to some extent spans the political divide between the Conservative, Liberal and Labour parties, and which they referred to in their earlier analysis of ideologies of welfare as *reluctant collectivism* (George and Wilding 1976). Other Conservative supporters of the Middle Way include the prominent post-war architect of the reform of state education, R. A. B. Butler, and more recently Gilmour (1978). All of them were supporters of the positive role of state welfare within advanced capitalist economies, and this of course distanced them significantly from the neoliberals of the New Right.

However, the Middle Way is more than just the ideology of the centrist wing of the Conservative Party. Through the views of Butler, in particular, it is associated with the supposed cross-party consensus on the role of state welfare that dominated politics in the period immediately following the Second World War, and is captured in the term *Butskellism* (see Chapter 1). It is thus the ideological perspective that informed Beveridge and Keynes in their recommendations for the social and economic reforms that formed the basis of post-war policy development. Both Keynes and Beveridge were Liberals, and this perspective has also therefore been referred to as *liberal collectivism*.

The common theme that unites both left and right adherents to the Middle Way, therefore, is their commitment to the collective provision of social services and the planning of economic development, through the use of the power and legitimacy of the state. They do not believe that the free market alone can be relied upon to protect all citizens. However, as the phrase 'reluctant collectivists' implies, Middle Way supporters are concerned about the principles of collectivism espoused by socialist perspectives to the left. In particular, they justify the role of collective provision because of the practical benefits that it provides for a market economy, not because of the alternative to this that it might represent. In other words, reluctant collectivists stress the advantages of partnership between state and market rather than the opposition between them that those to the right and left foresee.

This partnership between state and market is based upon the practical benefits that state intervention can provide for the development and growth of a capitalist economy. Keynes envisaged state intervention as a means of ensuring growth and profitability in a market economy and his commitment was to state intervention, rather than merely state planning, as we discuss in Chapter 15. It is also a partnership that is based upon the obligations that the government in a market economy carries to ensure the social protection of all citizens. Thus, where the market cannot provide, the state must (perhaps reluctantly) be moved in. This is predicated upon a holistic vision of social structure and social obligations, captured in the phrase *One Nation*, which was the title adopted by a backbench group of Conservative Middle Way MPs in the 1950s. However, it is not a vision based on only one model of social protection. Middle Way support for a political partnership between the market and the state was also expected to be replicated within welfare provision; as Beveridge (1942, 1948) himself envisaged, the presumption was that a mixed economy of welfare agencies would continue to operate in which the state would rarely be a monopoly provider.

The Middle Way is thus an ideological perspective forged out of pragmatism rather than principle. Social needs are recognized and acknowledged to be a public responsibility; but so, too, is private investment and economic growth. Middle Way theorists, such as Keynes, argued that both were inextricably interlinked. Economic growth is needed to ensure social needs can continue to be met; but economic growth will not be achieved in a society where social problems and social divisions are permitted to continue unchecked.

It might be argued that (albeit with mixed success) such a pragmatic perspective has dominated policy development in Britain since the welfare reforms of the 1940s, although it certainly came under threat from the New Right during the Thatcherite governments of the

1980s. A similar picture can also be found in many other European welfare capitalist countries. In Germany, France, Belgium, the Netherlands and Italy, for example, welfare state protections have been supported, and introduced, within capitalist market economies and have contributed to continuing growth within these economies too. For example, within Germany the Christian Democratic party has allied support for state welfare and capitalist development to employment-based welfare and support for 'traditional' family structures, and has enjoyed significant political support, often encouraged by an electoral system that produces more frequent coalition governments.

At the beginning of this century in both Britain and Germany, however, Conservative and Christian Democrat governments gave way to social democratic parties, under Blair and Schröder, which also made an appeal to a centre ground, state and market, approach to welfare policy, which they referred to as the *Third Way* (in Germany, *Die Neue Mitte*, or the new middle). There is much debate over the extent to which this new Third Way was an attempt to capture the old Middle Way ground of the liberal collectivists, or even the New Right (see Driver and Martell 2002 and 2006; Powell 1999 and 2008). Since then in Germany a new Coalition government led by the Christian Democrats under Merkel have pursued similar policies to those developed by Schröder; and in Britain the Conservatives under Cameron initially claimed to have returned to some extent to the centre ground – although the austerity policies of the Coalition government have led in practice to significant attacks on comprehensive public provision. So the question now perhaps is how far there is still a significant difference between the reluctant collectivists and the social democrats.

COMPREHENSION QUESTIONS

- Why are Middle Way supporters sometimes referred to as 'reluctant collectivists'?
- To what extent is the Middle Way a pragmatic compromise between the state and the market rather than a principled alternative to both?
- Have the Conservatives under Cameron moved back to the Middle Way?

SOCIAL DEMOCRACY

Social democracy is the main ideological perspective to the left of the Middle Way. In Britain it has traditionally been associated with the Fabian tradition on the left of the Labour Party, although it was centre-left Labour members (to the right in party terms) who left Labour in the early 1980s to set up a separate Social Democratic Party (which subsequently merged with the Liberals). After that Blair's 'New Labour' party of the 1990s was based on an attempt to adapt social democratic principles to twenty-first century social issues. In many continental European countries parties going explicitly under the title of Social Democrats have frequently constituted the main political opposition to the centre right and have often been in government themselves, in particular in Scandinavia.

There has sometimes been debate, however, about the extent to which the social democratic perspective can (or should) be separated from *democratic socialism*, the term used by George and Wilding in 1994. For instance, it can be distinguished on the grounds that democratic socialism implies a commitment to radical socialist change, albeit achieved by democratic means, whereas social democracy implies support for existing democratic structures but the use of these to pursue policies that are more interventionist and socially responsible. However, such a distinction is not consistently borne out in practice; and, even if there might be potential theoretical disagreement between the two perspectives over *ends*, there is substantial ideological and political consensus across them over *means*.

The common ground that social democrats and democratic socialists share here is the pursuit of social justice through the gradual reform of the – predominantly capitalist – market economy. As the early Fabians openly claimed, all social democrats are gradualists rather than revolutionaries; and, although they frequently identify major social problems within capitalist economies, they are committed to using the existing structures of power to seek a resolution, or amelioration, of these problems within immediate social circumstances. For social democrats, reform is very much a case of bread today rather than jam tomorrow.

The social democrat belief in the pursuit of social justice within a capitalist economy, however, is based both on practical politics and moral principles. The *practical politics* is the use of working-class power, both through the industrial muscle of the trades union movement and through the electoral success of the Labour Party (formed by the trade unions), to force the capitalist holders of wealth and control to concede to a redistribution of these privileges, under the implicit threat of otherwise more revolutionary or disruptive social change. Social democracy in Britain, therefore, has traditionally sought a political home in the Labour Party. The *moral principles* are those of collectivism and solidarity; in other words, the desirability of mutual support. These principles have also sometimes been linked to Christian values of care and concern for one's fellow man, or woman. Many leading social democrats, such as Tawney (and more recently Blair), have been Christians, although of course many have not.

Perhaps the earliest theoretical exposition of the major themes of social democracy can be found in Tawney's (1931) discussion of the *strategy of equality*, in which he argued that social justice could, and should, be pursued within a capitalist economy through the introduction of state welfare services and redistributive tax and benefit policies. Fifteen years later the post-war welfare state reforms could be seen as an attempt by the left-wing Labour government, under the leadership of Attlee, to engage directly in such a strategy. Subsequent criticisms of the achievements of state welfare, in particular in securing greater equality in access to services, have cast doubt upon the viability of such a strategy (Le Grand 1982). However, during the early post-war years, Fabian politicians and academics such as Crosland (1956) and Titmuss (1958) argued that, despite remaining inequalities, the welfare state had resulted in an irreversible transfer of power and resources to the lower classes and had therefore fundamentally altered the character of the social and economic structure of society.

Despite the later criticisms – and the anti-state reforms of the 1980s – there can be little doubt that Crosland and Titmuss were, in part at least, correct in their assessment of the impact of the welfare state. The introduction of state provision for health, education and social security did effectively displace much private market provision in these areas, and of course this is why the New Right later opposed such measures. The universal welfare state is often claimed by social democrats as the embodiment of their ideological support for the pursuit of social justice, and they contrast this with the grudging support for more limited state welfare advanced by the Middle Way.

In twentieth-century Britain it is arguable that social democratic ideology only achieved any real political influence during the brief period of Labour Party government from 1945 to 1951, although even then by no means all members of the Labour government could be called social democrats. However, in some other European countries, notably in Scandinavia, social democratic governments were in power for the major part of the latter half of the century, and here the gradual transformation of capitalism and the pursuit of a strategy of equality through universal state welfare has been more consistently attempted and achieved (Baldwin 1990; Kautto et al. 2001).

Scandinavian social democrat theorists such as Esping-Andersen (1985) and Korpi (1983) have argued openly for the pursuit of a 'democratic road' to socialism through the transformatory politics of state welfare. In countries such as Sweden and Denmark universal state provision has led to more extensive welfare protection and to greater social equality than in other welfare capitalist countries, such as Britain. Electoral support for social democracy in Scandinavia suggests that such an ideological perspective can in practice be popular and, although more right-of-centre governments have enjoyed short periods of office in both Sweden and Denmark in more recent years, there has been no significant departure from the social democratic approach to welfare policy there.

Another Scandinavian theorist, Therborn (see Therborn and Roebroek 1986), has argued further that, once achieved, the welfare state becomes an irreversible feature of any modern democratic society, both because it is functional for the economy and because the protection that it provides will guarantee its electoral popularity (or rather the popularity of those parties that claim to protect it). This may suggest that the democratic road to social reform is more than just an ideological vision: it is a social fact. For instance, research in Britain in the 1980s and 1990s demonstrated that popular support for state welfare services remained high even during periods of right-wing Conservative government (Taylor-Gooby 1991); and more recently it was a significant factor in the securing of three election victories for Labour and in the shift to the centre by the Conservatives in their coalition with the Liberal Democrats.

However, towards the end of the last century the popularity and desirability of the social democratic approach to welfare began to be questioned, at least within the Labour Party in the UK. In part this was a product of the electoral successes of the New Right Conservative governments of the 1980s and early 1990s and the need for Labour to mount a credible opposition to these; but in part it was the outcome of a more fundamental review of the central role that state welfare (and the 'welfare state') had traditionally played within social democracy.

These questions were raised by some Fabian critics in the 1980s (Plant 1988). However, they became more prominent in the early 1990s when, after the 1992 election defeat, the then Labour leader, John Smith, established a *Commission on Social Justice*, chaired by Gordon Borrie, to review past approaches to social policy and make proposals for future development. Its report (Borrie 1994) distinguished three different approaches to policy development:

- The *deregulators*, in effect the neoliberals, who favoured private markets over public provision
- The *levellers*, who were the supporters of old-style social democratic justice through redistribution and tax-financed public services
- The *investors*, who linked social justice to support for, and investment in, economic growth within a market economy.

It was clear that the Commission favoured the third of these; and, although it never achieved any formal status (in part because before it was completed Smith had died and been replaced as Labour leader by Tony Blair), this 'investor' approach became central to the 'Third Way' rhetoric that was championed by Blair's 'New Labour' governments after the 1997 election. Blair himself wrote a Fabian pamphlet extolling the virtues of the Third Way (Blair 1998). In this he drew on the work of the academic, Tony Giddens (1998, 2002), who had also used the concept and argued that such a 'new' approach was necessary to adapt policy development to the changed social and economic climate of the 1990s and the new century.

Many of the policy statements of the Labour administrations of 1997–2010 referred explicitly or implicitly to the need for a new approach within social democracy, between the state and the market and emphasized individual and community responsibility as well as public support (see Powell 1999, 2002, 2008). Labour also drew on similar policy approaches that were being promoted elsewhere, including Schröder's 'new middle' in Germany and, in particular, the 'New Democrats' under Clinton in the USA (see Jordan 1998). At the beginning of this century, therefore, social democratic politics in Europe and North America had moved to embrace a new, and more explicit, compromise between state support and capitalist market economy. However, as critics such as Page (2007) have argued, this has also resulted in the abandonment of some of the core principles of state welfare and a consequent shift towards a pragmatist approach to policy development and an undesirable level of compromise with capitalist market principles.

MARXISM

Opposition to the inequities of the market and to the ineffectiveness of the welfare state in challenging or combating these has for some time come from the far left of the political perspective, and has been voiced by critics who sometimes trace this opposition back to the theoretical analysis of capitalist economies developed in the nineteenth century by Karl Marx (Marx 1970). Marx's claim was that capitalism was an inherently oppressive economic structure in which the working class were exploited by the capitalist class through the labour market (see Chapter 15). The conflict to which this oppression gave rise would lead eventually to the overturning of capitalist power and its replacement with a socialist state in which all the people would own all the means of production, and all social needs could therefore be met. Marxists are thus also usually *socialists*. However, some also made a distinction between socialism and *communism*, which is a situation reached after state socialism when all production is in the hands of the people and the need for central state control has 'withered away'.

Socialism, or communism, is argued by Marxists to be the logical, and desirable, alternative to the failures of both capitalist markets and state welfare. However, their visions of socialist society are generally rather utopian, and usually contain no clear view of the route to be taken to achieve such equilibrium and harmony, except for the claim that revolutionary, rather than gradual, social change would be necessary, involving the overthrow of existing democratic governments (which in effect support capital) and the seizure of power by the representatives of the working class.

This is not a political programme that has ever attracted much effective support in Britain or in any other Western European country; thus its political potential here has been pretty limited. However, socialist revolution, inspired by Marx, did take place in Russia at the beginning of the twentieth century. Throughout most of the last century state socialism, under Communist Party rule, was practised in the USSR (including Russia) and, after the Second World War, was extended to the countries of Eastern Europe too.

Despite some of the advances and achievements of state socialism in these countries, the collapse of the Eastern European and Soviet communist regimes at the end of the 1980s, and the exposure of continuing inequalities and hardships within them, cast a deep shadow over the aspirations of the supporters of Marxism. It seemed to many that in the only countries in which revolutionary socialism had been attempted as a solution to the problems of capitalism, it had failed. Some supporters of Marxism have of course pointed to the continuation of communist rule in a few other countries, such as China and Cuba, although here, too, traditional state communism has been much diluted. Others have suggested that perhaps state socialism was not proper socialism in any case, and that without international change to replace capitalism on a global scale it was bound to fail.

Despite such expressions of continued revolutionary optimism, the collapse of Eastern bloc socialism has severely undermined the appeal and the influence of Marxist perspectives on welfare, because it has appeared to give a lie to their prescriptions for a revolutionary utopia. In contrast to such prescriptive visions, however, much Marxist debate and scholarship has in fact been directed not so much at making out the case for socialist revolution as at pointing out the failings and limitations of capitalism in meeting the needs of all citizens. Marx himself, of course, was primarily known for his critical analysis of capitalism, including analysis of early examples of welfare reform such as the factory legislation of the mid-nineteenth century, rather than for his ideas on the future of socialism. Many Marxist critics have continued this tradition into the analysis of welfare capitalism, although ultimately their message is a negative one.

In the 1970s Gough and Ginsburg produced cogent critiques of the British welfare state from within a Marxist perspective. Ginsburg (1979) argued that institutions of welfare operated within British society to control and suppress people as well as to provide for them: for instance, arguing that the social security scheme in practice stigmatized benefit claimants and forced them into low-waged employment. Gough's (1979) more extended analysis took this further, pointing out the *dual* character of the welfare state, which – although it was in part a product of the success of working-class struggle, as the democratic socialists claimed – was also an adaptation of capitalism to meet changed economic and social circumstances. He argued, for example, that state education and health services operated in practice to prepare workers for skilled employment and to keep them healthy for work.

The strength of the Marxist critique of state welfare within capitalism is its ability to demonstrate the contradictory nature of social policy as providing at one and the same time both social *protection* and social *control*. Some commentators, such as O'Connor (1973), have referred to these contradictory goals as the *accumulation* and *legitimation* functions of welfare. Through its support for the continued operation of the market, state welfare permits capital to continue to accumulate; and yet, through its provision of social protection, it also legitimates capitalist power by providing protection for all its citizens. However, in times of crisis – for example, during the recession of the 1970s and 1980s, and now the 2010s – these two functions can come into conflict; continued support for accumulation requires cutbacks in the costs of legitimation. Indeed, cuts in welfare spending were introduced in Britain, and in other welfare capitalist countries, during these periods. The welfare state within capitalism is thus not only contradictory, it is also inherently unstable.

This Marxist critique of the development and operation of welfare within capitalist societies is considerably more plausible, and influential, than the appeal to support for a communist revolution; and, as a critique of capitalist welfare, the Marxist perspective has survived despite the collapse of the socialist regimes to which it might have been seen to have allegiance. However, the continuing changes in production processes, class structures and political activity in modern capitalist countries make the legacy of Marx, on which some commentators have claimed to draw, an ever more distant one.

Many such commentators, who continue to point to the contradictory and unstable nature of social and economic policies in welfare capitalist countries, no longer refer to themselves as Marxists, and some have begun to suggest that the perspective must now be called *post-Marxism* or *neo-Marxism*. This, they argue, is because the social and economic changes that have divided the workforce and produced a large group of unemployed and marginal workers have rendered the role of the working class in the transformation of capitalism obsolete; as a result of this, they suggest that revolutionary change will therefore take a different form in the future. In particular, it will no longer involve taking the means of production into the hands of the workers but rather will be based upon a post-industrial economy in which work and production are no longer at the centre of material life (Gorz 1982).

The development of post-Marxism and the changed emphasis of former Marxists demonstrate that, despite its links to the past, this perspective, too, is constantly changing and adapting as new ideas develop and as social circumstances change. Marxism may have lost the concrete appeal of Soviet communism to oppose the inequities of capitalism, and it may have had to adapt to the restructuring of labour markets and class allegiances, but its ability to link a critique of the failings of welfare to the development of the structural forces of the capitalist economy retains a powerful ideological appeal. Thus, to the left of the social democrats, Marxist critics of welfare can still be found (Jones and Novak 1999; Ferguson et al. 2002).

NEW SOCIAL MOVEMENTS

One of the consequences of the declining size and influence of the traditional working class in modern societies and the growing fragmentation of labour market relations with more flexible (part-time and temporary) employment has been a growing recognition of the existence, and importance, of other social divisions as bases for conflict and political change in society, and of political and ideological issues other than exploitation within the labour market as a focus for critical comment and action. These include, for instance, gender differences and feminist politics, racial conflict and anti-racism, disability awareness and action, environmentalism and Green politics and the anti-nuclear movement. Of course, social divisions, such as gender and race, are not new sources of ideological and political conflict, even if widespread recognition of their importance has only relatively recently developed within social policy (Williams 1989). However, the recognition of this wider range of differences and divisions has challenged the dominance of those ideological perspectives which have sought to contain debate, and policy development, on a left/right continuum within which state welfare and redistribution of resources are seen as either the causes or the solutions of all social problems.

In part these changes are the product of political activity rather than ideological debate. New social movements grew up within many welfare capitalist countries in the latter part of the twentieth century, aiming to push new issues and different forms of discrimination and disadvantage on to the policy agenda, for example, the 'women's movement', anti-racist campaigns, and the Green Party and other environmental activists. Of course all of these different movements were quite distinct, pursuing particular political issues through different forms of organization and political practice. However, their very difference and disparity distinguished them from the more traditional labour market and state welfare politics of the old right and left, and so they were sometimes collectively referred to as *new social movements* (Williams 1989), although in practice some were rather 'newer' than others and many are not new at all, except perhaps in the eyes of some commentators. And there have even been some attempts to bring together these different movements into a more coherent political force: for instance, through the so-called *Rainbow Alliance* in the USA in the 1980s and 1990s, which suggested the coming together of different colours (or political perspectives) across the spectrum.

Nevertheless, there are serious political and ideological problems involved in trying to lump together the very different movements and perspectives of feminism, anti-racism, environmentalism, and others. Where some of these address social divisions, the divisions they focus on are very different (and sometimes mutually conflicting), as the disagreements over the allegiances of black women, for example, have demonstrated. What is more, not all movements focus on social divisions: for example, environmental and anti-nuclear politics are responding to very different social and economic forces. There is thus no real common ground across the new social movements, even though some radicals might wish there were.

These new social movements are discussed together here, therefore, not out of a misguided belief in their common features, but because the pressures of time and space do not permit adequate discussion of them all separately, although clearly some are more important than others, with feminism in particular having had a far-reaching impact on the study and practice of social policy (Pascall 2012). George and Wilding's (1994) text on ideologies of welfare makes something of a compromise in containing extended discussion of feminism and Greenism; and Williams's (1989) social policy text focuses on feminist and anti-racist critiques of welfare, whilst Lister (2010) considers these and environmentalism. We will return to discuss the problem of the failure of past social policy development to recognize the important social divisions of gender and race in Chapter 17. These are clearly two of the more influential perspectives, though they are not the only important ones, and a number of other divisions that also impact significantly on social policy development and delivery are discussed in Platt (2011).

Environmental politics presents – potentially at least – an even more fundamental critique of social welfare, for Green ideologists argue that current welfare protection is based upon the continuation of forms of economic growth that are unsustainable in the world in the longer term because of their environmental destructiveness. However, this environmental argument is a complex one. For a start, both commentators and activists themselves often make a distinction between different perspectives within environmental politics. In particular, a distinction is made between the reformists (the *light* Greens), who argue for change within existing economic structures, and the revolutionaries (the *dark* Greens), who argue that only a fundamental transformation of socioeconomic planning can guarantee a long-term future for welfare. Despite these differences, however, the focus of environmental politics upon sustainable economic policy in order to support viable social policy is now an influential perspective within social policy debate (Huby 1998; Cahill 2001; Fitzpatrick 2011).

COMPREHENSION QUESTIONS

- To what extent do new social movements present a coherent ideological perspective on the development of welfare policy?
- What is the difference between light and dark Greens?

POSTMODERNISM

The challenge to the traditional left/right ideological debate over state welfare does not come only from new political activity, however. At the theoretical level too there have been critiques of the ideological frameworks outlined earlier from those who have argued that they are no longer adequate to provide an understanding of the changing world in which we now live, or a model for how policies should be developed within that, and that previous analyses based upon class conflict in capitalist labour markets must also embrace other forms of difference and disadvantage. Actually, of course, some of these critiques are not all that new, either; and the theoretical challenge they pose is not only based upon the premise that it is changing social circumstances that have invalidated other ideological approaches. Underlying much discussion here are more fundamental questions about how our knowledge, and our ideologies, are constructed and whether it is at all possible to produce ideological frameworks which can provide a comprehensive guide to social structure and social policy in complex modern societies: to use their terminology, these critiques reject the notion of such 'meta-narratives' (Lyotard 1984).

However, much of the writing on social policy from within such a perspective has been relatively recent and has been based in part upon a critique of previous ideological frameworks. It has also frequently linked its theoretical criticism to a broader temporal shift from modernity (the modern, welfare capitalist world of class conflict) to *postmodernism*. Much has been written about postmodernism both as a social condition (has the world changed so that old relations and conflicts have been replaced by new ones?) and as a theoretical approach (should we reject all past attempts to theorize about social relations?). Some have welcomed the alternative and radical perspective that it provides for social policy debate (Leonard 1997), although others are more sceptical and argue much of postmodernist writing is a distortion or abandonment of key policy issues (Taylor-Gooby 1994). The debate is a complex one, however, and much of the theoretical literature is rather dense and jargon-ridden.

In addition, many of the core tenets of postmodern thinking seem to be based on a negative critique of what has gone before rather than a coherent framework for future development. Fitzpatrick (2012) provides a useful summary of the role of postmodernist thinking within social policy in which he points out that postmodernists generally reject universalism, do not believe in absolute truth or essentialist explanations, and celebrate difference and identity. Rather than seeking to identify shared social problems and promote universal policy responses to these, therefore, postmodernist approaches to social policy emphasize relativity, diversity and particularity. They also focus on the way in which different (and diverse) understandings (and experiences) are constructed by people through discourse, and this applies to social theorists as well as ordinary individuals.

This draws on the theoretical work of Foucault and his analysis of how punishment and sexuality were constructed (and changed) by the professionals and experts who controlled prisons and medicine in the nineteenth and twentieth centuries (Foucault 1977, 1979). It is sometimes referred to as 'constructivism'. Postmodernist thinkers drawing on Foucault (also sometimes called 'post-structuralists') argue that no one construction can be correct or agreed, and those that have dominated policy development have done so only because of the powerful positions occupied by their protagonists. Hence the role of ideological analysis is to explore the discourses (language) through which these arguments are constructed, and to expose the power that lies behind them to critical review.

O'Brien and Penna (1998) provided an early overview of the rise of postmodernist theorizing within the development of welfare theory more generally, while Lewis et al. (2000) gave examples of the ways in which such thinking impacts on different aspects of social policy analysis, including a chapter (by Watson) on the influence of Foucault. In the final chapter of that book Williams (2000) outlined how this could lead to 'a new politics of welfare' which 'extends beyond the redistribution of goods…[and] centres upon claims for the realisation of personhood and well-being, for cultural respect, autonomy and dignity'.

Many social policy analysts would no doubt agree with the importance of the issues of respect and autonomy that Williams identified in this chapter, and with some of the implications of this for social policy practice that she discussed, without necessarily sharing the more general postmodernist rejection of all past welfare theorizing and policy practice. Indeed it is not at all clear, as Fitzpatrick (2012) points out, what the policy implications of much postmodernist analysis are. As we said, postmodernists are stronger on critique and exposure than they are on explanation and prescription, and so coming to a conclusion about how such an approach has influenced the development of welfare in practice is not an easy task; although, of course, true postmodernists would probably point out that this is exactly their point: there can be *no* objective analysis of social circumstances and *no* agreed policy response to these.

Nevertheless, this radical rejection of the certainties of past welfare ideologies has provided a far-reaching and (to some) refreshing critical edge to policy debate over the last decade or so, and it has helped to extend the debate about the politics and ideology of welfare beyond a relatively narrow focus on class conflict and public policy practice. However, welfare policy and practice are not just shaped by ideologies and discourses and the power of those who hold them: they are also influenced by the material resources available to people and to policy-makers, and it is to this material context that we turn in Chapter 15.

COMPREHENSION QUESTIONS

- What are 'metanarratives' and why do postmodernists argue that they cannot provide an effective basis for understanding the ideological basis of welfare?
- To what extent can postmodernism provide us with an ideological basis for future welfare policy planning?

FURTHER READING

George and Wilding (1994) is still the most comprehensive guide to the major ideologies of welfare and George (2012) considers the ideas of a range of key welfare theorists. The chapters in Part 2 of Alcock et al. (2012) include short summaries of most of the major perspectives by expert authors. Lister (2010) offers an accessible coverage of a range of key concepts and perspectives and Daly (2011) provides a guide to recent theorizing. Fitzpatrick (2001) offers an accessible coverage of a number of key perspectives, and he extends this in 2005 to a range of new theoretical issues and perspectives. Williams (1989), although now rather dated, is still the best treatment of the impact of feminism and anti-racism on traditional perspectives within social policy. Pascall (2012) addresses more recent developments in feminist thinking on welfare and Annetts et al. (2009) contains a broad overview of different social movements in social policy development. Synopses of the main UK social policy think tanks can be found online in Brunsdon and May (2012) at www.blackwellpublishing.com/alcock4e/.

15 Economic Development

SUMMARY OF KEY POINTS

- Economic policy and social policy are closely interrelated, with changes in one resulting in changes in the other.
- The need to promote economic growth now lies at the heart of all economic policy planning.
- Capitalism is based on market exchanges of goods and services and on employment of workers in the labour market. However, modern economies also include non-market provision of some services and state intervention within markets.
- The *laissez-faire* approach of classical economics led to hardship and periods of recession in the late nineteenth and early twentieth centuries.
- Keynesian economic planning was based on government intervention to stimulate economic growth at times of low demand and was linked to social policy commitments to promote full employment.
- In the 1970s Britain's relatively weak international trading position led to problems of inflation and unemployment which could not be controlled by Keynesian economic management.
- Monetarists argue that reductions in public expenditure may be necessary to control the supply of money and so reduce inflation within the economy.
- In the 1980s rising unemployment and a deficit trading balance led to a shift from monetarism to supply-side economics with tax cuts and deregulation aimed at stimulating economic growth.
- High levels of borrowing in the early 1990s followed by rises in the interest rates charged on loans led to another recession in the British economy.
- Since the beginning of this century all advanced economies have had to adapt to the need to compete within a global economic context. This led the Labour governments to make control over inflation and the creation of a stable climate for economic growth the core features of its economic, and social, policy planning.
- In 2008 a global economic recession was triggered by the imminent failure of international banks due to speculation on risky loans and the unsustainable growth of credit.
- Since 2010 economic policy in the UK has been dominated by government commitment to reduce the future scale of public borrowing by cutting public expenditure. This has also taken even more extreme forms in a number of European countries within the *Eurozone*.

THE ECONOMIC CONTEXT

The study of social policy in Britain has traditionally focused on the development and structure of welfare services. More recently, however, concern has widened to include analysis of issues such as the ideologies and theories that have shaped the welfare policies and the political context in which these have evolved, as we saw in Chapter 14. However, welfare policies are not just the product of a particular political or ideological context; they are also affected by the economic forces that govern the development of the society within which they are located. Indeed, because they determine the resources that are available to meet all individual and social needs, it is arguable that economic forces are the *most* important factor influencing both the size and scope of all social policy.

At a simple level at least, this is certainly true. Welfare services cost money to deliver and, therefore, the economic circumstances of individuals and groups can dictate who pays for welfare and how much they pay (a question to which we shall return in more detail in Chapter 16). At a more complex level, however, social policy development is also closely dependent upon the economic structure of a society and the economic growth within it. Changes in both can have a direct impact upon social policy, as we discuss below.

However, it is not just the case that economic changes affect the development of social policy. In modern welfare capitalist societies social policies affect economic forces too. For instance, as we have seen, social security policies can maintain a reserve labour force during periods of low employment which is then ready to be re-employed when circumstances improve, and they can even operate to encourage employment through the subsidization of wages for low-paid employees. Policies for education and training can equip, or re-equip, the workforce with the skills they need to develop and implement new productive processes. In effect, in modern societies social and economic policies are inextricably intertwined, with changes in one inevitably leading to changes in the other.

An understanding of social policy thus requires an understanding of the economic policy context in which social policies develop and of the relationship between economic and social policy. The study of economic policy is a vast and complex field, however, with its own theories, concepts and literature. To understand it fully, therefore, we would first need to come to grips with the basic theories and concepts of economics, an enterprise that is well beyond the scope of this introductory book. Nevertheless we will look briefly at some of the major trends in economic policy that have influenced the study of social policy in Britain, and elsewhere, over the recent past, and discuss the implications of these for the development of social provision.

The early Fabian proponents of social policy in Britain at the beginning of the twentieth century argued that social policy was needed in order to counteract some of the undesirable consequences of economic development. In particular, they argued that the capitalist economic system, which was dominant in Britain, had resulted in the creation of significant social problems, most importantly high levels of poverty, and that social policy intervention was required by government in order to restructure socioeconomic conditions in ways that would eliminate or prevent these problems, for example, in order to redistribute resources from wealthy capitalists to poor workers, or would-be workers.

As we have seen, therefore, the social policies developed in Britain have been constructed within a capitalist economy, in order to mitigate some of the effects of the operation of capitalist economic forces. The consequences, however, have been to transform that capitalist economy, in particular through an enhanced role for the collective actions of the state in exercising some control over both production and distribution. In effect the crude (and cruel) capitalist forces, which were criticized by Fabians, have been supplemented, and in part replaced, by public provision and public ownership. This has led politicians and commentators to argue that Britain no longer has a capitalist economy but rather has a mixed economy, in which private capital plays only a partial role (albeit in practice a dominating one). Whether we conceive of Britain as a capitalist or a mixed economy, however, our understanding of the context this economy provides for the development of social policy requires an examination of the basic structures of capitalist economic systems and the processes by which these have developed, and have been changed and adapted.

CAPITALISM

We can trace the growth of capitalism back over at least 200 years of British history, although, in practice, its roots extend back much further than that as the earlier feudal system was gradually transformed into an economic structure based on monetary exchange and the market mechanism. Writing over 200 years ago, Adam Smith was one of the earliest, and most well-known, economic proponents of capitalism (Smith 1776). His argument was that the market mechanism was the most proper way in which society should be ordered because it ensured goods and services would be produced and distributed in the most efficient and effective manner. In simple terms this was because of the impartial operation of the laws of supply and demand. Goods and services would be produced and sold on the market, and consumers would go to the market to purchase what they needed or desired. Because consumers would only purchase what they wanted at a price they could afford, only those producers who were supplying such needs would be able to sell their products. Inefficient, or undesirable, production would thus be driven out of business and the market would produce a stable balance between the forces of supply and demand.

This is a persuasive model, in theory. However, economists quickly discovered that in practice such a comfortable balance was difficult to achieve as production processes changed and consumers' purchasing power fluctuated. Even its theoretical explanation of capitalist development was questioned in the nineteenth century by Karl Marx, who produced a far-reaching and highly influential critique of the basic structure of the capitalist economy (Marx 1970).

Marx's argument was that the basic structure of the capitalist economy was not the market mechanism of supply and demand but the wage–labour arrangement for the production of goods and services. This arrangement was founded upon the structural exploitation of the worker, who was paid less by the capitalist than the exchange (or market) value of the goods he or she produced, with the surplus value (or profit) being pocketed by the capitalist or reinvested through accumulation in further capitalist production, which would produce yet further profit. Therefore the capitalist, however morally righteous he or she might be, was inevitably motivated by the pursuit of profit for further production, with the result that the productive forces of capitalism were driven forward through the exploitation of the working class.

This process of the development of productive forces resulted in a growth in the range and scope of the production of goods and services; but it also, Marx suggested, led to an inevitable (and structural) conflict between the worker and the capitalist, or more generally between the representatives of the working class and the representatives of the capitalist class. Capitalists would pursue higher profits and workers would pursue higher wages; conflict between the two would be endemic. This conflict could lead to adjustments to profits or to wages as struggles were won or lost, or compromises reached; but the cause of conflict would always remain. Capitalism was not therefore, according to Marx, a stable economic order, but rather a fundamentally unstable one; and eventually, he predicted, it would collapse and be replaced by a more stable order: socialism.

However, in over 200 years of capitalist economic development in Britain there has been no fundamental collapse, or replacement, of capitalism with socialism. Indeed, where socialist economic systems have been introduced in Eastern Europe and the former Soviet states, these have now collapsed and capitalist market economies reintroduced. Thus, although Marx's explanation of the driving force behind capitalist development (and of the inevitable conflicts this produces) may have been a convincing one, his conclusions about its fundamental instability have proved unfounded.

Perhaps the reason why the conflicts generated by capitalist development have not led to its demise is because they have led instead to its transformation. Working-class demands for higher wages (and later for legal regulation and social protection of conditions of work) have, in part at least, been successful in securing changes in the private market economic order of capitalism. As we have already discussed, the development of social policy and welfare services have displaced private markets largely, or entirely, in the provision of some important goods and services: hence the reference to a mixed economy. Another phrase which is used to describe this mixture of private production and public welfare is *welfare capitalism*, and more recently still commentators have begun to refer to such societies as *social market economies*.

This does not mean that the exploitation, and resulting conflict, which Marx argued characterized capitalist society, has been removed; clearly exploitation and conflict both remain, as low wages and industrial disputes continue to demonstrate. However, the exploitation and the conflicts are more fractured and more complex than a basic head-on battle between the capitalists and the working class:

- Exploitation is fractured: some workers earn good wages and work in good conditions, and also many produce no direct profit for their employer; not all exploitation at work is wage-based, as those engaged in unpaid caring work often experience.
- Conflicts are complex: workers may be in conflict with each other (for instance, over a decision to close one plant to secure jobs at another) or with the state (teachers' and nurses' disputes over pay or work practices), or conflicts may be based on consumers' interests (tenants' campaigns against LA landlords).

However, British capitalism has also changed in other ways. In the early part of the twentieth century UK economic policy was largely a matter of national development, even though this relied in practice on the exploitation of a large empire. Now, however, economic development in Britain is significantly affected by international forces within a global capital economy, in which production processes are owned or controlled by worldwide corporations and goods and services are produced and marketed on an international level, as we shall discuss shortly. This international context has been further accentuated by Britain's membership of the EU. As we discuss in more detail in Chapter 7, the EU operates a single market for production and distribution throughout its member states, with a single currency operating in most countries, so economic policy planning increasingly takes place at a supranational level.

The British capitalist economy is no longer, therefore, based on the simple process of capitalist ownership and workers' exploitation described by Marx, or on the simple market of supply and demand advanced by Adam Smith. It is no longer exclusively *capitalist* and it is no longer only *British*. However, it is still in large part a market economy, and one in which capitalist investment by major private corporations is a significant determinant of economic growth. Furthermore, economic growth remains a crucial factor in securing improvements in standards for both capitalists and workers and in providing the resources for the social policy developments that seek to mitigate the market's harshest effects. All major economic commentators, and certainly all important political actors, are now agreed that it is the prospects for economic growth within Britain's complex and fractured economy which are the major focus of economic policy concern, and thus, indirectly, they are the major concern of social policy too. The need to secure growth has become at least as important as the question of what to do with the fruits of it.

CLASSICAL ECONOMICS

Policy based on classical economics drew on the relatively simple model of the capitalist market economy outlined by early economists such as Adam Smith. Classical economists believed that economic growth was the product of the free operation of market forces within society. Freedom did not imply anarchy, of course; there was a role for the state within society to provide a secure context in which the market could operate. Thus the government had a responsibility to protect property through law and contract, and to provide security through policing and national defence. Beyond this, however, the laws of supply and demand would determine investment, production and distribution, and therefore also prices and wages. Efficient producers of desirable products would survive and others would have to adapt or disappear; this was a process in which government could not, and should not, interfere.

This was referred to at the time as the *laissez-faire* approach (leave alone). In the late twentieth century the neoliberal economists of the New Right called for a return to the policies of *laissez-faire*, claiming the interventionist measures pursued earlier in the century (discussed below) had failed to secure growth. Neoliberal economists such as Hayek (1944) and Friedman (1962) argued for a return to the classical economic policies of the (supposedly) free market, through the removal of government controls over investment, credit and employment relations, with the claim that this would restore the equilibrium of the market forces of supply and demand, and reproduce the capitalist economic growth that Britain had enjoyed in the nineteenth century, although, as we shall see, this has not in practice been realized.

In nineteenth-century Britain capitalist production certainly grew in scope and scale but at a heavy cost in terms of low wages, poor conditions and frequently high levels of unemployment for the majority of the population. At the end of that century, when the British economy was arguably at its most powerful, the early social policy researchers, Booth (1889) and Rowntree (1901), found high levels of acute poverty even in London, the capital city of the British Empire; and in the early twentieth century the economy in Britain, and most other industrial nations, experienced a major economic recession leading to further high levels of unemployment and poverty.

The depression of the 1930s was seen by many social policy reformers as powerful evidence of the failure of the capitalist economy to provide adequately for the whole of the population. Beveridge's (1942) proposals for social security reform, which followed the depression, were intended to ensure that never again would economic change result in such social hardship. The depression was also seen by some economists as evidence of the failure of the *laissez-faire* approach to secure sustainable economic growth. Pressure for a change towards a more interventionist economic policy therefore began to develop. This was given greater impetus by the experience of 'total war' during the Second World War, during which government control over production and distribution throughout the economy in Britain and over relations with allied trading partners was essential to the success of the war effort.

KEYNESIANISM

The welfare state reforms of the post-war period, associated in particular with the recommendations of Beveridge's 1942 report, were the social policy response to the deprivations of the depression. At the same time as this change in the direction of social policy, however, the post-war period also saw a change in the direction of economic policy in Britain, associated with the recommendations of Beveridge's colleague, Keynes; indeed, the economic and social reforms of the period have sometimes been referred to as the establishment of the Keynes/Beveridge Welfare State (Cutler et al. 1986).

Keynes was an economic adviser to the wartime government and, although he died in 1946, his ideas dominated government economic policy in the two decades following the war. His recommendations had been formulated during the depression of the 1930s (Keynes 1936) and were based upon a belief that government could, and should, intervene in economic markets, in particular to ensure full employment was maintained. That full employment was a goal of both economic and social policy was a matter on which Keynes and Beveridge were firmly in agreement. Full employment was essential to Beveridge's recommendations for social security and family support, even though this was restricted to men's labour market participation. It was also the cornerstone of Keynes's prescriptions for future economic growth.

It was to be achieved, according to Keynes, by ensuring that growth was sustained in manufacturing production; and, as the depression had demonstrated, this could not be guaranteed by the free market alone. Classical economists had assumed that in a market economy supply would necessarily encourage demand: people would see goods and would want to buy them. In a depression, of course, many people could see goods that they wanted, but were unable to afford to buy them. However, if they could be given the resources to purchase the goods, they would do so, thus stimulating further production of these goods. This would lead to increased resources for those employed in the production of the goods, who themselves could then buy more goods, so stimulating yet more production elsewhere. In other words, Keynes argued that increased *demand* could stimulate *supply* and thus lead to economic growth.

This virtuous circle of increased demand leading to increased production is called by Keynesian economists the *multiplier effect*. The investment of an additional fixed sum of money into the economy will lead to further production, further spending and further investment that cumulatively will be of much greater value than the initial sum invested. Economists even claim that the growth potential of any particular investment can be calculated from the workings of this multiplier effect, thus giving economic planners a clear idea of how much to invest to secure any particular level of improved growth. Not surprisingly, advice along these lines would be likely to be warmly welcomed by governments, especially those promising to improve economic and social circumstances in the short term.

Keynes also argued that the means of securing such additional investment was in the hands of the government which, in times of reduced demand and supply, could afford to borrow money in order to increase government spending on public works and services, in the secure knowledge that the multiplier effect of this would be to stimulate economic growth from which the borrowed money could later be recouped and repaid. Such a period is called a *deflationary gap*, and at such times governments should increase spending or cut taxes to invest in economic growth. When full employment is achieved, however, continued growth in demand could lead to inflation (if more goods cannot be produced, prices go up: a problem to which we shall return shortly). This is called an *inflationary gap*, and at such times, Keynesians argue, governments should cut spending or increase taxes to reduce demand.

Through the application of Keynesian economic principles, therefore, it appeared that governments could control and manage economic growth through public spending and investment in the economy. This provided a great boost to the interventionist social and economic tendencies of the post-war Butskellite governments and, of course, a great boost to the profession of economists. Economic advisers were now much valued by government for the guidance they could provide on how to manipulate the economy. Mathematically constructed economic models could be used to simulate the performance of national economies and the effects of different economic policy measures could be estimated in advance. The Treasury began to use such a model to calculate the effects of government spending in Britain, further increasing its already powerful influence over more general policy planning.

Certainly during the first two decades after the war Keynesian economic policies did appear to be successful. Britain was experiencing one of its longest periods of sustained economic growth, wage levels were rising in value and employment levels were so high that immigrants were encouraged to come from the old imperial colonies to fill gaps in the labour market. In 1959 the Conservative Prime Minister, Harold Macmillan, entered the election campaign claiming that the British people had 'never had it so good'. However, in practice, the government's management of the economy fluctuated from deflationary gaps to inflationary gaps, characterized by what commentators called *stop/go* policies on spending and taxation. No attempt was made to control the rises in incomes and prices that resulted from the increased industrial power which full employment gave to organized workers in manufacturing industry.

Furthermore, in spite of the consensus on welfare, there were also problems within the mutual interdependence of social and economic policy planning. In social policy terms it was argued by critics such as Titmuss (1955) and Townsend (Abel-Smith and Townsend 1965) that, despite improved incomes and public services, not everyone was benefiting equally from the protection of the welfare state, and indeed some were still living in poverty. Economists talked about this as the trade-off between *efficiency* and *equity*, an issue that we discuss in Chapter 16. Efficiency could be achieved by economic growth if all were better-off, so that no one's gain meant somebody else's loss. However, equity required ensuring that all needs for protection were met and this might require some redistribution of resources to those who were poor, with consequent losses for the better-off. Keynesianism appeared to assume that greater efficiency would also lead to more equity but, as continuing inequalities revealed, this might not necessarily be the case.

COMPREHENSION QUESTIONS

- To what extent is the exploitation of the working class, identified by Marx, still at the heart of economic conflict?
- What is *laissez-faire* and why did critics argue that it failed to provide an effective basis for economic policy in the nineteenth and early twentieth centuries?
- What is the 'multiplier effect', and how did Keynesians argue it could be used to manage economic development in post-war Britain?

REFLECTIVE QUESTION

- Why do we need to understand economic policy in order to study social policy?

THE COLLAPSE OF KEYNESIANISM

During the euphoria of the long post-war boom, however, these contradictions within the Keynesian approach appeared to be minor issues when compared to the overall success of sustained economic growth in Britain. However, there were other problems with this sustained growth. Britain was not at this point a member of the European Economic Community (EEC, now the EU, see Chapter 7), and did not benefit from all of the economic development generated by the new community. Further, as part of the *Bretton Woods* agreement entered into in 1944 under the auspices of the International Monetary Fund (IMF), the country had committed to maintaining the international value of the pound in relation to the US dollar (the exchange rate).

The high value of the pound internationally meant that British exports were relatively expensive for foreign buyers. It also conversely meant that imported goods were relatively cheap in Britain. These two factors affected the performance of the economy and began to be revealed in new economic problems in the country in the 1960s.

The most obvious problem to flow from decreased exports and increased imports is a reduction in the *balance of payments*: that is, the overall surplus, or deficit, shown in Britain's trading with other nations within the world economy. A deficit in the balance of payments can be sustained for a short period as obviously not every trader can make a profit all the time. However, a sustained reduction in the balance is evidence of poor economic performance and thus a decline in the relative international economic standing of a nation's economy.

However, balance of payments reductions do not just lead to difficulties at an international level: they are manifested in economic problems at home too. Lower exports and higher imports can lead to a decline in manufacturing activity and this can lead to the creation and growth of unemployment. They can also lead to inflation, as British manufacturers seek to offset the loss of foreign sales by increased prices for goods sold at home. *Inflation* is a complex economic problem, and a much disputed one. In simple terms it means that the prices of goods and services, as measured by a national aggregation of the prices of a sample of major items, is rising faster than the production of them. There are two such aggregate measures in the UK: the *Retail Price Index* (RPI) and the *Consumer Price Index* (CPI), which use different samples of items to calculate average prices.

Any rise in prices, however, leads to workers demanding higher wages to pay for the more expensive goods and services. However, if wage rises are conceded, these result in yet further price increases to meet the higher wages, leading to a spiral of rising prices and wages. Once such an inflationary spiral has taken hold, the government is brought under pressure to print more money to meet the demand for higher prices and wages. This additional money (unlike the public spending investment foreseen by Keynes) does not contribute to increased demand and supply but rather is soaked up in meeting the higher prices of existing goods, simply adding to the amount of money circulating in the economy without any increase in production or economic growth.

Such inflation, with rises in prices and wages running ahead of economic growth, had not been foreseen as a significant problem by the early Keynesian economists, who assumed full employment and economic growth would ensure an equilibrium between prices and wages because increases in wages would inevitably flow from improved economic activity. Thus Keynesian economic policy focused upon using state intervention in the economy in order to secure full employment rather than to control inflation. However, in the mid-1960s Britain's balance of payments problems and declining international confidence were threatening this single-minded focus on the need for demand-led growth to boost manufacturing employment.

Britain's problems were serious enough at this time to encourage the Labour government to seek international financial aid from the IMF. However, the IMF were only prepared to provide this on condition that Britain devalued the pound within the Bretton Woods exchange rate agreement. This was done, and it was later followed by a withdrawal from the fixed exchange commitment to *float* the pound on the international currency market. This meant that the value of the pound would depend on its position in this market and would therefore fluctuate as confidence in the country's economy changed.

Britain's international position was expected to be strengthened, however, by the decision to join the EEC in 1973; and it was hoped that this would boost Britain's trade with its partner members, although of course it also opened up British markets more directly to penetration from Europe. But the British economy did not strengthen in the 1970s. Indeed the major economic indicators got worse. Unemployment began to increase, passing the one million mark; and inflation began to rise, reaching over 26 per cent a year by 1975. As if this were not enough, Britain's problems were further compounded – as indeed were those of all other industrial economies – by the massive increase in the price of oil introduced by the Organization of Petroleum Exporting Countries (OPEC) in 1973. Oil was by the 1970s the world's major fuel for economic production, and between 1972 and 1974 its price rose four-fold.

The oil price rise was a symbolic moment in the ending of the international economic boom that had followed the Second World War. In Britain, where problems were worse than in some other countries, it pushed the economy rapidly into recession (or, as the economists of the time called it, *stagflation*: high inflation in a stagnant economy). In the face of this, Keynesian demand management appeared to be impotent and the debate began for a shift in the focus of economic policy.

MONETARISM

Throughout the period of the post-war boom the social and economic policies of the Keynes/Beveridge welfare state had appeared to be successful in securing both economic growth and social protection in Britain; and the picture was the same in most other welfare capitalist countries. In this period welfare spending grew in cash terms but it also grew significantly as a proportion of *gross domestic product* (GDP). GDP and GNP (*gross national product)* are general measures of the activity of a national economy. They are an attempt to count together all goods and services produced *in* the country (GDP) or, in the case of GNP, including also those produced *abroad.* In a growing economy, therefore, GDP and GNP would be increasing each year.

In such an economy a growth in public expenditure may not be problematic: as the economy grows so we can afford better public services, and the taxes used to pay for these can be afforded relatively easily out of the improved profits and wages growth brings. Nevertheless, a growth in the *proportion* of public expenditure suggests a change in the balance of activity within the country, with more resources going into welfare services than industrial development. This again may not be a problem, especially in a growing economy. For example, much of the growth in public expenditure in the 1960s and early 1970s was the result of the rising numbers of public employees in welfare services, where employment increased by about one-third. This helped maintain high employment levels, as well as stimulating demand through the purchasing power that these workers brought into the economy more generally.

In a declining economy, however, growth in public expenditure is more problematic. Growing levels of expenditure still have to be financed out of increased taxation and now this will compete with private investment or private consumption within a restricted overall economic climate. This may make taxes, and thus spending, less popular; but, more seriously in economic terms, it may also compound economic recession by reducing investment in industrial production and curtailing consumer spending, and thus the demand for goods.

It is just such problems that new critics of Keynesian economic management began to suggest were the source of Britain's declining economic performance in the mid-1970s. Right-wing critics such as Bacon and Eltis (1976), in their book, *Britain's Economic Problem: Too Few Producers*, argued that growing public expenditure was crowding out private investment in the economy. The reduced size and scope of private manufacturing ('too few producers') thus led to economic decline, which was compounded if, at such a time, public expenditure and state employment continued to expand as a proportion of GDP.

The conclusion these critics were drawn to was that, at times of recession, it was not possible to stimulate economic growth through demand management, fuelled by public expenditure; and further that, if this were attempted, it would result only in growing inflation, which would make matters worse. To counteract Britain's accelerating economic decline, therefore, an alternative approach was required. This meant abandoning the policy commitment to full employment, which in any event had failed in practice, and seeking instead to control inflation in order to stabilize the economic climate and provide more security and encouragement for private investment, from which it was assumed growth would follow. Controlling inflation meant controlling the money supply and a move from Keynesianism to *monetarism* as the central plank of economic policy planning.

The *narrow* goal of monetarism was the control of inflation. This was to be achieved by restricting the supply of money within the economy, so counteracting the tendency for prices and wages to rise. The main factor leading to an increased money supply in the 1970s, it was argued, was government borrowing. Thus this had to be reduced and, in order to do this, public spending would have to be cut. The *broader* goal of monetarism, therefore, especially for some of its New Right proponents, was a general reduction of state expenditure, especially welfare expenditure, that otherwise seemed set to rise inexorably as yet more needs and demands for social protection were pressed on government.

A shift to monetarism in economic policy was not, therefore, merely a reaction to the limitations of Keynesianism in times of recession: it was a wholesale rejection of the Keynes/Beveridge welfare state partnership of social spending and demand-led economic growth. Thus the results of such a change in economic policy also had serious implications for the future development of social policy. This was not what the Labour government of the 1970s wanted to contemplate; but when they once again turned to the IMF for support, the IMF again insisted on economic policy changes. In particular they wanted the British government to implement monetarist controls over the escalating money supply and to reduce public expenditure; and reluctantly the government agreed. As Prime Minister James Callaghan explained to the Party Conference in 1976: 'We used to think that you could just spend your way out of a recession and increase employment by cutting taxes and boosting government spending. I tell you in all candour, that option no longer exists' (Callaghan 1987).

In practice Labour did not wholeheartedly embrace monetarism, and expenditure in some policy fields continued to rise. However, they also sought to control inflation through a voluntary restraint on pay and prices; and their ability to sustain this was challenged by the unions, especially those representing public sector workers, who went on strike for higher wages. The public sector strikes of 1978 and 1979, which halted many public services in LAs and hospitals, were dubbed the 'Winter of Discontent' by media critics; and they undoubtedly lost the government much political support. In the election that followed in 1979 the Labour Party was defeated, and a Conservative government, under the leadership of Margaret Thatcher, elected to power. Thatcher was an outspoken supporter of the policy prescriptions of the New Right and was much more willing than Labour had been to embrace the recommendations of the monetarists, and the rejection of Keynesianism.

The Conservatives sought to cut public expenditure more rapidly and to reduce inflation, and this was successful, with inflation reaching a low of 3.7 per cent in 1983 (Peden 1985). However, the economic growth that was supposed to follow from the shift towards financial constraint did not materialize. In the early 1980s the international recession was generally getting worse rather than better, in particular as a result of another OPEC oil price increase in 1979. By the 1980s though Britain was itself an oil producing and exporting nation and this did begin to provide much needed revenue for the country. Yet, despite it, the balance of payments began to decline dramatically, with manufacturing exports being particularly hard hit. Manufacturing industry in Britain experienced its worst ever period of decline during the early 1980s, with the effects of international recession being compounded by the government's policy of privatization and the withdrawal of public support for industry, aimed ostensibly at restoring private incentives within a free market. The effect of this was a shift into the red in the balance of trade in manufactured goods between Britain and the rest of the world by the mid-1980s, and a catastrophic decline in manufacturing employment and output, especially in the heavy staple industries such as steel and coal.

Thus in the 1980s, although inflation declined, unemployment rose to two, and then three, million, with many of those leaving (or seeking to enter) the labour market facing the prospect of never securing permanent employment again. This of course created pressure on government expenditure on social security to support the new army of unemployed and, ironically, despite the espoused aims of government, public spending continued to grow; in particular, it grew as a proportion of a now declining GDP (Peden 1985).

SUPPLY-SIDE ECONOMICS

Despite the rhetoric of financial control and the very real desire of the Thatcher governments of the early and mid-1980s to curtail public expenditure, at least on welfare services, their commitment to monetarism was in practice always rather faltering, and by 1985 had been officially abandoned. The government had been forced to face the reality that without economic growth, financial stringency was barely achievable and in any event was of debatable value. Thus the priority became the need to stimulate economic growth; and here the government was more inclined to follow the thinking of New Right thinkers such as Friedman (1962), who claimed that growth had been progressively prevented by Keynesian interventionism and welfare-state social protection. If economic growth was to be restored, therefore, freedom must be returned to the market. This was a twentieth-century return to *laissez-faire*, sometimes referred to as neoclassical economics or neoliberalism (see Chapter 14); following the terminology and the policy developments pursued along these lines by the Reagan administration in the USA in the 1980s, it was also called a *supply-side* approach.

Supply-side economics, as the name suggests, implies something of a reversal of the demand-led strategies for growth proposed by Keynes. Demand-led strategies required government manipulation of the economy in order to stimulate growth. This was now referred to as *macro* management and it was argued to be ineffective. Instead, the neoclassical economists contended, governments should withdraw from macro management and restrict public intervention in economic development to *micro* level strategies to respond only to particularly serious problems or blockages. Thus the Keynes/Beveridge control and protections should, as far as possible, be removed to restore the incentives to private capitalist investors to produce new goods and services in the expectation of making a profit. Incentives for profits would therefore stimulate supply, and increased supply would lead to a growth in employment, and thus greater demand, which would stimulate yet further production for supply: a virtuous circle operating in the reverse of the direction put forward by Keynes.

The withdrawal from macro management, however, included more than just limited privatization and cuts in subsidies. It required a removal of controls over the movement and investment of capital, the freeing-up of financial markets, the withdrawal of restrictions on credit, the repeal of protections and regulations governing employment conditions and wage levels, the reduction in the rights and powers of trade unions, the privatization of state assets, and (perhaps most importantly) cutting taxation levels. Critics and supporters referred to this as 'rolling back the boundaries of the state'; and, of course, it had implications for social, as well as economic, policy as significant cuts were implied in welfare services such as housing, education and social security benefits.

By the mid-1980s, moreover, it appeared the supply-side measures that had worked previously in the USA were also being successful in restoring growth to the British economy. British GDP began to rise reaching an average of 4 per cent growth a year in the mid- to late 1980s. As a result, although public expenditure itself continued to increase, it began to decline as a proportion of GDP after 1982–83 (see Figure 15.1). Unemployment, although still high by previous standards, also began to fall as new jobs were created, especially in the rapidly expanding service sector, which included areas such as banks, insurance, communication technology, catering and leisure (see Figure 13.1). At the height of the boom in 1988, the Chancellor, Nigel Lawson, continued the supply-side stimulation with wide-ranging tax cuts, especially for the wealthy from whom the higher rates of income tax were removed. Neoclassical economics appeared to have proved, finally, that Keynes was wrong after all.

COMPREHENSION QUESTIONS

- What is inflation, and why did it become a problem within the British economy in the 1970s?
- Why do monetarists believe that controlling public expenditure will promote economic growth?
- What was meant by a move from *macro* to *micro* state intervention in the economy in the 1980s, and to what extent did it involve a repudiation of Keynesianism?

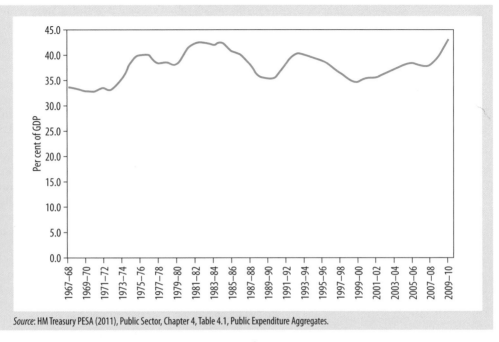

Source: HM Treasury PESA (2011), Public Sector, Chapter 4, Table 4.1, Public Expenditure Aggregates.

Figure 15.1 Public expenditure as a percentage of GDP 1967–2010

GLOBALISM AND RECESSION

Despite its apparent success there were serious problems, and indeed contradictions, at the heart of the supply-side boom in the British economy in the late 1980s. For a start, public expenditure growth had not been contained, even though it was no longer growing more rapidly than the economy itself. Furthermore, even this limited growth was being artificially restricted by the high revenue then being received from the sale of North Sea oil and the receipts the government was able to secure from its major privatizations of government monopolies in services such as gas, electricity and water supply. In this context tax cuts could be sustained as long as the economy continued to grow rapidly; but if it did not then public borrowing would be bound to rise again.

In addition, although unemployment fell, it still remained well above two million and the government continued to accept no responsibility for seeking to reduce it. Unemployment also was increasingly unevenly distributed throughout the country, with the highest levels being found in the still declining industrial areas of central and northern England, and in Scotland, Wales and Northern Ireland. This was because manufacturing industry was still producing much less than in the 1970s or 1960s and, even where production levels were increasing, this was usually a result of improved technology rather than a larger workforce. Much of the growth of jobs, therefore, was in the service sector and was concentrated in the South East of England. Although some of these jobs were well paid and highly skilled, many were menial tasks undertaken for very low pay in restaurants or shops and increasingly available only on a part-time or a temporary basis. Both socially and geographically, therefore, the economic trends of the 1980s produced only partial success with greater divisions within British society, growing affluence for some being mirrored by growing insecurity and poverty for others.

Britain's 1980s boom was not only partial, however; it was also very fragile. Increased supply of goods and services had been met by increased demand. But the growth in demand had been very rapid, and in practice much of it was fuelled by the private credit that was now much more widely available as a result of deregulation. Furthermore, this increased demand did not entirely support increased production at home. The result was a continuing, and growing, balance of payments deficit, which was made worse by the tax cut stimulation of the economy in 1988.

Ironically, the real problem was that the British economy was growing too rapidly and, in an international context, with a balance of payments deficit, this could not be sustained. The evidence for this non-sustainability was growing international pressure on the value of the pound, which was of course now floating on the international currency markets. As a result of these pressures the pace of change in British economic policy in the early 1990s was swift, in particular because the massive boom of the late 1980s came rapidly to an end. The increased cost of borrowing due to high interest rates halted the rise in credit, leading to a major reduction in demand. This was made worse, temporarily, when the government joined the EU's exchange rate mechanism (ERM) which *required* it to guarantee the value of the pound against other European currencies (in effect still primarily the Deutschmark) at a level which British economic performance did not justify.

This resulted in further interest rate rises, which further deflated demand; and in the end the pressure became too great. Following a shift of policy across the space of eight hours on one day in 1993 (dubbed 'Black Monday' by the press) Britain withdrew from the ERM and the pound was floated once again. After this interest rates were reduced, in the hope of stimulating demand once again, but without much success; especially as the government was forced to raise taxation levels, primarily through increased indirect taxes such as VAT.

Thus the boom of the 1980s was followed by a sharp recession in the 1990s, when GDP again declined and unemployment once more passed three million. While, however, it had been manufacturing workers in the Midlands and North who had lost their jobs in the 1980s recession, it was the service workers in the South who became redundant in the 1990s as the expansion in these jobs proved to be rather short term. Therefore, while many of those who remained in employment continued to enjoy relatively high standards of living, the social and economic divisions in society continued to widen. If the recession of the 1970s had proved Keynes wrong, and we could not *spend* our way out of a recession, the recession of the 1990s seemed to prove that neoclassical economics was also flawed, and that we could not *borrow* our way out of one either.

STABILITY AND PRUDENCE

In fact the major lesson to be learnt from the economic policy changes of the 1970s, 1980s and 1990s was that Britain had by then become a part of a much bigger, and more powerful, European and world market, on which the British government, no matter what policies it adopted, could have only limited impact. In this world market too this had been a period of rapid and far-reaching change, with manufacturing production moving increasingly to the Far East, and especially China, and Western countries, even those with strong welfare states such as Sweden, having to scale back planned growth in public expenditure and social protection.

The 'New Labour' government which came to power at the end of the century recognized, therefore, that economic development required all governments to adopt policies that would maximize economic competitiveness within the new global economy. The new Chancellor, Gordon Brown, made clear from the outset that he regarded the maintenance of low inflation and stable economic growth as the key to underpinning all aspects of private and public investment and expenditure. In other words, managing the economy to secure growth must come first, sometimes referred to by Brown, and his critics, as economic 'prudence'.

This was not Keynesian demand management, however. Brown also made clear that he accepted the importance of control over inflation as the key driver of economic stability, and that only from such stability could other goals, such as moves towards full employment or improvement in welfare services, be achieved. He also shared the view, common amongst many economists by the 1990s, that the most effective way to control inflation, and growth, was through the setting of appropriate levels for the rates in interest charged on borrowing in the economy. When inflation and growth were low, low rates of interest would encourage borrowing to support investment and expenditure; if rapid growth was leading to a rise in inflation, then higher interest rates would reduce borrowing and hence expenditure and so stabilize the economy.

What is more, Brown conceded that governments were not necessarily the best judges of the appropriate levels for interest rates, as they may be tempted (as most in the past had) to resort to interventionist actions to boost growth imprudently to meet short-term pressures to reduce unemployment, cut taxes or increase public spending, leading to the 'stop/go' policies of the 1950s and 1960s and the booms and recessions of the 1980s and early 1990s. Stability was best ensured, he argued, if decisions about interest rates were taken impartially by economists; and so, shortly after the 1997 election, he passed decisions on rates to a committee of the Bank of England, comprised of economic experts from different sections of the economy, which met on a monthly basis to set rates for the following month. The effect of this was to transfer a significant aspect of economic power outside government.

At the turn of the century Britain was experiencing slow but steady economic growth. Inflation remained low, and so interest rates were kept low, both in fact generally lower than at any time since the 1960s. Unemployment fell significantly, dropping below a million by 2001 for the first time in almost 30 years. The proud boast of the government was that by making economic management the key political priority (Brown's prudence) it had succeeded, where past Conservative and Labour administrations had failed, in providing a stable economic base for policy development. In this it also appeared that, unlike in the 1970s and 1980s, Britain was performing more effectively than many of its economic competitors, with higher growth and higher employment than most of its EU neighbours and a return to a positive balance of payments for the first time since the 1980s (Thomas 2001).

There was a price to be paid for such economic prudence, however. For a start, the policy priority accorded to economic management further increased the political power of the Treasury within government. Brown's powerful personal position within the government (which led him to succeed Blair unopposed as Prime Minister in 2007), and its determination to make all policy decisions conditional upon their not undermining the pursuit of stable economic growth, made this dominant position even stronger and further reaching.

For its first two years of government Labour pledged to remain within the public spending limits set by the previous Conservative administration, with the result that, in relation to a growing GDP, overall levels of public expenditure fell (Burchardt and Hills 1999). Brown sought to control and reduce public borrowing, and aimed to adhere to a 'golden rule' that over the economic cycle government would not borrow to finance current expenditure but only capital investment (such as new public buildings), and here only where such expenditure could be afforded (and in places matched by private investment). The effect of this initially at least was to reduce levels of public borrowing for the first time since the end of the 1980s (Thomas 2001).

Following the two years of fixed expenditure the government introduced a Comprehensive Spending Review (CSR) to plan public spending over a three-year cycle. The first of these in 1998 led to commitments to raise significantly public spending on health and education in particular, and this was followed by further such increases in the following CSR in 2002. By the early years of the new century, therefore, Labour was able to claim that its prudent approach to economic management had secured a major growth in public expenditure on welfare services, which was not financed by either public borrowing or major tax increases, although some tax increases were made, notably the increase in NI to fund new health spending in the 2002 budget.

However, even such prudent economic management remained in practice susceptible to changes in broader economic development. Significant downturns in economic growth in many advanced industrial countries (notably for a time in the USA) in the early years of the century led to reductions in growth in the UK too, and a consequent failure of the UK economy to meet the targets planned by government. In the short run this led to major extensions in government borrowing to meet public expenditure commitments, with these being maintained over a number of years in the mid-2000s, leading Brown in effect to abandon his 'golden rule'.

THE CREDIT CRUNCH

The impact of global economic forces in the new century has accentuated the shift of manufacturing and much economic power to China, which became the most rapidly growing economy in the world. With the exception of a few powerful exporters like Germany, therefore, economic growth in the established Western economies, such as the UK, is no longer driven primarily by traditional industries, and economic activity (and employment) here has been transferred to new service industries such as finance, retail, leisure and catering (Hay and Wincott 2012).

In the UK in particular these new 'industries' had come to dominate the economy, and this applied most significantly to the financial sector based in the City of London. The banks and insurance companies in the City were by the beginning of the century providing new financial and legal services to a range of global markets, operating alongside (and to some extent in competition with) other major financial centres such as New York and Frankfurt, as well as offshore 'tax havens' where trading in large capital sums attracted less taxation from national governments.

For the most part the services these banks and other companies provided was credit. This included credit to commercial companies and private individuals, where provision and competition had been largely unregulated since the 1980s. It also, of course, included loans to national governments to provide the borrowing that underpinned growing public expenditure, including in the UK. Although the British economy, along with many others, was growing therefore, much of this growth was fuelled by the credit made available by the banks.

What is more the banks seemed willing to provide more and more credit, despite the fact their own holdings of capital could in no way underwrite all these potential debts. For the most part the banks covered these risks by taking out insurance against defaults on their loans. And these insurance policies themselves became valuable financial assets that could be bought and sold, assuming that continuing economic growth would ensure that no one would ever need to claim on them. The market for these increasingly more complex financial transactions was a global one, and a lucrative one, especially for the traders in the banks who could make vast fortunes by buying up loans or insurance policies cheaply and selling them on a profit the next day (or with the use of information technology, the next minute!).

Vast fortunes were made by bank traders in the early years of this century; and these seemed to be driving continuing economic growth. Governments therefore welcomed, and encouraged, them – and, of course, were borrowers from the banks themselves. This included the UK Labour administrations, which, under Blair and Brown, were quick to praise the successes of the growing financial sector in Britain. However, what was underpinning all of this rapid growth was credit; and credit requires borrowers to repay their loans. The rapid growth in credit in practice, however, involved banks in lending more and more money to more and more borrowers, some of whom might not be so easily able to repay all their debts.

Economists call such rapid economic growth a 'bubble'. The metaphor is apt because at some point a bubble is bound to burst, and in 2007 to 2008 that is just what happened. One of the causes of this was argued to be the US mortgage market, where loans to buy houses had been offered by banks to purchasers who did not have the incomes needed to repay the loans – referred to as 'subprime mortgages'. This was assumed not to be a problem since, if the borrowers defaulted, the houses could be sold to repay the debts; but this is only possible if the houses can be sold – and if too many people default there may be insufficient buyers in the market. In this case the value of the houses falls, and the loans cannot be recouped. So the banks no longer have these assets. They therefore cannot lend any more and indeed may try to claim on the insurance they have taken out to cover themselves against the losses. But these may not be able to provide cover as they themselves are dependent upon income from other lenders.

The effect of the subprime crisis in the US was to undermine the whole basis of financial trading leading to a near total breakdown of confidence in the financial system and the collapse of many of the leading institutions within it. The most high profile casualty was Lehman Brothers, which was heavily exposed to the subprime market and went bankrupt in 2008. However, other leading financial institutions also faced ruin with the two major US mortgage providers, Fannie Mae and Freddie Mac, and the insurance giant AIG having to be bailed out, and in effect taken over, by the US government. The collapse in business confidence in 2007 and 2008 was the greatest international economic disaster since the Great Depression of the 1930s, and it came to be referred to by commentators as the *Credit Crunch*.

Not surprisingly the Credit Crunch also hit the UK economy, ironically for Brown just after he had taken over from Blair as Prime Minister. The first sign of the problems to come was a run on the Northern Rock bank. This was a former building society that, like many others, had converted to a bank following the financial deregulation of the 1980s in order to allow it to engage in a wider range of financial dealings. Much of its business remained mortgages, however, and as in the US some of these were to buyers who were unlikely to be able to repay, and sometimes for 100 per cent or more of the supposed value of the property. Investors in Northern Rock feared their savings might not be secure therefore, and many tried to withdraw them – leading to long queues outside local branches. Such a run on the banks had led to a collapse in the Argentinian economy two decades earlier, and the Labour government began to fear that this might be repeated in the UK. The new Chancellor, Darling, therefore provided public funding to shore up Northern Rock, to guarantee investors that their money was safe; making the Treasury its major shareholder and in effect nationalizing it.

This was only the beginning of such public intervention, however, as other major banks began to experience similar problems and the government stepped in to 'bail out' Lloyds TSB and the Royal Bank of Scotland too. This led to major new commitments on public funding, at a time when public borrowing was already rising, as explained above. The banks were 'saved', but the broader impact of the Credit Crunch on the UK economy was much more far-reaching. Credit, once so easy to secure, was now reined back and the banks became more and more cautious in lending. The result of this was a more general slowdown in economic activity and hence a decline in economic growth.

This led to a more general recession in the UK economy towards the end of 2008, defined technically as two or more quarters of negative economic growth, bringing to an abrupt end the stability that Labour had claimed to have achieved. The fall in output in the country was greater than at any time since the end of the Second World War. Unemployment also began to rise again, although initially at least not as rapidly as in the 1980s and 1990s recessions (Gregg and Wadsworth 2011). Employment levels were probably sustained in part by continuing government investment, which the Chancellor expanded, to counter the impact of economic decline.

The price of this continued government spending, however, was a more rapid increase in public sector borrowing, fuelled further by the tax revenues lost as a result of reduced economic activity. Such growth could not be sustained in the longer term, and this issue came into sharp political focus in 2010 when, after five years in office, Labour had to call a General Election.

PUBLIC AUSTERITY

The recession and its implications for the future of the British economy was the major issue underlying this election. In particular all parties had to explain how they would address the problem of the growing public sector deficit and the loss of growth in GDP. All agreed these were problems, but all were rather cagey about exactly how they would tackle them if in power (Smith 2010) – perhaps anticipating that this could only be seen as 'bad news'.

In the event no one party did win the election, and following several days of frantic negotiating, the Coalition government of the Conservatives and Liberal Democrats took over power in May 2010, led by the Conservative Prime Minister, David Cameron (Kavanagh and Cowley 2010). Once in office the Coalition did have to address the economic problems facing the country. This resulted in a public sector spending review in the autumn, led by the new Chancellor, Osborne. What underpinned the review was the new government's belief that central to the longer-term health of the British economy was the need to remove the pressure of public sector borrowing, which was by now rising rapidly in a stagnant economy. This deficit could be reduced by raising taxes or cutting public spending. The government promised both; but tax changes were projected to account for around a quarter (mainly through an increase in VAT to 20 per cent) with public expenditure cuts bearing the brunt of the challenge (see Lee 2011).

The spending review of 2010 outlined the government's plans for public expenditure from 2011 to 2015, when the next election was due; and in 2013 this was extended to include the year 2015–16. The plan was to aim to remove the public sector deficit over the period to 2015 through a total of £80.5 billion of expenditure savings, with totally managed expenditure falling from 47.3 to 41 per cent of GDP (Lee 2011). These cuts were not distributed equally, however, with the NHS and international development spared from the harshest treatment, meaning that other departmental budgets would have to fall by an average of around 25 per cent, with welfare benefits (social security) expected to save the largest amounts (see Chapter 8).

The government's view was that removing the deficit was essential to rebalance the British economy, and that, although this would mean major losses of public sector jobs, these would in time be replaced by growing private sector employment. Some critics, however, pointed out that the scale of the proposed changes was quite unprecedented and could lead to unanticipated social and economic problems in the future. For instance, Taylor-Gooby and Stoker (2011) pointed out that these projections would take public spending in the UK below the levels of major comparator OECD countries, including the USA, and would result in a new era of public austerity

Government resolve to follow through with its plans seemed firm though, with Osborne famously claiming that there could be no 'Plan B', if things did not seem to be working (Lee 2011). However, pinning all economic hopes on deficit reduction was risky, especially if things did not work out as planned; and to some extent this is what began to happen.

As we mentioned above, the British economy is now no longer a national affair. Economic prospects here are inescapably bound up with economic development elsewhere, and in particular within the EU, of which the UK is a member and with which it conducts much of its overseas trade. Within the EU other countries were also experiencing recession and inflated public sector borrowing, in particular Greece, but also Ireland, Portugal, Spain and Italy. What is more these countries were now part of the Euro, the common currency employed by most EU members states, which the UK had refused to join. Economic problems for one Eurozone member nation meant in effect economic problems for all the others too. The strongest economies, most notably Germany, were not themselves so badly hit, but as members of the Euro they came under pressure to support their weaker partners; and, albeit reluctantly, Germany and the other Eurozone countries agreed to commit billions of euros to 'bail out' the faltering Greek economy and provide a potential support for others too.

The problem with the Greek economy in particular was that its public borrowing had reached such high levels that it could no longer be repaid, and as a result, lenders were raising the interest rates charged for loans, making the situation even worse. This was much the same as the private credit crisis of 2007/08, although in this case the 'subprime' borrowers were national governments. It seemed to provide some support therefore for Osborne's argument that reducing the UK public sector deficit should be the country's major priority, and confirmation that the UK was wise to have remained outside the Eurozone. However, the crisis in the Eurozone also affected the UK, because at the beginning of the 2010s the Greek economy, and many others, were in recession, and even the German economy slowed down, in part under the pressure of bailout costs. This meant that UK trade with Europe was also depressed, hitting economic growth here particularly in the private sector industries that the government had hoped would step in to replace the jobs and spending lost through their public sector cuts.

The impact of the Eurozone crisis together with the deflationary effects of the spending cuts in the UK led to a further recession in the first two quarters of 2012, when GDP again showed negative growth. This was referred to by pundits as a 'double-dip recession', following a similar early return to decline in the mid-1970s, and was followed by a further 'dip' later in the year. Added to the public austerity flowing from the first full year of expenditure cuts this resulted in extensive economic gloom across the country. The government was pressed to relax its spending reduction plans and increase investment and/or cut taxes in order to stimulate economic growth, as to some extent had been attempted by the Democratic administration under Obama in the US, with some limited success.

The Coalition refused to budge from its overall spending plans, however, although some reductions in taxation were introduced, including delaying rises in fuel duties and (more controversially) a reduction in the top rate of income tax from 50 to 45 per cent; and spending on some infrastructure projects was increased. Whether these will be sufficient to reflate, and rebalance, the UK economy remains to be seen. However, beyond the major public expenditure cuts to be implemented by 2015, the government also found it necessary to plan for further reductions for the years up to 2018. So it seems that economic growth (or recession) and public austerity are likely to be major issues at the 2015 General Election, as they were in 2010.

COMPREHENSION QUESTIONS

- To what extent did the recession of the 1990s prove that the country could not *borrow* its way out of recession?
- Why did the Labour government transfer the setting of interest rates to the Bank of England Monetary Policy Committee?
- What is the 'golden rule', and why did Gordon Brown break it?
- Why did the UK government, and others, step in to bail out the banks in the Credit Crunch of 2008?
- What were the consequences of the 2010 spending review for public expenditure in the UK?

REFLECTIVE QUESTION

- To what extent is economic policy planning within the control of national governments?

FURTHER READING

An accessible and wide-ranging review of the British economy in the late twentieth century is provided by Hutton (1995). He extended this (2002) to an examination of the international context in which Britain is now operating, and later to a study of the future of the economy after recession (2013). Balls and O'Donnell (2002) and Balls et al. (2004) provide a discussion of the Labour governments' economic policy planning, and Lee (2011) is a good summary of the Coalition government's economic plans. For a longer-term historical analysis of Britain's economic problems and the political responses to these see Gamble (1994). Hay and Wincott (2012) provide an overview analysis of the political economy of European countries, including the UK.

16
Paying for Welfare

SUMMARY OF KEY POINTS

- Welfare services must be paid for, although patterns of spending, including public spending, vary widely across welfare capitalist countries.
- Some economists have argued that there is a 'trade-off' between the goals of equity and efficiency in the funding of welfare provision, although this is disputed by others.
- Public spending decisions are announced in the annual Budget, but they are also subject to longer-term planning by government as part of a regular Comprehensive Spending Review (CSR).
- Public expenditure redistributes resources *vertically* (between social groups) and *horizontally* (across the life course of citizens).
- Taxation includes both *direct* taxes on incomes and *indirect* taxes on the purchase of goods and services.
- Public spending includes subsidies paid to low-income earners, although where these take the form of tax credits they do not appear in public expenditure accounts.
- Fees are charged for most private welfare services, and charges also play a significant role in raising revenue from the users of some public welfare services.
- Charitable giving can take a number of forms. It is important to third sector welfare providers but may also be used to support public welfare services, and is now directly encouraged by government.

THE COST OF WELFARE

The economic context in which social policies are developed and implemented is important in determining the scale and the scope of welfare services. As we discussed in Chapter 15, economic trends influence both the need for social services and a country's ability to afford to provide them; and thus the shifting patterns of economic growth in Britain, and elsewhere, over the last century or more have had a significant impact in controlling the development of social policy. At the same time, however, it is now widely recognized that the provision of welfare services can also influence the patterns of economic growth: both directly, by providing employment in welfare services, and indirectly, by stimulating demand for goods and improv-

259

ing the quality of the workforce. Social and economic policy are interdependent; therefore they need to be planned and developed together and, in practice in Britain and elsewhere, this is just what happens.

This means recognizing the important role that welfare plays in securing economic growth; but it also means planning to ensure that the costs of welfare services are identifiable and measurable, and can be met from within current economic resources. For, even though welfare services may be desirable in both social and economic terms, they still have to be funded. Welfare costs money; or at least it consumes resources, whether or not those resources are provided in the form of cash. Thus the money, or the resources, must be identified and collected and must be distributed to those providing, or consuming, welfare services. In all cases, therefore, the study of social policy involves not just undertaking an examination of the structure and the use of welfare services but also understanding the means of *paying for* these.

Welfare services must be paid for in all countries; however, comparative analysis reveals that in practice the scale of resources allocated to welfare varies significantly across different countries. Table 16.1 compares the different proportions of GDP spent on social protection (education, health and social security) in a number of OECD countries. It reveals some stark differences across these developed nations. However, it is noticeable how the picture changes to some extent when total social expenditure is measured, taking account of private welfare transfers. Direct public expenditure is clearly a greater feature of welfare spending in some countries, such as Sweden and Denmark, whereas in others, such as the USA, there is less reliance on state provision. What the OECD data also reveal is that, although welfare spending had been more or less static as a proportion of GDP over the last two decades, it grew as a proportion of overall GDP during the recent recession and has not yet significantly declined (OECD 2012b).

Table 16.1	Public social expenditure in selected nations as a percentage of GDP, 2009								
Australia	*Denmark*	*Germany*	*Finland*	*Japan*	*Korea*	*New Zealand*	*Sweden*	*UK*	*US*
Gross Public Expenditure									
18	30	27	29	22	9	22	30	23	19
Total Social Expenditure									
20	25	27	24	25	13	19	26	27	29

Source: OECD (2012b), Social Expenditure Data update (SOCX), Chart 7.

Different countries are therefore paying different amounts for the welfare services that they have developed, and paying for these in different ways. What is more different models for financing and distributing welfare are likely to produce differences in the structure, and the effectiveness, of welfare services; and these are independent, at least in part, of overall costs. In other words, the same overall amounts of resources can be spent in different ways, some of which may deliver similar, or better, services for the same cost. Thus comparisons based only on overall expenditure may not tell us much about the extent of welfare; we need to look in addition at how effectively the money is spent.

The debate about the effective use of resources in providing welfare services has sometimes been presented as a balance, or a conflict, between 'equity' and 'efficiency' in paying for welfare:

- A concern with the *equity* of welfare services focuses attention upon whether services are provided adequately to consumers and, in particular, whether individual needs for social protection are being met.

- A concern with *efficiency* focuses attention upon whether the resources that are consumed in service delivery are being used for maximum effect and at minimal cost.

Economists have sought to evaluate the effectiveness of services in quantifiable terms, by contrasting equity gains with efficiency costs. They have sometimes suggested that pressure on efficiency resulting from the broader context of economic growth means that there is an inevitable 'trade-off' between the two, in which equity gains must be scaled back to meet the need for more efficient use of scarce resources for social protection (Okun 1975). However, as Le Grand (1990) pointed out, the inevitability of such a trade-off is in practice a misleading notion, for the goal of securing equity in the meeting of needs is rather different from the aim of ensuring that the delivery of services is cost-effective. Pursuing efficiency can result in the maintenance of quality at reduced cost (Le Grand 1993). Thus it does not necessarily prevent the securing of equity; indeed, arguably improved efficiency in service provision could contribute to greater equity.

Certainly attempts to contrast the two in quantifiable terms, and to set the costs of one against the other, are fraught with both conceptual and practical difficulties. Economists may argue that judgements about how, and how much, to pay for welfare should be subject to efficiency criteria; but efficiency alone cannot be the basis for making judgements about paying for welfare, for we also need to determine the social policy goals for which services are developed and delivered. Therefore efficiency and equity are twin goals for social policy that must be considered together, not mutually exclusive poles that we must choose between.

PUBLIC EXPENDITURE

Whatever the aims or the outcomes, however, economists all agree that public expenditure on welfare provision has been growing. As we saw in Figure 2.1 there has been a dramatic growth in welfare spending as a proportion of GDP in the UK over the past hundred years or so, despite a dip in the middle of the last century. This growth slowed to some extent towards the end of the last century, but this was a pattern common to most developed countries. In the first decade of the new century, however, expenditure levels increased again under Labour, though, as explained in Chapter 6, the devolved governments gained some discretion over aspects of public spending.

These levels were initially sustained following the 2008 recession, in part to use such expenditure to bolster economic performance. However, the Coalition government elected in 2010 moved quickly to fulfil its commitment to cut public expenditure significantly in order to reduce the growing demand for public borrowing to finance this expenditure and bring down the overall deficit in the public finances that this borrowing had produced. Its plans were outlined in a four-year Comprehensive Spending Review (CSR) published in autumn 2010, which, as we explained in Chapter 15, anticipated a total of £80.5 billion savings in public expenditure, with cuts in departmental budgets in England of around 25 per cent, and significant reductions in welfare benefit payments across the UK (see Chapter 8).

Taylor-Gooby and Stoker (2011) argued that these projections will take public spending in the UK below the levels of a number of comparator OECD countries and change the relative standing of the country in the chart which underlies Table 16.1. However, although major cuts in spending on many welfare services have been introduced since 2010, the overall targets for deficit reduction set by the government have not been achieved, in large part because economic growth has been less than forecast. In 2012 therefore the government announced an extension to the planned time frame for expenditure reductions through to 2018, although this time frame took such financial planning beyond the date of the next general election in 2015. The details of these future cuts were not explained in any revised CSR, although in 2013 figures were provided for projected reductions in spending in 2015–16.

Despite these recent planned reductions, however, over the longer term public expenditure growth has been a feature of the development of welfare provision. This has happened in large part because public expenditure is more effective, and more efficient, at providing for many social needs than the alternative provision within the private market or third sector: what economists sometimes call the effect of *market failure*. But it has also grown because a wider range of social needs and public services have resulted in demands for continuing improvements in collective welfare, creating pressures on government which cannot always be met: what economists sometimes call *government failure* (Glennerster 2009). Increased public expenditure thus reflects both growing demands for welfare services and limitations in the supply from other providers. In practice, however, this growth in expenditure has been a more complicated phenomenon than simply an increase in the scale of publicly provided services; and its relationship with private and voluntary welfare is also more sophisticated than a simple model of public take-over might imply.

Public expenditure can be used to cover the direct costs of providing services. This is the pattern for many well-known public services: schools and hospitals have been built with public money, and teachers, doctors and nurses are paid to deliver education and health services. Many of these services are not exclusively funded by the state, however. Private investment is now used in partnership with public funding in the building of new hospitals under private finance initiatives, and private investors contribute support to state schools, in particular where these are established as Free Schools under the new initiatives discussed in Chapter 12. Also charges are levied on users for some aspects of education, health and social care such as some school activities or, in England, medical prescriptions.

Within the public funding of welfare services there is also a distinction between the allocation of resources to the *providers* of the services such as schools or hospitals, and the distribution of resources to the *purchasers* of those services. As we saw in Chapter 3 the recent development of quasi-markets within state welfare has led to a shift in the distribution of public spending through purchasers rather than providers. There are some limits to this distribution, however. In education it is still schools, rather than children and their parents, who have the final power to allocate places. Indeed competition for places in popular schools has become a major political issue; and the idea of providing cash (or equivalent) vouchers to parents, which could be 'spent' in any public or private education setting, has only been taken up in early learning provisions. In health and social services it has generally been other state officers (doctors and social workers) rather than service users themselves who have controlled the funding, although the personalization of some health and social care funding, discussed in Chapter 11, could in time change this.

In other areas of spending public resources do go more directly to purchasers, however. For instance, HB and HLA paid to low-income tenants is a form of public spending on housing distributed to the purchasers of rented housing, in the public, third and private rented sectors. In effect such benefits are a form of state subsidy towards the cost of meeting housing needs for those without the means to purchase accommodation themselves either from state or non-state providers. Such subsidization extends to the provision of other forms of means-tested support for poor service users, for instance, the free school meals and, in England, the free prescriptions provided to low-income families and benefit claimants.

Benefits such as these usually go to those at the bottom of the income scale. However, the use of *tax credits* and tax allowances are also an indirect form of public subsidy, and they may extend more widely up the income scale. As we saw in Chapter 8 the use of tax credits was developed by the Labour governments of 1997–2010, particularly to subsidize the costs experienced by low-wage families, though its provisions have since been merged with certain social security benefits into the new UC scheme.

Governments have also used *tax allowances* (sometimes termed tax exemptions or reliefs) as a form of subsidy to enable individuals to meet particular costs or encourage certain activities. Currently the most crucial are the exemption on occupational and personal pension contributions. But in the past they included interest payments on private mortgages, and tax reliefs for married men and children. Traditionally such allowances have often been of most benefit to the better-off who are more likely to be paying tax and buying such services. Titmuss famously referred to this form of public spending as 'fiscal welfare' (Titmuss 1955), and argued it involved a disguised distribution of resources to these better-off taxpayers. More recently this skewing of tax allowances in favour of higher-earners has been described as having an 'upside down' effect (Sinfield 2013). It has also, moreover, often been hidden from analysis of public spending because, as income not received by the state rather than money spent, it is not included in official calculations of public spending.

Nevertheless, as forms of individual subsidy, tax allowances and credits are just as important as the benefits paid to people directly, and can be widely used by government. The use of public funding to purchase services outside the public sector extends beyond individual subsidization, however. Public funds are also allocated directly to those providing services within the private and third sectors. As we discussed in Part 1, this funding of non-state providers can take the form of *grants* of public money to organizations that offer to use this to provide particular services to citizens, a common form of funding for many third sector service providers in the past. It can also take the form of *contracts* between non-state providers and public funding agencies for the delivery of specific service packages.

Such contracts have become more common in recent years, with both for- and not-for-profit suppliers taking on an increasingly wide range of public services under contracts. There are now some large companies undertaking major areas of service delivery under contracts with government agencies, for instance, under the Work Programme, discussed in Chapter 13. The funding for these contracts has also increasingly been based on what is called 'payment by results' (PBR). Rather than a fixed contract price, non-state providers are paid a fixed fee for each individual served, based on the savings from other public expenditure budgets that result from the help being provided, for instance, to move them into employment or away from criminal reoffending. This shift towards 'outcome-based' funding has been heralded by some as an important means of moving public expenditure towards the achievement of direct benefits for service users; but whether it will work effectively in securing more effective services still remains to be seen.

It is not just where public expenditure takes place that matters to social policy, of course: there is also the question of what public money is spent on. Decisions on the distribution of public spending are taken by the UK government and, within the spending envelope allocated to them, by the devolved governments. At UK level this is done on an annual basis in the national Budget. This also contains decisions about the raising of revenue to pay for the planned spending; although in practice the Budget statement concentrates mainly on those decisions that involve major changes in planned spending or departures from past policy, for in large part future spending commitments are determined by past policy developments and the activities and organizations established to deliver these. We cannot just decide to stop funding schools or hospitals, and indeed any significant change in spending patterns is likely to take some time to implement. As a result the annual Budget statements often contain spending or taxation decisions which will not become operational for months or even years.

In the twenty-first century such longer-term planning has become more common in the UK. The Labour government initiated the CSR process in 1999 to outline funding plans over three years. Following the 2010 election the Coalition took an even longer-term perspective in its autumn spending review. This outlined spending plans through to 2015, as mentioned, primarily focused on the need to reduce expenditure significantly over this period, and in 2013 this was extended into the financial year 2015–16. Nevertheless annual budgets are still announced by the Chancellor of the Exchequer each spring for the coming financial year, from April to April. For 2013–14 this led to the distribution of funding revealed in Figure 16.1.

Despite the big increases in spending on health and education under Labour, social security (social protection) remains by far the largest single element of public spending on social

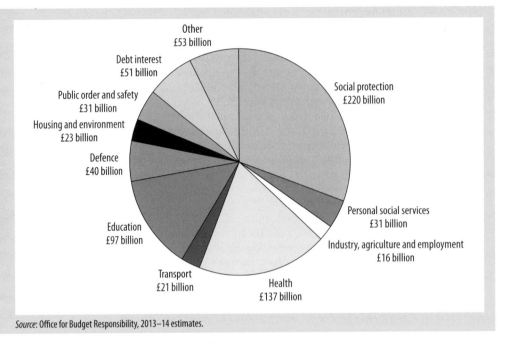

Source: Office for Budget Responsibility, 2013–14 estimates.

Figure 16.1 Public expenditure in the 2013 Budget

policy. It has also been growing consistently over the last two decades or so as the numbers of pensioners, unemployed and other claimants has generally increased. In this century the shift of some benefits to tax credits, and the growth in these discussed in Chapter 8, further inflated this figure, despite reductions in levels of unemployment. It is for this reason that the Coalition targeted much of its planned expenditure reductions on the 'welfare' budget. However, if levels of unemployment remain relatively high, it is debatable whether all the planned savings will be achieved, even with reductions in benefit rates.

As, also highlighted earlier, whilst social security policy is determined by the UK government most other welfare provision is the responsibility of the devolved administrations. They receive a block grant giving them a proportionate share of public expenditure calculated according to a long-standing arrangement, the Barnett Formula, and have discretion as to how this is spent. This system would of course change if Scottish voters decide on independence in 2014. In practice devolution has meant earlier spending differences between the countries of the UK have lessened (Parry 2012), though the Scottish and Welsh administrations have tended towards greater generosity and, especially since 2011, placed more emphasis on the role of the state.

The effect of public spending in redistributing resources within society is perhaps one of the main policy objectives of social policy planning. It was a key theme of Titmuss's early analysis of the role of public expenditure planning (see Alcock et al. 2001). Despite the assumption by many that such redistribution would generally benefit those at the bottom of the social scale, Le Grand (1982) produced a famous analysis of spending which suggested that much of it actually went to the middle classes. However, more recent analysis of the impact of a wide range of public spending commitments suggests that, despite the fact that key major services such as health and education continue to be available on a universal basis, overall there is significant redistribution of resources towards those in the lower parts of the income distribution within society, particularly if the effect of taxation is also taken into account (see Hills 2012).

Hills (2012) also pointed out that public expenditure operates to redistribute resources in another way, *horizontally* (over the life course of citizens) as well as *vertically* (between social groups). This is most obviously the case with payments such as pensions and child benefits, but it also applies to much education and health spending too. Horizontal redistribution is also affected by the impact of taxation with direct taxes, such as income tax and NI contributions, being paid predominantly by people during their working lives only. For all of us public spending is operating as a kind of 'savings bank', shifting resources across our life courses as our needs and circumstances change; and the overall impact of such horizontal redistribution is quite significant. Hills (2012) calculated that this 'savings bank' function accounted for nearly three-quarters of welfare spending. Some of these changes have been analysed in more detail by researchers using financial models to track the dynamics of life cycle redistribution (Evans and Williams 2009).

COMPREHENSION QUESTIONS

- Why is social security by far the largest area of public expenditure?
- What is 'fiscal welfare', and why has it been argued that it disguises disproportionate benefits for the middle class from the distribution of welfare services?

REFLECTIVE QUESTION

- Does is matter that significant elements of public spending are delivered by private and voluntary organizations?

SOURCES OF FUNDING

In his work on the funding of welfare services Glennerster (1997, 2009) argued that the sources of funding are as important in influencing the operation of social policy, and the distribution of resources and benefits, as are the ways in which money is spent. In this context he distinguishes between three main sources of funding: taxation, fees or charges, and gifts or charity. To some extent these different sources reflect the differences between the three organized sectors of welfare provision: the state, the market and the third sector. However, in practice, their use is more complex than such a simple three-way division, for funding of state services includes both charges and charity, and, as we have seen, taxation is used to support both private and third sector services. The mix of funding is thus as complex as the mix of services, if not more so, although state funding (financed through taxation) remains the most important source both in terms of its impact on taxpayers and its support for a wide range of service provision.

TAXES

Taxes are compulsory payments to the state that are used by government to fund public expenditure; and, though legislation in 2011 gave the Scottish government some independent tax raising powers, tax, or *fiscal*, policy is in practice determined by the UK government. The most widely known tax is probably *income tax*, which is fixed as a proportion of earned income. In most cases this is deducted at source from people's income by their employers, who then pay this to HM Revenue and Customs (the taxation arm of the Treasury). Income tax is a common form of taxation in most countries, and remains the largest source of taxation revenue in the UK; but it is not the only form of taxation – far from it. Figure 16.2 explains the relative size of different forms of taxation in the 2013 Budget and reveals that income tax comprises a minority of the total taxation income within government budget planning.

The total income from taxes is less than the expenditure outlined in Figure 16.1, however. Government borrowing is used to make up the difference. It this level of government borrowing, and the consequent overall deficit in the public finances that accumulates from it, that the Coalition government committed itself to removing, or at least significantly reducing. However, annual levels of borrowing have remained high, and the timetable for removing the overall deficit has been put back to 2018.

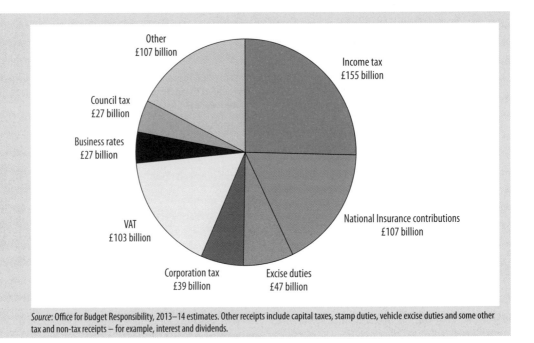

Source: Office for Budget Responsibility, 2013–14 estimates. Other receipts include capital taxes, stamp duties, vehicle excise duties and some other tax and non-tax receipts – for example, interest and dividends.

Figure 16.2 Distribution of tax funding in the 2013 Budget

Most commentators make a distinction between direct and indirect taxation. *Direct* taxation is tax on income and includes NI contributions. By and large this means that those with larger incomes pay more tax (sometimes referred to as progressive taxation), especially where higher rates of tax are levied on higher levels of income. Income tax in the UK is levied at 20 per cent, but taxpayers on higher incomes pay tax at the rate of 40 per cent on some of their income, and for top earners there is a higher rate of 45 per cent (reduced from 50 per cent in 2013). *Indirect* taxation is tax on the purchase of goods or services. The main indirect tax is Value Added Tax (VAT), which is levied at 20 per cent of the costs of most goods and services. Because everyone must buy such goods, indirect taxes fall more broadly across the income range and may even be *regressive*, comprising a larger proportion of the incomes of lower-paid people who generally spend all of their income rather than saving or investing it.

There are some other important distinctions within taxation. Although most taxes simply contribute to overall public expenditure, it is possible for taxes to be linked to specific areas of spending. This is called ear-marked or *hypothecated* taxation, and the only significant example in the UK is NI contributions, which are placed in the NI fund and used to fund insurance benefit expenditure, in particular state pensions. To some extent council tax is also hypothecated, or at least is restricted to those activities under the control of local government. Some indirect taxes are intended not only to raise revenue but also to influence social behaviour. This applies particularly to the additional taxation on tobacco and alcohol (much higher, for instance, in the UK than in most other European countries), but it also applies to taxation on fuel (especially petrol), which is intended in part to reduce road usage and atmospheric pollution. There is also now some political support for other 'green taxes', which aim to discourage environmentally damaging activities by penalizing them with higher rates of taxation, although in practice not many examples of these have been introduced in the UK.

Payment of taxes is compulsory and, in theory, should be popular for they supply the funding for the services the electorate has decided it wants the government to provide. There is, however, a strong ideological current of hostility to taxation; and this was encouraged in the 1980s and 1990s by Conservative government claims that there was a need to reduce tax burdens in order to 'return' control over spending to individual earners and so, it was argued, stimulate economic growth. This hostility to taxation is now widespread within the UK. It was influential on the Blair and Brown governments, which sought to avoid increases in (especially income) tax, even in order to pay for improved public service provision, although NI contributions were raised in 2003 to pay for increased spending on health and education. And, although the Coalition expected increases in taxation (most notably a rise in VAT) to contribute to its deficit reduction strategy, most of this is based on savings in public expenditure rather than increases in public income.

FEES AND CHARGES

The provision of most private welfare is based upon the payment of a fee, calculated to cover the cost of the service provided, and perhaps to include an element of profit for the owners of the service. However, access to public services too sometimes involves payment of a fee. For instance, fees are charged for the use of leisure services, such as public swimming pools; and sometimes for welfare services too, such as adult education classes. However, it is more common for payment by consumers of public services to take the form of a charge rather than a fee, the difference being that a charge is not intended to cover the full cost of providing the service but requires users to make a contribution towards such costs.

Charges have existed for a long time in state welfare services although their role was initially a minor one, with most services being provided free to users. The payment of charges for prescriptions for drugs was introduced in 1951, very soon after the NHS came into operation in 1948. This was a controversial measure at the time, leading to the resignation of the health minister and architect of the NHS, Aneurin Bevan. Nevertheless, charges for prescriptions have (apart from a brief period in the 1960s) remained; and in England more recently the level of the charge was significantly increased. However, devolution has led to changes here, with prescription charges being abandoned in Wales (2007), Northern Ireland (2010) and Scotland (2011).

Charges for other services, such as dentistry and optical treatment, also exist, though again with variations between the devolved administrations; and the use of charges within other areas of public provision, such as education and social care, has grown, especially in England. As we saw in Chapter 11 these include charges for residential, day and domiciliary care, the use of which again varies between the countries of the UK. Although the scope of charges has been increasing, however, the structure of charges and charging policies has remained uncoordinated and, as a result, somewhat complex. The types of charges used by public service providers vary, with some making flat-rate charges to all service users and others grading charges either according to the level of service use or according to the circumstances of the users. The levels charges are fixed at also vary widely. Some are based on an attempt to secure an approximate contribution to the cost of the service provided but some have been priced at quite nominal levels, perhaps not even recovering the cost of collecting them.

The growth in charges within state services has largely been the product of reductions in public funding for such services. However, the use of charges serves purposes other than revenue-raising. Charges can reveal the real preferences and priorities of consumers, by discouraging abuse of free services by those who do not really need or want them; and they can act to raise the status of service users by providing them with a feeling that they are paying for services and thus can expect more responsive delivery. On the other hand, even nominal charges can act to discourage genuinely needy, and often vulnerable, users from gaining access to services; and are likely to impact particularly harshly on poorer users who may not be able to afford to pay them out of their limited incomes.

The problem of the impact of charges on poor service users can be mitigated by the introduction of *rebates* for those with low, or no, incomes. Rebates may remove the charge altogether or reduce it according to the level of income received by the user and are widely used both by central and local government to mitigate the impact of charges on low-income users. For instance, NHS prescription charges are removed in England for children, pensioners and some people on low incomes; and, since these include the major users of health services, they mean that in practice most prescriptions in England too are provided free.

Most LAs also operate rebate schemes to reduce or remove the charges for education and social care for certain groups of poor people. One of the problems with such rebate schemes, however, is that they introduce a further layer of complexity into the provision of welfare services: users have to identify their right to the service, understand the nature of the charge, and then recognize and apply for any possible rebate. This can accentuate the already problematic issue of ensuring access to welfare services, a point to which we will return in Chapter 18; it can also lead to many people failing to identify and take up their entitlement to rebates. Fees, charges and rebates can therefore have negative as well as positive effects on the provision of social policy.

CHARITY

The other main area of funding identified by Glennerster (1997) was giving, or charity. Charitable actions and gifts are probably the oldest form of welfare funding, and there is a view amongst some supporters of public services that reliance upon charity is anachronistic in a modern welfare state. However, as our discussion of the third sector involvement in social provision in Chapter 4 revealed, giving remains a central feature of the modern welfare mix; and, although state support for the sector is often now an essential part of the resourcing of voluntary and community organizations, most of these still rely very largely on the time and money donated to them by voluntary activists or the public at large. Furthermore, it is not just voluntary organizations that benefit from charitable sources: gifts may also be made to public service providers perhaps through bequests in wills, which is quite common in education, especially to universities. Volunteer time is also utilized by public service providers. For example, volunteers of all ages, including school children, are used by local social care departments to work with vulnerable clients.

Charity and gift-giving also take a variety of forms across the third, private and public sectors. Volunteer time is obviously of particular importance as a resource for voluntary organizations, and can also include giving specialist skills, for instance, lawyers or accountants may have much to offer to voluntary agencies by way of unpaid professional advice and assistance. Gifts may also be made in kind: for instance, the provision of equipment, or computer software, or the use of a telephone or internet connection. Such gifts in kind are made by individuals, but they are often a form of corporate support for voluntary agencies provided by commercial companies. Gifts like this may even take the form of 'sponsorship', where a business provides goods or services in return for its name being publicized as a supporter of the voluntary welfare agency; and this 'corporate social responsibility' is an important aspect of the image which some companies seek to project.

Most such sponsorship arrangements take the form of cash donations made in return for publicity for the corporate, or individual, donor. Cash donations themselves take a wide variety of forms, including regular donations, one-off gifts and contributions to street collections, sponsored activities, jumble sales and charity shops. Such support is encouraged by government through the granting of exemptions from liability for direct taxation on money given as charitable donations under the Gift Aid scheme, as discussed in Chapter 4. However, this must be claimed by the charities involved, and might more accurately be seen as a form of state subsidy operating in addition to private decisions to give.

The very nature of charity, however – its unorganized and voluntary nature – can cause problems for welfare provision. It may prevent some from giving because in practice they have not been asked, and it may lead others to feel uncomfortable about this form of moral pressure to support welfare. What is more, people may give varying levels of support at different times and in different areas, and usually this bears little relation to individual income differentials, or social needs. Moral pressure may also apply in reverse to the recipients of gifts: users of charitable services may not feel that they have the rights and entitlements that the users of public services, or the purchasers of private welfare, can command, and thus may not use them so readily.

Charitable support for welfare is inevitably uneven in nature, therefore, both over time and across place, as we discuss in Chapter 4. However, the services that rely on such inequitable and uneven support require some level of consistency over time and equality across different places both to employ workers and to guarantee services to all users. Welfare services for the large part need to be predictable and comprehensive. Paying for welfare on a voluntary basis, therefore, cannot always operate to support regular service provision in the way that public taxation or private market fees can. As a result, charitable funding is often used to supplement other sources of support, in particular state funding, or to provide very specific, and adaptable, local services where flexibility and fluctuation in activity are not a limitation on provision – and may even, of course, be a virtue.

The funding of welfare in Britain, therefore, operates in practice on a mixed economy model with state, market-based and voluntary funding overlapping across the sectors and areas of provision; and, although state funding through taxation dominates in many areas (such as education, health and social security), throughout both state and non-state welfare varying mixtures of funding can be found. Thus the picture presented by a study of the means of paying for welfare is a complex one. It is also a dynamic one. Differing forms of funding and the balance between these in different sectors of welfare provision are constantly changing. In the latter part of the last century the role of direct state funding was transformed in some areas into indirect state subsidies through tax allowances and quasi-markets, and by a greater reliance on market-based fees and user charges, and these are being promoted again in the 2010s as government seeks to reduce the cost of public expenditure. Such changes affect the overall structure and delivery of welfare provision. But the delivery of welfare is also affected by a wide range of factors beyond money and it is to these that we will return in Chapter 18.

COMPREHENSION QUESTIONS

- What are 'hypothecated' taxes, and what are the advantages and disadvantages of using them to fund welfare services?
- What are the advantages and disadvantages of the use of charges for public services?
- What problems arise from the use of charitable donations as a source of income for the providers of welfare services?

- Why do you think that hostility to the payment of taxes is apparently so widespread in Britain?

FURTHER READING

Glennerster's texts (1997 and 2009), provide the best guides to the issues and sources of funding for different aspects of social policy. Hills (1993) is still the best guide to the issues underlying the public funding of welfare, and his chapter on the distribution of welfare in the *Student's Companion to Social Policy* is an excellent summary of key issues (Hills 2012). An example of analysis of the redistribution of welfare resources over people's lifetimes can be found in Evans and Williams (2009). Bennett (2012) and Sinfield (2013) provide overviews of fiscal policy; and a summary of the UK budget process can be found online in Brunsdon and May (2012) at www.blackwellpublishing.com/alcock4e/. Jordan and Drakeford (2012) examine some of the implications of social policy under austerity. Statistical data on UK population and spending patterns can be found at www.statistics.gov.uk; and the Treasury website, www.hm-treasury.gov.uk, contains information about public expenditure, taxation and other aspects of welfare spending and support.

17
Social Divisions

SUMMARY OF KEY POINTS

- Britain is a divided society within which the experiences and needs of different social groups are varied and diverse, and may even come into conflict.
- Class differences linked to economic status continue to divide British society, although social policy has acted to reduce some inequalities between classes and to promote mobility across classes.
- Gender inequalities within social policy have flowed in large part from the assumptions about the different roles of men and women in employment and family structures, which underpinned much of the welfare reform of the last century.
- Britain is a multicultural society with a wide range of different ethnic groups whose differing needs and circumstances have not always been recognized within the provision of welfare services.
- Racism directed at Britain's black population has led to discrimination and disadvantage within welfare provision.
- Families with children are disproportionately disadvantaged with around one-third of children in poverty compared to around a quarter of adults.
- Ageism within social policy planning has led to assumptions about 'dependency' in old age and to concerns that the growing proportion of older people in society will constitute a burden on future generations.
- Disability covers a wide range of different circumstances and needs, but generally means that people with disabilities need support to reach the standards of living enjoyed by others, yet disabled people are more likely to be unemployed and poor.

A DIVIDED SOCIETY

We usually conceive of British society, or indeed any society, as providing a uniform social structure in which we all live. Within this social structure we are bound together by a common democratic and political structure and by a shared cultural experience and heritage, exemplified perhaps most strongly in modern times by the national media (television, radio, newspapers and related social media) that provide us with so much of our knowledge of the rest of our social world. In particular, from the point of view of social policy, we are also subject to the same policy provisions and legal rights and responsibilities.

However, as some sociologists are quick to point out, this model of British (and other) societies as culturally and socially uniform is in fact a rather partial one, and in many senses a fundamentally flawed one. While there may be much that unites us as British citizens, there is also much that divides us. We have different histories, cultures and circumstances, which have shaped our individual lives and our social relations. As a result we do not all have similar needs and interests and our experiences of our supposedly shared welfare services can in practice be widely varying ones. Against the model of uniformity and harmony, therefore, it is argued that instead we should adopt a model of difference and even conflict, which highlights instead the varying circumstances and experiences of social groups within society in both the production and consumption of resources, and recognizes that the needs or interests of some will conflict with those of others. From such a perspective, the development and the consumption of welfare services itself may be a focus of social struggle.

In a broad sense, of course, both models have some truth in them. We do all share a social and cultural context as British citizens; yet at the same time we are members of different groups with different and sometimes conflicting interests. However, where there may have been a tendency in some of the more traditional social policy and social administration literature to emphasize the shared – even supposedly universal – nature of welfare services (Crosland 1956), there is now an increasingly widespread recognition in social policy debate of the fact that we live within a divided society (Platt 2011).

In understanding the development and operation of social policy, therefore, it is essential to recognize the importance of social divisions. The social groups to which people belong will structure their experience of social policies, and the political processes by which policies are developed will be determined by the differential power and influence of different groups. Furthermore, these experiences and processes are intertwined: marginalization or exclusion from the process of policy-making is also likely to lead to disadvantage or discrimination in the receipt of services. What is more, in Britain, as in most other advanced capitalist countries, welfare services have in practice been constructed largely by certain social groups, who have consequently benefited disproportionately from them. Advantage and disadvantage in society more generally can also be reflected in differential access to, and use of, welfare services.

The most widely recognized and debated social division is probably that of social class. This is also still the most important social division, although in modern welfare capitalist societies class differences have become ever more complex. Class divisions are a way of making sense of the inequalities of socioeconomic circumstances within society by reference to people's position within the labour market or production process and, as we shall see, such divisions have long been debated and argued about. However, inequalities are not just the product of the labour and production processes: class differences also arise from consumption patterns, and in addition there are broader aspects of inequality than simply cash income and access to material resources. Social status, life chances, life choices, and cultural freedom are also inequitably distributed, and differences here are not only structured by the economics of class.

Gender differences also affect all of these issues, as well as structuring economic inequality independently of class; and, in a multicultural and multiethnic society such as Britain, differences in racial or cultural background lead to further inequalities, although here, as we shall discuss, it is often the rac*ism* which reacts to such differences which is the primary cause of inequity and disadvantage. Gender and 'race' were discussed by Williams (1989) in her critical review of social policy, where she argued that they had largely been ignored by both academic analysis and policy development, though, as we shall see, consideration of both has developed since. However, there are other divisions, too, that were also hidden in – or hidden from – social policy debate.

Differences of age can also affect both involvement in, and experience of, welfare services, as do differences of physical ability, or disability, and we shall discuss these further below. Sexual orientation may also be a source of discrimination and influence experience of social policies. Family circumstances, language or geographical differences and many other circumstances also lead to varying needs and experiences. Indeed in all sorts of ways we are divided from each other through our membership of different social groups, with their different experiences and needs.

Furthermore, as mentioned above, welfare services are not only affected by social divisions, they also frequently reaffirm and reinforce these divisions. Indeed, the structure of welfare provision itself may *create* social divisions. For instance, as Dunleavy and Husbands (1985) argued, the consumption of welfare services can create *consumption cleavages* between user groups, such as the different material interests of owner-occupiers and tenants within different sectors of housing provision, discussed in Chapter 10. The receipt of services from different providers itself also creates divisions, such as those between pupils in 'public' (private) schools and pupils in the state sector. Finally, the very process of delivering services creates divisions and conflicts of interest between the providers of services and the consumers of them, starkly symbolized by the plastic screens once found in social security benefit offices separating staff from claimants who came to see them.

As we discussed in Chapter 14, recent *postmodernist* theorizing in social science has stressed the complex nature of such social divisions and social processes within welfare capitalist societies. Postmodern society, theorists argue, is characterized by complexity and diversity, and cannot be understood as a single unified entity with common social problems and services. This becomes clear when we consider the diverse social groupings to be found in current British society, some of which we summarize here.

COMPREHENSION QUESTIONS

- Why was it argued that the development of public welfare services in the twentieth century reinforced social divisions within British society?
- What are 'consumption cleavages'? How do they introduce further difference and conflict into the delivery of social policy?

CLASS

Theoretical and empirical debate about the structure of social class in Britain, and other modern societies, is both wide-ranging and longstanding. Indeed it is probably true to say that the concept of class is one of the most critical, and most contested, issues in social science, although useful guides to major perspectives in the UK are provided by Crompton (2008) and Roberts (2011). Theoretical differences over how to define, and how to determine, social classes have their roots in the major theoretical traditions stemming from the work of Marx and Weber over a century ago, the former arguing that social class is determined only through relationship to the means of production, and the latter arguing that differences of occupational status are also important in separating people into different classes (Sarre 1989). Since then sociological analysis has been taken further building on the work of Goldthorpe (Goldthorpe and Hope 1974), who developed a hierarchy of divisions based upon occupation, from managers to agricultural workers.

Within the UK there have also been a number of official classifications of class divisions, which in practice have been widely used for empirical measurement and to inform policy planning. These included the so-called Registrar General's scheme, which distinguished between six social groups ranging from professional and managerial to unskilled. However, these have been replaced since 2010 by a more complex model of occupational groups based on the National Statistics Socio-Economic Classification (NS-SEC); see Table 17.1.

Table 17.1 The ONS Socio-Economic Classification
1 Higher managerial and professional occupations
1.1 Large employers and higher managerial occupations
1.2 Higher professional occupations
2 Lower managerial and professional occupations
3 Intermediate occupations
4 Small employers and own account workers
5 Lower supervisory and technical occupations
6 Semi-routine occupations
7 Routine occupations
8 Never worked and long-term unemployed

Source: Office for National Statistics (2012b) .

The classes shown here are in a hierarchical order. Those at the top have most wealth, privileges and power; and the unemployed at the bottom are likely to have low incomes and little wealth. This reflects traditional Marxist and Weberian notions of differences in property and status. This hierarchy of categories is not watertight or fixed, of course. For instance, some factory workers are now paid more than some teachers; and in particular the relative size of different occupational groups has changed, with most commentators agreeing that over the latter part of the last century the size of the manual and unskilled classes (the working classes) declined and that of the non-manual and professional classes (the middle classes) increased (Crompton 2008). Furthermore, because the classification is based upon work it ignores those outside the labour market altogether, for instance, pensioners, students and carers.

What is more some commentators have argued that as a result of deindustrialization and the restructuring of the labour market a more or less permanent group of people who are unemployed or can only get limited part-time or temporary jobs has been created, and that this group now constitutes a separate social class, with little or no resources or power. The existence of such a group has, however, been much contested within sociology and social policy (see Morris 1994). Towards the end of the last century for instance some commentators, such as Murray described it as an *underclass*, suggesting its members had cut themselves off from the rest of society by their unwillingness to seek employment (see Lister 1996), although there was little evidence from sociological studies that this was the case (Smith 1992; Morris 1995). More recently others have used the term *precariat* to highlight the increasing numbers in insecure, irregular, unpredictable and low-waged forms of employment or without work (Standing 2011).

It is not only the case that categories of class are changing, however. Membership of social classes is also subject to change. In most societies there has been significant *class mobility*, with individuals moving up, and down, between classes. For instance, someone from a working-class family may, through achievement within the education system, secure a job in the professional middle class or start up a successful business; conversely, someone else may see their business fail, become unemployed and be unable to secure permanent work. Class mobility is, in part, the means by which such a hierarchical class structure retains a level of legitimacy within any society – as in the classic 'American dream', we might all one day hope to join the higher classes.

To some extent social policy has acted to promote such social mobility across classes. For instance, education can provide people with the knowledge and skills to secure high status and well-paid employment; indeed that is what many university students in particular expect to gain from their studies. However, in practice evidence suggests that such mobility has been limited, with the chances of people moving to a higher (or lower) social class than their parents remaining remarkably stable over time (Platt 2011). Further, despite significant commitments from the Labour governments of the 2000s to increasing expenditure on public services such as health and education in order to promote more equal opportunities for citizens, evidence suggests that social inequalities remained stubbornly high (Hills et al. 2013; National Equality Panel 2010). Indeed it appears that the gap between the most wealthy in the UK and the rest of the population has widened in recent years (Rowlingson and McKay 2011) and income inequality has increased (Brewer et al. 2012).

Furthermore, the development of welfare services themselves, while delivering benefits to users and securing (sometimes well-paid) employment for providers of services, has also created its own differences of power and privilege. Within the health service, for example, hospital consultants and managers have become influential arbiters of people's health needs, including decisions over life and death. Yet at the other end of the spectrum new sections of the lower working class, such as hospital cleaners and porters, have been created, often with lower pay and poorer conditions than those working in private industry.

Thus class differences may have been influential in creating pressure for the development of social policy in welfare capitalist societies; and class structures have been significantly affected by the development of welfare provision within all such countries. However, class differences have not been removed by social policy, and social mobility between classes has remained relatively stagnant.

COMPREHENSION QUESTIONS

- What is the Socio-Economic Classification, and how does it define social class?
- What is 'social mobility', and to what extent has it undermined the significance of class differences in determining life chances and welfare needs?

GENDER

Gender differences, in particular the greater power and privilege of men over women, are as deep-seated and longstanding as class differences in British society, and other countries too. These differences have not only survived but have also in part been accentuated by the development of welfare services, and they remain central to our understanding of the operation of these. However, unlike class, gender has not always been a central feature of debate about the development or the delivery of welfare services. In an early feminist critique Wilson (1977) argued that the different experience of welfare for women had frequently been marginalized in mainstream social policy debate, although concern with gender difference and inequality has been taken up by feminist writers and others since then (Daly and Rake 2003; Pascall 2012).

This is because, in a society in which men hold most of the dominant positions of power and influence, it is also men who have dominated the development, and the study, of social policy. But there has been a growth of academic interest in the gender dimension of policy development and delivery, and a growth in the political activity of women seeking to challenge male domination of our social services. Thus we now know much more about the different experiences, and needs, of men and women within welfare capitalist societies; and what we know confirms feminist suspicions that gender inequalities remain sizeable and significant, and that within this it is women who are disadvantaged.

The different circumstances and experiences of women and men are deep-seated features of society and extend far beyond the development and delivery of social policy. The context of social policy within the UK, and most other advanced industrial societies, has been in particular influenced by assumptions about family structure, labour market participation and the roles of women that underpinned the development of most services during the welfare reforms in the middle of the last century. These can be captured in the notion of the 'male breadwinner' model of work and family life.

In this model family life is presumed to be stable and based on married couples and their children. Within such families men work in the labour market and earn a wage that supports their wives and children, and women stay at home to care for the household and look after the children. This was the model that informed Beveridge's plan for social security. His assumption was that married women's main role would be as housewives and mothers within the family, and that they would therefore make 'marriage their sole occupation' (Beveridge 1942). He thus placed married women in a distinct insurance class in his social security proposals, providing for reduced contributions without an entitlement to benefits, because he assumed their husbands would be able to provide income support for them. In fact since then commitment to equal treatment, in part led by EU directives, has removed the separate treatment of married women within the social security system and ensured women and men have a formally equal status, although some older women who only paid the reduced contributions still experience exclusion from some National Insurance (NI) benefits such as pensions.

The assumptions Beveridge made about women's family 'responsibilities' extended beyond social security, however. The provision (or non-provision) of nursery education and care for young children and the organization of the school day and year for older children all assumed the availability of someone at home to care for children outside school hours, and in the vast majority of cases it has been women who have done this. And, as we discussed in Chapter 5, community care is predicated upon the availability of carers to provide informal support in cases of both acute need and chronic illness, and this burden too has fallen predominantly on women.

Of course, the male breadwinner model has always been a mythical characterization of family life, and of the roles and responsibilities of women and men. Even in the immediate post-war period when Beveridge's reforms were introduced, significant numbers of married women engaged in paid employment, and by and large did so because their income was critical for the survival of the family. Since then the participation of women within the labour market has been steadily growing, as we discuss in Chapter 13.

This has not been without its problems, however. For a start women do not enjoy equal status or equal pay within the labour market. In the 1970s women's average wages were only about 55 per cent of men's; and, despite the introduction of legislation to promote equal pay and prevent discrimination against women at work, the pay gap has remained relatively stable at around 16 per cent over recent times – that is women earn on average about 84 per cent of that earned by men (Platt 2011). The gap is greater if part-time work is taken into account as women are more likely than men to be working part-time and part-time wages are on average lower. This is largely because of occupational segregation. As we saw in Chapter 13, many of the jobs in which women typically work are different from those traditionally done by men, and often are lower paid.

Furthermore, the differences in women's employment circumstances have not been altered significantly by the development of welfare services. Indeed, to a large extent the growth of welfare provision, including in particular state welfare, has often reinforced occupational segregation through the creation of jobs that have been taken up almost exclusively by women, such as nurses, primary school teachers or social workers. In Britain these jobs have usually been associated with low status and low pay compared to those dominated by men, such as doctors, professors and service managers. Thus, while welfare services have created employment opportunities for women, they have also to some extent reinforced occupational segregation; although some women do of course achieve higher-status employment, and in some other countries (for example, Sweden) such occupational inequities are much less marked.

Women's position in different labour markets in part reflects their assumed responsibilities for family and community care. As we saw in Chapter 11, the costs of caring extend to disadvantage in other aspects of economic activity; and in practice, despite the false picture presented by the male breadwinner model, it is still predominantly women who forgo employment and career opportunities to undertake unpaid caring work, especially for children. As discussed in Chapter 13, this has been recognized to some extent through the promotion of family friendly employment and work–life balance provisions encouraging employers to recognize the caring commitments of women (and men), and financial support for some of the costs of childcare through childcare credits and nursery vouchers. But there is still some way to go before policies such as these reverse the disadvantage that women have experienced in labour markets or have much effect in shifting the burden of family responsibilities to men. Moreover, as in the 1980s, fiscal stringency and attempts to create a leaner welfare state are arguably likely to affect women more than men, with fewer public sector jobs and services, and increases in informal and voluntary care work.

The inequality and disadvantages that women experience in the labour market also have other consequences for their experience of social policy provision. With lower pay women are less able to purchase private welfare services, such as personal pensions or health care. They are also more likely to be dependent upon means-tested welfare services, notably social security benefits. Although the majority of benefit claimants are still men (because in family units it is still predominantly the man who claims benefit for the household), more women depend directly or indirectly on benefits and are more likely to be in those groups experiencing the lowest benefits and the longest periods of dependency, notably as lone parents and single pensioners.

Where women are dependent on the incomes received by their male partners, and where both are unemployed or where only the man is the breadwinner, there is an additional potential problem of dependency. As Research by Pahl (1989) revealed, within family units resources are not always equally distributed between women and men, with women generally receiving less; and this includes those in families on benefits (Goode et al. 1998). What is more, as some of the commentators in Glendinning and Millar (1992) demonstrated, this has sometimes resulted in greater risk of poverty for women. This can be continued, and even compounded, where women are separated from their partners, especially where they have dependent children, because of the difficulties many experience in getting maintenance payments from former partners. Women's experience of poverty and deprivation is therefore different from men's, in particular because of the different dimensions of dependency that frequently underpin it.

In other areas of welfare, too, women's circumstances and needs may sometimes be different from men's. In education there have always been a significant number of schools providing single sex education on the grounds that the educational needs of boys and girls are different, although here, and in co-educational schools, the prevailing evidence is now that in school achievement girls generally do significantly better than boys. In health some of women's different needs are self-evident (for instance, around fertility and child bearing); here too women-only services have been developed, sometimes extending to a wider range of women's health needs as in 'well women's clinics'. These latter examples are more positive indicators of the role of gender difference within social policy provision. More generally, however, the picture is one of inequalities and disadvantages within which women generally lose out to men, both in the development and delivery of services as policy-makers or providers, and in receipt of services as benefit claimants or home carers.

COMPREHENSION QUESTIONS

- What is the 'male breadwinner' model and how accurate a picture was it of the employment and family structures of the last century?
- What are 'family friendly' policies and to what extent do they challenge the roles of men and women assumed within much welfare provision?

RACE AND ETHNICITY

The importance of racial or ethnic differences in the experience of welfare services, like those of gender, has often been marginalized within mainstream social policy. This marginalization is now being exposed, and challenged. Like class, however, debates over divisions of 'race' depend to some extent upon how racial and ethnic differences are perceived and defined and, more importantly perhaps, upon how the whole issue of race – or racism – is approached.

Britain is, and always has been, a multiracial and multicultural society, as flows of immigrants and emigrants have altered the composition of the population. In the nineteenth and early twentieth centuries people came to Britain from Ireland, and Jewish emigrants arrived, in particular from Eastern Europe. Following the Second World War Europeans, notably Poles, established themselves in Britain, and immigration was encouraged from Britain's former imperial colonies, such as the West Indies, India, Pakistan and Bangladesh. Immigrants have also arrived at different times from Africa, the Middle East and the Far East. Since Britain's membership of the EU, significant numbers of people have come to this country from other member states; and particularly over the last decade this has included relatively large numbers from Eastern European states such as Poland and Romania. Instability in a number of countries in Africa and the Middle East has also led to increased numbers of migrants from these countries, often refugees and people seeking asylum in the UK (Bloch 2002; Jones Finer 2006).

This growing diversity was highlighted in the 2011 Census which showed that 13 per cent of the population of England and Wales was born overseas, rising to 37 per cent in London. There is thus a wide range of ethnic minority groups in the UK, some of whom have retained, or developed, relatively close community ties among themselves; and as the range of migration has extended it has led to a new terminology: *super-diversity*. Many of these different ethnic minority groups have also been subject to discrimination and ill-treatment by other sections of the indigent population. The Irish, Jews, Poles, Pakistanis, and others, have all been the victims of negative attitudes and hostile reactions; and this is now often extended to any ethnic minority groups suspected of being 'asylum seekers'.

These ethnic differences have also sometimes been reflected in disadvantage within welfare services. However, there has been a difference between some of these disadvantages and the discrimination experienced by the immigrants who came from Britain's former colonies to settle in the UK in relatively large numbers in the 1950s and 1960s. These immigrants were readily identifiable because of their different skin colour and this became a source of hostility – and identity – that was independent of, or additional to, any other cultural or ethnic differences.

The hostility to black people coming to live in Britain is *racism*; it extends not only to immigrants but to all black people living here, an increasing proportion of whom, of course, have been born and brought up as British citizens. The racism black people in Britain experience is not the same thing as reaction to ethnic differences, in part of course because it is quite independent of any such differences. The distinction that it creates is one between black people and white people, in which the former, whatever their origins, are seen as undeserving interlopers. Despite the differences of ethnic and cultural background that have always existed within the country, therefore, this racist distinction between black and white became a major force dividing the British population on the basis of race in the latter half of the twentieth century, and remains important for our understanding of the continuing divisions within welfare services. It means that the focus of our analysis needs to include not just *race*, but racism (Solomos 2003; Craig et al. 2012; Bloch et al. 2013).

This racism is in large part a product of the recent history of black immigration to the country. Although immigration from the former British colonies in the Commonwealth was encouraged in the 1950s in order to boost the labour force, including filling (mainly low-paid) jobs in the growing welfare services; in the mid-1960s recruitment even to low-paid jobs in Britain began to decline and, after legal changes in 1962, immigration was restricted to those who could first demonstrate a guarantee of a job on arrival. As the boom turned to recession in the 1970s, it was mainly only spouses and children joining their relatives here who were able to secure entry to the country. This process of restrictions on immigration in itself created many problems for black people who had difficulty proving their rights of entry into Britain (Moore and Wallace 1975). However, it also compounded the problem of anti-black racism, which was already present among the white British population, providing fuel for the suspicion that black people did not 'belong' in the country.

The exclusion of black service users from welfare provision in Britain is not, however, just a product of racist discrimination fuelled by suspicion of illegal immigration; at a more general ideological level it runs deeper than that. The development of services within the 'welfare state' of the post-war era was very much a product of the national (and nationalist) politics of the time. The political struggles which underpinned the reforms were dominated by the political parties and campaigning organizations of the white British population. The welfare state was a (white) British achievement, and most of the black people resident in Britain in the 1960s and 1970s arrived in the country after the establishment of these national welfare services. This invited an assumption by some that Britain's black population had not contributed to the development of the country's welfare services and thus were not *entitled* to use them.

This does not apply to most of the black population of the UK, however, most of whom now were born here and have contributed to British society in the same way as other citizens. But the ideology of (non)entitlement remains, and indeed has been more recently extended to refugees and asylum seekers, and immigrants from the new EU states in Eastern Europe, who are sometimes stigmatized as coming to Britain in order to access public welfare services here.

In the case of entitlement to some welfare services, however, such exclusion has been reinforced by the eligibility criteria for access to provision. For instance, as we discussed in Chapter 8, entitlement to NI benefits, in particular pensions, was based upon past contributions made through employment. Immigrants coming to Britain late in their working lives would be unable to establish full contribution records and so would not secure full benefit entitlement. Similar indirect exclusion has also occurred in housing policy where waiting lists for public sector tenancies can disadvantage those who have only recently moved into the area; and this has had the effect of channelling new immigrants into poorer and less secure properties in the private sector. In both of these cases the rules and practices controlling access to welfare services did not *directly* discriminate against people on the basis of ethnicity or skin colour: NI contribution conditions and council house waiting lists technically applied equally to all. However, they did constitute a form of *indirect* (or *institutional*) racism, because of the much greater likelihood that certain groups would experience reduced access as a result of them.

One of the effects of such institutional discrimination was that Britain's new black and minority ethnic population of the 1960s and 1970s was unable to benefit equally from the social services which had been developed within the national welfare state, and thus were forced into greater dependency on means-tested benefits and greater reliance upon poor quality inner-city housing. Together with their concentration in certain sectors of the labour market, this meant that black and ethnic minority populations were thus not evenly distributed on a social or geographical basis throughout Britain; and this has remained the case even though most communities are well-established here and comprise mainly British born people. In practice these groups are more prevalent in particular urban areas, such as London, the Midlands, Lancashire and West Yorkshire; and within these urban areas have been concentrated in poorer, inner-city districts where housing conditions, and other service provisions, are often below the average.

This pattern of concentration and exclusion has also been experienced by more recent groups of migrants, in particular refugees and asylum seekers, who sometimes have been placed within particular areas or neighbourhoods under policies of dispersal, and may also remain close to friends and family in communities comprised of those from similar geographic or cultural backgrounds (Bloch 2002; Bloch et al. 2013). Such race, or ethnic, concentration is common in most other welfare capitalist countries, too; and it is particularly stark, for example, in the USA. However, it also further compounds the discrimination and disadvantage experienced by the black and ethnic minority groups living in such inner-city 'ghettos'. The discrimination and exclusion flowing from immigration has thus become a structural feature of the disadvantage that many people experience in the UK, as well as a continuing the source of racist suspicion of them (Bloch et al. 2013).

In addition to the problems of direct and indirect racism there are some other examples of disadvantage within welfare services linked to ethnic and cultural differences. For instance, Muslim religious requirements for children to have halal meat in school meals and to subscribe to particular dress codes in girls' clothing have sometimes not been recognized in mainstream schools. And more generally, particular dress codes can be a source of discrimination against and stigmatization of particular religious and cultural communities.

Some of these forms of exclusion have therefore led some black and ethnic minority communities to develop separate welfare services, designed to meet the particular needs to which public welfare services cannot, or will not, respond. Separate provision can often be found in voluntary and community activity, where there are significant numbers of black and ethnic minority organizations providing for both distinct ethnic communities and particular service needs. Separate provision has also been sought within state welfare services, most notably in attempts to use the provisions for Free Schools and Academies to opt out of LA control, discussed in Chapter 12, to provide education in schools specifically targeted on certain religious or cultural communities.

There are problems with the development of separatist provision for black and other ethnic minority communities within welfare services, however. In general they can operate to confirm, rather than reduce, divisions between different groups of users within welfare services, for instance, in the case of separate 'religious schools'; and this can further fuel racist suspicions of 'difference' amongst the wider population. They can also perhaps promote the misleading assumption that, because of the existence of separate provision, changes in existing public services are either unnecessary or not worthwhile. The real issue here perhaps is how to secure an appropriate balance between exposing and combating the racism within existing welfare services, whilst at the same time recognizing and supporting separate provision where this is actively sought by different communities. However, this is a balance which is difficult to achieve, and one which is constantly challenged by the changing dimensions of 'super-diversity'.

COMPREHENSION QUESTIONS

- What is 'institutional racism', and to what extent is there evidence of this within the delivery of welfare services in Britain?
- What are the advantages and disadvantages of the separate development of black and ethnic minority voluntary activity to meet the particular needs of different ethnic groups?

AGE

Discrimination by age adversely affects both the young and the old. Children, of course, are unable to provide for themselves and so must be supported by others; they thus need welfare services. In Britain, as in many other countries, the expectation is that these services will be provided predominantly on an informal basis through the family, and this is largely what happens in practice, except for the provision of state education. However, families need support to care for their children, especially where income is low; and the cost of providing for children is likely to push some families into deprivation.

The costs of providing for children within families were a major focus of social policy campaigning in Britain in the years between the wars, resulting in the introduction in the 1940s of family allowances to cover some of the costs of family child-rearing (Macnicol 1980). Family allowances, and the former tax allowances for children, have now been replaced by *Child Benefit*, a direct subsidy towards the additional costs of children. However, this does not (and is not intended to) cover all of the additional costs that families face in providing for their children. Additional support is now provided for lower-income families by the Universal Credit and remaining tax credits and other measures discussed in Chapter 8; and Child Benefit has been withdrawn from families with higher-income earners since the beginning of 2013.

Families with children therefore still experience higher rates of poverty and social exclusion than adults, and this is a longstanding problem (Platt 2005; Ridge 2002). It resulted in the development of a policy concern with family poverty, taken up most notably by the campaigns of the *Child Poverty Action Group* (CPAG). Since 2000, however, there has been a government commitment reducing levels of child poverty and removing it altogether by 2020 (Walker 1999), although in practice, as noted in Chapter 8, progress towards this goal has been rather limited, and has been cast into further uncertainty by debates under the Coalition government about how child poverty should be measured, which may in practice 'move the goalposts' on this.

Disadvantage experienced by the young has been accompanied in British social policy by that encountered by, and even discrimination against, the elderly too. Older people experience a range of disadvantages within policy development and delivery that are the direct result of assumptions that younger policy-makers make about their circumstances and needs. It is only relatively recently that the particular problems experienced by older people as a result of 'ageism' within social policy have been widely debated and analysed, however. This has now developed as a specific area of study called *gerontology* and, in their influential collection of papers on ageing and social policy, two leading gerontologists (Phillipson and Walker 1986) discussed a number of the important aspects of age discrimination within welfare, in particular the myths about dependency and need in old age; and Macnicol (2006) has more recently developed a historical and comparative analysis of age discrimination.

The myth of dependency is based upon a fear among policy-makers that the growing numbers of elderly people will constitute a financial burden upon the rest of the population. Certainly the numbers of older people had been growing in Britain, and in most other developed countries, throughout the twentieth century, and are set to increase further (see Table 17.2). This is in large part, of course, a product of the success of other social policies in prolonging life expectancy. At an individual level it is no doubt welcomed by all; but at a collective level it changes the age balance within the population.

Table 17.2 Projected proportions of UK population at age last birthday 2010 (%)						
Ages	2010	2020	2030	2041	2051	2060
0–14	17.5	18.2	17.2	16.2	16.5	16.2
15–29	20.0	18.1	17.9	18.3	17.0	17.0
30–44	20.4	19.6	19.8	18.3	19.2	18.5
45–59	19.5	19.6	17.3	18.4	17.1	17.4
60–74	14.7	15.4	16.5	15.1	15.6	15.9
75 & over	7.9	9.1	11.3	13.6	14.7	15.0
All ages	**100.0**	**100.0**	**100.0**	**100.0**	**100.0**	**100.0**

Source: Office for National Statistics, National Population Projections, Table A1-1, UK Summary, 2010 (ONS, 2012c).

What Table 17.2 reveals is that proportions of people over 60 is projected to rise over the first half of the next century, in relation to those of working age and younger; and the proportion over 75 is projected to rise even more. This has led to debates about the affordability of pensions for growing numbers of older people, and is one of the reasons for the shift towards a greater reliance on personal and occupational provision discussed in Chapter 8. It is also the reason both for the planned rises in the state pension age from 60 to 65 for women by 2018 (it is already 65 for men), and to 66 for both men and women by 2020 and provisions for further rises beyond that.

Reliance on pensions amongst older people may also be reduced by the abolition of the requirement to retire at state pension age, introduced in 2011. Many older people do work beyond retirement already, although it is too early to tell how many will use this as an opportunity to defer their entitlement to state pensions. For those with significant occupational or personal pensions, retirement onto a reasonable income may be an attractive option; and, hitherto, occupational provision in particular has led to growing numbers of such better-off pensioners – sometimes referred to as *Woopies* (well-off older persons).

In fact, however, such better-off pensioners are only a minority of older people in Britain today. Many have little or no private pension income and depend entirely on the state benefits to which they are entitled; and, although the value of the Basic State Pension (BSP) has risen in relation to average earnings in recent years. For those reliant on it overall income will be low, and they are likely to be living in or near poverty and may be entitled to means-tested supplements through pensions credits. For some pensioners at least, therefore, old age is still associated with a heightened risk of poverty and financial disadvantage, and this is likely to be greater for older pensioners (the over 75s) who are also less likely to have access to significant private pension income.

The other disadvantage that older people may face within social policy is a greater need to rely on welfare services, in particular for health and social care. Most older people do not need to rely significantly on health or care services and are able to live independent lives in the same way as those of working age. For some, especially amongst the 'older old', however, increased ageing can be associated with frailty and disability, leading to an increased need for day care services, and in more extreme cases residential or full-time nursing care.

As we discussed in Chapter 11, there is much concern amongst policy-makers about how to finance the costs of such care particularly given the potentially larger demand for this likely to flow from the increasing proportion of older people revealed in Table 17.2, and the pressures that may be placed on younger age groups. However this is resolved it is likely to mean that in the medium term at least those relying on public support for such services are likely to be faced with reductions in their capital savings and low levels of benefit support. For many older people, and especially women, therefore, ageing remains associated with reduced income and greater dependence on limited public services.

COMPREHENSION QUESTIONS

- Why is child poverty an important policy issue?
- Why are the growing numbers of older people in the UK a concern for social policy?

DISABILITY

Discrimination and disadvantage experienced by people with disabilities is, like that experienced by the other social divisions discussed above, a longstanding feature of policy development and delivery in Britain (Roulston and Prideaux 2012). Like race and age, however, disability has frequently been absent from mainstream social policy debate and analysis, even in relatively recent times; and as a result the policy implications of recognizing the importance of disadvantage among the disabled are still sometimes overlooked in the study of social policy.

As in the case of older people, too, the numbers of people with disabilities has been growing, although again this is largely a product of more general successes within social policy more generally, which should be welcomed. Furthermore, the increased consciousness of disabled people of their disadvantaged state, and their more vocal demands for services, have challenged the paternalistic approach towards disability that had often accompanied service provision in the past (Campbell and Oliver 1996; Oliver 1996). Such paternalist approaches have generally characterized disabled people as the clients of welfare services, whose needs are provided for by others on the basis of professional assessment. More recently, however, political campaigners for disability have presented themselves as citizens with rights, which they are demanding, but are being denied by discriminatory practices among service providers. Disability has thus been forcing itself into a different place on the social policy agenda (Barnes and Mercer 2006; Lister 2010).

From a policy perspective, however, there are some definitional problems of both an analytical and a practical nature that complicate the debate about policy development for people with disabilities. Most fundamentally, there is no clear agreement about what constitutes a disability, or what degree of disability is likely to lead to disadvantage. Clearly degrees, and consequences, of disability vary widely from a minor loss of functions or physical features, which may often be undetected by others, to complete paralysis and dependency. This has resulted, for instance, in attempts to classify degrees and types of disability, such the detailed definitions of care and mobility needs used to determine entitlement to benefits intended to meet the extra costs associated with such disabilities.

These issues were explored in the 1980s by the then Office of Population Censuses and Surveys, which distinguished between different categories of disability and found over 6.5 million people in Britain with some disability and almost 250,000 in the most dependent category (see Dalley 1991). In 2010/11 data from the Family Resources Survey revealed that the overall number had increased to 11.5 million, with 6.6 million reporting problems with mobility (DWP 2012). Part of the disadvantage of much disability is obviously a result of the loss or impairment of function that disabled people experience: for instance, blindness or paralysis can mean that people cannot readily move around without guidance or assistance. Of course there are aids, such as guide dogs or wheelchairs, that can help to overcome such problems, but they cost money to purchase and maintain; in effect they mean that people with disabilities frequently require a larger income to enjoy the same standard of living, or quality of life, as others.

These extra costs of disability were recognized and discussed in the OPCS survey in the 1980s (Large 1991). They were also the focus of a study by Smith et al. (2004) which estimated at the time that the weekly budget needs for people with disabilities could range from £389 to £1,513 a week. More recent studies have also emphasized the additional costs arising from disability, often termed the 'conversion disadvantage' faced in trying to achieve the same standard of living as non-disabled people (Wood and Grant 2010).

These higher weekly costs suggest that people with disabilities will need to receive relatively high incomes, or significant support in the form of cash benefits or service provision, to maintain a similar lifestyle to others. In fact, however, people with disabilities generally have lower, not higher, incomes than the rest of the population, primarily because they experience inequality and discrimination in the labour market. Legislation to outlaw discrimination against disabled people was introduced in the 1990s, along similar lines to that applying to gender and race discrimination. But this has not had much effect in shifting the balance of employment opportunities; and in 2012 46 per cent of disabled people were in employment compared to 76 per cent of non-disabled people (DWP 2012).

Their relative exclusion from, and disadvantage within, employment thus means that people with disabilities are more likely than others to be dependent upon benefits. There are specific benefits targeted at the needs and costs experienced by disabled people. In the past this has included higher rates of standard benefits for those out of work due to chronic sickness or disability, although, as we discussed in Chapter 8, entitlement to these is now much restricted with disabled people being expected to seek appropriate employment wherever possible. In addition, as part of the Coalition's welfare cutbacks, the main additional non-contributory benefit aimed at meeting the extra costs of disability, the DLA, which included payments for the costs of providing mobility and home care, has been replaced by the Personal Independence Payment (PIP) based on tighter eligibility criteria.

Though the government claims PIP will increase claimants' benefit rates, like their predecessors none of these current benefits are paid at a very generous level, and they do not bring the majority of people with disabilities anywhere near the average income levels enjoyed by the bulk of the rest of the population. Moreover evidence suggests that in the past a significant proportion of disabled people did not claim the benefits to which they were entitled, in part because of their highly selective focus on specific disability needs and the complex process of claiming them; and there are fears that recent reforms will do little to redress this.

Inadequate incomes could be compensated, in part at least, by the provision of services for people with disabilities. Statutory requirements are placed on LAs for the provision of services for disability through the Chronically Sick and Disabled Persons Act 1970 and the Disabled Persons Act 1986. In the 1990s much of this provision was restructured as part of the planning of community care, as we discussed in Chapter 11. Where community care practice has given disabled people the ability to shape the development and delivery of packages of care and support for them this has increased their power as service users to some extent, and may even have improved their quality of life.

Whether the extension of personal budgets now under way will, as is hoped, enhance the control disabled people have over their lives remains to be seen. However, the limited financial resources available for social care has often resulted in reliance being placed on informal providers, further accentuating the family pressures that many disabled people and their caring relatives experience; and in greater expectations being placed on disabled people to purchase services from commercial or third sector suppliers, or pay charges for public services, out of their (generally low) incomes.

The disadvantages flowing from inadequate incomes and lack of services are compounded for many disabled people by their daily experience of the frustrations and exclusions of living within an able-bodied world. Lack of wheelchair access can keep many disabled people out of public buildings; lack of communication in other than written form means that blind people may be under-informed about events and services. Other barriers and exclusions exist throughout all public and private service provision. But, of course, it is quite wrong to conclude from this that it is necessarily their disability that prevents people from participating equally with their able-bodied colleagues and neighbours. The Houses of Commons and Lords, the main seats of government in Britain and the most powerful policy-making institutions in the country, contain members in wheelchairs and members who are blind and deaf: these politicians are no less capable or effective than their colleagues as a result of these disabilities, because they have the resources to ensure that, with appropriate support and assistance, they are able to avoid or overcome many of the barriers they face. These policy-makers are high-profile examples of the fact that it is often the barriers to participation, and not the conditions of disabled people, that are the primary cause of the disadvantage and discrimination experienced by them – and that these barriers can be overcome, by some.

COMPREHENSION QUESTIONS

- Why do disability campaigners argue that much welfare provision for disabled people is paternalistic?
- Why, despite the existence of services and benefits for people with disabilities, do many continue to experience disadvantage as a result of their disability?

FURTHER READING

A general guide to the different social divisions in British society is provided by the contributions to Payne (2013), and more detailed analysis of the empirical data on stratification and inequality is contained in Platt (2011). Williams (1989) was the first comprehensive analysis of the role of gender and race in structuring the experience of welfare. More recent overviews of gender issues in welfare can be found in Pascall (2012). Craig et al. (2012) and Bloch et al. (2013) examine patterns of racism and ethnic minority disadvantage. Though dated Phillipson and Walker (1986) is still a good introduction to ageing and social policy; Macnicol (2006) provides a useful historical dimension; and the compilation by Walker and Maltby (2013) contains a good coverage of many contemporary issues. Oliver (2009) provides an excellent introduction to understanding different models of disability and their policy consequences. Roulston and Prideaux (2012) provide a guide to recent policy, and Shah and Priestley (2011) examine this from the perspective of disabled people.

18
Delivering Welfare

SUMMARY OF KEY POINTS

- Provision of welfare services is made on both *universal* and *selective* bases.
- Social policy analysis in the past often concentrated upon the *providers* rather than the *users* of welfare services.
- Access to welfare services is 'rationed' by a range of formal and informal mechanisms.
- The bureaucratic and paternalistic nature of some public services has sometimes operated to exclude users from having much control over these services through lack of *exit* or *voice*.
- *New Public Management* practices imported business management ethos and methods into public service delivery in the late twentieth century.
- Performance management has sometimes led to a focus upon *inputs* and *outputs* within public services, rather than the *outcomes* of these.
- Independent audit and inspection of service providers has developed as a means of ensuring public accountability of services as an alternative to individual complaints or appeals.
- Modernization of public services under Labour led to new commitments to partnership working between agencies both within the state and across different welfare providers.
- The replacement of government with *governance* involved a shift from electoral to 'deliberative' democracy.
- Personalization and co-production are being promoted to give users more control over the services they receive.
- Public service reform now embraces a shift to encouragement of and support for commercial and third sector providers of welfare services.
- Commissioning of services from non-state providers has been shifting towards an outcome focus and more emphasis on 'payment by results'.

ACCESS TO WELFARE

It is a common assumption, shared especially by the protagonists of state welfare, that the provision of public services means the benefits of such services will be enjoyed by all those who are the intended recipients of them. If health services, for instance, are provided free at the point of demand, those who need health care will go and use them. As a result of this the development, and the study, of social policy traditionally concentrated predominantly on the structure and the funding of welfare provision rather than on the access to and use of the services themselves. The focus was more on the *producers* than the *consumers* of welfare, a distinction to which we shall return below.

This producer domination is understandable. It reflects both the powerful influence of major service providers within social policy and the concern of social policy analysts to influence service provision. However, it is in practice only a part of the picture of social policy; and has not prevented some commentators questioning whether service provision is in itself a guarantee of service use or benefit; and this is a concern that began to attract growing attention within social policy towards the end of the last century. What is more, there is an increasing body of evidence to suggest that the provision of welfare – including, in particular, public services provided through the state – does not in reality mean that all do benefit from these services, or benefit equally from them.

Most social policy commentators make a distinction between two contrasting approaches to access to welfare services:

- *Universal* services are intended to be used by, and equally available to, all who need, or expect, to benefit from them. State education in schools and most NHS services are universal, and so too was child benefit until it was withdrawn from higher-rate taxpayers in 2013. It is argued by some that in providing for all these provisions are in practice wasting limited resources on many users who could afford to pay for such services privately. However, universal access should mean that publicity about services can be easily disseminated and that there is no stigma attached to those using them. Also, because all use them, all have an interest in their quality and availability.
- *Selective* services restrict access to those identified as having particular needs that could only be provided for by direct access to particular services. Selection can be made in a number of ways: for instance, by focusing service provision on a specific geographical area or on a designated social group. Such geographical or social methods of targeting are widely used both by central and local government and by private and third sector providers. However, perhaps the most common form of selectivity in service allocation is the use of *means-testing* to target resources to those who have undergone some test of their inability to provide for themselves, usually because of low income. This ensures that resources are concentrated on those most in need, but also requires these people to come forward and demonstrate their need and may therefore lead to negative stigma being associated with 'dependency' upon such provision.

There are problems with access to both universal and selective benefits, in part associated with their different strengths and weaknesses. As we discuss in Chapter 17, some social divisions may mean universal services that are in theory provided equally to all are not in practice equally available to, or appropriate for, all social groups. There is also the evidence from Le Grand's (1982) study of the use of education and health services, which revealed that in practice better-off sections of society were more likely to use and benefit from these because, despite the principle of universal access, they were more informed about service provision and more able to negotiate with professionals and providers to get the best schools and most effective treatments.

Conversely, there is a danger that those services that are available only to those who are poor come to be seen as 'poor services'. And, in addition to this, although means-tested benefits are ostensibly targeted at the poorest groups in society, there is considerable evidence that not all those who might be entitled to such benefits take up their rights to these, as we saw in Chapter 8 in relation to social security. This non-take-up of selective services is in part a product of the stigma associated with benefits 'for the poor', but it is also due to the fact that many potential consumers do not know about their rights or how best to pursue these.

Whether services are provided on a universal or selective basis, therefore, there are problems of potential users failing to recognize their right to use them and so not getting the services that they may need. This ignorance or misunderstanding is in effect operating as a significant barrier to effective service delivery and, more importantly, to the meeting of acknowledged social needs. However, there are other barriers that also operate to restrict access to public services within service provision itself. Some of these are an intrinsic feature of provision, working in effect as a form of 'rationing' device to reduce demand on service providers (Foster 1983), particularly in periods of austerity, although other barriers may be less formal or intentional in their operation and in their effect on potential service users (Maybin and Klein 2012).

At the more formal level any procedures that are used to administer the delivery of services can act in effect to ration access to them. For example, reception procedures in health care practices may be used to determine, and to prioritize, appointments with medical staff. Here the receptionist is operating as a kind of *gate-keeper*, restricting the use of professional resources. Professionals may also operate as gate-keepers themselves, both to their own services (putting off some clients and encouraging others) and to the services offered by others. Doctors in general practice act as important gate-keepers to a wide range of NHS services, and social workers operate a significant gate-keeping role over both public and private social care provision.

Gate-keeping describes an organized and relatively well-planned way of using the process of application as a means of rationing access to welfare. However, procedural factors operate to ration access much more widely than this, and sometimes in ways that may not have been intended, or predicted, by service providers. Most obviously, the physical location and design of service delivery points may exclude many. For instance, the town centre location of the local social care or housing department may mean that it is out of reach for those whose mobility is restricted or who simply cannot afford to travel a long distance to make an appointment. Even where it does not keep people at home, physical disability may prevent them from entering certain buildings if appropriate access points are not provided – the grand staircase up to the Town Hall doors, for instance, is a barrier to all people in wheelchairs.

Working practices, as well as physical design, can exclude potential service users. Where there is a relatively high demand for inquiries about or applications for services many organizations operate queuing systems for potential clients. The experience of waiting in seemingly never-ending queues has often been a common one associated with access to services such as hospitals, housing departments and social security offices. Queuing alone may deter some from pursuing potential access but it is particularly problematic where the time spent queuing is preventing someone meeting other needs or is taking them away from paid employment. It is sometimes said that 'time is money', and this is perhaps most keenly felt by the self-employed or by those in insecure and poorly protected employment where absence from work means direct deduction of wages for time lost. This is a problem that is compounded by service offices and access points which are only open during the working day on a Monday to Friday, and which therefore effectively exclude all those who work these hours and cannot negotiate, or afford, time off.

Trips to offices may be avoided by use of telephone access. Telephone inquiries to call centres are often used as the first point of contact for those inquiring about potential service use and to provide advice and assistance, for example, the health service line *NHS Direct*. However, even telephone line access like NHS Direct has more recently often been replaced by online access to web pages, where not only can information be found but formal applications for services or support made. However, telephone and internet access are not available to those who do not have access to telephones or computers, or cannot afford to use these.

Furthermore, telephone and internet access – and indeed written information and application procedures too – are also often only provided in *English*. And those who have difficulty with spoken or written English may be excluded from services by such a language barrier. Thus language, location, design and working practices all operate in practice to restrict, and so to ration, access to welfare services; yet these barriers are often unplanned and generally unintended, and their effects are not monitored or even considered by most service providers. They tend to reflect a lack of concern within the planning and delivery of welfare services for the circumstances of the users of those services; and this is an absence that has been challenged more recently by critics of what has come to be called a 'provider culture' within social policy.

WHOSE WELFARE?

The design and implementation of most public services has largely been based on the assumption that both the producers and consumers of those services would have a coinciding interest in their development and delivery. For instance, teachers would want to teach children useful and important knowledge and children would want to learn everything teachers had to tell them. To some extent of course this is true; but, as all of us no doubt found during our own school education, this process of teaching and learning is not without its frustrations and conflicts. However, critics from both the right and left wing of the ideological spectrum have challenged the assumed coterminous interests of the producers and consumers of public welfare services, and suggested the conflicts which sometimes occur here may in fact represent real tensions within the process of delivery between the power and control of providers and the needs and rights of users.

Challenges to the alleged producer control in public welfare were a major feature of New Right criticisms of state welfare services in the 1980s and 1990s (Green 1988; Barry 1990). As we discussed in Chapter 14, the essence of the New Right argument was that market provision of services, including welfare services, was preferable to state provision, because markets provide for choice for consumers and, through the exercise of choice in the market, consumers can acquire sovereignty over providers; whereas within state services most providers are monopolies and under no pressure to respond to consumer demands or preferences.

Criticisms of a provider culture in state welfare provision have not only come from right-wing supporters of private markets; social policy academics have also pointed out that public services users have often been 'unequal partners' in the development and delivery of those services (Barnes et al. 1999), and organizations representing service users have also sought to challenge provider control over welfare services and to seek to influence the processes of social policy planning and delivery (Beresford et al. 2011). In an early review of some of the issues involved in *Consuming Public Services*, Deakin and Wright (1990) commented on the failure of many providers to recognize the need to develop services *for* the public rather than delivering services *to* them, as exemplified in the creation of 'bleak, unresponsive and inefficient bureaucracies'.

The *bureaucratic* structure of state welfare services is of course to some extent an inevitable consequence of the development and maintenance of national standards and the need to secure economies of scale through the organization of service delivery on a large-scale basis. However, as Weber's classic discussion of bureaucracy in the early twentieth century first revealed (Weber 1968), bureaucratic organizations eventually acquire their own logic; and the internal logic of the bureaucracy can sometimes come to overbalance the external demand for use of its services. For instance, social security claimants or LA housing tenants seeking to challenge – or even find out about – the processing of their cases have often experienced immense difficulties in understanding and negotiating the procedures that the officers dealing with them seem to be trapped within. It may seem to the users of these services – perhaps with some justification – that this bureaucracy is often presented as an *excuse* for inaction ('your file has been sent to another section') rather than as an *explanation* of what is (or is not) being done.

It is not just the process of bureaucracy that alienates consumers and perpetuates the power of producers, however. These bureaucracies employ workers whose job it is to deliver services within the procedures laid down; and these workers thus acquire a vested interest in maintaining their employment, and so indirectly in maintaining the bureaucratic structures and procedures within which they work, even where these may be in conflict with the needs of potential service users: for example, in maintaining nine-to-five office hours, which can prevent users with similar commitments from attending appointments.

It might be assumed that professionally qualified workers would have a more altruistic interest in the needs of the users of their services. However, the activities of the professionals in public service delivery can also have the effect of disempowering the consumers of services. Professional power can be seen most clearly in the work of the medical profession: doctors and hospital consultants think they know what their patients need and they expect patients to follow the recommendations they make without question. In fact, of course, doctors may not always know best what is in the interests of their patients' health; and in some cases patients do challenge the opinions of doctors, for example, women who wish to choose their own method of childbirth.

These professionals are not acting in their own self-interest in making judgements about their people's needs in this way, of course, nor indeed in most cases are other workers who seek to defend the procedures and structures within which they work. The problem is not one of self-interest, rather it is one of *paternalism*: that is, the assumption that the professionals or the bureaucrats know best, and therefore that the clients, or the users, should accept what they have to offer. It is this paternalism that is behind many of the problems of the provider culture within welfare services because, to adopt the terminology of the American critic, Hirschman (1970), such services do not give users the rights of 'exit' or 'voice'.

There is no right of *exit* for public service users because such services are in most cases a monopoly. The state provides services universally to all (in theory at least); but it is also the only provider of such services. Potential consumers are thus left with a 'take it or leave it' choice to engage with the bureaucracy and follow the professional advice, or to go without. In these circumstances people cannot take their business, or their needs, anywhere else (that is, exit). So, if they are unable or unwilling to use the state services available, they will fail to secure the welfare services that they need, and to which indeed in theory they are entitled.

It is this lack of exit that was behind many of the right-wing criticisms of state welfare services in the 1980s and 1990s and which led to the encouragement by the Conservative governments of private market alternatives to state services and the establishment of quasi-markets to introduce some element of choice into remaining monopoly services. It was also a feature of the Labour support between 1997 and 2010 for a mixed economy of service providers in many areas of welfare provision in England with profit and not-for-profit providers operating alongside state agencies.

The lack of a right of exit from such monopoly state services might be more acceptable if there was a right for consumers to have a *voice* within them. In other words, if the users of these services were able to influence provision to ensure their needs were met in ways that they experienced as appropriate and accessible. However, the paternalism of many state services has sometimes militated against the development of any mechanisms for a consumer voice, because of the belief that it is professionals and service providers who know best what potential users need. In paternalistic monopolies it is the producers, and not the consumers, who hold the power to determine the structure of service provision.

This lack of voice was also taken up by Labour, particularly by Prime Minister Tony Blair. He often accompanied his statements about the need to support and invest in public services with a commitment to challenge the provider culture within those services to offer more 'choice, equality, opportunity and autonomy' (Blair 2002) to service users. Labour referred to this challenge to the provider culture as the *modernization* of public services (DoH 1998; HMT 1998; Cabinet Office 1999), a development that was also taken up by the devolved governments.

However, as Miller (2004) discussed, the modernization agenda provided a series of challenges to the producers of welfare, both professionals and policy-makers, to which they were not easily able to respond. For instance Clarke et al. (2007) argued that the extension of choice to users was based on an 'unstable' model of citizen-consumers which sought to empower them to exercise their voice; but did not always provide viable institutional bases for the pursuit and achievement of such organizational change. In practice, therefore, users were given little power, and no ready mechanisms for implementing it; and, in England under the Coalition government, the focus of policy has shifted more to promoting the idea of exit, by facilitating competition between alternative providers of publicly funded services, as we discuss below. However, there have been other changes to the administration and management of state services in recent times, which have sought to alter the balance of decision-making and make services more accountable both to those who use them, and those who pay for them (generally taxpayers through the government). The result has been a broadening in the involvement of a range of different interests in the delivery of welfare services.

COMPREHENSION QUESTIONS

- What is 'gate-keeping', and why is it widely used to ration access to welfare services?
- Why do the critics of the 'provider culture' of public welfare services argue that the problem with such services is the lack of *exit* and *voice* for users?

REFLECTIVE QUESTION

- Is there a conflict of interest between the providers and the users of welfare services?

NEW PUBLIC MANAGEMENT

Underlying many of the changes that took place in the delivery of social policy towards the end of the last century was the influence of management, or managerialism, on public service delivery. In simple terms this can be characterized as a shift from the administration to the management of public services, now widely referred to as the 'New Public Management', or NPM (Pollitt 1990; Flynn 2012):

- *Administration* is concerned with the operation of established procedures that ensure users know how services operate and professionals are able to provide the services, which they judge their clients need. Power over services lies primarily with professionals, and administrators operate to service them.
- *Management* is concerned with the effective delivery of services; it requires the establishment of clear goals which providers are then made accountable for meeting. The setting of goals is determined by the needs of consumers, but also by the need for accountability to funders who have to be assured that resources are being used efficiently. Managers are responsible for delivering these assurances and making sure the professionals delivering the services are working towards them. Power over services lies primarily with the managers who direct the work of professionals.

In part this managerialist shift was based on an attempt to import into public service delivery ideas that were judged to have been effective in management in commercial settings. It was particularly attractive to the New Right critics of bureaucratic state welfare in the late twentieth century, who argued that competition in markets was the best way to ensure improved standards, and that where this could not be established directly then private market ideas should still be taken on. In an influential book written in the early 1990s two American authors (Osborne and Gaebler 1992) argued that the introduction of 'entrepreneurial spirit' was transforming the nature of the public sector. Much of the theory and practice of NPM was developed in the USA; but it was also embraced in the UK, initially by the Thatcher governments of the 1980s, with the Secretary of State, Michael Heseltine, saying as early as 1980 that: 'Efficient management is a key to the [national] revival . . . And the management ethos must run right through our public life' (quoted in Pollitt 1990).

Other supporters of NPM argued it was based on a concern to promote the 'three Es': economy, efficiency and effectiveness. Services should be effective in meeting the needs of citizens for which they were established, but they should also meet these in the most efficient way and at the least cost to public funders. These goals challenged the ideals, and the practices, of some public service professionals and bureaucrats, and it was the job of the new public service managers to ensure that where appropriate these practices changed. Not surprisingly therefore NPM was not always popular with existing public service providers, and to some extent the introduction of NPM ideas and personnel led to power struggles between professionals and managers, for instance, hospital consultants and trust managers in the NHS.

These conflicts were part of a broad cultural shift within public services both in the UK and elsewhere that was examined by academic commentators, who were sometimes critical of some of the effects of this 'new managerialism' (Clarke et al. 1994; Clarke and Newman 1997; Greener 2009). For a start, they argued, the influence of powerful managers seeking economy and efficiency could lead to reductions in the work of some professionals and in the services they were providing, in particular those which were not directly specified in legislation or guidance which provided the statutory basis for the service. More generally, however, managerialism imposed a concern with rationalization and productivity on public service provision, sometimes referred to as *neo-Taylorism*, from the Taylorist tradition of productivity management in manufacturing (Newman and Clarke 1994). In such an approach the concern was with *inputs* (what is done) and *outputs* (whether it has been done), rather than *outcomes* (whether service provision improved citizens' lives). Many also questioned the extent to which forms of management based on private-sector organizations were appropriate for public service provision or attuned to its underlying ethos (Greener 2009).

This rather mechanistic orientation to service delivery reached a particular peak in the use of 'performance management' processes to monitor and control service practices. Here the concern with the goals of service provision is translated into a set of targets for the delivery of predetermined outputs (numbers of clients interviewed or waiting time for appointments), perhaps also with 'milestones' to be reached in a move towards those targets (40 minutes' waiting in six months, 20 minutes' in a year's time). Achievement of performance in reaching these targets is then reported to managers, whose job it is to ensure they are met. Performance management had become widespread across many aspects of public service delivery by the beginning of the new century, with both new initiatives and established services being expected to set, and meet, milestones and targets.

Of course, this raises questions about the appropriateness of these targets and about who sets them, and how. It can also have other worrying consequences for service delivery, however. The setting and monitoring of targets itself consumes time and resources that cannot then be spent on direct service delivery, so performance management can be expensive. More significant still, targets and milestones can become substitutes for more direct and ongoing assessment of citizens' needs and professional expertise. At it crudest this can restrict service delivery to a concern *only* with meeting targets (when the waiting time is down to 20 minutes then the job is done), and encourage the setting of (soft) targets that providers know are actually easy to achieve. More generally, however, it can stifle innovation and change, especially where this comes from the knowledge and skills of professionals and other providers rather than the targets set by managers. The limitations of such performance targets were trenchantly criticized by Boyle (2001) in his book *The Tyranny of Numbers*, where he argued that numerical targets could never capture social needs or provide a sustainable basis for service development.

Despite some of these perverse, and perhaps unintended, consequences, however, the principles behind performance management, and NPM more generally, have become widely accepted, and even welcomed, by many concerned with the development and delivery of public services (Flynn 2012). It is important, if not essential, to have established goals for service provision and to monitor the extent to which these are being met; and this can lead from performance management being seen as a bureaucratic imposition towards a recognition that all public bodies should aim to be 'learning organizations'. In this context managers can play a critical role in ensuring that services are run efficiently and effectively since few professionals have the skills or training to make good managers. However, particularly under the Coalition government in England and its counterparts in the rest of the UK, there has been something of a backlash against this managerialist culture, and some attempt to shift power over service outcomes back to providers and users, as we discuss below. However, it is also not only public service managers who have become involved in monitoring the effectiveness of many public services.

AUDIT AND INSPECTION

The concern of the proponents of NPM that public services should meet the three objectives of economy, efficiency and effectiveness meant the responsibility for delivering this fell upon the new managers of those services. However, making these the responsibility of public service managers is not in itself a guarantee that they will be achieved in all cases. If these objectives are important to public provision, and services are to be held accountable for their achievement of them, then some independent assessment of their attainment is also arguably needed. This logic has led to the growth of a range of agencies concerned to assure users and citizens, service providers themselves, and the government, that service delivery is meeting the requirements set for it by its managers and paymasters.

Of course, users and citizens themselves are able to make independent judgements about the effectiveness of public services, and can act on these when problems occur. For a start citizens can use the democratic process to register their approval (or not) by voting out those national governments or LAs that are not delivering on their promises to provide acceptable public services. But this is a rather general response to particular service problems. It is also only accessible on a five-yearly cycle and citizens might need more than the occasional use of the ballot box to hold providers to account.

People can complain directly to service providers when problems occur, and many do of course do this. Informal complaints can lead to changes in provision and even to redress for complainants. More formal procedures are often also made available to service users and these can lead to a formal response recommending service improvements and/or compensation for aggrieved users. The *Citizen's Charters* introduced by the Major government in the 1990s provided such a procedure for complaints to be made about public services, requiring public service providers to publish details of service provision and giving individual citizens a right of redress when these were not met: for instance, financial compensation where train services were delayed for more than a minimum period. However, these charters were never effective in practice and were quickly abandoned, in part, of course, because financial compensation does not make trains run on time.

Such formal procedures extend to appeals and legal actions too. For instance, claimants have a right of appeal against decisions taken by benefits officers denying them entitlement; and users of services such as education and health can sue where they have suffered loss as a result of faulty provision. Bringing a legal action is expensive and time consuming, however, and requires a significant commitment on the part of the aggrieved service user. Not all users have the resources to pursue such avenues of redress, and many may find that even following through with a formal complaint seems more trouble than it is worth. Although individual citizens are generally the main losers when services fail, they may not be the people best equipped to take on the mantle of litigants or complainants.

Furthermore, service users may not be aware that mistakes have even been made. In many areas of service provision the practices and procedures of providers are complex, detailed and specialist – for instance, social security regulations and medical diagnoses – and individual users may not always understand these. It is partly for this reason that an independent source of support for individual complaints was established with the creation from the 1960s of government *ombudsmen* (though they may sometimes be women). The ombudsman's task is to explore complaints about maladministration reported by service users. They do not have the power to enforce action by, or changes in, service providers; but their reports are published and can carry significant weight in creating pressure for change.

The ombudsman model has been much developed and extended in recent times, however, as a result of concern by government to introduce further-reaching independent reviews of the management and delivery of public services, and ones not reliant solely upon the initiative of individual service users. These review procedures are based upon the audit and inspection of public service providers; and underlying them is the assumption that, as the funders and users of such services, the public, through the government, has a right to some independent assessment of the effectiveness of these services in meeting agreed goals.

Audit is not quite the same as inspection. It involves in particular a financial, or accountancy, assessment of the proper use of public funds, exemplified by the work of the *National Audit Office* (NAO) in its auditing of the accounts of government departments in England and its counterparts in the rest of the UK. Judgement of the proper use of public funds can extend beyond simply ensuring that account ledgers are accurate, however; it can also involve assessment of the economy, efficiency and effectiveness of those providing public services. For instance the *Audit Commission* established in 1982 had wide-ranging powers to investigate and report on the provision by LAs and other public agencies of services such as education and social care, roles that in varying phases were later transferred to the devolved administrations. In practice, however, its work was largely set by the government, and mainly directed at governmental and LA providers, suggesting how improvements in services might be made. However, the Coalition judged this to be an unnecessary, and expensive, bureaucratic layer of intervention into service provision in England, and abolished the Commission in 2012.

Inspection of public services has a rather broader remit than this, and a wider public appeal. The idea behind inspection is the presumption that the achievement of service targets by public service providers should be subject to independent verification. Thus service requirements are established for providers (for example, the national curriculum for school pupils), and regular inspections carried out by government-appointed visitors to ensure these requirements are being met. The titles and remit of these inspection agencies have changed over time and there are now parallel bodies responsible for scrutinizing services in the four administrations of the UK. The best known is the Office for Standards in Education (OFSTED) which is responsible for school inspection in England (see Chapter 12). Its regular inspections for instance have become an established feature of education service culture, and its reports, posted on its website, are available for all pupils, parents and other citizens to see.

The supporters of audit and inspection argue that in principle it is right that those responsible for delivering services to the public and spending public resources should be independently assessed on their discharge of these responsibilities. They also argue that in practice audit and inspection reporting has led to improvements in overall standards of public service delivery and to the dissemination of good practice. Audit and inspection are not without their critics, however. In England the Coalition has seen a number of these agencies as unnecessary extensions of public interference in service provision, and abolished or merged some. And others have argued, in similar vein, that what may be going on here is something of a power struggle between the providers of public services (who deal directly with users and citizens) and the managers and auditors (in most cases appointed by government and drawn from the ranks of other professional groups). So that whether or not this top-down process of accountability leads to genuine improvements in service provision is debatable (see Newman and Clarke 2009).

MODERNIZATION AND GOVERNANCE

The Labour governments of the early twentieth century took a number of measures in England to challenge the provider culture of the monopoly services established by the welfare reforms of the 1940s. As noted earlier this was referred to as the *modernization* of public services (Margetts et al. 2010). This included managerialism and inspection, but it also extended to more general 'reinvention' of the public domain, which also entailed new forms of partnership and collaboration in service delivery, a more active engagement with users and citizens, and a rethinking of the role of democracy in policy planning (Newman and Clarke 2009). Building on earlier shifts in the role of the state in public policy planning, it has also been characterized as a move from government to governance (Newman 2001), aspects of which also characterized policy-making in the devolved administrations though in Scotland and Wales within a less marketized approach to service provision.

Partnership was one key element of Labour's modernization agenda and that of public service reform in the rest of the UK. One of the criticisms of the state welfare services of the last century was the claim that the structures set up to administer those services had led to departmental cultures in the way services were provided – sometimes referred to as a 'silo mentality'. Officers were employed by their department in central or local government to deliver their services, and this they did without any real knowledge of, or contact with, providers of other services within the area. By contrast citizens and communities often made use of several of these local services, sometimes for similar and interrelated needs: notably, for instance, for care needs in hospitals or at home in the community. The experience of citizens was one of having to liaise between different officers in different departments with different procedures and practices, most of whom did not understand anything about the work of others. At best this was a frustrating experience; at worst it meant needs were met by neither. To use the phrase coined by the government, service provision was not *joined-up*; and part of the commitment to modernizing services was a commitment to secure this.

Joining-up was achieved in large part by encouraging, or requiring, service providers to work in partnership. As we discussed in Part 2 partnership planning is now required of education, health and social care agencies in both children's and adult services. However, partnership working extended beyond this to include, for instance, social and economic development, early learning and childcare provision, health promotion, and others; and it also extended beyond public sector agencies to include third and private sector providers in joint planning and delivery of public services. At a local level in England this cross-sector partnership planning was formalized through the creation of the Local Strategic Partnerships (LSPs), discussed in Chapter 6, to bring public, private and third sector agencies together in a formal body to coordinate economic and social development activity in the area.

LSPs were initially linked to neighbourhood investment funding targeted on LAs with high levels of deprivation. This funding has since been withdrawn; but the partnership bodies that it spawned have continued as forums for bringing together local agencies to promote and plan local economic and social development. The LSPs also provided a vehicle for encouraging participation in service planning by local citizens and communities, another important dimension of Labour's modernization agenda.

Participation in policy development was encouraged by Labour and policy-makers in the devolved administrations in order to combat the lack of voice that users and citizens were recognized to have in service delivery. This involved not just an acceptance of the failures of past policy providers to include user perspectives, but also recognition of the limitations within existing mechanisms for citizens to voice their concerns about policy priorities. In particular this meant tackling the limitations of electoral democracy as a means of engaging with the views of citizens. The increasingly low turn-out in local, and even national, elections has undermined the claim that these can be a vehicle for ensuring the democratic process means that the voices of citizens are heard. This has led proponents of participation to argue that such representative democracy was only one means of engaging citizens in the political process, and that we should also look to 'deliberative' (or 'associative') democracy to provide new means for citizens to influence policy-making (Hirst 1994; Stoker 2006). This means establishing ways for citizens to engage directly with politicians and policy-makers over issues that concern them, and requiring policy-makers to establish and respond to such association.

A wide range of such ways has in fact been developed within welfare services across the UK over recent years, including surveys and questionnaires, user forums, local focus groups and citizens' juries (panels of local people consulted on key policy issues). Some have provided a new forum for local people to establish direct contact with decision-makers, although they still encounter the problems of combating distrust and apathy amongst users and citizens that are the legacy of bureaucracy and paternalism. They also have to avoid the accusation of tokenism which some attempts at engagement have encountered in the past. Local citizens get invited to meetings but they are then swamped with incomprehensible paperwork and jargon by service providers and find that the agenda has been set by those who already hold most of the power and information. There is more to deliberative democracy than sitting round a table with policy-makers (Barnes et al. 2007).

For deliberative democracy to work of course it must lead to a real shift in the power over decision–making, moving away from politicians and government policy-makers and towards service users and local communities. As Miller (2004) discussed, there are different models of user engagement that may require rather different structures; but the real problem with all of this is that power is what economists call a 'positional good'. It cannot be expanded, as there is only so much available, and for some to have more others must have less. In other words power cannot be *extended*, it must be *transferred*; and this involves not just a change in the nature of service development and delivery, but a change in the very nature of government itself.

As we discussed in Chapter 6, some political scientists have explored this change in the structure of government and, as noted earlier, it is captured in the talk of a move from government to *governance*, which according to Rhodes (1997) involved a 'new method' of governing society. Some commentators, drawing on a boating analogy, have referred to governance as a move from 'rowing to steering' – government no longer determining and delivering, but rather guiding, policy development. Others talk of a 'hollowing out' of the state in which less and less is decided at government level and more and more devolved to local agencies and partnership bodies (Newman 2001). For Labour particularly, this meant state agencies should recognize that they could not do everything themselves, as the monopoly and paternalist state services of the post-war era had perhaps sought to do. Rather the task of such agencies – and indeed of government itself – was to coordinate different providers meeting different needs, engage with citizens and communities in policy planning, and, more generally, act as power brokers rather than decision takers.

Behind all of this, of course, was a belief that such 'modernization' would lead to improvement in public services through ensuring that users and citizens had a voice within the new structures of governance (Newman and Clarke 2009). Since coming to power in 2010, however, the Coalition government has seen the route to public service improvement in England lying less in participation and deliberative democracy, to give users 'voice', and more in competition and choice, to give users 'exit'.

OPENING UP PUBLIC SERVICES

To some extent the Coalition's policies on the provision of public services involve a continuation of a number of the core themes developed under Labour. Like Labour it has been critical of the paternalism and bureaucracy of past welfare provision, particularly its relative exclusion of users from service development and delivery. It has thus continued to promote the moves towards personalization in areas such as adult social care, discussed in Chapter 11, a development also pursued elsewhere in the UK though in Wales and Scotland with a less marketized emphasis.

Personalization involves passing control over the resources for the provision of care services to service users in the form of personal budgets, which users can then spend to purchase the particular services they need – rather than relying on professionals to determine this. Personal budgets can be 'spent' on public service providers, but they can also be used to purchase services from commercial or third sector agencies; and indeed a large part of the attraction of them is intended to be the freedom which they give users to 'shop around' for the provider who best meets their particular needs. Of course, this requires users to be able to understand their needs and the potential of different providers to meet these, and requires them to be able to manage their budgets appropriately to secure the best services (Needham 2011), although, as discussed in Chapter 11, a White Paper in 2010 proposed that LAs be obliged to ensure universal access to information and advice services (DoH 2010c). The extension of personal budgets to users is thus a challenging, and a gradual, process, and was still being developed in social care in 2013. It is also recognized that professional support and advice will still be required to make personal budgets work in practice (Glasby and Littlechild 2009).

Linked to this, aspects of personalization in service delivery can also be achieved by devolving budgets to 'front line' providers, working with service users to help customize provision to their particular needs. This builds on another dimension of public service reform developed under Labour, but taken up by the Coalition and the devolved administrations: the role of *co-production* in the improvement of public service delivery. Co-production has been championed by campaigners for public service reform as essential to the transformation of public services (Boyle and Harris 2009). It is based on the idea that service providers should work (equally) alongside users to shape services to meet the particular needs of individuals or groups, who through their contribution to this process will co-produce the services they need.

Such co-production delivers the participation in the policy process which Labour sought, but goes further to improve services by ensuring they are tailored to user needs (Bovaird 2007). It is not confined to traditional public service providers either. Indeed commentators have argued that alternative providers, especially in the third sector, may be particularly appropriate to deliver co-produced services because of their closer engagement with service users and their mission to work with particular user groups (Brandsen and Pestoff 2012).

Expanding the role of alternative providers of public services is also more generally at the centre of the Coalition's strategy for public service reform in England. Like Labour, it welcomed the growing recognition that welfare services come from a mixed economy of providers in the public, private and third sectors. This means service users can have more choice over who to approach to meet their service needs, and can use the power of exit to leave providers who are not responding appropriately to these. Personalization and co-production promise to put users at the heart of the process of choosing service providers, but in practice most of the development of alternative provision in recent years has come more directly from the role of government policy-makers in commissioning services from non-state providers.

Labour included private providers in a number of welfare services in England, and promoted the role of third sector organizations as alternatives to public agencies, as we discussed in Chapter 4. However, the Coalition has taken the drive to shift public service provision away from the state much further. In a White Paper published in 2011 on public service reform (HMG 2011b) it argued the case for 'opening up' public service provision in England to commercial and third sector providers so that choice and competition between different providers could drive up standards and improve efficiency.

To some extent this new reform agenda was simply a return to the market logic of competition, but now extended to a wider range of public welfare services; and, of course, it was implemented at the same time as the wide-ranging cuts in public service budgets discussed in Chapter 15. Market competition was expected to reduce the costs of public welfare by drawing in more efficient private providers. However, the government also saw this as an opportunity to increase the role of third sector agencies in public service provision and to promote the creation of new forms of organization to meet particular service needs. This included offering public service workers the 'right to provide' services themselves by opting out of their departments and creating new mutual enterprise agencies to deliver the services under contract from their former employers. This *mutualization* has been promoted as a radical new departure for public service provision, with a taskforce established to support groups of public service workers looking to move to this form of provision.

Mutualization will only work, however, if these new organizations can secure the contracts to deliver their services from the public agencies that will be commissioning these. This will be aided by new legislation requiring public service commissioners to take account of the social value offered by new providers, as well as the price they are planning to charge. But social value has not been defined, and the increased involvement of some large companies in public service provision may mean that despite this they are in practice better placed to secure contracts. This was certainly the case in the largest example of public service contracting introduced by the Coalition in the first half of its term in office, the Work Programme, discussed in Chapter 13, where almost all of the main prime provider contracts went to large private sector companies.

What this reveals is the important role that the commissioning of services plays in a mixed economy of welfare, where competition is being promoted between a range of public, private and third sector providers. Commissioners are buying public services from external providers, and thus are subject to regulations on competition in public law. However, they are also designing (and even co-producing) new models of welfare services to respond to the needs of users and citizens. The tension between the formalities of managing competition and the flexibility and innovation of redesigning public services is not easy to resolve, in particular where the commissioners themselves may have little training or experience in these new welfare arrangements.

The development of more sophisticated procedures for commissioning is part of the agenda for public services reform, and some training is now provided for commissioners to drive improvements in this. However, commissioners are still purchasing within competitive markets of providers, where price and efficiency (rather perhaps than quality) are likely to remain key determinants of success. This has been accentuated further by recent moves towards outcome-focused commissioning and payment by results (PBR).

The concern with the outcomes of, rather than the inputs to, public services arises out of some of the concerns with performance management discussed above. Surely what matters is not whether an unemployed person has been on a training course but whether, as a result, they have secured a job? If providers are going to be commissioned to deliver services for unemployed people, therefore, it is the desired outcome of the service (employment) that should form the basis of the contract. Traditionally, however, public sector contracts have focused on the activities of the providers and have been based on the costs of delivering these, rather than the longer-term outcomes for service users. The shift from cost-based pricing to outcome-based pricing required an alternative means for determining contract value; and this has been attempted by the use of PBR.

The idea behind PBR is that public service providers should be paid for the outcomes that they achieve, in the case of employment services the number of unemployed people securing jobs (for at least a minimum period of time). The contract price is based on a fee for each job secured, and the providers base their bids on their estimate of how much this is likely to cost them. What is significant here is the passing of the risk of performance from the contractor to the provider, for if the providers do not deliver the number of jobs contracted for they will not be paid the fees for these. It is largely for this reason that the contracts in the Work Programme were largely won by private sector providers, for only these large companies had the capital base and organizational scale to take on such risks over a contract period of several years. As a result it has been suggested that PBR will in practice favour large private sector providers over smaller third sector organizations, and the initial evidence from the Work Programme seemed to support this (Rees et al. 2013).

PBR is also attractive to government policy-makers as it shifts the costs of public service from direct public expenditure commitments (to provide employment training) to the future savings on overall expenditure flowing from successful outcomes (reductions in social security benefits paid to unemployed people). If successful this could help government to reduce public expenditure commitments significantly; and for this reason PBR has also been trialled in other areas, such as support to reduce reoffending amongst convicted criminals and treatment therapy for drug addicts. In principle outcome-focused commissioning could be the centrepiece of the major reforms of public service championed by the Coalition: introducing competition and choice amongst providers, gearing services to meet the longer-term needs of service users, and making savings in key areas of public expenditure. However, it all depends on providers being able to deliver the results for the fees negotiated; and, if this is not possible, it may be that service users once again have to rely on traditional public service agencies to pick up the pieces.

COMPREHENSION QUESTIONS

- What is 'joining-up', and why did Labour promote it in the delivery of public welfare services?
- What is the difference between *government* and *governance*, and what are the implications of the shift to the latter in public service policy-making?
- How do personalization and co-production aim to offer greater control to the users of public services?
- What is 'payment by results' and how does it aim to achieve savings in public expenditure?

REFLECTIVE QUESTION

- What are the advantages and disadvantages of opening up public services to private and third sector providers?

FURTHER READING

Deakin and Wright's (1990) collection remains a seminal review of the need to recognize the role of the consumers of welfare services. Though focused on the NHS, Maybin and Klein (2012) offer a helpful overview of rationing processes. Butcher (2002) provides a broader discussion of the issues involved in delivering welfare, and Miller (2004) explores some of the changes flowing from the impact of Labour's modernization agenda. Newman (2001) is a comprehensive guide to the broader issues of government and governance under Labour, and Newman and Clarke (2009) is a critical assessment of the Labour governments' efforts to transform public services. Stoker (2006) is a good introduction to the importance of politics in the policy-making process. Needham (2011) discusses the moves towards personalization and user engagement in public services.

19
The Future of Social Policy

SUMMARY OF KEY POINTS

- The last century saw the establishment of state welfare in Britain and the transformation of the country into a 'welfare capitalist' economy.
- Social policy provision extends beyond state welfare and is best described as a *welfare mix*.
- The development of social policy is affected by the political, ideological and economic contexts in which it is located.
- The impact of economic recession and the public sector deficit have led the government to plan for major changes to British social policy over the coming decade.
- Analysis of the future of social policy must balance contextual analysis with practical policy planning.

PAST ACHIEVEMENTS

The story of the development of social policy in Britain in the twentieth century was the story of the development of the welfare state. At the beginning of the century academics and campaigners such as the Fabian Society were arguing that state welfare was needed to combat the social problems created within an inequitable and exploitative capitalist economy. Throughout the early part of the century a range of measures was introduced to extend public provision of welfare, culminating in the wide-ranging reforms of the post-war period characterized by many at the time, and since, as the establishment of a welfare state. In the latter part of the century these reforms were taken further as services were expanded and new forms of protection introduced. Existing services were also subject to critical appraisal and review, however; and in the 1980s in particular the sustainability, and desirability, of state welfare services were called into question by a government which was seeking to control and contain public expenditure on welfare and to encourage alternative forms of protection on the private market or through voluntary provision.

The reforms of the 1980s did not significantly reverse the broad commitments to public welfare provision developed in earlier decades, however; and at the end of the century the establishment of state welfare in Britain remained as the outstanding policy achievement of the previous hundred years. Commentators have even argued that it led to a transformation of the social and economic structure of the country to create a new 'welfare capitalist society'. This was a development that was not confined to Britain: similar transformations took place in most other Western European countries, and in the advanced industrial nations of North America and Australasia. Public welfare reform was also rapidly pursued in the growing capitalist economies of the Far East and former communist nations of Eastern Europe. State welfare had become a global phenomenon.

There is also no doubt that the public welfare reforms of the last century have transformed the lives of the citizens of Britain, and other countries. Social security protection, the NHS and free public education, for instance, have lengthened and enriched the lifetimes of all, and expanded the expectations that we hold both of ourselves and the society in which we live. Nevertheless it is now recognized that state welfare services have only ever been a part of welfare provision within Britain and other welfare capitalist countries. As we saw in Part 1, private markets have provided welfare on a commercial basis, for some at least; and such market-based provision has in practice expanded, not declined, since state services became established. Third sector activity too has remained, and continued to grow. Informal welfare support, through families and communities, has consistently been the basis upon which many of the most basic social and individual needs have been provided for. As we stressed in Chapter 1, therefore, it might now be more accurate to refer to public welfare provision constituting part of a *welfare mix* rather than a *welfare state*, and social policy analysis has increasingly begun to recognize and respond to this.

Identification of a welfare mix has also directed attention to the different means by which service provision is paid for and supported. The assumption that social services are provided out of public expenditure, drawn from direct taxation, has always been a very partial picture of the complex and interlocking ways in which public and private funding for welfare operate together, and of the different ways in which resources are both collected and distributed. Paying for welfare encompasses financial and non-financial contributions from a wide range of sources and involves a mixture of fees, charges, contributions and rebates that in practice govern access to services in both public and private sectors. What is more, in recent years this complex mixture of funding sources and models of resource distribution has become still more complicated as market principles have been imported into the state sector and non-state providers have grown in scale.

The focus on the redistribution of public resources through state welfare services as the main feature of social policy is also, in another sense, a narrow one. It has sometimes led students and policy-makers to identify the *redistribution* of resources as the main goal of social policy activity, either through the payment of benefits to people or through the provision of services to them (the so-called '*social wage*'). Recognition of the economic and social context of individual needs, on the other hand, focuses our attention also on the role that policy may play in influencing the initial *distribution* of resources (sometimes called 'predistribution') from which many individual needs flow, and on the *production* of the resources that may be available to meet such needs. When we focus on these, too, the policy field broadens to include the control of wages and employment protection, and the control of wealth holding and capital movement; and analysis is extended to include economic trends and investment decisions affecting the growth and development of the wider economy.

As we have seen in Chapter 18, concern within social policy planning and analysis has also been extended to include the management and delivery of services to users and citizens, as well as the structure and funding of them. It is now widely accepted that we need to ensure that the policies that have been developed do deliver the benefits which users are entitled to expect from them, and that we need to develop effective mechanisms to ensure this is the case. It is also no longer possible to examine welfare provision only from the perspective of service providers. Academic analysis and policy practice must focus also upon the experiences, and the opinions, of users and the roles that they can play in co-producing the services that they rely on. Since the beginning of this century therefore the concern of much analysis and policy planning in social policy has shifted from a focus upon *what* we do, to *how* we do it.

As the chapters in Part 2 reveal, however, the range and scale of social policy provision in Britain is extensive, and ever changing. Even the inevitably limited coverage that could be included here tells a story of expansion, refinement and continuing reform that since devolution can also diverge in varying ways across the UK. However, these developments in welfare provision have been shaped by the economic, political and ideological context in which they operate, and these provide no guarantee of continued expansion. Despite the increased support for social policy under the Labour governments and its counterparts in the 2000s, the economic recession and political change in recent years have challenged the future development of state welfare in Britain.

FUTURE PROSPECTS

The global economic recession of 2008 provided a major challenge to the assumptions behind a continued expansion of investment in welfare services. As we discussed in Chapter 15 the primary cause of the recession was the credit crunch: a realization that credit could not continue to provide the resources to underpin economic expansion. This had particular consequences for governments who had themselves borrowed to maintain or expand public expenditure. It was the cause of the economic and political crisis in Greece and a number of other Eurozone countries, who had very large public sector deficits and had to be 'bailed out' by the EU and European Central Bank. It was a problem for Britain too, however, who under Labour had expanded public sector borrowing in order to maintain public services in the early years of the recession, and also to use this public expenditure to counteract the decline in growth resulting from the economic collapse.

The need to repay this borrowing and reduce the public sector deficit was the major issue in the general election in 2010. All parties agreed that this would be needed, but disagreed on the pace and scale of the reduced spending which would be required. For the Coalition government formed after the election, the need to remove the public sector deficit by 2015 became an overriding economic and political priority, and, as we have discussed throughout this book, this has led to significant reductions in public expenditure on welfare services, with more planned over the coming years – now through to 2018 at least and, possibly, beyond

For economic reasons, therefore, the future prospects for social policy look rather different to past developments, and it will be some time before future governments are likely to be able to countenance any return to major expansion in public welfare provision. However, the political complexion of the Conservative-led Coalition government is significantly different to the New Labour one that preceded it. As mentioned above, the Conservative governments of the 1980s called into question the desirability, as well as the sustainability, of state welfare services and sought to promote alternative market and voluntary provision. These themes have been taken up again by the Coalition, in particular in the *Big Society* agenda promoted by the Conservative Prime Minister, David Cameron.

As we discussed in Chapter 4 the Coalition has upheld the Big Society as a supposed alternative to the 'big state' policies of Labour, and of the post-war welfare settlement. Cameron himself has pointed out that this agenda is not just the product of the economic pressures that are forcing reductions in public expenditure, but is based upon core political beliefs in the need to replace the paternalism and bureaucracy of state welfare with choice and competition and to 'return' control over service provision to citizens and users. Whether the changes introduced by the Coalition both across the UK and, more particularly in public services in England, will lead to a Big Society of empowered citizens and competitive providers is open to question, of course. But, as Taylor-Gooby and Stoker (2011) have pointed out, the changes that flow from the planned reductions in public expenditure could change the whole nature of the welfare regime in the UK, with spending planned to fall below the levels of major comparator OECD countries, including the USA. The politics of welfare are also likely to take a turn away from the model of publicly led expansion that dominated the last century therefore.

In addition to economic and political pressures ideological changes are also likely to influence the future prospects for social policy in Britain. As we discussed in Chapter 14, ideologies of welfare do not map directly onto political and economic forces, but they do underpin policy planning and, more importantly perhaps, the ways in which the needs for planning are perceived. As we saw in Chapter 18 in particular, there has been a significant shift over the past two decades or so away from a provider culture of welfare services, dominated by monopoly state agencies, towards greater recognition of the need to gear service provision to the needs, and preferences, of users. As we have also seen there has been a parallel shift involving an increased reliance on self-provisioning.

These have had contradictory impacts on social policy over this time, from the increased managerialism and performance measurement of New Public Management to the personalization, co-production, competition and choice of more recent public service reform. Nevertheless some of the major forces for change have remained consistent: welfare provision, in England particularly, is now based on a plurality of providers, competing for contracts to deliver services and gearing their provision to the outcomes that will benefit individual users. The desirability of further movement towards an outcome focus for service planning, a greater mix of public, private and third sector providers and increased self-provisioning are likely to continue to dominate ideological debate within social policy over the foreseeable future, and to drive further departures from the welfare state model of comprehensive public services.

As this book also makes clear, however, social policy in Britain is no longer the single welfare regime that it was in the last century. Devolution of powers to the separate administrations in Scotland, Wales and Northern Ireland now means that there is increasing diversity of provision across these three countries; and the political differences which have now emerged following the elections in 2010 and 2011 are likely to create further political and policy distance between the UK government in England and the separate Parliaments and Assemblies in the other three countries. What is more the UK itself will no longer be a single political entity if Scottish voters opt for independence in 2014; and its relationship to the EU too is potentially under consideration.

As the recent changes in economics and politics have revealed, however, it is not easy to predict the future direction of policy planning; and students and practitioners of social policy may say, with some justification, that they cannot be expected to embrace such broader uncertainties, especially where they are focusing upon the development of particular welfare needs or welfare services. However, the study and practice of social policy requires us all to embrace both contextual understanding and practical policy action; and managing this balance is what drives both policy analysis and political debate. It is what makes the study of social policy both challenging and rewarding too.

REFLECTIVE QUESTIONS

- Will the welfare reforms of the early twenty-first century lead to the end of the British Welfare State?
- What would be your main priorities for the development of social policy provision over the next ten years?

References

Abel-Smith, B. and Townsend, P. (1965) *The Poor and the Poorest*, London: G Bell & Sons.

Acheson, Sir D. (1998) *Independent Inquiry into Inequalities and Health*, London: The Stationery Office.

Abu Sharkh, M. and Gough, I. (2010) 'Global welfare regimes: a cluster analysis', *Global Social Policy*, 10(1).

Adamson, P. (2012) *Report Card 10: Measuring Child Poverty*, Florence: UNICEF.

Addison, P. (1975) *The Road to 1945: British Politics and the Second World War*, London: Jonathan Cape.

Alakeson, V. (2011) *Making a Rented House a Home: Housing Solutions for 'Generation Rent'*, London: Resolution Foundation.

Alcock, P. (1999a) 'Poverty and social security', in Page, R. and Silburn, R. (eds) *British Social Welfare in the Twentieth Century*, London: Macmillan.

Alcock, P. (1999b) 'Development of social security', in Ditch, J. (ed.) *Introduction to Social Security: Policies, Benefits Poverty*, London: Routledge.

Alcock, P. (2006) *Understanding Poverty* (3rd edn), Basingstoke: Palgrave Macmillan.

Alcock, P. (2010) 'A Strategic Unity: Defining the Third Sector in the UK', *Voluntary Sector Review*, 1(1).

Alcock, P. (2012) 'New Policy Spaces: The Impact of Devolution on Third Sector Policy in the UK', *Social Policy and Administration*, 46(2).

Alcock, P., Beatty, C., Fothergill, S., Macmillan, R. and Yeandle, S. (2003) *Work to Welfare: How Men become Detached from the Labour Market*, Cambridge: Cambridge University Press.

Alcock, P. and Craig, G. (eds) (2009) *International Social Policy: Welfare Regimes in the Developed World* (2nd edn), Basingstoke: Palgrave Macmillan.

Alcock, P., Glennerster, H., Oakley, A. and Sinfield, A. (eds) (2001) *Welfare and Wellbeing: Richard Titmuss's Contribution to Social Policy*, Bristol: The Policy Press.

Alcock, P., May, M. and Wright, S. (eds) (2012) *The Student's Companion to Social Policy* (4th edn), Chichester: Wiley-Blackwell.

Alcock, P. and Powell, M. (eds) (2011) *Welfare Theory and Development*, London: Sage.

Aldridge, H., Parekh, A., McInnes, T. and Kenway, P. (2011) *Monitoring Poverty and Social Exclusion 2011*, York: Joseph Rowntree Foundation.

All Parliamentary Group for Runaway and Missing Children and Adults and the APPG for Looked After Children and Care Leavers (APPG) (2012) *Report from the Joint Inquiry into Children Who Go Missing from Care*, London: APPG.

Allen, G. (2011) *Early Intervention: The Next Steps*, London: DfE.

Andrews, D., Caldera Sanchez, D. and Johanssen, A. (2011) *Housing Markets and Structural Policies in OECD Countries*, OECD Economics Department Working Papers, no. 836, Geneva: OECD.

Annetts, J., Law, D., McNeish, W. and Mooney, G. (2009) *Understanding Social Welfare Movements*, Bristol: The Policy Press.

Appleby, J., Crawford R. and Emmerson, C. (2009) *How Cold Will It be? Prospects for NHS Funding 2011–17*, London: King's Fund.

Arksey, H. and Glendinning, C. (2012) 'Informal welfare', in Alcock, P., May, M. and Wright, S. (eds) *The Student's Companion to Social Policy*, (4th edn.) Chichester: Wiley-Blackwell.

Arksey, H. and Kemp, P. A. (2006) 'Carers and employment in a work-focused welfare state', in Glendinning, C. and Kemp, P. A. (eds) *Cash and Care: Policy Challenges in the Welfare State*, Bristol: The Policy Press.

Arnott, M. and Ozga, J. (2012) 'Education policy and social justice', in Mooney, G. and Scott, G. (eds) *Social Justice and Social Policy in Scotland*, Bristol: The Policy Press.

Association of Chief Executives of Voluntary Organizations (ACEVO) Commission on Youth Unemployment (2012) *Youth Unemployment: The Crisis We Cannot Afford*, London: ACEVO.

Atkinson, A. B. (2011) 'The case for universal child benefit', in Walker, A., Sinfield, A. and Walker, C. (eds) *Fighting Poverty, Inequality and Injustice: A Manifesto Inspired by Peter Townsend*, Bristol: The Policy Press.

Audit Commission (2008) *Are We There Yet?*, London: The Stationery Office.

Audit Commission (2010) *Against the Odds*, London: Audit Commission.

Audit Commission (2011) *Joining-up Health and Social Care: Improving Value for Money Across the Interface*, London: Audit Commission.

Bacon, R. and Eltis, W. (1976) *Britain's Economic Problem: Too Few Producers*, London: Macmillan.

Baggott, R. (2004) *Health and Health Care in Britain* (3rd edn), Basingstoke: Palgrave Macmillan.

Baggott, R. (2010) *Public Health Policy and Politics* (2nd edn), Bristol: The Policy Press.

Baggott, R (2012) 'Public health and policy success in England', *Journal of Social Policy*, 41(2).

Bailey, M. (2011) 'Foreword', in Lavalette, M. (ed.) *Radical Social Work Today*, Bristol: The Policy Press.

Baldock, J. (2003) 'The Personal Social Services and Community Care', in Alcock, P., Erskine, A. and May, M. (eds) *The Student's Companion to Social Policy* (2nd edn), Oxford: Basil Blackwell.

Baldock, J., Mitton, L., Manning, N. and Vickerstaff, S. (eds) (2011) *Social Policy* (4th edn), Oxford: Oxford University Press.

Baldwin, P. (1990) *The Politics of Social Solidarity*, Cambridge: Cambridge University Press.

Ball, S. (1896) *The Moral Aspects of Socialism*, London: Fabian Tract No. 72.

Ball, S. J. (2013) *The Education Debate* (2nd edn), Bristol: The Policy Press.

Balls, E., Grice, J. and O'Donnell, G. (eds) (2004) *Microeconomic Reform in Britain: Delivering Opportunities for All*, Basingstoke: Palgrave Macmillan.

Balls, E. and O'Donnell, G. (eds) (2002) *Reforming Britain's Economic and Social Policy: Towards Greater Economic Stability*, Basingstoke: Palgrave Macmillan.

Barnes, C. and Mercer, G. (2006) *Independent Futures: Creating User-led Disability Services in a Disabling Society*, Bristol: The Policy Press.

Barnes, M., Bauld, L., Benzeval, M., Judge, K., MacKenzie, M. and Sullivan, H. (2005) *Health Action Zones: Partnerships for Health Equity*, London: Routledge.

Barnes, M., Harrison, S., Mort, M. and Shardlow, P. (1999) *Unequal Partners: User Groups and Community Care*, Bristol: The Policy Press.

Barnes, M., Newman, J. and Sullivan, H. (2007) *Power, Participation and Political Renewal*, Bristol: The Policy Press.

Barry, N. (1987) *The New Right*, London: Croom Helm.

Barry, N. (1990) *Welfare*, Milton Keynes: Open University Press.

Bartlett, W., Roberts, J. and Le Grand, J. (1998) *A Revolution in Social Policy: Quasi-Market Reforms in the 1990s*, Bristol: The Policy Press.

Bell, D. (2010) *The Impact of Devolution: Long-term Care Provision in the UK*, York: Joseph Rowntree Foundation.

Benn, M. (2011) *School Wars: The Battle for Britain's Education*, London: Verso.

Bennett, F. (2012) 'Taxation and welfare', in Alcock, P., May, M. and Wright, S. (eds) *The Student's Companion to Social Policy* (4th edn), Chichester: Wiley-Blackwell.

Beresford, P., Fleming, J., Glynn, M., Bewley, C., Croft, S., Branfield, F. and Postle, K. (2011) *Supporting People: Towards a Person-Centred Approach*, Bristol: The Policy Press.

Bevan Commission (2011) *2008–2011 NHS Wales: Forging a Better Future*, Cardiff: Welsh Assembly Government.

Beveridge, Sir W. (1942) *Report on Social Insurance and Allied Services*, Cm. 6404, London: HMSO.

Beveridge, Sir W. (1944) *Full Employment in a Free Society*, London: George Allen & Unwin.

Beveridge, Sir W. (1948) *Voluntary Action*, London: Allen & Unwin.

Billis, D. (ed.) (2010) *Hybrid Organisations and the Third Sector: Challenges for Practice, Theory and Policy*, Basingstoke: Palgrave Macmillan.

Birrell, D. (2009) *The Impact of Devolution on Social Policy*, Bristol: The Policy Press.

Black, C. (2008) *Working for a Healthier Tomorrow*, London: DoH/The Stationery Office.

Black Report (1980) *Inequalities and Health*, London: DHSS.

Blair, T. (1998) *The Third Way*, London: Fabian Society.

Blair, T. (2002) *The Courage of our Convictions: Why Reform of Public Services is the Route to Social Justice*, London: Fabian Society.

Bloch, A. (2002) *The Migration and Settlement of Refugees in Britain*, Basingstoke: Palgrave Macmillan.

Bloch, A., Neal, S. and Solomos, J. (2013) *Race, Multiculture and Social Policy*, Basingstoke: Palgrave Macmillan.

Blunkett, D. and Green, G. (1983) *Building from the Bottom: The Sheffield Experience*, London: Fabian Society.

Blunkett, D. and Jackson, K. (1987) *Democracy in Crisis: The Town Halls Respond*, London: Hogarth Press.

Bochel, H. (ed.) (2011) *The Conservative Party and Social Policy*, Bristol: The Policy Press.

Boddy, M. and Fudge, C. (eds) (1984) *Local Socialism? Labour Councils and New Left Alternatives*, London: Macmillan.

Bonoli, G. (2010) 'The political economy of active labour-market policy', *Politics and Society*, 38(4).

Bonoli, G., George, V. and Taylor-Gooby, P. (2000) *European Welfare Futures: Towards a Theory of Retrenchment*, Cambridge: Polity Press.

Booth, C. (1889) *The Life and Labour of the People*, London: Williams & Northgate.

Borrie, G. (1994) *Social Justice: Strategies for National Renewal – The Report of the Commission on Social Justice*, London: Vintage.

Bovaird, T. (2007) 'Beyond engagement and participation – user and community co-production of public services', *Public Administration Review*, 67(5).

Bovaird, T. and Loffler, E. (eds) (2009) *Public Management and Governance* (2nd edn), London: Routledge.

Boyle, D. (2001) *The Tyranny of Numbers: Why Counting Cannot Make Us Happy*, New York: Flamingo/Harper Collins.

Boyle, D. and Harris, M. (2009) *The Challenge of Co-production: How Equal Partnerships between Professionals and the Public are Crucial to Improving Public Services*, London: New Economics Foundation/NESTA.

Boyson, R. (1971) *Down with the Poor*, London: Churchill.

Brandsen, T. and Pestoff, V. (eds) (2012) *New Public Governance: The Third Sector and Co-production*, London: Routledge.

Brenton, M. (1985) *The Voluntary Sector in British Social Services*, London: Longman.

Brewer, M., Browne, J. and Joyce, R. (2011) *Child and Working Age Poverty from 2010 to 2020*, IFS Commentary 121, London: IFS.

Brewer, M., Dickerson, A., Gambin, L., Green, A., Joyce, R. and Wilson, R. (2012) *Poverty and Inequality in 2020: The Impact of Employment Changes*, London: UKCES/JRF.

Brewer, M. and Shephard, R. (2005), *Employment and the Labour Market*, London: IFS.

Brown, F. Lauder, H. and Ashton, D. (2011) *The Global Auction, The Broken Promises of Education, Jobs and Income*, Oxford: Oxford University Press.

Brown, W. (2011) 'International review; industrial relations under New Labour, 1997–2010: a post mortem', *Journal of Industrial Relations*, 53(3).

Brown, W. and Marsden, D. (2010) 'Individualization and growing diversity of employment contracts', in Marsden, D. (ed.) *Employment in the Lean Years*, Oxford: Oxford University Press.

Browne, J. (2010) *Sustaining a Future for Higher Education. Independent Review of Higher Education and Student Finance in England*, www.independ.gov.uk/brownreport.

Brunsdon, E. and May, M. (2007) 'Occupational welfare', in Powell, M. (ed.) *Understanding the Mixed Economy of Welfare*, Bristol: The Policy Press.

Brunsdon, E. and May, M. (2012) *The Student's Companion to Social Policy – online resources*, www.wiley.com/go/alcock

Buchanan, J. (1986) *Liberty, Market and the State*, Hemel-Hempstead: Harvester Wheatsheaf.

Buck, D. and Frosini, F. (2012) *Clustering of Unhealthy Behaviours Over Time Implications for Policy and Practice*, London: King's Fund.

Buchs, M. (2008) 'The open method of coordination as a two-level game', *Policy and Politics*, 36(2).

Bulmer, M., Lewis, J. and Piachaud, D. (eds) (1989) *The Goals of Social Policy*, London: Unwin Hyman.

Burchardt, T. and Hills, J. (1999) 'Public Expenditure and the Public/Private Mix', in Powell, M. (ed.), *New Labour, New Welfare State? The 'Third Way' in British Social Policy*, Bristol: The Policy Press.

Butcher, T. (2002) *Delivering Welfare* (2nd edn), Milton Keynes: Open University Press.

Cabinet Office (1999) *Modernising Government*, Cm. 4310, London: The Stationery Office.

Cabinet Office (2010a) *Building the Big Society*, London: Cabinet Office.

Cabinet Office (2010b) *Applying Behavioural Insight to Health*, London: Cabinet Office.

Cahill, M. (2001) *The Environment and Social Policy*, London: Routledge.

Callaghan, J. (1987) *Time and Chance*, London: Collins.

Campbell, J. and Oliver, M. (1996) *Disability Politics: Understanding our Past, Changing our Future*, London: Routledge.

Care Quality Commission (CQC) (2011) *The State of Health Care and Adult Social Care in England, An Overview of Key Themes in Care in 2010/11*, London: CQC.

CQC (2012) *Learning Disabilities Service Inspection: National Overview*, London: CQC.

Castles, F. (1999) *Comparative Public Policy: Patterns of Post War Transformation*, Cheltenham: Edward Elgar.

Castles, F. (2004) *The Future of the Welfare State*, Oxford: Oxford University Press.

Castles, F., Leibfried, S., Lewis, J., Obinger, H. and Pierson, C. (2010) *The Oxford Handbook of the Welfare State*, Oxford: Oxford University Press.

Castles, F. and Mitchell, D. (1991) *Three Worlds of Welfare Capitalism or Four?*, Discussion Paper 21, Australian National University.

Chartered Institute of Public Finance and Accountancy (CIPFA) (2008) *UK Health: A Report into Diverging Structure and Policy Under Devolution for the National Health Service in England, Scotland, Wales and Northern Ireland*, London: CIPFA.

CIPFA (2011) *Smart Cuts? Public Spending on Children's Social Care*, London: CIPFA.

Chitty, C. (2009) *Education Policy in Britain* (2nd edn), Basingstoke: Palgrave Macmillan.

Chitty, C. (2010) 'Education policy and policy-making 1997–2009', in Greener, I., Holden, C. and Kilkey, M. (eds) *Social Policy Review 22*, Bristol: The Policy Press.

Chowdry, H. and Sibieta, L A. (2011) *Trends in Education and Schools Spending*, IFS Briefing Note BN 121, London: IFS.

Churchill, H. (2011) *Parental Rights and Responsibilities; Analysing Social Policy and Lived Experiences*, Bristol: The Policy Press.

Clark, J., Kane, D., Wilding, K. and Bass, P. (2012) *The UK Civil Society Almanac 2012*, London: NCVO.

Clarke, J., Cochrane, A. and McLaughlin, E. (eds) (1994) *Managing Social Policy*, London: Sage.

Clarke, J. and Newman, J. (1997) *The Managerial State*, London: Sage.

Clarke, J., Newman, J., Smith, N., Vidler, E. and Westmarland, L. (2007) *Creating Citizen-Consumers: Changing Publics and Changing Public Services*, London: Sage.

Clarke, M. and Stewart, J. (1988) *The Enabling Council*, London: Local Government Management Board.

Clarke, M. and Stewart, J. (1999) *Community Governance, Community Leadership and the New Local Government*, York: Joseph Rowntree Foundation.

Clasen, J. (2011) *Converging Worlds of Welfare? British and German Social Policy in the 21st Century*, Oxford: Oxford University Press.

Clasen, J. and Clegg, D. (2011) *Regulating the Risk of Unemployment. National Adaptations to Post-Industrial Labour Markets in Europe*, Oxford: Oxford University Press.

Clery, E. (2012) 'Are tough times affecting attitudes to welfare?', in Park, A., Clery, E., Curtis, J., Phillips, M. and Utting, D. (eds) *British Social Attitudes: the 29th Report*, London: National Centre for Social Research.

Cockburn, C. (1977) *The Local State*, London: Pluto Press.

Cole, I. and Furbey, R. (1994) *The Eclipse of Council Housing*, London: Routledge.

Commission on Social Justice (CSJ) (1994) *Social Justice: Strategies for National Renewal*, London: IPPR

Compton, J. (2011) *Transforming Your Care: A Review of Health and Social Care in Northern Ireland*, Belfast: Northern Ireland Executive.

Connolly, S., Bevan, G. and Mays, N. (2011) *Funding and Performance of Healthcare Systems in the Four Countries of the UK Before and After Devolution*, Summary Briefing July, London: Nuffield Trust.

Cooke, G. (2011) *National Salary Insurance Reforming the Welfare State to Provide Real Protection*, London: IPPR.

Coote, A. (2010) *Cutting it: The 'Big Society' and the New Austerity*, London, New Economics Foundation.

Craig, G., Atkin, K., Chattoo, S. and Flynn, R. (2012) *Understanding Race and Ethnicity: Theory, History, Policy, Practice*, Bristol: The Policy Press.

Craig, G., Taylor, M., Wilkinson, M. and Monro, S. (2002) *Contract or Trust? The Role of Compacts in Local Governance*, Bristol: The Policy Press.

Crawford, R. and Emmerson, C. (2012) *NHS and Social Care Funding: The Outlook to 2021/22*, London: Institute of Fiscal Studies.

Crompton, R. (2006) *Employment and the Family*, Cambridge: Cambridge University Press.

Crompton, R. (2008) *Class and Stratification: An Introduction to Current Debates* (3rd edn), Cambridge: Polity Press.

Crosland, C. (1956) *The Future of Socialism*, London: Jonathan Cape.

Cutler, T., Williams, K. and Williams, J. (1986) *Keynes, Beveridge and Beyond*, London: Routledge & Kegan Paul.

Dale, J. and Foster, P. (1986) *Feminists and State Welfare*, London: Routledge & Kegan Paul.

Dalley, G. (ed.) (1991) *Disability and Social Policy*, London: Policy Studies Institute.

Daly, M. (2010) 'Shifts in family policy in the UK under New Labour', *Journal of European Social Policy*, 20(5).

Daly, M. (2011) *Welfare*, Bristol: The Policy Press.

Daly, M. and Rake, K. (2003) *Gender and the Welfare State*, Cambridge: Polity Press.

Davies, C. (2011) *Reforming the NHS: Reflections on Four Decades of NHS Care*, London: Adam Smith Institute.

Davis Smith, J. (2001) 'Volunteers: Making a Difference?', in Harris, M. and Rochester, C. (eds) *Voluntary Organisations and Social Policy in Britain: Perspectives on Change and Choice*, Basingstoke: Palgrave Macmillan.

Deacon, A. (2000) 'Learning from the USA? The Influence of American Ideas on New Labour Thinking on Welfare Reform', *Policy and Politics*, 20(1).

Deacon, A. (2002) *Perspectives on Welfare: Ideas, Ideologies and Policy Debates*, Buckingham: Open University Press.

Deacon, A. and Bradshaw, J. (1983) *Reserved for the Poor: The Means-Test in British Social Policy*, Oxford: Basil Blackwell and Martin Robertson.

Deacon, A. and Patrick, R. (2012) 'Employment', in Alcock, P., May, M. and Wright, S. (eds) *The Student's Companion to Social Policy* (4th edn), Chichester: Wiley-Blackwell.

Deacon, B. (2007) *Global Social Policy and Governance*, London: Sage.

Deacon, B. (2011) 'Global social policy responses to the economic crisis', in Farnsworth, K. and Irving, Z. (eds) *Social Policy in Challenging Times*, Bristol: The Policy Press.

Deacon, B., Castle-Kanerova, M., Manning, N., Millard, F., Orosz, E. and Szalai, J. (1992) *The New Eastern Europe: Social Policy Past, Present and Future*, London: Sage.

Deacon B., with Hulse, M. and Stubbs, P. (1997) *Global Social Policy: International Organisations and the Future of Welfare*, London: Sage.

Deakin, N. (1994) *The Politics of Welfare: Continuities and Change*, Hemel Hempstead: Harvester Wheatsheaf.

Deakin, N. (1996) *Meeting the Challenge of Change: Voluntary Action into the 21st Century*, Report of the Commission on the Future of the Voluntary Sector in England, London: NCVO Publications.

Deakin, N. (2000) *The Treasury and Social Policy: The Contest for Control of Welfare Strategy*, Basingstoke: Palgrave Macmillan.

Deakin, N. (2001) *In Search of Civil Society*, Basingstoke: Palgrave Macmillan.

Deakin, N. and Wright, A. (eds) (1990) *Consuming Public Services*, London: Routledge.

Dean, H. (1996) *Welfare Law and Citizenship*, Harlow: Prentice Hall.

Department for Business, Innovation and Skills (BIS) (2010a) *Skills for Sustainable Growth Strategy Document*, London: BIS.

BIS (2010b) *Further Education – New Horizon: Investing in Skills for Sustainable Growth. Strategy Document*, London: BIS.

BIS (2011a) *Skills Investment Statement 2011–2014*, London: BIS.

BIS (2011b) *New Challenges, New Chances: Further Education and Skills System Reform Plan: Building a World Class Skills System*, London: BIS.

BIS (2011c) *Consultation on the Future of the Right to Request Time to Train Regulations*, London: BIS.

BIS (2011d) *New Challenges, New Chances: Next Steps in Implementing the Further Education Reform Programme*, London: BIS.

BIS (2011e) *Higher Education: Students at the Heart of the System*, London: BIS.

BIS (2012) *European Structural and Cohesion Funds*, London: BIS.

Department for Children, Schools and Families (DCFS) (2010) *Support for All: The Families and Relationships Green Paper*, Cm. 7787, London: DCFS.

Department for Communities and Local Government (DCLG) (2006) *A Decent Home: Definition and Guidance for Implementation*, London: DCLG.

DCLG (2007a) *Homes for the Future: More Affordable, More Sustainable*, Cm. 1791, London: The Stationery Office.

DCLG (2007b) *Delivering Housing and Regenerating Communities in England and the Future of Social Housing Regulation*, London: DCLG.

DCLG (2007c) *Mechanisms for Setting Guideline Rents in Housing Revenue Account Subsidy 2008–09 and 2009–10*, London: DCLG.

DCLG (2010a) *Household Projections 2008–2033, England*, London: DCLG.

DCLG (2010b) *Final HRA Subsidy Determination*, London: DCLG.

DCLG (2010c) *Local Decisions: A Fairer Future for Social Housing*, London: DCLG.

DCLG (2011) *Vision to End Rough Sleeping: No Second Night Out Nationwide*, London: DCLG.

DCLG (2012) *English Housing Survey: Homes Report 2010*, London: DCLG.

Department for Education (DfE) (2010) *The Importance of Teaching*, London: DfE.

DfE (2011a) *A New Approach to Child Poverty: Tackling the Causes of Disadvantage and Transforming Families' Lives*, Cm. 8061, London: DfE.

DfE (2011b) *Support and Aspiration: A New Approach to Special Educational Needs and Disability*, Cm. 8027, London: DfE.

DfE (2011c) *Wolf Review of Educational Provision Government Response*, London: DfE.

DfE (2011d) *Schools, Pupils and Their Characteristics*, SFR12/2011.

DfE (2011e) *Looked After Children in England year ending 31 March 2011*, London: DfE.

DfE (2011f) *A Child-Centred System: the Government's Response to the Munro Review of Child protection*, London: DfE.

DfE (2012a) *Supporting Families in the Foundation Years*, London: DfE.

DfE (2012b) *Reforming Key Stage 4 Qualifications Consultation*, London: DfE.

DfE (2012c) *Wolf Review of Education Provision Government Response*, London: DfE.

DfE (2012d) *More freedom and Flexibility – a New Approach for Children's Trust Boards*, London: DfE .

DfE (2012e) *An Action Plan for Adoption: Tackling Delay*, London: DfE.

Department for Education and Employment (DfEE) (1998) *The Learning Age: Further Education for the New Millennium*, Kennedy Report, London: The Stationery Office.

Department for Education and Skills (DfES) (2001) *Schools – Achieving Success*, London: HMSO.

DfES (2003a) *Every Child Matters*, Cm. 5860, The Stationery Office.

DfES (2003b) *Twenty First Century Skills: Realising Our Potential – Individuals, Employers, Nation*, Cm. 5810, London: HMSO.

DfES (2005) *Higher Standards, Better Schools for ALL: More Choice for Parents and Pupils*, Cm. 6677, London: The Stationery Office.

DfES (2006) *Care Matters: Transforming the Lives of Children and Young People in Care*, Cm. 6932, London: DfES.

Department for Employment and Learning (DEL) (2010) *Success Through Skills 2: The Skills Strategy for Northern Ireland*, Belfast: DEL.

DEL (2012) *A Strategy for Those Not in Education, Employment or Training (NEET)*, Belfast: DEL.

Department for Social Development (DSD) (2010) *Building Sound Foundations*, Belfast: DSD.

DSD (2012) *Facing the Future: Housing Strategy for Northern Ireland 2012–2017*, Belfast: DSD.

Department for the Environment, Transport and the Regions (DETR) and DSS (2000) *Quality and Choice: A Decent Home for ALL. The Housing Green Paper*, London: DETR and DSS.

Department for Work and Pensions (DWP) (2002) *Building Choice and Responsibility: A Radical Agenda for Housing Benefit*, London: DWP.

DWP (2006a) *Opportunity for All*, Eighth Annual Report 2006, London: DWP.

DWP (2006b) *A New Deal for Welfare: Empowering People to Work*, Cm. 6730, London: DWP.

DWP (2007) *In Work, Better off: Next Steps to Full Employment*, Cm. 7130, London: The Stationery Office.

DWP (2009a) *Supporting People into Work: The Next Stage of Housing Benefit Reform*, Cm. 7769, London: Stationery Office.

DWP (2009b) *Building Britain's Recovery: Achieving Full Employment*, Cm. 7751, London: The Stationery Office.

DWP (2010a) *Income-related Benefits: Estimates of Take-ups*, London: DWP.

DWP (2010b) *Universal Credit: Welfare that Works*, Cm. 7957, London: DWP.

DWP (2010c) *Twenty-First Century Welfare*, Cm. 7913, London: DWP.

DWP (2010d) *The Work Programme Prospectus*, London: DWP.

DWP (2011a) *A State Pension for the 21st Century*, Cm. 8053, London: DWP.

DWP (2011b) *The Work Programme*, London: DWP.

DWP (2012) *Office for Disability Issues, Disability Facts and Figures*, London: DWP.

DWP (2013) *The Single-Tier Pension: A Simple Foundation for Saving*, Cm. 8528, London: The Stationery Office.

DWP/HWW (2011) *Health, Work and Wellbeing Indicators Progress Report*, London: DWP.

Department of Education and Science (DES) (1985) *Education for All. The Report of the Committee of Inquiry into the Education of Children from Ethnic Minority Groups*, London: HMSO.

Department of Health (DoH) (1989) *Working for Patients*, London: HMSO.

DoH (1992) *The Health of the Nation*, Cm. 1986, London: HMSO.

DoH (1997) *The New NHS. Modern. Dependable*, London: The Stationery Office.

DoH (1998) *Modernising Social Services: Promoting Independence, Improving Protection, Raising Standards*, Cm. 4169, London: The Stationery Office.

DoH (1999) *Saving Lives: Our Healthier Nation*, London: Stationery Office.

DoH (2000) *The NHS Plan: A Plan for Investment, a Plan for Reform*, Cm. 4818, Stationery Office.

DoH (2001) *Your Guide to the NHS*, London: DoH.

DoH (2003a) *Tackling Health Inequalities: A Programme for Action*, Cm. 6374, London: DoH.

DoH (2003b) *Fair Access to Care Services – Guidance on Eligibility Criteria for Adult Social Care*, London: The Stationery Office.

DoH (2004a) *The NHS Improvement Plan, Putting People at the Heart of Public Services*, Cm. 6268, London: The Stationery Office.

DoH (2004b) *Choosing Health – Making Healthier Choices Easier*, London: The Stationery Office.

DoH (2005) *Independence, Well-being and Choice: Our Vision for the Future of Social Care for Adults in England*, London: DoH.

DoH (2006) *Our Health, Our Care, Our Say: New Directions for Community Services*, Cm. 6736, London: The Stationery Office.

DoH (2007a) *Personal Social Services Statistics: Finance*, London: DoH.

DoH (2007b) *National Service Framework for Children, Young People and Maternity Services, Core Standards*, London: DoH.

DoH (2007c) *Putting People First*, London: DoH.

DoH (2008) *High Quality Care for All: NHS Next Stage Review Final Report*, Cm. 7432, London: The Stationery Office.

DoH (2009a) *From Good to Great – Preventative, People-Centred, Productive*, Cm. 7775, London: The Stationery Office.

DoH (2009b) *The NHS Constitution for England*, London: The Stationery Office.

DoH (2010a) *Equity and Excellence: Liberating the NHS*, Cm. 7881, London: The Stationery Office.

DoH (2010b) *The NHS Outcomes Framework 2011/12*, London: DoH.

DoH (2010c) *A Vision for Adult Social Care: Capable Communities and Active Citizens*, London: DoH.

DoH (2010d) *Think Local, Act Personal Partnership Agreement Between the Government and Social Care Sector*, London: DoH.

DoH (2011a) *NHS Future Forum, Summary Report on Proposed Changes to the NHS*, London: DoH.

DoH (2011b) *Government Changes in Response to the NHS Future Forum*, London: DoH.

DoH (2011c) *Changing Behaviour, Improving Outcomes: A New Social Marketing Strategy for Public Health*, London: DoH.

DoH (2011d) *The Public Health Responsibility Deal*, London: DoH.

DoH (2011e) *Working for Personalised Care: A Framework for Supporting Personal Assistants Working in Adult Care*, London: DoH.

DoH (2011f) *Statement of Government Policy on Adult Safeguarding*, London: DoH.

DoH (2012a) *Government Accepts New Recommendations from NHS Future Forum*, London: DoH.

DoH (2012b) *Improving Outcomes and Supporting Transparency*, London: DoH.

DoH (2012c) *Transparency in Outcomes: A Framework for Adult Social Care – A Consultation on Proposals*, London: DoH.

DoH (2013) *Caring for Our Future Consultation on Reforming What and How People Pay for Their Care and Support*, London: DoH.

DoH/DfES (2004) *National Service Framework for Children, Young People and Maternity Services: Our Health, Our Care, Our Say – New Direction for Community Services*, London: DES/DoH.

Department of Health and Social Security (DHSS) (1976) *Prevention and Health: Everybody's Business*, London: DHSS.

Department of Health, Social Services and Public Safety (DHSSP) (2012) *The Strategic Implementation Plan*, Belfast: DHSSP.

Department of Social Security (DSS) (1998a) *New Ambitions for our Country: A New Contract for Welfare*, Green Paper, Cm. 3805, London: The Stationery Office.

DSS (1998b) *A New Contract for Welfare: Partnership in Pensions*, Cm. 4179, London: The Stationery Office.

Deputy Prime Minister (DPM) (2011) *Opening Doors, Breaking Barriers A Strategy for Social Mobility*, London: DWP.

Dickens, L. and Hall, M. (2009) 'Legal regulation and the changing workplace', in Brown, W., Bryson, A., Forth, J. and Whitfield, K. (eds) *The Evolution of the Modern Workplace*, Cambridge: Cambridge University Press.

Dilnot, A. (2011) *Fairer Care Funding, The Report of the Commission on Funding Care and Support*, London: The Stationery Office.

Dilnot, A. (2012) *Letter to John Hunt, Secretary of State for Health December 12th*, London: UK Statistics Authority.

Dixon, A. and Ham, C. (2010) *Liberating the NHS: The Right Prescription in a Cold Climate?*, London: King's Fund.

Dodds, A. (2013) *Comparative Public Policy*, Basingstoke: Palgrave Macmillan.

Dolowitz, D. (1998) *Learning from America: Policy Transfer and the Development of the British Workfare State*, Brighton: Sussex Academic Press.

Dolowitz, D. with Hulme, R., Nellis, M. and O'Neill, F. (2000) *Policy Transfer and British Social Policy: Learning from the USA*, Buckingham: Open University Press.

Dolowitz, D. and Marsh, D. (1996) 'Who Learns What from Whom? A Review of the Policy Transfer Literature', *Political Studies*, 44.

Dolphin, T. and Griffith, M. (2011) *Forever Blowing Bubbles? Housing's Role in the UK Economy*, London: IPPR.

Donnison, D. (1994) 'Social Policy Studies in Britain: Retrospect and Prospect', in Ferris, J. and Page, R. (eds) *Social Policy in Transition*, Farnham: Avebury.

Donzelot, J. (1980) *The Policing of Families: Welfare versus the State*, London: Hutchinson.

Dorling, D. (2013) *Unequal Health: The Scandal of Our Times*, Bristol: The Policy Press.

Drakeford, M. (2000) *Privatisation and Social Policy*, Harlow: Longman.

Drakeford, M. (2008) 'Going private', in Powell, M. (ed.) *Modernising the Welfare State: The Blair Legacy*, Bristol: The Policy Press.

Drakeford, M. (2012) 'Wales in the age of austerity', *Critical Social Policy*, 32(3).

Driver, S. and Martell, L. (2002) *Blair's Britain*, Cambridge: Polity Press.

Driver, S. and Martell, L. (2006) *New Labour* (2nd edn), Cambridge: Polity Press.

Duffield, M. (2002) 'Trends in female employment 2002', *Labour Market Trends*, November.

Dunleavy, P. (1984) 'The Limits of Local Government', in Boddy, M. and Fudge, C. (eds) *Local Socialism? Labour Councils and New Left Alternatives*, London: Macmillan.

Dunleavy, P. and Husbands, C. (1985) *British Democracy at the Crossroads*, London: Allen & Unwin.

Durose, C., Greasley, S. and Richardson, L. (eds) (2009) *Changing Local Governance: Changing Citizens*, Bristol: The Policy Press.

Dutton, D. (1991) *British Politics Since 1945: The Rise and Fall of Consensus*, Oxford: Basil Blackwell.

Edwards, K., Hiscocks, V. and Nicholas, J. (2012) *Welsh Housing Review 2012*, Cardiff: CIH Cymru.

Elcock, H .(1982) *Local Government: Politicians, Professionals and the Public in Local Authorities* (2nd edn), London: Methuen.

Ellis, H. (2011) *Policy Analysis of Housing and Planning Reform*, London: Town and Country Planning Association.

Ellison, N. (2006) *The Transformation of Welfare States?*, London: Routledge.

Enthoven, A. (1985) *Reflections on the Management of the NHS*, London: Nuffield Provincial Hospitals Trusts.

Equalities and Human Rights Commission (EHRC) (2011) *Close to Home Report: An Inquiry into Older People and Human Rights in Home Care*, London: EHRC.

Esping-Andersen, G. (1985) *Politics against Markets: The Social Democratic Road to Power*, Harvard: University of Harvard Press.

Esping-Andersen, G. (1990) *The Three Worlds of Welfare Capitalism*, Cambridge: Polity Press.

Esping-Andersen, G. (ed.) (1996) *Welfare States in Transition: National Adaptations in Global Economies*, London: Sage.

Esping-Andersen, A., with Gallie, D., Hemerijck, A. and Myles, A. (2002) *Why We Need a New Welfare State*, Oxford: Oxford University Press.

Evans, M. and Williams, C. (2009) *A Generation of Change: A Lifetime of Difference*, Bristol: The Policy Press.

European Commission (EC) (1993) *Growth, Competitiveness, Employment: The Challenges and Ways Forward into the 21st Century*, COM (93) 700, Brussels: European Commission.

EC (1994) *European Social Policy: A Way Forward for the Union*, COM (94) 333, Brussels: European Commission.

EC (2010) Europe 2020: *A European Strategy for Smart, Sustainable and Inclusive Growth*, Brussels: The European Commission.

Evers, A. and Laville, J.-L. (eds) (2004) *The Third Sector in Europe*, Cheltenham: Edward Elgar.

Farnsworth, K. and Irving, Z. (eds) (2011) *Social Policy in Challenging Times: Economic Crisis and Welfare Systems*, Bristol: The Policy Press.

Ferragina, E. and Seeleib-Kaiser, M. (2011) 'Thematic review: welfare regimes past and present', *Policy and Politics*, 39(4).

Ferguson, I., Lavalette, M. and Mooney, G. (2002) *Rethinking Welfare: A Critical Perspective*, London: Sage.

Ferrera, M. (1996) 'The "Southern Model" of welfare in Social Europe', *Journal of European Social Policy*, 6(1).

Field, F. (2010) *The Foundation Years: Preventing Poor Children Becoming Poor Adults: The Independent Review on Poverty and Life Chances*, London: HM Government.

Financial Services Authority (FSA) (2009) *Mortgage Market Review 09/3: Discussion Paper*, London: FSA.

FSA (2012) *PS12/16 Mortgage Market Review: Feedback on CP11/31 and Final Rules*, London: FSA.

Finch, J. (1984) *Education as Social Policy*, Harlow: Longman.

Finch, J. and Groves, D. (eds) (1983) *A Labour of Love: Women, Work and Caring*, London: Routledge & Kegan Paul.

Finlayson, G. (1994) *Citizen, State and Social Welfare in Britain 1830–1990*, Oxford: Clarendon Press.

Finn, D. (2011) 'Welfare to work after the recession: from the new deals to the work programme', in Holden, C., Kilkey, M. and Ramia, G. (eds) *Social Policy Review 23*, Bristol: The Policy Press.

Fitzpatrick, S., Pawson, H., Bramley, G. and Wilcox, S. (2012) *The Homelessness Monitor: Great Britain 2012*, London: Crisis/Heriot-Watt University/The University of York.

Fitzpatrick, T. (2001) *Welfare Theory: An Introduction*, Basingstoke: Palgrave Macmillan.

Fitzpatrick, T . (2005) *New Theories of Welfare*, Basingstoke: Palgrave Macmillan.

Fitzpatrick, T. (2011) *Understanding the Environment and Social Policy*, Bristol: The Policy Press.

Fitzpatrick, T . (2012) 'Postmodernist Perspectives', in Alcock, P. May, M. and Wright, S. (eds) *The Student's Companion to Social Policy* (4th edn), Chichester: Wiley-Blackwell.

Flynn, N. (2012) *Public Sector Management* (6th edn), London: Sage.

Forest, R. and Murie, A. (2010) *Selling the Welfare State*, London: Routledge.

Foster, P. (1983) *Access to Welfare: An Introduction to Welfare Rationing*, London: Macmillan.

Foucault, M. (1977) *Discipline and Punish: The Birth of the Prison*, London: Allen Lane.

Foucault, M. (1979) *The History of Sexuality*, London: Allen Lane.

Francis, R. (2013) *Report of the Mid-Staffordshire NHS Foundation Trust Public Inquiry*, London: The Stationery Office.

Fraser, D. (2009) *The Evolution of the British Welfare State* (4th edn), Basingstoke: Palgrave Macmillan.

Friedman, M. (1962) *Capitalism and Freedom*, Chicago: University of Chicago Press.

Friends Provident/Future Foundation (2012) *Visions of Britain 2020: Health and Wellbeing*, London: Friends Provident/Future Foundation.

Freud, D. (2007) *Reducing Dependency, Increasing Opportunity: Options for the Future of Welfare to Work*, Independent Report, London: DWP.

Frost, N. and Parton, N. (2009) *Understanding Children's Care*, London: Sage.

Gamble, A. (1994) *Britain in Decline* (4th edn), London: Macmillan.

Garnham, A. (2007) *Work over Welfare: Lessons from America?*, London: CPAG.

George, V. (2012) *Major Thinkers in Welfare*, Bristol: The Policy Press.

George, V. and Page, R. (eds) (1995) *Modern Thinkers on Welfare*, Hemel Hempstead: Harvester Wheatsheaf.

George, V. and Taylor-Gooby, P. (eds.) 1996, *European Welfare Policy: Squaring the Circle*, London: Macmillan.

George, V. and Wilding, P. (1976) *Ideology and Social Welfare*, London: Routledge & Kegan Paul.

George, V .and Wilding, P. (1994) *Welfare and Ideology*, Hemel Hempstead: Harvester Wheatsheaf.

Giddens, A. (1998) *The Third Way: The Renewal of Social Democracy*, Cambridge: Polity Press.

Giddens, A. (2002) *What Next for New Labour?*, Cambridge: Polity Press.

Giddens, A. (2007) *Europe in the Global Age*, Cambridge: Polity Press.

Gilmour, I. (1978) *Inside Right*, London: Quartet.

Ginsburg, N. (1979) *Class, Capital and Social Policy*, London: Macmillan.

Glasby, J. (2012) *Understanding Health and Social Care* (2nd edn), Bristol: The Policy Press.

Glasby, J. and Littlechild, R. (eds) (2009) *Direct Payments and Personal Budgets: Putting Personalisation into Practice* (2nd edn), Bristol: The Policy Press.

Glendinning, C. (1992) *The Costs of Informal Care: Looking Inside the Household*, London: HMSO.

Glendinning, C. and Bell, D. (2008) *Rethinking Care and Support: What Can England Learn from Other Countries?*, York: Joseph Rowntree Foundation.

Glendinning, C. and Means, R. (2006) 'Personal social services: developments in adult social care', in Bauld, L., Clarke, K. and Maltby, T. (eds) *Social Policy Review 18*, Bristol: The Policy Press.

Glendinning, C. and Millar, J. (eds) (1992) *Women and Poverty in Britain: The 1990s*, Hemel Hemsptead: Harvester Wheatsheaf.

Glendinning, C., Powell, M. and Rummery, K. (eds) (2002) *Partnerships: New Labour and the Governance of Welfare*, Bristol: The Policy Press.

Glennerster, H. (1988) 'Requiem for the Social Administration Association', *Journal of Social Policy*, 17(1).

Glennerster, H. (1997) *Paying for Welfare: Towards 2000* (3rd edn), Harlow: Prentice Hall.

Glennerster, H. (2003) *Understanding the Finance of Welfare*, Bristol: The Policy Press.

Glennerster, H. (2006) *British Social Policy: 1945 to the Present* (3rd edn), Oxford: Basil Blackwell.

Glennerster, H. (2009) *Understanding the Finance of Social Policy: What Welfare Costs and How to Pay for It* (2nd edn), Bristol: The Policy Press.

Glennerster, H. (2012) 'Paying for Welfare', in Alcock, P., May, M. and Wright, S. (eds) *The Student's Companion to Social Policy*, (4th edn.) Chichester: Wiley-Blackwell.

Goldthorpe, J. and Hope, K. (1974) *The Social Grading of Occupations: A New Approach and Scale*, Oxford: Clarendon Press.

Goode, J, Callender, C. and Lister, R. (1998) *Purse or Wallet? Gender Inequalities and Income Distribution within Families on Benefits*, London: Policy Studies Institute.

Goodin, R., Headey, B., Muffels, R. and Dirven, H. (1999) *The Real Worlds of Welfare Capitalism*, Cambridge: Cambridge University Press.

Gordon, D., Adelman, L., Ashworth, K., Bradshaw, J., Levitas, R., Middleton, S., Pantazis, C., Patsios, D., Payne, S., Townsend, P. and Williams, J. (2000) *Poverty and Social Exclusion in Britain*, York: Joseph Rowntree Foundation.

Gorz, A .(1982) *Farewell to the Working Class*, Pluto Press.

Gough, I. (1979) *The Political Economy of the Welfare State*, London: Macmillan.

Gove, M. (2011) *Speech to the World Forum, January 12th 2011*, London: DFE.

Graham, H. (2007) *Unequal Lives: Health and Socio-economic Inequalities*, Maidenhead: Open University Press.

Gray, A. M. and Birrell, D. (2012) 'Coalition government in Northern Ireland: social policy and the lowest common denominator thesis', *Social Policy and Society*, 11(1).

Green, D. (1987) *The New Right: The Counter Revolution in Political, Economic and Social Thought*, Hemel Hempstead: Harvester Wheatsheaf.

Green, D. (1988) *Everyone a Private Patient*, London: IEA.

Green, F. (2009) 'Job quality in Britain', *Praxis*, No 1, London: UKCES.

Greener, I. (2009) *Public Management: a Critical Text*, Basingstoke: Palgrave Macmillan.

Greer, S. (2004) *Territorial Politics and Health Policy – UK Health Policy in a Comparative Context*, Manchester: Manchester University Press.

Greer, S. and Rowland, D. (eds) (2008) *Devolving Policy: Diverging Values? The Values of the United Kingdom's National Health Services*, London: Nuffield Trust.

Gregg, P. and Wadsworth, J. (2011) *The Labour Market in Winter*, Oxford: Oxford University Press.

Griffiths, Sir R. (1983) *NHS Management Inquiry*, London: DHSS.

Grover, C. (2011) *The Social Fund 20 Years On*, Farnham: Ashgate.

Guillebaud Committee (1956) *Report of the Committee of Enquiry into the Cost of The National Health Service*, Cmd. 9663, London: HMSO.

Hackett, L., Shutt, L. and Maclaclan, N. (2012) *The Way We'll Work: Labour Market Trends and Preparing for the Hourglass*, London: University Alliance.

Hadley, R. and Hatch, S. (1981) *Social Welfare and the Failure of the State: Centralised Services and Participatory Alternatives*, London: George Allen & Unwin.

Halsey, A. H., Lauder, H., Brown, P. and Wells, A. S. (eds) (1997), *Education: Culture, Economy and Society*, Oxford: Oxford University Press.

Ham, C. (2009) *Health Policy in Britain* (6th edn), Basingstoke: Palgrave Macmillan.

Hantrais, L. (2007) *Social Policy in the European Community* (3rd edn), Basingstoke: Palgrave Macmillan.

Hantrais, L. (2012) 'Social policy and the European Union', in Alcock, P., May, M. and Wright, S. (eds) *The Student's Companion to Social Policy* (4th edn), Chichester: Wiley-Blackwell.

Harris, B. (2004) *The Origins of the British Welfare State: Society, State and Social Welfare in England and Wales 1800–1945*, Basingstoke: Palgrave Macmillan.

Harris, B. (2010) 'Voluntary action and the state in historical perspective', *Voluntary Sector Review*, 1(1).

Harris, J. (1989) 'The Webbs, The Charity Organisation Society and the Ratan Tata Foundation: Social Policy from the Perspective of 1912', in Bulmer, M., Lewis, J. and Piachaud, D. (eds) *The Goals of Social Policy*, London: Unwin Hyman.

Hay, C. and Wincott, D. (2012) *The Political Economy of European Welfare Capitalism*, Basingstoke: Palgrave Macmillan.

Hayek, F. (1944) *The Road to Serfdom*, London: Routledge & Kegan Paul.

Hayek, F. (1960) *The Constitution of Liberty*, London: Routledge & Kegan Paul.

Hayek, F. (1982) *Law, Legislation and Liberty*, London: Routledge & Kegan Paul.

Headlam, S (1892) *Christian Socialism*, London: Fabian Tract No. 42.

Health and Social Care Information Centre (HSCIC) (2009) *Personal Social Services: Expenditure and Unit Costs – England 2007–08*, London: Health and Social Care Information Centre.

HSCIC (2012) *Personal Social Services: Expenditure and Unit Costs – England 2010–11*, London: Health and Social Care Information Centre.

Heenan, D. and Birrell, D. (2011) *Social Work in Northern Ireland, Conflict and Change*, Bristol: The Policy Press.

Henderson, J. and Karn, V. (1987) *Race, Class and State Housing*, Farnham: Gower.

HM Government (HMG) (2010a) *Healthy Lives, Healthy People: Our Strategy for Public Health in England*, Cm. 7985, London: The Stationery Office

HMG (2010b) *Our Health and Wellbeing Today*, London: The Stationery Office.

HMG (2010c) *Building a Safe, Confident Future: Implementing the Recommendations of the Social Work Task Force*, London: DCFS and DoH.

HMG (2011a) *A New Approach to Child Poverty; Tackling the Causes of Disadvantage and Transforming Family Lives*, Cm. 8061, London: The Stationery Office.

HMG (2011b) *Open Public Services*, Cm. 8145, London: The Stationery Office.

HMG (2011c) *Laying the Foundations: A Housing Strategy for England*, London: The Stationery Office.

HMG (2011d) *Consultation on Modern Workplaces*, London: The Stationery Office.

HMG (2012a) *Caring for Our Future: Reforming Care and Support*, Cm. 8378, London: The Stationery Office.

HMG (2012b) *Europe 2020: UK National Reform Programme*, London: The Stationery Office.

HMG (2013) *The Coalition: Together in the National Interest, Mid-term Review – Programme for Government Update*, London: The Stationery Office.

HM Revenue and Customs (HMRC) (2011) *Child Benefit, Child Tax Credit and Working Tax Credit Take-up Rates 2007–2008*, London: HMRC.

HM Treasury (HMT) (1998) *Modern Public Services for Britain: Investing in reform*, Cm. 4011, London: The Stationery Office.

HMT (2010) *Spending Review 2010*, Cm. 7942, London: The Stationery Office.

HMT (2012a) *Autumn Statement 2012*, London: HMT.

HMT (2012b) *Budget 2012*, HC1853, London: The Stationery Office.

Hill, M. (2009) *The Policy Process* (5th edn), London: Pearson.

Hills, J. (1993) *The Future of Welfare: A Guide to the Debate*, York: Joseph Rowntree Foundation.

Hills, J. (2007) *Ends and Means: the Future Roles of Social Housing in England*, CaseReport 34, London: LSE.

Hills, J. (2012) 'The distribution of welfare', in Alcock, P., May, M. and Wright, S. (eds) *The Student's Companion to Social Policy* (4th edn), Chichester: Wiley-Blackwell.

Hills, J., Bastagli, F., Cowell, F., Glennerster, H., Karagiannaki, E. and McKnight, A. (2013) *Wealth in the UK: Distribution, Accumulation and Policy*, Oxford: Oxford University Press.

Hills, J., Le Grand, J. and Piachaud, D. (eds) (2002) *Understanding Social Exclusion*, Oxford: Oxford University Press.

Hirschman, A. (1970) *Exit, Voice and Loyalty: Responses to Decline in Firms, Organisations and States*, Harvard: Harvard University Press.

Hirst, P. (1994) *Associative Democracy*, Cambridge: Polity Press.

Hirst, P., Thompson, G. and Bromley, S. (2009) *Globalization in Question* (3rd edn), Cambridge: Polity Press.

Holden, C. (2009) 'Exporting public–private partnerships in health care: Export strategy and policy transfer', *Policy Studies*, 30(3).

Holden, C. (2012) 'Commercial welfare', in Alcock, P., May, M. and Wright, S. (eds) *The Student's Companion to Social Policy* (4th edn), Chichester: Wiley-Blackwell.

Holman, B. (1990) *Good Old George*, Oxford: Lion.

Holton, R.J. (2011) *Globalization and the Nation State* (2nd edn), Basingstoke: Palgrave Macmillan.

Home Office (HO) (1998) *Compact on Relations between Government and the Voluntary and Community Sector in England*, Cm. 4100, London: Stationery Office.

HO (2011) *More Effective Reponses to Anti Social Behaviour*, London: Home Office.

HO (2012) *Putting Victims First: More Effective Responses to Ant-social Behaviour*, Cm. 8367, London: The Stationery Office.

Hood, A., Johnson, P. and Joyce, R. (2013) *The Effects of the Welfare Benefits Uprating Bill*, London: IFS.

Horgan, G. and Gray, A. M. (2012) 'Devolution in Northern Ireland: A Lost Opportunity?', *Critical Social Policy*, 32(3).

House of Commons Health Select Committee (HoCHSC) (2010) *Social Care*, Third Report (session 2009–10), House of Commons Health Select Committee, London: House of Commons.

House of Commons Public Accounts Committee (HoCPAC) (2011), 62nd Report, *Means Testing*, London: The House of Commons.

Howarth, P. (2005) 'Dealing with Complexity', *Benefits*, 13(1).

Huby, M. (1998) *Social Policy and the Environment*, Buckingham: Open University Press.

Hudson, B. (2006) 'Children and young people's strategic plans: we've been here before haven't we?', *Policy Studies*, 27(2).

Hull, A. and Cooke, G. (2012) *Together at Home*, London: IPPR.

Humphries, R. (1995) *Sin, Organised Charity and the Poor Law in Victorian England*, London: Macmillan.

Humphreys, R., Foder, J. and Fernandez, J.-L. (2010) *Securing Good Care for More People: Options for Reform*, London: Kings Fund.

Hunter, D. J., Marks, L. and Smith, K. (2010) *The Public Health System in England*, Bristol: The Policy Press.

Hutton, W. (1995) *The State We're In*, London: Jonathan Cape.

Hutton, W. (2002) *The World We're In*, London: Little Brown.

Hutton, W. (2013) *The State to Come*, London: Vintage Books.

Independent Commission on Social Services in Wales (ICSS) (2010) *From Vision to Action*, Cardiff: Welsh Assembly Government.

International Labour Office (ILO) (2011) *Global Employment Trends for Youth: 2011 Update*, Geneva: ILO.

Jin, W. Levell, P. and Phillips, D. (2010) *A Survey of the UK Benefit System*, London: IFS.

Johnson, N. (1987) *The Welfare State in Transition: The Theory and Practice of Welfare Pluralism*, Brighton: Wheatsheaf.

Johnson, N. (1990) *Reconstructing the Welfare State: A Decade of Change 1980–1990*, Hemel Hemsptead: Harvester Wheatsheaf.

Jones, C. (1993) 'The Pacific Challenge: Confucian Welfare States', in Jones, C. (ed.) *New Perspectives on the Welfare State in Europe*, London: Routledge.

Jones, C. and Novak, T. (1999) *Poverty, Welfare and the Disciplinary State*, London: Routledge.

Jones, K. (2002) *British Education 1944–2001*, Cambridge: Polity Press.

Jones Finer, C. (ed.) (2006) *Migration, Immigration and Social Policy*, Oxford: Blackwell.

Jordan, B. (1998) *The Politics of Welfare*, London: Sage.

Jordan, B. and Drakeford, M. (2012) *Social Policy and Social Work Under Austerity*, Basingstoke: Palgrave Macmillan.

Joshi, H. (1988) *The Cash Opportunity Costs of Childbearing*, Discussion Paper 208, London: Centre for Economic Policy Research.

Joshi, H. (1992) 'The Cost of Caring', in Glendinning, C. and Millar, J. (eds) *Women and Poverty in Britain: The 1990s*, Hemel Hempstead: Harvester Wheatsheaf.

Joyce, R. and Sibieta, L. (2013) 'An assessment of Labour's record on inequality and poverty', *Oxford Review of Economic Policy*, 29.

Kautto, M., Fritzell, J., Hvinden, B., Kvist, J. and Uusitalo, H. (2001) *Nordic Welfare States in the European Context*, London: Routledge.

Kavanagh, D. and Cowley, P. (2010) *The British General Election of 2010*, Basingstoke: Palgrave Macmillan.

Keating, M. (2009) 'Social citizenship, devolution and policy divergence', in Greer, S. L. (ed.) *Devolution and Social Citizenship in the UK*, Bristol: The Policy Press.

Keep, E., Payne, J. and Rees, G. (2010) 'Devolution and strategies for learning and skills: the Leitch report and its alternatives', in Lodge, G. and Schmuecker, K. (eds) *Devolution in Practice 2010*, London: Institute for Public Policy Research (IPPR).

Kelly, E. and Tetlow, G. (2012) *Choosing the Place of Care: The Effect of Patient Choice on Treatment Location in England 2003-2-11*, London: IFS/Nuffield Trust.

Kemp, A. (1997) *Heart and Hand, Report of the Commission on the Future of the Voluntary Sector in Scotland*, Edinburgh: Scottish Council for Voluntary Organisations Publications (SCVO).

Kemp, P. (2006) 'Housing benefit: Great Britain in comparative perspective', *Public Finance and Management*, 6(1).

Kendall, J. (2003) *The Voluntary Sector: Comparative Perspectives in the UK*, London: Routledge.

Kendall, J. (2009) (ed.) *Handbook of Third Sector Policy in Europe: Multi-level Processes and Organised Civil Society*, Cheltenham: Edward Elgar.

Kendall, J. and Knapp, M. (1995) 'A Loose and Baggy Monster: Boundaries, Definitions and Typologies', in Davis Smith, J., Rochester, C. and Hedley, R. (eds), *An Introduction to the Voluntary Sector*, London: Routledge.

Kendall, J. and Knapp, M. (1996) *The Voluntary Sector in the UK*, Manchester: Manchester University Press.

Kennett, P. (2008) *Globalization, Governance and Social Policy*, Cheltenham: Edward Elgar.

Keogh, B. (2013) *Review Into the Quality of Care and Treatment Provided by 14 Hospital Trusts in England, Overview Report*, London: DoH.

Ketels, C. and Porter, M. (2003) *UK Competitiveness Moving to the next Stage*, London: DTI Economics Paper No 3.

Keynes, J. M. (1936) *The General Theory of Employment, Interest and Money*, London: Macmillan.

King, D. (1987) *The New Right: Politics, Markets and Citizenship*, London: Macmillan.

King, D. and Stoker, G. (eds) (1996) *Rethinking Local Democracy*, London: Macmillan.

Klein, R. (2010) *The New Politics of the NHS, From Creation to Re-invention* (6th edn), Abingdon: Radcliffe Publishing.

Korpi, W. (1983) *The Democratic Class Struggle*, London: Routledge & Kegan Paul.

Kramer, R. (1990) *Voluntary Organisations in the Welfare State: On the Threshold of the 1990s*, London: Centre for Voluntary Organisation, LSE.

Laing & Buisson (2012) *Laing's Healthcare Market Review 2011–12*, London: Laing & Buisson.

Laming, Lord (2003) *The Victoria Climbié Inquiry Report*, Cm. 5730, The Stationery Office.

Laming, Lord (2009) *The Protection of Children in England: A Progress Report*, HC 330, London: The Stationery Office.

Large, P. (1991) 'Paying for the Additional Costs of Disability', in Dalley, G. (ed.), *Disability and Social Policy*, London: PSI.

Law Commission (2011) *Adult Social Care, Law Com No326, HC 941*, London: The Stationery Office.

Le Grand, J. (1982) *The Strategy of Equality*, London: Allen & Unwin.

Le Grand, J. (1990) 'Equity Versus Efficiency: The Elusive Trade-off', *Ethics*, 100.

Le Grand, J. (1993) 'Paying for or Providing Welfare', in Deakin, N. and Page, R. (eds) *The Costs of Welfare*, Farnham: Avebury.

Lee, S. (2011) 'No Plan B: The Coalition Agenda for Cutting the Deficit and Rebalancing the Economy', in Lee, S. and Beech, M. (eds) (2011) *The Cameron–Clegg Government: Coalition Politics in an Age of Austerity*, Basingstoke: Palgrave Macmillan.

Lee, S. and Beech, M. (eds) (2011) *The Cameron–Clegg Government: Coalition Politics in an Age of Austerity*, Basingstoke: Palgrave Macmillan.

Leibfried, S. (1993) 'Towards a European Welfare State?', in Jones, C. (ed.) *New Perspectives on the Welfare State in Europe*, London: Routledge.

Leitch, S. (2006) *Leitch Review of Skills: Prosperity for All in the Global Economy – World Class Skills*, London: The Stationery Office.

Leonard, P. (1997) *Postmodern Welfare: Reconstructing an Emancipatory Project*, London: Sage.

Lewis, G., Gewitz, S. and Clarke, J. (eds) (2000) *Rethinking Social Policy*, London: Sage.

Lewis, J. (1992) 'Gender and the Development of Welfare Regimes', *Journal of European Social Policy*, 2(3).

Lewis, J. (1995) *The Voluntary Sector, the State and Social Work in Britain*, Aldershot: Edward Elgar.

Lewis, J. (2005) 'New Labour's Approach to the Voluntary Sector: Independence and the Meaning of Partnership', *Social Policy and Society*, 4(2).

Lewis, J. (2009) *Work–Family Balance, Gender and Policy*, Cheltenham: Edward Elgar.

Lindsay, C. (2007) 'The United Kingdom's "work first" welfare state and activation regimes in Europe', in Serrano Pascual, A. and Magnusson, I. (eds) *Reshaping Welfare States and Activation Regimes in Europe*, Brussels: Peter Lang.

Lipset, S. (1963) *Political Man*, London: Heinemann.

Lister, R. (ed.) (1996) *Charles Murray and the Underclass: the Developing Debate*, London: IEA.

Lister, R. (2010) *Understanding Theories and Concepts in Social Policy*, Bristol: The Policy Press.

Listowel, Earl of (2012) Hansard, 21 June: column 1873 (www.parliament.uk).

Local Government Association (LGA) (2012) *Budget Survey 2011*, London: LGA.

Lodemel, I. and Trickey, H. (eds) (2001) *'An Offer you can't Refuse': Workfare in International Perspective*, Bristol: The Policy Press.

Lodge, G. and Schmuecker, K. (eds) (2010) *Devolution in Practice 2010*, London: Institute for Public Policy Research (IPPR).

Lowe, R. (1990) 'The Second World War: Consensus and the Foundations of the Welfare State', *Twentieth-Century British History*, 1(2).

Lowe, R. (2005) *The Welfare State in Britain since 1945* (3rd edn), Basingstoke: Palgrave Macmillan.

Lowe, S. (2011) *The Housing Debate*, Bristol: The Policy Press.

Lund, B. (2011) *Understanding Housing Policy* (2nd edn), Bristol: The Policy Press.

Lyotard, J.-F. (1984) *The Postmodern Condition*, Manchester: Manchester University Press.

Macmillan, H. (1938) *The Middle Way*, London: Macmillan.

Macmillan, R. (2010) *The third sector delivering public services: an evidence review*, Birmingham: Third Sector Research Centre, Working Paper 20.

Macnicol, J. (1980) *The Movement for Family Allowances 1918–1945; A Study in Social Policy Development*, London: Heinemann.

Macnicol, J. (2006) *Age Discrimination: An Historical and Contemporary Analysis*, Cambridge: Cambridge University Press.

Macrory, I. (2011) 'Social protection', in Beaumont, J. (ed.) *Social Trends 41*, London: ONS.

Malpass, P. and Murie, A. (1999) *Housing Policy and Practice* (5th edn), London: Macmillan.

Margetts, H., 6, P. and Hood, C. (2010) *Paradoxes of Modernisation: Unintended Consequences of Public Policy Reform*, Oxford: Oxford University Press.

Marmot, M. (2010) *Fair Society, Healthy Lives*, London: The Marmot Review, available at www.marmotreview.org.

Marshall, T. H. (1950) *Citizenship and Social Class*, Cambridge: Cambridge University Press.

Marx, K. (1970) *Capital*, Vol. 1, London: Progress Press.

May, M. (2006) 'Employment policy', in Hill, M. (ed.) *Social Policy in the Modern World, a Comparative Text*, Oxford: Blackwell.

May, M. (2012) 'Comparative analysis', in Alcock, P., May, M. and Wright, S. (eds) *The Student's Companion to Social Policy* (4th edn), Chichester: Wiley-Blackwell.

May, M. and Brunsdon, E. (2007) 'Health, safety and employee well-being', in Bloisi, W. (ed.) *An Introduction to Human Resource Managements*, Maidenhead: McGraw Hill.

Maybin, J. and Klein, R. (2012) *Thinking About Rationing*, London: King's Fund.

McCormick, J. (2007) *Contemporary Britain* (2nd edn), Basingstoke: Palgrave Macmillan.

McCormick, J. (2011) *Understanding the European Union* (5th edn), Basingstoke: Palgrave Macmillan.

McKay, S. and Rowlingson, K. (1999) *Social Security in Britain*, London: Macmillan.

McKee, K. and Phillips, D. (2012) 'Social housing and homelessness policies: reconciling social justice and social mix', in Mooney, G. and Scott, G. (eds) *Social Justice and Social Policy in Scotland*, Bristol: The Policy Press.

Means, R. and Smith, R. (2008) *Community Care: Policy and Practice* (4th edn), Basingstoke: Palgrave Macmillan.

Merrett, S. (1979) *State Housing in Britain*, London: Routledge.

Millar, J. (ed.) (2009) *Understanding Social Security Issues for Policy and Practice* (2nd edn), Bristol: The Policy Press.

Millar, J. and Haux, T. (2012) 'Family policy', in Alcock, P., May, M. and Wright, S. (eds) *The Student's Companion to Social Policy*, (4th edn.) Chichester: Wiley-Blackwell.

Miller, C. (2004) *Producing Welfare: a Modern Agenda*, Basingstoke: Palgrave Macmillan.

Mishra, R. (1984) *The Welfare State in Crisis*, Brighton: Wheatsheaf.

Mishra, R. (1989) 'The academic tradition in social policy: The Titmuss years', in Bulmer, M., Lewis, J. and Piachaud, D. (eds) *The Goals of Social Policy*, London: Unwin Hyman.

Mishra, R (1990) *The Welfare State in Capitalist Society*, Hemel Hempstead: Harvester Wheatsheaf.

Mishra, R .(1999) *Globalisation and the Welfare State*, Aldershot: Edward Elgar.

Monitor (2012a) *Review: Fair Playing Field – For the Benefit of Patients*, Consultation, Monitor, available at www.monitor-nhsft.gov.uk.

Monitor (2012b) *Introduction to Monitor's Future Role*, Monitor Briefing Sheet, 20 June, available at www.monitor-nhsft.gov.uk.

Montague, A. (2012) *Review of the Barriers to Institutional Investment in Private Rented Homes*, London: DCLG.

Moore, R. and Wallace, T. (1975) *Slamming the Door*, London: Martin Robertson.

Moran, M. (2011) *Politics and Governance in the UK*, Basingstoke: Palgrave Macmillan.

Morel, N., Palier, B. and Palme, J. (2011) *Towards a Social Investment Welfare State*, Bristol: The Policy Press.

Morris, L. (1994) *Dangerous Classes: The Underclass and Social Citizenship*, London: Routledge.

Morris, L. (1995) *Social Divisions: Economic Decline and Social Structural Change*, London: UCL Press.

Mortimore, P. (2013) *Education Under Siege Why There Is a Better Alternative*, Bristol: The Policy Press.

Moser, C. (1998) *Improving Literacy and Numeracy: a Fresh Start*, London: DFES.

Mulgan, G. and Bury, F. (2006) *Double Devolution: the Renewal of Local Government*, London: the Smith Institute.

Mullins, D. (2011) *Housing Scoping Papers – Housing Associations*, Birmingham: Third Sector Research Centre, Briefing Paper 16.

Mullins, D. and Murie, A. (2006) *Housing Policy in the UK*, Basingstoke: Palgrave Macmillan.

Mullins, D. and Murie, A. (2012) 'Housing', in Alcock, P., May, M. and Wright, S. (eds) *The Student's Companion to Social Policy* (4th edn), Chichester: Blackwell-Wiley.

Muncie, J. (2009) *Youth and Crime: A Critical Introduction* (3rd edn), London: Sage.

Munro, E. (2011) *The Munro Review of Child Protection: Final report: A Child-Centred System*, London: DfE.

Murray, C. (1984) *Losing Ground: American Social Policy 1950–1980*, New York: Basic Books.

Murray, C. (2006) *In Our Hands: a Plan to Replace the Welfare State*, Cambridge, Mass.: American Enterprise Institute for Public Policy Research.

Murie, A. (2012) 'Housing, the welfare state and the coalition government', in Kilkey, M., Ramia, G. and Farnsworth, K. (eds) *Social Policy Review 24*, Bristol: The Policy Press.

Muriel, A., Phillips, D., Sibieta, C. (2010) *Living Standards, Inequality and Poverty: Labour's Record*, IFS Briefing Note, London: IFS.

National Assembly for Wales (2001) *Improving Health for Wales: A Plan for the NHS with its Partners*, Cardiff: National Assembly for Wales.

National Association for the Prevention of Cruelty to Children (NSPCC) (2011) *Child Protection Register Statistics*, London: NSPCC.

National Audit Office (NAO) (2011) *Means Testing*, HC 1464, London: NAO.

NAO (2012) *Healthcare Across the UK: A Comparison of the NHS in England, Scotland, Wales and Northern Ireland, Report by the Comptroller and Auditor General*, HC 192, Session 2012–13, London: NAO.

National College for Leadership of Schools and Children's Services (NCSL)/ Association of Directors of Children's Services (ADCS) (2011) *The Changing Shape of Children's Services: A Survey Conducted by the National College and the ADCS*, London: NCSL.

National Equality Panel (2010) *An Anatomy of Inequality in the UK, Report of the Independent National Equality Panel*, London: Government Equalities Office.

National Housing Federation (NHF) (2011) *Home Truths 2011: England*, London: NHF.

NHF (2012) *Home Truths 2012: England*, London: NHF.

Needham, C. (ed.) (2011) *Personalising Public Services Understanding the Personalisation Narrative*, Bristol: The Policy Press.

Newman, J. (2001) *Modernising Governance: New Labour, Policy and Society*, London: Sage.

Newman, J. and Clarke, J. (1994) 'Going about Our Business? The Managerialization of Public Services', in Clarke, J., Cochrane, A. and McLaughlin, E. (eds), *Managing Social Policy*, London: Sage.

Newman, J. and Clarke, J. (2009) *Publics, Politics and Power: remaking the public in public services*, London: Sage.

Northern Ireland Assembly (NIA) (2008) *New Housing Agenda*, Belfast: NIA.

Northern Ireland Executive (NIE) (2006) *Children and Young People – Our Pledge: Ten Year Strategy for Children and Young People*, Belfast: NIE.

NIE (2011a) *Improving Children's Life chances, The Child Poverty Strategy*, Belfast: OFMDFM.

NIE (2011b) *Transforming Your Care: A Review of Health and Social Care in Northern Ireland*, Belfast: NIE.

NIE (2012) *Improving and Safeguarding Social Wellbeing: A Strategy for Social Work in Northern Ireland 2012–2022*, Belfast: NIE.

Northern Ireland Housing Executive (NIHE) (2012a) *2011 House Conditions Survey*, Belfast: NIHE.

NIHE (2012b) *Homelessness Strategy for Northern Ireland 2012–2017*, Belfast: NIHE.

O'Brien, M. and Penna, S. (1998) *Theorising Welfare*, London: Sage.

O'Connor, J. (1973) *The Fiscal Crisis of the State*, London: St Martin's Press.

Office for National Statistics (ONS) (2010) 'Adoptions in England and Wales 2009', *Statistical Bulletin*, November.

ONS (2011a) *Life Expectancy at Birth and at Age 65 by Local Area in the United Kingdom, 2004–06 to 2008–10*, Statistical Bulletin, London: ONS.

ONS (2011b) 'Adoptions in England and Wales 2010', *Statistical Bulletin*, July.

ONS (2012a) *What Are the Chances of Surviving to Age 100?*, London: ONS.

ONS (2012b) *Statistical Bulletin: 2011 Census: Key Statistics for England and Wales, March 2011*, London: ONS.

ONS (2012c) *Population Ageing in the United Kingdom: Its Constituent Countries and the European Union*, London: ONS.

Office for Standards in Education, Children's Services and Skills (Ofsted) (2012) *Framework for the Inspection of Local Authority Arrangements for the Protection of Children*, London: Ofsted.

Office of Health Economics (OHE) (2012) *Expenditure Data Table 2.5 NHS Sources of Finance 1949–2009*, London, OHE.

Okun, A. (1975) *Equality and Efficiency: The Big Trade-Off*, Washington, DC: Brookings Institute.

Oliver, M. (2009) *Understanding Disability: From Theory to Practice*, 2nd edn, Basingstoke: Palgrave Macmillan.

Organisation for Economic Co-operation and Development (OECD) (2008) *OECD Indicators of Employment Protection*, Paris: OECD.

OECD (2009) *Health at a Glance OECD Indicators 2009*, Paris: OECD.

OECD (2012a) *Education at a Glance OECD Indicators 2012, United Kingdom Country Note*, Paris: OECD.

OECD (2012b) *Social Expenditure Data update (SOCX)*, Paris: OECD.

Osborne, D. and Gaebler, T. (1992) *Reinventing Government: How the Entrepreneurial Spirit is Transforming the Public Sector*, Harlow: Addison-Wesley.

Page, R. (2007) *Revisiting the Welfare State*, New York/Maidenhead: McGraw Hill/Open University Press.

Pahl, J. (1989) *Money and Marriage*, London: Macmillan.

Pantazis, C., Gordon, D. and Levitas, R. (eds) (2006) *Poverty and Social Exclusion in Britain: the Millennium Survey*, Bristol: The Policy Press.

Parker, G .(1990) *With Due Care and Attention: A Review of Research on Informal Care*, London: Family Policy Studies Centre.

Parry, R. (2012) 'Social Policy and Devolution', in Alcock, P., May, M. and Wright, S. (eds) *The Student's Companion to Social Policy* (4th edn), Chichester: Wiley-Blackwell

Pascall, G. (2012) *Gender Equality in the Welfare State*, Bristol: The Policy Press.

Patterson, L. (2003) *Scottish Education in the Twentieth Century*, Edinburgh: Edinburgh University Press.

Pawson, H. and Mullins, D. (2010) *After Council Housing: Britain's New Social Landlords*, Basingstoke: Palgrave Macmillan.

Pawson, H. and Wilcox, S. (2011) *UK Housing Review 2010/2011*, Coventry: Chartered Institute of Housing.

Paxton, W., Pearce, N., Unwin, J. and Molyneux, P .(2005) *The Voluntary Sector Delivering Public Services: Transfer or Transformation?*, York: Joseph Rowntree Foundation.

Payne, G. (ed.) (2013) *Social Divisions* (3rd edn), Basingstoke: Palgrave Macmillan.

Peattie, K. and Morley, A. (2008) *Social enterprises: diversity and dynamics, contexts and contributions*, London: Social Enterprise Coalition and Economic and Social Research Council.

Peden, G. (1985) *British Economic and Social Policy: Lloyd George to Margaret Thatcher* (2nd edn), London: Philip Allan.

Perry, J. (2012) 'Who really gets government subsidized housing?', *Guardian Housing Network*, 27 January.

Phillipson, C. and Walker, A. (eds) (1986) *Ageing and Social Policy: A Critical Assessment*, Aldershot: Gower.

Pierson, P. (ed.) (2001) *The New Politics of the Welfare State*, Oxford: Oxford University Press.

Plant, R. (1988) *Citizenship, Rights and Socialism*, London: Fabian Society No. 531.

Platt, A. (1969) *The Childsavers: The Invention of Delinquency*, Chicago: University of Chicago Press.

Platt, L. (2005) *Discovering Child Poverty: The Creation of a Policy Agenda from 1800 to the Present*, Bristol: The Policy Press.

Platt, L. (2011) *Understanding Inequalities: Stratification and Difference*, Cambridge: Polity.

Pollitt, C. (1990) *Managerialism and the Public Services*, Oxford: Basil Blackwell.

Poole, L. (2012) 'Health policy and health inequalities', in Mooney, G. and G. Scott, G. (eds) *Social Justice and Social Policy in Scotland*, Bristol: The Policy Press.

Powell, M. (ed.) (1999) *New Labour, New Welfare State? The 'Third Way' in British Social Policy*, Bristol: The Policy Press.

Powell, M. (ed.) (2002) *Evaluating New Labour's Welfare Reforms*, Bristol: The Policy Press.

Powell, M. (ed.) (2007) *Understanding the Mixed Economy of Welfare*, Bristol: The Policy Press.

Powell, M. (ed.) (2008) *Modernising the Welfare State: the Blair legacy*, Bristol: The Policy Press.

Powell, M. and Barrientos, A. (2011) 'An audit of the welfare modeling business', *Social Policy and Administration*, 16(1).

Powell, M. and Hewitt, M. (2002) *Welfare State and Welfare Change*, Buckingham: Open University Press.

Putnam, R. (1993) *Making Democracy Work: Civic Traditions in Modern Italy*, Princeton: Princeton University Press.

Putnam, R. (2000) *Bowling Alone: The Collapse and Revival of American Community*, London: Simon & Schuster.

Qureshi, H. and Walker, A. (1989) *The Caring Relationship: Elderly People and their Families*, London: Macmillan.

Randall, C. (2011) 'Housing', in Beaumont, J. (ed.) *Social Trends 41*, London: ONS.

Rees, G. (2007) 'The impacts of parliamentary devolution on education policy in Wales', *Welsh Journal of Education*, 14(1).

Rees, J., Taylor, R. and Damm, C. (2013) *Does Sector Matter? Understanding the Experiences of Providers of Work Programmes*, Birmingham: Third Sector Research Centre, Working Paper 92.

Reid, M. (2011) 'The Glasgow effect', *Bulletin of the World Health Organisation*, 89(10).

Ridge, T. (2002) *Childhood Poverty and Social Exclusion: from a Child's Perspective*, Bristol: The Policy Press.

Rhodes, R. (1997) *Understanding Governance*, Buckingham: Open University Press.

Roberts, K. (2011) *Class in Modern Britain* (2nd edn), Basingstoke: Palgrave Macmillan.

Rochester, C. (2001) 'Regulation: The Impact on Local Voluntary Action', in Harris, M. and Rochester, C. (eds), *Voluntary Organisations and Social Policy in Britain: Perspectives on Change and Choice*, Basingstoke: Palgrave Macmillan.

Rossiter, C. and Wicks, M. (1982) *Crisis or Challenge? Family Care, Elderly People and Social Policy*, London: Family Policy Studies Centre.

Roulston, A. and Prideaux, S. (2012) *Understanding Disability Policy*, Bristol: The Policy Press.

Rowlingson, K. and McKay, S. (2011) *Wealth and the Wealthy: Exploring and Tackling Inequalities between Rich and Poor*, Bristol: The Policy Press.

Rowlingson, K., Orton, M. and Taylor, E. (2010) 'Do we still care about inequality', in Park, A., Curtice, J., Clery, E. and Bryson, C. (eds) *British Social Attitudes: the 27th Report*, London: Sage.

Rowntree, B. S. (1901) *Poverty: A Study of Town Life*, London: Macmillan.

Rugg, J. and Rhodes, D. (2008) *Review of Private Rented Sector Housing*, York: The Centre for Housing Policy, University of York.

Rummery, K. (2006) 'Disabled citizens and social exclusion: the role of direct payments', *Policy and Politics*, 34(4).

Ryan, P. (1978) 'Poplarism 1893–1930', in Thane, P. (ed.) *The Origins of British Social Policy*, London: Croom Helm.

Sainsbury, R. (2003) 'Understanding social security fraud', in Millar, J. (ed.) *Understanding Social Security Issues for Policy and Practice*, Bristol: The Policy Press.

Salamon, L. and Anheier, H. (1997) *Defining the Nonprofit Sector: A Cross-National Analysis*, Manchester: Manchester University Press.

Salamon, L., List, R., Toepler, S., Sokolowski, S. and associates (eds) (1999) *Global Civil Society: Dimensions of the Non-profit Sector*, Baltimore: Johns Hopkins Centre for Civil Society Studies.

Sarre, P. (1989) 'Recompostition of the Class Structure', in Hamnett, C., McDowell, L. and Sarre, P. (eds), *Restructuring Britain: The Changing Social Structure*, London: Sage.

Saville, J. (1983) 'The Origins of the Welfare State', in Loney, M., Boswell, D. and Clarke, J. (eds) *Social Policy and Social Welfare*, Buckingham: Open University Press.

School Curriculum and Assessment Authority (SCAA) (1996) *Nursery Education: Desirable Outcomes for Children's Learning on Entering Compulsory Education*, London: SCAA.

Schroder, M. (2013) *Integrating Varieties of Capitalism and Welfare State Research A Unified Typology of Capitalism*, Basingstoke: Palgrave Macmillan.

Schwartzmantel, J. (1994) *The State in Contemporary Society: An Introduction*, Hemel Hempstead: Harvester Wheatsheaf.

Scott, G. and Wright, S. (2012) 'Devolution, social democratic visions and policy reality in Scotland', *Critical Social Policy*, 32(3).

Scott, J. and Crompton, R. (eds) (2010) *Gender Inequalities in the 21st Century*, Cheltenham: Edward Elgar.

Scottish Executive (2006) *Changing Lives: Report of the 21st Century Social Work Review*, Edinburgh: Scottish Executive.

Scottish Government (SG) (2007a) *Skills for Scotland: a Lifelong Skills Strategy*, Edinburgh: Scottish Government.

SG (2007b) *Firm Foundations: The Future of Housing in Scotland*, Edinburgh: Scottish Government.

SG (2008) *Equally Well: Report of the Ministerial Task Force on Health Inequalities*, Edinburgh: Scottish Government.

SG (2010a) *Skills for Scotland: accelerating the recovery and increasing sustainable economic growth*, Edinburgh: Scottish Government.

SG (2010b) *Equally Well Review*, Edinburgh: Scottish Government.

SG (2011a) *Child Poverty Strategy for Scotland*, Edinburgh: Scottish Government.

SG (2011b) *Putting Learners at the Centre*, Edinburgh: Scottish Government.

SG (2011c) *Homes Fit for the Twenty-First Century: The Scottish Government's Strategy and Action Plan for Housing in the Next Decade: 2011–2020*, Edinburgh: Scottish Government.

SG (2011d) *Self-Directed Support: A National Strategy for Scotland*, Edinburgh: Scottish Government.

SG (2011e) *Renewing Scotland: The Government's Programme for Scotland 2011–2012*, Edinburgh: Scottish Government.

SG (2012a) *Report of the Review on Higher Education Governance in Scotland*, Edinburgh: Scottish Government.

SG (2012b) *Housing Statistics for Scotland*, Edinburgh: Scottish Government.

SG (2012c) *Integration of Adult Health and Social Care in Scotland Consultation on Proposals*, Edinburgh: Scottish Government.

Scottish Parliament (2008) *Getting g it Right for Every Child*, Edinburgh: Scottish Parliament.

Secretary of State for Education and Science and Secretary of State for Wales (1977) *Education in Schools: A Consultative Document*, Cm. 6860, London: HMSO.

Secretary for State for Health (1998) *Our Healthier Nation*, Cm. 352, London: The Stationery Office.

Shah, S. and Priestley, M. (2011) *Disability and Social Change: Private Lives and Public Policies*, Bristol: The Policy Press.

Shaw, M., Thomas, B., Smith G. D. and Dorling, D. (2008) *The Grim Reaper's Road Map: An Atlas of Mortality in Britain*, Bristol: The Policy Press.

Sinfield, A. (1981) *What Unemployment Means*, Oxford: Martin Robertson.

Sinfield, A. (2013) 'Fiscal welfare', in Greve, B. (ed.) *The Routledge Handbook of the Welfare State*, London: Routledge.

Skills for Care (SfC) (2010a) *The State of the Adult Social Care Workforce in England, 2010*, London: Skills for Care.

SfC (2010b) *Step by Step Workforce Commissioning in Adult Social Care – a detailed guide for Local Authorities and their partners*, London: Skills for Care.

SfC (2011) *Capable, Confident, Skilled: A workforce development strategy for people working, supporting and caring in adult social care*, London: Skills for Care.

Smith, A. (1776) *An Enquiry into the Nature and Causes of the Wealth of Nations*, Edinburgh: Adam & Charles Black.

Smith, D. (ed.) (1992) *Understanding the Underclass*, London: PSI.

Smith, G .(1988) 'A Paen for the Social Policy Association: A Response to Glennerster', *Journal of Social Policy*, 17(3).

Smith, K. and Hellowell, M. (2012) 'Beyond rhetorical differences: a cohesive account of post-devolution developments in UK health policy', *Social Policy and Administration*, 46(2).

Smith, M. (2010) 'From Big Government to Big Society: Changing the State–Society Balance', *Parliamentary Affairs*, 63(4).

Smith, N. , Middleton, S., Ashton-Brooks, K., Cox, L., Dobson, B., and Reith, L. (2004) *Disabled People's Costs of Living: 'More than you would think'*, York: Joseph Rowntree Foundation.

Solomos, J. (2003) *Race and Racism in Contemporary Britain* (3rd edn), Basingstoke: Palgrave Macmillan.

Spence, A. (2011) 'Labour Market', in Beaumont, J. (ed.) *Social Trends 41*, London: ONS.

Spicker, P. (2011) *How Social Security Works*, Bristol: The Policy Press.

Staetsky, L. and Mohan, J. (2011) *Individual voluntary participation in the United Kingdom: an overview of survey information*, Birmingham: Third Sector Research Centre, Working Paper 6.

Stafford, A., Parton, N., Vincent, S. and Smith, C. (2011) *Child Protection Systems in the United Kingdom*, London: Jessica Kingsley Publishers.

Standing, G. (2011) *The Precariat: The New Dangerous Class*, London: Bloomsbury Academic.

Stephens, M. (2011) *Tackling Housing Volatility in the UK*, York: Joseph Rowntree Foundation.

Stephens, M., Whitehead, C. and Munro, M. (2005) *Lessons from the Past, Challenges for the Future for Housing Policy*, London: ODPM.

Stoker, G. (1991) *The Politics of Local Government* (2nd edn), London: Macmillan.

Stoker, G. (2003) *Transforming Local Governance: from Thatcherism to New Labour*, Basingstoke: Palgrave Macmillan.

Stoker, G. (2006) *Why Politics Matters: Making Democracy Work*, Basingstoke: Palgrave Macmillan.

Sullivan, M. (2005) 'Wales, devolution and health policy: policy experimentation and differentiation to improve health', *Contemporary Wales*, 17(1).

Sutherland, Sir S. (1999) *With Respect to Old Age: Long Term Care Rights and Responsibilities, Report by the Royal Commission on Long Term Care*, Cm. 4192, London: The Stationery Office.

Sutherland, Sir S. (2008) *Independent Review of Free Personal and Nursing Care in Scotland*, Edinburgh: Scottish Government.

Swank, D. (2010) 'Globalization', in Castles, F., Leibfried, S., Lewis, J., Obinger, H. and Pierson, C. (eds) *The Oxford Handbook of the Welfare State*, Oxford: Oxford University Press, 318–30.

Tawney, R. H. (1931) *Equality*, London: Allen & Unwin.

Taylor, S. and Emir, A. (2009) *Employment Law: an Introduction* (2nd edn), Oxford: Oxford University Press.

Taylor-Gooby, P. (1991) *Social Change, Social Welfare and Social Science*, Hemel Hempstead: Harvester Wheatsheaf.

Taylor-Gooby, P. (1994) 'Postmodernism and Social Policy: a great leap backwards?', *Journal of Social Policy*, 23(3).

Taylor-Gooby, P. (ed.) (2004) *Making a European Welfare State? Convergences and Conflicts over European Social Policy*, Oxford: Basil Blackwell.

Taylor-Gooby, P. (2013) *The Double Crisis of the Welfare Stet and What We Can Do About It*, Basingstoke: Palgrave Macmillan.

Taylor-Gooby, P. and Dale, J. (1981) *Social Theory and Social Welfare*, London: Edward Arnold.

Taylor-Gooby, P. and Stoker, G. (2011) 'The Coalition Programme: A New Vision for Britain or Politics as Usual?', *Political Quarterly*, 82(1).

Teasdale, S. (2012) 'What's in a name? Making sense of social enterprise discourses', *Public Policy and Administration*, 27(2).

Thane, P. (1996) *The Foundations of the Welfare State* (2nd edn), Harlow: Longman.

Therborn, G. and Roebroek, J. (1986) 'The Irreversible Welfare State', *International Journal of the Health Services*, 16(3).

Thomas, R. (2001) 'Economic Policy: The Conservative Legacy and New Labour's Third Way', in Savage, S. and Atkinson, R. (eds) *Public Policy under Blair*, Basingstoke: Palgrave Macmillan.

Thorlby, R. and Maybin, J. (eds) (2010) *A High Performing NHS? A Review of Progress 1997–2010*, London: King's Fund.

Timmins, N. (2001) *The Five Giants: A Biography of the Welfare State* (new edn), London: HarperCollins.

Timmins, N. (2012) *Never Again: The Story of the Health and Social Care Act 2012*, London: Institute for Government/King's Fund.

Titmuss, R. (1955) *The Social Division of Welfare: Some Reflections on the Search for Equity*, Liverpool: Liverpool University Press.

Titmuss, R. (1958) *Essays on 'the Welfare State'*, London: Allen & Unwin.

Titmuss, R. (1970) *The Gift Relationship*, London: Pelican, and reprinted 1997, London: LSE books.

Titmuss, R. (1974) *Social Policy: An Introduction*, London: Unwin Hyman.

Tomlinson, S. (2005) *Education in a Post Welfare Society* (2nd edn), Buckingham: Open University Press.

Townsend, P. (1962) *The Last Refuge: A Survey of Residential Institutions and Homes of Old People*, London: Routledge & Kegan Paul.

Townsend, P. (1979) *Poverty in the United Kingdom: A Survey of Household Resources and Standards of Living*, Harmondsworth: Penguin.

Townsend, P., Davidson, N. and Whitehead, M. (eds) (1988) *Inequalities in Health: The Black Report and the Health Divide*, Harmondsworth: Penguin.

Trades Union Congress (TUC) (2012) *Labour Market Report 23*, London: TUC.

Turner, A. (2006) *Implementing an Integrated Package of Pension Reforms: The Final Report of the Pensions Commission*. London: The Stationery Office.

Twigg, J. (1989) 'Models of Carers: How do Social Care Agencies Conceptualise their Relationship with Informal Carers?', *Journal of Social Policy*, 18(1).

UK Commission for Employment and Skills (UKCES) (2010) *Ambition2020: world-class skills and jobs in the UK; key findings and implications for action: the 2020 report*, London: UKCE.

United Nations Children's Fund (UNICEF) (2007) *The State of the World's Children 2007*, UNICEF.

Ungerson, C. (1987) *Policy is Personal. Sex, Gender and Informal Care*, London: Tavistock.

Van Berkel, R. and Borghi, A. (2008) 'Introduction: the governance of activation', *Social Policy and Society*, 7(3).

Van Oorschot, W. (1995) *Realising Rights: A Multi-Level Approach to the Non-Take-Up of Means-Tested Benefits*, Farnham: Avebury.

Van Oorschot, W. (ed.) (1996) *New Perspectives on the Non-Take-Up of Social Security Benefits*, Tilburg: Tilburg University Press.

Vasagar, J. (2011) 'Weaker schools face squeeze as Gove unleashes academies', *The Guardian*, 23 May, 1.

Veit-Wilson, J. (1998) *Setting Adequacy Standards: How Governments Define Minimum Incomes*, Bristol: The Policy Press.

Waldfogel, J. (2010) *Britain's War on Poverty*, New York: Russell Sage Foundation.

Walker, A. and Maltby, T. (2013) *The Political Economy of Ageing and Later Life: Critical Perspectives*, Cheltenham: Edward Elgar.

Walker, R. (1999) *Ending Child Poverty: Popular Welfare for the 21st Century*, Bristol: The Policy Press.

Walker, R. (2005) *Social Security and Welfare: Concepts and* Comparisons, Buckingham: Open University Press.

Wanless, D. (2002) *Securing Our Future: Taking a Long-Term View*, London: HMT.

Wanless, D. (2004) *Securing our Future Health: Taking a Long-Term View, Final Report*, London: HMT.

Wanless, D. (2006) *Securing Good Care for Older People: Taking a Long-Term View*, London: King's Fund.

Weber, M. 1(968) *Economy and Society*, New York: Bedminster Press.

Webster, C. (2002) *The National Health Service: A Political History*, Oxford: Oxford University Press.

Welsh Assembly Government (WAG) (2000) *Children and Young People: A Framework for Partnership*, Cardiff: Welsh Assembly Government.

WAG (2003a) *The Learning Country: The Foundation Phase*, Newtown: Welsh Assembly Government.

WAG (2003b) *Health, Social Care and Wellbeing Strategies*, Cardiff: Welsh Assembly Government.

WAG (2004) *Children and Young People: Rights to Action*, Cardiff: Welsh Assembly Government.

WAG (2005) *A Review of Low Cost Housing in Wales*, Cardiff: Welsh Assembly Government.

WAG (2008a) *Skills that Work for Wales: a Skills and Employment Strategy and Action Plan*, Newtown: Welsh Assembly Government.

WAG (2008b) *Transforming Education and Training Provision in Wales: Delivering Skills that Work for Wales*, Caerphilly: Welsh Assembly Government.

WAG (2009a) *Ten-Year Homelessness Plan for Wales 2009–19*, Cardiff: Welsh Assembly Government.

WAG (2009b) *A Strategy for Social Services in Wales Over the Next Decade*, Cardiff: Welsh Assembly Government.

WAG (2010a) *Child Poverty Strategy for Wales*, Cardiff: Welsh Assembly Government.

Walsh Government (WG) (2011a) *Programme for Government*, Cardiff: Welsh Government.

WG (2011b) *Together for Health*, Cardiff: Welsh Government.

WG (2011c) *A New Policy for Social Housing Rents*, Cardiff: Welsh Government.

WG (2011d) *Sustainable Services for Wales: A Framework for Action*, Cardiff: Welsh Government.

WG (2012a) *Review of Qualifications for 14 to 19-year-olds in Wales, Final Report and Recommendations*, Cardiff: Government.

WG (2012b) *Dwelling Stock Estimates*, Cardiff: Government.

WG (2012c) *Homes for Wales: A White Paper For Better Lives and Communities*, Cardiff: Government.

WG (2012d) *Reforming Social Services in Wales – Consultation*, Cardiff: Welsh Government.

Watts, A.G. (2010) 'National all-age career guidance services: evidence and issues', *British Journal of Guidance & Counseling*, 38(1).

Whitehead, C., Williams, P., Tang, C. and Udagawa, C. (2012) *Housing in Transition: Understanding the Dynamics of Housing Change*, London: Resolution Foundation/ Shelter.

Wilcox, S. and Fitzpatrick, S. with Stephens, M., Pleace, N., Wallace, A. and Rhodes, D. (2010) *The Impact of Devolution Housing and Homelessness*, York: Joseph Rowntree Foundation.

Williams, F. (1989) *Social Policy: A Critical Introduction*, Cambridge: Polity Press.

Williams, F. (2000) 'Principles of Recognition and Respect in Welfare', in Lewis, G., Gewitz, S. and Clarke, J. (eds) *Rethinking Social Policy*, London: Sage.

Wilkinson, R. and Pickett, K. (2009) *The Spirit Level: Why More Equal Societies almost always do Better*, Harmondsworth: Penguin Books.

Wilson, D. and Game, C. (2011) *Local Government in the United Kingdom* (5th edn), Basingstoke: Palgrave Macmillan.

Wilson, E. (1977) *Women and the Welfare State*, London: Tavistock.

Wolfenden, Lord J. (1977) *The Future of Voluntary Organisations*, London: Croom Helm.

Wood, C. and Grant, E. (2010) *Counting the Cost*, London: DEMOS.

World Health Organization (WHO) (2008) *Closing the Gap in a Generation: Health Equity through Action on the Social Determinants of Health, Final Report of the Commission on the Social Determinants of Health*, Geneva: WHO.

Wright, K. (1987) *The Economics of Informal Care of the Elderly*, York: Centre for Health Economics, University of York.

Wright, S. (2012) 'Welfare- to- work, agency and personal responsibility', *Journal of Social Policy*, 4(2).

Yeates, N. (ed.) (2008) *Understanding Global Social Policy*, Bristol: The Policy Press.

Yeates, N. and Holden, C. (eds) (2009) *The Global Social Policy Reader*, Bristol: The Policy Press.

Index